D0181341

Roadfood

Also by Jane and Michael Stern

Amazing America

Ambulance Girl (by Jane Stern)

American Gourmet

Auto Ads

Blue Plate Specials and Blue Ribbon Chefs

Blue Willow Inn Cookbook

Carbone's Cookbook

Chili Nation

Cooking in the Lowcountry from The Old
Post Office Restaurant

Dog Eat Dog

Douglas Sirk (by Michael Stern)

Durgin-Park Cookbook

Eat Your Way Across the USA

El Charro Café Cookbook

Elegant Comfort Food from the Dorset Inn

Elvis World

Encyclopedia of Bad Taste

Famous Dutch Kitchen Cookbook

Friendly Relations

Goodfood

Happy Trails

Harry Caray's Restaurant Cookbook

Horror Holiday

Jane and Michael Stern's Encyclopedia of
Pop Culture

Louie's Backyard Cookbook

Real American Food

Roadfood Sandwiches

Southern California Cooking from the Cottage

Sixties People

Southern Country Cooking from the
Loveless Cafe

Square Meals

Taste of America

Trucker: A Portrait of the Last American
Cowboy

Two for the Road

Two Puppies

Way Out West

BROADWAY BOOKS ✳ New York

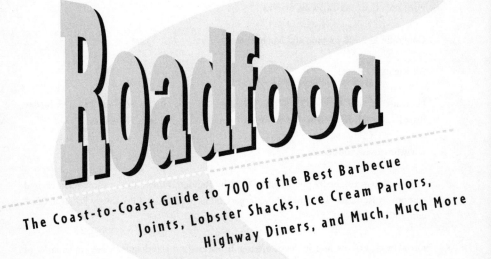

Roadfood

The Coast-to-Coast Guide to 700 of the Best Barbecue
Joints, Lobster Shacks, Ice Cream Parlors,
Highway Diners, and Much, Much More

Jane and Michael Stern

BROADWAY

PUBLISHED BY BROADWAY BOOKS

Copyright © 2008 by Jane and Michael Stern

All Rights Reserved

Published in the United States by Broadway Books, an imprint of The Doubleday Broadway Publishing Group, a division of Random House, Inc., New York.

www.broadwaybooks.com

This book was originally published in 1978 by Random House and in subsequent revised editions by Random House in 1980, HarperCollins in 1992, and Broadway Books in 2002 and 2005.

BROADWAY BOOKS and its logo, a letter B bisected on the diagonal, are trademarks of Random House, Inc.

Book design by Caroline Cunningham
Maps designed by Jeffrey L. Ward

Library of Congress Cataloging-in-Publication Data

Stern, Jane.
   Roadfood : the coast-to-coast guide to 700 of the best barbecue joints, lobster shacks, ice cream parlors, highway diners, and much, much more / Jane and Michael Stern.
      p. cm.
   Includes bibliographic references.
   1. Restaurants—United States—Guidebooks. I. Stern, Michael, 1946– II. Title.

TX907.2.S84 2008
647.9573—dc22
2007028239

ISBN 978-0-7679-2829-8

PRINTED IN THE UNITED STATES OF AMERICA

10   9   8   7   6   5   4   3   2   1

Acknowledgments

Roadfood is the story of our two appetites. We ate everything in this book and wrote all the reviews. But when we travel, we are never alone. Alongside us in the car, at the diner counter, or in the hash house booth are *Gourmet* magazine's Ruth Reichl, James Rodewald, John "Doc" Willoughby, and Larry Karol. When we size up a place, we do so with the inspiration of our comrades at Roadfood.com—Steve Rushmore and Stephen Rushmore, Jr., Kristin Little, Marc Bruno, Cindy Keuchle, and Bruce Bilmes and Sue Boyle. And whenever we converse with a cook, waiter, customer, butcher, baker, or farmer, we think of our friends at public radio's *The Splendid Table*—Sally Swift, Lynne Rosetto Kasper, and Jen Russell.

Our editor, Jennifer Josephy, along with Kristen Green and Stephanie Bowen, has graciously shepherded this book through from manuscript to completion, and our literary agent, Doe Coover, enables us to spend the vast majority of our time eating and writing rather than worrying about the intricacies of publishing.

Finally, it is crucial that we acknowledge the fact that these pages would be blank if it weren't for all the thousands of good people who keep *Roadfood* restaurants thriving across the country: cooks and proprietors and customers, too, who make traveling as much about meeting great people as eating good meals. It has been a joy of our lives to spend some time with these people all around the country. To do justice to their achievements has been a guiding principle all along.

Contents

Mid-South 139

Deep South 211

Midwest 289

Great Plains 383

Southwest 423

West Coast 517

It is torture writing a new edition of *Roadfood* with over 175 restaurants that weren't in the last one. Because we need this book to be wieldy, we had to cut out nearly that many old favorites. If a place included in a previous edition of *Roadfood* is not here, you should not assume we no longer like it. Yes, it may have gone out of business or hit the skids and thus deserved its excision; but it may have been removed only to make space for new discoveries that we believe merit your attention.

Foremost among criteria for inclusion in *Roadfood* is that a place be memorable, offering the kind of eating experience that we travelers hold dear as the highlight of a trip. We especially seek out restaurants that sing of their region and community and serve a meal that is part of locals' sense of self and of place. There may be a fantastic Cajun restaurant in Sioux City, but it is our belief that the experience of eating gumbo in the bayous, elbow to elbow with the people who live there, listening to their music and hearing their unique way of talking, cannot be tasted in full measure anywhere else.

Roadfood is edible folk art; the cooks, pitmasters, pancake makers, and hot dog vendors who create it are not celebrity chefs. We've met amazingly few bloated egos in our travels around the country in search of those good folks who, whether they know it or not, are carrying on a precious cultural heritage. Like folk art, Roadfood isn't the work of a single creative genius or television personality; it grows out of tradition and out of the brilliantly spiced ethnic, global, regional, and religious diversity that makes this nation such an eater's adventure.

No one can deny the soulless homogenization of the American road in recent decades; the blight of corporate sameness surely does endanger these distinctive eateries. It is heartbreaking to see a one-of-a-kind favorite driven out of business when the monotonous franchises come to town. But we are not glum about Roadfood's future. An appreciation of regional food, local farms, sustainable foodways, and quirky town cafés has grown tremendously in recent years. More and more of us have come to realize that food isn't just something to eat. It can be an essential and very delicious part of who we are.

We are optimistic about the future of good eats because we have seen so many old restaurants passed on to new generations who treasure the legacy, as well as brand-new ones that honor food as soul sustenance. Whenever we hit the road, we are armed with more good tips and suggestions from readers than time and appetite will allow us to sample. At the Web site Roadfood.com a burgeoning community of passionate eaters has come together to share their knowledge, enthusiasm, and experience, and to help one another savor this country's best food. Please join us there, where users are welcome to post reviews, to participate in discussion forums about all good-eats topics, and to partake of the best recipes from Roadfood restaurants all around the country. If you have a particular restaurant you want to review or recommend or if you have a comment on one that we have recommended, please visit Roadfood.com and let the world know or get in touch with us directly at jane&michael@ roadfood.com.

Until then, we hope to see you at the lunch counter or in a diner booth or parked at the drive-in somewhere down the road!

Notes about Using This Book

✳ If you are planning a special trip to any restaurant in this book, *please* call ahead to make certain it is open and is serving what you want to eat. Hours of operation change over the course of the year and proprietors sometimes go fishing. Our notation of BLD, meaning breakfast, lunch, and dinner, can mean different times in different places. For instance, many heartland restaurants do serve dinner, but dinner hour can end as early as seven o'clock. Also, some specialties are seasonal. (When calling, be aware that telephone area codes are changing all the time.)

✳ The vast majority of *Roadfood* restaurants require no reservations and are come-as-you-are. A few pricier ones do require a reservation. We've made note of which ones get insanely crowded and what you can do about it. But again, if in doubt, please call ahead.

✳ Our approximate cost guide is as follows:
  ✦ $ = one full meal is under $10
  ✦ $$ = one full meal is between $10 and $30
  ✦ $$$ = one full meal is over $30

* We welcome tips for inclusion in future editions, comments, and even complaints. Please address any such correspondence to us c/o Broadway Books, 1745 Broadway, New York, NY 10019. Or contact us via our interactive Web site: www.roadfood.com.

New England

Connecticut * Maine * Massachusetts *

New Hampshire * Rhode Island * Vermont

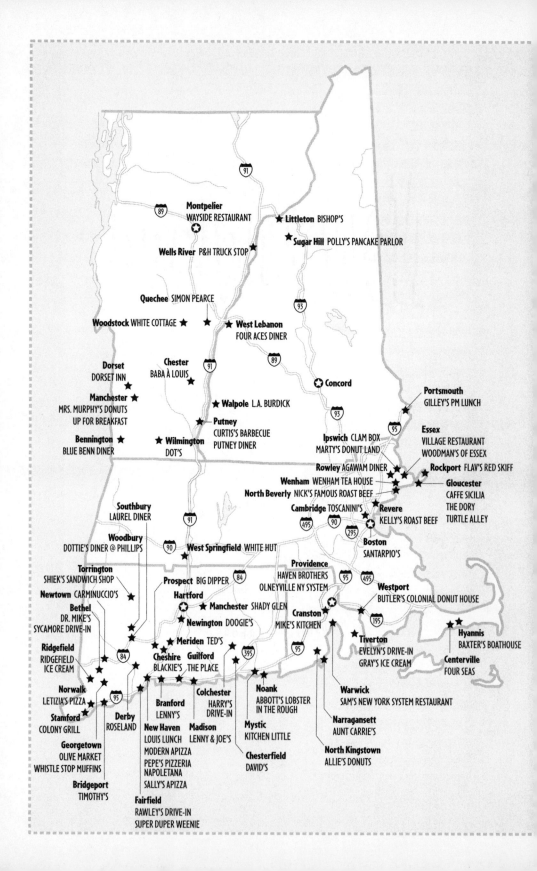

Montpelier WAYSIDE RESTAURANT

★ Littleton BISHOP'S

Sugar Hill POLLY'S PANCAKE PARLOR

Wells River P&H TRUCK STOP

Quechee SIMON PEARCE

Woodstock WHITE COTTAGE ★

West Lebanon FOUR ACES DINER

Dorset DORSET INN

Chester BABA À LOUIS

Concord

Manchester MRS. MURPHY'S DONUTS UP FOR BREAKFAST

Walpole L.A. BURDICK

Portsmouth GILLEY'S PM LUNCH

Putney CURTIS'S BARBECUE PUTNEY DINER

Essex VILLAGE RESTAURANT WOODMAN'S OF ESSEX

Bennington BLUE BENN DINER

Wilmington DOT'S

Ipswich CLAM BOX MARTY'S DONUT LAND

Rockport FLAV'S RED SKIFF

Rowley AGAWAM DINER

Wenham WENHAM TEA HOUSE

Gloucester CAFFE SICILIA THE DORY TURTLE ALLEY

North Beverly NICK'S FAMOUS ROAST BEEF

Cambridge TOSCANINI'S

Revere KELLY'S ROAST BEEF

Southbury LAUREL DINER

Boston SANTARPIO'S

Woodbury DOTTIE'S DINER @ PHILLIPS

West Springfield WHITE HUT

Torrington SHIEK'S SANDWICH SHOP

Providence HAVEN BROTHERS OLNEYVILLE NY SYSTEM

Prospect BIG DIPPER

Newtown CARMINUCCIO'S

Westport BUTLER'S COLONIAL DONUT HOUSE

Hartford

Bethel DR. MIKE'S SYCAMORE DRIVE-IN

Manchester SHADY GLEN

Cranston MIKE'S KITCHEN

Newington DOOGIE'S

Ridgefield RIDGEFIELD ICE CREAM

Hyannis BAXTER'S BOATHOUSE

Meriden TED'S

Tiverton EVELYN'S DRIVE-IN GRAY'S ICE CREAM

Centerville FOUR SEAS

Norwalk LETIZIA'S PIZZA

Cheshire BLACKIE'S

Guilford THE PLACE

Stamford COLONY GRILL

Colchester HARRY'S DRIVE-IN

Noank ABBOTT'S LOBSTER IN THE ROUGH

Warwick SAM'S NEW YORK SYSTEM RESTAURANT

Derby ROSELAND

Branford LENNY'S

Georgetown OLIVE MARKET WHISTLE STOP MUFFINS

New Haven LOUIS LUNCH MODERN APIZZA PEPE'S PIZZERIA NAPOLETANA SALLY'S APIZZA

Madison LENNY & JOE'S

Mystic KITCHEN LITTLE

Narragansett AUNT CARRIE'S

Chesterfield DAVID'S

North Kingstown ALLIE'S DONUTS

Bridgeport TIMOTHY'S

Fairfield RAWLEY'S DRIVE-IN SUPER DUPER WEENIE

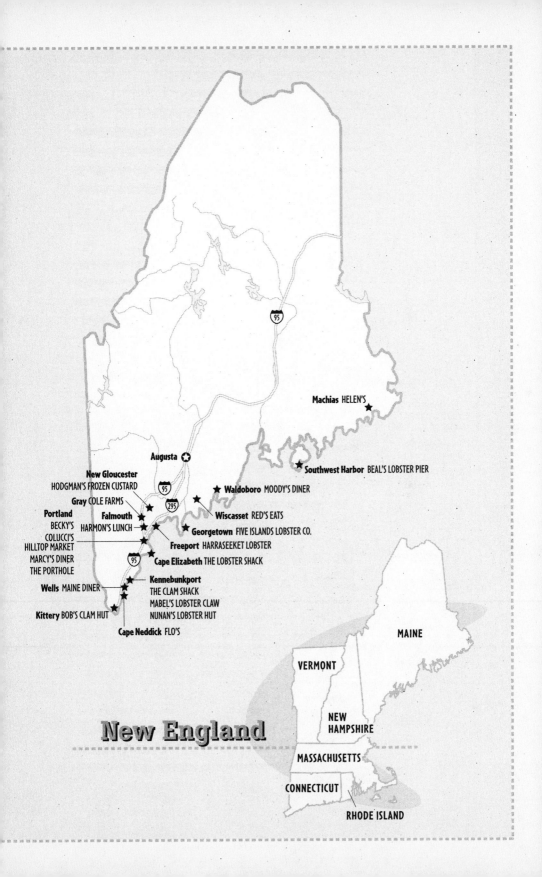

Machias HELEN'S

Southwest Harbor BEAL'S LOBSTER PIER

Augusta

New Gloucester
HODGMAN'S FROZEN CUSTARD

Gray COLE FARMS

Waldoboro MOODY'S DINER

Portland
BECKY'S
COLUCCI'S
HILLTOP MARKET
MARCY'S DINER
THE PORTHOLE

Falmouth
HARMON'S LUNCH

Wiscasset RED'S EATS

Georgetown FIVE ISLANDS LOBSTER CO.

Freeport HARRASEEKET LOBSTER

Cape Elizabeth THE LOBSTER SHACK

Wells MAINE DINER

Kennebunkport
THE CLAM SHACK
MABEL'S LOBSTER CLAW
NUNAN'S LOBSTER HUT

Kittery BOB'S CLAM HUT

Cape Neddick FLO'S

New England

MAINE

VERMONT

NEW
HAMPSHIRE

MASSACHUSETTS

CONNECTICUT

RHODE ISLAND

Connecticut

Abbott's Lobster in the Rough

117 Pearl St.   860-536-7719
Noank, CT   LD May to Labor Day, then weekends
                                  through mid-Oct | $$

Hugely crowded on nice summer evenings, Abbott's specializes in warm-weather shore dinners. Start with bracing, steel-gray chowder (milkless), then littlenecks on the half shell and/or steamers or mussels by the bucket with broth and butter for dripping. If you arrive with a big appetite, you will need to eat many hors d'oeuvres because the lobsters, cooked to order, can take a while. They are beauties, available in whatever size you need. If you don't have the energy to crack, pick, suck, and pluck your way through a whole one, this is a grand place to have a hot lobster roll—hunks of pink sweet meat bathed in butter, sandwiched inside a warm bun. Cold lobster salad rolls are also available, as are hot and cold crab rolls.

Abbott's is one of the prettiest places in Connecticut to dine al fresco. Seating is at bare wooden tables, either in the open or under tents. Civilized sorts actually bring their own tablecloths as well as their own wine. The air is filled with the salty smack of shore breezes, and background music is provided by gulls screeching in the sky (but kept away from the tables by invisible netting).

Big Dipper

91 Waterbury Rd.   203-758-3200
Prospect, CT $

Two words to the wise: toasted almond. Inspired by the traditional Good Humor bar but infinitely more delicious, this creamy, nutty stuff has the luxuriousness of marzipan and the all-American appeal of a sunny Independence Day. It is but one of a multitude of Big Dipper flavors, which include plain vanilla, silky chocolate, silly cotton candy, and a shockingly sophisticated cinnamon-coffee Cafe Vienna. Because it is not cloyingly rich, Big Dipper ice cream begs to be eaten in large quantities or in such indulgences as a triple-dip fudge sundae. The line stretches far out the door on a pleasant night; and the staff is famously fun to deal with.

Blackie's

2200 Waterbury Rd.   203-699-1819
Cheshire, CT   LD (closed Fri) | $

Blackie's just may serve the best hot dog in Connecticut, a state with high hot dog standards. While there are a couple of other items on the menu (hamburgers, cheeseburgers), hot dogs are so entirely the specialty of the house that regular customers sit down at the counter and simply call out a number, indicating how many they want.

They are pink Hummel-brand plumpies that are boiled in oil to the point that they literally blossom with flavor as their outside surface bursts apart from heat. They are served plain in barely toasty buns, and it is up to each customer to spoon out mustard and relish from condiment trays that are set out all along the counter. That's the really good part about dining at Blackie's: dressing the dogs. The mustard is excellent, and we recommend a modest bed of it applied to the top of each wiener, all the better for the relish to cling to. The relish is transcendent: thick, luxurious, dark green, and pepper-hot enough that your lips will glow after lunch. Blackie's—and its customers—are so devoted to this formula for frankfurter perfection that the kitchen doesn't even bother to offer sauerkraut or chili.

Blackie's is a charming dog house, especially in good weather when the long counter offers semi–al fresco seating. Service is nearly instantaneous, so if your preference is *hot* hot dogs, it is entirely practical to order them one by one until you can't eat any more.

Note that Blackie's is closed on Friday, a policy that dates back to when customers observed the Catholic prohibition against meat-eating.

Carminuccio's

76 S. Main St. (Route 25)   203-364-1133
Newtown, CT   LD | $

Located in a yellow clapboard house by the side of the road, Carminuccio's doesn't look like one of the great pizzerias of the Northeast, but it is. At the small array of bare-topped tables or on the patio to the side, customers eat pizzas on a level with New Haven's best.

The underside of the crust is a mouth-watering fright, tawny dough smudged and blackened and speckled with crumbs. "Sometimes right after we clean the oven, customers get mad because their pizza has none of that good grit," says Eddie Martino, who, with former partner David Kennedy, opened the pizzeria ten years ago. Their ovens are common—no wood fire or brick floor—nor do they use a screen to keep air flowing underneath. And yet the crust on a Carminuccio's pizza—patted out to about two-thirds the thickness of a traditional Neapolitan pie—has such a sturdy crunch that you can hold a hot slice by the edge and the center will not wilt. Even with meat and vegetables on top it stays sturdy from the outer edge almost to the point, and no matter what ingredients you get, topping slippage is rare. "Nobody wants a pizza where the cheese is floating in oil and the crust droops," Martino declares.

He tells us that New Haven–made sausage, strewn edge-to-edge in countless little pinches, is cooked and well-drained of fat before a pie is assembled and baked, thus ensuring the cheese stays cheesy and the crust dry. Vegetables are precooked in a convection oven, a process that not only saps crust-threatening moisture but dramatically intensifies the flavor of such toppings as spinach, onions, and tomatoes. Garlic especially benefits from the process, each whole clove caramelized to its soft essence. Before learning how it is done, we would have sworn the brilliant flavor of the kitchen's supple red pepper strips came from marinade and/or seasoning. But they are unadulterated red peppers roasted to a sunny concentrate. Combine the peppers with roasted garlic and you have a magisterial combo, one of the nation's essential pizza-eating experiences.

Colony Grill

172 Myrtle Ave.   203-359-2184

Stamford, CT   LD | $$

Stamford's Colony Grill wins our vote as the most unlikely source of excellent pizza. Opened as a speakeasy during Prohibition and run by Irishmen ever since, it is a neighborhood tavern in the shadow of I-95, where there isn't much neighborhood left. Modern life seemingly has had scant effect here. A sign above the dining room door still advises, "No Stags Allowed," referring to the bygone policy of not allowing single men to walk from the bar into the room where respectable people have supper. The wood-paneled walls are decorated with hundreds of portraits of servicemen from decades past and black-and-white group photos commemorating moments of camaraderie among patrons and staff. Still a hangout where many come just for shots and beers and conversation, Colony's elbow-bending personality was established by Eugene "Bobo" Bohannan, who bought it in 1961 after working as a waiter following his discharge from the U.S. Navy after World War II. "He used to know everyone who came in," says his son Gary James, who now runs it with his brother Jim Screwse. Gary notes that Bobo and Robert "Fitzy" Fitzmaurice, who was a waiter from 1946 to 2005, are the only two people who know the identity of every one of the portraits on the wall. "Guys come in with their kids to show them pictures of their fathers," he says.

Pizza is the only food on the menu, available in one size, about a foot-and-a-half in diameter with crust as thin as a saltine. Nobody recalls how the recipe was developed, sometime in the late 1940s, and no one will share its secrets, other than Jim Screwse's joke that "It must be the good Stamford water." Gary said that the process of making dough begins very early every morning about three hours after the bar closes at night, and he told us that the original ovens are sacrosanct. Aside from the wild crunch of their crust, Colony pizzas are known for sweet sausage made across the street at another neighborhood survivor, DeYulio's Sausage Co., and for the optional topping called "hot oil": peppery olive oil that imbues them with zest and lusciousness unlike any other.

Pizzas—one per person, please—arrive on age-dented metal trays along with paper plates so flimsy they are useless, except as an emergency order pad when a waitress can't find anything else to write on. Each slice is crisp and yet so sumptuously oily that your fingers are guaranteed to glisten, even if you forgo the wonderful hot oil. Postprandial wreckage on the table is a giddy bedlam of severely battered trays piled with count-less balled-up, twisted paper napkins. Napkins are the only essential utensil for eating a Colony Grill pizza.

Doogie's

2525 Berlin Turnpike	860-666-6200
Newington, CT	LD | $

Doogie's used to boast that it was "Home of the 2-foot hot dog," but price increases have reduced the size of the jumbo dog to a mere sixteen inches. Firm-fleshed and with a chewy skin that gets slightly charred on the grill, it has a vigorously spicy flavor that holds up well not only under any and all extra-cost toppings, but does well when spread with Doogie's superb homemade hot relish or just ordinary mustard. For those of meek appetite, the same good frank is available in a mere ten-inch configura-tion, too.

Doogie's hamburgers, cooked on the charcoal grill where the hot dogs are made, have a delicious smoky flavor. The top-of-the-line ham-burger is described on the menu as "the ultimate," and while not as awe-some as the elongated hot dog, it is quite a sight: two five-ounce patties with bacon, cheese, grilled onions, and sautéed mushrooms. Its formal name on the menu is the Murder Burger.

Beyond hot dogs and hamburgers, Doogie's makes a heck of a good Philly cheesesteak as well as all sorts of other sandwiches, New En-gland–style clam chowder, a hot lobster roll, and that junkiest of junk foods, so beloved hereabouts—fried dough. Doogie's fried dough, a plate-size disc of deep-fried dough, is available veiled in cinnamon sugar or under a blanket of red tomato sauce. Either way, it is a mouthful!

Dottie's Diner @ Phillips

740 S. Main St. (Route 6)	203-263-2516
Woodbury, CT	BL | $$

We were sad to hear in 2006 that the Phillips family was getting out of the restaurant business. Phillips Diner, along Antiques Row in Wood-bury, had been hunger's destination for decades, its donuts and chicken pies without peer. We miss Bud and his daughters and in-laws and the late Mrs. Phillips and the kibitzing they encouraged around the counter, especially early in the morning.

But for donut lovers and chicken pie lovers, the news is good. New owner Dotty Sperry is on the beam. "I knew I had to keep the best of the old place," she told us, "but I wanted to add my personality, too." The chicken pie is an example. Traditional farmhouse chicken pie is still available, and still made by the Phillips family: a savory crust, top and bottom, loaded with warm, moist chicken meat. Dottie's own version, which includes gravy, peas, and carrots, is an option for $1 more. The gravy has changed from the old-style white cream to a darker, spicier sauce. The mashed potatoes are the genuine article; they and cranberry sauce have been supplemented on the plate with a sprig of al dente broccoli and a few thin, buttery slices of cooked squash.

As for the donuts, they remain excellent; on some occasions, better than ever. Cinnamon donuts are creamy inside with a crunchy exterior; chocolate donuts come loaded with vast amounts of the glossy dark glaze that so perfectly complements the cake within.

Dottie has spiffed things up with retro aqua upholstery in the booths and a new counter, but the community feeling essential to the soul of a diner still can be felt. During a recent visit, we had a hard time sidelining Dottie to have a chat with, she was so busy schmoozing with her customers.

Dr. Mike's

158 Greenwood Ave. 203-792-4388
Bethel, CT LD | $

Forget psychotherapy and medication! The best antidepressant we know is a visit to the good Dr. Mike of Bethel. The cones and cardboard cups dished out year-round by this little shop are a miracle cure. As hopeless ice cream addicts, we must tell you that there is nothing quite like Dr. Mike's, and there are occasions when its ultrarichness is actually too, too much. If you like lots and lots of ice cream, this is the wrong stuff. A single scoop can be overwhelming.

The longtime standard-bearer, Rich Chocolate, for example, is stunningly flavored, cocoa brown, and more deliriously chocolaty than a pure melted Hershey's bar, but with the added luxury of all that high-butterfat cream. Chocolate Lace and Cream is another Dr. Mike's invention, made with a chocolate-covered hard candy produced by a local confectionery. The candy is broken into bite-size pieces and suspended in a pure white emulsion of sweetened cream: another dreamy experience, but in this case our warning is to get it in a cup. The crunch of the candy conflicts with the crunch of a cone.

We've named our two favorite flavors. Don't hesitate, though, if you find your personal favorite among the approximately six varieties available on any particular day. Each one is made the old-fashioned way, using cream from dairy buckets, in five-gallon batches, and we have fond memories of Dr. Mike's coffee, coconut, cinnamon, Heath Bar crunch, even prune, dazzling vanilla, and some real tongue-stunners made with fresh fruits in the summer.

After you have tasted the ice cream in its unadulterated state, please return to Dr. Mike's for a milk shake or a hot fudge sundae. Sundaes are huge, made so they literally fill up pint ice cream containers. The fudge is dark and dense, faintly granular, and a glorious complement to any of the light colors and fruit flavors. And the freshly whipped cream is heaped on with a trowel.

Harry's Drive-In

104 Broadway   860-537-2410
Colchester, CT   LD (summer only) | $

A completely al fresco eat-place with wood-slat picnic tables arrayed under groves of flowering trees, Harry's has been a favorite stop for people on their way to and from the beach for more than eighty years. One of the best things about coming here is waiting for a meal to be assembled. There is no curb service. Exit your vehicle and stand in line; place an order and pay, then slide sideways to the pickup window. The view is breathtaking: two dozen hamburgers lined up on a glistening hot grill, sizzling and sputtering and oozing juice. They are formed from spheres of meat that get slapped onto the grill and lightly squished so they flatten a bit, but the craggy patties remain unspeakably luscious inside their rugged crust. With a mantle of melted cheese and a few strips of bacon, garnished with slices of summer tomato, lettuce, pickle, and mustard, sandwiched inside a lovely bakery bun and held together with a long toothpick, this might be the best drive-in hamburger anywhere. Hot dogs are grill-cooked, too, and are especially excellent when bedded in a split-top bun atop a spill of Harry's chili sauce.

Kitchen Little

135 Greenmanville Ave.   860-536-2122

Mystic, CT   BL | $

"Kitchen Little" isn't just a cute name. This place on the road to historic Mystic Seaport really is minuscule: 400 square feet, including the kitchen, with tiny tables packed so close together you need to keep an eye on your plate to make sure a neighbor doesn't accidentally fork up a piece of your linguiça sausage.

Because this little eating hut has exactly twenty-three indoor seats, including a handful at a counter with a view of the closet-size kitchen, plus a handful of picnic tables on a deck out back, you must expect to wait almost any day, especially on weekends. If the weather is pleasant, the delay can be delightful. There are a couple of wood-slat benches out front under a tall pole topped with the U.S. flag, and the steel-blue water lapping up against the grassy shore just beyond the café is hypnotic.

"AM Eggstasy" is the house motto, and the omelets are stupendous, as is the Mystic Melt, which is eggs scrambled with crabmeat and cream cheese served with raisin toast on the side. There are Benedicts, heart-healthy egg-white omelets, and sizzled-crisp corned beef hash. If you don't come for breakfast, there is a whole menu of fried clams (strips or whole bellies), a beautiful hot buttered lobster roll, and a half-pound hamburger, plus excellent clam chowder. It is southern New England–style chowder—creamless, steel-gray, and briny—a great winter warm-up meal.

Laurel Diner

544 Main St. South   203-264-8218

Southbury, CT   BL | $

Table seating is available, but we highly recommend a seat at the counter facing the Laurel Diner's pint-size grill. Here you have a spellbinding vision of time-space management as two short-order chefs fry, scramble, and flip eggs, fold omelets, butter toast, pour pancakes, and squish down patties of the diner's legendary corned beef hash.

The hash is a coarse-cut mélange of spicy beef shreds and nuggets of potato cooked on the griddle until a web of crust begins to envelop the tender insides. If you ask, the grill man will cook the hash until it is brittle-crisp nearly all the way through, which is a great idea if textural excitement supersedes succulence in your hierarchy of culinary pleasure, but we personally enjoy it the regular way: forkfuls of corned beef that are brick red and moist, their pickled zest balanced perfectly by the soft pieces of potato.

As for the potatoes that come on the side, there are two choices: chunky home fries, which are excellent, and hash browns, which are even better than that. While the chefs regularly scrape debris into the grill's front gutter, their touch is light enough that the flavors of bacon, ham, sausage, and hash linger, ready to be sucked into heaps of shredded potatoes piled on the hot surface. A broad cake of three or four servings is flattened and remains untouched long enough for the underside to turn gold, then the still-soft top is crowned with a scoop of butter. As the butter melts, the potatoes are flipped and worried so that by the time they are plated, they have become mostly crunchy, but with enough tender white tips to sop up at least two sunnyside yolks.

Adjacent to the Laurel Service Station, the Laurel Diner opens every day at 5:30, and by midmorning, sections of Connecticut's daily papers are strewn almost everywhere, providing easy-reach reading no matter where you sit. The menu is written daily in multicolored marking pens directly on the diner's white wall. If you are hungry and also need an oil change, call ahead to the service station (where the pumps open at seven and the garage at nine) and make an appointment. Your vehicle can be in and out in thirty minutes, which is about as long as it takes to order and enjoy breakfast next door. The service station number is 203–264–9100.

Lenny & Joe's Fish Tale Restaurant

1301 Boston Post Rd. (Route 1)   203-245-7289
Madison, CT   LD | $$

Also at 86 Boston Post Road (Route 1), Westbrook, CT (860-669-0767), and 138 Granite St., Westerly, RI (401-348-9941)

Lenny & Joe's opened as a roadside fried-clam stand in 1979. It has since become three restaurants with vast seafood menus that range from all-you-can-eat Wednesday fish fries (winter months) to whole lobster dinners (summertime) and include virtually every kind of fried seafood known to the human race.

Whole-bellied fried clams are big and succulent with golden crusts. We also love the fried shrimp and scallops, even simple fried fish. All fried items are available in an ample regular-size configuration as well as a "super" plate with double the amount of fish. This is one restaurant where the undecided customer who craves the crunch of fresh-fried seafood will be happy ordering a variety platter with some of everything. It is a gargantuan meal, including crinkle-cut French fries and a little cup of sweet coleslaw. The only other necessary item would be an order of fried onions; Lenny & Joe's are wicked good!

Lobster fanatics know Lenny & Joe's as a reliable source for a hot lobster roll, meaning chunks and shreds of lobster meat drenched in butter and heaped into a butter-toasted long roll. This is pure bliss, with none of the whole-lobster hassle of shell cracking and meat extraction. In season, the kitchen also offers a soft-shell crab roll that is almost as luscious.

Lenny's

205 S. Montowese St. 203-488-1500
Branford, CT LD | $$

A fixture of the Indian Neck section of Branford's coast well known to local cognoscenti, this excellent restaurant is a neighborhood place with a menu that ranges from hamburgers and hot dogs to full shore dinners. The latter includes chowder (either creamy New England–style or clear-broth shoreline-style), a couple of cherrystone clams on the shell, a lobster, a heap of steamers, sweet corn, and a thick slice of watermelon for dessert.

Good as both kinds of chowder are, one should never begin a meal at Lenny's without zuppa d'clams: six steamed-open cherrystones in a bowl of briny, lemon-laced broth, with a half-loaf of bread on the side for dunking. Delicious! Many of Lenny's best meals are fried: whole-belly clams, succulent oysters, scallops, fish 'n' chips, and huge butterflied shrimp. Crunch-crusted and clean-flavored, these are consummate fried seafood, and proof that a crisp, clean crust can be the ideal complement to seafood's natural sweetness.

Throughout the summer, strawberry shortcake is available for dessert. It is the true Yankee version, made from a sideways-split, unsweetened biscuit layered with sliced berries in a thin sugar syrup, and a mountain of whipped cream. "I make it myself," our waitress boasted, suggesting that one might be enough for the both of us. "It's big!" she said. Yes, it is, but it is so good we recommend getting your own.

Letizia's Pizza

666 Main Ave. (Town Line Shopping Center) 203-847-6022
Norwalk, CT LD | $$

"I wish I had some of that New Haven aura," says Dan Letizia from be-hind the counter of the restaurant he runs with his brother Dennis in a Norwalk strip mall wedged in among Wal-Mart, Outback, Staples, and Starbucks. Letizia's physical aura, such as it is, is that of a modest family-owned deli, walls decorated with heirloom photos of "Uncle Joe" (their grandfather), mementoes of the Brooklyn Dodgers (Papa Letizia's fa-vorite team), and a collage of hockey-player trading cards faded blue from exposure to sunlight. "I put up the cards because the store looked like a hospital room when we moved in," Dan says. "I wanted people to have something to look at while they waited for their pizza."

While the setting isn't much, Letizia's name is part of northeast pizza history, one of the first in the region to serve it—as a weekend-only item—when Joe Letizia opened his restaurant down on Norwalk's Wall Street in 1937. Well after his death in 1962, Uncle Joe's was still known as a source of fine red-sauce meals at rock-bottom prices. The family sold the old place in 1985 (it is now in others' hands), but today's Letizia's, opened by grandson Dan in 1992, still offers baked ziti and manicotti, spaghetti with marinara, and hot-parm grinders on made-here rolls. Those things are fine; however, with pizza this good, they're immaterial.

As is true of New Haven's greats, crust matters immensely. Baked on a screen then further toughened on the oven's brick floor, it is medium-thin Neapolitan-style, chewy more than brittle, with a full, earthy taste. Traditional mozzarella and sauce—the same food service brands the fam-ily has used since the beginning—meld into a creamy Italian-American slurry with veins of tomato tang. Add disks of pepperoni weeping oil into the mix, and you've got a mighty bite that is outrageously juicy. It is best consumed the New York City way, by pulling one triangular slice from the circle and folding it in half along the radius—the crust is pliable enough to bend, not break—creating a trough that holds everything like an open-top calzone.

Louis Lunch

261 Crown St.	203-562-5507
New Haven, CT	L	$

A small brick building with school-desk seats and an ancient wooden counter with years' worth of initials carved into it, Louis Lunch cooks hamburgers in fat-reducing metal broilers that predate George Foreman's Lean Mean Grilling Machine by almost a century. The result is a plump, moist patty with a crusty edge. Ken Lassen, grandson of founder Louis and now a very senior citizen himself, happened to drop by one day in the summer of 2005 to watch his progeny cook burgers and we got into a conversation with him about what makes his hamburgers taste special. He assured us with a straight face that when he was a young man he developed a formula of grinding different cuts in exact proportion to replicate beef from the good old pre-hormone days of full-flavored, range-fed longhorn cattle.

Louis burgers are served on toast because when Louis Lassen began serving them in his little lunch wagon over a hundred years ago, there was no such thing as a hamburger bun. In fact, it is possible that there was no such thing as a hamburger. Some culinary historians believe that this is where the hamburger was invented. Others attribute it to the Tartars or to the Earl of Salisbury or to sailors from Hamburg, Germany, but Louis Lunch devotees contend that it was born of Louis Lassen's thrifty nature. The hamburger was his way of doing something useful with the leftover trimmings from the steak sandwiches he sold at his lunch wagon.

Whichever origin is true, Louis Lunch is an essential stop on America's burger trail. The hamburgers are moist and crusty, available with a schmear of Cheez Whiz, if desired, and the place itself, now run by a fifth generation of the Lassen family, is a taste of culinary history.

Modern Apizza

874 State St.	203-776-5306
New Haven, CT	LD	$$

While it is less famous than Pepe's and Sally's, Modern Apizza, a 1930s-era pizzeria on State Street in New Haven, is one of the earth's best pizza parlors. In addition to its superb pies, it is especially likable for the fact that you will not have to wait forever for a table.

"Our brick oven reaches temperature in excess of 700 degrees,"

Modern's menu warns. "Some pizzas may blacken around the edges, and even lose their perfect shape due to contact with the brick floor of the oven." Okay with us! While a few places around the edge may be charred, the whole pizza has a swoonfully appetizing smoky taste, and you see why when you devour slices off the paper on which the pizza rests atop its round pan. The paper appears strewn with charred little bits of semolina from the oven floor, most of which cling to the underside of the crust, creating a slightly burned hot-bread flavor that no wussy metal-floored pizza oven could produce.

Modern's specialty toppings include broccoli, sliced tomato, arti-choke, and clams casino, which is clams, bacon, and peppers. It is known for the Italian Bomb, which is a joy to eat despite the fact that it totally overwhelms its crust: sausage, pepperoni, bacon, peppers, onions, mush-rooms, and garlic. There is also a Vegetarian Bomb topped with spinach, broccoli, olives, peppers, mushrooms, onion, and garlic. As for the New Haven favorite, white clam pizza (hold the mozzarella, please), Modern uses canned clams, not fresh, meaning there is less soulful marine juice to infuse the pizza; nevertheless, it is delicious—ocean sweet and powerfully garlicky, and built on a crust that puffs up dry and chewy around the edges, but stays wafer thin all across the middle.

The Olive Market

19 Main St.   203-544-8134
Georgetown, CT   BLD | $$

Full disclosure: We live around the corner from the Olive Market and we're good friends with the guys who run it. When we are home in the morning and need to grab a cup of really good strong coffee or a bacon, egg, and cheese sandwich, the Olive Market is where we go. So, although its main specialty—Uruguayan food—doesn't exactly fit the definition of Roadfood as an expression of local culture, and although its inventory includes hoity-toity olive oils, imported cheeses, and boutique pasta, we do love it enough to recommend it to anyone passing through.

In fact, it is a swell place for a quick breakfast or lunch that's fairly easy on the wallet. The menu ranges from French toast and pancakes to exotic grilled sandwiches and ultra–thin crust pizzas. Grilling things is the house forte. Pizzas and flatbread sandwiches inhale a smoky savor from being cooked on the grill. Especially notable is a sandwich known as a *chivito*. That's a protein-eater's delight of sliced steak with thin layers of ham and provolone cheese plus a fried egg, all on a beautiful hunk of bread crowned with a single olive.

On weekend nights the Olive Market goes from casual to awesome. That is when co-owner Fernando Pereyra shows off the cooking of his native Uruguay by offering, among other things, a stupendous "Gaucho dinner" for two or four people: an immense platter crowded with skewers of filet mignon, individual pork ribs, spicy chicken wings, teriyaki chicken skewers, and unbelievably luscious little lamb chops. In the center of this feast are ramekins of peanut dipping sauce, garlicky chimichurri sauce, and, of course, olives.

By the way, the coffee upon which Jane insists here is a specialty known as a *cortado*—strictly for those who like it ultra strong. Normal coffee and espresso drinks are also available.

Pepe's Pizzeria Napoletana

157 Wooster St.   203-865-5762
New Haven, CT   LD | $$

Also at 238 Commerce Dr., Fairfield, CT (203-333-7373)

Dating back to 1923, Pepe's Pizzeria Napoletana is a brash neighborhood joint on New Haven's pizza parlor row that makes what we have long considered to be the best pizza on earth. Any toppings are fine (pepperoni especially so), and the crust is sensational—brittle at its edges, ruggedly chewy where it puffs up, scattered on its crisp underside with burned grains of semolina from the oven's brick floor. The best pizza of all is white clam, which Frank Pepe created sometime midcentury after discussing the idea with a vendor selling littlenecks in a Wooster Street alley near the pizza parlor. It is an elementary pie strewn with freshly opened littleneck clams and their nectar, a scattering of grated sharp Romano, a salvo of coarsely minced garlic, and a drizzle of oil. No mozzarella, no tomato sauce: pure elegance.

In 2006, Pepe's Pizzeria opened a second store in Fairfield, Connecticut, where the family has almost exactly duplicated the old New Haven kitchen and oven and where, to our amazement, the pizza can be every bit as excellent if not, on occasion, even better. One big difference is the Fairfield waitstaff, which actually is courteous rather than New Haven brusque. Still, they're all business. Our waiter virtually sprinted to the table three minutes after we were seated. We hadn't looked at the wall-mounted menu but he nevertheless demanded to know what we wanted. "Order now," he commanded. "They're backed up on pizzas in the kitchen." Toward the end of the meal, after he decided we were okay because we ordered the right things and ate them all, he confided, "We must have a lot of good New Haven people here today. They're ordering the classics—white clam, plain tomato. You know someone is a novice when they ask for bacon with their clams or for extra mozzarella."

The Pepe's dining experience has no amenities. Pizzas arrive on metal trays and silverware is flimsy and useless. When two people order the same soft drink, the waiter suggests a quart, which is brought to the table, along with tumblers full of ice, for customers to pour for themselves.

The Place

891 Boston Post Rd.   203-453-9276
Guilford, CT   D (summer only) | $$

Harold "Whitey" Miller was a Connecticut clam digger who sold littlenecks off the back of a truck in New Haven County. One cold day in the mid-1940s, he laid some clams on a metal grate and put the grate over a hardwood fire he had lit in an oil drum to keep warm. As heat opened the shells and the air filled with a briny smell, passersby offered to pay Whitey to eat some of his fire-cooked clams. Soon, he set up shop as a grilled-clam stand, and in 1966 he opened an al fresco restaurant in a grove of trees by Route 1 in Guilford. Informality ruled. Plates were paper; customers had to bring not only their own wine and beer, but also bread and salad if they wanted some. In lieu of chairs around the picnic tables, Whitey offered seats made of tree stumps cut smooth on top. To let passersby know he was there, he put up a sign that said, "There's no place anything like this place anywhere near this place so this must be the place."

Route 1 has gone from an ambling country road to a congested, mall-lined shopping strip, but at The Place, you still sit on tree stumps in the open air and eat clams, lobsters, and corn-on-the-cob cooked over an open fire. "Magic happens when you roast clams on a wood fire," says Vaughn Knowles, who began working for Whitey as a high-school student and, with his brother Gary, bought the business in 1971. It is such an appetizing moment when the clams pop open on the grate above the flames that many customers stand around the 20-foot-long fireplace just to watch. The Place's Specials are to die for: as soon as the clam opens, the hollow half of its shell is removed and the clam is dabbed with cocktail sauce and margarine. It is then returned to the fire long enough for the sauce to darken and the clam to free itself from the shell. Specials are served with a wooden fork to pluck the clam. Once the meat is eaten, true joy is slurped from the bottom of the shell: an elixir of clam broth, sauce, and margarine.

Corn also is transformed by direct-fire cooking. The husk turns dark and brittle; its surface dimples from the imprint of the kernels inside. The charred husk and silk easily slip away and the whole cob gets a quick dip in butter before being served.

"This is nothing like a normal restaurant, where customers walk in with long faces expecting a serious meal," Vaughn says. "It is not unusual for half our tables to be occupied by birthday or anniversary parties or even wedding rehearsal dinners. Late at night, Yale teams come to enjoy themselves and toast marshmallows over the fire. Eating here is fun. When people think of The Place, they smile."

Those who become regulars earn a special honor. Vaughn inscribes their name in white paint on one of the tree stumps that serve as chairs. "It makes sense," he explains. "Over many years, returning families come to think of The Place as *their* place, so it's only right to honor them. I tell them they have become stumpworthy."

Rawley's Drive-In

1886 Post Rd.	203-259-9023
Fairfield, CT	LD | $

Rawley's defined a way of cooking hot dogs that has become gospel for many of the important frank emporia in southwestern Connecticut. Here a dog gets deep-fried. When plump and darkened, it is pulled from the hot vegetable oil and rolled around on the griddle with a spatula—a finishing touch that strains off excess oil and gives the exterior a delectable crackle. The dog is then bedded in a high-quality roll that has been spread open, brushed with butter, and toasted on the griddle until its interior surfaces are crisp, in contrast to the outside, which remains soft and pliant. The kitchen does the dressing, the most popular configuration being mustard and relish topped with sauerkraut and garnished with a fistful of chewy bacon shreds. To our taste, it is a perfect combination, although "heavy bacon"—twice as much—is a popular option.

The restaurant is pint-size: four booths plus a six-stool counter on what used to be a front porch, where an open picture window provides a scenic view into the lively short-order kitchen. As plebeian as can be, Rawley's is known for attracting celebrities who live or summer in the area. Paul Newman, Meg Ryan, and David Letterman have all been spotted eating these fine hot dogs, and Martha Stewart used to be a regular.

Ridgefield Ice Cream Shop

680 Danbury Rd.   203-438-3094
Ridgefield, CT $

A former Carvel stand, the Ridgefield Ice Cream Shop makes quintessential soft-serve ice cream by using machines from Carvel's early days when the formula was not pumped full of air. The resulting lick—our favorite ice cream anywhere—is not sinfully rich or weird-flavored or in any way surprising. It is smooth, dense, and pure, and while it is available with all sorts of toppings, coating, nuts, and fruits, we like ours au naturel: a swirly mound of it piled up on an elegant wafer cone. For those who live nearby, there are also extraordinary ice cream cakes made from the same frozen manna and layered with icing and crumbled cookies.

Although it has a sunny, summertime feel, Ridgefield Ice Cream is open year-round, rain or shine. In good weather, customers lick their cones leaning on their cars in the lot or at one of the picnic tables out front.

Roseland Apizza

350 Hawthorne Ave.   203-735-0494
Derby, CT   D Tues–Sun | $$$

Roseland Apizza (pronounce that second word the Neapolitan way, "ah-BEETS") started as a bakery in 1934. Today, it has a menu of hand-cut ravioli, four-star lasagna, and a board full of nightly specials featuring shellfish and pasta, but it is most famous for its brick-oven pies. The crust is what connoisseurs know as New Haven–style—thin but not quite brittle, with enough brawn to support all but the weightiest combinations of ingredients and to allay the pizza eater's primal fears: slice collapse and topping slippage.

Baker Gary Lucarelli uses two ovens to cook pizzas, one that runs hot for those made with the sturdy meats and vegetables typical of pizzeria menus, the other slower for white pizzas topped with fragile seafood. Roseland makes some spectacularly lavish pies, such as a shrimp casino topped with bacon, mozzarella, fresh garlic, and too many jumbo shrimp to count, but for us, the one must-eat specialty is the relatively uncomplicated Connecticut classic, white clam pizza. Recommended configuration: no mozzarella, no tomato sauce, just a crowd of freshly shucked Rhode Island clams strewn across a crust slicked with olive oil and scattered with bits of basil, parsley, and oregano, thin-sliced garlic, a twist of cracked black pepper, and a scattering of grated Parmigiano-Reggiano. The nectar of the whole clams insinuates itself into the surface of the crust, giving every crunch exhilarating marine zest.

Sally's Apizza

237 Wooster St.   203-624-5271
New Haven, CT   D | $$

"Sally" was Sal Consiglio, the nephew of Frank Pepe, and in 1938, about a dozen years after Frank Pepe opened New Haven's first pizzeria, Sal broke away and started his own just down Wooster Street. Sal himself is gone, but his wife, Flo, still runs the old pizza parlor. So Sally's and Pepe's are still in the same extended family. There are some aficionados who love one much more than the other; but in truth, each has its charms, and both make superb pizza.

Sally's has soul. The place glows with old-neighborhood feel: wood-paneled walls, booths with well-worn Formica-topped tables, ubiquitous images of Frank Sinatra (a fan of Sal's cooking) all over the walls. And the pizza packs a wallop. It is generously topped, well-oiled, and comes on a thin crust that is smudged and gritty underneath. While the kitchen's version of the New Haven specialty, white clam pizza, is second-rate (made using canned clams), it does turn out two outstanding pizzas that are Sally's alone: fresh tomato pie (made only when good fresh tomatoes are available) with thick circles of tomato, creamy mozzarella, and hails of garlic, and broccoli rabe pie, heaped with bitter greens when they are available at the Long Wharf produce market. Although it is not formally listed on the menu, Sally's multimeat "Italian bomb" (sausage, pepperoni, bacon, plus lots of onions) is also significant.

Old friends of Sally's are treated like royalty. Newcomers and unknowns might feel like they have to wait forever, first for a table, then for their pizza, and they will likely endure a staff who are at best nonchalant, but no one comes to Wooster Street for polished service or swank ambience. It's great, thin-crust pizza that counts, and on that score, Sally's delivers the goods.

Shady Glen

840 East Middle Turnpike   860-649-4245

Manchester, CT   BLD | $

Shady Glen makes some of the most dramatic cheeseburgers you ever will see. On a high-temperature electric grill, each circular patty of beef is cooked on one side, flipped, then blanketed with several square slices of cheese. The cheese is arranged so that only one-quarter to one-third of each slice rests atop the hamburger. The remainder extends beyond the circumference of the meat and melts down onto the surface of the grill. At the exact moment the grilling cheese begins to transform from molten to crisp, the cook uses a spatula to disengage it from the grill and curl it above the meat like some wondrous burgerflower—still slightly pliable, but rising up in certain symmetry. The petals of cheese, which may be topped with condiments and are crowned by a bun, are crunchy at their tip but chewy where they blend into the soft parts that adhere to the hamburger.

The restaurant originally was opened in 1948 by John and Bernice Reig in order to put something on the menu of their dairy bar other than homemade ice cream. The ice cream is fantastic, including such seasonal flavors as mince pie, cranberry, and pumpkin in the fall and the outstanding February specialty, bing cherry and chocolate chip. Our personal flavor faves include Grape-Nuts and Almond Joy.

Shiek's Sandwich Shop

235 E. Elm St.   860-489-5576

Torrington, CT   BL | $

Roadfooder Charles Cramer is the angel who directed us to Shiek's Sandwich Shop in Torrington, Connecticut. He wasn't the first tipster to sing its praises, but the former Torringtonian, now living in the orbit of Boston, made us an offer we couldn't refuse: "If you try it out and feel as though I've led you astray, I will gladly and willingly reimburse you for your meals."

We wound up paying our own way, with pleasure. This little joint is a treasure, and not only for sandwiches. Since visiting the first time, we have returned for excellent fresh salads, top-notch diner breakfasts, and serious Yankee chili. It is strictly a breakfast-and-lunch operation, closing midafternoon six days a week, and at mealtimes, the counter and scattering of tables tend to be mobbed. Since so many people who know about Shiek's are regulars, it's not at all uncommon for conversations to take place table to table, table to counter, in front of and behind the counter, and all across the cozy dining area.

The ringmaster of the whole affair is Gary Arnold, who manages to carry on at least a couple of conversations at the same time as he works the grill, builds sandwiches, and packs lunches to go for the takeout trade. One day we were seated at the counter with a mother and her adult son who explained that whenever the son returns home to Torrington, this is where they go, not only to eat but also to feel very much a part of the community that is theirs.

Charles Cramer said the sandwich to eat at Shiek's is "hot" roast beef, which means slices are cut to order from the roast and tossed on the grill to heat, then sandwiched in a grinder roll with provolone, romaine lettuce, roasted green peppers, grilled onions, and mayonnaise and/or mustard. Delicious!

The other specialité de la maison is hot dogs. They are big plump ones available with all the usual condiments, plus a hot relish that is nearly as addictive as that served at Blackie's in Cheshire (p. 6). There's a good meaty chili available as a topping, too.

Super Duper Weenie

306 Black Rock Turnpike	203-334-DOGS
Fairfield, CT	LD | $

A former dog wagon, now a stationary restaurant with indoor seating, Super Duper Weenie is without peer. Its hot dog is a firm-fleshed, locally made sausage that is split and cooked on the grill until its outside gets a little crusty but the inside stays moist. It is sandwiched in a lovely fresh-baked roll and adorned with utterly amazing condiments—homemade condiments, including relish made from pickles that Chef Gary Zamola has himself made from cucumbers! The sauerkraut, the hot relish, the meat chili, the onion sauce are *all* made from scratch.

You can get whatever you like on a hot dog, but Super Duper Weenie makes it easy (and fast) by offering certain basic configurations. These include the New Englander, which Gary devised based on his own fond memories of the superior franks served at Jimmie's of Savin Rock in West Haven and at Rawley's in Fairfield: it's a dog topped with sauerkraut, bacon, mustard, sweet relish, and raw onion. The New Yorker, Gary says, was inspired by what is served from Gotham's street-corner carts (but we dare say it is 1000 percent better than any dirty water weenie we've eaten in Manhattan): sauerkraut, onion sauce, mustard, and hot relish. There is a Chicagoan topped with lettuce, tomato, mustard, celery salt, relish, and a pickle spear; a dynamite Dixie dog that is topped with hot meaty chili and rests atop a bed of sweet homemade coleslaw (inspired by a North Carolina hot dog Gary likes); and there is a Georgia red hot, which is a spicy sausage with the works.

Whatever you order, you must have French fries. These are beautiful, fresh-cut twigs of potato that are served fresh from the fry-basket and made extra-delicious by a perfect sprinkle of salt and pepper.

Sycamore Drive-In

282 Greenwood Ave.   203-748-2716
Bethel, CT   BLD | $

Hamburgers at the Sycamore Drive-In are made in an unusual way known as French-style. What that means here in Bethel, Connecticut, is that the grill man slaps a thick circle of beef onto the grill then uses his spatula to flatten it out so far that the edges are nearly paper thin. As the burger cooks, the middle gets juicy while the circumference turns into a crusty web of beef. You can get it plain, doubled, or topped with all sorts of ingredients, but the connoisseur's choice is the Dagwood burger. That's a pair of patties with cheese and nearly every garnish known to mankind piled into a bun.

Beyond hamburgers, the Sycamore also offers frankfurters topped with bacon and sauerkraut, a fine "pot o' beans" (baked), and good chili. It is famous for root beer, made on premises from a top-secret recipe and served in frosty glass mugs. The root beer varies from sweet to dry, depending on where in the barrel your serving comes from, but whatever its nature on any day, it always makes the perfect basis for a root beer float.

The Sycamore is a genuine drive-in with carhop service (blink your lights) and window trays for in-car dining. Indoors, there are booths and a long counter. And in the summer, on weekend evenings, Cruise Nights attract hordes of vintage car collectors in their finest restored and custom vehicles. It's a true blast from the past!

Ted's

1046 Broad St.	203-237-6660
Meriden, CT	L	$

Central Connecticut is home to about a half-dozen restaurants that all make steamed cheeseburgers, a regional specialty so geographically focused that even people in eastern and western Connecticut have never heard of it. A steamer, as served at Ted's (since 1959), is cooked not on a grill or grate, but in a steam cabinet, the meat held inside a square tin as it browns. Adjacent to the beef in the cabinet are tins into which are placed blocks of Vermont cheddar. The cheese turns molten and is ladled atop the burger in a hard roll (preferably with lettuce, tomato, pickle, and mustard). Curiously, this dish was created in the 1920s, when eating steamed food was a health fad.

Ted's is a tiny place with four booths, but the best place to sit is at the counter—a short slice of Roadfood heaven. Here the seats provide a view of the twin steam boxes, the bin of chopped meat from which fistfuls are grabbed for burgers, as well as a pile of hard rolls and big blocks of cheese ready to be melted.

Timothy's

2974 Fairfield Ave.	203-366-7496
Bridgeport, CT	$

The antique hand-cranked, salt-and-ice churners in the windows of Timothy's are now only for display purposes, but the ice cream you will eat here does have the kind of extreme purity and goodness you'd expect from a farm-churned brand. We adore the elemental Sweet Cream (dulcet white with no flavor other than dairy sweetness) and supercharged Black Rock (French vanilla studded with chocolate-covered almonds), and the Dutch Chocolate is simply the most chocolaty ice cream possible. Waffle cones are made on premises in irons behind the counter, and they are broad mouthed enough to hold multiple scoops dolloped with fudge and whipped cream.

Dining facilities include tables inside and a few chairs out on the sidewalk that are good for watching traffic pass on Fairfield Avenue. A big bonus of Timothy's location is the fact that it is around the corner from both Super Duper Weenie (p. 24) and the Fairfield location of Pepe's Pizzeria Napoletana (p. 18).

Whistle Stop Muffins

20 Portland Ave.   203-544-8139
Georgetown, CT   BL | $

Located inside the Branchville, Connecticut, train station where commuters hop Metro North on their way to the city, Whistle Stop caters to people with little time to sit and eat. We aren't commuters, but even when we buy a couple of sticky buns to take home, which is a mere two miles away, it is not likely both will arrive at the kitchen table. They're too much fun to eat while still warm, and frankly, licking the caramel goo off one's fingers is part of the pleasure. When Whistle Stop originally opened, muffins were the only thing on the menu; there are still about a dozen varieties baked every morning, as well as rich-textured scones, biscotti, and other sweet coffee companions.

While most customers get their breakfast to go, it is a pleasure to take your muffin and a cup of coffee to the adjoining "waiting room," where there are a few tables for those in no hurry to eat, sip, and read the morning paper.

Beal's Lobster Pier

182 Clark Point Rd.   207-244-7178
Southwest Harbor, ME   LD (summer only) | $$

Beal's is on a working lobster pier. Picnic tables overlook the harbor; from them, you can see the mountains of Acadia National Park in the distance and listen to the water rippling against the hulls of berthed fishing boats. At sunset, it is magic.

Inside, select a lobster from the tank; while waiting for it to boil, eat your way through a bucket of steamer clams or dip into a cup of chowder. Lobsters come pre-cracked for easy meat extraction, but it's still some work. If a handsome whole one is too challenging a proposition, you can also get a lobster roll—tightly packed, with plenty of fresh, cool meat atop a cushion of shredded lettuce. Burgers and a few other non-lobster meals also are available. Desserts vary; we have enjoyed blueberry cake and ice cream.

Becky's

390 Commercial St.   207-773-7070

Portland, ME   BLD | $

To say Becky's is a friendly place only hints at its sociability. If you are a newcomer and walk in the door any time after 5:00 A.M., you might think you have suddenly crashed some sort of predawn party of ravenous coffee hounds. Becky loves her varied clientele. "No matter who you are 'out there,' when you walk into Becky's Diner, you are one of us," she says. "Side by side at my counter sit fishermen and captains of industry, college professors and paranoid schizophrenics. They talk to each other and they talk to those who work here. We are all family."

The breakfast menu includes homemade muffins, French toast made from locally baked Italian bread, and "loaded" hash brown potatoes, which are mixed with peppers and onions and blanketed with melted cheese. There is a full array of the usual breakfast sandwiches, and one sandwich that isn't usual at all: peanut butter and bacon. "I guess it's a breakfast sandwich," Becky chuckled. We love the "Titanic omelet," loaded with all three breakfast meats, cheese, onions, and peppers, and accompanied, preferably, by Portland's favorite morning breadstuff, toasted Italian bread. Home fries come plain, with onions, with green peppers, with cheese, or with all of the above.

Lunch and supper are swell. Baked beans and franks is as classic a platter as you'll find anywhere in New England, as is the frequent special of pot roast, which is basically an old-fashioned boiled dinner. We've savored hot turkey plates, seafood chowder (every Friday), fish and chips, and Italian sausage sandwiches, as well as handsome slices of Becky's jumbo layer cake.

Bob's Clam Hut

315 US Route 1   207-439-4233

Kittery, ME   LD | $$

What Roadfood adventurer could say no to Bob's simple motto: "Eat Clams"? Fried clams, clam cakes, clam chowder, and clamburgers are all wonderful, but in fact they are just the headliners on a long menu of excellent Downeast seafood.

Seafood rolls are showpieces, and not just those piled with fried whole-belly clams or clam strips. You can have them loaded with scallops, shrimp, and oysters (all fried) or with crab, shrimp salad, or lobster. The lobster roll, a high-ticket item at about $12, is a beaut, served in a nice warm bun that is buttered and grilled until toasty golden brown on both sides; the lobster meat inside is faintly chilled, but not so much that any of the taste has been iced. In fact, this lobster blossoms with bracing ocean flavor when you sink your teeth into the good-size pieces. There is plenty of meat, bound with enough mayo to help it hold together. The taste that lingers, though, is not the mayonnaise. It is lobster and its butter-sopped bun. On the side of most seafood dishes comes Bob's excellent tartar sauce, a perfect balance of richness and zest.

The method of ordering and getting food at Bob's is the immemorial Yankee clam hut ritual. There is no table service. Either outdoors or at the indoor counter, you read the posted menu, then place your order and pay in advance. If it is summer and you are outside in the bright sun, you will not see anything in the darkened interior, including the person taking your order, and it is all done so fast your eyes don't adjust. No matter. The order-taker hands you a number, then you dawdle outside around the pickup window (different from the order window) until your number is called over a loudspeaker. Dine either from the dashboard of your car, indoors at utilitarian tables and counter, or at one of Bob's blue-checked picnic tables outside.

The Clam Shack

Route 9 at the bridge   207-967-2560
Kennebunkport, ME   LD (summer only) | $$

The Clam Shack anchors one end of the bridge that connects Kennebunk to Kennebunkport. Fried clams, sold by the pint, are some of the best anywhere—crisp-crusted and heavy with juice-bursting marine succulence—but it's lobster rolls that are stratospheric. Big hunks of fresh-picked meat are arrayed across the bottom of a very nice round bakery roll. It is your choice to have them bathed in warm butter or dolloped with cool mayonnaise before the roll's top is planted. It is not a huge sandwich, dimensionally speaking, but its flavor is immeasurable: a Maine summer pleasure to make any lobster-lover weak-kneed.

Whole lobsters are boiled and sold from an adjoining store that is also a seafood market and bait and tackle shop. Upon receiving a cooked lobster, and maybe a half-pound of steamer clams, it is the customer's job to find a place to eat. There are benches on a deck in back and seats facing the sidewalk in front, where fish crates serve as makeshift tables. (Town zoning forbids proper seating here.) Potatoes? Rolls? Corn? Dessert? None are available. You are on your own. The store does sell bottles of beer and wine.

Cole Farms

Route 100   207-657-4714
Gray, ME   BLD | $

Inland Maine, east of Sebago Lake, waitress Dawn Ross grieved as she arrived at our booth with a steaming hot plate of lipstick-red franks and beans; "The red hot dog is going the way of beef liver," she declared. We had come to Cole Farms looking for vintage Downeast meals. Of all the nation's regional cooking styles, none is as endearingly candid and so ir-redeemably unfashionable as what you get in an old Maine diner. Forget such culinary values as creativity and sensual delight. What matters here are parsimony and plainness. Opened as a farmland diner in 1952, Cole Farms still can be relied on to serve such parochial arcana as boiled dinner and mince pie in the autumn, corn chowder every Wednesday, and a choice of sweet beverages that includes both milk shakes (no ice cream, just milk and flavoring) and frappes (what the rest of the world knows as a milk shake, made with ice cream).

We want to call the kidney beans on the lunch platter puritanical: no syrup, minimal sugar, only hints of spice. Each distinct one is a sturdy packet with silk-smooth skin and flavor that is nothing but bean. (Pea beans also are available: smaller, firmer, and more elegant.) With these forthright legumes come a brace of blubbery frankfurters with skin as enthusiastically red as a maraschino cherry. Such naughty weenies have long been a favorite at lunch counters and in cheap-eats shops throughout the region, where they are more commonly sold in steamed-soft buns and embellished with bright yellow mustard, but red franks seem to be as scarce on local menus as the once-popular liver and onions, which, like franks and beans, is part of the Cole Farms repertoire every day.

It must be noted that Cole Farms is not preserved in amber. Remodeled and expanded at least a dozen times, the building is now huge and features a gift shop as well as a banquet room. Lunch choices include wraps and modern salads with fat-free raspberry vinaigrette dressing alongside such longtime kitchen specialties as clam cakes and chicken potpie. Even morning muffins aren't quite as dour as they used to be.

"We've tweaked them over the years," says proprietor Brad Pollard. "People want their muffins sweeter. You have to keep up." Such changes notwithstanding, a Cole Farms muffin is demure, nothing like a cloying cake-batter pastry.

A good measure of Cole Farms's personality is American chop suey, a *déjeuner maudit* listed on the menu side by side with "Campbell Soups." Rarer than the red hot dog, it is an archaic New England staples-stretcher once popular in institutions and on the supper tables of frugal housewives: ground beef mixed with elbow macaroni and vaguely Italian tomato sauce. It is bland as can be—closet comfort for those of us who sometimes wax nostalgic for school lunch.

The enduring regional value we like best at Cole Farms is the importance of pudding. The lineup is the same every day: tapioca, bread, Indian, and Grape-Nuts. Indian pudding, the rugged cornmeal samp sweetened with molasses, is served hot under a scoop of melting Cole Farms vanilla ice cream. Grape-Nuts pudding comes as a cool block of custard topped by a ribbon of sweetened cereal that has an amber crust reminiscent of a swanky crème brûlée. Swanky, it is not; Yankee, it is.

Colucci's Hilltop Market

135 Congress St.   207-774-2279

Portland, ME   L | $

Portland, Maine, loves Italians. Although Italians are similar to hoagies, heroes, grinders, blimps, zeps, wedges, and submarines elsewhere, the Downeast version has character all its own. We remained ignorant of this regional passion for years because Italians tend not to be served in places people go to eat. They are a specialty of convenience stores, delis, and butcher's counters in groceries, where they are made to order, wrapped, and carried out. We have never seen one listed on a sit-down restaurant menu. It was a letter from Italian loyalist Bettie Shea, describing its "marvelous taste and texture," that diverted us from our usual Portland chowder diet to go hunting for a real Italian.

The best one we found was at Colucci's Hilltop Market. As proprietor Dick Colucci expertly assembled one for us behind the counter of his corner store, he told us that his place has been a source of Italians since the end of World War II, and that the big issue among those who make them is not lunch meat or seasoning, but bread. "A good, fresh roll is the key," he counseled, reeling off the names of bakeries known for making the long buns on which Italians are made.

The uniqueness of Portland's Italian is not owed to the meats and cheeses, which are commonplace, but to the toppings and the bread. Thick-cut tomatoes, crunchy strips of pepper, briny olives, and a surfeit of spiced oil give the upper layer a brilliant sparkle. And the bread below, completely unlike the muscular, chewy lengths typical of Mid-Atlantic sub sandwiches, is tender and light, something like a gigantic version of the split-top buns in which Yankee wieners typically are served. The layers of salami or ham and cheese form a barrier between the bread and the oily vegetables above, but once that barrier is breached (generally at first bite), the bread quickly absorbs what's on top and loses its ability to hold anything. The experience is similar to eating a hot buttered lobster roll: midway through, the absorbent bun has transformed from a foundation into just one element among the stuff it originally contained. By the time you near the end of an Italian, the ingredients on the folded-open butcher paper no longer resemble a sandwich at all. They have become a deliciously messy cold cut salad, laced with fluffy tufts of oil-sopped bread.

We also recommend Colucci's for the big, gnarled blueberry muffins set out each morning on the counter in muffin tins, for cheeseburgers made from just-ground beef, and for such démodé hot lunches as mac and cheese, beef chili, and American chop suey. There is no place to eat in this family-run market; any meal you get is takeout. From the outside, it looks like any other corner grocery, its sign advertising, "Meats—Produce—Groceries—Lottery Tickets—Ice—Deli." Inside, shelves are stocked with a high-low cultural array of groceries that includes Twinkies and imported olive oil.

Five Islands Lobster Co.

1447 Five Islands Rd.   207-371-2990
Georgetown, ME   LD (summer only) | $$

There is no finer place to eat lobster than Five Islands, at the end of the road on a dock from which a couple of dozen lobster boats sail. Seating is at picnic tables on a wooden deck overlooking blue waters and five small islands tufted with pine trees.

How to dine at Five Islands can be a little confusing, nothing like a restaurant with waiters or even an eat-in-the-rough seafood shack. The first thing to do is go into the red clapboard building where a sign above the open door says "lobsters." In here, confer with one of the ladies about the size you want—they'll happily hoist lobsters out of the seawater tank for inspection—and let them know whether you want clams, corn, or potatoes thrown into the net and boiled alongside. You can buy a soft drink (or bring your own wine or beer), although we had to convince one old salt to sell us a bottle of Moxie, which she promised was too bitter for travelers unaccustomed to the Yankee beverage that was originally marketed as nerve tonic. Slices of blueberry cake and brownies are sold on the honor system. Leave a dollar for each one you take.

After arranging for dinner in the red building, head outside and find a picnic table or, if too hungry to wait foodless for the twenty to twenty-five minutes it takes for everything to boil, go next door to the Love Nest Grill (so named because fishermen and their paramours used to tryst there) and pick up an order of fried clams that are Ipswich-good, their briny marine essence encased in micro-thin crust. The Love Nest menu also features lobster rolls, fish and chips, crab cakes, even hamburgers and hot dogs.

When we told Chris Butler, who, with his wife, Jenny, bought Five Islands only a few years ago, that his lobsters were the best we ever have eaten, he explained that the water around here is the deepest and coldest on the coast, meaning lobsters yield meat that is firm and radiant with clean marine flavor. Ours fairly burst out of the shell when we took a nutcracker to it, and the juices that dripped on corn and potatoes added saltwater radiance to the whole meal.

Tranquility reigns when you look out at the islands in the distance, even when all the picnic tables are crowded with happy eaters chattering with the joy of their sleeves-up meal. As we devoured our shore dinners, savoring the beautiful scene every bit as much as the food, a fishing boat glided into the harbor and tied up at the wharf a few yards from our table. We ate Maine blueberry cake while watching two lobstermen offload crates full of lobsters just trapped in the deep.

Flo's

Route 1
Cape Neddick, ME

No phone
L (closed Weds) | $

We're the first to admit that Flo's is not for everyone. Its blubbery little weenies are by no stretch of the imagination gourmet sausages, and the place itself feels like a crowded garage. Nonetheless, there are many roadside hot dog fans (ourselves included) who would put this wacky little place on any all-American top-ten hot dog list.

Hot dogs are the one and only thing on the menu, so when you enter the low-slung, six-seat diner and peer through the pass-through window into the kitchen, proprietor and chef Gail Stacey (the late Flo's daughter-in-law) will ask simply, "How many?" They are small, so most regulars have a large number in mind. Three or four will sate a modest appetite. We've seen normal-size men consume a dozen at lunch, allotting no more than two good bites per dog. Like the wieners, buns are steamed to order, and these gentle buns, fresh out of the heat box, have a fine, silky texture that is itself a vital component of the singular culinary experience of dining at Flo's.

Hot sauce, which is technically optional but culinarily essential, is Flo's secret weapon. Nothing like the beefy chili on a chili dog, it is meatless, a devilishly dark sweet/hot relish of stewed onions, glistening with spice, and customarily finished with a sprinkle of celery salt. A "special" at Flo's is a hot dog with this sauce and a thin line of mayonnaise, a magic combination that makes the modest dog unspeakably lavish. If instead of mayo you get mustard, the sauce/mustard interaction gives every bite a wicked kick.

Note: Flo's has no phone! It is open only for lunch, from 11:00 A.M. daily except for Wednesday, when it is closed.

Harmon's Lunch

144 Gray Rd. 207-797-9857
Falmouth, ME L | $

We are indebted to Portland writer Elizabeth Peavy (author of *Maine and Me* and *Outta My Way*), who told us that when we headed out of town toward Gray, it was our duty to stop at Harmon's Lunch. We make the same recommendation to anyone who loves hamburgers and burger joints with character aplenty.

A sign behind the counter warns, "This is not Burger King. You don't get it your way. You take it my way, or you don't get the damn thing." In our estimation that's fine, because Harmon's hamburgers are just right. Doneness is not an issue. They are all cooked medium—nice and moist but not oozing juice or pink inside. They are lunch counter patties par excellence, sizzled on a seasoned old griddle and sandwiched inside soft

Portland-bakery buns that are buttered and heated just enough to become ultra-tender mitts, perfect for hamburger holding.

Among the options you do have when you order a hamburger is a slice of cheese melted on top and, better yet, grilled onions. The onions are fried until melting soft, and they add sweet, smoky luxury to the little package. Also available are mustard and a vivid red relish. Lettuce and tomato? Forget about them. "They are not available on a Harmon's hamburger!" proprietor Peter Wermell informed us. "Never were, never will be."

The only other entree is a hot dog—of which we saw no evidence on anybody's table or in the small open kitchen behind the counter. The one side dish is French fries, and they're super: thick cut and delivered too hot to handle. However, when this little shop gets crowded, as it so often does, ordering French fries can delay delivery of the meal. You see, while fifteen hamburgers will fit on the grill at one time, the fry kettle has room for only four orders of potatoes. Therefore people who come only for burgers sometimes have their order put to the head of the line while potato-eaters wait. On a busy summer Saturday, it's not uncommon to wait a half-hour for a meal.

The little wood-frame diner was opened in 1960 by Marvin Harmon, a former Air Corps cryptographer, and current boss, Mr. Wermell, maintains the unforgiving attitude for which the place became known. He only reluctantly agreed to allow us to take pictures of the wonderful décor—row after row of old-fashioned glass milk bottles from long-gone Maine dairy farms—and he did not seem at all pleased when we started asking him about the source of his good-tasting beef. Nonetheless, after we paid at the press-button, nondigital cash register and walked out the front door heading for our car in the dirt parking lot, Mr. Wermell came running out behind us—leaving a griddle full of hamburgers sputtering—just so he could give us a small magnetic calendar, the kind you slap onto a refrigerator door, that featured the restaurant's name, address, and phone number, as well as the pacific motto, "Let's Get Harmonized!"

Harraseeket Lobster

Town Landing	207-865-3535
Freeport, ME	LD May-Oct | $$

Dine at a picnic table overlooking the Freeport town harbor, the meal perfumed by the salt smell of the ocean and serenaded by the sound of an

American flag flapping overhead. This is one of the nicest places west of Bath to plow into a shoreline meal and enjoy the view. The specialty is boiled-to-order lobsters (also available live, to go), but don't ignore the seafood baskets. Whole-belly clams are giants, hefty gnarled spheres of golden crust enveloping mouthfuls of ocean nectar. On the side, you want onion rings: puffy circles of brittle, sweet batter around a hoop of onion that still has crunch. Clam cakes are good, too, their puffy dough holding dozens of little nuggets of marine goodness. The chowder is wonderful, but best of all is the lobster roll, served splayed open in a broad cardboard dish and packed with briny-sweet chunks of meat. Have it with onion rings or an order of fried onion middles (sweet, slick nuggets that are to fried rings what holes are to donuts), and conclude with a fudgy, hand-fashioned whoopie pie.

Now that the management has put an awning up over the picnic tables, you can dine outdoors even when it rains. They tell us that it does rain in Freeport, but every visit we have made to town in search of our favorite clam baskets and o-rings, the sun was shining brightly and gulls were swooping overhead through the blue, blue sky. It is almost painfully picturesque, this eat-in-the-rough jewel of a clam shack overlooking the South Freeport Harbor. But even if it were not so attractive, we would recommend it for the seafood baskets and the lobsters.

Helen's

28 East Main St.   207-255-8423
Machias, ME   BLD | $

Helen's is deservedly famous for blueberry pie. And oh, what a great pie it is. A dense slurry of cooked and fresh tiny wild Maine blueberries—one-fifth the size of the big ones you buy by the pint at the supermarket—is piled onto a nice flaky crust and heaped with whipped cream. If all you know are the store-bought ones, the flavor of these berries is astonishing: intensely fruity, sweet but not sugary, bright as the sun. You can get Helen's blueberry pie year-round, but the best time to have it is late summer, when fresh-picked lowbush blues are abundant.

The same fine blueberries find their way into morning muffins, and pies made from raspberries, strawberries, and boysenberries should not be ignored, nor should brownies, cakes, and turnovers. But Helen's is not merely a pastry shop. It is a dandy small-town restaurant that serves a lunch of elegant fried clams or fried haddock, broiled halibut, hot turkey and mashed potatoes, a whole boiled lobster dinner, or a simple and unimprovable bowl of fresh-picked lobster meat sopped with butter.

Hodgman's Frozen Custard

1108 Lewiston Rd.	207-926-3553
New Gloucester, ME	Mother's Day to Labor Day (closed Mon & Tues) | $

A fair-weather destination north of Portland, Hodgman's is the sort of place that calls out to anyone with a sweet tooth and a love for old-fashioned Americana. It is a roadside custard shop where they make their own in only the basic flavors—vanilla and chocolate—plus one special each day. There are no mix-ins, swirls, chunks, chips, cookie dough, or candies polluting this dairy-pure manna. It's just custard. But oh, what good custard it is: thick and creamy, totally unlike bland brands pumped full of air.

We like vanilla best, just plain. Nothing is more perfectly satisfying on a warm summer day, whether perched on a cone or served in a cup. Of course, you can doll it up if you wish. Hodgman's menu lists sundaes, frappes and floats, banana boats and thunderstorms, hot fudge royals, tin roofs, and tin lizzies. Whole custard pies are also available.

There is no indoor dining area, but facilities include a large covered picnic area to the side of the stand, where you can sit and lick in the shade.

Lobster Shack

225 Two Lights Rd.	207-799-1677
Cape Elizabeth, ME	LD (closed in winter) | $$

Here is the most dramatic possible setting for lobster-eating—the water's edge, framed by a pair of lighthouses at the entrance to Casco Bay. A restaurant has perched here since the 1920s, and while you might find better fried clams and lobster rolls along the coast, you will find no more inspired place to eat them than at one of the picnic tables marshaled on a flat patch of sandy land between the takeout counter and huge rocks where the ocean splashes in. When the sea is rough and wind is gusting, a foghorn sounds nearby and a fine mist of salty air blows across your meal, causing hot lobster meat to exude puffs of aromatic steam as you crack claws, vent the tail, and unhinge the back.

Beyond whole lobsters, the menu includes some pretty fair fried clams and onion rings, a lovely lobster roll dolloped with a dab of mayonnaise, lobster stew, and clam cakes. For dessert there are Yankee puddings and pies and the unique Downeast chocolate-crème sandwich known as a whoopie pie (but here spelled "whoopy" pie).

There is indoor seating, too, but as far as we're concerned there is no point in coming to the Lobster Shack unless you plan to eat outdoors.

Mabel's Lobster Claw

124 Ocean Ave.   207-967-2562

Kennebunkport, ME   LD | $$

Mabel's wood-paneled walls are decorated with autographed pictures of the many celebrities who favor her restaurant, including local householders George and Barbara Bush (he likes baked stuffed lobster; she goes for eggplant parmesan). You don't have to be famous to feel at home in this comfy dining room, which has an old-fashioned, summer-resort ambience. Paper placemats explain how to eat a lobster, and a staff of swift waitresses all suggest that any piece of pie you order ought to be had à la mode.

The lobster roll is as deluxe as they come, served with fries and slaw on an actual china plate. The meat in the roll, glazed with a thin film of mayo, is juicy, fresh, and copious, some chunks so large that you feel a little embarrassed picking it up and eating it out of hand; a knife and fork seem more suited to the task. Mabel's lobster stew is legendary, and the shore dinner is swell: start by spooning into creamy chowder crowded with pieces of clam and potato, then tackle a good-size lobster perched atop a pile of steamers and accompanied by broth and butter. Corn, potatoes, and beets are available on the side. If you spy fudge cake on the counter, it must not be ignored, but the essential dessert is peanut butter ice cream pie.

Maine Diner

2265 Post Rd.   207-646-4441

Wells, ME   BLD | $

It has been a quarter-century since the Henry brothers bought this old diner in Wells and turned it into one of the great culinary attractions of the lower Maine coast. Using family recipes and their own know-how, as well as occasional suggestions from friendly customers, they cooked up a menu that is equal parts Downeast and diner, with a dash of modern savoir faire. (Lobster benedict, for heaven's sake!)

For us, no trip up Route 1 is complete without a visit to the Maine Diner, whether it's for a plate of homemade baked beans at dawn, chowder and meat loaf at noon, or lobster pie at supper time. Daily specials are truly special, including classic New England boiled dinner every Thursday and red flannel hash (made from leftover boiled dinner) on Saturday . . . while supplies last. We are especially fond of the fried clams, which are vigorously oceanic, just a wee bit oily, so fragile the crust seems to melt away as your teeth sink into them. If you are a serious clam lover, you can order the clam-o-rama lunch, which includes clam chowder, fried whole-belly clams, fried clam strips, and a clam cake!

Seafood rolls are outstanding—split buns piled with clams, haddock, scallops, or shrimp. And the lobster rolls are not to be missed. Yes, we said rolls, plural; for the Maine Diner is one of the few places that offer two kinds—a lobster salad roll, of cool meat and mayo, or a hot lobster roll of warm meat with plenty of melted butter to drizzle on it. Either one is terrific; for us, the hot lobster roll is heaven on earth.

The menu is vast, including such all-American items as buffalo wings and barbecued pork sandwich, plus a superb chicken potpie. When we visit, we stick to Maine cuisine, which the Henry brothers do so well, the best of which is lobster pie. Made from their grandmother's recipe, lobster pie is a casserole containing plump sections of lobster—soft claw and chewy tail meat—drenched in butter, topped with a mixture of cracker crumbs and tomalley. It is a strange, punk-colored dish, monstrous green and brown and pink, shockingly rich.

Marcy's Diner

| 47 Oak St. | 207-774-9713 |
| Portland, ME | BL \| $ |

In this 1930s urban hash house, décor is not exactly that of a fine-dining restaurant. Walls are hung with Harley-Davidson posters and pictures of the Three Stooges. The well-worn counter is occupied mostly by a blue-collar crowd drinking coffee from thick mugs and plowing into hearty plates of corned beef hash, pancakes, and chili-cheese omelets.

Of the many available omelets, chili-cheese won our hearts. Rib-sticking Yankee chili is blended with creamy melted cheese inside an envelope of egg that is thin as a crêpe. Morning luxury! Fried potatoes that come on the side of egg dishes are the supreme ideal of hash-house home fries, lacing the air with alluring Parfum de Spud. They sizzle in a pile on the grill, where they are pushed around, stacked, and restacked. A few pieces stick to the griddle and get brittle. Some chunks develop a leathery skin over creamy insides; still others are as squishy as white bread. Because potatoes are a Downeast crop, Mainers tend to pay them serious attention. "Sometimes our potatoes are from Canada," proprietor Joely Sparks confessed. "But the Maine ones are best. We boil and cut them every day. And we cook them in a butter-margarine mix. No oil."

As is Portland custom, when you order an egg dish, the choice of toasts to go with it includes not only white, rye, and whole wheat, but also Italian toast. Buttered and grilled, it's a tender slice of comfort food. When we ordered our chili-cheese omelet and hesitated about what kind of toast to have with it, the waitress explained to us, "You will be having Italian toast. I don't know why, but Italian toast goes with that. It's the only choice." In addition to good toast, Marcy's offers fresh-baked muffins every morning.

Moody's Diner

1885 Atlantic Highway (Route 1)   207-832-7785
Waldoboro, ME   BLD | $

Percy Moody started Moody's Diner west of Duckpuddle Pond, in Waldoboro, Maine, in the early 1930s so the people spending $1.50 per night to stay in his cabins on old Route 1 would have a place to eat. His son Alvah recalls windows being covered with black gauze during World War II to prevent sighting by enemy airplanes. That was when the diner was an open-all-night waystation for truckers hauling fish out of Rockland or Belfast who used to stop for pie and coffee at two in the morning.

Although it has grown over the decades, it remains a place where hidebound ritual reigns. Alvah Moody delights in telling of the time the family was expanding the diner and considered replacing the severe straight-back wood booths with modern seating. "Everyone complained," he says. "Even the carpenters who were going to make the booths complained. So we had them make new ones exactly like the old."

Moody's is no longer open around the clock, but it remains one of the top spots along the coast route for predawn breakfast. When the doors open at 4:30, morning muffins have been out of the oven long enough that you can pull one apart without searing fingertips; through the cloud of steam that erupts, a constellation of blueberries glistens in each fluffy half. "It's a good thing you came on Thursday," advises waitress Cheryl Durkee when we occupy a booth. "I think the girl who comes in today makes the best cinnamon rolls. They're the tallest." Cheryl also warns that the 1.36-ounce jug of maple syrup that costs $1.50 is enough for only two pancakes, so anyone who gets a stack of three should consider purchase of a second jug.

Thrift is a pillar of traditional New England cooking and a big part of Moody's echt-Maine character. This is not the place you come to splurge on a full-bore shore dinner or a $12 lobster roll; in fact the restaurant's 208-page cookbook, *What's Cooking at Moody's Diner*, doesn't contain a single recipe for lobster. But it does offer "mock lobster bake" made with haddock fillets. Haddock, which costs less than just about any other edible fish, has been served with egg sauce every Friday for as long as any of the Moody family can remember. (At last count, over two dozen Moodys worked in the restaurant and at the motel and cabins just up the hill.)

The menu is a primer of Northeast diner fare: meat loaf and mashed potatoes; hot turkey sandwiches; a panoply of chowders, stews, and soups; red flannel hash; baked beans with brown bread; and a fabulous selection of pies, including a legendary walnut pie that is actually a gloss on Southern-style pecan pie but, as Alvah Moody proudly notes, "not sickening sweet."

Nunan's Lobster Hut

9 Mills Rd. 207-967-4362
Kennebunkport, ME D (summer only) | $$

The best thing about Nunan's Lobster Hut, other than the lobster, is the plumbing. In particular, the sinks. Should you desire to wash your hands before, during, or after eating, the sinks are right there, out in the open dining room, ready for immediate action. They are serious, proletarian sinks, like you'd want to have next to your workbench in the basement. For drying hands, Nunan's supplies rolls of paper towels.

In some restaurants, this arrangement might not be so appealing, but at Nunan's Lobster Hut—which really is a hut—the sanitary accommodations are exactly right because this place is designed for serious lobster eating. Tables have easy-wipe surfaces with ribs around the edge to keep the inevitable mess from falling to the floor. The floor is painted battle-ship gray, which makes it easy to swab at the end of the day. Overhead lights are unadorned tubes. A touch of romance is provided in the form of a utility candle stuck in a thick cork on every table.

Lobsters are brought to tables on pizza pans, accompanied by bags of potato chips and store-bought rolls. Coffee is served in mugs. Water comes in paper cups. Bring your own wine or beer.

There are no frills at Nunan's to distract you from the perfection of the lobster (except maybe the view, when the panels on the sides of the dining room are raised and reveal a pleasant vista of Cape Porpoise marshlands). Each lobster is steamed to order in a couple inches of salty water for exactly twenty minutes, emerging with silky tender claw meat, its knuckles and tail succulent and chewy.

The Nunan family have been lobstering for three generations, so by now they have the process of enjoying their catch down to its essence. Af-ter you've polished off the lobster, there are homemade brownies or a slice of pie, the recipes for which have been perfected over the last thirty years. Blueberry and apple are memorable, their subtly sweetened fruits encased in sugar-dusted crusts.

The Porthole

| 20 Custom House Wharf | 207-780-6533 |
| Portland, ME | BLD \| $$ |

Nearly fifteen years ago, Portland's Elizabeth Peavy, author of *Maine and Me* and *Outta My Way* and regular columnist for www.thebollard.com, described The Porthole as "the real thing, untouched by trends." It has since changed hands and there is evidence of modern foodways on the menu, including breakfast sandwiches on focaccia and wrapped in tor-tillas, but for an excellent and authentic home-cooked breakfast on the waterfront, this old fisherman's bar (since 1929) is still the real deal.

Corned beef hash has a soft, almost creamy consistency with only a few crusty edges, rich with the flavor of garlic and onions blended into the beef along with tender nuggets of potato. Atop it are a couple of lovely poached eggs and bread of choice (I chose sourdough). Jane had blueberry pancakes, which were great (although served without maple syrup: BYOMS).

We were smitten by the place itself with its creaky floors and seafoam green walls decorated with old posters and just the right amount of nautical bric-a-brac. It was a cold morning, but the deck outside, overlooking the water along Custom House Wharf, looked mighty inviting. Among available libations are ales brewed just yards away.

Red's Eats

Water and Main Sts.   207-882-6128
Wiscasset, ME   LD | $$

Red's opened in Boothbay in 1938, moved to the north end of Wiscasset in 1954, and has since become a summertime legend. Many people believe that this shack serves the best lobster roll anywhere: meat from a one-pound lobster is extracted in great hunks and piled into a toasted split-top bun that is accompanied by a cup of drawn butter or, if you wish, mayonnaise to garnish it. It is lobster-eater's nirvana.

"Look how beautiful!" says the waitress when she presents ours through the window on its picnic tray. Her enthusiasm is that of someone who has never seen one of these amazing sandwiches ever before. In fact, she is dishing out dozens, probably hundreds on this pleasant summer day. Crowds of people line up for lobster rolls at Red's so that the wait just to get to the window can be up to an hour.

Once you receive your food—the large menu also contains fried seafood of all kinds, burgers, onion rings, French fries, and Round Top ice cream—you carry it to one of the plastic tables in back of the restaurant and dine in the sun alongside Route 1.

Agawam Diner

US Routes 1 and 133   978-948-7780
Rowley, MA   BLD | $

A worthy alternative to the great fried clam shacks of Massachusetts's North Shore, Agawam is a shipshape, pint-size Fodero Company diner (circa 1954) that is all silver sunbursts, pink laminate paneling, and red-upholstered booths. The menu is pure and traditional diner fare, including beef stew, hot hamburger plates, crunchy-skinned grilled hot dogs, and luscious grilled cheese sandwiches for less than the cost of a junk-food hamburger, and breakfast that arrives moments after you order it.

We have enjoyed hearty beef and bean chili in a sweet-hot tomato sauce and we have savored a daily special of lamb shank, which was so tender that it slipped from its bone with ease. A double-layer banana nut cake gobbed with whipped cream was a memorable dessert.

Baxter's Boathouse

177 Pleasant St.   508-775-7040

Hyannis, MA   LD April to Columbus Day | $$

After studying the posted menu at Baxter's, place an order at the counter then loiter nearby as the kitchen puts it together in about two minutes. You then carry your own tray to a varnished table indoors or a picnic table overlooking Hyannis Harbor. Or you can enjoy table service on the *Governor Brann*, a ferry boat converted into a floating dining room with seating for a few hundred customers. Or, if you choose, you can arrive in Lewis Harbor by boat, tie up at Baxter's dock, and be waited on without going ashore!

However you experience Baxter's, the thing to eat is summertime Yankee shore fare: crisp fried clams served with decent fries or indecently tasty clam fritters, which are deep-fried doughballs dotted with morsels of clam and served with honey for dipping. The lobster rolls are good, as is the Yankee-style (creamy) chowder. Or you can eat fine scallops, shrimps, or oysters. Steaks are available for fish-frowners.

Baxter's is a restaurant and a club, and it is popular pastime among the local drinking set to occupy the club long into the night, knocking back shots and beers. For us, the beverage of choice with our seafood dinners is the drink known here as "tonic," which is simply an eastern Bay State word for what the rest of us know as soda pop.

Butler's Colonial Donut House

461 Sanford Rd.   508-672-4600

Westport, MA   BL | $

We were worried a few years ago when we learned that donut-maker Alex Kogler had sold his little bakery gem in Westport. What would happen to his superior donuts?

As soon as we saw the long johns on the shelf, we breathed great sighs of relief. Under the new management, they are as beautiful as ever: long, lightweight rectangles that are cut in half and filled with a thin ribbon of black raspberry jelly and freshly whipped cream. Mr. Kogler used to call these the ultimate donuts, and in our book, they still are.

You'll find whipped cream filling in hole-less donuts, too. Each one is a big featherweight cream puff sliced in half and filled. Made from raised yeast dough, it is so fragile that you want to hold it very gently, lest you dent the surface with a heavy thumb. The cool filling is pure and white, and the counterpoise of silky whipped cream with ethereal cake, crowned by a spill of powdered sugar on the top, is out of this world. Butler's shelves are also stocked with a vast array of sticky apple fritters, tarts, and glazed and frosted donuts, even PB&J donuts for childlike tastes. Nothing in this little bake shop is ordinary!

Caffe Sicilia

40 Main St.   978-283-7345

Gloucester, MA   BL | $

Paul Ciaramitaro is a man you need to meet if you come to Gloucester. A former fisherman, he is a huge guy with huge enthusiasms, and his presence fills the tiny espresso and pastry shop that is his domain down near the waterfront. He holds court behind the counter, where he makes espresso for friends who drop by for morning chats among the four small tables that barely fit in the store, and he loves to show off his cornetti to newcomers. Cornetti resemble featherweight croissants, but they have a ribbon of lemon filling inside and a dusting of powdered sugar. He also makes featherweight sfogliatelle, semolina bread, cakes, marzipan candies, and a Downeast-Italian "lobster tail" pastry—ultra-thin sheaves of dough shaped like a lobster tail, sugar-dusted, and filled with cream.

Mr. Ciaramitaro's gelati are delightful. He recommended the *nocciola* (hazelnut) and also *zuppa inglese*, for which he had no proper English translation. "Marsala wine and fruit!" he rhapsodized, and when we didn't seem to comprehend quite how wonderful it is, he quickly dipped spoons into the freezer case to offer us each a hearty taste. When we smacked our lips at its creamy sweet goodness, he beamed with satisfaction, then, bursting with pride, he pointed us to a newspaper story displayed on the wall. "From the *Financial Times* . . . of London!" he said, stepping over to run his finger underneath a line that says his pastries put those of New York's Little Italy to shame. "No more need be said!"

Clam Box

246 High St.   978-356-9707

Ipswich, MA   LD (summer only) | $$

It's hard to believe that we ever wondered where the best fried clams are made. One taste of those served at the Clam Box is irrefutable evidence that there are none better. The whole-belly clams are not overly gooey and not too large, offering a subtle ocean sweetness that is brilliantly amplified but not the least bit overwhelmed by the crusty sheath outside. A whole clam plate is a magnificent meal that includes not only the native beauties sheathed in their fragile red-gold envelope, but also elegant onion rings, French fries, and bright, palate-refreshing coleslaw. Even the tartar sauce is a cut above. The lobster roll is loaded with meat, and Jane declares the clam chowder to be among New England's best.

The place itself is a gas, shaped like a clam box, the trapezoidal container in which fried-clams-to-go are customarily served. It is a genuine roadside attraction that dates back to the 1930s and would be of interest for its looks alone. There is indoor seating, but across the parking lot are choice seats for whenever the weather is nice: sunny picnic tables for al fresco dining. Throughout most of the summer, expect a wait in line at mealtimes. The Clam Box is famous, deservedly so.

The Dory

| 29 Commercial St. | 978-283-2408 |
| Gloucester, MA | B | $ |

A pint-size breakfast-only nook on the waterfront, the Dory has a sign on its wall that says "Fishing Spoken Here." This is where commercial and sport fishermen come before dawn for coffee, conversation, hearty breakfast, and more coffee. Repeat customers keep their own coffee mugs on pegs to the right of the counter.

The menu is big and fundamental, including egg sandwiches on white, wheat, Italian bread, or giant English muffins; stacks of pancakes with or without blueberries; and three-egg omelets with toast and home fries or hash browns. On the side you can get bacon, Canadian bacon, sausage, honey ham, Portuguese linguiça sausage, or a meal-size order of corn beef hash. The gals behind the counter will even make you eggs Florentine with hollandaise sauce or eggs Benedict further gussied up with pieces of asparagus.

What we like about the Dory more than its repertoire of breakfast, plain and fancy, is its attitude. A true blue-collar café, it seems always populated by at least a few gents (and a few ladies) whose profession and passions are guided by the tides, and who apparently are delighted to share with newcomers their devil-may-care philosophy of life. Over one breakfast at the Dory counter, we discussed omelet cookery, the fine points of food photography, bait strategies, swordfishing, and the worst storms of the twentieth century, and on every subject, we gleaned the wisdom of genuine experience.

Flav's Red Skiff

15 Mt. Pleasant St.   978-546-7647

Rockport, MA   BL | $

Flav's Red Skiff, named for proprietors Mark and Victoria Flavin, is a tiny café with cute pastel-checked cloth-covered tables and décor that consists of old magazine advertisements, a glowing review or two, and the paper napkin Tom Selleck signed for proprietor Mrs. Flavin the day he stopped in for breakfast while filming the movie *The Love Letter* on the oh-so-picturesque streets of Rockport. It is a hang-out for locals as well as visitors, and during the busy summer months, you can expect to wait for a precious table or seat at the counter any time after eight in the morning.

The restaurant is small enough that early in the morning, before the crowds arrive, conversations tend to include diners at the counter and tables and the staff behind the pass-through window to the kitchen. By midmorning, Flav's is so crowded that you might have a hard time hearing your tablemate talk.

The most interesting regional item on Flav's menu is anadama bread, which was supposedly invented in Rockport, when a fisherman grew so angry at his lazy wife, Anna, that he baked his own loaf of bread from wheat flour, cornmeal, and molasses . . . all the while muttering, "Anna, damn her." Whatever its origins, Flav's makes a dark, sweet, and highly flavored anadama loaf that tastes just great when toasted and buttered. (Whole loaves are available to take home.) The unique bread is used to make interesting French toast, available plain or topped with strawberries, but in truth, we like simple toasted anadama bread better. The egg dip, frying, and strawberry topping tend to detract from the solid Yankee character of the bread itself. Other good breakfasts include elegant, plate-wide pancakes (buttermilk, blueberry, or chocolate chip) and a warm pecan roll that is served adrip with caramel frosting.

Four Seas

360 S. Main St.

Centerville, MA

508-775-1394

LD (summer only) | $

Long inventories on the inside and outside walls enumerate which of several dozen flavors are available that day: vanilla, chocolate, strawberry, of course; maple walnut, black raspberry, and other fairly familiar names; plus such curious house specialties as penuche pecan and frozen pudding; and, on occasion, fresh cantaloupe. Likewise, the list of sundae sauces ranges from the familiar—hot milk chocolate (aka hot fudge) and hot butterscotch—to such soda-fountain Victoriana as claret, wild cherry, and soft walnuts in maple syrup. Frappes and milk shake flavors are also itemized—all are available plain, minted, or malted—and if you're not from around here, you need to know that a milk shake means nothing but a flavored syrup and milk; a frappe is what most of the rest of us know as a milkshake: flavoring, milk, and ice cream blended together.

Sundaes are a delight; claret sauce on chocolate ice cream is our undoing. Frappes are expertly blended. But the pride of Four Seas are the cones: small (one generous globe), large (one extra-big triangle-shaped scoop), or double (two globes); the last is the maximum amount of ice cream any ordinary-size cone can bear. It is a pleasure to watch the boys and girls behind the counter construct the cones. They have perfected the correct circular scooping motion to retrieve just the right amount from the bucket, packed tight and even, and they know exactly how to use the scoop to force it onto the cone for maximum adherence and minimum drippage.

Kelly's Roast Beef

410 Revere Beach Blvd.

Revere, MA

781-284-9129

LD | $

There are a couple of other Kelly's branches, but there is no comparison to the charm of the Kelly's at Revere Beach, especially on a warm spring weekend when gulls screech overhead and occasionally panhandle from the sky over diners who don't closely guard their meals. The salty air of the ocean wafts in to add ineffable savor to the roast beef sandwiches, and the sun shines down, making the roast beef's special sauce glisten. While there is no indoor dining at Kelly's, the pavilions at the broad beach across the street are one of the nicest dining areas a Roadfood devotee could hope for.

The beef sandwich is one of the North Shore's finest. There are many toppings available but the primary trio—and a fine combo—is cheese, sauce, and mayo. If the beef tends to be a little bit dry—and in our experience, sometimes it is—the sauce and mayo are superb compensation, and the cheese, of course, adds extra fatty luxury to beef that is fundamentally very lean. We're also fans of the tender sesame seed bun.

Beyond the signature beef, Kelly's menu is mostly beach cuisine: fried clams, lobster rolls, scallops, shrimp and, of course, French fries and onion rings.

Marty's Donut Land

8 Central St.   978-356-4580
Ipswich, MA   B | $

Marty's makes big, hefty donuts. They include the honey dew, which is a simple raised, glazed sinker with a substantial sweet cake texture that is perfect for dunking, as well as a honey dipped, which is an airy raised round of which we can easily eat half a dozen with a few cups of coffee. Chocolate-frosted donuts are weighty with a crunchy exterior, and there are jelly-filled and powdered and coconut-spangled donuts, too. Many regular customers come for big goopy coffee rolls.

A simple storefront with scarcely any decoration other than a wonderful oil portrait of Marty hanging on the back wall, Marty's has a counter where take-out dozens are sold and where customers sit and converse. And there are counter seats in the front window that afford a view of passing traffic on Route 133. It is a true local hangout; one Cape Ann native told us that when he or his friends go on a ski trip, they stop by Marty's long before the doors officially open to get boxes of hot donuts to go. Although the donuts are ready—and especially delicious while still hot!—the counter gals haven't yet arrived, so the boys help themselves to what they need and leave their money on the counter. (Not a recommended strategy for out-of-towners!)

At the register after a satisfying Marty's breakfast, we asked the cashier if she had a business card she could give us with the address, phone number, etc., of the establishment for our records. "This is Marty's, hon'," she informed us. "We don't do business cards."

Nick's Famous Roast Beef

139 Dodge St. 978-922-9075

North Beverly, MA LD | $

Roast beef is huge north of Boston. You can hardly drive a mile without passing a restaurant that advertises beef sandwiches. Some are chains, many are mediocre. Nick's, where the motto is "We're the Only One," is in the top tier of excellence.

Like all the local roast beef houses, it is a self-service joint where you place your order and wait for your number to be called, then carry your own tray to a table somewhere in the small strip-mall storefront eatery. The choices include a large beef sandwich, a junior beef sandwich, and a super beef sandwich on an onion roll. (There are also many other kinds of sandwiches available.) Super beef is the one we recommend. It is a well-stacked pile of moist, tender, full-flavored pink beef inside a giant rectangular roll that is egg-yellow and studded with squiggles of onion. Many condiments and add-ins are available, including horseradish, cheese, mayo, and mustard, but the people's choice is barbecue sauce, which has a spicy sweetness that makes it beef's good companion. And speaking of companions, you definitely want onion rings! Nick's onion rings are beautiful—golden brown and wickedly crunchy—requiring only a hail of salt to attain perfection.

Decoration at Nick's consists of hundreds of snapshots taken of roast beef fans all over America and the world that show them standing in front of famous places holding up a Nick's Beef bumper sticker.

Santarpio's

111 Chelsea St. 617-567-9871

Boston, MA LD | $$

Many Bostonians consider Santarpio's the city's premier pizza place. Arriving on battered metal trays carried by a staff of take-no-prisoners waitresses (who are as efficient as they are brusque), this kitchen's thin-crusted pies are a joy to eat. The outer rim of the pizza is a balance of bready crunch and chew, featuring an occasional blistered-black spot from the oven, and while the inside of the circle tends to soften and become unwieldy under a lot of toppings—leading to the heartbreak of cheese slippage—even the flexible part of the crust has a taste that makes you want to keep on eating, then ordering more. Curiously, the most powerhouse toppings (garlic, onions, anchovies) do not seem to pack a really wicked flavor wallop on Santarpio's pizzas; these are tomato and cheese pies with plenty of soul, but with a mild, creamy disposition. In our experience, one pie, ranging from simple cheese or cheese and garlic (the latter with a blizzard of oregano on top) to a deluxe combo of sausage, mushrooms, etc., is just about enough to satisfy one normal appetite.

But if your appetite is like ours—bigger than normal—then you need to know about Santarpio's barbecue. For if this establishment's reputation rides on pizza, it is barbecue that will lure us back again and again. Barbecue in Boston? you ask. In this case, "barbecue" is not the Southern ritual of slow-cooked meat in a metal pit. It refers to meat cooked on a grate over charcoal—lengths of homemade Italian sausage and skewered hunks of lamb, or what Italians know as *spiedini.* That sausage is spectacular—a long, taut tube with the flavor of the charcoal fire permeating its succulent, high-spiced insides. Many folks get it as a pre-pizza hors d'oeuvre—one long char-crusted sausage on a plate with hot cherry peppers and some crusty Italian bread. The barbecue lamb has a vivid flavor—for lamb lovers only—and it ranges from a pleasant chew to a serious chaw. Plates of sausage and lamb, with peppers and bread, are the *only* thing other than pizza on Santarpio's menu.

The barbecue adds immeasurably to Santarpio's atmosphere. Literally. The meat is cooked on a grill that is just inside the front door, and its wonderful aroma harmonizes with the smell of tomato sauce, cheese, and crust from the pizza ovens in back to make this place the most appetizing bar we've ever found. And make no mistake, it is a bar: smoky, raucous, a little unkempt, with boxing posters on the wall and 1960s Motown tunes setting a sassy beat.

Toscanini's

899 Main St.	617-491-5877
Cambridge, MA	$

First, let us say that the vanilla ice cream made by Gus Rancatore at Toscanini's is some of the best there is: pure, uncomplicated, satisfying. And the regional favorite, Grape-Nuts, is as good as it gets, the familiar breakfast cereal blended into sweet cream so it becomes flavorful streaks of grain. We love such flavors as Cocoa Pudding and Cake Batter. But the true call to glory is Burnt Caramel. If you are one who enjoys the preciousness of the crust on a flawlessly blowtorched crème brûlée, you, too, will understand how a controlled sugar burn creates an ice cream that transcends sweetness and makes taste buds buzz.

Turtle Alley

| 91A Washington St. | 978-281-4000 |
| Gloucester, MA | L \| $ |

Step into Hallie Baker's candy store, named Turtle Alley, and behold a school of terrapin: big, knobby candy rounds of dark, white, and milk chocolate, each as unique as a snowflake, and each bristling with nuts that poke out from the caramel like multiple turtle flippers from underneath the chocolate shell. Hallie makes them with pecans, almonds, peanuts, and macadamias, as well as cashews, which she believes are the ideal nut, at least cosmetically, because cashews most resemble turtle flippers. Hallie's turtles, you see, are not totally enrobed in chocolate. She makes them one by one, by hand, so that the nuts stick out the side, for the sake of turtle foot verisimilitude. And while she may be right about cashews looking best and white chocolate tasting richest, the turtles we like best are the more traditional pecan-footed ones, dark or milk chocolate.

Turtles are just one of many things available in this joyous candy land. There are brittles and clusters and butter crunches, chocolate-coated candied fruits, snowflakes, nonpareils, and simple hunks of uncomplicated chocolate. The confectionery is a joy to visit, for Hallie's pleasure at running it is contagious—she is the proverbial kid in a candy store, but in this case grown up and running it. Turtles and chocolate samplers are available by mail order.

The Village Restaurant

| 55 Main St. | 978-768-6400 |
| Essex, MA | LD \| $$ |

Dark, wood-paneled, comfortable, and staunchly middle-class, the Village has been a town fixture for nearly half a century. One veteran staff member recalled to us that when it opened as a five-booth café, the owner used to leave the door open so that before the staff arrived in the morning, regulars could let themselves in and cook their own breakfasts on the grill!

Menus from those early days are posted in the vestibule, and they are a joy to read, not only for the prices (a dollar for a full dinner), but because they list so many of the very basic items that are still on the Village menu and that still make this such a true regional eating experience. "We serve Essex clams" boasts a menu from 1956. The Village still serves Essex clams, fried to golden perfection. For dessert, you can have a dish of baked Indian pudding, Grape-Nuts custard, or strawberry shortcake on an old-fashioned biscuit.

Nowadays, the menu has something for everyone, and we must confess that there have been occasions, after long days of eating fried clams up and down Cape Ann, we have come to the Village because we needed a sirloin steak or even, on one occasion, vegetarian pasta! But still, it's local seafood that stars on these tables, simply fried or broiled, or in more deluxe configurations such as haddock Rockefeller. Lobsters are available boiled, fried, or as a luscious lobster pie that is baked in a casserole dish with seasoned bread crumbs.

Among desserts, we recommend the Indian pudding, a true Yankee dessert. It is grainy with a powerful molasses kick, and it is served piping-hot with a scoop of vanilla ice cream melting on top. A bit fancier, but true to local character, is blueberry bread pudding, made of cornmeal and molasses bread and set afloat in a pool of sweet rum sauce.

Wenham Tea House

4 Monument St.	978-468-1398
Wenham, MA	L&T (closed Sun) | $

A real ladies' lunchroom going back nearly a century, Wenham Tea House is part of a philanthropic enterprise that sells books, antiques, china, and handwork to benefit the community. Also on sale in the front room are bakery cases full of dainty cakes, pies, muffins, casseroles, and hors d'oeuvres one can buy to take home. Beyond the prepared foods is the tea room, open only midday (and for afternoon tea), where a lovely lunch is served six days a week.

Much as we like two-fisted diner grub, these gentle meals are irresistible. Of course, there are several main-course salads, including a terrific Caesar salad and a chicken Waldorf cut into tiny bite-size pieces. Crab cakes, available as an appetizer or main course, are demure little disks with a nice sweet flavor and the soft texture of good white bread. There are club sandwiches, a cheddar crab melt on eight-grain bread, and even a modern vegetable wrap. Count on a quiche of the day as well as a soup; we love the creamy, smooth lobster bisque. Meals are accompanied by warm, fresh-baked muffins.

Delicate foods are what you expect in such a setting (lace-curtained windows, decorative plates on the wall), but do not underestimate the satisfaction of such full meals as Yankee pot roast or turkey with trimmings that include moist sage dressing, mashed potatoes, whipped butternut squash, and cranberry-orange sauce, followed by hot milk sponge cake for dessert.

Custom decrees that all able ladies (and the occasional gentleman visitor) help themselves to coffee and tea at the sideboard, where a sign advises, "No cell phones, please." Service is swift and efficient, provided by a staff of waitresses in crisp uniforms with white aprons that remind us of the golden days of New York's fabled Schrafft's.

The White Hut

280 Memorial Ave. 413-736-9390
West Springfield, MA BLD | $

The White Hut is quintessential Roadfood. Not a lot of different choices are available from this brash, open kitchen, but the two for which it is known are unbeatable: cheeseburgers and hot dogs.

The cheeseburger is a modest-size patty cooked through on a grill and sandwiched in a tender white bun. It is a likable lunch-counter burger, but what puts it in a class by itself is grilled onions. Look at the grill, next to the frying beef patties, and there you see a veritable mountain of onions cooked until soft and limp and nearly caramel sweet. Heaped atop the cheeseburger, they complete a simple but perfect study in burger excellence.

The hot dogs are good, too. Sizzled on the grill alongside the hamburgers, they are medium-size tube steaks that blossom under a mantle of mustard, relish, and raw onions (applied by the waitress, as you specify), and they are served in a bun that is soft on the inside, but buttered and toasted to a luxurious golden brown on the outside.

Seating inside is limited to a few counter stools, but there is plenty of standing room at a counter that runs around the back of the room, as well as at a broad metal table where the lunch crowd can gather and scarf down weenies by twos and threes.

When finished with this fine feast, walk over to the cash register at the far end of the counter, tell the man what you ate, and he charges you accordingly. It is truly fast food: you can be in and out, and well-fed, in less than five minutes.

Woodman's of Essex

121 Main St.	978-768-6451
Essex, MA	LD | $$

Woodman's claims to be the place where the fried clam was invented—on July 3, 1916, when Lawrence Woodman tossed clams into the deep fryer along with the Saratoga chips he was selling at his clam bar. Who knows if the story is true? Who cares? If you are interested in the subject of fried clams in particular or fried seafood in general, this place is essential.

Overlooking a scenic marsh in the heart of the clam belt, where towns have bivalvular names like Ipswich and Little Neck, Woodman's epitomizes a whole style of informal Yankee gastronomy, known as "eat in the rough." That means you stand at a counter, yell your order through the commotion, then wait for your number to be called. The food is served on cardboard plates with plastic forks. Carry it yourself to a table (if you can find one that isn't occupied).

A chart we made a few years ago comparing and contrasting the top clam shacks along the North Shore evaluated Woodman's clams as follows: Crust crunch = crusty. Chew = resilient. Belly goo = overflowing. Flavor = clamorama! Quantity = substantial. Whole platter presentation = merry jumble. In our experience, Woodman's clams tend to be somewhat larger and gooier than those served in other local places, sometimes a bit too large. But there is no faulting the frying, which results in big mouthfuls that are shatteringly crisp. Also on the must-eat fried-food roster are onion rings and French fries, and big, spherical clam fritters. Nor is creamy clam chowder to be ignored.

Woodman's gets bonus points for being the one North Shore clam shack that is open year-round.

New Hampshire

Bishop's

183 Cottage St.	603-444-6039
Littleton, NH	Apr to Columbus Day | $

Bishop's ice cream flavors range from the baroque—Bishop's Bash is chocolate chips, nuts, and brownie chunks in dark chocolate—to basic. Vanilla is pure and creamy-white; chocolate is like iced chocolate milk more than some ungodly rich chocolate mousse cake; the coffee is reminiscent of HoJo's—smooth and creamy more than ultra-caffeinated. Here, too, you can savor the old Yankee favorite, Grape-Nuts ice cream, in which the little specks of cereal soften into grainy streaks of flavor in pudding-smooth ice cream.

There is something unusually civilized about coming to Bishop's for ice cream. You'd think that such a happy-time product would stimulate yelps of exuberance and that the interior of the shop would ring with rapture. On the contrary, there is a reverential hush about it, even when Bishop's is jammed and every little table is occupied with ice cream eaters and a hundred are waiting to get inside. Perhaps it's due to the polite aura of the stately old house in which the business is located, or maybe to the captivating charm of the ice cream servers, who are extraordinarily solicitous as you choose between a S'more sundae and a maple sundae, and who want to know, if you order a sundae with buttercrunch and coffee ice cream, which flavor you want on top.

Four Aces Diner

23 Bridge St.   603-298-6827
West Lebanon, NH   BLD (B & L only on Sun & Mon) | $

"Nothing Beats a Home Cooked Meal . . . Except Four Aces!" boasts the menu in this 1950s diner that seems to have been partially ingested by a large Colonial house surrounding it on three sides. Breakfast is served from predawn until mid-afternoon and includes interesting pancakes (with blueberries, bananas, chocolate chips, or walnuts). For an extra $1.50, you'll get real maple syrup to pour on them. We are partial to the pork chop and egg plate with home fries and a grilled biscuit, as well as to "the joker," a meal of pancakes, eggs, potatoes, sausage, and bacon. Also on the menu are such traditional morning meals as hot oatmeal, corned beef hash, and creamed chipped beef on toast.

We automatically like any restaurant that makes a big deal out of franks and beans. Here, epicures in search of local tradition can come for a mighty handsome plate of genuine baked beans—al dente, not too goopy or sweet—with a brace of hot dogs and a biscuit. Other old-time favorites include chicken and dumplings and macaroni and cheese with hot dogs. The menu even lists that locally beloved supper specialty, fried tripe—in our opinion, a taste that needs to be acquired at an early age. Among traditional diner fare, you'll find superb liver and onions and bacon, meat loaf with a choice of either brown gravy or tomato gravy, and pork chops served with potatoes and applesauce.

Gilley's PM Lunch

175 Fleet St.   603-431-6343
Portsmouth, NH   LD | $

Gilley's is an old-fashioned night-owl lunch wagon made by the Worcester Dining Car Company, now semipermanently anchored on Fleet Street in Portsmouth. It was named for Ralph "Gilley" Gilbert, an employee who slung hash here for over fifty years. If it is the wee hours of the morning, and all the normal restaurants are closed and even the bars are shut, you can count on this joint to be serving up hamburgers with chocolate milk on the side to a rogue's gallery of city folk who range from derelicts to debutantes.

Many dine standing on the sidewalk, but there is limited indoor seating at a narrow counter opposite the order area and galley kitchen. Gathered here under some of the most unflattering lighting on earth are insomniacs, die-hard partiers, and late-shift workers with no other place to eat, feasting on such quick-kitchen fare as chili dogs, French fries gobbed with cheese, and fried egg sandwiches with ultra-strong coffee on the side. The best dish in the house, or at least the one that seems most appropriate in this reprobate restaurant, is the hamburger, actually the cheeseburger . . . no, make that a double cheeseburger, with bacon and onions, too.

L.A. Burdick

47 Main St.   603-756-2882
Walpole, NH   BLD | $$

We're not quite sure how to describe L.A. Burdick, but let us start with "ohhhh. . . ." That would be a chocolate-induced moan of pleasure. Here is a magnificent chocolatier, specializing in the highest-quality bonbons. Among the stars are truffles with flavors that range from mint and honey-caramel to Scotch whisky (single-malt, of course); full-size dessert tortes, chocolate fondue, marzipan, nougat, and pâte de fruits. The signature chocolate is a mouse—a small rodent-shaped delicacy (complete with ribbon tail) filled with dark ganache, milk chocolate and mocha, or dark chocolate and cinnamon. Ourselves, we get weak-kneed over the chocolate-enrobed thin-sliced candied ginger. It has a sweet-spicy kick with a just a hint of saltiness that amplifies its confectionery intensity. Thin-sliced candied pears are another of our heartthrobs.

All these sweets are available in beautiful boxes to take home or to buy via mail order—check out www.burdickchocolate.com—but there is far more to this wonderful place than chocolate. It is also a café where you can come for coffee and amazing pastries (Viennese gugelhupf, anyone?) any time after 7:00 A.M. as well as for lunch and supper. The full-scale meals are swank indeed, featuring such upscale offerings as salad of arugula with truffled fennel and Parmesan and pepper-crusted yellowtail. The prices for these items are relatively high on the Roadfood scale, maybe $15 for lunch, twice that for supper. But for all its certified excellence, the eatery has the comfy, casual air of a town café, which is what it is.

Polly's Pancake Parlor

Route 117
Sugar Hill, NH

603-823-5575
BLD (closed in winter) | $$

New England boasts prolific maple sugar trees and a long tradition of grain cookery, and thus it is home to some mighty fine pancakes. Top of the line is Polly's Pancake Parlor in the White Mountains of New Hampshire. Polly's was opened in 1938 by "Sugar Bill" Dexter because he thought a tea room would provide him the opportunity to show passersby all the good things that could be done with the maple harvest on his farm. Named for his daughter and now run by his progeny, Polly's remains maple paradise.

Of course, pancakes are the specialty of the house; they are made from stoneground flours or cornmeal, either plain or upgraded with shreds of coconut, walnuts, or blueberries. One order consists of a half a dozen three-inchers, and it is possible to get a sampler of several different kinds. They come with the clearest and most elegant fancy-grade maple syrup, as well as maple sugar and mouthwatering maple spread. You can also get maple muffins, sandwiches made with maple white bread, a gelatinized dessert called maple Bavarian cream, ice cream with maple hurricane sauce (syrup and apples stewed together), and all sorts of maple candies to take home.

Polly's is a beautiful restaurant in a breathtaking location. It is surrounded by maple trees hung with taps and buckets in the spring, but the most wonderful time to visit is autumn, as the sugarbush starts to turn colors. The dining room has a glass-walled porch that overlooks fields where horses graze, and its inside walls are decorated with antiques and tools that have been in the family since the late eighteenth century, when Sugar Bill's ancestors began farming this land.

Allie's Donuts

3661 Quaker La. (Route 2)   401-295-8036
North Kingstown, RI   B | $

Allie's is Rhode Island's premier donut stop, so popular that it has two doors, funneling into two lines of people who wait at two separate counters to place their orders. The waiting area is fairly small, but the open kitchen behind it is an immense workspace where powerful mixers whir and deep-fryers bubble.

The variety of donuts made each morning is vast, including honey-dipped, glazed crullers, raised jelly sticks, plain cake donuts, coconut-strewn solid chocolates, and colorful jimmies-topped extravaganzas. None are fancy-pants pastries; these are big, sweet, pretty things to eat. Regular customers love them so much that it is common to see people buy a dozen in a box (to take to the office), plus a bag of two or three to eat in the car—or in the parking lot on the way to the car—before the dozen is opened.

Aunt Carrie's

1240 Ocean Rd.　　　　　　　　　401-783-7930

Narragansett, RI　　　　　　　　LD (summer only) | $$

Aunt Carrie's, at Point Judith on the ocean, has been a summertime destination since the 1920s. It remains one of the few places in Rhode Island
that still lists a full shore dinner on its menu. It starts with chowder: your
choice of white, red, or Rhode Island–style, which is clear and bacon-
flavored. That's accompanied by crusty gold balls of deep-fried clam-
flavored dough called clam cakes as well as steamers with broth and
butter for dipping. Then come fillet of sole with corn on the cob and
French fries, accompanied by homemade bread and butter. After that you
get a whole lobster and finally warm Indian pudding topped with ice
cream or a slice of pie. Abbreviated versions of the big feed are available
(without the lobster or without the fish), or you can order à la carte and
get whatever combination of chowder, clam cakes, fish, or lobster you
like.

We enjoyed our shore dinners on occasions when we visited last summer, but weren't happy with the other eat-in-the-rough shoreline fare.
Fried clams were thick and drab, and the tired meat in the lobster roll
was a sorry contrast to the fresh meat we picked from the whole lobster
in the shore dinner. Desserts, however, were as good as ever: swell sweet-
tart rhubarb pie, seriously good Indian pudding, and, at the very end of
the summer, pumpkin pie. We missed visiting during strawberry season,
when Aunt Carrie's traditionally offers Yankee strawberry shortcake.

Evelyn's Drive-In

2335 Main Rd.　　　　　　　　　401-624-3100

Tiverton, RI　　　　　　　　　　BLD (summer only) | $$

Evelyn's is a fair-weather drive-in with the nicest possible outdoor dining
area: a row of covered picnic tables perched over Sakonnet Bay with a
view of pleasure boats and the Newport shores. The outdoor dining is
strictly self-service—carry your own food from the order window. We actually saw one couple spread a tablecloth and open their own wine to accompany lobster plates.

Regular customers tend to eat inside at tables and a short counter,
where the view is of one another and the tight quarters are filled with

conversation and the hum of air conditioning (rather than the lap of water and the screech of seagulls). We noted that many of the locals order non-seafood meals from the broad menu: meat loaf, burgers, chicken pie, and one oddity we couldn't resist trying: a chow mein sandwich. It is a plate of frizzled-crisp chow mein noodles, soy-sauce gravy, and vegetables (beef optional) with a hamburger bun floating in it. Weird!

Evelyn's is at its best being a seafood shack, where the blackboard menu lists market prices for fried clams, scallops, and lobster. Scallops and clams are available in small- and large-size plates, the large being immense. In our experience, the clams are extraordinarily uniform in shape—the classic diamond-ring formation, with a chewy hoop and a gooey belly. The lobster roll, available with a choice of butter or mayonnaise served on the side, is only pretty good—more shredded meat than chunked. Chowder and clam cakes make a nice single-digit-priced meal—those market prices for seafood can take the better part of $20 for a single lunch. You want to have a little cash to splurge on the Rhode Island favorite for dessert: Grape-Nuts pudding.

Gray's Ice Cream

16 East Rd. at Four Corners   401-624-4500
Tiverton, RI $

On a summer day in Tiverton, Gray's parking lot is packed with people who come from miles around to indulge in the time-honored ritual of standing in line at the order window and getting cups and cones of ice cream that ranges from normal flavors to that Yankee oddity, Grape-Nuts. Gray's also is proof of our contention that Rhode Island is one of the most coffee-conscious places in the nation. (Where else do you find coffee milk—like chocolate milk but coffee flavored—sold by the cup and pint?) Coffee ice cream here is robust and just-right sweet. The other great Gray's flavor is ginger, made with bits of fresh root that give the creamy scoops a brilliant spicy bite.

Haven Brothers

Fulton and Dorrance Sts. at Kennedy Plaza   401-861-7777
Providence, RI   D late night | $

From the time the Haven Brothers truck pulls up alongside City Hall at 5:00 P.M. sharp to its 3:00 A.M. closing, there is always a colorful parade of Providence characters, inside and outside the movable diner, who carry on continuous conversation with the staff, with customers, or—if no one will listen—with the voices inside their own heads. To say that the clientele at this 1888-vintage late-night haunt is diverse is a ridiculous understatement. Among the regulars are big-shot city politicians, police officers, drunks who need to sober up when the bars close, and street people who range from wildly entertaining early in the evening to wild and scary after midnight.

There is a full menu of sandwiches, including lobster rolls and a great steak and cheese sandwich on toast, but most orders are for hot dogs or hamburgers. The dogs are plump and pink, served in soft steamed buns, available with chili and all the usual condiments. The hamburgers are modest-size patties, available from plain to deluxe (lettuce, tomato, mayo, etc.), but devotees of junk food get a double cheeseburger with the works, which includes every condiment in the house plus bacon, cheese, and chili. Side that with cheese-glopped French fries and you have a seriously satisfying sidewalk feast.

The most popular beverage at Haven Brothers is coffee milk, which is like coffee, but with much more milk than coffee. Or you can get what Rhode Islanders call a frappe (known elsewhere as a milkshake) made from ice cream, milk, and the flavoring of your choice.

Mike's Kitchen

At Tabor-Franchi VFW Post 239
170 Randall St.   401-946-5320
Cranston, RI   LD | $$

If you happen to drive past Mike's Kitchen, you won't notice it's a restaurant. Located in a VFW hall with no sign outside other than the post number, Mike's doesn't need to advertise. To those who seek out great Italian food at low prices, it is an appetite-stirring magnet. At mealtimes, its tables are always crowded. (Tuesday, Saturday, and Sunday nights, it is generally closed to the public; that's when the vets meet and when private functions generally are held.)

The menu, posted on the wall, is extremely appetizing: a catalog of dishes that are mostly Italian, a little Portuguese, and very Rhode Island. You can begin a meal with a stuffie (a stuffed quohog clam) or the unique Ocean State snail-salad appetizer, then move on to perfectly broiled swordfish or scallops, or indulge in such delectable old world favorites as sautéed broccoli rabe (or a rabe and provolone sandwich), sole Florentine, and chicken with cannellini beans. On the side of anything, you want polenta—a cream-soft block of steamy cooked cornmeal available with fennel-spiked sausage, meatballs, or a blanket of thick marinara sauce.

Many of the Italian dishes are familiar: veal cutlets in a variety of sauces, parmesans galore, scampis, and even spaghetti and meatballs and linguine with nothing but oil and garlic. Seafood pastas are especially wonderful, offered with a choice of red or white sauce; the top of the line is seafood diablo—lobster, scallops, and shrimp in spicy tomato sauce on a bed of noodles.

To drink with your meal, wine and cocktails are available from a bar at one side of the dining room. You will pay for these separately, as the bar is run by the veterans who own the building.

Olneyville N.Y. System

20 Plainfield St. 401-621-9500
Providence, RI LD | $

Rhode Island's distinctive New York System hot dog, known also as a hot wiener, is a small, pink, natural-casing, pork-beef-veal frankfurter nestled in an untoasted bun, topped with yellow mustard, chopped raw onions, and a dark sauce of ground beef plus a sprinkling of celery salt. It's the sauce that makes the dog unique—spicy but not hot, the meat ground as fine as sand, the flavor vaguely sweet, reminiscent of the kaleidoscopic flavors that give Greek-ancestored Cincinnati Five-Way chili its soul.

Indeed, most New York System restaurants are Greek-run. Olneyville was opened in the 1930s by the Stevens family, Greek immigrants who came to Rhode Island by way of Brooklyn, New York. It is still a Stevens-family operation, now with a second location on Reservoir Avenue in Cranston. The countermen use the old-time wiener-up-the-arm technique of preparing the hot dogs, lining up six to eight bunned ones from wrist to elbow and spreading sauce, onions, and mustard on all of them in the blink of an eye.

One very curious item on the short menu is beef stew, which is not beef stew at all. It is an order of salted French fries spritzed with vinegar and ribboned with ketchup. The beverage of choice is the Rhode Island favorite, coffee milk—like chocolate milk, but coffee flavored.

Baba à Louis

Route 11   802-875-4666
Chester, VT   BL | $

While scarcely a restaurant—no hot meals are served in the morning, and only sandwiches at lunch—Baba à Louis in Chester is one of Vermont's most noteworthy breakfast stops. Since he opened his bakery a quarter century ago, John McLure has won a reputation for masterful yeast breads. If you are serious about bread, you can stop in any day after 7:00 A.M., find a seat at one of the tables opposite the bakery shelves, and enjoy a cup of coffee while you tear off pieces from a warm baguette, anadama loaf, or sourdough rye. Morning-specific pastries are breathtaking, especially Mr. McLure's sticky buns. Ribboned with a walnutty brown-sugar glaze, these buttery cylinders are so fragile and fine that they verge on croissanthood.

Lunch is served cafeteria-style. There is pizza on the weekends, and Tuesday through Saturday, you can have a panini, open-face, or regular sandwich, quiche or soup or salad.

The place itself is beautiful: a sun-bathed baking cathedral with a full view of the open kitchen where doughs are kneaded and hot breads pulled from ovens.

Note: The bakery is closed during April and most of November, but opens again at Thanksgiving.

Blue Benn Diner

314 North St.   802-442-5140

Bennington, VT   BLD | $

The Blue Benn, an original Silk City dining car, was planted on this site along Route 7 in 1949. To this day, it remains a true-blue hash house with a menu that includes such square meals as pot roast, turkey dinner, and meat loaf and mashed potatoes. In addition to the expected, there are international dishes including Syrian-bread roll-ups and vegetarian enchiladas, and such modern fare as a grilled salmon Caesar salad. In fact, the interior is plastered everywhere with literally hundreds of kitchen specials, plain to fancy. Breakfast delights include corn bread French toast and stacks of Crunchberry pancakes with turkey hash on the side, as well as eminently dunkable locally made donuts.

Curtis's Barbecue

Route 5 (exit 4 off I-91)   802-387-5474

Putney, VT   L&D Apr-Oct (closed Mon) | $$

Pitmaster Curtis Tuff's self-proclaimed "Ninth Wonder of the World" serves fine ribs and chicken in high roadside style. By that we mean that this place is not actually a restaurant at all. It is a picnic. Place your order at the window of one of the blue-painted school buses that are permanently anchored in the meadow. When you have paid and it is ready, you will be pointed to a stack of cardboard cartons that are useful in toting the plates to a table, either in the sun or shade. Dine al fresco, then toss your trash in a can and be on your way.

Of the two things Mr. Tuff smoke-cooks, we go for ribs. They are available as slabs, half-slabs, medium orders and small. A half-slab is a hearty meal. The ribs are cooked so the meat pulls off in big, succulent strips that virtually burst with piggy flavor and the perfume of smoke. To dress these dandy bones, Mr. Tuff offers two sauces: mild and spicy, both of which are finger-licking good. On the side you want a nice baked potato, a cup of terrific beans, and/or ears of sweet corn.

Note that Curtis's Barbecue closes in October and reopens in April.

It is open for lunch and supper in the summer from Tuesday through Sunday, and fewer days of the week in the late spring and early fall.

The Dorset Inn

8 Church St.	802-867-5500
Dorset, VT	BLD | $$$

The Dorset Inn sings of Green Mountain character. Its two-century history, its setting on the village green, its broad front porch just right for rocking, its inviting hearth and broad-plank floors all contribute to an enveloping sense of place that could be nowhere else. When you eat here—breakfast, lunch, or dinner—you are savoring Vermont at its very best.

Chef-owner Sissy Hicks calls the meals she makes comfort food, and they are. But like the town of Dorset itself, this is a very fine kind of country comfort with an unmistakable air of elegance. Yes, you can have meat and potatoes for supper, but the meat may be pot roast Provençale and the potatoes may be roasted reds stuffed with pureed yams. Not that there is anything ostentatious about the food service here. The dinner tables, especially in the tavern, are as cozy as a club room. While the Dorset Inn is a destination for travelers in search of good food (and traditional accommodations for the night), it is also where locals come for lunch and supper to enjoy one another's company as well as the delicious meals.

It is not easy to define the Dorset Inn's cuisine. It is local in terms of ingredients, from Green Mountain maple syrup for morning waffles to small-farm beefsteak and wild-picked fiddlehead ferns at dinner. But Chef Hicks doesn't make a fetish of Vermont cuisine. "I pick up ideas here and there," she says. "I throw stuff together; I always find ways to put leftovers to good use. I cook the way it feels right. I never ventured off into nouvelle cuisine or anything like that. My mentors are James Beard and Julia Child. Like them, my joy comes from sharing good food. If there is a theme to what I do, it is 'natural simplicity.' " While she can dazzle guests with such culinary tours-de-force as breast of chicken stuffed with brie and coriander with pear and cider sauce, her repertoire is replete with masterful renditions of such down-to-earth dinners as braised lamb shanks, corned beef and cabbage, and turkey croquettes. Her own favorite dish—and, amazingly, the most popular meal at the inn—is liver and onions. There is none better, anywhere.

Dot's

3 West Main St.
Wilmington, VT

802-464-7284
BLD | $

If there are small towns in heaven, every one will have a place like Dot's: open for three square meals a day starting before dawn, with a staff of seasoned pros who are as welcoming to strangers passing through as to every-day regulars. The building itself—on Main Street, of course—has character galore. It was built in 1832 and has been a post office and a retail store. Current proprietors John and Patty Reagan told us, "We believe it started operating as a restaurant sometime after the turn of the twentieth century."

Dot's is a favorite of skiers on their way to or from Mt. Snow, and there's no place better to stop for a really hearty breakfast. We love the kitchen's French toast made from cracked wheat bread; the berry-berry pancakes poured from a batter positively loaded with blackberries, strawberries, raspberries, and blueberries; and the McDot's breakfast sandwiches, which are based on the Yellow Arches' version but are really, really good.

Year after year Dot's takes the People's Choice First Prize in the New England chili cook-off, and while Southwest chiliheads wouldn't even recognize it as their beloved bowl of red, this Yankee chili is terrific. It is listed on the menu as "Jailhouse Chili," but it's most respectable. Beefy, thick with beans, spicy but not ferocious, it comes as a cup or bowl under a mantle of melted cheese.

Mrs. Murphy's Donuts

Route 30
Manchester, VT

802-375-9387
BL | $

If a donut and a cup of coffee are all you need to start the day, there's no better place than a counter stool at Mrs. Murphy's Donuts in Manchester. You can get deluxe donuts—Boston creams, jelly-filled, iced and jimmie-sprinkled—but we'll take plain sinkers every time. They are the polar opposite of the frivolous fat puffs sold by Krispy Kreme in other parts of the country (but *not* in Vermont). These hefty boys have a wicked crunchy exterior and cake insides that love to sop a while in coffee; at Mrs. Murphy's, you'll see a virtual dough-si-donut line of dunkers sitting at the counter bobbing theirs in and out of mugs.

The storefront café is a locals' favorite; it occurred to us one breakfast hour that most customers didn't tell Cheryl, the waitress, what they wanted; she brought them the usual. One banker-looking guy in striped suit and brogues left his sedan idling outside, stepped to the take-out counter, grabbed a bag and flapped it open for Cheryl to load with six sour cream donuts. As she rang him up, he nodded thanks to her and she nodded thanks to him, then he left and drove away; not a word was spoken between them.

P & H Truck Stop

Exit 17 off I-91   802-429-2141
Wells River, VT   BLD | $

P & H, a real truck stop, is not for the fastidious epicure. You need to pass through the aroma of diesel fuel outside to get to the smells of fresh-baked bread and of pot roast with gravy in the dining room. Enter past shelves of whole loaves of white and cinnamon-raisin bread for sale. This is a kitchen that means business.

Soups and chowders are especially inviting: tomato-macaroni soup is thick with vegetables, ground beef, and soft noodles; corn chowder is loaded with potatoes and corn kernels and flavored with bacon. We love the falling-apart pot roast and any kind of sandwich made using thick-sliced P & H bread, but the mashed potatoes (*puree de pommes de terre* on the bilingual menu, written for French-Canadian truckers) taste like they were made from powder, and the meat loaf is strictly for die-hard diner fans.

The homemade dessert selection is huge, including fruit pies, berry pies, custard pies, meringue pies, Reese's pie (a peanut-cream), a few types of pudding, and maple-cream pie thick as toffee and topped with nuts.

Putney Diner

82 Main St.   802-387-5433
Putney, VT   BLD | $

"We're ready for our pies," we tell Ellie, the waitress at the Putney Diner.

"No, you're not!" she responds, noting that we haven't totally cleaned our plates of foot-long hot dogs with baked beans, macaroni and (cheddar) cheese, a meat loaf sandwich with cheese and cranberry sauce, shepherd's pie, and split pea soup with ham.

We implore her, and she relents, cutting big, unwieldy slices of apple pie, crumb-top berry pie, and maple walnut pie. The maple walnut is especially hefty. "You want ice cream or whipped cream with that?" Ellie asks. "You need one or the other because that pie is so sweet."

Although the logic of her recommendation escapes us, we do as Ellie says and have our maple pie topped with whipped cream. She is the kind of waitress who makes you want to behave right. "Can't you tell I used to be a mother?" she says. Then comes the punch line: "But I gave it up due to lack of interest."

So it goes at the Putney Diner, a delightful little town eatery just minutes away from I-91 at Exit 4. Although it doesn't look like a classic diner, this place has the spirit . . . and the menu. In the morning, plates of plain or buckwheat pancakes come with only-in-Vermont maple syrup. Eggs can be had with kielbasa or corned beef hash. And broad-topped muffins are split and toasted on the grill. At lunch, you can count on square meals of meat loaf or roast turkey and stuffing or the arcane Yankee favorite, American chop suey.

Simon Pearce Restaurant

1760 Main St.	802-295-2711
Quechee, VT	LD | $$

Quechee is a magical New England village, known best for the nearby Quechee Gorge, "Vermont's Grand Canyon," and for the legendary Simon Pearce Restaurant. Originally opened in 1985 as the Glassblower's Cafe, the restaurant is part of the Simon Pearce glassblowing factory that is still downstairs. An airy dining room is perched high above the rushing waterfall that powers the glasswork's furnaces and has large windowed walls that look out over Quechee's covered bridge. The setting is New England at its most picturesque.

Pearce himself is Irish, and his kitchen offers such homeland comfort-food specialties as soda bread scones and Ballymaloe brown bread, beef and Guinness stew, and an unspeakably delicious shepherd's pie made from local grass-fed beef and topped with a savory cheese-enriched crust. Many dishes are a creative ode to favorite Yankee groceries, such as horseradish-crusted cod, Maine salmon in phyllo dough with Vermont chèvre cream, Vermont cheese soup, and house-smoked trout. And there is a grand Caesar salad garnished with crusty fried oysters.

Available libations include a choice from an astonishing 900-label wine list, locally brewed beers and ales, and hot mulled cider. For dessert, we favor the old-fashioned Irish apple cake and pumpkin bread pudding, served warm with cranberries and caramel sauce and a dollop of rich vanilla ice cream.

Up for Breakfast

710 Main St.   802-362-4204
Manchester, VT   BL | $$

Seats can be scarce in this cozy café, but if you are looking for something extraspecial in the morning, Up for Breakfast is a gold mine. You really do go *up* for breakfast. It is a second-story restaurant with window views of Main Street. There is pleasant art on the walls, and if you sit toward the back, you can enjoy watching goings-on in the semi-open kitchen.

Pancakes are a true taste of Vermont, especially when glazed with pools of maple syrup. You can have them with or without blueberries, made from sunny-hued buttermilk batter, dark and serious buckwheat batter, or sourdough. Sourdough 'cakes make a faint crunching sound when you press the edge of a fork to their surface. Inside the lacy web that encloses them, they are thin but substantial, with the vigorous disposition of a starter with character.

Muffins are excellent, available hot from the tin or sliced, buttered, and grilled. More elaborate meals include multi-ingredient frittatas, French toast made using big slabs of spice bread, and chicken-duck-cilantro sausage. Wild turkey hash—wildly assembled, not made from wild turkeys—is a cook's tour-de-force that combines big shreds of roasted turkey with peppers, onions, potatoes, and pine nuts, all griddle-cooked until crusty brown on the outside and topped with poached eggs and a film of fine hollandaise. If you like omelets, let us suggest "The Metropolitan"—smoked salmon, chopped red onions, melting-warm cream cheese, capers, and a sprinkle of dill.

Wayside Restaurant

1873 US Route 202   802-223-6611
Montpelier, VT   BLD | $$

The Wayside Restaurant has been an oasis of regional cooking since it opened in 1918. The true-Vermont menu has traditionally included salt pork and milk gravy, fresh native perch, old-fashioned boiled dinner, and several kinds of hash, including red flannel hash (so named because beets dye it the color of a farmer's long johns). Most of these things are still available at the Wayside, although not every day. Perch can be had only during ice-fishing season, when it is lightly breaded and fried to a crisp; salt pork covered with creamy white gravy has become a Thursday-only tradition; boiled dinner and shepherd's pie are cold-weather specials; fiddlehead ferns are offered only a few weeks in the spring. Every supper is complemented by fresh-baked Parker House rolls.

Whatever the daily specials, and regardless of seasonal shortages, you will eat well any time you come to this cheerful town lunchroom. You begin to sense that fact when you smell warm rolls being toted to the tables. They have a just-baked, yeasty perfume that promises great things to come. What joy it is to tear off a shred from a roll and submerge it into a bowl of Wayside beef barley soup—a hearty brew so thick with meat and pearly grain that a spoon literally stands up in it—or dip it in the vegetable soup, a jumble of hand-cut carrots, squash, onions, tomato, and beans.

Please note that Wednesday is traditionally chicken pie and meat loaf day. What a feast the chicken pie is: piled into a big crockery boat with dressing and a crusty biscuit, with a great heap of gravy-dripping mashed potatoes on the side. The meat loaf is superb, too: a two-inch-thick slab with a sticky red glaze along the rim and rivulets of stout brown gravy dripping down its sides.

In addition to such classic north country lunch-room desserts as tapioca pudding, Grape-Nuts custard, mince pie, and homemade ginger snaps, the dessert repertoire includes apple pie made with densely packed hand-cut apples in a fork-crimped crust and maple cream pie. Low and flat with barely whipped cream dolloped on top, the filling of the maple pie is too delicious for words. Its radiant band of amber cream is complex, powerful, and elegant the way only pure maple can be, and it resonates on your taste buds after a Wayside meal like a Yankee cordial.

White Cottage

Route 4	802-457-3455
Woodstock, VT	LD (summer only) | $

It was the summer of 1957 when the White Cottage opened on Route 4 at the edge of the pretty Vermont town of Woodstock, and the menu is still a vivid expression of midcentury drive-in tastes. Residents and summer visitors come to these breezy tables for excellent made-to-order hamburgers, hot dogs, and foot-longs served Yankee-style in grilled rolls and fried clams, available whole bellied or as strips.

On the side of the classic vacation meals, you can drink a soda, a lemonade, a milkshake, or a frappe. Ever curious about the obscure taxonomy of New England soda fountain beverages, we asked the person behind the order window to explain the difference between a milkshake and a frappe. Here, a frappe is made with hard ice cream, a milkshake with soft ice cream.

In fact, ice cream is big in this place. (Vermont is a dairy state.) They serve Gifford's brand, available in several dozen flavors, in cones and cups, in floats and freezes, and in handsome banana splits made with three ice cream flavors and three toppings, plus whipped cream, nuts, and a cherry.

Mid-Atlantic

Delaware * District of Columbia * Maryland *

New Jersey * New York * Pennsylvania

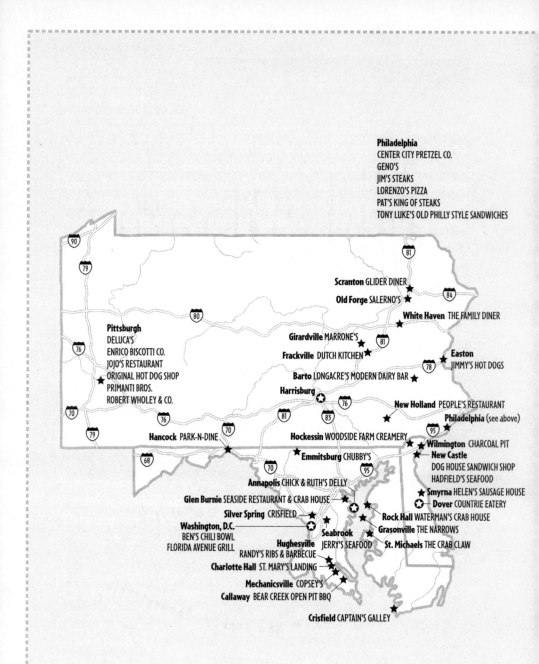

Philadelphia
CENTER CITY PRETZEL CO.
GENO'S
JIM'S STEAKS
LORENZO'S PIZZA
PAT'S KING OF STEAKS
TONY LUKE'S OLD PHILLY STYLE SANDWICHES

Scranton GLIDER DINER ★
Old Forge SALERNO'S ★

White Haven THE FAMILY DINER

Pittsburgh
DELUCA'S
ENRICO BISCOTTI CO.
JOJO'S RESTAURANT
ORIGINAL HOT DOG SHOP
PRIMANTI BROS.
ROBERT WHOLEY & CO.

Girardville MARRONE'S ★
Frackville DUTCH KITCHEN ★

Easton
JIMMY'S HOT DOGS

Barto LONGACRE'S MODERN DAIRY BAR ★

Harrisburg

New Holland PEOPLE'S RESTAURANT ★

Philadelphia (see above)

Hancock PARK-N-DINE ★

Hockessin WOODSIDE FARM CREAMERY ★

Wilmington CHARCOAL PIT ★
New Castle ★
DOG HOUSE SANDWICH SHOP
HADFIELD'S SEAFOOD

Emmitsburg CHUBBY'S ★

Annapolis CHICK & RUTH'S DELLY

Smyrna HELEN'S SAUSAGE HOUSE ★
Dover COUNTRIE EATERY ✪

Glen Burnie SEASIDE RESTAURANT & CRAB HOUSE

Silver Spring CRISFIELD ★

Rock Hall WATERMAN'S CRAB HOUSE ★

Washington, D.C. ✪
BEN'S CHILI BOWL
FLORIDA AVENUE GRILL

Seabrook

Grasonville THE NARROWS ★

Hughesville ★
RANDY'S RIBS & BARBECUE

Jerry's Seafood JERRY'S SEAFOOD

St. Michaels THE CRAB CLAW ★

Charlotte Hall ST. MARY'S LANDING ★

Mechanicsville COPSEY'S ★
Callaway BEAR CREEK OPEN PIT BBQ ★

Crisfield CAPTAIN'S GALLEY ★

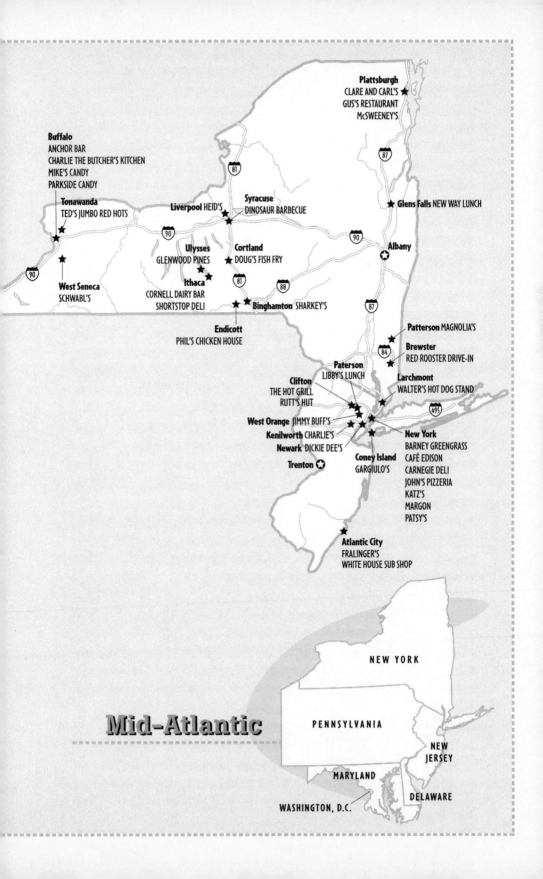

Plattsburgh
CLARE AND CARL'S
GUS'S RESTAURANT
McSWEENEY'S

Buffalo
ANCHOR BAR
CHARLIE THE BUTCHER'S KITCHEN
MIKE'S CANDY
PARKSIDE CANDY

Tonawanda
TED'S JUMBO RED HOTS

Glens Falls NEW WAY LUNCH

Liverpool HEID'S

Syracuse
DINOSAUR BARBECUE

Ulysses
GLENWOOD PINES

Cortland
DOUG'S FISH FRY

Albany

West Seneca
SCHWABL'S

Ithaca
CORNELL DAIRY BAR
SHORTSTOP DELI

Binghamton SHARKEY'S

Endicott
PHIL'S CHICKEN HOUSE

Patterson MAGNOLIA'S

Brewster
RED ROOSTER DRIVE-IN

Paterson
LIBBY'S LUNCH

Clifton
THE HOT GRILL
RUTT'S HUT

Larchmont
WALTER'S HOT DOG STAND

West Orange JIMMY BUFF'S
Kenilworth CHARLIE'S
Newark DICKIE DEE'S

New York
BARNEY GREENGRASS
CAFÉ EDISON
CARNEGIE DELI
JOHN'S PIZZERIA
KATZ'S
MARGON
PATSY'S

Trenton

Coney Island
GARGIULO'S

Atlantic City
FRALINGER'S
WHITE HOUSE SUB SHOP

NEW YORK

PENNSYLVANIA

NEW JERSEY

MARYLAND

DELAWARE

WASHINGTON, D.C.

Mid-Atlantic

Charcoal Pit

2600 Concord Pike (Route 202)   302-478-2165
Wilmington, DE   LD | $

We were tipped off to the Charcoal Pit by a Roadfooder who believed they hadn't changed their recipes since opening in 1952: "Everything has all the cholesterol and great taste from the old days." He recommended malts, sundaes, burgers, and fries.

Sure enough, the hamburger exudes midcentury Americana: a modest patty with a charcoal taste served on a spongy bun either plain or in the deluxe configuration, which adds lettuce, tomato, and pickle. For those who crave extra meat, there is also a double-size eight-ounce hamburger, but in our opinion, that's too late twentieth century, not really 1950s in spirit. The fries on the side are savory, normal-size twigs with a nice tough skin and soft potato flavor. And the milkshakes come in their big silver beakers that hold at least two glasses full. (The shakes are so thick that a long-handled spoon is provided to help you get it from the beaker into your glass.) We even enjoyed the crab cakes, which were a couple of hardball-shaped spheres with crusty outsides and a fair measure of crab filling the interior.

It's an old-fashioned kind of place with comfy maroon booths and vintage menus decorating the wall. Waitresses go about their job with aplomb and attitude that make customers feel part of a cheap-eats ritual that has gone on forever.

There are other Charcoal Pits at 5200 Pike Creek, in the Fox Run Shopping Center, and in Prices Corner at Kirkwood Highway and Greenbank Road.

Countrie Eatery

950 N. State St.	302-674-8310
Dover, DE	BLD | $

Breakfast is swell at the Countrie Eatery: buttermilk pancakes or shillings (silver dollar 'cakes) filled with bananas or blueberries, or hefty biscuits topped with sausage gravy. The gravy, like creamed chipped beef, is also available on regular toast or an English muffin. There are two noteworthy styles of French toast, one made with cinnamon bread, the other with seed-dotted sunflower bread. The latter is served as three long, thick pieces that are soft, moist, and nearly as eggy as pudding, dusted with powdered sugar. We got ours with a side order of scrapple—two thick slices from the loaf, fried until crunchy on the outside, but moist and porky within.

At lunch you can have a sirloin burger, a hot sandwich made with turkey, pork, or beef and *real* mashed potatoes, or a terrific crab melt loaded with hunks of pearly sweet Chesapeake Bay crab meat. Every day the Countrie Eatery offers one all-you-can-eat special. Monday = chicken 'n' dumplings, Tuesday = stuffed peppers, Wednesday = lasagna, Thursday = beef stew, Friday = fried chicken, Saturday = chicken livers.

Ambience is country-craftsy Colonial with primitive art and old-time farm implements on the wall.

Dog House Sandwich Shop

1200 DuPont Hwy. (Route 13)	302-328-5380
New Castle, DE	LD | $

"Our dogs go out with the nicest people!" is the house motto here, where a large percentage of business is take-out. Placing and picking up to-go orders in the vestibule is an adventure unto itself, not for anyone too timid to push through a crowd to get what they want. Nor is the Dog

House a restaurant to which you want to come for a calm, quiet meal or even for a normal-level conversation. This joint is loud and a little looney and lots of fun. Dining accommodations are limited to counter seats with a view of sandwich makers at work.

The hot dogs are excellent—bisected and grilled, served in soft buns and available with terrific hot peppers—and the cheesesteaks are near-Philly quality, loaded with griddle-cooked, thin-sliced meat and soft sweet onions. About the only other item on the menu we care about is the turkey sandwich. This is the real thing, made from a bird roasted on premises using meat that is, as the sign above the counter boasts, "hand-picked for easy eating."

Hadfield's Seafood

192 N. DuPont Hwy. (Route 13) 302-322-0900
New Castle, DE LD | $

You will have no trouble spotting Hadfield's as you travel north on Route 13. It is the shop with a crab statuette the size of a minivan hovering over the front door. While many people buy crabs and other raw seafood to take home and cook, Hadfield's makes a specialty of selling whole meals to go. There used to be makeshift tables where you could sit down and eat here, but they are gone, so finding a place to eat is your responsibility.

Beyond whole crab, fried fish is the star of the show—scallops, flounder, oysters, whiting, and shrimp—but it is also possible to get broiled crab cakes, stuffed flounder, a pair of shells filled with creamy crab imperial, and hot chicken wings by the ten-count, up to 100 for $35.99, including blue cheese and celery. Dinners include coleslaw, French fries, a roll and butter, and tartar sauce. It is also possible to get just about anything the kitchen makes by the pound or dozen.

We love browsing Hadfield's cases and studying all the seafood on display, especially the bounty of the Chesapeake Bay. Last time we visited, it was the height of crab season and the counter contained a visual demonstration of different-size hard-shell crabs, from itty-bitty hardly worth cracking to the kind we all want to eat, here labeled "Texas monsters" and selling for $49 per dozen, live or cooked, and $189 a bushel (live) or $193 a bushel (cooked).

Helen's Sausage House

4866 N. Dupont Hwy. (Route 13)　　302-653-4200
Smyrna, DE　　　　　　　　　　　BL | $

If you are hungry and rushing north toward the Delaware Valley Bridge any time between four in the morning and lunch (or on Sunday, starting at 7:00 A.M.), call Helen's and place a sandwich order. That's the way the truckers do it, and in this case, the truckers are onto a very good thing. Helen's Sausage House is a roadside eatery with huge sandwiches at small prices.

The sausages Helen serves are thick and crusty giants with plenty of Italian zest. They spurt juice when you bite them, and a normal sandwich is two in a roll (although wimpy appetites can get a single). With fried green peppers and onions, this is a truly majestic arrangement of food— a little messy to eat with one hand while driving, but nevertheless, one of the great sausage sandwiches anywhere.

Helen's offers all manner of breakfast sandwich on bread or rolls, made with eggs, bacon, scrapple, and fried ham, as well as lunchtime sandwiches of steak, cheesesteak, burgers, hot beef, and hot ham. Other than the sausage, the one must-eat (and must see!) meal is Helen's pork chop sandwich. When the menu says jumbo pork chop, you better believe it. This slab of meat is approximately three times larger than the puny pieces of white bread that are stuck on either side of it. It isn't all that thick a chop, but it is tender, moist, and mouth-wateringly spiced.

While most of Helen's clientele stop by for sandwiches wrapped to go, it is possible to dine here. Place your order at the counter and carry it to one of a few tables on ground level opposite the instant-order counter, or proceed up a couple of steps into a dining room decorated entirely with pictures of Elvis. Roadfood extraordinaire!

Woodside Farm Creamery

1310 Little Baltimore Rd.　　　302-239-9847
Hockessin, DE　　　　　　　　$ (closed in winter)

Rebekah Denn, now of Seattle but formerly of Delaware, tipped us off to this ice cream bonanza out in cow country at Stuyvesant Hills Park. It is a working farm open to the public daily from early April through late October, and while schoolkids may come to it as a place to learn about how a dairy operates, about conservation of woodlands and pasture, and about raising sheep for wool, serious eaters, young and old, think of it as home of the Hog Trough Sundae. That's five flavors of ice cream—two scoops of each—topped with three different toppings, a fresh banana, whipped cream, and a cherry.

Ice cream is made the really old-fashioned way, by taking high-butterfat milk from Jersey cows and turning it into sweet cream. The sweet cream is mixed with fruit, flavorings, and nuts and frozen in small batches to be sold at the farm's stand. Jim Mitchell, whose family settled here in 1796, likes to tell visitors, "Two weeks ago, our ice cream was grass."

The flavors range from chocolate and coffee to pumpkin pecan and butter brickle toffee, all available in quarts and pints as well as cones, cups, and sundaes. It is wonderful normal ice cream, by which we mean it is not sickeningly butterfatty or cloying with too many mix-ins. The ingenuous true-farm flavor is especially welcome in varieties made with fresh fruit: peach, strawberry, black raspberry, and black cherry. Turtle ice cream is choco-caramel-cream ecstasy. African vanilla is vanilla squared.

Ben's Chili Bowl

1213 U St. NW   202-667-0909

Washington, DC   LD | $

"Mustard and onions?" is the question you will be asked when you order a half-smoke at Ben's Chili Bowl. The correct answer is yes. The snappy-skinned, slightly smoke-flavored tube steak that is unique to the DC area benefits beyond measure from both condiments.

This is Ben's Chili Bowl, and so a chili smoke is another essential thing to eat. That is a half-smoke smothered with Ben's dark, lively chili sauce. You can also get the chili atop French fries, which in our opinion is a bad decision. Ben's fries are especially crisp and a great companion for half-smokes and chili smokes. Good as the chili tastes, it mitigates the fries' crispness.

Half-smokes, chili smokes, and French fries are familiar elements of Ben's exalted reputation among Roadfooders. Less famous, but well worth knowing about, are Ben's soulful cakes and pies. The last time we visited, the menu included both sweet potato cake and sweet potato pie, the former a spicy layer cake encased in luxurious cream cheese frosting, the latter creamy and not too sweet—true essence of sweet potato.

Big as its reputation is, Ben's remains a relaxed and easygoing diner, part of the neighborhood since 1958, surviving urban unrest and economic ups and downs. In 2001, its founders, Ben and Virginia Ali, were inducted into the Washington, DC, Hall of Fame. Today the restaurant is run by their sons.

Florida Avenue Grill

1100 Florida Ave.   202-265-1586
Washington, DC   BLD | $

Aside from its good eats, we love the Florida Avenue Grill because it never changes. Open now for fifty years, and on our Roadfood map for about half that time, the only things we've seen change are the celebrity photos and endorsements on the wall. A lot of retired representatives and members of White House staffs have been supplanted by current office-holders. Curiously, though, the big name sports stars never seem to go out of style and their images remain long past their glory days.

If by our preceding description of its famous clientele, you've gotten the notion that the Florida Avenue Grill is highfalutin or high priced, please reconsider. It is anything but. A humble diner with a counter and booths, it serves meals that generally cost well under $10, some under $5. And, as for being fancy, you'll see taxicab drivers and blue-collar workers here shoulder to shoulder with the capital's power players. Good meals like these aren't the privilege of any one class.

You can come for seriously soulful soul food such as pigs' feet or chitterlings, but unless you are a feet aficionado already, we suggest you begin with more familiar things to eat—spare ribs, for example, glazed with breathless hot sauce, rugged and satisfying. These are not yuppie baby back ribs; they are food that makes you work, and when you do, they deliver tidal waves of flavor. Pork chops are like that, too: highly seasoned, meaty, and substantial. For a tender meal, how about meat loaf? This meat loaf, particularly with a side of mashed potatoes and a heap of pungent collard greens, is one of the kitchen's unexpected triumphs, its coarse-textured meat shot through with brilliant spices. True to Southern custom, there are lots of vegetables to accompany the entrees: candied sweet potatoes, rich macaroni and cheese, lavish potato salad, rice, beans, peas, and always sweet corn bread for mopping up a plate.

For many devotees of the Florida Avenue Grill, the best meal of the day is breakfast. That's when you can have stacks of pancakes, onion-laced corned beef hash, cornmeal muffins, squares of scrapple, crusty fried potatoes, stewed spiced apples, buttermilk biscuits, and grits and gravy.

This humble restaurant with its sprung-spring booths, pink counter, and red plastic stools is cheap, fast, and satisfying. Its motherly waitresses make even us strangers feel right at home.

Bear Creek Open Pit BBQ

21030 Point Lookout Rd.   301-994-1030

Callaway, MD   LD | $

Callaway is way south in Maryland, and while the Chesapeake Bay is best known (and rightfully so) for its excellent seafood, it is also a place where you'll find fine true-South barbecue. One of several smokehouses in the region, Bear Creek is unique for its huge open pit. You'll see it on the left as you walk in the door. Here, pitmaster Curtis Shreve cooks pork and beef so tender that if you look at it hard, it falls apart. We are especially fond of the pork, either hand-pulled into shreds or sliced into pieces soft as velvet. It has a fine smoky flavor and a piggy richness that defies description. It is, in fact, so good that we like it without any sauce whatsoever, all the better to savor the flavor of the meat. (Mr. Shreve's sauce, we should say, is excellent: sweet and a wee bit hot.)

Beyond barbecue and the St. Mary's County specialty, ham stuffed with spiced greens, you can expect Bear Creek to have interesting game on the menu. Curtis Shreve is a hunter, and while he cannot serve what he kills (health department regulations forbid it), he does have a fondness for such meats as venison, alligator, and frog legs. When we stopped in, the day's special was rabbit stew—a hearty meal that included big hunks of carrot and potato and easy-to-eat pieces of breaded and fried rabbit. On the side of the stew we had a block of homemade corn bread.

Mr. Shreve originally hails from the Louisiana-Texas borderland, so his cooking reflects Southwest roots, too. The kids' menu contains corn dogs reminiscent of those at the Texas State Fair, and here also is that miraculous Texas twist on chili known as Fritos pie: a bed of crisp corn chips topped with chili and spangled with cheese. Shreve remembered, "When I was a kid years ago, they used to take a scoop of chili and put it right in the bag of Fritos and you ate it just like that. Now the bags are made of plastic that does not withstand the heat. So we serve our Fritos pie in a dish."

Captain's Galley

1021 W. Main St.   866-576-6412
Crisfield, MD   LD | $$$

Dining at the Captain's Galley can be expensive by Roadfood standards. An order of rockfish is $14. Broiled lump crabmeat is $18. And while there are some very nice-looking sandwiches in the under-$10 range, including oyster fritters on a hoagie roll and fried soft-shell crabs, the dish we recommend will set you back $20. That's a pair of crab cakes, available fried or broiled. Many Mid-Atlantic seafood aficionados think these are the best. They are creamy-sweet and fresh as ocean spray, tender but with a nice little snap to their golden crust, even if you get them broiled.

The restaurant, which is a family-friendly outfit with enough elbow room to host banquets and offer frequent weekend entertainment, claims "the best view on the Eastern Shore." That's hard to dispute, especially looking west at sunset, but it's those superlative crab cakes that will keep us coming back.

Chick & Ruth's Delly

165 Main St.   410-269-6737
Annapolis, Maryland   BLD | $

Chick & Ruth's is a wild, fun place to eat breakfast, lunch, dinner, or a late-night snack. In the heart of old Annapolis, it is a Jewish-style (but not strictly kosher) deli that is so cramped that if you sit in one of the booths opposite the counter, you will be within inches of the person next to you. This is not the place to come for a quiet, private, or intimate conversation!

The menu is wide-ranging, from creamed chipped beef on toast to spiced steamed shrimp by the pound. At breakfast, you can have a bagel with lox, pancakes with a ham steak, or a seasoned crab omelet with a heap of Delly fried potatoes. At lunch, there are sandwiches, hot plates, foot-long dogs, and fantastic hamburgers ranging from two-ouncers to one-pounders. The homemade soup repertoire is grand, including matzoh ball, chicken noodle, French onion, Maryland crab (spicy!), and cream of crab.

Being near the District of Columbia, Chick & Ruth's Delly has its own twist on the kosher-style restaurant theme of giving celebrity monikers to sandwiches. Here the house specialties have the names of politicians ranging from George W. Bush (turkey breast, lettuce, and tomato on whole wheat toast) to George Nutwell, the registrar of wills (turkey, bacon, lettuce, and tomato on rye toast). Big as regular sandwiches are, there is a whole separate section of the menu that boasts "The Biggest Sandwiches in Annapolis." Someday we shall order a foot-and-a-half-long sub titled USS Annapolis, loaded with with hams, salamis, cheeses, lettuce, tomato, onions, and special Italian sauce.

Chubby's Southern Style Barbeque

Route 15N at Old Frederick Rd.   301-447-3322
Emmitsburg, MD   LD | $$

A plain place in the beautiful countryside south of Gettysburg, Chubby's has become a destination dining spot for lovers of barbecued pork. Smokemeister Tom Caulfield marinates and dry rubs ribs, cooking them low and slow until drippingly tender, then serving them with a choice of sauces that includes South Carolina mustard–style, North Carolina vinegar-pepper, and the most familiar, sweet-tangy tomato. Caulfield's pulled pork is soft and smoky, and baked beans are liberally laced with shreds of it. Even the barbecued brisket is excellent, albeit more Texan than Southern.

The menu is broad and also includes non-barbecued daily specials. About five years ago Washington Redskins lineman Randy Thomas made pig-out history by consuming six pounds of Chubby's food in less than an hour. His menu included a pound of brisket, two-and-a-half pounds of ribs, a pound of shrimp scampi, a pound of chili, three-quarters of a pound of crab dip, cheese-garlic toast, cheesecake, and pumpkin parfait. His beverage of choice was iced tea, of which he ingested a gallon.

Copsey's

Route 5	301-884-4235
Mechanicsville, MD	LD | $$

Copsey's is an all-purpose stop along Route 5: it is a liquor store, a raw seafood market, a take-out seafood shop, and a sit-down restaurant, as well as a place fishermen and friends hang around having a few tall cool ones and discussing whatever needs to be discussed. The primary attraction for those of us eating our way along the Western Shore is spiced, steamed, hard-shelled crabs, served by the dozen on tables covered with brown paper and outfitted with mallets and picks for getting at the crustaceans' elusive meat.

Beyond whole Maryland crabs, Copsey's is a source of big, plump crab cakes, pounds of you-peel-'em steamed shrimp (infused with the same peppery orange spice mix that is used on the crabs), and raw oysters by the dozen. It is a distinctly local kind of place, and we have observed that many of the regular patrons come to eat fried chicken dinners; they are apparently that blasé about their great local seafood.

The Crab Claw

Route 33 West	410-745-2900
St. Michaels, MD	LD (closed in winter) | $$

The great meal of Maryland's shore is a crab feast. Hard-shelled blue crabs, steamed in spice, are served in a great heap upon the table along with pick, mallet, piles of napkins, and plenty of beer. It is a royal mess, and crab-eating novices will expend nearly as many calories as they consume pulling and prying meat from the crustaceans' shells. But oh, what delicious meat it is! Soft and sweet yet laced with spice, it is as addictive as food can be.

Perched high on a pier overlooking the Miles River, the Crab Claw of St. Michaels opened for business about a half a century ago as a wholesale crab business. It is now one of the top places to indulge in such a feast, and it has customers who arrive by boat as well as by car. Some come to take away bushels full of crabs for waterside picnics; many come to sit at the Crab Claw tables with rolled-up sleeves and dig in. The dining room clatters with the sounds of hammering, cracking, and slurping that are a crab feast's happy tune. Written instructions are provided telling exactly how to extract meat from a cooked hard-shelled crab, but if you find all that work a little daunting, the kitchen here has a full roster of other crab-centric meals to offer, including crab cakes, soft-shell crabs, crab claws, crab soup, and crab cocktail.

Oysters, clams, shrimp, and scallops are also available on the Crab Claw menu, as are filet mignon and chicken for crustacean-frowners. But if you don't like crabs, this is the wrong part of the world for you to be in.

Crisfield

8012 Georgia Ave.　　　　　　301-589-1306
Silver Spring, MD　　　　　　LD | $$$

Crisfield's is expensive, but no-frills. The room you enter is like a bar, with a long counter running along both sides and stools where people sit to eat and drink. The adjoining dining room has walls covered with white tile and cinder blocks, with all the charm of a locker room. Service is brusque and efficient and a full dinner can run over $20; even "light fare" meals are close to $15 and sandwiches are just under $10.

We'll happily pay these prices because some of the food served here is top-drawer. Crisfield's is a fish house with regional specialties you simply don't find many places anymore. For example, seafood Norfolk–style (i.e., swimming in butter), and huge filets of flounder, broiled or fried or heaped with mountains of fresh lump crabmeat, as well as oysters and soft-shell crabs in season.

We have found the Crisfield special (lump crabmeat mixed with a bit of mayo and baked until golden brown) to be erratic: one time fresh and sweet, another kinda tired, but the crab-stuffed flounder has never been a disappointment. It is a gigantic, milky-white fillet covered with a full-flavored crown of crab. We also liked the Combination Norfolk—hunks of crab, whole shrimp, and pieces of lobster all crowded into a skillet up to their waistlines in melted butter. It's a simple preparation, but unbeatable.

(A second, more stylish Crisfield is located at Lee Plaza, 8606 Colesville Rd., in Silver Spring. The number there is 301–588–1572.)

Jerry's Seafood

9364 Lanham-Severn Rd.   302-645-6611

Seabrook, MD   L Mon-Fri, D Tues-Sat | $$$

Surefire tipster Joe Heflin described Jerry's Seafood to us as the "best overall Maryland seafood restaurant without a view." He warned that the ambience is nondescript—Jerry's is located in a strip mall—and we should expect long lines any evening, especially on weekends.

No problem. We'll gladly wait for this extraordinary DC-area seafood treasure. Nor do we need to be soaking up ambience when we have one of Jerry's crab bombs on a plate in front of us. This is a fairly gigantic (ten ounce) and very expensive ($34) crab cake that is nothing more than fresh jumbo lump meat, Old Bay seasoning, and enough mayonnaise to make it cling together, baked until a painfully fragile crust develops all around the edges but the inside is still moist and sweet. Even better for those with a yen for spice thrills is the firecracker crab bomb, to which mustard and pepper are added. Jerry's also makes a six-ounce Baby Bomb ($26) and ordinary-size crab cakes.

Mr. Heflin's other recommendation was crab soup, which is a virtuoso balance of creaminess, crabbiness, and sharp spice. You can also eat velvety crab imperial perked up with peppers, crab dip, and crab bisque made with sherry. Those who are anti-crab can revel in fried shrimp, scallops, and oysters, all with a delicate crust, as well as good side dishes that include what the menu promises are made from Jerry's mom's recipes: stewed tomatoes and coleslaw.

The Narrows

3023 Kent Narrows Way S.   410-827-8113

Grasonville, MD   LD | $$$

Here is an extraordinarily handsome Eastern Shore restaurant in a breathtaking setting overlooking the Kent Narrows, where local watermen come and go and pleasure boaters drop anchor and relax. The menu is broad, including $30 and up steak dinners, sandwiches, and salads for lunch, hamburgers, cioppino, and barbecued quail with polenta, blackberries and Smithfield ham in a balsamic glaze.

Great stuff, what little of it we have sampled, but we likely wouldn't include this place in Roadfood if it weren't for the crab cakes. Here is the Eastern Shore delight done to perfection—crab cakes so perfect that any traveler in search of the best regional specialties needs to dive in with a fork.

As the fork touches the cake, chances are good it will begin to disintegrate, for there isn't much here other than pearly lump crabmeat, a little mayo, and some seasoning. The outside is baked to faint brownness, but beyond minimal crust is only moist, warm, sweet ocean goodness. And by the way, the cream of crab soup is sensational, too—loaded with hunks of crab.

Park-n-Dine

189 East Main St.	301-678-5242
Hancock, MD	BLD | $

If you are driving—or riding your bicycle—through the narrowest part of western Maryland in Hancock and find yourself hankering for meat and potatoes, pull up to Park-n-Dine. Located alongside I-70 and on the bike trail from Indian Springs along the C&O Canal, this venerable establishment is a blast from the past where uniformed waitresses are pros and where the kitchen still practices the craft of from-scratch cooking.

High kudos to the old-fashioned roast turkey dinner with mashed potatoes, stuffing, and gravy, followed, of course, by wedges of apple pie or actual from-scratch pudding (banana, tapioca, chocolate). Yes, that's pudding, not mousse! Sandwiches and hamburgers are available, and breakfast is fine and dandy, but the charm of Park-n-Dine for us is its seven-day-a-week roster of Sunday dinner, i.e., pork chops, meat loaf, and plates of steaming-pink corned beef and cabbage. Portions are vast and prices are low.

Randy's Ribs and Barbecue

Leonardtown Rd. (Route 5) at Gallant Green Rd.	301-274-3525
Hughesville, MD	LD | $

Randy's opened in 1981 as a weekend-only roadside stand, and while its catering business has become large, the eatery remains small and charming. The sweet perfume of slow-smoking pork fills the air seven days a week throughout the year, and if you are one who considers barbecue foremost among the food groups, you will love what you find.

Sandwiches and platters are available: minced or sliced pork, ribs and ham, whole chickens, and slabs of ribs. "Slaw on that?" the order taker will ask if you get a sandwich. "Yes!" we say, and then unwrap the foil around a big bun loaded with chunks of moist, full-flavored pork bathed in Randy's excellent spicy sauce, with which sweet slaw sings happy harmony. Ribs are large and chewy, their luscious meat infused with smoke, and on the side, we relished collard greens, macaroni and cheese, and baked beans.

Randy also offers a mighty fine half-smoke, which is the locally preferred variant of a hot dog: an extra-fat sausage bisected lengthwise and smoke-cooked until its skin is taut and dark red, its insides dense and succulent. All the usual hot-dog condiments are available, but we recommend topping it with only one thing: Randy's sauce. That good sauce is available by the pint and gallon: an excellent investment in one's future culinary happiness.

Seaside Restaurant and Crab House

224 Crain Hwy. N	410-760-2200
Glen Burnie, MD	LD | $$

Beautiful crabs, especially big, come to the table stuck with a peppery, salty spice mix and too hot to handle. Grab your knife to pry away the outer shell, pick up the mallet to start pounding, and soon you will be rewarded with fat nuggets of the sweetest meat any crab ever delivered. Toss your shells into paper bags on the floor and hoist an ice cold beer to quench the thirst that spicy crabs inevitably provoke: this is a true finger-licking feast, a royal mess, and incomparably fun.

Beyond beautiful blue crabs, the Seaside Restaurant has a menu of other local specialties, well worth sampling, especially if crabmeat-extraction is too daunting a task (it *is* hard work!). There are beautiful broiled shrimp, scallops, and flounder, and zesty crab cakes, plus as good a crab soup as we've had anywhere along the Chesapeake Bay.

A busy place, especially on weekends. Expect to wait at mealtime.

St. Mary's Landing

29935 Three Notch Rd.	301-884-3287
Charlotte Hall, MD	BLD | $$

St. Mary's County stuffed ham is a seasonal dish, generally served between Thanksgiving and Easter, but you can get it year around at St. Mary's Landing. It's wonderful stuff: a corned ham packed with heaps of kale, cabbage, onions, and spice, served for breakfast on a plate with delicious potato cakes or for supper as a main course.

Lucky for us, they were out of stuffed ham one December night when we came for supper. That meant we discovered the kitchen's marvelously crabby crab cakes, a plate of big, snapping-firm spiced boiled shrimp, and barbecued ribs that had a delicate crunch to their outermost edges and meat that slid right off the bone.

This is a fascinating restaurant, a serious tavern as well as an eatery, with a wall-mounted TV monitor that displays Keno numbers and a countdown to the next game. One morning when we arrived at 7:00 A.M., we were the first customers to take seats in the restaurant, but bar stools in the adjoining tap room were already occupied by ladies and gentlemen having shots and beers to start their day. Contrary to general principles of detecting good Roadfood, St. Mary's County stuffed ham is almost always found in places where drinking and gambling are featured attractions.

Waterman's Crab House

Sharp St. Wharf   410-639-2261
Rock Hall, MD   LD | $$

A big, breezy eatery with an al fresco deck overlooking Rock Hall Harbor and shuttle service for those who arrive by boat at one of the nearby marinas, Waterman's is a good-time place. Live blues, rock, and 1950s oldies bands perform on weekends, and at dusk merrymakers gather at the 40-foot-long bar to savor cocktails, beer, and a spectacular sunset.

Tuesday and Thursday nights, customers come for an all-you-can-eat Chesapeake Bay crab feast, and that is probably the one meal a first-timer ought to have, but Waterman's menu is broad and inviting. Other seafood temptations include crab soup served with a shot of sherry alongside, crusty-creamy crab cakes (fried or broiled), stuffed flounder, spiced steamed shrimp, soft-shell crabs, and a gorgeous broiled rockfish available with or without a side of crab imperial. Even fish-frowners will find plenty here: baby back ribs, prime rib, and Maryland fried chicken that the menu promises is "just like grandma's."

Charlie's

18 S. Michigan Ave.   908-241-2627
Kenilworth, NJ   LD | $

While you can order what the menu calls a "push cart dog"—an ordinary street weenie on a blah roll with mundane condiments—Charlie's raison d'être is its Italian hot dog: one or preferably a pair of deep-fried, crisp-skinned, bursting-with-flavor franks stuffed into a half-circle of what's known hereabouts as pizza bread. It's a sizable, hearth-baked round loaf that vaguely resembles a pita pocket with muscle. The bread is chewy, soulful, and absorbent, that last quality essential for engulfing all the traditional garnishes that an Italian hot dog demands. These include a good measure of glistening fried peppers and onions and a fistful of crisp-fried potato discs. The same ingredients can be used to accompany a sausage sandwich, also packed into pizza bread, and while we do like the sausage, it's the hot dog that has earned Charlie's landmark status in the Roadfood pantheon.

Service is do-it-yourself, and while there are a few tables for dining here, a majority of business is take-out.

Dickie Dee's

380 Bloomfield Ave.   973-483-9396
Newark, NJ   LD | $

No ordinary weenie, Dickie Dee's specialty is an Italian-style (aka Newark-style) hot dog, meaning it is deep-fried and stuffed deep inside half a loaf of Italian bread along with fried peppers and onions and big chunks of crisp-edge, soft-center fried potatoes. All the ingredients are cooked in the same vat of oil next to the order counter, and they are plucked from the oil and inserted directly into the bread (no draining!), making for a wondrously oily double-handful of food.

Be prepared for serious attitude from behind the counter of this brash lunchroom. When it's crowded—it usually is—the line moves fast, and woe to he who hesitates when placing an order. As the sandwich is made, the cook will demand to know what you want on it in the way of condiments, and this is another time you don't want to be slow responding. (We suggest that a spritz of ketchup is a nice complement for the potatoes that go atop all the other ingredients in the sandwich.)

Carry your tray to a table and ease into a permanently attached molded plastic chair. Lay out plenty of paper napkins for the inevitable spillage, and dig into a great hot-dog meal that is a true North Ward original.

Fralinger's

1325 Boardwalk   1-800-93-TAFFY
Atlantic City, NJ $

Our Atlantic City ritual has remained pretty much the same for a few decades now. First we eat subs at the White House, then we find the cross street, South Ocean Ave., quite a ways down from where all the corporate casinos are located, and enjoy a taste of old Atlantic City . . . at one of the best candy stores here or anywhere.

Fralinger's is most famous for its salt water taffy. And if you are a taffy person, you'll be in heaven with its sixteen different flavors, each as smooth and creamy as taffy can be. Ourselves, we go for the hard stuff: chocolate, in the form of molasses paddles that are coated with the darkest, most delicious chocolate imaginable. With its stick handle, a molasses paddle makes for great sucking and eating while on a Boardwalk stroll. Also irresistible is Fralinger's crunchy molasses sheathed in chocolate. There are dozens of other candies available at this old store, which as far as we are concerned is the real jackpot in Atlantic City.

The Hot Grill

669 Lexington Ave.   973-772-6000

Clifton, NJ   BLD | $

Texas weiners (spelled *e-i,* not *i-e)* are a big deal in this part of New Jersey, the word "Texas" being vintage hash-house code for chili. One of the best places to sample this Garden State specialty is the Hot Grill of Clifton.

Step up to the order counter, where empty trays await, and order a pair. *Nobody* gets just one Texas weiner! The counterman will holler out to the back kitchen, "Two, all the way!" And within ninety seconds, a pair of handsome little hot dogs will appear on the tray in front of you. Each is a deep-fried pup with rugged skin nestled in a too-short bun topped with mustard, onion, and spicy/sweet beef-chili sauce. Exemplary eats! On the side you can get French fries topped with gravy, sauce, cheese, or any combination of the three, and the preferred beverage with a Texas weiner is always root beer.

It's fun to dine in the Hot Grill's vast, modern dining room where, instead of music, you listen to the calls of the countermen back to the kitchen, and instead of sports, the overhead TV is tuned to the "Hot Grill Channel," which is a continuous program of hosannas to the hot dog.

Jimmy Buff's

60 Washington St.   973-325-9897

West Orange, NJ   LD | $

James Racioppi, proprietor of Jimmy Buff's, believes it was his grandparents, James and Mary Racioppi, who created the Newark hot dog. Mr. Racioppi says, "He played cards there every week. My grandmother served sandwiches to him and his associates. After a while, people started coming just to eat." As for the name of the store, James explains: "My grandfather Jimmy was an excellent card player. He was known for his talent to bluff, but with their Italian accents, they used to call him Jimmy Buff."

A Newark hot dog is built in a round of fresh, tawny-crusted Italian bread that is nothing at all like an ordinary, sponge-soft hot dog bun. It is sturdy, chewy, and delicious in its own right. It *needs* to be tough to hold all the ingredients that get piled into it. The bread is cut in half, forming two half circles. Each gets squeezed open to become a pocket like a huge, spongy pita. Into the pocket go a pair of all-beef hot dogs that have been fried in hot fat until crunch-crusted, a heap of onions and peppers that have been sautéed until limp, and a handful of crisp-fried potato disks. The ingredients are forked directly from the frying cauldron into the sandwich, which is why the bread needs oomph—to absorb drippin's from the garlicky dogs and sweet vegetables. Options include ketchup and/or mustard and/or marinara sauce, and fire-hot onion relish.

There are three other Jimmy Buff's locations: in Castle Ridge Plaza in East Hanover, in Irvington, and in Scotch Plains.

Libby's Lunch

98 McBride Ave.   973-278-8718

Paterson, NJ   LD | $

Texas weiners were invented in New Jersey prior to 1920 by John Patrellis, who worked at his father's hot dog stand at the Manhattan Hotel in Paterson. According to hot dog historian Robert C. Gamer of Wyckoff, Mr. Patrelis devised the formulation of a deep-fried frankfurter in a too-short bun topped with mustard, onions, and spicy meat sauce, traditionally accompanied by French fries and a mug of root beer. In 1920 the hot dog stand was renamed the Original Hot Texas Weiner because Mr. Patrelis believed the sauce to be like Texas chili. In fact, it is more Greek than Texan, but the Lone Star moniker stuck, and today Paterson is rich with Texas weiner shops.

Libby's Lunch, since 1936, is the best of the best. Here in a dog house with no pretense but with impeccable pedigree, countermen dish out dogs "all the way," meaning topped with mustard, chopped onions, and sauce. Good as the spicy chili sauce is (you can buy it by the pint), it is the hot dog itself that makes this a memorable eating experience. Its insides are tender and succulent, while the exterior is blistered and chewy because of its hot-oil bath. Extra-large dogs (and cheese dogs) are available, but we believe the original size works best. A pair of these tube steaks with a side of crisp French fries blanketed with gravy is a grand plate of food: true New Jersey, and uniquely American fare.

Rutt's Hut

417 River Road   973-779-8615
Clifton, NJ   BLD | $

Fans of Rutt's know the magnificent hot dogs served here as rippers because their skin tears and crinkles when they are deep-fried. The oil bath
turns the pork-and-beef links rugged, dark, and chewy on the outside,
while the interior remains soft and juicy. Weenie wimps can ask for an
"in and outer," which gets plucked from the fat more quickly and remains thoroughly pink and plump; while those who crave maximum succulence can get one well-done, which is so porcine that it reminds us of
fried pork rind.

The one stellar addition for a ripper is Rutt's spicy-sweet relish, a
dense yellow condiment made from onions and finely chopped carrots
and cabbage. Hamburgers and hot-from-the-kettle French fries are nice,
too, and we are especially fond of Rutt's chili: a chunky Mid-Atlantic
brew of clods of ground beef suspended in a vividly spicy tomato emulsion. With crumbled crackers on top, it's a formidable meal.

Rutt's serves hot-lunch meals as well as real drinks in an adjoining
taproom with its own separate entrance. Here, amid wood-panel décor,
one can quaff many beers with platters of such blue-plate fare as chicken
croquettes, stuffed cabbage, Jersey pork chops, and bean-heavy chili by
the cup or bowl. Prices are low, and the food we have tasted is mighty satisfying. But if you are coming to Rutt's only once, eat hot dogs at a
counter. It's a Roadfood experience to remember. Dine in a wide-open
mess hall with high counters at the windows that provide a view of the
parking lot. Stand and eat off paper plates, and for entertainment, enjoy
the calls of the countermen as they sing out, "Twins, all the way," meaning a pair of rippers with mustard and relish.

White House Sub Shop

2301 Arctic Ave.   609-345-1564
Atlantic City, NJ   L | $

Each White House sub is a good two feet long, requiring a brace of paper
plates to hold it. Ingredients range from fancy white tuna fish to meatballs and sauce, and the Philly cheesesteak (arguably a subcategory) is
excellent. The go-to variation is known as the White House Special—
Genoa salami, ham, capicola, and provolone cheese all rolled and tightly

packed inside the loaf, lubricated with olive oil, decorated with lettuce and bits of sweet pepper.

The ingredients are excellent, but submarine connoisseurs know that it's what's outside that counts. White House bread, obtained throughout the day from a local bakery, is robust and soulful, not nearly as dainty as the loaves used to make po-boys in the South, but similar to what's used for Italian beef sandwiches in Chicago.

This place is a landmark for sandwich connoisseurs, and like the cheesesteak shops of Philadelphia, it likes to boast of a stellar clientele. Pictures of celebrity customers line the walls, inscribed with praise for the excellence of the cuisine. News clippings tell of the time the astronauts came to scarf down subs, and of Frank Sinatra once having a bunch of them shipped from New Jersey across the world to a movie location. For all its stardust, the White House remains a humble Naugahyde-and-neon eatery with a row of booths along the wall and a counter up front. The lighting is harsh, the napkins are paper, and the service is lightning fast: it would be a sin to sell subs any other way. Expect a long wait at high noon.

Anchor Bar

1047 Main St.   716-886-8920

Buffalo, NY   LD | $$

The Anchor Bar was established in 1935, but it wasn't until July 29, 1977, officially proclaimed by the City of Buffalo to be Chicken Wing Day, that anyone other than its loyal local clientele gave a hoot about it. In the last quarter century, chicken wings have become an American obsession.

Teressa Bellissimo, who ran the bar with her husband, Frank, invented wings as we know them in 1964. Mrs. Bellissimo's genius was to cut the wings into two wieldy sections (drumettes and bows) and, after deep-frying them, stir them up in buttery hot sauce. Her presentation is now classic: they are served under an upside-down bowl (for bones) with a few stalks of celery and a bowl of creamy blue cheese dressing. The wings are crisp, a lovely orange-yellow, not dripping sauce, but imprinted with it. They are available hot or mild. Hot is fiery and will burn your lips; mild is more butter-flavored.

Mrs. Bellissimo's invention has proven to be a sublime combination of tastes and textures, as well a significant thirst-inducer, hence ideal bar food.

Barney Greengrass

541 Amsterdam Ave.
Between 86th and 87th 212-724-4707
New York, NY BL | $$

Food trends come and go, great New York bakeries have vanished, and it is harder and harder to find a good babka on the Upper West Side. Barney Greengrass still has these dense, sweet cakes that go so well with coffee, and although babka is not the main attraction, we cannot come to this storefront restaurant without taking one home.

The food that put Barney Greengrass on the map is not pastry; it is smoked fish. In the glass case of this restaurant and take-out store, you will find lean, silky sturgeon, salty cured salmon (known as lox), not-so-salty cured salmon (novie, short for Nova Scotia), snow-white white-fish, and luscious sable. In the dining room adjacent to the take-out counter, the fish are available on platters, with bagels and/or bialys, cream cheese, onions, tomatoes, and olives. These are the makings of a grand New York breakfast, and there isn't a restaurant in town that does it with the aplomb of bare-tabled Barney Greengrass.

Good as the smoked fish platters are, the single best dish in the house is the one known as eggs-and-novie. If you come in the morning, especially on a weekend, you will smell plates of it being carried from the kitchen to customers as soon as you enter. It is eggs scrambled with plush morsels of Nova Scotia salmon and onions nearly caramelized by frying. The combination is salty and sweet, and the textural range from the eggs' soft curds to the firm nuggets of fish they enfold to the slippery bits of onion is perfection. The aroma of this omelet, as well as smells of freshly toasted bagels and of cold cuts, salamis, and garlic pickles from the take-out side of the restaurant, makes walking into Barney Greengrass one of the most appetizing experiences New York City has to offer.

Café Edison

228 W. 47th St. 212-840-5000
New York, NY BLD | $$

Known to regulars as the Polish Tea Room, Café Edison offers a delicious taste of old New York that seems utterly unaffected by the corporate takeover of Times Square. Prices are moderate, the food is good, and the experience is unforgettable. In particular, we highly recommend ordering borscht, matzoh ball soup, braised brisket, kasha varnishkes (bowtie pasta and kasha groats), and homemade gefilte fish. Experts consider the cheese blintzes among the city's best, and we think the matzoh brie is superb.

Way back in the 1920s, this used to be a ritzy spot. Today, while it's no flophouse, the Edison Hotel is far from ultraluxurious. The café, which used to be the hotel's grand ballroom, still shows evidence of the glamour that once was, including bas-relief salmon-colored walls and elegant chandeliers. But now the walls are taped with signs advertising daily specials and the staff of weary waiters and waitresses will give any crabby deli help a run for their money in an angst-on-a-tray contest.

Carnegie Deli

854 Seventh Ave. 212-757-2245
New York, NY 10019 BLD | $$

Expensive, rude, loud, uncomfortable, and overrun with tourists, the Carnegie Deli is one of the great restaurants of New York City. Its pastrami and corned beef are among the best anywhere; the kaleidoscopic menu of sandwiches, coffee shop hot lunch, and Jewish comfort food is definitive. Merely walking in from Seventh Avenue is a gastronomic blast as the aroma of cured deli meats and sour pickles assaults your nose. A host points you to the back, and as you walk toward the tables, you pass a counter full of meats and smoked-fish salads behind which sandwiches are made. Salamis hang like a curtain over the counter, adding their garlicky perfume to the air. At the back of the restaurant, or in the adjoining dining room, you will be directed to a place at a table where you sit elbow-to-elbow with strangers.

The Carnegie is best known for immense sandwiches made of cured meat, brisket, turkey, chopped liver, and triple-decker combinations of ingredients. Beyond sandwiches, culinary highlights include blintzes and potato pancakes, gefilte fish and pickled herring, borscht and kreplach soup.

Although purists gripe that the meat is no longer available handsliced, we have no complaints about the Carnegie's machine-sliced pastrami. It is mellow and not too zesty, utterly tender and infused with fatty savor. It is ridiculously large—so tall that the top piece of rye bread appears to be merely an afterthought applied to the tower of meat. In fact, it is difficult to eat the ordinary way, by picking it up in your hands and taking a bite. Many customers go at it by piece-by-shred, directly from the plate. To accompany the monumental sandwiches, the Carnegie supplies perfect puckery accouterments—half-sour and sour dill pickles arrayed in metal bowls along the tables.

Aside from the food, one of the pleasures of dining at the Carnegie is eavesdropping, which you do whether or not you want to, because you are seated so close to other people. We remember a visit several years ago when one little old lady sitting near us shouted to her friend across the table, "Today I saw the doctor." The sparrow-size woman actually had to crane her head high to see over her sandwich—a mountain of pastrami combined with an inch-and-a-half of chopped liver sandwiched in rye. "His office is nearby. I make my appointment in the morning, so I can come here when I am through." She expertly hefted half of the mighty sandwich in her two tiny hands, inhaling steam wafting up from the warm pink meat. Before taking that first delicious bite, she proclaimed loud and clear for all the table to hear: "First I have my treatment . . . then I have my treat!"

Charlie the Butcher's Kitchen

| 1065 Wehrle Dr. at Cayuga | 716-633-8330 |
| Buffalo, NY | LD \| $ |

According to Charlie Roesch, proprietor of Charlie the Butcher's Kitchen, it was beer that inspired the invention of beef on weck. He believes that back in the 1880s a now-forgotten local tavern owner decided to offer a sandwich that would induce a powerful thirst in his patrons. He had plenty of coarse salt on hand for the pretzels he served, so he painted a mixture of the salt and caraway seeds (known in German as *kummelweck*) atop some hard rolls, cooked a roast and sliced it thin, and piled the meat inside the rolls. As a condiment, he served hot horseradish. Slaking the thirst these sandwiches induced, beer sales soared. And Buffalo's passion for beef on weck—customarily served with fiery fresh horseradish and accompanied by schooners of cold beer—was born.

As Mr. Roesch stands at his butcher block rhapsodizing about his favorite subject—the cuisine of western New York—an attentive patron waiting at the order window of his restaurant offers support: "If Charlie the Butcher says it's so, it's so!" declares the loyal customer before ordering a beef on weck with a smoked Polish sausage on the side.

Charlie the Butcher's fans consider him the ultimate authority on meat of all kinds. Although he is a young man who has operated this restaurant only since 1993, he is hardly a Johnny-come-lately on the Buffalo beef scene. His father was a butcher, as was his grandfather (their slogan: "You know it's fresh if it comes from Roesch"), and he still manages a butcher shop and food kiosk at Buffalo's century-old Broadway Market. To honor the family trade, he wears a white hard hat on his head and a butcher's smock over his shirt and necktie as he works at counters in the open kitchen at the center of his restaurant. His menu, we should note, extends well beyond beef on weck, and everything else we've sampled is first rate: Buffalo-made hot dogs and sausages grilled over coals, chicken spiedie (a boneless breast that is marinated and grilled), and such daily-special sandwiches as meat loaf (Tuesday) and double-smoked ham (Monday). The beverage list includes the local favorite, loganberry, as well as Charlie's personal favorite, birch beer.

Clare and Carl's

4731 Lake Shore Dr.   518-561-1163
Plattsburgh, NY   LD (summer only) | $

A Michigan is a small, porky frank bedded in a cream-soft bun and topped with mustard, onions, and a sauce made from a little tomato, a lot of spice, and finely ground beef. Where do you find one? Not in Michigan, where similarly configured weenies are known as Coney Islands. The Michigan is unique to New York's North Country between the Adirondacks and Lake Champlain. It resembles not only the Coneys of the Midwest, but also the New York Systems of Rhode Island and the Texas weiners of New Jersey and Pennsylvania. Someday, someone has got to create a chili-dog map of America, which we imagine would be more complicated than the sequence of nucleotides on a DNA strand.

At Clare and Carl's, the oldest Michigan stand in Plattsburgh (since 1943), a newspaper story posted on the wall says that the region's unique weenies owe their name to a Michigander named Eula Otis who came to work for Clare Warn in the early days and went around to area restaurants saying, "I'm from Michigan. Would you like to try one of our chili dogs?" The state's name clung to the hot dog topped with Warn's sauce, which she had invented because New York–style hot dogs with mustard and sauerkraut weren't selling well. The Michigan became a local passion—served at summertime stands, in grocery stores, and even in the cafeteria at the Champlain Valley Physicians Hospital Medical Center.

Clare and Carl's presents its Michigans in an ineffably tender bun that is similar to the traditional northeast split-top, but is thicker at the bottom and closed at both ends, forming a trough to shore in the sloppy topping. The chili is thick with minced meat, kaleidoscopically spiced, not at all sweet, and just barely hot. It is intriguing and addictive.

There is another Clare and Carl's in town, but the original is a wonderful vision of long-gone roadside Americana, its clapboard walls so old that they appear to have settled deep into the earth. Carhops attend customers in a broad parking lot, and there is a U-shaped counter with padded stools inside. A menu posted above the open kitchen lists Michigans first, but signs outside advertise the house specialty as Texas red hots.

Cornell Dairy Bar

At the Cornell Dairy Store, corner of Tower and Judd Falls Rds. 607-255-3272
Stocking Hall   L | $
Ithaca, NY

If you believe that food is best when it is close to the source, have a dish of ice cream or, for that matter, a glass of milk at the Cornell Dairy Bar. All the cow-sourced products served in this on-campus eatery are produced by the College of Agriculture and Life Sciences; even the maple syrup sold in the little grocery store upstairs comes from the Natural Resources Department, the apple cider from the Pomology Department.

The Dairy Bar is, as the name suggests, a casual joint with scattered tables inside and a few seats outdoors by the sidewalk. Although there are a limited number of other things to eat and drink, including soup from a Knorr Soup Bar and hot drinks from a cappuccino machine, it's ice cream that stars. Step up to the counter and browse among such flavors as Kahlua Fudge (coffee flavored with a fudge swirl), Mexican Sundae (with peanuts and fudge chunks), Espresso Chunky Chip, Sticky Bunz, even Green Tea! Order a cone, cup, or sundae and carry it to a seat. This is excellent ice cream: just rich enough to fully satisfy without cloying, and without the complications you find in boutique ice creams that sell for $4 a pint in supermarket freezers.

In addition to praising the good ice cream, we must also note that the whipped cream that goes atop sundaes is superb: thick, sweet, and dairy-fresh. And finally: chocolate milk. It's a beautiful thing, so smooth, so gently chocolaty, so perfectly juvenile.

Doug's Fish Fry

206 West Rd.
Cortland, NY

607-753-9184
LD | $$

Fried fish sandwiches are common throughout much of upstate New York, appreciated by locals but little known by outsiders. A visit to Doug's is convincing evidence that this is regional food to take seriously. Your choice is a sandwich, a fish dinner, or a fish onion dinner. The titles are misleading because the sandwich is in fact two or three large hunks of fried fish piled in and around a modest bun that in no way is large enough to hold even half its ingredients. Like a tenderloin from the southern Midwest, the presentation pushes the envelope of what, exactly, a sandwich is. A fish dinner adds beautiful chunky French fries to the pseudo-sandwich. A fish onion dinner means onion rings.

The fish is moist, sweet, and mild-flavored, encased in a sandy crust with just the right amount of crunch. It comes with pickly tartar sauce that is surprisingly unsweet. Sweetness comes in the form of Doug's superb coleslaw, which is finely chopped and fetchingly spicy.

Service is eat-in-the-rough style. Place your order at the stand-up counter (from which you have an appetizing view of fish and fries coming out of the hot oil), pay for the meal, and wait for your name to be called. Fetch your own utensils from a table in the center of the dining room that holds plastic forks and knives, ketchup and mustard, and malt vinegar for spritzing on fries.

Bonus: Doug's is a source for excellent soft-serve custard, dense and alabaster-pure. Throughout the warm-weather months the custard is a foundation for warm fruit sundaes. The available compote, made right here from the fruit of the season, begins with strawberries and blueberries early in the summer, then moves to peaches, and finally to apples in the fall. Glorious!

Gargiulo's

2911 West 15th St.
Coney Island, NY

718-266-4891
LD | $$$

Here is a style of big-city dining that gastronomes have come to know as Italian-American but is, in fact, unique to the Northeast United States, its repertoire as humble as spaghetti and meatballs and deluxe as lobster tail *fra diavolo*. Indeed, lobster is very important at Gargiulo's (which happens to be only yards from the Atlantic Ocean); big ones are held in a tank in the vestibule opposite the bar. Between ten-dollar spaghetti entrees and thirty-dollar lobster are a vast number of preparations of veal, chicken, seafood, sausage and steak . . . and—oh, wow—glorious pastas.

For the pasta alone, we would list Gargiulo's as a great Coney Island destination. Whether meaty ribbons of linguine or slim strands of spaghettini, the noodles are al dente delicious. On the linguine, we savored a luxurious white Bolognese sauce ("You get your meat and Alfredo in one!" declared our friend George, the Brooklyn native who took us here), and the fine spaghettini was served Sorrento-style, which means laced with nuggets of juicy sirloin steak and chicken and sauced with nothing but garlic and oil.

Veal is big here, with twelve different varieties of cutlet on the menu, not including veal chops and the daily specials. After a barrage of appetizers that included mighty pasta e fagioli soup, baked clams, and manicotti, we appreciated the simplicity of veal Milanese—thin, crisp, and flavorful.

Located in an otherwise honky-tonk section of Coney Island (across the street from Nathan's and a short distance away from one of the nation's last remaining freak shows), Gargiulo's is quite deluxe, its waiters outfitted in tuxedos, its tables covered with thick white linen. It's a special-occasion weekend date place and a regular dinner haunt for people from surrounding neighborhoods. We love it on a Saturday night when the pageant of customers is a great cross-section of New Yorkers, young and old, tough and tender, all gathering for a good time and a fabulous meal in a party atmosphere.

Glenwood Pines

1213 Taughannock Blvd. (Route 89)   607-273-3709
Ulysses, NY   LD | $

Glenwood Pines has been a destination diner for Cornellians since it opened in 1946. The primary attraction of this friendly roadhouse overlooking Cayuga Lake is a Pinesburger. That's a six-ounce beef oval topped with a couple of slices of cheese wedged into a length of Ithaca Bakery French bread with lettuce, tomato slices, onion slices, and your choice of Thousand Island dressing or mayonnaise. Connoisseurs told us that we had to have it with the Thousand Island, and it would be hard to argue against that. The sweetness of the dressing is a grand complement to the smoky meat and all its dressings. On the side, good companions include ultra-crunchy fried onion rings and creamy coleslaw.

We said the Pinesburger was the primary reason to visit. The secondary one is the fish fry. A huge, thick length of haddock is breaded and fried crisp and served with either tartar sauce or cocktail sauce. It is sweet, moist, flavorful fish, and a giant meal.

Ambience at Glenwood Pines is old-time tavern. When you walk in, you see a few pinball machines and a bowling game on the right, a pool table ahead of you, and, beyond that, the bar where some folks sit and imbibe beers with (or without) their Pinesburgers as a TV in the upper right corner delivers sports broadcasts. To the left are tables and a small separate dining room; also a small case of trophies—for baseball, bowling, and volleyball—earned by teams that Glenwood Pines has sponsored.

Gus's Restaurant

3 Cumberland Head Rd.   518-561-3711
Plattsburgh, NY   BLD | $

In the same phylum as the Coney Islands of the heartland and New York Systems of Rhode Island, the Michigan of New York's North Country is primarily summertime food, but Gus's serves it year-round. As to why this only–in–New York specialty is called a Michigan, our waitress at Gus's didn't have a clue.

Nomenclature aside, Michigans are addictive little porkers, and Gus's is a good place to try them. It started as a dog stand in 1951, but it has grown to a three-meal-a-day restaurant with a full menu that boasts, "The restaurant features just about everything [even Lake Champlain perch], including their famous 'Michigan red hot,' which they invite you to try while dining." One Michigan costs $1.85 and is presented in a cardboard boat. The heft of the sauce contrasts with the fluffy bun and fatty frank, and while each separate ingredient is inarguably ignominious, the combo is taste-buds magic—especially when topped with a judicious line of yellow mustard and a scattering of crisp, chopped raw onions.

Heid's of Liverpool

305 Oswego St.   315-451-0786

Liverpool, NY   LD | $

Heid's has been around since before the hot dog was formally invented, but for as long as any living human can remember, hot dogs have been its claim to fame. For a while there were branches of the original, but today only this one remains: a fast-food dog house with some tables inside and picnic tables outdoors under a tent.

The menu is totally wiener-centric. Hofmann-brand franks, made in Syracuse of beef, pork, and veal, are quickly grilled, a process you can watch after placing your order. They are handsome sausages with a delicate casing and plump, muscular insides. In the old days the one and only available condiment was mustard. But since John and Randall Parker started running Heid's back in 1995, the topping choices have expanded to include chili, onions, and ketchup.

As always, the beverage list is a short one, including milkshakes, sodas, beer, and chocolate milk.

John's Pizzeria

278 Bleecker St.   212-935-2895

New York, NY   LD | $$

Pizzerias all over New York call themselves "Original." While John's of Bleecker Street (and three offshoots on E. 64th, W. 65th, and W. 44th) makes no such claim of primacy, it is a Greenwich Village original and a source of true New York–style pizza in a setting that could be nowhere else. John's is such a landmark that one time when we ate there, on a Sunday afternoon, a tour group of about a dozen Europeans came in off the sidewalk, did a walk around the dining room, and exited. They were sightseeing . . . and the pizza-eaters of Lower Manhattan were the attraction.

John's looks extremely well lived-in and well eaten-in, its walls and the wooden backs of its rickety booths covered with a dense thicket of graffiti that represents the countless enthusiastic visitors who have dined here since 1934, when John's moved to Bleecker from its original location (opened in the '20s) on Sullivan Street. At the back of the front dining room, where two Italianate murals decorate the walls above the scarred wood, photographs of famous fans of John's are displayed. They include former mayor Rudy Giuliani and the Chairman of the Board, Frank Sinatra.

Pizzas come large (eight slices) or small (six slices). There are no surprises on the ingredient list, except that the sausage is especially delicious, the mushrooms are fresh, and the mozzarella has a creamy goodness that makes magic with the brightly herbed red sauce. What makes John's pizza taste special is its crust. Cooked in a coal-fired wood oven, it has a dough that turns almost brittle at its outer edges in places where it blisters and blackens from the heat, and yet just fractions of an inch inside that circumference, it has a wondrous chew. The best part of it is the underside. Take a peek at the bottom of a slice, and notice how it is charred from its stay on the floor of the old oven. Nearly black and on the verge of ashy, the crunchy bottom surface of this pizza is an intoxicating eating sensation. For serious bread-and-pizza lovers, it verges on a spiritual experience.

Katz's

205 E. Houston St.	212-254-2246
New York, NY	BLD | $$

This relic of bygone New York operates like an old-time urban deli: you get a ticket when you enter and gather food at different stations along the counter, while the ticket is marked accordingly. Pay on your way out. It is a cavernous eating hall with lines of tables, the air filled with the noise of shouted orders and clattering carving knives and the aroma of the odoriferous garlicky salamis hanging along the wall. Pictures of happy celebrity customers ranging from comics Jerry Lewis and Henny Youngman to Police Commissioner Raymond Kelly are everywhere.

Ordinary table service by waiters is available, but the better way to do it is to personally engage with a counterman. Here's how: make eye contact with one of the white-aproned carvers who is busy slicing meats and making sandwiches behind the glass. Once you've gotten his attention, be quick and tell him what you want: pastrami on rye or on a club roll; or corned beef or brisket. They slice meat and assemble sandwiches with the certainty and expertise of Dutch diamond cutters.

Even if you don't enjoy the sometimes exasperating process of getting your food, all will be forgiven when you heft a Katz's pastrami sandwich: three-quarters of a pound of meat that has been expertly severed into pieces so chunky that the word "slice" seems too lightweight to describe them. Each brick red, glistening moist hunk is rimmed black, redolent of garlic, smoke, and pickling spices, as savory as food can be. You can pay a dollar extra to have it cut extra-lean, but it is hard to imagine these taut, pink slices any leaner than they are.

Beyond superb cured meat: Katz's hot dogs just may be the city's best all-beefers; omelets are made deli-style, meaning open-face and unfolded; there is matzoh ball soup and chicken noodle soup as well as potato latkes (pancakes) and blintzes. French fries are large-cut, creamy inside with skins that range from crunchy to leathery to parchment-tender. To drink you can have a classic New York egg cream, chocolate or vanilla.

Magnolia's

21 Front St.   No phone
Patterson, NY   BL | $

Before K. C. Scott opened up the original Magnolia's in Carmel in April 1999, it took a long while to come up with the right name. Then one day, standing in her kitchen, she found herself looking at one of the antique signs she had collected . . . for Magnolia Dairy Products. "I like Magnolia because it has a slow, Southern feel," she explains, noting that her goal in starting this seductive little restaurant was to create a place that provided quality food at a reasonable price in a setting that was as relaxed as a friend's kitchen.

"We have an aversion to anything pre-made," K.C. says, noting that all the breads, the salad dressings, and the pastries are made right here in the semi-open kitchen. They smoke barbecue brisket and pork butts for hours, then bathe the meats in a house sauce that will snap taste buds to attention. At breakfast, the repertoire includes omelets, French toast, pancakes, an egg-potato-cheese-salsa burrito, and waffles (weekends only).

Sandwiches are swell, especially the "Local Hero" portobello mushroom and pepper sandwich on focaccia bread and the "Ludington" cheese and tomato sandwich on hearth bread (named after Revolutionary War hero Sybil Ludington). We are fond of two always-available wraps: the Catalina, which is an assortment of vegetables, including delicious roasted peppers, in an herb wrap, and the Cortland, which is grilled chicken and Havarti cheese and pieces of locally grown Cortland apple.

Margon

136 W. 46th St. 212-354-5013

New York, NY BLD | $

Margon is a personality-plus hole in the wall around the corner from otherwise Disneyfied Times Square. Plush, it is not. A ramp leads downward to a long, narrow space with four stools jammed up against an impossibly uncomfortable counter near the front; tables are lined up on the right of an aisle that leads to the back.

On the left of the aisle is a buffet counter where arriving customers stand and place orders. Here is how it works: Walk to the back with your eyes looking left. This allows a full view of what's to eat, including pork chops smothered in gravy, glistening roast chicken, rice and beans, sweet plantains, and octopus salad. Place your order and have a seat. When it's ready, one of the counter help will call you to pick it up, or on occasion, they will bring it to your table.

The octopus salad can be a meal or a lip-smacking appetizer: tender leaves of meat glistening in a garlic marinade. While daily lunch specials include such exotica as tripe and pigs' feet (Monday and Thursday) and fried chicken chunks known as *chicharron de pollo* (Tuesday), everyday entrees include stews and chops and roast chicken that are beautiful to see and a delight to eat.

The Cuban sandwich is first-rate, a crisp-toasted length of bread enveloping roast pork, salami, ham, melted cheese, a surfeit of pickle slices, mustard, and mayo. Actually, any sandwich made on the good Cuban bread, then pressed and heated, is excellent. We love the plain roast pork that is anything but plain tasting.

On your way out, have a shot of espresso. It's dark, syrup-rich, and delicious, just about the best cup we've had anywhere in New York.

McSweeney's

535 N. Margaret St. 518-562-9309

Plattsburgh, NY 12901 LD | $

It was only recently that we learned about Michigans, thanks to Roadfooders David Scheinberg, who used to spend summers in the Adirondacks, and Adam Graham, and Cynthia Potts, all of whom alerted us to a style of chili dog unique to New York State's northland. Michigans go back to the early 1940s and have remained very popular in and around

Plattsburgh, but virtually unknown elsewhere. Each place that makes Michigans has its own formula, but the basic idea is a piggy pink wiener in a split-top bun, topped with dark-orange chili sauce in which the meat is sandy smithereens.

McSweeney's, which bills itself as "Plattsburgh's Red Hot Car Hop Stop," is a relative newcomer to the area, opened in 1991 and now boasting three locations in Plattsburgh. We visited the one on Route 9 North (Margaret St.), which features old-time carhop service and an inside counter as well as comfortable sit-down tables indoors. Michigans are listed on the menu as chili dogs, but our waitress assured us they are indeed Michigans. She also explained the bun crisis of 2002, when long buns became unavailable, thus wreaking havoc on the eating habits of those who order their Michigans with buried onions. "Buried means underneath the weenie," she said. "That makes the weenie stick up above the bun and the sauce will fall off."

McSweeney's makes excellent sauce: luxuriously beefy, flecked with pepper that kindles a nice glow on the tongue. The package is substantial enough that Michigans come with a fork. Looking around the dining room and at people eating off trays hung on car windows, it appeared to us that most customers forgo the utensil. A few people we observed had perfected a technique of hoisting the entire cardboard boat to chin level with one hand, then using the other hand to ease the Michigan from boat to mouth, bite by bite.

McSweeney's sells Michigan sauce by the pint ($11.50) and offers a Michigan without the hot dog: mustard, onions, and plenty of sauce in the unique, hollowed-out bun. This configuration is known, strangely enough, as a sauceburger, and as much as we like the sauce, we much prefer it in concert with a weenie.

New Way Lunch

54 South St.   518-792-9803

Glens Falls, NY   BL | $

Hungry in Glens Falls, we pulled to the curb to investigate a storefront diner on South Street. "You looking for the hot dog place?" a pedestrian asked. "It moved." He pointed up the street. Interesting as the diner was, we figured that the unsolicited tip was worth following. So we drove a few hundred yards to New Way Lunch, which has a sign outside boasting that it has been world famous since 1919.

While the interior may be modern, the hot-dog cookery is timeless. New Way griddle cooks slim, non-kosher franks and slips them into soft, warm buns. The fundamental dressing formula is a trio of mustard, diced onions, and a finely textured beef sauce that has a peppery tang. It is a small package, costing all of $1.15, and we observed that big guys ordered them by fours or sixes. Take-out customers come in for dozens.

Hot dogs are the claim to fame, but there's a small menu of other items, too: char-cooked burgers, a Philly cheesesteak, fried fish and chicken, and a Greek salad. For a quick lunch not far from the New York Thruway, New Way is an easy detour.

Parkside Candy

3208 Main St.   716-833-7540
Buffalo, NY   LD | $

This gorgeous 1920s-era confectionery is ringed with cases all around the perimeter of the room displaying creams and chews, truffles and cordials, clusters, dixies, and barks all made in the candy factory just behind the store. Best of them all is that Buffalo favorite, sponge candy, a chocolate-coated, spun-molasses wonder that is like no ordinary bonbon. It literally melts in your mouth, creating a delirious harmony of chocolate and molasses. In the room where candies are displayed are little ice-cream-parlor tables, where you can order from a menu of fountain delights that range from frappes, parfaits, and sundaes to the lovers' indulgence, Old Granada Special, which is eight scoops of ice cream, four toppings, and two varieties of toasted nuts under a mountain of whipped cream, served with two spoons.

There is a short sandwich menu, too, but we've never tried it. The aroma of chocolate when we walk in the Parkside door is a siren's call.

Patsy's

2287 First Ave.   212-534-9783
New York, NY   LD | $

New Yorkers think nothing of picking up a slice of pizza for eating on the go. Patsy's is the Italian landmark in the midst of Spanish Harlem where street slices were first served back in the 1930s. To this day, customers stand around on the sidewalk outside or lean on an open-air counter facing First Avenue wolfing down slices of elegant pizza.

Whole pies are served at tables and booths inside. While all sorts of toppings are available, we like the most basic tomato-cheese combo: easy to hoist slice by slice, built on a marvelous fragile crust with charred spots all along the edge that have the smoky flavor that only a coal oven delivers. Two versions of plain cheese pizza are available: fresh mozzarella, with thin pools of creamy sliced cheese spread out within the microthin layer of tomato sauce, and regular mozzarella on which saltier, slightly oilier shredded cheese is spread evenly all across the surface. They both are built upon that marvelous wafer-thin charcoaled crust.

Patsy's is a true destination restaurant, way uptown in a place that is not exactly "restaurant row." It's ancient, going back to 1933 when Pasquale Lancieri first opened for business, and it has the well-aged character of a neighborhood restaurant that hasn't changed even as the neighborhood around it has. We were especially charmed by waiter Victor, who advised us that in his opinion, "98 percent of the pizza places in New York aren't worth walking past."

Phil's Chicken House

1208 Maine Rd.   607-748-7574
Endicott, NY   LD | $

Phil's Chicken House was opened some forty years ago by Phil Card, who learned his skills at Endicott's Chicken Inn. His folksy wood-paneled restaurant is decorated to the hilt with country-crafty knick-knacks (souvenir plates, angel statuettes, lighthouse miniatures) and it attracts customers that range from local families to well-armed state police SWAT teams (who practice marksmanship nearby).

As you might guess by the name of the restaurant, the featured attraction here is chicken—slow cooked and relentlessly basted on a rotisserie until the skin is glazed gold and the meat drips juice. The breast meat is velvet soft; thighs and drumsticks pack a roundhouse flavor punch; and wings are bathed in the regionally favored marinade.

Mr. Card told us that his chicken recipe is no secret; in fact it is well known throughout the southern Finger Lakes. "It's your basic Cornell chicken," he said, referring to a formula developed by Cornell professor Dr. Robert Baker back in the early 1950s. Dr. Baker's tomato-free vinaigrette, enriched with eggs and shot through with poultry spice, is now used as a marinade and/or basting sauce by cooks throughout the region.

While nine out of ten customers come to Phil's for a half or a quarter barbecued chicken, there are plenty of other square meals on the menu, including pot roast, meat loaf, grilled ham, and steak. There's a lunch buffet every day and a breakfast buffet on weekends.

Red Rooster Drive-In

1566 Route 22	845-279-8046
Brewster, NY	LD daily | $

Although a roadside archeologist would definitely categorize the Rooster as a drive-in, there is no car service and there are no carhops. Still, there is a vast parking lot and plenty of people eat in their cars (or in one of three improbably small two-person booths in the cramped interior), and the service, cuisine, and ambience are pure mid-twentieth-century America.

The hamburgers are especially satisfying: not too big, not odd in any way, just fine handfuls fashioned by proprietor Jack Sypek or Andy the grill chef from freshly ground beef that is sizzled on a smoky charcoal grill. We are particularly fond of cheeseburgers gilded by an order of onions grilled until limp and slippery. They are served on tender buns—deluxe, please, with lettuce and tomato!—and accompanied by French fries, milkshakes, ice cream floats, or expertly made egg creams in a variety of flavors beyond the traditional chocolate.

In nice weather, customers can choose to eat at one of several picnic tables spread across the lawn in back. Adjacent to this open-air dining room is a miniature golf course where kids and carefree adults while away pleasant evenings in the Red Rooster's afterglow.

Schwabl's

789 Center Rd.	716-674-9821
West Seneca, NY	LD | $$

Now operated by former waitress Cheryl Staychok and her husband, Gene, Buffalo's best-known beef house didn't miss a beat when the Schwabl family left the business. Here is a definitive version of that glorious Buffalo specialty, beef on weck. The beef itself is superb: thin, rare slices severed from a center-cut round roast just before the sandwich is assembled. The pillow of protein is piled high inside a roll heavily crusted with coarse salt and caraway seeds (known as *kummelweck*, German for caraway seed), the roll momentarily dipped in natural gravy before it sandwiches the meat. The only thing this package could possibly want is a dab of horseradish, which is supplied on each table and along the bar.

That is all you need to know about Schwabl's, except for the nice hot ham sandwich on white bread in a pool of tomato-clove gravy, served with warm potato salad. The ham is an interesting alternative to the beef, although it has none of the famous local sandwich's authority.

Schwabl's is a casual, well-aged eatery, attended by business people at noon and families at suppertime. "We Cater to Nice Homey Family Trade," the menu announces, and a dry, nonalcoholic birch beer with the faint twang of spearmint is always available on draught.

Sharkey's

| 56 Glenwood Ave. | 716-729-9201 |
| Binghamton, NY | LD \| $$ |

Larry Sharak's father started making spiedies at a cookfire in the window at the family's tavern over fifty years ago. Skewered, marinated hunks of lamb were cooked on a charcoal grill and served with broad slices of bread. The custom was to grab the bread in one hand and use it as an edible mitt to slide a few hunks off the metal rod, thus creating an instant sandwich. Spiedies are still served and eaten this way at the bar and tables of Sharkey's. Lamb has grown too expensive, however, so today's spiedies are made from either pork or chicken. When you bite into a piece, it blossoms with the flavorful juice of a two-day marinade that tastes of garlic and vinegar, peppers and oregano, and, according to Larry Sharak, for whom the recipe is a family heirloom, "a lot of pinches of many spices."

Beyond the spiedie, Sharkey's serves Eastern European fare made by experts: *holupkis* (stuffed cabbage rolls) are the work of Larry's sister-in-law, Marie. Around Easter and Christmastime, the menu features homemade kielbasa sausages. And you can always count on buttery pierogi filled with seasoned mashed potatoes.

Sharkey's is a local institution to which families have come for generations. Old-timers know to enter through the back door rather than the front. Here, you walk into a dark dining room outfitted with ancient wooden booths and long family-style tables formed from pushed-together dinettes. Between courses, the young folks get up to play a few lines on the old Tic Tac Strike game, a pre-electronic diversion that seems at home in this historic tavern.

Shortstop Deli

204 W. Seneca St.   607-273-1030

Ithaca, NY   Always open | $

Any hearty eater who attended Cornell University in Ithaca, New York, in the last four decades knows about Hot Truck, the mobile food wagon that invented French bread pizzas in the early 1960s. As served from the campus truck starting every night at 11:00 P.M. during the school year, these fusions of pizza and submarine sandwich are piled with ingredients, then baked open-face until the bread is shatteringly crisp, the cheese bubbles, and the meats sizzle.

The Hot Truck's hours are extremely limited, which is why we love the Shortstop Deli, to which proprietor Albert Smith and his son Michael have brought Hot Truck cuisine. More a big convenience store than a sit-down eatery, the Shortstop features shelves of snack foods, countless varieties of coffee, and a counter where you write your own order for Hot Truck. There are no tables or chairs, just some concrete benches outside the front window where it is possible to bring your wrapped sandwich and your cup of soda (ten cents with a meal!) and dine al fresco.

The pizza subs are made on loaves of Ithaca Bakery French bread, and they range from the basic PMP (Poor Man's Pizza), which is nothing but bread, sauce, and cheese, to the extravaganza known as a Suicide (garlic, sauce, mushrooms, sausage, pepperoni, and mozzarella). These sandwiches have inspired a language all their own. For example, a Triple Sui, Hot and Heavy, G and G is a full Suicide with a sprinkle of hot red pepper, three extra homemade meatballs, extra garlic, mayonnaise, and lettuce (G and G = grease and garden, i.e., mayo and lettuce). An Indy includes link sausage, pepperoni, onion, sauce, and cheese, hot and heavy. A Flaming Turkey Bone (which contains no turkey and no bones and is not served on fire) includes chicken breast, tomato sauce, cheese, onions, extra hot and heavy, plus "spontaneous combustion" (double-X hot sauce).

Ted's Jumbo Red Hots

2312 Sheridan Dr.   716-836-8986

Tonawanda (Buffalo), NY   LD | $

Ted's began as a horse-drawn hot dog cart in Buffalo in the 1920s. It became a permanently anchored hot dog stand under the Peace Bridge in

1927, and opened as a bigger store on Sheridan Drive in 1948. There are now eight Ted's in western New York, and one in Tempe, Arizona, but the one to which we always want to return is Ted's of Tonawanda. It's modernized since 1948 and is as clean and sanitary as any fast-food franchise, but the hot dogs are something special.

Sahlen's-brand frankfurters, available regular, foot-long, or jumbo, are cooked on a grate over charcoal that infuses each one with pungent smoke flavor and makes the skin crackling-crisp. As they cook, the chef pokes them with a fork, slaps them, squeezes them, and otherwise abuses them, thus puncturing the skin and allowing the dog to suck in maximum smoky taste.

As the dogs cook, you must make some decisions. In consultation with a person behind the counter known as "the dresser," you decide how you want to garnish your tube steak. The stellar condiment is Ted's hot sauce, a peppery-hot concoction laced with bits of relish. You also want onion rings, sold as tangled webs of crisp fried batter and limp onion. To accompany a foot-long and a basket of o-rings, the beverage of choice in these parts is loganberry juice, which is like exotic Kool-Aid.

Walter's Hot Dog Stand

937 Palmer Ave.   No phone
Larchmont, NY   L | $

Walter's is one heck of a roadside attraction. Built in the 1920s (although the business began in 1919), it resembles a pagoda, complete with lanterns hanging off the edges of the roof. On a sign over the road, letters that spell out "Walter's" at first appear to be the elegant brushstrokes of Chinese calligraphy. On close inspection, the "brushstrokes" turn out to be facsimilies of hot dogs.

Yes, hot dogs are the thing to eat—the only entree on the menu—and they are dandies. Diminutive tubes of pork, beef, and veal made from an original recipe developed by founder Walter Warrington, they are split nearly in half and grilled until brown and light-crusted. The iron on which they grill is spread with Walter's secret sauce, a clear, buttery dressing that gets sucked into the pink meat of the wiener and gives it a taste that many East Coast frankfurter connoisseurs consider to be the world's best. The grilled dogs are nestled in toasted buns, and there is only one condiment to consider: mustard. This is Walter's own mustard, a dark blend dotted with tiny bits of pickle. Two or three hot dogs and a side of

French fries (or spicier curly fries) are a perfect little snack. Soft drinks are available, but do note that behind the counter is a vintage malt powder dispensing machine; Walter's chocolate malts are superb.

Service is walk-up, rain or shine; seating is limited to a grove of picnic tables and a grassy lawn adjacent to the restaurant.

Center City Pretzel Co.

816-18 Washington Ave.   215-463-5664
Philadelphia, PA $

Bad-tasting water = good-tasting food. There is no other good explanation for the excellence of Philadelphia soft pretzels.

We reached that conclusion when the Roadfood.com team went to Philadelphia on a cheesesteak-eating expedition a few years ago. Between sandwiches, we cleansed our palates at Rita's Water Ice stand with cups of finely shaved ice saturated with bright red cherry syrup that was dotted with little bits of fruit. It was especially delicious (was that because of the water from which it was made?), so good that we all ate fast enough to suffer serious brain-freeze.

The other break in our cheesesteak hunt was at Center City Pretzel Company, where we picked up a half-dozen freshly made soft pretzels. By this point in the day, we had all eaten enough cheesesteaks that appetite was becoming a distant memory. But the aroma, then the taste of these big soft pretzels proved irresistible. There is a certain brackish tang to the flavor of the pretzel, especially to its tan skin, that is like no other—a flavor that many experts attribute to the Philadelphia water in which they are boiled before being baked. Whatever the cause, these pretzels, hot from the factory, are superb. They are supplied to vendors throughout the city, but by the time they get to where they're going, in most cases they have lost their freshness and their sparkle.

When you get a pretzel at Center City, it will likely be warm, especially if you arrive early in the day (doors open at 4:00 A.M.). It is dense, chewy, and full flavored—a true bread-lover's pretzel—and it is, of course, sprinkled with coarse salt. Some connoisseurs like to have a little yellow mustard as a condiment. As far as we're concerned, one (or a few) of these big softies need nothing to attain street-food perfection.

DeLuca's

2015 Penn Ave.   412-566-2195
Pittsburgh, PA   BL | $

If you need a really satisfying breakfast in Pittsburgh, we recommend a visit to DeLuca's. Located in the Strip District (an eater's paradise by any measure), this fine storefront café serves mighty morning meals. There are frittatas, pumpkin pancakes, extra-large egg sandwiches, and a show-stopper called mixed grill: sausage or ham sizzled with a huge heap of peppers, onions, tomatoes, mushrooms, and zucchini, crowned with a couple of eggs (the eggs are optional) and sided by hunky home-fried potatoes and a couple of slabs of toast. Among the available varieties of toast are an aromatic cinnamon-raisin, rye, wheat, and white.

"Ordinary" omelets are jumbo, too, stuffed with giant hunks of fresh vegetables and/or your breakfast meat of choice. For many visitors, DeLuca's is an opportunity to indulge in one of the really outrageous breakfast items, such as the chocolate chip hotcake sundae, which is a stack of pancakes choc-a-bloc with melted and melting chocolate chips, topped with ice cream and strawberries. We are especially fond of blueberry French toast.

DeLuca's is open for lunch as well as breakfast, with a nice menu of hamburgers, cold-cut hoagies, and such square meals as meat loaf or pork chops with potatoes. Milkshakes are served in bright metal beakers . . . and topped with a dab of whipped cream.

Expect to wait for a seat at peak mealtime hours, especially on weekends, when Pittsburghers throng to the Strip on a kind of eaters' holiday. For us, the choice place in DeLuca's is at the counter with a good view of the short-order chefs flipping eggs and hotcakes at lightning speed.

Dutch Kitchen

Exit 36W off I-81   570-874-3265

Frackville, PA   BLD | $

The Dutch Kitchen is really convenient. It always seems to be just where we need it to be when hunger strikes south of the I-81/I-80 junction. It is a big, friendly place, a former dining car (still intact inside) to which has been added a whole dining room that is decorated to the max with country crafts, speckleware, homily plaques for kitchen walls, and souvenirs of Pennsylvania.

As for the food, it's wonderful. Start with the salad bar, which goes way beyond ordinary salad ingredients with a spectacular array of vegetables that reflect co-owner Jennifer Levkulic's Pennsylvania Dutch ancestry. Here are breathtaking pickled vegetables, seriously dark apple butter, chow-chow, beets, beans, and fresh-baked bread to add to your plate of real daily roasted turkey, hearty bread filling (aka stuffing), genuine mashed potatoes (with an occasional reassuring lump in the smooth, swirly spuds), and gravy.

The Dutch Kitchen is a traditional diner, and it is possible to stop here for bacon and eggs in the morning or a nice hamburger or sandwich at lunch, but we are always drawn to such hearty traditional dishes as smoked pork chops, turkey croquettes, and a stupendously good potpie with homemade noodles, chicken and turkey, potatoes and vegetables. One of our favorite daily specials is a stew of ham, cabbage, and potato sided by a block of brown-top corn bread nearly as sweet as cake. For dessert, of course, we choose shoofly pie, this of the wet-bottom variety: crustless, with a ribbon of molasses at the bottom and a faintly eggy thickness to the crumbly coffee-cake top.

Enrico Biscotti

2022 Penn Ave.   412-281-2602

Pittsburgh, PA   BLD | $

One of the fringe benefits of coffee's ascendance in recent years is the discovery of biscotti, the firm Italian cookie that dunks so well. Alas, like coffee itself, there are a lot of lame versions around. While biscotti are supposed to have a good crunch, too many simply feel stale. We didn't even think we liked them . . . until we visited Enrico Biscotti Co. in Pittsburgh's historic Strip district. Here baker Larry Lagattuta makes them by hand using the finest ingredients, turning out such flavors as anise-almond, apricot-hazelnut, and pineapple-vanilla with white chocolate.

Attached to the bakery is a European-style café where you can eat individual-size brick-oven pizza, torta rustica, soup, or a "big fat salad." Here too is the espresso machine, as well as a handful of tables both inside and outdoors in a sort of makeshift patio along the sidewalk. We know of no nicer place to start the day with strong coffee and biscotti or to have a leisurely lunch of expertly made true-Italian food. Bring your own wine.

The Family Diner

302 Main St.   717-443-8797
White Haven, PA   BLD | $

Interstate 80 through Pennsylvania is a challenging route for people who like to eat. There are plenty of truck stops and restaurants at every exit, but many are mediocre. That is why we treasure the Family Diner, just a few minutes off the highway. There is something for everyone in this friendly place, from blue-plate liver 'n' onions or meat loaf and mashed potatoes to one spectacular super-duper burger with the works to which the menu attributes a "college degree."

As in so many diners, breakfast is deeply satisfying, served here from dawn until the middle of the afternoon. The pancakes, while not what you'd call elegant, are colossal, so wide that they nearly eclipse the plate on which they're served. To add even more avoirdupois to this seriously high-caloric feast, you can get them blanketed with gooey, supersweet hot apple or blueberry topping. A real Pennsylvania favorite, creamed chipped beef, comes sided by hearty home fries or bite-size potato cakes. Eggs are available any way (including soft boiled and poached) with a choice of bacon, ham, sausage, pork roll, or scrapple. Scrapple, as any true Pennsylvanian can tell you, is a local passion—thin slices from a loaf of ground pork and cornmeal that are sizzled in a pan until crisp.

Geno's

1219 S. 9th St.   215-389-0659
Philadelphia, PA   LD | $

Anybody on a cheesesteak-eating expedition through South Philly needs to put Geno's on the short list. Virtually across the street from Pat's King of Steaks (page 134), it is brash and sassy, perfumed by sizzling meat and onions, and patronized by a motley crew of neighborhood wisenheimers, compulsive sandwich eaters, and visiting Roadfood fanatics.

Whichever cheesesteak shop we happen to consider our favorite at any particular time, we have always appreciated a certain classicism about Geno's. It seems that here the meat is cut a little thicker than at other places (although it's still thin enough to be cooked through almost instantly when it hits the griddle), the rolls are sturdy, and the cheese choice includes provolone, American, or Whiz. Open into the wee hours of the morning, Geno's is a magnet for night owls who eat standing under carnival-colored neon, leaning forward at the waist so shreds of beef that fall from the sandwich hit the sidewalk rather than their shoes.

Be sure to order your steak properly: first give your choice of cheese then say the word "with" or "without," indicating your decision on whether or not you want onions. In other words, "Whiz without" means a cheesesteak made with Cheez Whiz but no onions. Red sauce is another option, but for most aficionados, sauce is not an essential cheesesteak ingredient. On the other hand, you must have fries—or cheese fries—on the side.

Glider Diner

890 Providence Rd.	570-343-8036
Scranton, PA	Always open | $

Named because it originally was built from the packing crates that held a glider airplane, the wood-sided Glider Diner was replaced by a shiny silver Mountain View dining car in 1952. A large annex known as the Fireside Lounge was added in the early 1960s, but for blue-plate traditionalists, the old silver streamliner is the place to be. Here breakfast is served 24 hours a day and lunch and supper specialties include Gliderburgers and milkshakes and comforting hot sandwiches of roast beef, meat loaf, Virginia ham, and turkey.

Roadfood stalwarts Bruce Bilmes and Sue Boyles clued us in to the real specialty of the house, listed on the menu as porketta (*porchetta* in Italian) and available either in a toasted hard roll or as the centerpiece of a hot platter surrounded by slices of white bread, accompanied by mashed potatoes, and blanketed with gravy. Porketta is well-seasoned roast pork, sliced thin and moist as can be: delish!

For dessert, there are fruit and cream pies, but we never can resist the specialty old diner cooks know as cat's eye—tapioca pudding.

Jimmy's Hot Dogs

2555 Nazareth Rd.   610-258-7545
Easton, PA   LD | $

We're not cheapskates, but we must confess that there is something ir-resistibly alluring about a decent meal that costs considerably less than coffee at Starbucks. Maybe "decent" isn't exactly the right term to des-cribe what's served at Jimmy's Hot Dogs, for these dogs are sinful little franks—piggy and juicy from their steambath, and simply addictive.

Last we looked, the price of one was seventy cents! So you can have two hot dogs, dressed, of course, the Jimmy's way, with mustard, onions, and pickle spears, along with a bag of potato chips and a Coke or choco-late milk, for under three dollars. If you've got a big appetite, you might want three or four hot dogs, but even if you and a friend indulged in five apiece, you could still walk out with change from a ten-dollar bill.

Want something other than a hot dog and chips? Too bad, because that is the extent of Jimmy's menu. There is no extra charge to kibitz with members of the Apostopolous family, who have run the joint, without changing a thing, for decades . . . and who have perfected the art of freez-ing and overnight-shipping their beloved weenies to ex-Eastonites des-perate for a taste of home.

Note: There are no seats. Business is take-out only.

Jim's Steaks

400 South St.   215-928-1911
Philadelphia, PA   LD | $

Opened in 1939, Jim's is Philadelphia's second-oldest cheesesteak shop (after Pat's), and it's definitely the sharpest looking with its deco black-and-white tile décor.

It's a very popular place, which is a good thing, because your wait in line will provide ample time for deciding how you like your steak gar-nished—"wit'" or "wit'out" (onions), and whether you want the stan-dard Cheez Whiz or optional American or provolone. The wait in line also takes you past the back of the store where an automatic slicer pro-duces heaps of rosy-colored beef ready to be fried.

The steaks are made by hacking up the meat on the grill (with onions, preferably!) so it becomes a kind of onion-flavored steak hash. If you get sliced cheese, it is layered in the roll before the meat and melts underneath it. Whiz is ladled atop the meat. Pizza sauce and peppers are optional condiments. The bread is excellent, the fried onions are appropriately slippery, and the optional hot peppers are breathtaking. Have a Dr. Brown's soda on the side, and you've got a cheap-eats meal to remember.

JoJo's Restaurant

110 24th St.

Pittsburgh, PA

412-261-0280

B&L (from 11:00 P.M. to just after noon) | $

A word of warning about JoJo's hours: although its motto is "Breakfast Served All Day, Every Day," what that means here in Pittsburgh's produce market is that it is open from 11:00 P.M. until noon. The schedule is made to jibe with that of truck drivers who haul produce up from the South and arrive shortly after midnight. They unload their reefers (refrigerated trucks) then come for the JoJo Special, an impossibly overstuffed three-egg omelet containing peppers, onions, mushrooms, provolone and American cheese, bacon and/or sausage and/or ham, plus a spatula-load of hot fried potatoes. Unless you have the appetite of Gargantua, consider this plateload a meal for two. French fries are popular, too, ordered on the side of a meat loaf sandwich in lieu of home fries, and frequently served underneath a blanket of dark brown gravy.

JoJo's is located at the far end of Pittsburgh's Strip District (where the all-night produce market thrives), and it gets mighty colorful at the counter and long tables of this former gas-station café about 2:00 A.M. As the music clubs close and truckers arrive to conduct business at the produce terminal a few blocks away, the late and early shifts come together to eat huge breakfast omelets cooked in individual skillets and served with pre-buttered slabs of Italian toast.

While the majority of JoJo's customers are sober, responsible folks who simply happen to be out late at night, chances are good you will meet a handful of, shall we say, eccentric types who drink too much. One superfan of the big omelet very carefully and precisely explained that he comes to the restaurant every morning about four for the purpose of drinking a JoJo omelet after eating beer all night.

Longacre's Modern Dairy Bar

1445 Route 100   610-845-7551

Barto, PA   BLD (closed Sun) | $

The rolling land of eastern Pennsylvania, dotted as it is with black-and-white bossies roaming farm fields, is a perfect appetizer for one of Longacre's excellent milkshakes or malts, or an old-fashioned ice cream soda in a tall tulip glass. If you need an ice cream dish that is more substantial, choose a sundae made from your choice of over a dozen flavors of ice cream and nearly two dozen toppings, including the usual fudge and marshmallow and butterscotch as well as such old-time fountain oddities as wet maple walnut and crushed cherries. The supreme such concoction is known as the Longacre Special (aka Garbage Sundae) and features ten scoops of ice cream, ten toppings, whipped cream, and a cherry, all served in a thirty-two-ounce goblet.

It is also possible to come to Longacre's for a handy-size hamburger or hot dog, accompanied, of course, by a cherry Coke, vanilla Coke, or Hadacol (today, that's a Coke and root beer combo; early in the twentieth century, it was an elixir loaded with alcohol).

We like the fact that Longacre's little eating area—a short counter and a handful of booths—opens at 7:30 A.M., a time when most ordinary customers come for coffee and an egg sandwich. But the waitress assured us that it is not uncommon for the doors to open at dawn for customers who grab a booth or a stool at the counter and order up a cookie dough sundae or a CMP (chocolate marshmallow peanut sundae) for breakfast. Humankind's fundamental need for excellent ice cream is a craving that cannot be controlled by the hands of a clock.

Lorenzo's Pizza

900 Christian St.   215-922-3808

Philadelphia, PA   LD | $

Despite the name of this restaurant, we can tell you nothing about its pizza. We went there on a cheesesteak-eating expedition with the Roadfood.com team for the purpose of comparing it to the better-known shops around town. Located on a corner near the Italian market, it is a real neighborhood place with none of the tourist trade found elsewhere.

The steaks are made from frozen sheets of meat, which is not really a bad thing. After all, we are not talking about prime beef here. Anyway, the frozen sheets get thrown onto the grill along with a pile of raw onions. As the meat and onions sizzle together, the chef hacks away at them with a spatula, winding up with a hodgepodge of meat and soft-cooked onions. The aromatic combo is shaped into an oval about the length of the Italian bread for which it's destined, and the oval is generously dolloped with molten Cheez Whiz. The cheese is insinuated into the hash, then the lengthwise-sliced bread is used to shovel up the whole mess and finally enclose it. We like this sandwich plenty; our Roadfood.com colleague Stephen Rushmore declared it the cheesiest steak in the city.

Marrone's

31 W. Main St.   570-276-6407
Girardville, PA   LD | $

Pennsylvania has a pizza culture unlike any other place. There's Philadelphia, of course, with many excellent examples of classic Neapolitan-American, thin-crust pie; and there is Old Forge, outside of Scranton, where the pizzas are thick-crusted and rectangular, available with toppings that range from bacon and eggs in the morning to Monterey Jack cheese and meatballs to Polish pizza with kielbasa and onion topping.

Marrone's of Girardville, down in Schuylkill County, serves its own unique variation of Old Forge pizza. Presented on a thin sheet of paper in a metal pan, it is rectangular with a lightweight crust that is about a half-inch thick and crisp around the edges but chewy-bready toward the middle. Most regular pizza toppings are available in addition to the gobs of cheese that are standard, and on the side comes a plastic cup full of bright-red, crushed-pepper hot sauce. A plastic spoon is provided to spread the sauce atop the pizza, and it is a brilliant addition. The pizza is mild-mannered, the sauce packs a punch. What a nice duet!

Marrone's is a seventy-plus-year-old, brick-front tavern where many people come only to drink in the bar next to the dining room. The ideal beverage for its distinctive pizza is a pitcher of locally brewed Yuengling beer, known here in coal country as Pottsville Punch.

Original Hot Dog Shop

3901 Forbes Ave.   412-621-7388 or 687-8327 for delivery
Pittsburgh, PA   LD late night | $

The Original Hot Dog Shop has quite a large menu, including pizza, hoagies, fish sandwiches, and hamburgers, but if the name of the place doesn't clue you in to what's good, the view behind the counter will. There on a broad grill are row upon row of lovely hot dogs—pale pink ones barely warm and darker ones cooked through and ready to be bunned, as well as a formation of deep red all-beef kosher dogs. Regular or all-beef, these are fine franks with a seriously meaty flavor, available plain or gooped with cheese or in a "Super" configuration with cheese and bacon, and with a full array of condiments that include ketchup, mustard, relish, onion, pickle, chili, mayo, and kraut.

On the side of whatever hot dog suits your taste, you must get French fries. Big O fries are legendary, crisp and dark gold with a clean flavor and a wicked crunch that makes them a good companion for just about any sandwich. Even a small order is a substantial dish. Although cheese for dipping is available, as are gravy, hot sauce, and ranch dressing, these exquisite potatoes want only a sprinkle of salt.

Aside from great fast food and past-midnight hours, one reason Pittsburghers are so fond of the Original Hot Dog Shop is that it can trace its heritage back to the Original Famous Sandwich Shop, where the foot-long hot dog was introduced in 1928. Syd Simon, who opened the Original Hot Dog Shop in 1960, worked fifteen years at the old Famous.

Pat's King of Steaks

1237 E. Passyunk Ave.   215-468-1546
Philadelphia, PA   Always open | $

Street-food historians believe that Pat Olivieri invented the cheesesteak in Philadelphia in 1930. His family continues to operate the restaurant he began, and while aficionados of the cheesesteak enjoy debating the merits of the city's many cheesesteak restaurants (some operated by renegades from Pat's own family), this joint's shaved-beef-and-cheese sandwiches on serious Italian bread have stood for over three-quarters of a century as the benchmark. Pat's sandwich is oily, salty, meaty, i.e., everything nutrition prigs dislike. Thin flaps of less-than-prime beef are sizzled on a grill alongside onions and hefted into a roll (with or without some of those onions), then a trowel of melted Cheez Whiz is dripped on top. Peppers, mushrooms, pizza sauce, and extra cheese are all extra-cost options, and if you wish to dude it up further, there are big glass jars with hot sauce and peppers near the take-out windows.

The combination of plebeian ingredients transcends its lowly status and becomes something . . . if not aristocratic, then certainly distinguished. Side your sandwich with a cup full of cheese fries (French fries blanketed with more of that melted Whiz), and eat standing up on the sidewalk under harsh lights. Observe the splattered hot sauce and dropped and crushed French fries underfoot. Listen to the rumble of trucks going past on their way to or from the Italian market. Smell the mingling of cheap after-shave lotion and fancy fragrances on customers in line—both aromas overwhelmed, as the line approaches the take-out window, by the powerhouse aroma of steak and onions sizzling on a hot grill. For our money, even at ten times the price, there is no meal in Philadelphia that can top this one.

People's Restaurant

140 W. Main St. 717-354-2276
New Holland, PA BLD Sun-Fri | $$

People's Restaurant is a civilized café on Main Street where locals and tourists come for home-style food. Accommodations include tables with upholstered chairs and a counter toward the middle of the restaurant where townsfolk gather and exchange sections of the newspaper as they discuss current events.

Suppers include such local delights as fresh-roasted pork with sauerkraut, smoked country ham steak, and lengths of light-bodied Lancaster sausage, as well as all-American meals, including tuna-noodle casserole and fried chicken. Alongside main courses, you choose from an inviting list of freshly prepared vegetables: whipped potatoes, cheddar-macaroni salad, three-bean salad, pepper cabbage, etc. And dessert is a reminder of just how seriously Lancaster County takes its sweets. There are pies aplenty, including apricot crumb, coconut cream, French apple, strawberry Boston cream, shoofly (wet-bottom, of course), grasshopper, and peanut butter silk. Plus, there are always cakes, custards, and pudding.

Sunday is a great day to dine at People's if you don't mind crowds and a wait, for locals and visitors fill the place with the joy of family weekend dining. We also love coming when only a few regulars occupy the counter seats, very early in the morning, when we feast on either old-fashioned oatmeal or "baked oatmeal," which is like a coarse-textured bread pudding made with cooked oats and brown sugar. Another excellent breakfast, and a true Mid-Atlantic specialty, is creamed chipped beef. This is the real stuff—spicy shreds of brined beef in a rich cream sauce, ladled over a plate of crusty fried potato discs. Of course, you can also get a dish of expertly crisped scrapple, and eggs are guaranteed to be from local hens.

Primanti Bros.

46 W. 18th St.   412-263-2142
Pittsburgh, PA   Always open | $

If you like big sandwiches, you need to eat around Pittsburgh. In this brawny city, where the Big Mac was invented in 1968 by a local McDonald's franchise, "the more the merrier" is the basic rule of sandwich-making. The city's champion of huge sandwiches is Primanti Bros., a raucous open-all-night beer-and-sandwich joint that throbs with the play-by-play broadcast of whatever local team is in action. Opened in 1933, the original Primanti's down in the Strip District is a city shrine where walls are painted with caricatures of native sons who range from Andy Warhol to Mr. Rogers and Tom Mix to Roberto Clemente. (There are three other Primanti Bros. around town; none of those is open round the clock.)

The astonishing sandwiches were originally designed for truckers who hauled produce to the nearby wholesale market. While their trucks were being unloaded, they dashed over to Primanti Bros. with a big appetite but little time to eat a dagwood, slaw, and potatoes separately. The solution was to load hot French fries directly into the sandwich atop the customer's meat of choice, then top the fries with Pittsburgh-style (no mayo) coleslaw and a few slices of tomato. The sandwiches are assembled at the grill behind the bar at the speed of light, so when the sandwich is delivered, the fries and grilled meats are still steaming hot, the slaw and tomato cool.

Weird as this combination sounds, the regulars at Primanti's tables assert that such combinations as double-egg and pastrami (both sizzled on the grill) or steak and cheese simply do not taste right without a layer of crisp-fried potatoes and another of slaw. The barely hoistable meal is presented wrapped in butcher paper so that when appetite flags, the paper's edges can be gathered to pick up the spillage.

Robert Wholey & Co.

1501 Penn Ave.	412-261-3377
Pittsburgh, PA	LD | $

Located in Pittsburgh's appetite-inducing Strip District, Robert Wholey & Co. seems more like a culinary amusement park than a mere store. It has a toy train and singing mechanical pigs to amuse children and an extensive kitchenware department to amuse recipe-obsessed adults.

Once strictly a wholesale fish market, Wholey now carries a vast inventory of foodstuffs that range from baked ham by the haunch (or sliced superthin, aka chipped, the way Pittsburghers like it) to sides of tuna that are cut into steaks to order. For those of us who demand immediate gratification, there are a few makeshift tables for sit-down meals at the end of a cooked food line, and more tables upstairs in the Pittsburgh Room. The meal most people come to eat is a fish sandwich on a tender, butter-rich bun. It is made of cod sizzled in the bubbling fry kettles toward the front, where waiting in line is almost always de rigueur. It is common to see grocery-browsers munching a sandwich as they peruse this fabulous market.

Salerno's

139 Moosic Rd.	570-457-2117
Old Forge, PA	LD | $$

Salerno's is a tavern where many people come only to drink. We recommend a visit for Old Forge pizza, a style of pie unique to this area around Scranton. Most of the Old Forge pies are squared off rather than round, airy crusted, and topped with sweet marinara sauce and a mild blend of Italian and American cheese. It's an easy-to-eat pizza, simple and friendly.

At lunch you can get only red pizza, which is a twelve-slice pie big enough for two healthy appetites. At dinner, Salerno's better-known creation is a white pizza—a double-cruster made with a blend of several cheeses between the crusts.

There is a broad menu beyond pizza in this neighborhood tavern: sausage and peppers, chicken parmesan sub sandwiches, pasta e fagiole.

Many customers eat at the bar, where they can knock back draft beers and watch the wall-mounted TV.

Tony Luke's Old Philly Style Sandwiches

39 E. Oregon Ave.   215-551-5725

Philadelphia, PA   BLD | $

Tony Luke's is an old-time city haunt where it is easy to believe that the Delaware Valley in general and Philadelphia in particular is America's great sandwichland. Tony Luke's is a small restaurant with uncomfortable counter seating for only a few dozen people (there's a lot of take-out business), open from dawn until late at night. It is decorated in the traditional South Philly style, i.e., with autographed 8 X 10's of celebrities. In this case, many of the glitterati are club boxers who apparently enjoy meals here between bouts.

The sandwich menu is huge, ranging from hot dogs (aka Texas Tommies) to traditional Philly cheesesteaks topped with Cheez Whiz, and even cheesesteaks made from ostrich meat. The greatest of them all is roast pork, which is garlicky slices and shreds of juicy meat piled inside a long Italian loaf along with cooked-soft broccoli rabe. Chicken and veal cutlets are also particularly wonderful, with or without provolone and either a heap of broccoli rabe or spinach so well-cooked it is more like a condiment than a vegetable.

Service is brash and fast. When you place your order and pay for it, they take your name; and when the sandwich is ready, they call you to the counter, front and center.

Mid-South

Kentucky * North Carolina * Tennessee *

Virginia * West Virginia

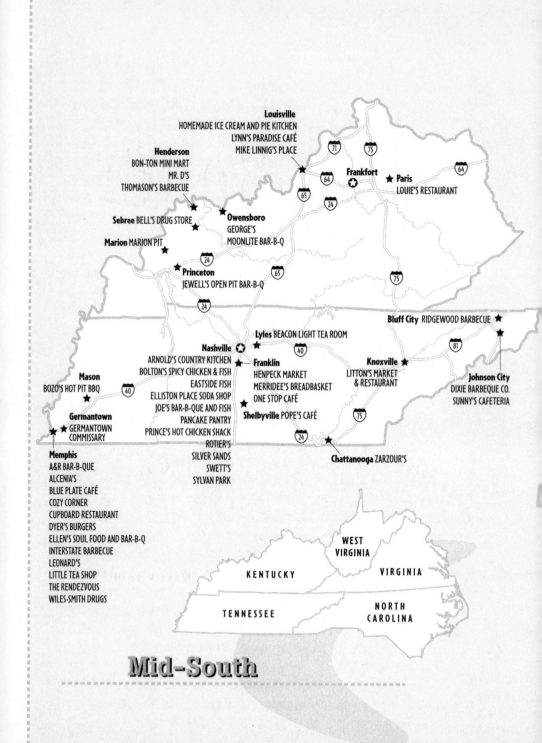

Louisville
HOMEMADE ICE CREAM AND PIE KITCHEN
LYNN'S PARADISE CAFÉ
MIKE LINNIG'S PLACE

Henderson
BON-TON MINI MART
MR. D'S
THOMASON'S BARBECUE

Frankfort

Paris
LOUIE'S RESTAURANT

Sebree BELL'S DRUG STORE

Owensboro
GEORGE'S
MOONLITE BAR-B-Q

Marion MARION PIT

Princeton
JEWELL'S OPEN PIT BAR-B-Q

Lyles BEACON LIGHT TEA ROOM

Bluff City RIDGEWOOD BARBECUE

Nashville
ARNOLD'S COUNTRY KITCHEN
BOLTON'S SPICY CHICKEN & FISH
EASTSIDE FISH
ELLISTON PLACE SODA SHOP
JOE'S BAR-B-QUE AND FISH
PANCAKE PANTRY
PRINCE'S HOT CHICKEN SHACK
ROTIER'S
SILVER SANDS
SWETT'S
SYLVAN PARK

Franklin
HENPECK MARKET
MERRIDEE'S BREADBASKET
ONE STOP CAFÉ

Shelbyville POPE'S CAFÉ

Knoxville
LITTON'S MARKET
& RESTAURANT

Johnson City
DIXIE BARBEQUE CO.
SUNNY'S CAFETERIA

Mason
BOZO'S HOT PIT BBQ

Germantown
GERMANTOWN
COMMISSARY

Memphis
A&R BAR-B-QUE
ALCENIA'S
BLUE PLATE CAFÉ
COZY CORNER
CUPBOARD RESTAURANT
DYER'S BURGERS
ELLEN'S SOUL FOOD AND BAR-B-Q
INTERSTATE BARBECUE
LEONARD'S
LITTLE TEA SHOP
THE RENDEZVOUS
WILES-SMITH DRUGS

Chattanooga ZARZOUR'S

WEST
VIRGINIA

KENTUCKY

VIRGINIA

TENNESSEE

NORTH
CAROLINA

Mid-South

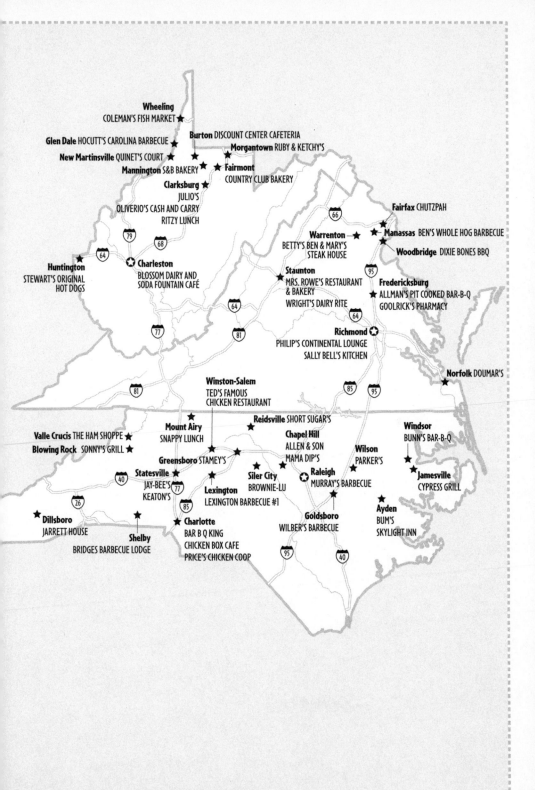

Wheeling COLEMAN'S FISH MARKET ★

Glen Dale HOCUTT'S CAROLINA BARBECUE ★

Burton DISCOUNT CENTER CAFETERIA

New Martinsville QUINET'S COURT ★

Morgantown RUBY & KETCHY'S

Mannington S&B BAKERY ★

★ **Fairmont**
COUNTRY CLUB BAKERY

Clarksburg ★
JULIO'S
OLIVERIO'S CASH AND CARRY
RITZY LUNCH

Fairfax CHUTZPAH

Warrenton ★
BETTY'S BEN & MARY'S
STEAK HOUSE

★ **Manassas** BEN'S WHOLE HOG BARBECUE

Woodbridge DIXIE BONES BBQ

Huntington ★
STEWART'S ORIGINAL
HOT DOGS

✪ **Charleston**
BLOSSOM DAIRY AND
SODA FOUNTAIN CAFÉ

Staunton ★
MRS. ROWE'S RESTAURANT
& BAKERY
WRIGHT'S DAIRY RITE

Fredericksburg ★
ALLMAN'S PIT COOKED BAR-B-Q
GOOLRICK'S PHARMACY

Richmond ✪
PHILIP'S CONTINENTAL LOUNGE
SALLY BELL'S KITCHEN

Norfolk DOUMAR'S ★

Winston-Salem
TED'S FAMOUS
CHICKEN RESTAURANT

Reidsville SHORT SUGAR'S ★

Mount Airy ★
SNAPPY LUNCH

Chapel Hill ★
ALLEN & SON
MAMA DIP'S

Wilson ★
PARKER'S

Windsor ★
BUNN'S BAR-B-Q

Valle Crucis THE HAM SHOPPE ★

Blowing Rock SONNY'S GRILL ★

Greensboro STAMEY'S ★

Statesville ★
JAY-BEE'S
KEATON'S

Lexington ★
LEXINGTON BARBECUE #1

Siler City ★
BROWNIE-LU

✪ **Raleigh**
MURRAY'S BARBECUE

★ **Jamesville**
CYPRESS GRILL

Dillsboro ★
JARRETT HOUSE

Shelby ★
BRIDGES BARBECUE LODGE

Charlotte ★
BAR B Q KING
CHICKEN BOX CAFE
PRICE'S CHICKEN COOP

Goldsboro ★
WILBER'S BARBECUE

Ayden ★
BUM'S
SKYLIGHT INN

Bell's Drug Store

Main St.   270-521-7187

Sebree, KY   L | $

As we drove into the small town of Sebree on a backroads eating tour in the company of Kentucky food authority Louis Hatchett, Louis suddenly called out, "Orangeade!" We pulled into a parking place across from the sturdy old brick-façade building that is Bell's Drug Store. It is a working pharmacy with shelves of patent medicines and knickknacks for sale and a short soda fountain counter up front. Here is where milkshakes are whirled, sundaes and floats constructed, and cherry Cokes brewed to order.

We placed our orangeade orders and then, a moment later, the soda jerk turned to us with a tragic look on his face. "We have run out of oranges," he lamented. But there was still a good supply of lemons, so we ordered lemonade and lemon ice and watched him go to work squeezing juice to make them. We ordered one lemonade made with an extra lemon (50¢ surcharge): what a mighty sweet-tart wallop! And the lemon ice was something different: nothing but fresh lemon juice poured over crushed ice and seasoned with a dash of salt. When the mixologist handed it to us, he pointed to a large sugar dispenser that had been filled with salt (and conspicuously so labeled!). "There's more salt if you'd like," he said. To our taste, it was just right as presented, the sprinkle of salinity enriching the pure citrus power.

While sipping and slurping at one of the small tables opposite the soda fountain, we struck up a conversation with Charles Davis, a gent in well-worn overalls who was savoring a fountain beverage while standing near the counter. He confessed that he was diabetic, but the pure pleasure of a cherry Coke, which he has been enjoying at Bell's for the last four decades, made it easy to throw caution to the wind.

Bon-Ton Mini Mart

2036 Madison St.   270-826-1207
Henderson, KY   L | $

West of Louisville is fried chicken country. Nearly every restaurant, plain or fancy, has its own special version. One of the most humble—and the very best—is to be found at the Bon-Ton Mini Mart. In this former convenience store snack shop, white and dark meat are marinated before being fried, resulting in pieces that are wickedly crunchy outside, dripping moist inside, and fairly exploding with flavor. With the chicken come savory biscuits, French fries, and coleslaw.

The chicken is so incredibly good that it is all too tempting to eat until you can't eat another thing. But the Bon-Ton demands you save room for dessert. Banana pudding is a big bowl of comfort, coconut cream and chocolate pie are deeply satisfying, and the chess pie just may be the best one we have ever tasted. It is sweet, but has a buttery richness that goes beyond sweetness. What a brilliant dessert!

George's

1346 E. 4th St.   502-926-9276
Owensboro, KY   LD | $

Of all the burgoo we have eaten in western Kentucky, we like George's best. It is thick with vegetables and resonant with the gamy flavor of mutton, and has just enough pepper kick to make every spoonful a thrill. Technically speaking it is a soup, but you could eat it with a fork.

Good as the burgoo is, the main reason to come to George's is for a full barbecue meal. Mutton is the foremost meat in these parts: dark, full-flavored, with a tang that is nothing like pork or beef. Whether you choose a plate of mutton "off the pit" (sauceless) or regular mutton sopped with the natural gravy that is unique to this region or mutton ribs or more familiar items such as pork ribs, chopped pork, chicken, ham, or beef, the smoky meat is accompanied by very good side dishes: sweet coleslaw, creamy potato salad, or goopy baked beans. If you're not quite so hungry, you can have any of the barbecued items on a tray, which includes only pickles, onion, and bread. Bread, by the way, is available white or rye, the rye looking like Wonder Bread with a slight tan, bearing no resemblance whatsoever to tough-crusted deli rye. All the barbecues in this part of Kentucky serve it.

George's is an inconspicuous café with booths and tables and a sweet-as-honey waitress named Trish who confided to us that although born and raised in western Kentucky, she had spent ten years in Memphis where she was not happy: Memphis barbecue is legendary, but nobody there serves mutton.

Homemade Ice Cream and Pie Kitchen

2525 Bardstown Rd.   502-459-8184
Louisville, KY   LD | $

We arrived at the Louisville airport in the company of three sophisticated palates from New York, and before heading into Kentucky on a barbecue-eating expedition, we took them to one of America's great places to sate a sweet tooth, this modest-looking ice cream and pie kitchen. Our friends were flabbergasted by the variety of pies and cakes available, many of which are virtually unknown outside the South: chocolaty red velvet cake encased in thick white cream cheese frosting, chess pie that is purity itself, hummingbird cake that we guess was named because it would please a nectar-crazed avian. In addition to regular chess, which is little more than cream, sugar, and eggs, there are lemon chess and chocolate chess. And of course there are literally dozens of more universally known pies and cakes, including key lime, lemon meringue, banana cream, apple, apple crunch, and Dutch apple with caramel.

Many of the handsome layer cakes come swirled with sweet-smelling buttercream frosting. A few of our favorite varieties include banana-pecan cake, coconut cake, mandarin orange cake with pineapple-flavored whipped cream, and jam-spice cake with caramel frosting.

Because we visit Louisville for only short periods of time, coming to this little shop is inevitably frustrating. There is no way two people or even five people can begin to sample most of the lovely desserts available any one day. Nearly everything is sold by the slice as well as the whole cake, and there are dining tables scattered about inside and on a front patio for drop-ins who require instant gratification.

Jewell's Open Pit Bar-B-Q

730 US 62E

Princeton, KY

270-365-5415

LD | $

"I watch the food shows on TV when they go all over the place looking for barbecue," opined pit master Lowell Jewell. "And I'm saying, 'Why don't you come to western Kentucky and eat the real thing?' "

Good advice. Following the barbecue trail west of Louisville and south toward the Land Between the Lakes you will find an open-pit culture unlike anywhere else and radically diverse from county to county. Local barbecue preferences vary in large ways and small, from the meat of choice—mutton around Henderson, pork in Crittenden County—to what the wet stuff is called—dip to the north, sauce to the south. Around the Ohio River, if you don't want any dip at all, you ask for your meat off the pit, meaning sauceless.

Around Princeton in Caldwell County, barbecue has a flavor all its own. At Lowell Jewell's place, the meat to eat is pork shoulder torn into variegated strips and nuggets, some variations soft as velvet, others threaded with crusty shreds of skin. In this area, you make an important decision that is seldom an issue up in mutton country: hot or mild sauce. Unlike the meats of Henderson, where pork is generally served pre-sauced, here it is bunned or plated, and only then topped with hot or mild sauce.

Princeton-style sauce, at Heaton's Citgo & BBQ as well as at Jewell's, is unique—rich and red with a compelling citrus zest. A pile of Jewell's unbelievably juicy pulled pork gilded with sizzling hot sauce and sided by a circle of earthy griddle-cooked corn bread, followed by the family-recipe French coconut pie, is a taste-buds joy ride. (French coconut pie is a chess pie laced with coconut, and we take the opportunity of this parenthesis to note that Kentucky's barbecue byways also happen to traverse one of the nation's premier pie lodes, from Derby pie up in Louisville to lemon icebox pie farther south.)

Jewell's is a comfy wood-paneled dining room across the road from a huge factory and just down from a Wal-Mart. It has a casual rustic air, its walls decorated with antique farm implements, its tables occupied by regulars who come to chat and chew over barbecue and endless cups of coffee.

Louie's Restaurant

1000 Pleasant St.   859-987-6116
Paris, KY   BL Mon–Sat, D Weds–Sat | $

Louie's is a favorite haunt of the horsey set that populates this beautiful section of Kentucky. They include not only the occasional owner or investor but also the hands-on folk of the upper-echelon equine world: grooms, handlers, and stable personnel who tend to some of the most expensive horseflesh on earth at surrounding barns.

The town café is staffed by waitresses who are quick with the coffee refills and the snappy repartee. We love Louie's fried chicken at lunch, which is served with good southern-style vegetables, and the Kentucky "hot brown" open-face sandwich (turkey, melted cheese, and bacon) is a classic, as are caramel pie and Woodford pudding, the latter a vintage local recipe laced with jam. But our favorite time to claim a seat is breakfast, for a three-egg omelet sided by biscuits and gravy or one of the house-special Big Sire breakfasts, built around a meat of choice—fried country ham or sugar-cured ham, sausage patties, bacon strips, pork tenderloin, or a rib-eye steak, plus, of course, a couple of eggs, hash browns, and toast or biscuits and gravy.

The front wall is adorned with racing silks and the exterior façade bears a swell motto—almost always a sign of an interesting Roadfood restaurant. Louie's watchwords are "We Treat You □ The Year ○."

Lynn's Paradise Café

984 Barret Ave.   502-583-3447
Louisville, KY   BLD | $

Lynn's Paradise Café is about the most whimsical restaurant we know. Décor is wild and kitschy, and the gift shop up front sells a panoply of useful appliances as well as silly souvenirs. For all its sense of fun, this is a place that serves some seriously good food. We love breakfast the most, from lovely local eggs with grits and biscuits on the side to bourbon-ball French toast and banana split pancakes. There is also a good ol' plate of

Kentucky country ham with eggs and warm Granny Smith apples. This is true country comfort food!

Not that we want to slight lunch and dinner. Lynn Winter's "Mom's Meatloaf" is a square-meal knock-out made with marinara sauce, sided by real mashed potatoes and al dente lima beans. Louisville's own hot brown sandwich is built on sourdough bread, its turkey, bacon, and tomato slices fully blanketed by a mantle of sizzling broiled cheese. Hamburgers are available with French fries or one of several side dishes. These include creamy polenta, braised rosemary cabbage, crusty blocks of mac 'n' cheese, and grilled asparagus. Last visit, we relished a dinner of hot turkey, dressing, and cheese grits.

The beverage selection includes a "gigantic mimosa" and a "world famous bloody Mary," made from Lynn's own mix and garnished with a skewer of peppers and olives.

Marion Pit

728 S. Main St. 270-965-3318
Marion, KY LD | $

Marion Pit is open every day of the year except Christmas, Thanksgiving, New Year's Day, and Easter. Proprietor Jack Easley said that he usually cooks an especially large number of pork shoulders on Saturday because so many local churches purchase meat by the pound for Sunday suppers. At thirty-plus years in business, his is the oldest smokehouse around, and certainly the most unpretentious—a tiny hut on the outskirts of town with a few picnic tables for dining al fresco or inside a screened patio.

Place your order at a window in the small building to which hickory-cooked shoulders are brought from an adjoining building and readied for eating. Mr. Easley told us that he cooks his meat for seventeen hours, using no seasonings and no sauce whatever. The long roast at low temperatures results in pork that is unspeakably tender, so soft that it cannot be sliced because it would fall apart. You can buy it by the pound to go, by the sandwich, or by the plate (billed here as a "big pile of bar-b-q"). It is some of the best Q anywhere, served with a delicious sauce, the recipe for which is known only to Mr. Easley, his wife, and his son.

Mike Linnig's Place

9308 Cane Run Rd. 502-937-9888
Louisville, KY LD (closed Mon) | $$

"Fried fish and bottled beer under the trees down by the Ohio River!" is how our tipster described Mike Linnig's, a destination eatery that dates back some eighty years to when it opened as a fruit and vegetable stand on Mike Linnig's farm. Sweet as it is to eat outdoors, inside accommodations are pretty swell, too. It's a huge place with cavernous dining space in back and a smaller front room opposite the bar where you step up to place your order (table service is available in back). Here the wood-paneled walls are crowded with trophies of creatures from the land, sea, and air, as well as nostalgic photos, clippings, and knickknacks.

The menu includes just about every kind of seafood that can be fried, including sea scallops, crawfish, and salmon, but its highlights are such fish camp specialties as catfish, white fish, and frog legs, all served in immense portions. We are especially fond of the spicy fish nuggets and the freshly breaded shrimp. The fish, the frog legs, the scallops, and the oysters have a seriously nice crunch to their crust, but are not otherwise memorable.

Onion rings are a specialty. They are big chunky things, extremely brittle and mostly crust, with just a hint of onion flavor emanating from the slick ribbon within. By the way, the tartar sauce and cocktail sauce, while served in the sort of individual cups typical of institutional meals, are Mike Linnig's own recipe, and both are outstanding.

Among the beverage choices beyond bottled beer are iced tea (sweet or not), lemonade (which tastes a lot like the tea), and genuine Kool-Aid, listed on the menu as fruit punch.

Moonlite Bar-B-Q

2840 W. Parrish Ave. 270-684-8143
Owensboro, KY LD | $$

There's not a lot of waitress contact at Moonlite Bar-B-Q, where everyone avails themselves of a spectacular buffet. But we have to say that the interaction we have had is a pleasure. Last time we dined here, we arrived a good half-hour before the people we were joining. We were famished. We explained the situation and our waitress suggested we go fill some plates at the buffet and eat awhile. "I'll have your plates cleaned and places set again, so when they arrive you can act like you haven't et yet."

Good plan, for a mere single trip to the Moonlite buffet doesn't provide nearly enough plate space to enjoy everything that needs to be tasted. The array of foods occupies one large room with salads and desserts on one side, vegetables and meats on the other. There are barbecued chicken, ribs, pulled pork, spectacularly succulent beef brisket, and even a pan of non-barbecued sliced country ham that is firm and salty, as well as a tray of ready-made ham biscuits. And there is western Kentucky's favorite barbecue meat, mutton. Cooked until pot-roast tender, it is set out on the buffet two ways: chopped or pulled. Chopped mutton is pulverized to nothing but flavor: tangy lamb and wood smoke in a bold duet. The pulled version is a textural amusement park—rugged and chunky with a lot of hard outside crust among soft, juicy chunks of interior meat. Apply your own sauce at the table from the pitchers the waitress brings. One is a dark orange emulsion with gentle vinegar-tomato zest; the other is known as "mutton dip," an unctuous gravy that is used to baste the mutton as it cooks. For those who need heat, Moonlite also supplies bottles of "Very Hot Sauce," which is brilliantly peppered and will set your lips and tongue aglow.

Beyond meats, we need to mention the impressive deployment of vegetables, including cheesy broccoli casserole, macaroni and cheese, creamed corn niblets, ham and beans, and butter-drizzled mashed potatoes, plus the western Kentucky soup-stew of mutton and vegetables known as burgoo (pronounced BUR-goo) and crusty corn muffins. Last visit, we also sampled a retro banana salad made with Miracle Whip and chopped nuts. And there are a couple of tables of terrific Kentucky pies.

Mr. D's

1435 S. Green St.
Henderson, KY

270-826-2505
LD | $

A fiberglass chicken about as tall as a grizzly bear stands outside of Mr. D's beckoning customers to drive in. While Mr. D's is a full-menu drive-in with a repertoire of hamburgers, hot dogs, and sandwiches, chicken rules. It is fried chicken made from a recipe popularized decades ago by a legendary chicken man named Colonel Jim, and like the stupendously good chicken at the nearby Bon-Ton Mini Mart (p. 144), it has a crunchy crust that is spicy enough to make your eyes water.

Because Mr. D's is a quick-service drive-in with car service only, the chicken you order will be delivered to your window in five minutes or less, meaning that the kitchen cooks it ahead of time rather than to order. This is good if you are really, really hungry, but not so good if you are a crisp-skin connoisseur, because the crust loses its crunch. Make no mistake: this is four-star fried chicken, and puts just about any non-Kentucky fried chicken to shame. But the next time we order some, we are going to do as Henderson tipster Louis Hatchett advises, request that the kitchen cook it to order. If that twenty-minute wait means crust that cracks when bitten, we'll happily endure it.

Thomason's Barbecue

701 Atkinson St.   270-826-0654
Henderson, KY   LD | $

Kentucky tipster Louis Hatchett IV brought us to Thomason's for barbecue beans, which are magnificent—rich and smoky, laced with shreds of meat and so vividly spiced you could make a meal of them—but the barbecue itself is worth a trip, too.

Thomason's barbecues everything: pork, mutton, beef, spare ribs, baby back ribs, chicken, ham, and turkey. You can get your choice of meat on a plate, which includes pickle, onion, bread, and beans; on a tray, which includes only pickle, onion, and bread; or in a sandwich. Like all other sandwiches in this area, Thomason's can scarcely be picked up by hand because juice from the meat saturates the lower piece of bread, causing it to disintegrate. The pork is velvet-soft, moist, and seductively smoky; mutton is sopped with gravy and mild tasting. We'll have to return to sample the other choices.

A simple, freestanding eatery with an order counter and a scattering of tables, Thomason's does a big carry-out business, selling its specialties by the pound and gallon. On a shelf below the order counter are bottles of dip for sale. Dip is sauce with natural, au jus character.

Allen & Son

6203 Millhouse Rd.   919-942-7576

Chapel Hill, NC   LD | $

Cinder-block walls, plastic tablecloths, and pork slow-smoked over hickory coals: here is a definitive North Carolina barbecue parlor. Sandwiches are available, but we recommend getting Allen's meat on a plate, which includes a pile of sparkling coleslaw and about a half-dozen crisp-skinned hush puppies. The hush pups are arranged like a sculptor's work, on top of the pork. It is a field of spheres atop a heap of meat: a lovely, aromatic, and absolutely mouthwatering sight. Meat is served sauceless, but you can dress it up with Allen & Son's butter-rich, vinegar-based hot sauce loaded with spice and cracked pepper.

If you get the combination plate known to some locals as "stew and que" (highly recommended), the pile of good smoked meat is supplemented by a bowl of Brunswick stew, another traditional companion to smoked pork in these parts. Unlike the meatier Brunswick stews of southern Virginia, this luscious stuff is mostly vegetables with a few shreds of meat, all cosseted in a tomato-rich sauce. It is a hearty, rib-sticking food that makes a wonderful contrast to the exquisite pork.

For dessert, choose among peanut butter pie, fruit cobbler, key lime pound cake, and chess pie.

Bar B Q King

2900 Wilkinson Blvd.   704-399-8344

Charlotte, NC   LD | $

Bar B Q King has no indoor seating. It is a building in the middle of a parking lot with two rows of car slips, order-matic menus, and trays mounted on articulated arms so you can pull dinner right up to the side of your vehicle when it is delivered by the carhop. While many customers eat in their cars, phone-ahead service is popular, too: call in your order, then arrive to pick up meals packed in the sturdy cardboard boxes that have become the BBQK trademark.

On our first visit, we made the mistake of asking the carhop for a "pork sandwich." What we got was a perch sandwich. We ate it anyway, and it was marvelous—moist, sweet white meat so satisfying it reminded us of the best pork, but encased in a golden crust. In fact, the perch was so good, we subsequently ordered trout, shrimp, and oysters—all fried in that only-in-the-South soulful way that's guaranteed to convert even a die-hard fish-frowner.

What we learned from our experience—other than to recommend BBQK as a fine fried-fish restaurant—is that if you want smoked pork hereabouts, you don't say "pork"; you say "barbecue." Pork is the only pit meat there is. It is available sliced or minced (the latter really is pulverized, the former "hacked"), and it, too, is superb—tender, succulent, veiled in a subtle sauce that does not overwhelm the meat's fundamental fineness.

Bridges Barbecue Lodge

US 74   704-482-8567

Shelby, NC   LD (closed Mon-Tues) | $

Bridges has no written menu, just the slip of paper used by the waitress to take orders: sandwich, tray, or plate. A tray is barbecue and barbecue slaw; a plate also holds French fries, lettuce, tomato, and pickle. Both are accompanied by hush puppies, and whether you select sandwich, tray, or plate, you must decide if you want your meat (pork shoulder) minced, chopped, or sliced. It is a major decision, for they are almost like three different foods. Bridges is one of the few places that offers minced barbecue, an old-time configuration from traditional pig-pickin's. It is pulverized into moist hash with some little shreds of darkened, chewy crust amid the distressed pork. The mound is held together by a good portion of uniquely North Carolinian sauce—tomato-based, but with a strong vinegar punch. Chopped is the more typical way modern North Carolinians like it—chunky and easily chewable, and with only a smidgen of sauce. Sliced barbecue comes as big, soft flaps. All three kinds of Q are delightfully tender with a truly inspired smoky tang. With the pork comes a Styrofoam cup of warm sauce for dipping.

The hush puppies are curious: elongated crescents with a wickedly brittle, sandy-textured crust. The slaw is strange, too, if you are expecting anything like typical coleslaw. This is barbecue slaw, meaning finely chopped cabbage bound together with—what else?—barbecue sauce! It's got a brilliant flavor and a pearly-red color that handsomely complements your pork of choice. The small tray, by the way, is only about three by five inches and an inch-and-a-half deep, but it is astounding how much meat and slaw get packed into it.

Bridges's dining room is plain and soothing, with the kind of meditative atmosphere unique to the finest pork parlors of the mid-South. Square wooden chandeliers cast soft light over green-upholstered booths and a short counter up front where single diners chat quietly among themselves as they sip buttermilk or iced tea and fork into barbecue. During our first meal here, five police officers with gleaming automatics in their patent leather holsters occupied a table toward the back. Even they spoke in hushed tones, as if it would be sacrilegious to be raucous in this upstanding eat-place.

Brownie-Lu

919 N. Second Ave.   919-663-3913

Siler City, NC   BLD | $

Brownie-Lu chicken is Broasted, meaning that it is cooked in Broaster equipment, a unique combination of frying and pressure-cooking that goes back to the mid-1950s. The result is chicken that is shockingly tender, so gentle that it tends to slide off the bone of its own accord, encased in crunchy-brittle skin so thin you can practically see through it. The meat has a full but mellow flavor, like something an ideal grandma might make. It is served with nice rolls and such laudable side dishes as butter beans cooked with ham and genuine mashed potatoes. In fact, there are enough good vegetables on the menu that a health-food type could come here and have a totally meatless, delicious meal. A full breakfast is served—country ham is a must—and lunch and supper demand a slice from one of the kitchen's homemade cream pies.

Bum's

115 E. Third St.	252-746-6880
Ayden, NC	BL | $

Many people think of Bum's as a barbecue restaurant, and that in itself is a high compliment considering its "competition" in Ayden is the Skylight Inn (p. 164), which any sane person must agree is one of the best barbecue restaurants anywhere in the state. Some others think of it as a chicken restaurant. You'll wait a good twenty minutes for the bird to fry, but the reward for your patience is crisp-crusted chicken on a par with North Carolina's finest. We relish the barbecue and the chicken, but we love Bum's most for its vegetables and side dishes.

It's small torture to go through the cafeteria line and have to choose among corn sticks and corn bread, luxuriously porky boiled cabbage, pieces of crisp pork skin, butter beans, and collard greens. The last, those greens, are actually grown by proprietor Latham "Bum" Dennis in his home garden, and they are cooked to a point of supreme tenderness and savor at the restaurant. There are a few desserts from which to choose; banana pudding is the one not to be missed.

Bum's breakfast buffet features excellent biscuits (with or without gravy) and a choice of pig meats that includes homemade sausage, pork tenderloin, and fried ham.

Bunn's Bar-B-Q

127 N. King St.	252-794-2274
Windsor, NC	L | $

Bunn's building started life in the mid-1800s as a doctor's office. It became a filling station in 1900, and in 1938 barbecue was added to the menu of gasoline and motor oil. There's still an old Texaco pump outside, and the place is decorated with vintage signs, ads, and ephemera. The atmosphere is vaguely similar to what the Cracker Barrel chain aims to create, but in this case, it is real.

When you enter, you have a choice of sitting on a bench at a counter in a room to the left or at a table in a room to the right, in back. Whichever place you sit, service is lightning-fast. That's because there is virtually no choice on this menu. What you eat is pork, with or without Brunswick stew, on a plate or sandwich, accompanied by tart, tangy coleslaw. The pork is chopped ultrafine, a mix of soft white meat from the inside of the roast laced with chewy brown shreds from its surface. It comes ever-so-lightly sauced with what the locals like—vinegar and spice—but if you want it moister or hotter, other sauces are provided on the counter and tables. Plates are topped with a lovely square of thin, extremely luscious corn bread that has a serious chew and is the ideal medium for pushing around Brunswick stew on the plate.

Chicken Box

3726 N. Tryon St.   704-332-2636
Charlotte, NC   LD | $

When hungry for fried chicken in Charlotte, we always headed for Price's Chicken Coop (p. 163) or the Coffee Cup. Nothing wrong with either choice, nothing at all. But there's another contender for chicken supremacy, a very humble eatery named the Chicken Box. Located in a drab setting that used to be a fast-food eatery, this place serves chicken with crust that crackles with savory flavor. Wings, drumettes, drumsticks, thighs, and breasts are sold by the plate with French fries or soul food vegetables (mac and cheese and collard greens are especially noteworthy) or in party-size quantities to take home. Just because this is the cheapest fried chicken in the fried-chicken-crazy city of Charlotte does not mean it isn't the best.

Amenities are minimal. Carry a tray with your food from the counter to a molded seat in the dining area. And it would be appreciated if you cleaned up the table when you are done.

Cypress Grill

1520 Stewart St.

Jamesville, NC

252-792-4175

D Jan–Apr | $$

For those of us who grew up thinking of herring as a pickled hors d'oeuvre, North Carolina river herring is a shock. For one thing, it looks like a fish. And for another, it really tastes like a fish. Not the least bit like chicken or anything else. If you like fish, you will love it. And there is no better place to love it than at the Cypress Grill on the banks of the Roanoke River. Here is the last of the old-time herring shacks, quite literally a cypress wood shack, open only for the herring run, January through April.

There is nothing on the Cypress Grill menu other than fish. In addition to herring, you can have rock (striped bass), perch, flounder, shrimp, oysters, devil crab, clam strips, trout fillet, or catfish fillet. Tuesday, Thursday, and Saturday, roe is available. Not even a gesture is offered for fish-frowners. No hamburgers or grilled cheese sandwiches here! Side dishes include a choice of vegetables, which are fine but not particularly interesting: boiled potatoes, fried okra, slaw.

The herring are spectacular, heads lopped off but not the tails, each one veiled in the thinnest possible sheath of cornmeal, its flesh scored with notches so that when it is tossed into the boiling oil, it cooks quickly deep down to the bone.

The big issue among river herring lovers is degree of doneness. Some ask for it sunny-side-up, meaning minimal immersion in the fry kettle, resulting in a fish from which you can peel away the skin and lift moist pieces of meat off the bones. The opposite way to go is to ask for your herring cremated: fried until hard and crunchy and so well cooked that all the little bones have become indistinguishable from the flesh around them. The meat itself is transformed, its weight lightened so the natural oiliness is gone but the flavor has become even more intense. The crust and the interior are melded, and they break off in unbelievably savory bite-size pieces, finally leaving nothing but a herring backbone on the plate.

While some herring-crazed patrons fill up on four, five, six, or more of the plush fish, we must advise first-time visitors to the Cypress Grill to leave appetite for dessert. That's the one non-fish item on the menu worth singing about. Every morning, proprietors Leslie and Sally Gardner make pies. When we stopped to visit one day around 10:00 A.M., Mr. Gardner led us right over to the pie case—a wooden cupboard built by a neighbor to be so sturdy, he says, "you could dance on it." He insisted we feel the bottom of a pie pan, still nearly too hot to touch. We sat down then and there and forked up a piece of chocolate pie that was modest-size but intensely fudgy.

Mama Dip's

408 W. Rosemary St.
Chapel Hill, NC

919-942-5837
BLD | $$

Mama Dip is Mildred Council, founder-owner-chef at Chapel Hill's beloved soul-food restaurant. Ms. Council, nicknamed "Dip" by her siblings because she was such a tall kid, wrote *Mama Dip's Kitchen* in 1999, and it is a valuable cookbook that includes many of the recipes she has used in her restaurant.

Three meals a day are served in the nouveau rustic quarters to which Dip's moved a few years ago, and while lunch and dinner offer great southern classics—fried chicken, chitlins, Brunswick stew—we love to start the day with eggs, pork chops, and gravy, sided by biscuits and grits. Other hearty wake-up meals include salmon cakes, brawny country ham, and blueberry pancakes.

Later in the day, what we love most about Dip's meals, aside from the lumpy, crunchy, brightly salty crust of the fried chicken, are the vegetables. The daily list includes long-cooked greens, blackeyed peas, crunchy nuggets of fried okra, mashed potatoes and gravy, porky string beans, okra stew with tomatoes, corn-dotted coleslaw, always a sumptuous vegetable casserole, broccoli, squash, stewed tomatoes, and cool sweet potato salad. For mopping and dipping, there are buttermilk biscuits, corn bread, and yeast rolls.

The Ham Shoppe

132 Broadstone Rd.
Valle Crucis, NC

828-963-6310
BL | $

For a quick sandwich or a piece of cake while passing through the mountains, or to stock up on southern-style grits and groceries, the Ham Shoppe is the place to go. Country hams are sold whole, halved, and by the slice, ready to fry, and the shelves offer a wide array of jellies, preserves, and put-up vegetables.

What we most appreciate about this full-service country store is the fact that you can walk in and grab a hot ham biscuit ready-to-eat. Regarding the ham sandwich, Roadfooder T. Jeffries wrote us a while back to say, "I have never found a better sandwich . . . stacked high on fresh bread with all the fixin's." Or if you are in the mood for something sweet, there are cut-and-wrapped slices of apple, blackberry, and peach pie, as well as sundrop lemon cake and blackberry pound cake.

The most intriguing thing we found to eat was a blueberry biscuit. Yes, it is real biscuit dough with its distinctive baking powder flavor, studded with soft sweet berries and topped with the sort of icing you'd find on a sweet roll. It is weird, no doubt about it, and biscuit purists will likely have a fit over this iconoclastic piece of pastry. But we each managed to eat a whole one and drive away with satisfied smiles.

Jarrett House

Dillsboro, NC

828-586-6251

LD (closed in winter) | $$

Hoo-eee, talk about country cooking! How about a skillet-fried, center-cut slice of country ham with red-eye gravy and biscuits on the side? Or chicken and dumplings with fried apples, and locally grown beans and squash? Catfish and fried chicken are also on the lunch menu; battered and fried mountain trout is available at supper. And for dessert? A nice slice of vinegar pie ("like pecan pie without the pecans") or warm peach cobbler. Yes, this is the real thing, all right, served in the gracious dining room of a Smoky Mountain inn built in 1884.

Lunch is swell, served by the plate, but full enjoyment of this grand restaurant is found at dinnertime or on Sundays, when meals are served by the platter and bowl, family-style, and guests are welcome to keep eating until it's time to lean back and let out the belt a notch or two.

Jay-Bee's

320 Mocksville Hwy.

Statesville, NC

704-872-8033

LD | $

Jay-Bee's has the feel of a drive-in, but technically it is a drive-through, like the soulless franchised places that crowd so many roadsides. But the menu is fetching, and the brash personality of this car-friendly (or dine-in) eat-place is irresistible. "This Ain't No Fast Food Joint!" a sign outside brags. "We Proudly Make All Our Menu Items to Order and It Takes a Little More Time." That would be about a three-minute wait until you are presented with a ready-to-eat Prairie Dog topped with barbecue sauce, chopped onions, and melted cheese or a Northerners' Fancy Dog under sauerkraut and mustard.

Although Jay-Bee's pride is hot dogs, hamburgers are very impressive. Available in quarter-pound or half-pound configurations, they are hand-formed from beef ground daily and sizzled to appealing succulence, particularly good when dressed with a heap of sautéed onions.

The beverage menu ranges from sweet tea and milkshakes to Dr Pepper and Mountain Dew, and if you dine inside, a refill of any soda is free. One-quart-size drinks—yes, thirty-two ounces—are available at the drive-through window.

Keaton's

Woodleaf Rd.	704-278-1619
Statesville, NC	LD Weds-Sat | $

A cinder-block bunker in North Carolina cattle land between the High Country's natural beauty and High Point's unnaturally low-priced furniture outlets, Keaton's serves some of the best fried chicken you ever will eat.

Step up to the counter and order an upper or a lower (the polite country terms for breast and wing or thigh and drumstick). Pick side dishes from a soulful repertoire of mac and cheese, baked beans, hot-sauce slaw or white-mayo slaw, choose iced tea (sweet, of course) or beer, then go to your assigned table or booth, to which a waitress brings the food.

In Keaton's kitchen, the chicken is peppered and salted, floured and fried, at which point it is simply excellent country-style pan-fried chicken. Then comes the distinctive extra step: just-fried pieces are immersed in a bubbling vat of secret-formula red sauce, a high-spiced, opaque potion similar to what graces High Country barbecued pork. This process takes only seconds, but the hot and spicy sauce permeates to the bone. You eat this chicken with your hands, pulling off crisp strips of sauce-glazed skin, worrying every joint to suck out all the flavor you can get.

Lexington Barbecue #1

10 Hwy. 29-70 South   336-249-9814
Lexington, NC   LD | $

Welcome to Lexington, North Carolina, a small city with more than one barbecue restaurant per thousand citizens! Of the nearly two dozen eateries that specialize in hickory-cooked pork, Lexington Barbecue, which opened in 1962, is definitive. Monk's Place, as locals know it (in deference to founder Wayne "Honey" Monk), looks like a barn with some smelters attached to the back. From those smelters issues the tantalizing aroma of burning hickory and oak wood and the sweet smell of slow-cooking pork, one of the most appetite-inducing aromas in the world. Honey Monk's is a straightforward eatery with booths and tables and little in the way of décor other than pictures of rural life on the wall. Much business is take-out.

There are no complicated techniques or deep secrets about Lexington barbecue. After about ten hours over smoldering smoke, pork shoulders are shredded into a hash of pieces that vary from melting soft (from the inside) to burned crisp (from the "bark," or exterior). The hacked meat is served on a bun with finely chopped slaw or as part of a platter, on which it occupies half a small yellow cardboard boat, with slaw in the other half. Like the meat, the slaw is flavored with a vinegar–sweet red barbecue sauce. As part of the platter with the meat and slaw, you get terrific, crunch-crusted hush puppies with creamy insides.

Historical note: in 1983 the North Carolina General Assembly designated Lexington as the "Hickory-Cooked Barbecue Capital of Piedmont North Carolina"; that same year the White House asked Mr. Monk to cook barbecue for President Reagan and other heads of state at the Williamsburg International Economic Summit.

Murray's Barbecue

4700 Old Poole Rd.   919-231-6258
Raleigh, NC   LD Mon-Fri only | $

Murray's is on the wrong side of town and looks like a rambling gas station. In other words, it has the appearance of a four-star house of barbecue. Further proof of its legitimacy can be found in the piles of green hickory wood outside. This wood is made into coals for the pits, which send a sweet haze wafting through the air.

Hogs are cooked for six hours, then chopped into chunks that are subtly flavored, moist, and tender. This is the sort of refined Carolina barbecue for which any sort of heavy, sweet, or too-hot sauce would be anathema. Murray's sauce is merely a condiment; it is not overbearing, adding only an accent to the meat. The truly vital companions on a plate of pulled pork at Murray's are the crusty, tubular hush puppies and peppery coleslaw. For a special treat, get an order of yam sticks—like French fries, but made with sweet potatoes. There is excellent banana pudding for dessert.

Parker's

Hwy. 301   252-237-0972
Wilson, NC   LD | $

The popularity of Parker's goes back to the 1940s, when Wilson was the place many tobacco farmers sold their crop. A big barbecue meal was how tobacco men celebrated the harvest; buyers ate here and spread the word up and down Highway 301, which was the main north-south road prior to I-95. Still, the highway is only seven miles away, making Parker's an extremely convenient stop for those traveling along the interstate.

It's a vast eating hall with multiple dining rooms where customers crowd the lined-up tables for family-style combo platters of chopped pork, fried chicken, Brunswick stew, boiled potatoes, corn sticks, and coleslaw. Cooked over hardwood and chopped into hash, the pork is a mix of lean inside meat and crunchy shreds from the outside of the loins and hams from which it has been cut. There is scarcely any sauce on it at all, just a hint of vinegar and peppers to accentuate the wood-smoke savor. If you need to doll it up, tables are set with plain vinegar and a hot sauce that has a vinegar base. As for the fried chicken, we like it even better than the pork. Its seriously crunchy crust encloses juice-dripping meat; the dark pieces are especially luscious.

From the moment it opens each day, Parker's always seems to bustle. As you enter, it's an adventure maneuvering your way to a table as waiters zoom past toting platters piled high with food.

Price's Chicken Coop

1614 Camden Rd.   704-333-9866

Charlotte, NC   LD (take-out only) | $

Ask anyone in Charlotte where to find four-star fried chicken, and expect to be directed to Price's Chicken Coop. This longtime favorite, take-out-only chicken shack is known for fried chicken that smells so good it causes hungry people to salivate as soon as they exit their vehicle and head for the food. There will be a line of customers—there is almost always a line, often leading out the door—but it moves quickly; and once you get a cardboard box of hot, just-fried bird in your hand, our suggestion is to open the box and eat immediately—sitting in your car. If you like fried chicken, it will be love at first bite. The shattering crunch of the salty crust is itself a joy; the meat inside, white or dark, drips with flavor. On the side come tater tots, coleslaw, and a spongy white dinner roll.

If fried chicken isn't quite rich enough for you, Price's also fries up some dramatically delicious chicken livers. And if you need a pop-in-the-mouth snack a whole lot easier to eat than juice-oozing chicken parts, gizzards are a tasty, chewy alternative.

Short Sugar's

1328 S. Scales St.   336-342-7487

Reidsville, NC   BLD | $

Carhop service is still available at Short Sugar's, which opened as a hamburger joint in 1949. It now serves three meals a day, but its fame rests on barbecue. The whole-ham meat comes sliced, chopped, or minced in a sandwich or as half of a tray with coarse-grated coleslaw. Sauce is dark and intriguing, slightly sweet and a little spicy with a long afterglow. If you like your barbecue with a more direct pepper kick, hot sauce is available to goose it up. French fries and/or hush puppies are available on the side. For dessert: cool lemon pie.

Next time we visit Short Sugar's, we are going to try to pull ourselves away from the fine barbecue to have a few chili dogs. One morning during an early barbecue lunch, we saw two guys laying waste to braces of them, which sure looked good.

Skylight Inn

S. Lee St.   919-746-4113
Ayden, NC.   LD | $

You know that pig meat is serious business the moment you enter the Skylight Inn, for just behind the counter is a window where big hunks of pork from the pit are being chopped with a heavy cleaver on a cutting block. The sound of pork being hacked to pieces is sweet music to accompany a Skylight meal.

Known to one and all as Pete Jones's Skylight Inn, after its late pitmaster, it is now run by his progeny, and still dedicated to whole-hog barbecue. Pork is cooked for up to fifteen hours over oak wood coals until it is moist, tender, and laced with smoke. It is hacked into meat of nearly infinite variety, including tender inside shreds and crunchy skin from the outside of the pit-cooked meat, all tossed together and dressed with just enough vinegar and hot sauce to make the natural sweetness blossom. Sandwiches include coleslaw atop the meat, or you can have it in a cardboard tray with corn bread and slaw.

You can't miss this place. It has a dome like the Capitol in Washington, D.C., with the U.S. flag flying overhead. Not by looks alone can the Skylight Inn claim primacy. It is one of the best—if not the best barbecue in North Carolina. And in North Carolina, that is saying a lot!

Snappy Lunch

125 N. Main St.   910-786-4310
Mount Airy, NC   BL | $

As Yankees, we never heard of a pork chop sandwich until we traveled south. Even in Dixie, it is not all that common, but you'll find it on menus in various configurations ranging from a bone-in chop with superfluous bread that serves merely as a mitt so you can eat the meat without utensils to the boneless beauty at Snappy Lunch. Surely this is the king of pork chop sandwiches. It is a broad slab of meat that is breaded and fried, similar to the tenderloins of the Midwest, but with more pork, and with more cushiony breading. It is luscious and tender.

Few customers of Snappy Lunch get a plain pork chop sandwich. The ritual here in Mount Airy (Andy Griffith's hometown, and the inspiration for TV's Mayberry) is to have it all the way, which means dressed with tomato, chopped onion, mustard, meaty/sweet chili, and fine-cut cabbage slaw speckled with green peppers and onions. The total package is unwieldy in the extreme. Served in booths or at the counter in a wax paper wrapper, this is a sandwich that requires two big hands to hoist and eat. There are no side dishes available other than a bag of potato chips, and the beverage of choice is tea—iced and presweetened, of course.

There are, however, other items on the menu, including a weird Depression-era legacy known as the breaded hamburger, for which ground beef is extended by mixing it with an equal portion of moistened bread. The result is a strange, plump hamburger that resembles a crab cake. Definitely an acquired taste!

Sonny's Grill

1119 Main St. 828-295-7577
Blowing Rock, NC BL | $

In the heart of the Smoky Mountains, less than an hour north of the furniture outlets in Hickory, Blowing Rock was named for a huge cliff over Johns River Gorge, where the wind blows so hard that it snows upward in the winter. The town itself is a quiet hamlet with a charming café on Main Street named Sonny's Grill, and in this three-table, eight-stool eatery you will find one of the most delicious quick-bites of the South: a ham biscuit. It is a stunning harmony of two dramatically disparate ingredients: complex, zesty cured country ham and a pillowy biscuit with creamy insides that readily absorb the ham's savory drippin's. A pair of these and a few cups of coffee or sweet iced tea are an utterly simple and totally satisfying meal. We also love Sonny's sweet potato pancakes, with a silky-soft texture and faint potato sweetness that almost makes syrup redundant. They, too, are a good companion for country ham.

Breakfast at Sonny's is especially wonderful off-season, when the tables and counter are occupied by locals who carry on room-wide conversations, read the paper, and keep each other posted on news and gossip. At lunch, it is a more hurried scene (and during tourist season it can be a madhouse). But we do recommend lunch at Sonny's. It is the best place in town to have a hamburger. A real, short-order kind of burger, handmade and grilled to crusty succulence, served on a bun with lettuce, tomato, and mayonnaise. The hot dogs are excellent, too: all-beef beauties with a snapping-taut skin, available plain or in true southern style, topped with chili and coleslaw.

Stamey's

2206 High Point Rd.   336-299-9888

Greensboro, NC   LD | $

Stamey's serves Lexington-style North Carolina barbecue, which means that the meat of choice is pork shoulders that are pit-cooked over smoldering hickory wood until ridiculously tender, then chopped or sliced. "Chopped" means chopped so fine it is nearly pulverized. Slices are actually more like shreds of varying sizes, some soft, others edged with crust from the outside of the meat. The sauce is peppery with a vinegar tang, and thin enough to permeate the soft, sweet pork rather than blanket it. If you get a platter (as opposed to a sandwich), it will be accompanied by a powerfully zesty coleslaw and odd-shaped, deep-fried corn squiggles that are Stamey's version of hush puppies. This is a Piedmont meal that connoisseurs consider the best barbecue in a big state that is fanatical about barbecue and has at least six different regional variations from the coast to the western mountains.

Warner Stamey started the business in the 1930s; his descendants have tended it ever since, and many of the other good barbecue pitmasters in the area learned their trade from him. Although the restaurant started as a rustic shack, a modern barnboard building was erected in the 1980s, and today customers dine in country comfort.

The barbecue pit outside is one of the wonders of the culinary world—the largest pit we've ever seen, actually more like a vast barbecue factory . . . but where everything is done the old-fashioned way. Wood is burned down to coals in fireplaces; the coals are shoveled into huge brick pits; and in the pits, the shoulders bask in smoke on grates two feet above the coals, where they are turned periodically with a pitchfork by the pitmaster.

Oh, yes, one more thing: try to leave room for dessert. Stamey's warm peach cobbler is nearly as famous as the barbecue.

Ted's Famous Chicken Restaurant

4695 S. Main St.   336-650-0290

Winston-Salem, NC   LD | $

Ted's cooks chicken the same way they do at the venerable Keaton's (p. 160): after being pan-fried, each piece is briefly dipped in sassy, vinegar-based, hot-pepper barbecue sauce that quickly soaks into the skin and meat down to the bone. The result is chicken that is permeated with flavor and heat, and is impossible to stop eating. It is known as Kickin' Chicken.

The menu is minimal. You order an upper (breast and wing) or a lower (leg and thigh), and there is such a thing as a chopped chicken sandwich. Wings are available in counts of 10, 25, 50, or 100. Side dishes are unremarkable beans, slaw, and potato salad; tables are outfitted with rolls of paper towels, which are a necessity when eating this stuff.

Last we looked, Ted's had a second location in North Wilkesboro and a franchise operating in Pfafftown. A sign in the restaurant noted that franchises were currently available in all fifty states.

Wilber's Barbecue

4172 US 70 East   919-778-5218
Goldsboro, NC   BLD | $

Pilots who take off from Seymour Johnson Air Force Base have flown the fame of Wilber's far and wide, and legends abound regarding the pounds of barbecue carried aboard strategic flights. Even if it weren't at the end of the runway, Wilber's reputation for serving first-class Lexington-style North Carolina barbecue could never have remained merely local. This place is world class! Since 1962, when Wilber Shirley stoked the oak and hickory coals in old-fashioned pits, he has been known for whole-hog barbecue, chopped and judiciously seasoned with a peppery vinegar sauce. After eight hours over coals, the meat is soft as a sigh, its natural sweetness haloed by the indescribably appetizing tang of hardwood smoke. It is served with potato salad, coleslaw, Brunswick stew (a pork hash with Veg-All type vegetables) and squiggle-shaped, crunch-crusted hush puppies.

Beyond terrific barbecue, the original Wilber's has the added attraction of serving breakfast, in the form of a buffet with smoky sausages, thick-cut bacon, chewy cracklin's, biscuits and gravy, grits, and sweet muffins. By late morning, chopped barbecue reigns, and it is served until about nine at night . . . or until the day's supply runs out. When that happens, the management locks the door and hangs up a sign that advises, "Out of Barbecue!"

A&R Bar-B-Que

1802 Elvis Presley Blvd.   901-774-7444
Memphis, TN   LD | $

E-mail correspondent sdakin tipped us off to A&R and its pulled pork sandwich, which he declared to be "simply the best in the USA." As we drove up to the ramshackle smokehouse a few blocks north of Graceland, we had very good vibes. All the signals were right: the parking area outside smelled of smoking pork; a big, happy pig was painted on the exterior wall; and customers were walking out the front door with arms full of to-go containers.

At the counter where you stand and place your order you can hear the blissful smokehouse lullaby coming from the kitchen: chop-chop-chop on the cutting board as hickory-cooked pork gets hacked into mottled shreds and pieces for plates and sandwiches. The sandwich is the classic Memphis configuration: pork mixed with tangy red sauce piled in a bun and crowned with a spill of coleslaw. It occurred to us as we plowed through a jumbo that the slaw in a Memphis barbecue sandwich is as important for its texture as for its pickly sweet taste. The cabbage provides such nice little bits of crunch among the velvety heap of pork.

Beyond pig sandwiches, the A&R menu is full. You can have ribs (wet or dry), catfish dinner, hot tamales, meatballs on a stick(!), and that only-in-Memphis treat, barbecue spaghetti. That's a mound of soft noodles dressed not with ordinary tomato sauce, but with—of course—barbecue sauce, laced with shreds of pork. It's weird, but in this city, where restaurants also offer barbecue pizza and barbecue salad, it makes sense.

The ambience of A&R is unadulterated barbecue parlor: quiet enough so you can hear the chopping in the kitchen while you concentrate on enjoying the meal. It is a big place with a lot of elbow room. Raw brick walls and fluorescent lights set a no-nonsense mood, and however hot it is outside, you can count on the air conditioning system to be running so high that it's practically like going into hibernation. Or is the trance we experienced a result of hypnotically good food?

Alcenia's

317 N. Main St.   901-523-0200

Memphis, TN   L | $

Everyone who eats at Alcenia's gets a hug from proprietor B. J. Lester-Tamayo, either on the way in or out, or both. "I feel so guilty if I haven't hugged you, I'll chase you down the street when you leave," she laughs. Her restaurant, named for her mother and granddaughter, is a modest lunchroom decorated in a style that is an intriguing mix of 1960s psychedelic beaded curtains, primitive folk art, odes to African-American culture, and white wedding-veil lace strung up across the ceiling over the large table.

B.J. learned to cook from her mother, who lives in Meridian, Mississippi, but comes to visit and makes tea cakes and egg custard pie and coaches B.J. on the phone when she is making chowchow or pear preserves. B.J.'s turnip greens are extraordinary, flavored not with pork but with what she calls turkey "tails." Even more wondrous is cabbage, which, when we first saw it, we assumed was steamed with greens because dark leaves were laced among the white ones. B.J. explained that those are the cabbage's outer leaves. "The best part!" she declared. "Most people throw them away because they are tough. They need an hour extra steaming; that makes them soft and brown." Flavored with a hail of spice that includes jerk chicken seasoning and lots of pepper, this is cabbage with tongue-searing punch. On the side comes a basket of hot-water corn bread: cushiony-moist, griddle-cooked cakes that are the perfect foil for ecstatically seasoned vegetables.

Aside from Alcenia's exemplary southern vegetables, dining delights here include a delicious fried pork chop that is crisp-crusted and dripping with juice, crunch-crusted fried chicken, and bread pudding that the *Memphis Commercial Appeal* declared to be one of the ten best desserts in the city.

Beacon Light Tea Room

6276 State Route 100   931-670-3880
Lyles, TN   D Tues–Fri, BLD Sat & Sun | $

Opened in 1936 by Lon Loveless, who went on to open the renowned Loveless Café in Nashville, the Beacon Light Tea Room is a lesser-known gem of Tennessee country cooking. Loveless fans will have déjà vu upon opening the menu, for it is the same as the Loveless's used to be. Brittle-crusted fried chicken and country ham with red-eye gravy are the only entrees to know about, and among essential sides is the sumptuously rich mid-twentieth-century Home-Ec triumph, hash brown casserole. Potato shreds are mixed with cheese, sour cream, and—you guessed it—a can of cream of chicken soup, then baked until bubbly with a crust on top.

Meals are sided by biscuits with homemade peach and blackberry preserves, which are set out on the table in spoon-it-yourself crocks. There are whole, soft hunks of peaches in the amber one, and the blackberries have a sultry flavor that is a brilliant counterpoint to super-salty country ham.

Although it was originally named for the revolving spotlight that directed planes flying mail between Memphis and Nashville, the term "Beacon Light" now has another meaning. For the proprietors of this upright restaurant, the beacon is Jesus, and his image is everywhere in art on the old wood-paneled walls. Each table, which is clad in a leatherette cloth, is outfitted with a "Scripture Bread Box," a small plastic loaf hollowed out to contain cards about the size of fortune-cookie fortunes, but in this case with scriptural advice on each side.

Blue Plate Café

5469 Poplar Ave.   901-761-9696
Memphis, TN   BLD | $

Listen up, waffle-hounds! If, like us, you are perpetually on the lookout for slim, small-tread waffles (as opposed to the thick Belgian plumpies), put the Blue Plate Café of Memphis on your itinerary. They make plate-size round ones, crisp and golden brown, with plenty of little holes to hold gobs of butter and syrup. While it is possible to order one filled with pecans or topped with apple compote, blueberries, or other fruits, we like ours plain and hot from the griddle . . . with a huge slab of salty country ham on a separate plate.

In this cheery café that was once a private home, the menu goes way beyond waffles. Breakfast (served any time) includes pancakes, omelets with great hash browns or grits on the side, and flavorful knobby-top biscuits served with silky cream gravy dotted with bits of sausage.

Lunch is good ol' meat-and-three, with such entrees as pot roast, baked pork chops, chicken and dumplings, and fried shrimp (that last one is every Friday). The vegetable roster is about twenty items long, including real mashed potatoes, turnip greens, creamed corn, mac 'n' cheese, etc., etc. If you want something simpler than meat-and-three, there are salads, soups, and sandwiches, including a fried peanut butter and banana sandwich. Apparently, that one is health food: it is served on whole wheat bread.

Bolton's Spicy Chicken & Fish

624 Main St.   615-254-8015
Nashville, TN   LD | $

Bolton's manager Dolly Graham once said, "Our chicken is hot, but it won't cause you to lose your composure." That depends. The fact is that if you don't like really hot food, Bolton's chicken might indeed be reason for a meltdown, especially if you ask for it hot. What's great about it, for those who do like ferocious food, is that the heat is deep in the meat, right down to the bone itself. It is much more spicy than it is salty, making each bite a taste-buds adventure.

This is some beautiful chicken with a thin crust that flakes off in delicate strips. You can get breast, leg, or wings, and side dishes include vigorous turnip greens, sweet coleslaw, strangely soupy mac 'n' cheese, and that Nashville soul-food favorite, spaghetti. In addition to chicken, Bolton's sells a whiting sandwich that is available garnished in the locally favored way, with mustard, onion, pickles, and enough hot sauce to make your tongue glow.

A tiny east Nashville shop with a carry-out window to its side and a dining room with a handful of tables (oilcloth-covered), Bolton's is an essential stop for anyone in search of a true taste of the Music City.

Bozo's Hot Pit BBQ

342 Hwy. 70   901-294-3405
Mason, TN   LD Tues-Sat | $$

In the eighty-five years since it opened, Bozo's has earned a sterling reputation for barbecue. Slow-smoked shoulder is served white or dark, the
former unspeakably tender shreds, the latter more chewy and crusty outside meat. (Many savvy eaters get a combination of the two.) You can
have it the classic Memphis way, in a sandwich with slaw (although here
the slaw has a pronounced vinegar tang), or on a plate with beans and/or
onion rings. Sandwiches are immense, loaded with more meat than any
bun could possibly contain. Tables are armed with three sauces, mild,
sweet, and hot. The hot is *very* hot.

Although barbecue is the must-eat meal, Bozo's menu also includes
steaks, shrimp, and wicked pies, including pecan, coconut, and chocolate.

Named for founder Thomas Jefferson "Bozo" Williams, the restaurant was engaged in a trademark battle with Bozo the Clown back in the
1980s that went all the way to the U.S. Supreme Court. But Bozo's is still
Bozo's, its well-worn Formica tables showing only about a half-century
of use. (The original Bozo's was destroyed by fire in 1950.)

Cozy Corner

745 N. Parkway   901-527-9158
Memphis, TN   LD | $$

When we come to Memphis hungry for barbecue, the Cozy Corner is the
first place we go. The spare ribs are big and deep-flavored; baby back ribs
are nearly too tender, their meat virtually evaporating on your tongue.
Pork shoulder is our favorite meat, sliced into thick pieces that have a
devilishly blackened crust that is blanketed with spice, their centers velvet soft, sweet, and moist. We're also fond of barbecued bologna, a thick
oinky disk bathed in profound red sauce, available on a platter or on a
bun with coleslaw dressing. The best-known specialty of the house, and
an item found in few smoke pits anywhere, is barbecued Cornish hen—a
small bird with burnished skin and meat of ineffably delicate texture.

The beeline we make for the Cozy Corner isn't only for its food; we
love the place, which has the quiet, colorful character of a truly grand
barbecue parlor. Its front room clouded with haze from the smoker be-

hind the self-service counter, it is a storefront that does a lot of take-out business but also has a small dining room to the side where Memphis blues provide a suitable beat for pork-eating. The place was established back in 1977 by Raymond Robinson with $2,500 he borrowed from his mother; and until his death early in 2001, Mr. Robinson presided over his small, sweet-smelling empire from behind the order counter, haloed by the glow of his smoke pit. When we first stopped in, over a decade ago, his mother was holding court on the couch near the order counter. Mrs. Robinson rhapsodized about the health benefits of eating barbecue as often as possible, pointing to a row of effulgent aloe vera plants growing in plastic spice buckets along the window. "They have been here for years," she said. "Look how healthy they are. They thrive on barbecue smoke!"

The Cupboard

| 1400 Union Ave. | 901-276-8015 |
| Memphis, TN | LD \| $ |

The Cupboard is a hugely popular restaurant in what used to be a Shoney's, where a sign outside boasts, "Freshest Veggies in Town." Proprietor Charles Cavallo is a fresh-food fanatic, a joy he credits to his uncle, who sold watermelons. "One day when I was twelve, he gave me a few he had left over. I sold them by the side of the road, and from that moment, I had the passion." He drove a produce delivery truck for ten years, and in 1993 bought the Cupboard with the goal of making it a showcase for vegetables. Tomatoes direct from the field in Ripley, local squash, crowder peas, onions, cabbage, and sweet potatoes appear not only on the menu (which features a five-vegetable, no-meat meal), but also on the floor of the restaurant, in the vestibule and around the cash register, from which they are sold by the peck and bushel when they are in season.

One of the best cooked vegetables here is the simplest: a whole baked sweet potato, starchy sweet and soft as pudding. And the Cupboard's full-flavored turnip greens are made without pork or poultry, just boiled and seasoned. "My greens taste like greens," Charles states the obvious. "Sometimes I have people who come in and say, 'You've changed the recipe. These are different.' Yes, they are different, I say: maybe younger, maybe winter greens, which have a softer taste, maybe they are from Georgia instead of Tennessee. Every bunch has a flavor of its own."

Non-vegetable notables at this high-spirited eatery include fantastic corn bread gem muffins and yeast rolls, warm fruit cobbler, and brilliant lemon icebox pie.

Dixie Barbeque Co.

3301 N. Roan St. (Kingsport Hwy.)   423-283-PIGS
Johnson City, TN   LD | $$

Dixie Barbeque's menu notes that its ribs are "meaty pork ribs (not wimpy baby backs)." They are hefty bones with a real chew to their meat, and a deep satisfying character that only hours over a smoldering pit can produce. When we asked proprietor Alan Howell what kind of wood he prefers for his barbecue, he answered "tree wood . . . whatever blows down . . . hickory, mostly." Other than ribs, there's pulled pork (inside white and outside dark), smoked chicken, and pulled beef.

To gild the meats, Dixie Barbeque offers a dizzying array of sauces: East Tennessee Red, classic Carolina Vinegar, Devil's Dew, South Carolina Gold, Alabama White, Texas/Oklahoma Style, and Sauce from Hell, all of which are made on premises, plus Richard Petty brand sauce and Maurice's Gourmet Sauce from South Carolina. Any or all of them are brought to the table by your waitress, who patiently explains the fundamental qualities of each. We like most (except the bizarre mayonnaise-based white sauce: fie on it!), but for a true local experience, try the cinnabar-red East Tennessee sauce. Unless you say otherwise, this is what comes on sandwiches.

Although barbecue is serious business in this establishment, the ambience is plenty goofy, including sports-team pennants and amusing vanity license plates plastered all over the walls and a rack of fabulous rebel-themed bumper stickers for sale. (We could not resist plastering our bumper with one that says "Don't Make Me Open This" next to a can of "Whoop-Ass.") Loud shag music blasts over the sound system, providing perpetual-party atmosphere, and dual television sets run continuous tapes of *The Andy Griffith Show*.

Dyer's Burgers

205 Beale St.   901-527-3937
Memphis, TN   LD | $

A modest-size round of raw ground beef is held on the cutting board under a spatula and the spatula is whacked a few times with a heavy hammer, flattening the meat into a semicompressed patty at least four inches wide. Now, the good part: the patty is submerged into a deep, black skillet full of bubbling-hot grease, grease that the management boasts has not been changed since Dyer's opened in 1912! It's the grease that gives a Dyer's burger a consummately juicy interior while it develops a wickedly crusty outside and a unique, shall we say, intriguing flavor.

Our waitress explained that the grease is carefully strained every night after closing hour (usually about 4:00 A.M.; this is Beale Street, after all), and besides, the really old grease is always burning off, so the supply that supposedly never changes is, in fact, always changing. Whatever. The fact is that this is one heck of an interesting hamburger. We are especially smitten by the many ways in which it is served: as a double or triple, or as a double or triple combo (with layers of cheese), and with really good hand-cut French fries on the side. The menu boasts that each hamburger is served "Always on a Genuine Wonder Bread bun."

If hamburgers are not your passion, allow us to suggest another Dyer's specialty: the Big Rag Baloney sandwich. That's a half-inch thick slab of bologna that is fried to a crisp in the same skillet, and in the same vintage oil as the burgers.

Eastside Fish

2617 Gallatin Pike   615-227-8388

Nashville, TN   LD | $

The Giant King, signature dish at Eastside Fish, is immense. A pair of whiting fillets, each at least a half-pound, are dredged in seasoned cornmeal and crisp fried, then sandwiched between four slices of soft supermarket white bread. The fish is cream-moist and delicate, its brittle crust mottled with splotches of four-alarm Louisiana hot sauce and enveloped in a harmony of crunchy raw onion, dill pickle chips, and smooth yellow mustard.

Hot fish sandwiches are a staple at soul-food restaurants throughout the South, but the tradition is strongest in Nashville, where they are the specialty of shacks, stands, and drive-throughs. Donald "Bo" Boatright, who started Eastside Fish in 2003, grew up eating them as part of what he calls "summer nights of fun"—evenings when neighbors gather to play cards and to eat hot fish. Standard companions for the fish are white bread, hush puppies, coleslaw, and, strangely enough, meat-sauced spaghetti.

The small storefront tucked back from Gallatin Pike has a single tall table with a couple of stools for those who need a place to eat, but Eastside's business is virtually all take-out. Whiting is traditional; you also can get catfish, tilapia, or trout. There is no heat lamp to keep fish on hold, so from the time an order is placed, it takes a good ten to fifteen minutes to get it. The brown paper bags in which customers receive their fish from the order window are steaming hot and splotched with oil; the sandwich inside is wrapped in wax paper and held together with toothpicks.

We also recommend Eastside's hot wings: jumbo drumettes fried so the skin turns luxuriously chewy. They are served sauceless, so they don't look hot, but they will clear your sinuses.

Ellen's Soul Food and Bar-B-Q

601 S. Parkway E.   901-942-4888
Memphis, TN   LD | $

"Call your pieces," says the waitress if you've come for fried chicken, meaning tell her which parts you like best. We are especially fond of thighs, an embarrassment of juices packed inside skin that crunches with brio. Favorite side dishes include stewed cabbage flecked with fire-hot pepper, fried corn dotted with bits of green pepper, and a stack of griddle-cooked corn cakes that tear easily into pieces well-suited for mopping gravy.

A south Memphis storefront café with a tired, timeworn appearance, Ellen's is nothing but energetic when it comes to cooking consummate soul food. Ever since Memphis's beloved Four Way Grill closed, this is the place we happily go whenever we crave a plate of neck bones, catfish, or fried pork chops sided by candied yams, purple hull peas, and a stack of corn bread. And that fried chicken, which may be the best in town.

"You do want to eat here?" asked the hostess in a friendly sort of way as we entered the dining room for the first time, gazing around at a clientele that was, on this occasion, 100 percent African American. Apparently, we looked a little shocked. We nodded yes, and she said, "You are very welcome," pointing us to a table where we sat in molded laminate seats and perused the handwritten menus. Yes, that's right, every single menu at Ellen's was written out on a piece of 8½ X 11-inch paper, by hand in ballpoint pen, then enclosed in plastic to protect it from spills and drips. It looked to us as though more than one person had done the writing. Jane's menu listed *pigs' feet*. Michael's, in totally different hand-writing, spelled out *pig feets*.

Elliston Place Soda Shop

2111 Elliston Pl.	615-327-1090
Nashville, TN	BL | $

Elliston Place is one of Nashville's top meat-and-three spots. Choose sugar-cured ham, salt-cured country ham, southern-fried chicken (white or dark meat), a pork chop, or liver 'n' onions, then select three vegetables from a daily roster of at least a dozen. On Mondays and Thursdays the house special is turkey and dressing, a casserole of shredded roasted white and dark meat with steamy corn bread dressing: delicious! Or if you want to skip the meat altogether (Elliston Place vegetables are so good, such a strategy makes sense), there is a four-vegetable plate, accompanied by hot bread, for about three dollars. Among the vegetable repertoire you will likely find whipped potatoes, turnip greens, baked squash, fried bite-size rounds of okra, black-eyed peas, baked squash, and congealed fruit salad (the local name for Jell-O).

For breakfast, biscuits are crunchy brown on the outside with a soft interior that begs to wrap itself around a slice of salty country ham. Many locals ignore the excellent ham and choose fried bologna as their breakfast meat of choice. On the side comes a bowl of firm, steamy white grits—an excellent gentle-natured companion for full-flavored breakfast meat.

A city fixture since 1939, this is a restaurant with personality! Its tiny-tile floor is well weathered and its tables wobble. Above the counter, vintage soda fountain signs advertise banana splits, fruit sundaes, sodas, and fresh fruit ades. Each green-upholstered booth has its own jukebox with selections that are, suitably enough, country classics.

Germantown Commissary

2290 S. Germantown Rd.	901-754-5540
Germantown, TN	LD | $$

Here's well-made down-home food, served in decorator-rustic surroundings in an upscale neighborhood. The Germantown Commissary has barnboard walls choc-a-block with old tin signs, wind-up telephones, and vintage advertisements. Many of its tables wobble as much as those in a juke joint and the air has the unmistakably seductive aroma of a working smoke pit.

It is best known for ribs, which truly are first rate: crusted with sauce, scented by hickory, meaty as hell with enough chew to provide maximum flavor. You can order them by number of bones, from five to twelve (a full rack), or as part of a half-and-half plate with another barbecued meat. We suggest the latter, because it would be a crime to come to the Commissary and *not* have pulled pork. It is shoulder meat, pulled into slightly-more-than-bite-size strips and hunks, some edges crusty, some parts velvet-soft. You can also get the meat chopped, which is okay, but deprives your tongue of the pleasure of worrying those long strips of meat you get when it's pulled.

For dessert, there are smokehouse classics: banana pudding with softened vanilla wafers in the custard and tongue-soothing lemon icebox pie.

Henpeck Market

1268 Lewisburg Pike	615-794-7518
Franklin, TN	BLD | $

A gas station, grocery store, live bluegrass venue, and café serving the finest possible versions of classic mid-South fare, the Henpeck Market is a Roadfood vision. Simply getting to it is a pleasure, for the rolling-pasture landscape around Franklin is achingly bucolic.

Service is cafeteria-style, which is a good thing because it allows you to study the beautiful desserts and to see other people's meals get plated. Casual though it may be, there is a refinement about the experience that makes this charming place something much more compelling than any other gas station/convenience mart that happens to serve hot meals. Yes, it is a country store and the menu items are mostly familiar, but the food is a cut above.

For us, the standout dish was a pimiento cheese sandwich. It's fine on white bread, better when grilled, best when smoky bacon is included. A few other standouts were corn bread salad (a crumble of greens and corn bread), biscuits and country ham, and fried grits squares. Desserts are a sight to behold, and there are so many that choosing only one or two is a real challenge. We like the seven-layer carrot cake, meringue-topped banana pudding, and cream cheese–chocolate brownies.

The last Saturday of each month, the Henpeck Market features a live bluegrass jam that includes a supper of catfish, turnip greens, white beans, and slaw, and every Tuesday night meals are served family-style.

Interstate Barbecue

2265 S. Third St.   901-775-2304
Memphis, TN   LD | $$

Inside and out, Interstate is perfumed by smoke from slow-sizzling barbecue round the clock. That is because proprietor Jim Neely puts his pork shoulders in the pit at 5:00 P.M. for the next day's lunch and he starts the day's ribs every morning. Mr. Neely is a master, and in the city of Memphis, to be a true pitmaster is to be a god.

His restaurant is a modest pork house serving four-star ribs, shoulder meat, sausages, and bologna with all the proper fixin's, including addictive barbecue spaghetti (soft noodles in breathtaking sauce). You eat at a table in the simple dining room where a "Wall of Fame" boasts critics' accolades and 8 X 10s from celebrity fans, or enter next door and get it to go, by the sandwich, plate, or whole slab of ribs.

When you lift a rib and merely poke it hard with a finger, the meat slides off the bone. It is chewy with a deep savor haloed by the perfume of wood smoke; chewing it generates massive infusions of flavor that literally exhaust taste buds after a while. Chopped pork shoulder is a magnificent medley of shreds, chunks, wisps, and ribbons of smoky meat, all crowned with Neely's spicy-sweet red sauce. A chopped pork sandwich is the most Memphian dish on the menu, made as per local custom with a layer of cool coleslaw atop the well-sauced meat. It is a total mess that disintegrates as you eat it, but the most delicious mess imaginable!

Joe's Bar-B-Que and Fish

3716 Clarksville Pike   615-259-1505
Nashville, TN   LD | $

Joe's just might be the world's slowest fast-food restaurant. It looks quick. No indoor seating, just a drive-through line with a large menu to study and a microphone to speak into when the time comes to place your order. A few yards beyond the menu is the window where you pay and receive the food. We were third in line for lunch, and based on the timing, we almost believe that each car's order is started from scratch, bagged, and served before the next car's order is taken.

The thirty-minute wait was well worth it! This food is indeed made to order. Whiting is crisp and hot from the deep-fryer, served the Nashville way with mustard, dill pickle chips, raw onion, and plenty of hot sauce. The corn bread that enfolds pulled pork in Joe's wonderfully soulful pork-on-corn-bread sandwich comes off the grill so steamy that the unwieldy sandwich is almost too hot to handle. Rib tips are succulent and sauced with gusto.

Dining amenities? There is a small gazebo in back with a few tables where customers are welcome to bring their bagged meals. The only problem is that the quickest way to get there is to drive from the pick-up window out onto Clarksville Pike—against the flow of traffic—then quickly cut back into the drive-through line. Or it is possible to pull out and make a legal U-turn in one of the parking lots across the road. That's the slower way, and at Joe's, slow is good.

Leonard's

5465 Fox Plaza Dr.	901-360-1963
Memphis, TN	LD | $$

Since 1922, Leonard Heuberger's pit has set the pork standard in Memphis. In fact, barbecue historians credit Mr. Heuberger with configuring the barbecued pork sandwich that has become a local signature dish: shreds of smoked shoulder meat topped with tomato-sweet, vinegar-tangy sauce, festooned with a heap of creamy, cool coleslaw. It is a mesmerizing confluence of sugar and spice, meat and bread and sauce.

Choices range far beyond the famous sandwich. There are slabs of ribs, platters and plates, barbecued bologna, and even a roster of Italo-Dixie combo plates that include spaghetti with ribs and barbecue with ravioli.

Leonard's is worth visiting not only for its pork, but also for its sign, which is one of the great images in porklore: a neon pig, all decked out in top hat and tails, wielding a cane, captioned "Mr. Brown Goes to Town." Years ago, a waitress explained its significance: "Mr. Brown was the term used for brown-meat barbecue. It is the outside of the shoulder that gets succulent and chewy from the sauce and the smoke in the pit. The inside part of the roast, which is moist but has very little barbecue flavor, is known as Miss White. People in Memphis used to ask for plates and sandwiches of 'Mr. Brown and Miss White.' "

Little Tea Shop

69 Monroe Ave.   901-525-6000
Memphis, TN   L | $

Memphis is our favorite place to eat pork, but there's none served at the Little Tea Shop down by old Cotton Row. Proprietor Suhair Lauck is Muslim, and yet despite her religion's prohibition against pigs, she serves some of the most soulful eats in the city. We were aghast when Sue told us that her greens were in fact completely meat-free. It had always seemed to us that the opulent "likker" in which they wallow in their serving bowl—a spruce-green broth retrieved from the pot in which they have boiled—gets its intoxicating character at least as much from the hambone as from the collard, turnip, or mustard leaves that the boiling process turns soft and mellow.

But tasting is believing, and let us tell you that a serving of pork-free turnip greens with pot likker at the Little Tea Shop is positively tonic. If a flavor can be verdant, here it is: the heady soul of a plant with leaves that marinate in sunlight. Turnip greens are the centerpiece of Sue's most popular lunch, on the printed-daily menu every day of the week. For $6.50, you get a bowl filled with sultry dark greens sodden in their likker, the once-tough leaves cooked so limp that you can easily separate a small clump of them with the side of a soup spoon and gather it up with plenty of the liquid. Atop the greens are slices of raw onion, leaching pungent bite into the leaves, and atop the onions are bright red slices of tomato, which are shockingly sweet compared to everything below. On the side are crisp-edged, cream-centered corn sticks well suited for crumbling into the bowl.

We love the do-it-yourself ordering process at the Little Tea Shop. Every customer gets a one-page printed menu of the day—there is a different menu for each day of the week—with a little box next to each item. Like voting with an old-fashioned ballot, you put a check mark in the box next to each dish you want to elect for your lunch. Other than pot likker, some of the outstanding dishes are the Lacy Special (named for a cotton trader), in which corn sticks sandwich a chicken breast topped with gravy, and such vegetables as sliced candied yams, fried corn, baked squash, black-eyed peas, and scalloped tomatoes.

Sue is the life force of the Little Tea Shop, working the dining room with relentless enthusiasm. Old friends who enter get a buss on the cheek;

newcomers are instant Sweetie and Dear; and she manages to introduce parties of strangers if she thinks they'd get along. We shake hands with three gents who have been eating at the same table for over thirty years— "No one else would dare sit there," Sue says. As for the lack of pork in her greens, she sums up her reasoning as she whisks past our table carrying chocolate-draped ice cream pecan balls for somebody's dessert: "It is dietetic, it is delicious, it is religious."

Litton's Market & Restaurant

2803 Essary Dr.	423-688-0429
Knoxville, TN	LD | $

With a catalogue of burgers that range from minimalist beef patties to a Thunder Road burger (named for the movie about moonshining in these parts) topped with pimiento cheese, onions, and hot peppers, Litton's is the most famous hamburger restaurant in the mid-South. For each burger, meat is hand-formed into a patty that is nearly a half-pound and is cooked to order, then sandwiched in a made-here bun, preferably with at least lettuce, tomato, and onion, and, at most, bacon, pickles, or chili. Hamburgers—and other sandwiches—are available with onion rings, French fries, or, best of all, a potato-cheese casserole known as Arizona spuds.

At least as famous as the hamburgers are Litton's desserts: coconut cream pie, old-fashioned red velvet cake, creamy banana pudding, and five kinds of freshly baked cookies every day. The one dessert that brings us to our knees is Italian cream cake, a creamy, buttery concoction with old-fashioned simplicity that goes perfectly with a lingering cup of after-meal coffee.

Litton's has been around for years and its walls are covered with mementoes of old Knoxville. It is a fun place to eat, but for those who prefer to dine rather than merely eat, there is a classier "Backroom" with its own upscale menu of Continental fare. For a seat in either place, expect a wait at peak mealtimes.

Merridee's Breadbasket

110 Fourth Ave. S.	615-790-3755
Franklin, TN	BL | $

Our friend Roger Waynick, a Franklin resident who first brought us to Merridee's, described it as the kind of place where locals go not only to eat but also to chat with each other throughout the day. Opened in 1981 by Merridee Erickson, it is situated in an old building that used to be a harness shop, and it is now run by Jim and Marilyn Kreider. Merridee's is a casual kind of place where people come early in the day to buy breads and pastries to take home or to sit down for breakfast of ham-egg-cheese breakfast braids or biscuits and gravy. Lunch is served between 11:00 A.M. and 3:00 P.M. each day, and it is available packed and ready to go for picnics, or on plates to eat here.

Place your order at the counter, and they call your name when it is ready, by which time, hopefully, you have found a table. It's a large menu that includes hot breakfasts and a vast array of oven-fresh rolls (almond swirl, cinnamon twist, sticky bun, muffins, biscuits, scones, etc.) as well as lunch of sandwiches, salads, and crescents ("No, not croissants!" says the menu), which are homemade bread doughs wrapped around turkey and honey mustard, spinach and feta cheese, or roast beef and Swiss. While the choice of sandwiches is vast, pimiento cheese is an essential.

Pimiento cheese is a passion in the mid-South. It is not dramatically different from any ordinary cheese spread, but that subtle difference is just the point. Pimiento cheese is all about nuance: the slight zip of chopped pimientos and sweet relish and their red and green sparkle in the orange cheese. While hearty and satisfying, it has a refined character that sings of ladies' lunchrooms, afternoon tea, and Dixie finesse.

For dessert: cake, pie, fudge brownies, and sugar tea cakes, available with espresso coffee drinks.

One Stop Café

901 Columbia Ave.	615-794-3881
Franklin, TN	BL | $

One Stop Café is a locals' favorite stop for breakfast and lunch. We came for lunch on Monday, which is chicken and dumplings day. This was about the best chicken and dumplings imaginable: big chunks of soft meat floating in creamy gravy with tender drifts of dumpling. Other daily specials include fried chicken Tuesday, meat loaf Wednesday, chicken and dressing Thursday, and catfish Friday. Every day you can get One Stop's magnificent pork barbecue, served in a heap of big, fall-apart shreds that are so moist and smoky-good that you hardly want any sauce (although each table is set with squeeze bottles of hot and mild for squirting).

With an entree, choose from a large menu of such sides as turnip greens, cream corn, hash brown casserole, mac and cheese, baked cinnamon apples, etc. The menu lists twenty-four different side dishes! Along with any of these full meals, you want a big slab of light corn bread, which is sweet and dense as cake.

Service is cafeteria-style. Tote your own tray and fill your own cups with iced tea (sweet, of course).

Pancake Pantry

1796 21st Ave. S.   615-383-9333
Nashville, TN   BL | $$

We suffer from anxiety at the Pancake Pantry. First we worry about getting in. For years, Nashvillians have stood in line for a precious seat in this singular restaurant that transcends generic pancake-house dining. Warm maple syrup, anyone? Caribbean buttermilk pancakes? Just looking at the menu induces paroxysms of indecision. If we order sweet potato pancakes that are so good drizzled with cinnamon cream, then it doesn't make sense also to eat onion-laced potato pancakes. And if we get stacks of pancakes, how much appetite can possibly remain to enjoy what are surely the best hash browns in the South? We don't know if they're cooked on the same griddle as the pancakes, or if it's just pancake scent in the air, but Pancake House potatoes are as buttercream-fluffy as the best flapjack. Fried to a golden crisp, they are the perfect way to balance the salty punch of a brick-red slab of griddled country ham.

A few other favorites from the broad and inviting menu: Smoky Mountain Buckwheat Cakes, which appear dark and somber, but are in fact featherlight, arriving in a stack of five with plenty of butter and a pitcher of very warm syrup to pour on top, and thin and eggy Swedish pancakes wrapped around lingonberry preserves. No syrup is necessary.

The Pancake Pantry is a big restaurant with plenty of space among the tables and a high-spirited ambience throughout the dining room. What's not to be happy about when you are eating excellent pancakes with plenty of butter and syrup and good coffee on the side? The only dark cloud to mention is the frequent long line that can signal up to an hour's wait to be seated.

Pope's Café

120 East Side Sq.   931-684-7933

Shelbyville, TN   BL | $

Pope's Café has been a fixture on the town square of Shelbyville (the Walking Horse capital of the World) since 1945. It is a well-weathered place with a half-dozen tables along one wall and a long counter with stools, jukeboxes arrayed every few seats so customers can play tunes while they eat.

For breakfast, the thing to eat is ham: salty, chewy, resonantly flavorful ham with (or sandwiched inside) buttery tender biscuits. If such ham is too powerful, try Pope's good sausage, or even gentler (and more succulent), there are tenderloin patties that are made to slip inside a biscuit.

Lunch is classic meat-and-three: about a dozen deluxe vegetables and side dishes every day, including fried apples, buttered corn niblets, spinach and eggs, spiced peaches, even baked spaghetti. These accompany main courses of roast pork, roast beef, country-style steak (that's like chicken-fried), ham, pork barbecue, or an ultra-luxurious heap of crisp-fried chicken livers.

Then there's only-in-the-Southland pie, including baby-food-gentle chess pie, fudge pie, meringues of all kinds, pecan pie, and a rich chocolate pie with nuts named after a walking horse (who was named after the singer), Charlie Pride.

Prince's Hot Chicken Shack

123 Ewing Dr.   615-226-9442

Nashville, TN   Tues-Sat

Pay attention to the name: Prince's *Hot* Chicken Shack. You can take that to the bank. The fried chicken is available mild, medium, hot, and extra hot. Even the mild packs a punch. We tried hot and it had us tearing up . . . with joy! What's great about this crisp-fried wonder is that it isn't merely hot. It is radiant with flavor; its chewy skin has soulful character; the meat is moist and luxurious. To say it is addictive is not hyperbole. We met several customers who told us they come to Prince's five times a week (it's closed Sunday and Monday), and any day they didn't get their extra-hot was a sad one. If we lived in Nashville, we would easily get hooked.

Chicken is all you need to know, except for the French fries, which are terrific, too. The chicken comes in halves and quarters. It is delivered in a paper bag near the window where you placed your order and paid. There are a handful of tables in the restaurant and many people simply step outside to dine on the walkway of the small strip mall where Prince's is located. Beverages are sold from vending machines inside.

The Rendezvous

52 S. Second St.	901-523-2746
Memphis, TN	D	$$

Famous as they are as an icon of Memphis barbecue, the Rendezvous's ribs are not actually barbecued. They are charcoal broiled rather than slow smoked and instead of being bathed in sauce, which is the more traditional Memphis way, they are dry. Dry, but not drab. Indeed, these are some of the most flavorful ribs you will eat anywhere. Instead of sauce, the meaty bones arrive at the table encased in a crusty blanket of spice in which they have been cooked. The spice accentuates the sweetness of the pork and also seems to contain and concentrate its succulence. These ribs are ultra-lean yet moist, unbelievably tender, and flavorful beyond description.

Unique ribs put the Rendezvous on the map, but the kitchen's more traditionally Memphian pork shoulder is worth eating, too, as is the charcoal-cooked chicken. To go with the beer you must drink before (as well as during) any meal, there are plates of sausage and cheese as hors d'oeuvres. Sound like a lot of food? Eating large is part of the Rendezvous experience; of all the restaurants in town, we nominate this one as the worst to visit on a diet.

The Rendezvous reminds us of a cross between an old southern speakeasy and a beer hall in *The Student Prince*. It is a rollicking, semi-subterranean place decorated with antique bric-a-brac and thousands of business cards left behind by decades of happy customers.

Ridgewood Barbecue

900 Elizabethton Hwy. (old Hwy. 19 E)	423-538-7543
Bluff City, TN	LD	$$

Ridgewood Barbecue has defined excellence for decades. Pork is hickory cooked in a pit adjacent to the restaurant, sliced into fairly thin pieces, then reheated on a grill when ordered. It is sauced with a tangy, dark-red, slightly smoky brew (available by the pint and quart near the cash register) and served as a platter, under a heap of terrific dark-gold French fries, or in a giant sandwich that spills out all sides of the bun.

We love the platter presentation, because it allows one to fork up a French fry and a few flaps of sauced meat all at the same time, making for what we believe to be one of the world's perfect mouthfuls. Prior to the arrival of the platter, you will be served a bowl of coleslaw—cool, crisp, sweet—surrounded by saltine crackers. We also recommend ordering a crock of beans. They are soft, laced with meat, and have a fetching smoky flavor.

A word of warning: if you arrive at a normal mealtime, expect to wait. Despite its fairly remote location, this place attracts barbecue lovers from far away, some of whom come to take vast party platters home; but there are almost never enough seats. We like to arrive at about 4:00 P.M., when chances are good we will get one of the really choice booths adjacent to the open kitchen in the old dining room. From here, the view is magnificent. You see the cooks heating meat on the grill, making sandwiches and platters, and immersing potatoes into the bubbling-hot deep-fryers. Once a meal is plated and ready to be sent to the table, it is set on a holding counter just inches from your booth, separated only by a short glass partition. If you arrive hungry and are waiting for your food to be delivered, this sight—and its accompanying aromas—is tantalizing beyond description.

Rotier's

2412 Elliston Pl.   615-327-9892
Nashville, TN   LD | $

A Rotier's hamburger, served on French bread, is monumental. Piled with lettuce, tomato, pickle, and mustard (and preferably crowned with a slab of bright orange cheese, too), the rugged-textured meat patty is held inside its two bread halves with a long toothpick. It is a beautiful sight, and once the toothpick is removed, the diner faces a significant challenge keeping the sandwich intact as it is lifted from plate to mouth. To go with this hamburger are fresh, crisp French fries . . . and a choice from a list of several dozen beers.

Although everyone in town knows Rotier's as the hamburger place, it also happens to be one of Nashville's premier hot-lunch restaurants, and every day at lunch and supper, you can choose from a menu of such entrees as pork barbecue, country-fried steak, fried chicken, and meat loaf. On the side you pick two vegetables from a list of southern classics: blackeyed peas, turnip greens, fried okra, baked squash casserole, crowder peas, white beans. Or, it is possible to get a plate of nothing but vegetables—an excellent strategy even if you aren't a vegetarian. With the vegetables come good rolls or warm corn bread, and if you don't want beer to drink, the menu lists chocolate milk, sweet milk, and buttermilk.

Silver Sands

937 Locklayer St.   615-742-1652
Nashville, TN   BL | $

Silver Sands is a soul-food cafeteria known for its great breakfast and its meat-and-three lunch. Meals are portioned out from a short cafeteria line that gives customers a view of what's to eat as well as the opportunity to discuss options with one of the team of servers behind the counter: What's good with smothered pork steak? (Answer: stewed apples and fried potatoes with onions.) Don't be surprised if the helpful gals dipping plates refer to you as Honey, Darlin', Sweetheart, and Baby.

We recommend the country ham, but when the kitchen runs out of it, a good fallback meat is fried bologna, which is served under a mantle of sweet, soft fried onions. Grits are thick, full-flavored, and especially wonderful when ladled with plenty of butter. Huge chicken wings are dished out with brown gravy, and among the worthy vegetables at lunch are porky greens, green beans, and luxurious macaroni and cheese.

Silver Sands is a low-slung cinder-block building tucked into a corner in an otherwise residential neighborhood just west of the Farmers Market in North Nashville. There are about a dozen tables—much business is carry-out—and despite circulating overhead fans, air in the cream-colored dining room is thick with the homey aromas of good cooking.

Sunny's Cafeteria

1000 S. Roan St.   423-926-7441
Johnson City, TN   LD Mon-Sat, L only Sun | $

Pick up a tray, select your silverware, and work your way along the line. First comes dessert. Pies galore adorn the shelves: peach, coconut meringue, lemon meringue, chocolate chip pecan, plain pecan, custard. Also on the dessert shelf is banana pudding—great banana pudding!—

and near that are the Jell-Os and salads, a kaleidoscopic array of sweet things that makes us week-kneed with desire.

After salads, you are at the main-course and entree station, where a nice lady asks what you want. This is the moment of truth, for sometimes we look down at our tray and realize that we have taken so many desserts and salads that there isn't room left for a main course. Somehow, though, we manage, and choose a beautiful hunk of fried chicken or a plate of ul-timate comfort-food chicken and dumplings, or steak and gravy topped with sautéed onions, and accompany that with a few choices from the cornucopic vegetable selection. Pungent collard greens, real mashed po-tatoes, crunchy fried okra, silky boiled cabbage: all are recommended, but if squash casserole is available when you push through the line, we implore you to have a bowl. It is laced with buttery bread crumbs and rich as top cream.

To drink? Presweetened iced tea, of course. Now find a place in the good-size dining room, partitioned into cozy sections where fans spin overhead and music is provided by the local radio station.

"Y'all doin' all right?" asks the man at the end of the line when he tallies up the bill for trays of food. Seldom do we feel as all right as when we sit down to enjoy Sunny's fine food.

Swett's

2725 Clifton Ave.   615-329-4418
Nashville, TN   LD | $

Swett's is a visible success story: opened in 1954 as a small soul-food meat-and-three café, it became a large, modern cafeteria, burned down, and was built again. Portraits of the founding Swetts adorn the walls, and their legacy is well reflected by a kitchen that continues to serve hearty soul-food meals at reasonable prices.

Like so many cafeteria lines, this one starts with dessert: lovely slices of pie ranging from low-profile chess to lofty meringues, plus a couple of hot fruit cobblers. Beyond the sweets are the meats: magnificent fried chicken, spice-encrusted baked chicken, sausages, country steak, and beef tips. Now comes the real fun: vegetables. Swett's repertoire is a southern symphony of steamed or fried okra, fried corn, squash casse-role, candied yams, mashed potatoes, mac 'n' cheese, stewed cabbage, candied apples, baked beans, turnip greens, rice and gravy. Most cus-tomers get one meat and two or three vegetables. Some fill their tray with nothing but four or five vegetable dishes . . . accompanied, of course, by corn bread, either baked as a loaf and sliced or in the more typical local formation, as a cake fried on a griddle.

Draw your own iced tea (sweet or unsweet) at the end of the cafeteria line.

Sylvan Park

4502 Murphy Rd. 615-292-9275

Nashville, TN LD | $

With all the ambience of a prison cell, Sylvan Park remains one of the most charming meat-and-threes in Tennessee. Serenaded by the loud hum of an ice cooler, you sit at one of the dozen tables scattered through the small cinder-block dining room and order off a short menu that includes such entrees as country ham, fried steak, and salmon croquettes, as well as a long list of vegetables and side dishes. The standard meal is one meat and three vegetables, but we often forgo the meat and get a four-vegetable plate.

For dipping and mopping the juices and for serving as uncomplicated punctuation among the assertive flavors of the vegetables, Sylvan Park offers tender little biscuits with great absorbent qualities as well as tangy corn bread muffins with a rough texture that crumbles nicely over a serving of creamy white beans.

Sylvan Park is known also for its pies: chocolate, butterscotch, egg custard, sweet potato. They aren't pretty. Cut to order in the kitchen, a slice often arrives half-fallen-apart on the plate. That's because these pies are very, very delicate, with fragile meringue on top of the creamy ones. A highly recommended alternative to pie, when available, is banana pudding. Its flavor is huge, and it is made the classic southern way, with softened vanilla wafers and streaks of meringue throughout the custard.

Note: there is a second, larger Sylvan Park at 330 Franklin Road.

Wiles-Smith Drugs

1635 Union Ave. 901-278-6416

Memphis, TN BL | $

Just up the road from the Sun Records studio, where Elvis made his first recording, is a drugstore that opened when the King was nine years old. Wiles-Smith has been remodeled, so it doesn't look ancient, but its culinary values are tradition itself. You can sit at the boomerang-pattern Formica counter and enjoy a nice breakfast or lunch sandwich or meal-size beef stew for about $3. Ice cream concoctions are classic, including perfectly blended sodas, cherry and chocolate sundaes, and milkshakes that come in tall silvery beakers so you can refill your glass approximately 1½ times. When Memphis sizzles in the summer, this is the place to come for an icy fruit freeze.

Zarzour's

1627 Rossville Rd.   423-266-0424
Chattanooga, TN   L Mon-Fri | $

When you get lost trying to find Zarzour's, don't bother looking in the phone book to call and ask driving directions. There is no evidence of it in the Yellow Pages; its number is in residential listings, under the name of the manager's mother-in-law. And if you do finally locate the no-man's-land café, you will not be able to eat unless you arrive during the fifteen hours a week that it's open for business: Monday through Friday from 11:00 A.M. to 2:00 P.M.

When we first visited, we encountered two women dressed in business suits and heels coming out the front door. Apparently noting the bewildered looks on our faces—watching these two fancy executives coming out of a building that looks like a bail bondsman's office—one said to us, "This is the place!"

"The best hamburger in the world!" added her companion.

The two of them stood at the door, effectively blocking our way and, sotto voce as if imparting a secret code, they went back and forth issuing a litany they believed we needed to hear: "Turnip greens . . . creamed potatoes . . . butter beans . . . black-eyed peas . . . and, oh! fried chicken livers today . . . and peanut butter pie and banana pudding."

When you walk in, chef Shannon Fuller will call out, "Are you having a cheeseburger or dining off the menu today?" The burgers are hand-pattied, thick and juicy and satisfying, but we prefer the menu, a 5 X 7-inch piece of paper with three entrees handwritten every day above a printed list of vegetables. The murky turnip greens are especially delicious: pork-sweet, as tender as long-steamed cabbage, and heavy with tonic pot likker.

Certain menu items are immemorial, including roast beef every Friday. We adore the antediluvian baked spaghetti, which is timidly sauced, toothless pasta laced with crumbled beef, chewy shreds of cheese scraped from the edge the casserole, and a web of hardened noodles from the top. No hot meal is more popular than the every-Wednesday salmon croquettes. "I make twenty-five or thirty plates of them," Shannon says, showing how she forms each one from a mix of salmon, egg, onion, flour, and milk, then pan-fries it so the luxurious pink mash inside is encircled by a good crunch.

It was Charlie Zarzour, great-grandfather of Shannon's husband, Joe, who established the café in 1918, making it Chattanooga's oldest family-run restaurant. At that time, Main Street was the thriving heart of the city and Zarzour's lunchroom on Rossville Road was in the thick of it. Charlie had come from Lebanon via Syria, and shortly after opening day his wife died of influenza. He raised five children in the restaurant's back room, which has since become the smoking section. After Prohibition was lifted, Zarzour's was the place to go for hamburgers and beer.

Joe's mother, Shirley—Charlie's granddaughter—took over the café back in the 1950s from her Aunt Rose and Uncle George, and she continues to make the desserts. These include such exemplary southern-kitchen sweets as lemon icebox pie, banana pudding, and millionaire pie. Millionaire pie is named for its abundance: pineapple chunks, walnut pieces, green grapes, and mandarin orange slices suspended in a mix of frozen Cool Whip and sweetened condensed milk.

Allman's Pit Cooked Bar-B-Q

1299 Jeff Davis Hwy.   540-373-9881
Fredericksburg, VA   LD | $

For over fifty years, Allman's has been building a reputation on smoke-cooked pork shoulder, sliced or minced. Sliced is more like pulled—irregular shreds and nuggets that are soft and lean with a subtle flavor that can be amplified quite nicely by an application of sweet, thin sauce. You can have it on a plate or in a bun, or as the main ingredient in pork stew by the cup or bowl. Good fries and crisp coleslaw come alongside and milkshakes are made to order.

The pork is good, but to a large degree the allure of Allman's is the place itself: a brick storefront with a counter and stools and a scattering of bare tables in a room that feels untouched by time. (Thanks to Hetty Lipscomb for tipping us off to this place.)

Betty's Ben and Mary's Steak House

6800 James Madison Hwy.   540-347-4100

Warrenton, VA   D | $$

About the name: Betty was an employee of Ben and Mary when they opened their steak house along James Madison Highway about a half-century ago. Ben and Mary retired and sold the place to a third party who ultimately sold it to Betty. Betty was so devoted to the original restaurant concept that she simply added her name to the front of the old one. It's a cozy old place, frequented by locals as well as travelers who have staked it out as a serious stop for traveling carnivores.

B's B&M's boasts that it is "Home of the Fabulous Filet Mignon," and while we are admittedly smitten with any place claiming to be the home of anything, this declaration carries real weight. The filets mignon served here are big rounds of beef that run rivers of juice when cut. While they lack the protein tang of a sirloin, they pack plenty of flavor. Our medium-rare filets were perfectly grilled with velvet-red insides and a nice crust. On the side came good French fries.

The menu is vast, including other kinds of steak, seafood, and chicken cooked on the broiler, but we can't imagine coming to the Home of the Fabulous Filet Mignon and ordering anything else.

Chutzpah

12214 Fairfax Towne Center   703-385-8883

Fairfax, VA   BLD | $$

While Chutzpah is not by any means a regional restaurant, it had come highly recommended to us by members of Roadfood.com, and so one afternoon on the outskirts of DC, desperately in need of comfort food, we sought it out. Located at the far end of a nondescript Fairfax shopping center, it is a modest-size storefront with an immodest personality. Billing itself as a *real* New York deli, Chutzpah features gigantic sandwiches, smoked fish platters, bagel plates, hot and cold borscht, and a full repertoire of Dr. Brown's sodas.

Meals begin with bowls of sour and half-sour pickles and creamy coleslaw. We spooned into matzoh ball chicken noodle soup, which was as homey as can be, then feasted on wiener schnitzel, a big, thick slab of juicy meat in an envelope of crunchy, dark brown crust. It is served with lemon wedges and a large side dish of serious meaty gravy. We thought the gravy superfluous, but the latke (potato pancake) on the side was excellent. Of course, we also had to have a sandwich, but which to choose? Pastrami (annotated on the menu with the advice, "Please don't embarrass yourself and ask for mayonnaise"), hot brisket, or chopped liver? We went for a Reuben, which is an extremely unwieldy heap of steamy corned beef, sauerkraut, melted Swiss cheese, and Russian dressing between two crisp-grilled slabs of rye bread. It comes with thick-cut steak fries and it is delicious!

High on the list of must-try dishes for the future are matzoh brei, blintzes, corned beef hash, chicken in the pot with matzoh ball and kreplach, and noodle kugel. We walked out with a nice black and white cookie, forgoing the seven-layer cake, carrot cake, and genuine New York cheesecake.

Dixie Bones BBQ

13440 Occoquan Rd.	703-492-2205
Woodbridge, VA	LD | $$

Roadfood adventurer Laura Key tipped us off to Dixie Bones for its macaroni salad, iced tea (available sweet or unsweet), and hickory-smoked pork. As far as we've tasted, the pork is the best barbecue in the greater DC area and an essential Roadfood stop along I-95.

Cooked at least a dozen hours over smoking hickory logs, the meat is velvet soft, served in sandwiches heaped on a platter with such side dishes as Laura's favorite macaroni salad, French fries, baked beans, limp greens, and a terrific item known as muddy spuds. That last item is chopped-up baked potato dressed with barbecue sauce.

Dixie Bones offers three kinds of Carolina-style sauce (tomato-sweet/vinegar-tangy), the hottest of which is not incendiary. In addition to boneless pork, there are ribs sold by the rack and half-rack, pork sausage, beef brisket, pulled chicken breast, and fried catfish fillets.

Pies are made here, and we found the apple pie endearingly soulful, i.e., well-sweetened and cooked long enough that the pieces of apple inside were virtually as tender as the pork that preceded dessert. Thursday is lemon chess pie day. Friday and Sunday feature coconut cream. Saturday's pie is sweet potato.

Doumar's

20th St. and Monticello Ave.   757-627-4163
Norfolk, VA   BLD | $

Doumar's has been at the corner of 20th Street and Monticello Avenue in Norfolk since 1934, but it was thirty years before that and in the city of St. Louis that the Doumar name first gained fame. At the World's Fair of 1904, Mr. Doumar introduced a novel way of serving and eating ice cream: the cone. The cone made it possible for fairgoers to walk and eat ice cream at the same time, and without utensils—surely, one of the great ideas in culinary history.

Today's Doumar's of Norfolk is marked by a sign with two big ice cream cones on either side, but it's known also for pork barbecue, double-meat hot dogs, burger-and-French-fry plates, and flat grilled cheese sandwiches. As for ice cream, if you choose not to get a traditional waffle cone (still made in Doumar's kitchen), you can order what is here known as a Reggie (a chocolate milkshake with crushed cone chips), a June Bride (chocolate ice cream topped with strawberry sauce), a Scope (hot fudge atop vanilla ice cream and orange and lime sherbet), or a Kingston Flat (strawberry shortcake with bananas). Milkshakes are superb, served in glasses made of . . . glass!

Best of all, Doumar's delivers its classic drive-in fare in the classic drive-in manner—on trays that hang on the window of your car.

Goolrick's Pharmacy

901 Caroline St.   540-373-9878
Fredericksburg, VA   L | $

A while ago when we were on a Washington, DC–based NPR program, Jane bemoaned the fact that good, honestly made milkshakes were getting hard to find, what with all the machines that spew out chemically stabilized shakes that are big on thick but short on taste. A handful of listeners wrote and e-mailed us to cheer Jane up with the recommendation of Goolrick's, a vintage pharmacy lunch counter where shakes are still assembled from ice cream, syrup, and milk, whirred by wand, and served in the tall aluminum beaker in which they were mixed.

What a joy! Not only are the shakes great, so is the lemonade, which is freshly squeezed. And while nothing on the lunch menu will win huzzahs on the Food Network, we love a roster of nice, modest sandwiches such as BLT, chicken salad, grilled cheese, cream cheese and olive, and even peanut butter and jelly. If a shake or lemonade doesn't suit your fancy, how about a cherry Coke, vanilla Coke, or chocolate Coke—each made the time-honored way, of course, by squirting fountain syrup into the bottom of the glass before the Coke is drawn.

Naturally, ice cream desserts are a big deal: hot fudge sundaes and individual scoops are available with wet walnuts (60 cents extra) and rainbow sprinkles (40 cents).

Accommodations are limited to counter stools and a handful of tables along the wall. In back, a compounding pharmacist can actually fill prescriptions the old-fashioned way, by customizing medicines to meet patients' special needs.

Mrs. Rowe's Restaurant & Bakery

74 Rowe Rd. (Exit 222 off I-81)   540-886-1833
Staunton, VA   BLD | $$

In all candor, we need to say that we have received a handful of notes from travelers who were disappointed with their meals at Mrs. Rowe's over the last few years. On the other hand, we have heard from many happy customers, and our own experiences, which have included at least one visit per year, have been swell.

Of course it is not the same since Mrs. Rowe passed away, but we continue to love the biscuits and sticky buns, the crunchy fried chicken with mashed potatoes and/or mac 'n' cheese on the side, the pork chop and stewed apple plate, and the creamy, meringue-crowned banana pudding.

Opened decades ago as a small mom-and-pop café, Mrs. Rowe's has become a big roadside enterprise. Its fame and its location at the end of a highway exit ramp bring mobs on busy travel weekends (a million people per year!) and sometimes it can seem like an assembly-line eatery where customers are processed rather than served. But once you are seated— and more importantly, once the food starts coming—we are more than willing to forgive the ambience and eat hearty.

Philip's Continental Lounge

5704 Grove Ave.   804-288-8687
Richmond, VA   LD | $

A favorite haunt of students at the University of Richmond for seventy years, Phil's is famous for outsize sandwiches ranging from grilled cheese to Reubens and Reuben variants. The turkey club is tall and ravishing and the hamburgers, while not at all fancy, are diner delights, especially when topped with cheese and accompanied by an order of brittle-crusted beer-batter onion rings or French fries. Crunchy pickle wedges come alongside.

Beyond sandwiches, Phil's offers a broad menu of hot suppers: fried chicken, fried shrimp, even steak. Among libations, adult and otherwise, are terrific milkshakes, tart limeade, and the house signature cocktail, vodka limeade.

Ambience is that of a mid-twentieth-century college-town lounge with a décor of pennants and giant droopy inflated beer bottles hanging from the ceiling.

Sally Bell's Kitchen

708 W. Grace St.   804-644-2838
Richmond, VA $

Sally Bell's Kitchen was conceived in 1924 as a bakery, and that is what it is today—a charming little relic from the past with Sally Lunn muffins, pies, tarts, and that nearly lost icon of the Old South kitchen, beaten biscuits. The biscuits are crisp, tan rounds with silky tops that are an ideal companion for bisque or salad or Sally Bell's tomato aspic. Cupcakes are notable because they are iced all over, not just on top. We love the strawberry cupcakes, so pretty in pink.

There is no place to eat here, but you can get a boxed lunch that sells for a little over $6. Inside a white cardboard box, inscribed with the trademark feminine silhouette, you will find a sandwich on a made-here roll or bread, a cup of macaroni or potato salad, a cupcake . . . and this marvelous thing called a cheese wafer. It is delicate and fragile—a couple of bites and it is gone—a taste of a more refined era long before supersizing. Among available sandwich ingredients are, of course, pimiento cheese, as well as chicken salad, egg salad, Smithfield ham, and cream cheese with nuts.

While we travelers generally confine ourselves to cupcakes, little tarts (apple, peach, or pecan), muffins, and boxed lunches, people with a dinner table nearby come to Sally Bell's for full-size cakes. The devil's food and yellow batter cakes are picture-perfect.

Wright's Dairy Rite

346 Greenville Ave.   540-886-0435
Staunton, VA   LD | $

Three years before Ray Kroc began franchising McDonald's, Wright's Dairy Rite of Staunton, Virginia, started serving Superburgers. Two beef patties with cheese and lettuce, topped with special sauce and layered in a triple-decker bun, this monumental hamburger is still served as it was in 1952—by carhops at the window of your vehicle in a car slip at the side of the restaurant. Wright's added a dining room in 1989, so it is possible to eat inside, where décor includes a handsome Wurlitzer jukebox (with compact discs rather than 45s) and vintage Wright's menus from the 1950s and 1960s, but for us, the joy of this place is in-car dining.

If really, really hungry, forgo the Superburger for a Monsterburger. That is one-half pound of beef barely sandwiched in a bun, available in a basket, with French fries or, better yet, with Wright's homemade onion rings. To drink with this festive heap of food, one needs a shake. At Wright's, milkshakes are the real thing, available in chocolate, strawberry, or vanilla, as well as with real bananas or strawberries (mmmm!), and with or without malted milk for additional richness. While on the subject of dairy products, we should also note that this place knows how to make a fine banana split, a float (a big blob of ice cream set adrift in the soda pop of your choice), and a flurry (candy and/or cookies blended into soft-serve ice cream).

Wright's menu goes well beyond burgers. There are regular and foot-long hot dogs, pork barbecue on a bun, sandwich baskets with potato chips and a pickle, whole submarines, hearty chili with beans, even a veggie wrap with fat-free dressing. In addition to milkshakes and soda pop, the beverage list includes that drink known to connoisseurs of Dixie mixology as the champagne of the South—freshly brewed, presweetened iced tea, served in twenty-ounce cups.

Blossom Dairy and Soda Fountain Café

904 Quarrier St. 304-345-2233
Charleston, WV LD | $$

A 1933 art deco dairy bar that has been polished and restored to gleaming perfection, Blossom Dairy is a vast, high-ceilinged room with tables and plush blue-upholstered booths, and a long counter facing vintage mixological tools.

During the day you can come for a late breakfast of coffee and pastries; at lunch there is a wide-ranging menu of sandwiches and salads, including better-than-lunch-counter hamburgers; and at supper, the tables are covered with soft white linen and butcher paper and the menu is eclectic bistro fare. Beautiful filets mignon are a specialty, well-charred and with butter-tender insides, served on a bed of caramelized onions and accompanied by a timbale of pepper-and-mushroom-infused potato hash. An appetizer of creamy polenta is described to us by our waitress, and we quote, as "better than S-E-X" . . . and we wouldn't disagree! Other interesting items are seared tuna steak, crawfish étouffée with jerk-seasoned shrimp, and a vegetarian grilled eggplant steak with portobello mushrooms. To accompany these deluxe dishes, you can choose a fine wine . . . or a chocolate milkshake from the soda fountain.

The most interesting aspect of the menu is the build-it-yourself pasta selection. You choose penne, spinach fettuccine, angel hair, linguine, or bowtie noodles, then pick the kind of sauce you want on them: marinara, Alfredo, creamy marinara, herb-infused oil, or Thai barbecue. After making that configuration, you can then add any one or several accompaniments to the dish from a long list of such items as artichoke hearts, capers, roast Italian sausage, olives, pine nuts, shrimp, and scallops. We got angel hair pasta with marinara sauce, roasted peppers, and gorgonzola cheese: mmm-mmm!

For dessert in this awesome sweet shop, we need ice cream (although clever-sounding cheesecakes and pies are also available). The hot fudge sundae, made with creamy fresh ice cream, comes in a tulip glass with fudge spilling over the edge, whipped cream, and a cherry on top. A beautiful sight!

Coleman's Fish Market

2226 Market St.   304-232-8510
Wheeling, WV   LD | $

There are tens of thousands of loyal customers who believe that Coleman's Fish Market makes the best fish sandwich on earth. It is simplicity itself: two pieces of soft white bread holding a cluster of steaming hot fried fish fillets. If you want tartar sauce, you have to ask for it, and you pay a dime extra. The sandwich is delivered across a counter, wrapped in wax paper; it is your task to find a table somewhere on the broad floor of the renovated century-old Wheeling Centre Market House, unwrap it, and feast!

The golden crust on the North Atlantic pollock fillets is made of cracker meal, thin as parchment. When you break through it, your sense of smell is tickled by a clean ocean perfume, and as the pearl-white meat seeps its warm, luscious sweetness, you taste a brand-new food, like no other fish sandwich ever created.

After you've eaten several dozen over time, you might want to branch out and try some of the many other excellent foods Coleman makes, all delivered over the counter in a bag for toting to a table: Canadian white sandwich (a bit blander and "whiter" tasting than the regular fish), shrimp boats and baskets, fried clams, oysters, deviled crabs, and Cajun-spiced catfish. Coleman's really is a fish market, and if you wait in the "Special Line" (as opposed to the "Regular Sandwich Line"), you can ask the staff to cook up just about any raw fish in the case, and pay for it by weight. On the side of whatever fish you get, there are good French fries and Jo-Jo potatoes, and onion rings every day but Friday (when the deep-fryers are totally devoted to making only fish sandwiches).

Coleman's was started by John Coleman in 1914 in the old city market (which itself dates back to 1890). Joe Coleman, grandson of John, keeps things up to date with the latest advances in nutritionally virtuous cooking oils. And the iron pavilion in which the market is located was handsomely renovated about fifteen years ago. In the heart of a muscular city better known for steel and coal more than cooking, Coleman's is a thriving legend of American gastronomy.

Country Club Bakery

1211 Country Club Rd.   304-363-5690
Fairmont, WV   (Closed Wed) | $

Culinarily speaking, West Virginia has a curious character. At its best, it combines the rib-sticking taste of muscular immigrants who came to make steel and mine coal with the niceties of the Old Dominion plantation table, resulting in wondrous meals of stewed chicken and dumplings with spicy hot giardiniera relish on the side or country ham and red-eye gravy with sweet banana peppers.

As far as we can discern, there is but one single dish unique to the state, found mostly between Morgantown and Weston, but at its best in the old Italian-settled communities of Fairmont and Clarksburg. It is the pepperoni roll, a portable, self-contained meal similar to the Cornish pasty, but made of Italian-style dough wrapped and risen and baked around a fistful of pepperoni twigs scarcely bigger than matchsticks. Originally invented at the Country Club Bakery by Giuseppe Agrio in 1927, pepperoni rolls were a favorite food among miners, who could carry them underground without fear of spoilage and eat them with little mess.

Now pepperoni rolls are sold in every grocery store, convenience store, and gas station in the area, and not all of them are good to eat. But some of the best are still made by Country Club in a classic configuration. They are simple, small sandwiches, selling for fifty-nine cents apiece—a four-inch tube of warm, crusty dough with just enough pepperoni cushioned inside to add fetching zest to the bready wrap. It is not unusual for hungry locals to eat a half-dozen rolls as a snack.

Discount Center Cafeteria

US 250   304-775-7781
Burton, WV   BL | $

What do you need? A box of ready-to-make macaroni and cheese? A loaf of soft white bread? A genuine West Virginia pepperoni roll? A cast-iron skillet? Penny candy? A winter coat? A new carburetor? The Discount Center, by the side of Highway 250 in the tiny town of Burton, has it all . . . and then some. We stopped for brunch. (In fact, we stopped for a meal midway between breakfast time and lunchtime. It's a certainty the word "brunch" has never been spoken in this down-to-earth place.)

Adjoining the all-purpose dry goods/hardware/automotive/grocery store is a strange little fluorescent-lit eating shed where, among a hodge-podge of merchandise and posters for automobile parts, breakfast and lunch are served at low, low prices. Seating is at booths or one long communal table covered with oilcloth.

We arrived too early for the daily special of chicken breast, mashed potatoes, gravy, beans, applesauce, and a biscuit ($4.89), but were delighted with breakfast of biscuits and gravy and an all-purpose true-country meal of soup beans and corn bread. As we dined at one of the booths, the lady who made the food chitchatted with us and was horrified to learn that a good biscuit is hard to find in some parts of the country.

In truth these were not the best biscuits and corn bread we've ever eaten, but the latter crumbled mighty well into the soup beans, which were hammy and delicious. And the ragtag place itself is irresistible.

Hocutt's Carolina Barbecue

1724 Wheeling Ave.   304-845-7157
Glen Dale, WV   LD | $

Every once in a while, we walk away from a meal we've just found somewhere along the road and one of us declares to the other, "We do have the best job in the world." Travis Hocutt's place is where it most recently happened. The full name is Hocutt's Carolina Barbecue and Ice Cream, but the truth is that we ate no ice cream so we cannot tell you about that. But we can tell you that the barbecue, the hush puppies, the country ham, the collard greens, the macaroni and cheese, and the real home-brewed iced tea were all exemplary.

Travis does the cooking and his wife tends the dining room, and the two of them are a joyful duo. Even though it was a fairly busy lunch hour, Travis had plenty of time to pop out of the kitchen on several occasions to chat with us and old friends and regular customers who occupied the tables. Travis told us that the recipe for his hush puppies came from his grandmother, and oh, wow, what great hush puppies they are. Small and irregular-shaped, extremely crusty but with creamy insides, they come with a choice of honey butter, molasses butter, or just plain warm butter. We went crazy dipping ours and devouring them even before the meal arrived. Every meal at Hocutt's starts with hush puppies.

The barbecue is eastern North Carolina–style (that's where Travis is from): tender, smoky shreds of moist pork butt and shoulders infused with a peppery vinegar marinade. Sandwiches come with slaw included in the bun. Plates are sided by wondrous southern-style vegetables.

Be sure to call ahead if you are planning to visit Hocutt's. Travis sometimes takes his cooking skills on the road to festivals and fairs and, as he put it, "I don't let anybody do my cooking in my kitchen. If I'm not here and I can't cook, we ain't open."

Julio's

501 Baltimore Ave.   304-622-2592
Clarksburg, WV   LD | $$

Across from the train station in the old Elk Point section of Clarksburg, Julio's is a first-rate Italian restaurant with a tin ceiling, carved wooden bar, and plush leather booths that are, incongruously, outfitted with Lava Lites. While the food is excellent, and clearly prepared by a chef with culinary expertise, prices are reasonable and service is neighborhood-friendly.

A printed menu lists lots of inviting pastas including four different versions of pasta e fagiole—with cream sauce, with marinara, with potatoes and kale, and en brodo zesty with fennel—and primavera made with uncooked vegetables in red sauce. But some of the best dishes are not in print; waitresses recite extremely appetizing lists of the day's appetizers, entrees, and desserts.

For hors d'oeuvres, we loved our "paisano salad," a cold antipasto plate topped with the kitchen's jade-green garlic basil dressing, and roasted peppers with gorgonzola served atop slabs of garlic toast. We devoured entrees of vivid red peppers stuffed with hot ground sausage on a bed of al dente spaghetti, a supremely comforting bowl of pastae fagiole, and a stylish plate of tuna pomodoro. The meal commenced with a basket of swell garlic toast with a smoky taste and concluded with an outrageously rich house-made éclair loaded with pastry cream and blanketed with good chocolate.

Oliverio's Cash and Carry

427 Clark St.   304-622-8612
Clarksburg, WV $

"This was once *the* spot in Clarksburg," Angela Oliverio told us about seven years ago as she slid a long length of pig gut onto the spout of her hand-cranked sausage-making machine. "We had everything here in Elk Point [the Clarksburg neighborhood where her grocery is located]: prostitution, gambling, big business, street corner business, thriving industry. Now, there's not much left."

But Elk Point is coming back and, most important, Oliverio's is as wonderful as ever. What a gem: a vintage, family-run grocery store where Angela sits in back, and with the help of her brother John, cranks out lengths of coarse-textured Italian pork sausage seasoned with paprika, fennel seed, and plenty of hot pepper. She also prepares bowls full of peppered green and black olives that she will sell you by the pint. On the front shelves of the store are a wide assortment of roasted peppers and vegetable relishes that Angela's other brother, Frank, makes in his kitchen just down the street. Peppers are how Oliverio's has been best known, ever since mama Antoinette Oliverio began canning them in the back of this store in the early 1930s. Some of the choice varieties made by son Frank today include diced hot cherry peppers, a spicy giardiniera (garden mix), and peppers in hot red sauce.

We need to point out the rather obvious fact that Oliverio's is not a restaurant. It is a little grocery store, and unless Angela takes a liking to you and you happen to be lucky enough to arrive just when she's cooked up a batch of her zesty sausage for tasting purposes, you cannot eat here. But a new place called Tre Sorrelli, just around the corner, does use the sausage in tremendously good sandwiches, and if you are able to take some of this good food home, you will inscribe this charming little cash-and-carry in your must-visit book of West Virginia culinary treasures.

Quinet's Court

Main St. across from the courthouse   304-455-2110
New Martinsville, WV   BLD | $

"We use the area's finest hobby chefs' recipes often," boasts the printed menu of Quinet's Court, where the choice of items on multiple buffet tables is cornucopic. Although presented in big institutional pans on room-length steam tables, most of the dishes do indeed seem like home cooking at its finest—from cake-smooth corn bread to stuffed peppers to cream pies, cobblers, cookies, and pudding.

While we love the baby back ribs, kielbasa, chicken casserole, and ham loaf with pineapple glaze, we are even more smitten by vegetables. Indeed, this is a smorgasbord that vegetarians might pray to find in heaven. The selection is incredibly vast. Silk-tender butter beans, sweet hunks of carrot, scalloped potatoes, homemade noodles, five-cheese mac and cheese, and baked beans filled a plate with a variety of wonderful flavors that was a more than filling meal.

The buffet rule is that you pay one price ($7.95 for lunch) and help yourself to as much as you want. A sign at the beginning of the first table does warn, however, that a $1 surcharge will be added to the bill of anyone who wastes food. Our waitress was especially generous. As we walked in the door, early during lunch hour, we noted a couple of beautiful sticky buns in a pan left over from breakfast. When we asked her if we could have one, she brought it, no charge, and told us simply to consider it as part of our lunch buffet.

Accommodations are appropriately vast: big tables in several spacious dining rooms. Décor includes an awesome picture of prizefighter Jack Dempsey (who ate here in the 1940s) and a thousand of pictures of town history and local citizens. It is possible to dine non-buffet style: breakfast, lunch sandwiches, and a selection of hot meals listed on the menu under the heading, "Great Specials for Our Not-So-Hungry Friends."

Ritzy Lunch

456 W. Pike St.   304-622-3600
Clarksburg, WV   LD | $

"A hot dog without chili is not a hot dog!" proclaims John Selario, known in Clarksburg as Hot Dog John. Mr. Selario's parents opened Ritzy Lunch in 1933, and he shows us pictures of his father in front of the same storefront sometime in the 1940s when hot dogs are listed on the window for seven cents each, hamburgers a dime. "Ritzy Lunch has always been known for hot dogs," he tells us. "Clarksburg itself is an important hot dog town, not so much because of the weenies but because of the way we make our chili. There are so many immigrants and sons and daughters of immigrants—Greeks and Italians, mostly—that when we spice up our chili, we know how to do it right!"

Hot Dog John will get no argument from us. His dogs are lovely little pups, buried deep inside a steamed-soft bun and topped with a zesty ground beef sauce that is gently peppered and earthy. If you want to add a sweet note, ask for a layer of coleslaw to go atop the chili—a very popular configuration in this cute little diner.

Although hot dogs are the specialité de la maison, you should also consider sampling an unusual kind of hamburger in one of Ritzy's old wooden booths. Listed on the menu as a Giovanni, it is a patty of meat topped with melted cheese and roasted peppers served between two slices of butter-and-garlic-infused toast. Excellent!

Ritzy Lunch is an immensely happy place, a sort of nonalcoholic tavern where old friends and town characters hang out on the ancient counter stools to kibitz with each other and the waitresses and where, on any pleasant day, two or three wise-acres are likely to be found out on the sidewalk joshing with each other and making friends with newcomers.

Ruby and Ketchy's

2232 Cheat Rd.   304-594-2004
Morgantown, WV   BLD | $

Ruby and Ketchy's is a charming out-of-the-way diner in the Cheat Lake area east of Morgantown. It's open for three meals a day, and its knotty-pine booths and counter are favorite places for locals to come for good eats and conversation. Opened in 1958 by Ruby Nicholson, who was soon joined by husband Ketchy, it's still run by descendants of the beloved couple, and many of the recipes, including every-Tuesday meat loaf, vegetable soup, and chili, are Ruby's.

Today's menu is broad, including sandwiches, hot meals that range from crab cakes to sirloin steak, and such lunch specials as bean soup and corn bread (every Thursday) and salmon patties with mac and cheese on Friday. We enjoyed our ham dinner, of which the menu boasts "served over 30 years." The ham was pan-sizzled and had a good, rewarding chew. Hot roast beef was also good: pot-roast tender and accompanied by a sphere of mashed potatoes covered with gravy. We're not sure what to say about the potatoes, which didn't taste all that real to us, but were a fine gravy conduit.

Blackberry pie is the go-to dessert. It is dark purple and winey, with a rugged berry texture. The crust could have been flakier, but the filling was first rate.

S&B Bakery

720 E. Main St.   304-986-3247
Mannington, WV   L Tues-Sat | $

While the S&B bakery is open from 7:00 A.M. to 4:30 P.M., lunch is served at the handful of tables only midday, starting at 11:00. We arrived too early to sample the hoagies (made on S&B buns), hot dogs and sloppy joes, but even at 10:00 A.M. there were pepperoni rolls ready to eat. At lunch you can have one toasted and topped with sauce and peppers, but we were thrilled to pluck a couple off the shelf and eat them unheated. They were only hours out of the oven, so there remained a faint residue of warmth about them. What a joy to eat!

This is one of the best pepperoni rolls you will find in north-central West Virginia, where every bakery and most grocery stores make their own. The sticks of pepperoni are firm and mighty zesty, the tunnel of bread that completely envelops them is soft and fluffy and slightly sweet: a terrific contrast. Our cold one also contained cheese (an option), and while we no doubt would have liked it even better if the cheese had been molten and the pepperoni sticks hot enough to be weeping piggy moisture into the tender white bread around them, we hit the road whistling a happy tune as we ate them off the dashboard of our car.

By the way, on Fridays, S&B makes pizza.

Stewart's Original Hot Dogs

2445 Fifth Ave.   304-529-3647
Huntington, WV   LD | $

Like passionate eaters in almost every other place in the United States, West Virginians believe their hot dogs are the best. The place to test that claim is Stewart's, a curb-service drive-in since 1932. The formula includes local Logan hot dogs and Heiner's buns and, most important, all the trimmings: onions, mustard, and—drum roll, please—Stewart's secret-recipe chili sauce. The sauce is thick and pasty, not too hot. The basic configuration—in which the dog is set on top of its trimmings and presented wrapped in a paper napkin—will set you back all of $1.14. Most West Virginia hot dog connoisseurs will tell you that the picture is not complete unless you also get coleslaw as part of the trimming constellation; Stewart's is creamy and smooth.

To drink, nearly everybody swills renowned Stewart's root beer, available in quantities that range from a four-ounce mug for kids to a thirty-two-ounce drink to a gallon jug. Or you can enjoy it as the basis of an ice cream float.

Note: there are four other Stewart's locations in the Huntington area: First St. and Adams Ave. in West Huntington; in the Huntington Mall; 1025 Oak St. in Kenova; and 205 Towne Center Dr. in Ashland.

Deep South

Alabama * Arkansas * Florida * Georgia *

Louisiana * Mississippi * South Carolina

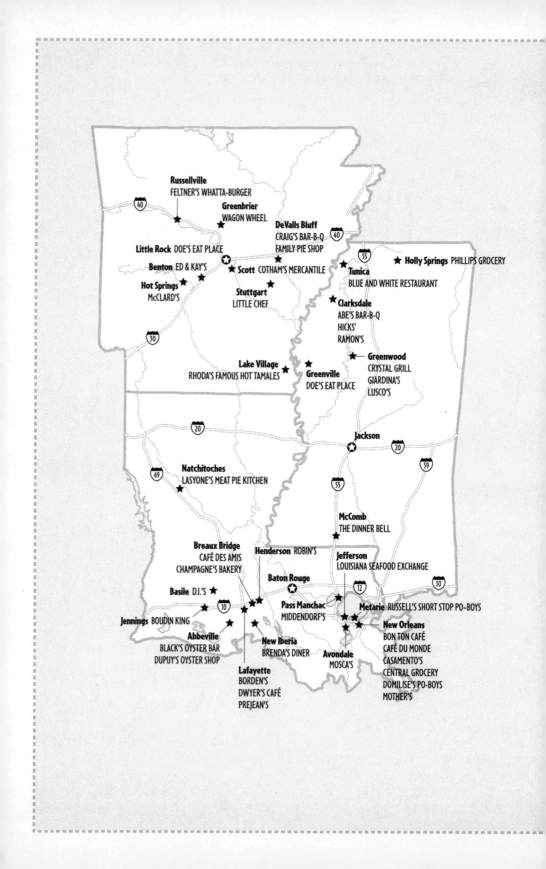

Russellville
FELTNER'S WHATTA-BURGER

Greenbrier
WAGON WHEEL

DeValls Bluff
CRAIG'S BAR-B-Q
FAMILY PIE SHOP

Holly Springs PHILLIPS GROCERY

Little Rock DOE'S EAT PLACE

Benton ED & KAY'S

Scott COTHAM'S MERCANTILE

Tunica
BLUE AND WHITE RESTAURANT

Hot Springs
McCLARD'S

Stuttgart
LITTLE CHEF

Clarksdale
ABE'S BAR-B-Q
HICKS'
RAMON'S

Lake Village
RHODA'S FAMOUS HOT TAMALES

Greenville
DOE'S EAT PLACE

Greenwood
CRYSTAL GRILL
GIARDINA'S
LUSCO'S

Jackson

Natchitoches
LASYONE'S MEAT PIE KITCHEN

McComb
THE DINNER BELL

Breaux Bridge
CAFÉ DES AMIS
CHAMPAGNE'S BAKERY

Henderson ROBIN'S

Jefferson
LOUISIANA SEAFOOD EXCHANGE

Baton Rouge

Basile D.I.'S

Pass Manchac
MIDDENDORF'S

Metarie RUSSELL'S SHORT STOP PO-BOYS

Jennings BOUDIN KING

Abbeville
BLACK'S OYSTER BAR
DUPUY'S OYSTER SHOP

New Iberia
BRENDA'S DINER

Avondale
MOSCA'S

New Orleans
BON TON CAFÉ
CAFÉ DU MONDE
CASAMENTO'S
CENTRAL GROCERY
DOMILISE'S PO-BOYS
MOTHER'S

Lafayette
BORDEN'S
DWYER'S CAFÉ
PREJEAN'S

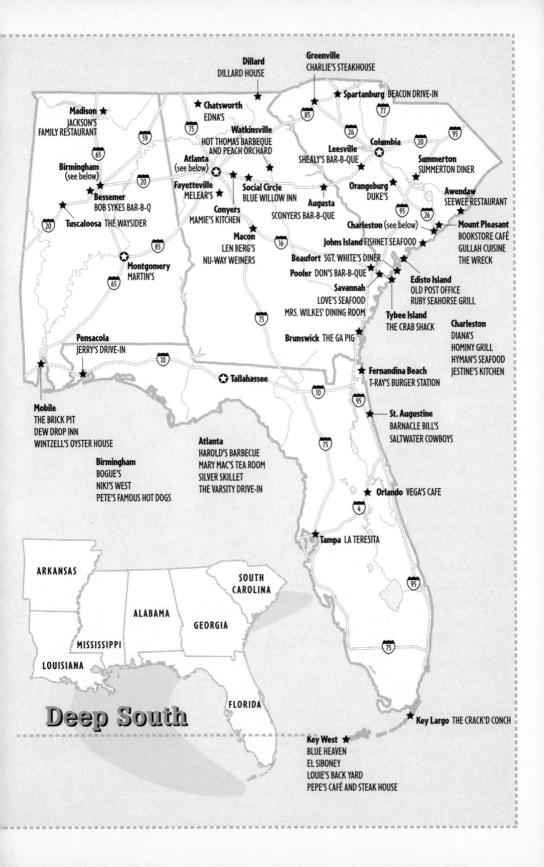

Dillard
DILLARD HOUSE

Greenville
CHARLIE'S STEAKHOUSE

Spartanburg BEACON DRIVE-IN

Madison
JACKSON'S
FAMILY RESTAURANT

Chatsworth
EDNA'S

Watkinsville
HOT THOMAS BARBEQUE
AND PEACH ORCHARD

Columbia

Leesville
SHEALY'S BAR-B-QUE

Summerton
SUMMERTON DINER

Birmingham
(see below)

Atlanta
(see below)

Bessemer
BOB SYKES BAR-B-Q

Fayetteville
MELEAR'S

Social Circle
BLUE WILLOW INN

Orangeburg
DUKE'S

Awendaw
SEEWEE RESTAURANT

Tuscaloosa THE WAYSIDER

Conyers
MAMIE'S KITCHEN

Augusta
SCONYERS BAR-B-QUE

Charleston (see below)

Mount Pleasant
BOOKSTORE CAFÉ
GULLAH CUISINE
THE WRECK

Macon
LEN BERG'S
NU-WAY WEINERS

Johns Island FISHNET SEAFOOD

Montgomery
MARTIN'S

Beaufort SGT. WHITE'S DINER

Pooler DON'S BAR-B-QUE

Edisto Island
OLD POST OFFICE
RUBY SEAHORSE GRILL

Savannah
LOVE'S SEAFOOD
MRS. WILKES' DINING ROOM

Tybee Island
THE CRAB SHACK

Charleston
DIANA'S
HOMINY GRILL
HYMAN'S SEAFOOD
JESTINE'S KITCHEN

Pensacola
JERRY'S DRIVE-IN

Brunswick THE GA PIG

Tallahassee

Fernandina Beach
T-RAY'S BURGER STATION

Mobile
THE BRICK PIT
DEW DROP INN
WINTZELL'S OYSTER HOUSE

St. Augustine
BARNACLE BILL'S
SALTWATER COWBOYS

Atlanta
HAROLD'S BARBECUE
MARY MAC'S TEA ROOM
SILVER SKILLET
THE VARSITY DRIVE-IN

Birmingham
BOGUE'S
NIKI'S WEST
PETE'S FAMOUS HOT DOGS

Orlando VEGA'S CAFE

Tampa LA TERESITA

ARKANSAS

SOUTH
CAROLINA

ALABAMA

GEORGIA

MISSISSIPPI

LOUISIANA

FLORIDA

Key Largo THE CRACK'D CONCH

Deep South

Key West
BLUE HEAVEN
EL SIBONEY
LOUIE'S BACK YARD
PEPE'S CAFÉ AND STEAK HOUSE

Bob Sykes Bar B-Q

1724 9th Ave.   205-426-1400

Bessemer, AL   LD | $$

Bob Sykes opened in 1957 as a hamburger stand. Bob soon built a pit and started cooking barbecue. At one time there were fourteen Bob Sykes barbecues in northern Alabama, but in 1977 the Sykes family decided to concentrate on one location only and moved into Bessemer, southwest of Birmingham. For the last thirty years, this smokehouse, now run by Van Sykes, has been a smoke signal of good eats.

Cooked over slow-smoldering hickory wood, the pork is finely chopped and succulent; ribs are beautiful burnished mahogany with great hefty ribbons of meat around each bone; chopped beef is particularly flavorful. "Big Bob" dinner plates include your barbecued meat of choice with baked beans, coleslaw, and French fries or potato salad, plus rolls. There is even a version of the barbecue salad so popular farther west: lettuce, tomatoes, carrots, cheese and croutons topped with your choice of pork, chicken, turkey, or ham. For those with a lot of hungry mouths to feed, Sykes's menu lists extra-large orders to feed five or ten (the latter is based on 2½ pounds of barbecue and comes with a gallon of tea). Carry-out meals and big feeds are sold at a drive-through window that the menu advises is ideal for "church functions . . . hunting trips . . . tired mothers . . . unexpected guest."

Pies are excellent, sold by the slice, whole pie, or mini-pie. You can get chocolate, pecan, and coconut, but the one that must be sampled is the meringue-topped lemon pie: sweet, creamy, and southern to its soul.

Bogue's

3028 Clairmont Ave.	205-254-9780
Birmingham, AL	BL | $

The house motto is, "It's vogue to eat at Bogue's," but if you are looking for an epicurean breakfast, for gracious service with a smile, or for the trendiest restaurant in town, Bogue's is *not* the place for you! In this hash house, you can expect plebeian food served by wiseass waitresses to a clientele who have been coming to eat the same meal for decades.

Generally, that meal ought to include biscuits. Bogue's breakfast biscuits are richly endowed with enough cooking grease that your fingers will glisten after you split one in half, and the bottom gets as crusty-brown as a deep-fried potato. These biscuits make great companions to breakfasts in which eggs are only minor players on plates of pork chops or country ham or just a huge spill of pepper gravy and, of course, lots of grits.

If for some reason you don't want biscuits, we highly recommend the sweet rolls. "Are they made here?" we ask our waitress.

"Every morning," she reassures us, speaking loud enough to be heard over the blast of Bogue's high-powered air-conditioning and, without being asked, bringing us Tabasco sauce for a plate of eggs.

No, the pea green walls and upholstered booths are not exactly glamorous, but to connoisseurs of stick-to-the-ribs cuisine and of the take-no-prisoners waitresses who serve it, Bogue's is a gem in the rough.

The Brick Pit

5456 Old Shell Rd.	251-343-0001
Mobile, AL	LD | $$

Legendary Texas pitmaster Sonny Bryan once explained the secrets of his delicious meats: "smoke and time." There is plenty of both involved in the barbecue of the Brick Pit, where Bill Armbrecht has built a room-size cooker into which he piles hickory and pecan logs and smokes meats at the lowest possible temperature for the longest possible time. Pork shoulder sizzles for some thirty hours; ribs for twelve; chicken for six. During the process, the meats' natural fat becomes their basting juices; and by the time they are done, each piece of pork and chicken is virtually fatless, yet moister than moist.

We think the best meat is pork shoulder, pulled from the cooked roast by hand. It is presented as a motley pile of chunks and shreds—some as soft as warm butter, others with crunchy crust from the outside of the roast. It is accented by a substantial film of house-made sauce that is thick and tomato-based, with laid-back character that does not distract from the fineness of the smoky meat. Ribs are blackened on the outside but extravagantly tender, with many areas so softened by the smoke pit that the lightest finger pressure causes pieces of meat to slide off the bone.

The low-slung dining room at the Brick Pit is painted white and completely covered in signatures, tributes, and other assorted happy graffiti. Orders are taken at a back window; once you've said what you want, you find a seat, and in no time, a waitress brings the meal in a partitioned plate that holds the meat of choice separate from the beans and coleslaw that come with it.

When most smokehouse devotees think of barbecue in Alabama, their thoughts turn to Birmingham and such legendary eateries as Dreamland. Birmingham is indeed a significant barbecue nexus, but we have a hard time disputing the sign above the breezeway that leads to the Brick Pit parking lot: "Welcome to the Best Damn Smoked Bar-B-Que in the Great State of Alabama."

Dew Drop Inn

1808 Old Shell Rd.   334-473-7872
Mobile, AL   LD | $

Hot dogs and cheeseburgers are the main reasons to come to the Dew Drop Inn, but there is a whole large menu of po-boys, gumbo, Gulf shrimp, and hot dinners accompanied by such good vegetables as turnip greens and rice and gravy. Coca-Cola is served the true-South way, in its shapely classic bottle alongside a glass full of ice. Banana pudding is the choice dessert.

Mobile's oldest restaurant (since 1924), the Dew Drop Inn is best known for hot dogs. In fact, local food historians believe that the hot dog was introduced to southern Alabama right here by original proprietor

George Widney. Dew Drop dogs are so beloved by natives that the waitresses here tell tales of former Mobilians now living in Memphis, Louisville, and even farther north who return like exiles so they can weep for joy over plates of Dew Drop dogs. The hot dogs themselves are merely bright red steamed franks of medium size, but the presentation is awesome—in toasted buns, topped with cool sauerkraut, a moist layer of sweet beefy chili, mustard, ketchup, and a pickle slice. A minority of hot dog connoisseurs order them "upside down" (the dog sits atop the condiments) and it is also possible to get them "shaved" (without kraut). The same unusual chili can be used as a topping for Dew Drop cheeseburgers.

The setting is cool and comfy, a wood-paneled roadhouse of laminate tables with little flower arrangements in Coke bottles on partitions between booths. Service is speedy and there is no waiting for the check, which arrives with the meal.

Jackson's Family Restaurant

234 Lime Quarry Rd.   256-772-0191
Madison, AL   BL | $

Halfway between Huntsville and Decatur, the small town of Madison is home to a great small-town restaurant. What a pleasure it is to ease into a Naugahyde booth and open up a menu to find a piece of paper clipped inside that lists all the various elements from which you can choose your fundamental southern plate lunch of meat-and-three. That means one meat and three vegetables from a choice that might include, among the former, country fried steak or barbecue, and among the latter, fried okra, vinegar slaw or mayo slaw, greens, beans, and hush puppies.

The star of the show is catfish, which is crusted with a fine, crumbly cornmeal coat and fried whole, meaning it is the customer's task to pull succulent hunks of flavorful meat from the bones (mighty easy with catfish). You get two catfish per order, obligatory sides being hush puppies, coleslaw, and French fries. To drink: Coke or iced tea. And for dessert, you'll want a slice of pie that is baked locally for the café, preferably either pecan or apple.

Meat-and-three is a ritual of lunchtime, but Jackson's is also a terrific place for an early morning breakfast of country ham and biscuits, and on weekends, it is open for dinner and the menu expands to include grilled (not country-fried) steak and slow-baked potatoes.

Martin's

1796 Carter Hill Rd.   334-265-1767

Montgomery, AL   LD | $

Oh, such biscuits begin supper at Martin's! Warm, flaky-crusted with gossamer insides, they would be insulted by the use of butter. The only thing better than the biscuits is corn bread, in the form of soft-textured muffins, also warm.

The dinner menu at Martin's is good-size, including such main-course choices as whole fried catfish, stuffed deviled crabs, and fried chicken livers. At lunch, choice is limited to daily specials: catfish fillets, smoked sausage, country-fried steak, chicken and dumplings. At either meal, you can count on a roster of side dishes that epitomize the southern way with vegetables: velvet-soft cooked cabbage, pot-likker-sopped collard greens, pole beans, buttery mashed potatoes, plus, of course, Jell-O salad in rainbow hues.

Of all the things to eat at Martin's, the one essential, at lunch or supper, is fried chicken. Fried chicken has been the main reason Montgomery citizens have favored Martin's for over half a century. It's crisp gold crust has a nice jolt of spice, it is easy to handle (i.e., grease-free), and it is juicy inside. One serving includes a meaty white breast and a dark-meat thigh. With biscuits, mashed potatoes, and greens, it makes a memorable meal . . . followed, of course, by a piece of Martin's coconut meringue pie.

A wood-paneled, colonial-themed restaurant that moved to its current location in a strip mall about ten years ago, Martin's is busier at lunch than at supper; in fact, at noon, you will likely wait, and watch, as early-arriving customers devour their plates of irresistible fried chicken with hedonistic gusto.

Niki's West

233 Finley Ave.   205-252-5751

Birmingham, AL   BLD | $

In the Deep South, vegetables are grown nearly year-round, and many of those vegetables are trucked to the produce center in Birmingham, where they are then shipped to destinations all over the East. Niki's West, surrounded by warehouses and loading docks, is where the produce-haulers come to eat. We counted more than three dozen vegetables along the steam table line—far too many to even contemplate sampling some of each; so prepare yourself to make some hard choices among the likes of yellow squash casserole, fried green tomatoes, black-eyed peas, and three different kinds of seasoned greens (turnip, collard, and spinach). Some items from the market are austere enough to please even the strictest dieter: unadorned sliced tomatoes, raw vegetable vinaigrette, and baby lima beans. But the more temptatious segment of Niki's produce repertoire is prepared according to voluptuous southern-café tradition. Broccoli is mixed with cheese and rice in a crazy-rich mélange; tomatoes are stewed with sugar and shreds of torn white bread until they become as sweet as cobbler; bright orange yams are infused with sugar; crunchy-fresh okra is sheathed in a deep-fried crust.

The decorative theme at Niki's is the Aegean sea (fish nets, scenic art of fishing boats, etc.), and when it comes to choosing an entree, we recommend baked fish Creole, broiled mackerel, and grilled amberjack. For fish-frowners, there is always a selection of beef and pork as well as baked Greek chicken that is terrific.

Our only disappointment was dessert. In so many southern cafeterias, desserts are really big: cobblers, puddings, pies, cakes. Niki's has all of them, but only the pleasantly balmy banana pudding stirred our passion.

Pete's Famous Hot Dogs

1925 2nd Ave. N   205-252-2905
Birmingham, AL   L | $

A hole-in-the-wall downtown hot dog shop that can feel as snug as an MRI machine, Pete's Famous has been dishing out cheap eats since 1915. We first learned about it thanks to a Roadfooder who goes by the handle "The Don." The Don described Pete's hot dogs as "the absolute best in the land, perfectly grilled every time, always on a fresh steamed bun." He said that Pete's hot dogs are "so good I have to hit myself in the head with a brick to stop eating them."

We can relate. Pete's hot dogs are addictive. They are modest-size crisp-grilled weenies, loaded into soft steamed buns, and almost always served "all the way"—with onions, sauerkraut, and tangy-sweet sauce, as well as a shot of mustard. Pete's "special" supplements the mix with dark, beefy chili. Cheese adds a whole other level of taste to the combo and is highly recommended.

Other than hot dogs and hamburgers, there is nothing on Pete's menu, not even French fries. If you need something on the side, bags of chips are available, and the beverages of choice are Coca-Cola and a curiously tangy grape-flavored bubbly bug juice known as Grapico. For dessert, choose from a selection of candy bars that includes Goo Goo Clusters. Expect to dine standing up.

The Waysider

| 1512 Greensboro Ave. | 205-345-8239 |
| Tuscaloosa, AL | BL \| $ |

Alabama's breakfast house for a half a century, the Waysider is the place to go for country ham with red-eye gravy and dainty-size, fluff-centered, crisp-topped biscuits and, of course, grits on the side. With the biscuits comes honey, a nice complement; the triple whammy flavor combo of salty ham, creamy biscuit, and sweet honey makes a taste experience that is, for us, as close to heaven as earthly food ever gets.

Another fine way to eat pork is streak o' lean, served with brown gravy and biscuits. It is a dish Elvis loved: bacon-lover's bacon. You get four pieces of it on a plate, each about a quarter-inch thick, fried crisp. The word "luscious" does not do justice to the overwhelmingly rich quality of this pork, streaks of which are chewy but most of which just melts away on your tongue.

Waysider lunch is good café fare: fried chicken or steak with slews of such satisfying southern vegetables as fried okra, field peas, collard greens, squash soufflé, candied yams, and fried corn. Warm fruit cobbler and cream pies top things off with a super-sweet exclamation mark.

Wintzell's Oyster House

| 605 Dauphin St. | 334-432-4605 |
| Mobile, AL | LD \| $$ |

Wintzell's is goofy but great. A downtown Mobile institution since Oliver Wintzell opened it as a six-stool oyster bar in 1938, it has survived hurricanes and floods, rebuilt and expanded into a modern, comfortable seafood restaurant with four other branches in the area and franchises available to entrepreneurs. The old place still has an oyster bar where you can sit and knock 'em back by the dozen; and it continues to keep score in the ongoing contest to see who can eat the most raw oysters in one hour. The walls are plastered with thousands of little signs offering bons mots and politically incorrect rules of life put there by the late Mr. Wintzell, starting in the 1950s. For example: "When a wife looks high and low for her husband at a party, she usually finds him high." *Bits of Wit and Wisdom (The Signs at Wintzell's Oyster House)* and *Oysters and Politics*, Mr. Wintzell's self-published books, are available for sale at the cash register.

Aside from impeccable, opened-as-you-watch raw oysters and the vintage bar-room charm, Wintzell's is a worthy place for sampling many of the dishes that define Gulf Coast cookery: seafood gumbo and crisp-fried crab claws, oyster po-boys, and crusty-fried catfish, and a definitive version of the unique Mobile specialty, West Indies salad. No one knows how West Indies salad became such a favorite dish of the city's, but it's one every visitor must try: hunks of crabmeat marinated in oil and vinegar with grated onions. It is simple, rich, and ocean-sweet—so addictive that many customers, rather than ordering it as an appetizer (its usual role), get a couple of large orders for their main course, accompanied by saltine crackers.

Cotham's Mercantile

5301 Hwy. 161 S   501-961-9284

Scott, AR 72142   L Mon-Weds, L&D Thurs-Sat | $

In the Grand Prairie about a half-hour southeast of Little Rock, Cotham's Mercantile is perched on stilts above a slow-flowing river. Built in 1917, it has been a general store, a jail, and a military commissary. Contemporary Arkansans know it as a plate-lunch destination.

The old wood building is fronted by a broad porch. Enter a swinging door into a dining room packed to the ceiling with vintage home and farm bric-a-brac, from garden tools to vintage television sets. Remote the restaurant may be, but it is rare to see an empty chair. Bare wood tables are surrounded by customers who come for hearty noonday meals built around catfish, chicken-fried steak, or chicken-fried chicken, and such daily specials as fried pork chops (Monday), chicken and dumplings (Tuesday), meat loaf (Wednesday), and southern-fried chicken (Thursday). Side dishes include corn fritters, hush puppies, collard greens, and fried green tomatoes. There is a long list of sandwiches, too, the king of which is known as a Hubcap Hamburger. That is an immense circle of cooked ground beef—close to a foot in diameter and a half-inch thick—that comes in a bun that nearly fits, dressed with a salad's worth of mustard, lettuce, tomato slices, pickles, and hoops of onion. Incredibly, it is possible to lift it with two hands from plate to mouth. The outlandish specialty has earned such renown that the store's push-pin map of the United States has no room left for any more pins to show where Hubcap-loving customers have come from; business cards from visitors around the globe are tacked up all around it.

Desserts include fine Arkansas fried pies and peach or blackberry cobbler.

Craig's Bar-B-Q

Hwy. 70 W	870-998-2616
DeValls Bluff, AR	LD | $

Craig's is a shack so unrepentantly dumpy that you've got to love it. Dim fluorescent lights hang over a half-dozen rickety tables. Pinned to faded wallpaper with a ducks-in-flight pattern are business cards and hand-penned ads who-knows-how-old: Lost Black Lab named Cache; 12 Gauge Steel Shot Cheap; Deer Processing; Emergency Gas and Rescue Assistance; Joyce's Beauty Salon. Diners' attire ranges from still-wet camouflage waders to pressed pinstripe suits, and includes an amazing number of giant-size overalls on great big farm folks. The close quarters mean that conversations are wide open among seated eaters as well as take-out customers hovering around waiting for their food. We shared thoughts with Arkansawyers about political vice and bird-dog virtue.

The chopped pork is spectacular, certainly the best between Memphis and Little Rock: alternately soft and crunchy, deeply smoked and brushed with thick, orange sauce that is big on spice and nearly sugarless. To balance the devilish sauce, which is available ultra-hot if specially requested, sandwiches are constructed with a layer of sweet coleslaw inside the bun; dinner plates include beans and slaw. The only other available side dish is a bag of chips. And the only proper thing to drink is iced tea—very sweet, of course.

Doe's Eat Place

1023 W. Markham St.	501-376-1195
Little Rock, AR	LD | $$$

Doe's is one of the worst-looking restaurants we love. It looks a little derelict from the outside, but inside is even worse: the linoleum floor is worn through; tables wobble; plates are flea-market quality.

Steaks are some of the best anywhere. Porterhouses, T-bones, and rib eyes are served family-style by weight. Family-style means that the cut of your choice comes hot from the kitchen already sliced, along with tongs for everyone to hoist their own from the serving plate. Are you stumped as to whether you need a three-pound porterhouse or a six-pound sirloin? No problem. The menu advises, "If you are a new customer at Doe's and wish assistance ordering, our experienced staff will be glad to help you." In fact, we want to mention that the staff at Doe's is amazingly friendly and obliging, even those times when the place is mobbed, as it is on weekend nights.

Along with succulent, charred-edge slabs of beef come skillet-cooked French fries. And before the arrival of the meat you get a bowl of memorable salad slick with garlicky, lemony, olive oil dressing. There are serious appetizers, too, and we highly recommend them for those of limitless appetite. Fried or broiled shrimp are available by the half-dozen, and Doe's hot tamales with chili are legendary (but also very, very filling).

Ed and Kay's

15228 I-30   501-315-3663
Benton, AR   BLD | $

Best known for its showstopping pies, Ed and Kay's also happens to be a great place for a hamburger with good onion rings or a yeomanly plate lunch. There may be only one or two hot entrees any day—stuffed peppers, fried chicken, ham, pork chops—but the list of side dishes is awesome, including mac and cheese, purple hull peas, creamed corn, and skillet fried potatoes. Most people get an entree and two or three vegetables, but it is possible to forgo the main course altogether and have a wonderful meal of four different side dishes.

Meringue pies are amazing-looking, their tops a perfect volcano shape that is two or three times the height of the filling itself. Of course there are chocolate cream, coconut cream, and lemon meringue. Our personal favorite from this phylum is peanut butter cream. But neither should one ignore the non-meringue pies. Pecan is masterful, and the one known as PCP is the ultimate, its initials standing for pineapple, coconut, and pecan. We recently received an e-mail from a Roadfood traveler who implored us to sample the cantaloupe cream pie on our next visit. Sounds dreamy!

Family Pie Shop

Hwy. 70 W   870-998-2279

DeValls Bluff, AR   Erratic hours; call ahead | $

Mary Thomas, who used to be a barbecue cook for Mr. Craig at Craig's Bar-B-Q on the other side of Route 70 (p. 224), opened her little bakery in 1977, and while it is merely a cinder-block garage hidden from easy view, aficionados consider Mary's the finest pie stop in the state: high honor hereabouts, where pie consciousness is as elevated as Iowa's.

Mary's dining facilities are minimal: four stools at a short counter in a disheveled storage room next to the kitchen. Most people get whole pies or small ones for two to eat in the car or at home. Mary told us that when Bill Clinton lived in Little Rock, he stopped in all the time and ate pie at the counter with his friends and family. He didn't have a favorite. "He liked them all!" she confides.

We love Mary's simple sugar cream pie and her luxurious "Karo nut," aka pecan, and the sweet potato pie is platonic. But filling almost doesn't matter; crust lifts these heavenward. Honey-brown, ready to flake with slight pressure from a plastic fork, the crust's savor is amplified in Mary's version of the Arkansas favorite, fried pie—apple, peach, or apricot filling inside a crescent of pastry dough that is deep-fried until brittle. "Lard! That is the secret," we proclaim as we crunch into a hot fried pie at the counter.

Mary shakes her head. "I will not speak of crust." She does allow that there is no lard in it. but she is mum about details of the recipe, a legacy from her husband, who was a Mississippi riverboat cook. Sitting at her counter, we ate two of Mary's individual-size meringue pies, then took one full-size egg custard pie to have in our Little Rock hotel room that night.

Feltner's Whatta-Burger

1410 North Arkansas   501-968-1410

Russellville, AR   LD | $

Feltner's serves the best hamburger in Arkansas. There are Whatta-Burger shops throughout the Southwest, but none like this one, known for "custom made hamburgers," gorgeous French fries, and milkshakes served in cardboard flagons that are more like buckets than cups.

In addition to big and good meals, Feltner's offers the kick of an only-in-America fast-food experience. The instant you enter the low-slung brick building, an order taker virtually accosts you at the door to find out what you want. At the head of the line, you convey the precise details of your order, from a simple Whatta-Burger (that's a quarter-pound patty on a five-inch bun) to a Whatta-Burger with double meat and double cheese. At the end of the line, you pay and receive your meal on a tray in a white bag, beverage on the side. Find a booth in the big dining room, where the walls are lined with humorous and inspirational homilies: "We guarantee fast service no matter how long it takes"; "The hurrier I go, the behinder I get"; "Cherish yesterday, dream tomorrow, live today."

Feltner's is *the* town burger joint, a favorite for families, teens on dates, and Arkansas Tech students. We well recall our first visit when we shared the dining room with a happy stampede of approximately three dozen fresh-faced six-footers attending basketball camp at the college, each of whom carried a tray with a brace of double-doubles (double meat, double cheese) and a heap of French fries.

Little Chef

1103 E. Michigan 870-673-7372

Stuttgart, AR BLD | $

The Little Chef is a Quonset hut in the Rice and Duck Capital of the World. It looks stark from the parking lot, but inside, it's cozy small-town café all the way. The dining room is decorated in antique memorabilia, and cakes of the day are appealingly set out on the counter. For breakfast, we've enjoyed biscuits with sausage gravy and pancakes with country ham. We've had excellent four-vegetable plates, including buttery mac 'n' cheese (such a swell vegetable!), greens, beans, and rice and gravy, and first-rate fried chicken, super moist inside its envelope of golden crust. All meals are accompanied by blocks of rugged corn bread.

The banana pudding is comfort in a dish, its custard interleaved with banana slices and plenty of vanilla wafers, some still firm, others softened into streaks of vanilla grain in the pudding. And who could resist hummingbird cake, the southern favorite that had to be named because hummingbirds like sweet things: spice cake chockablock with bananas and pineapple and spread with a thick layer of cream cheese frosting.

McClard's

505 Albert Pike   501-623-9665
Hot Springs, AR   LD | $$

If we had to select the best ribs in America (what an awesome task!), we'd think about Dreamland's smoky bones in Tuscaloosa, Alabama, and racks of velvet succulence at Van's Pig Stand in Shawnee, Oklahoma (p. 482). But our holy grail is McClard's in Hot Springs, Arkansas, a resort town named for its salubrious waters, and still a mecca for travelers in search of a mineral-water cure on Bathhouse Row.

Pork is king in this smokehouse, the pulled pork ineffably tender and moist, its smoky sweetness especially radiant when spread with hot sauce. The signature dish is a rib and fry plate. The ribs are a meat-heavy slab with a sticky glaze of peppery red sauce. They are presented under a pile of gorgeous honeytone French-fried potatoes and sided by fine, bright coleslaw to create a perfectly balanced barbecue meal.

A whole section of McClard's menu is devoted to tamale plates, ranging from plain tamales with beans to a full spread. A spread is McClard's term for a pair of tamales topped with sauce-sopped chopped smoked meat, beans, crisp Fritos chips, raw onions, and shredded orange cheese. Spreads remind us of the locally favored Fritos pie, but with the added zest of genuine pit barbecue.

The neon-lit 1942 stucco building that houses McClard's once offered toot-your-horn carhop service, but now hordes of happy eaters line up to fill the booths inside. The recipe for its sauce supposedly dates back to 1928, when a customer at the McClard family trailer court couldn't pay his bill and so offered his barbecue sauce recipe instead!

Rhoda's Famous Hot Tamales

714 Saint Mary St.   870-265-3108
Lake Village, AR   BL | $

The name of Rhoda Adams's café is no lie. The tamales are delicious, and well deserving of the fame they have earned up and down the Mississippi Delta. She makes them with a combination of beef and chicken; the meats combined with steamy cornmeal are wrapped in husks that, when unfolded, emanate an irresistibly appetizing aroma and are a joy to eat as a snack or meal any time of day.

Beyond tamales, the menu at James and Rhoda Adams's little eat-place by the side of the road is a full roster of great, soulful regional specialties. For fried chicken or pigs' feet, pork barbecue or catfish dinner, you won't do better for miles around. Early one morning Rhoda made us breakfast of bacon and eggs with biscuits on the side. Even this simple meal tasted especially wonderful. Rhoda is one of those gifted cooks who makes everything she touches something special.

We've always considered Arkansas one of America's top-seven pie states (along with Iowa, Wisconsin, Minnesota, Virginia, Texas, and Maine). Rhoda's pies are proof. She makes small individual ones as well as full-size pies. We've never tasted the coconut or the lemon pie, but we can say that her sweet potato pie and pecan pie are world-class.

Wagon Wheel

166 S. Broadview St.
Greenbrier, AR

501-679-5009
BLD | $

The best way to get to Bransom from Little Rock is up Highway 65, and if you pass through Greenbrier while hungry, you're in luck. At the Wagon Wheel, freshly baked, high-domed rolls envelop breakfast sandwiches of eggs and Petit Jean bacon; bread baskets come piled with white toast that is rich as cake; and tall meringue pies are Arkansas-excellent.

We were taken to the Wagon Wheel by our favorite Arkansas tipsters, Tony and Donna Perrin, and while they both sang the praises of the good pies and breads, Tony was particularly enthusiastic about the chocolate gravy. Yes, chocolate gravy! With your morning biscuits! Normal gravy is available, too, and it is excellent, but we had to try this extremely odd variation, and lo, it's pretty darn good. It's not as sweet as pudding and in fact it does seem to have a savory component, but there is no denying its chocolate essence. It's probably not for everyone, but if your taste buds want to go where few taste buds have gone before, we recommend it.

Despite its location on the road to Bransom, this is a cozy sort of place where locals hang out and discuss things over coffee every morning. We were especially charmed by veteran waitress Lynn Lockie, who, when she came to take our order, pulled up a chair and sat down to write on her order pad. "My legs are tired," she said. "I'm not; just my legs." Lynn confided that a few days before, the cook had put too much cornstarch in the pies, but that they were definitely up to snuff today. Yes, indeed, the tall meringues were Arkansas-excellent, and that is saying a lot, for Arkansas is one of this nation's premier pie places.

Barnacle Bill's

14 Castillo Dr.   904-824-3663

St. Augustine, FL   LD | $$

"Best fried shrimp in the world!" promised tipster Meg Butler, to which we would add a dazzling dessert titled Banana Delight, which is like banana pudding but with a crust of crunchy pecans, and excellent Minorcan clam chowder using the hot datil peppers unique to the area. (Datil peppers were brought to St. Augustine by settlers from the island of Minorca, off Spain, when they arrived generations ago. They are very, very hot.)

Barnacle Bill's is not exactly an undiscovered Roadfood hole-in-the-wall. It is big and popular and in fact there are two, the second location (dinner only) at 451 A1A Boulevard in St. Augustine (phone: 904-471-2434). But these two are no relation to the other Barnacle Bill's restaurant found along the Atlantic coast.

The shrimp indeed are something special: jumbo butterflies that are firm and juicy with a delicate crust. They are available just like that or with a coconut crust or, best of all, in a crust enhanced by the heat of datil peppers. Shrimp sauce and hush puppies are the shrimps' companions. When proprietor Chris Way opened the restaurant twenty-seven years ago, he put datil pepper hot sauce on the tables as a condiment. Lore says that customers came to like it so much they began to pocket the bottles. Way created the Dat'l Do-It line of hot sauces, now available at www.datildoit.com. For first-timers and those who have a hard time making up their mind, there are plates of a dozen shrimp, four of each variety.

There are all kinds of other seafood dishes on the menu and even a selection of "landlubber fare," but we agree with Meg Butler's recommendation, which was "I can't say much other than fried shrimp, fried shrimp, fried shrimp. . . ."

Blue Heaven

729 Thomas St.   305-296-8666

Key West, FL   BLD | $$

Off the beaten path in the Bahama Village area of the sunny never-never land known as the Conch Republic, Blue Heaven is a breakfast-lover's dream. Dining is al fresco on a broad outdoor patio under the shade of opulent banyan trees, where your companions include the café's flock of hens and roosters who hop and peck around tables and chairs. Their cock-a-doodle-doing is a natural companion for hefty omelets, but our favorite dishes are the tropical-tasting banana pancakes and a luxurious seafood benedict built upon ocean-fresh fish and topped with lime hollandaise. To drink? Who can resist a mimosa made with fresh-squeezed orange juice?

An incredibly colorful place to eat, Blue Heaven has been the home of a boxing ring (Ernest Hemingway sparred here), a bordello (the tiny rooms upstairs are now part of an art gallery), a bookmaking parlor, and a cockfighting pit (heroic roosters are buried in a little graveyard behind the dining area), as well as inspiration for Jimmy Buffett's song "Blue Heaven Rendezvous." It is delightfully disheveled, casual in the extreme, and one of Key West's most evocative dining experiences.

Starting at eight o'clock every morning, when neighborhood roosters are still greeting the sun with gusto, three meals a day are served. Much as we relish the jerk chicken and barbecued shrimp at lunch and supper, it's breakfast we like most: banana pancakes with maple syrup, nutty-flavored granola with fresh fruit, and coffee from mugs inscribed with the house motto: "Blue Heaven: you don't have to die to get there."

One other reason we like early breakfast best is that seats are usually available. In the evenings and on weekends, the wait for a table can be maddening. And true to its spirit of taking life easy, Blue Heaven does not take reservations.

The Crack'd Conch

Mile Marker 105, Ocean Side	305-451-0732
Key Largo, FL	LD | $$

Started as a fish camp in the 1930s, The Crack'd Conch remains a seafood shanty without airs, but with a big, brash personality. A white clapboard hut trimmed in violet and green with picnic tables on its front porch, a breezy back patio, and a helter-skelter dining room in which wall décor consists of customers' business cards and foreign currency, it is the most casual of restaurants, the type of place that makes travel along the Florida Keys toward the Conch Republic such a dreamy experience.

Fried 'gator, steamed shrimp, and house-smoked chicken are all long-time favorites, and the fried shrimp are startlingly light and crisp-crusted. The house specialty is, of course, conch. Nuggets of sweet, tangy mollusk meat, tender but with mouthwatering tooth resistance, are encased in breading and served in a great, tangled heap. On the side, we like oily fried bananas—a soft, hedonistic tropical food that has no comparables in the Northeast where we live. And for dessert, the key lime pie is a cool classic.

In addition to local seafood, The Crack'd Conch offers ambience that attracts a wide range of clientele from nice little white-haired ladies to clusters of leather-clad bikers, plus carloads of families on their way to or from vacation in America's Caribbean paradise.

El Siboney

900 Catherine St.	305-296-4184
Key West, FL	LD | $$

When you consider El Siboney is just ninety miles from Cuba itself—closer to Havana than to Miami—you understand why its Cuban food tastes so right. This is the best place we know in Key West to taste grilled garlic chicken, a half-bird with a crisp skin and meat so tender that it slides off the bone when you try to cut it. Plantains on the side are slightly crusty and caramelized around their edges. And yuca, a side dish served with roast pork, beans, and rice, is a revelation not quite like any other vegetable. Soft and glistening white hunks, reminiscent of a well-baked potato, but more luscious and substantial, are served in a bath of heavily garlicked oil and garlanded with onion slices.

The Cuban sandwich is a beaut, made on a length of fragile-texture toasted bread that is cut in half at a rakish angle and loaded with ham, roast pork, salami, and cheese, with pickles, lettuce, and tomato. Conch chowder is thick with conch meat, and provides a great opportunity for dunking shreds of the buttered Cuban bread that comes with every meal. The grandest dish in the house is paella Valenciana for two (call ahead; it takes an hour to prepare), a vast fisherman's stew served with rice, black beans, and plenty of Cuban bread for mopping juices. Dessert choices include key lime pie, flan, and rice pudding, accompanied of course by espresso or café con leche.

El Siboney is a clean, pleasant place with red-striped tables topped with easy-wipe plastic and silverware presented in tidy little paper bags. If you don't speak Spanish, the waitresses do their best to help you understand the menu. Ours explained that El Siboney was a Cuban Indian, and that the Indian-themed art on the walls is a tribute to him.

Jerry's Drive-In

2815 E. Cervantes St. 850-433-9910

Pensacola, FL BLD | $

Jerry's originally opened for business in 1939, and frankly, it doesn't look like it's changed much in the last sixty-plus years. It is a Formica-counter café with a few tables and booths and help-yourself rolls of paper towels for customers to use as needed. The walls are decorated with college pennants and graffiti going back decades.

Jerry's has character to spare . . . but it also has important hamburgers—hamburgers that local newspaper readers voted the best along the Gulf Coast. They are good-size, juicy patties of beef beautifully dressed with lettuce, tomato, chopped onions, mustard, and mayo, served with sweet coleslaw and crisp French fries. Not gourmet burgers, not unusual burgers: just good, satisfying hamburgers . . . in a classic lunch-counter setting.

Although many visitors to the "Redneck Riviera" know Jerry's as the hamburger place, regulars come for three square meals a day. The breakfast menu features all the usual configurations of eggs and luncheon meat (with grits and/or hash browns), plus an extraordinarily luxurious chicken liver omelet. At lunch, you can have such regional delights as smoked mullet, deviled crab, and broiled grouper, as well as big deep-fried oysters with hush puppies on the side.

La Teresita

3248 W. Columbus Dr.	813-879-4909
Tampa, FL	BLD, open all night Fri & Sat	$

A Cuban sandwich is a beautiful thing: ham, roast pork, and cheese along with mustard, mayonnaise, and pickles encased in elegant bread that is toasted to a crisp. There is no better place to eat one than Tampa, especially at the neighborhood café called La Teresita.

There are a few tables scattered about, but the choice seats (and swift service) are at the counters. Seats are arrayed along a sweeping serpentine surface where whole families line up on the rows of stools at dinnertime.

Regulars come for breakfast of buttered Cuban bread and café con leche; lunch favorites include carne asada, ropa vieja, vaca frita, and the best black beans and rice in town. Throughout the day, you'll see groups of happy gents gathering in the street after dining at La Teresita. Here they fire up big made-in-Tampa cigars and look like kings who have just enjoyed a royal feast.

Louie's Back Yard

700 Waddell Ave.	305-294-1061
Key West, FL	LD	$$$

When we visit Key West and think about dinner, we think of more than something to eat. We think of the ocean of warm breezes, of tropical beverages in a magical place. Those thoughts logically lead us to a table at Louie's Back Yard, where the best seats are located on a multileveled terrace overlooking the Atlantic. Here you dine while pleasure boats sail past and pelicans graze the waves.

In truth, this gracious pink classic-revival house could serve a TV dinner and it would be irresistible on a moonlit night, but it happens to be one of the innovators of Key West cuisine, known for such tropical delights as Bahamian conch chowder with bird-pepper hot sauce, grilled local shrimp with salsa verde, and cracked conch with pepper jelly and ginger daikon slaw.

We have since worked with chef Doug Shook on *The Louie's Back-*

yard *Cookbook,* which is filled with all kinds of recipes for Caribbean culinary pleasure. Still, the Louie's supper forever etched in our book of great culinary memories was our first: a pair of lovely grilled strip steaks glazed with hot chipotle chile sauce, sided by garlic mashed potatoes and red onion corn relish. To top things off, we had fancy coffee and feathery key lime tarts. Soft island breezes made hurricane lamps flicker. Bulbs strung among branches in overhead trees formed a radiant canopy above the patio. The ocean glowed cobalt blue when distant, soundless lightning storms at sea ignited over the horizon.

Pepe's Café and Steak House

806 Caroline St.   305-294-7192

Key West, FL   BLD | $$

"I could be you! You could be me!" exclaims our waitress with glee, setting down her ever-present pot of coffee to write an order that happens to precisely match what she likes to eat in the morning: an omelet of Jack cheese, Anaheim peppers, and smoked sausage sided by a creamy griddle-cooked mashed potato patty and a slab of bread du jour—warm coconut quick bread, nearly as sweet as cake. Breakfast at Pepe's, from 6:30 every morning, is heaps of fun, always featuring a bread of the day in addition to a big menu of omelets, pancakes, homemade granola, and creamed chipped beef on toast.

Later in the day, Apalachicola Bay oysters by the dozen make Pepe's a destination for insatiable oyster lovers who consume them raw, baked, or roasted Mexican-style. Weekly traditions include a Sunday night barbecue that features beefsteaks, pork ribs, tenderloin, chicken, salmon, and mahi-mahi. And who can resist a lunch menu that offers both a blue-collar burger and a white-collar burger? (The former is six ounces, the latter four.)

As attractive as Pepe's food may be, it's the place that's irresistible. It boasts of being "the eldest eating house in the Florida Keys," and it sure does have the feel of a place that's seen it all. The old wood dining room is covered with bric-a-brac as miscellaneous as the contents of grandma's attic, including pictures of famous people and nobodies, a nude painting, nautical bibelots, scenes of old Key West. Each varnished booth is outfitted with a shelf that holds about a dozen different hot sauces for oyster eating. Out back is a bar where locals congregate. (The bar opens at 7:00 A.M.!) And to the side, on an open patio strewn with mismatched tables, illumination is provided by an array of fixtures that includes a crystal chandelier, green-shaded billiard lamps, and year-round Christmas lights strung among the trees.

Saltwater Cowboys

Dondanville Rd.   904-471-2332
St. Augustine, FL   D | $$

Named for local founder Howard Dondanville, who was affectionately called Cowboy, and designed to look like a salt marsh fish camp from long ago, this way-too-popular restaurant serves excellent Minorcan clam chowder (a St. Augustine specialty) and a slew of southern seafood: freshly opened oysters and fancy-cooked ones, boiled crawfish with Cajun vibes, snapper, deviled crabs, soft-shells, and shrimp. A whole portion of the menu is headlined "Florida Cracker Corner" and devoted to frog legs, cooter (soft-shelled turtle), catfish, alligator tail, and even fried chicken with a vividly flavored bread-crumb crust. We suggest starting a meal with oysters Dondanville, served on the half-shell glistening with a mantle of garlic, butter, wine and finely chopped onions, then moving on to Cowboy's jambalaya, which is a profusion of shrimp, oysters, chicken, ham, and sausage on a pile of seasoned rice.

Fish-camp-fare-frowners come for open-pit barbecue, including ribs, chicken, and shrimp. What we saw on other people's plates looked good, but the opportunity to indulge in so much seafood precluded a sample.

When we said "too popular," we meant that chances are good you will have to wait for a table at any normal suppertime. It's a big place with four dining rooms, but reservations are not accepted. Waiting facilities are an open-air deck where cool frozen drinks (and sweet tea in mason jars) are served. The place is in a restored old home where the walls are decorated with antique fishing gear, snakeskins, stuffed animals, and cracker memorabilia, and where the outside view at the edge of the Intracoastal Waterway is an ideal background for a romantic dinner.

T-Ray's Burger Station

202 S. Eighth St.   904-261-6310
Fernandina Beach, FL   BL | $

It's easy to drive right past T-Ray's. It looks like every other Exxon station . . . except for the fact that there are a whole lot of cars circled around every day about breakfast and lunch times. That's because inside this ultra-casual eatery are some of the best down-home meals around, at prices that are rock-bottom.

As its name suggests, burgers are the house specialty. They come in two sizes and dressed in many ways. We like the Big T Bacon Burger—extremely juicy and full-flavored. For beef-frowners there is a portobello mushroom burger, and there are salads and fried chicken and delicious cheese grits, too. Locals know T-Ray's as the place to get superb chicken and dumplings every Thursday as well as classic banana pudding for dessert every day. And they flock here in the morning for masterful hot-from-the-oven biscuits.

Dine at the counter or one of the mismatched tables. Ray's the guy who does the cooking. His father, Terrell, runs the gas station.

Vega's Cafe

1835 E. Colonial Dr.   407-898-5196
Orlando, FL   BL | $

The place that is now Vega's started as a gas station. Today it is the best informal Cuban restaurant in central Florida. For the price of a soulless Happy Meal, you can walk into this friendly little fast-food shop and not only satisfy your hunger, but also uplift your spirit with the joy of real food and a staff of people who care.

There are soups and sandwiches of all kinds, as well as chicken and beef platters, but the one must-eat dish is a Cuban sandwich. Thin slices of sweet ham, moist fresh pork, and Swiss cheese (nearly melting from the warmth of the other ingredients) are combined with dill pickles and mustard in a length of glorious Cuban bread (baked in Tampa and imported daily) that is toasted until fragile-crisp and buttered while still warm so the butter simply becomes part of the fleecy interior. This magic combination of ingredients is simply one of the great sandwiches anywhere. A whole one is a giant meal. A half, with a side of black beans and rice, is a perfect lunch . . . with caramelized flan and a cup of high-octane espresso for dessert.

(Special thanks to Jerry Weeks of Nashville for tipping us off to this fine restaurant, which is all too easy to drive right past.)

Blue Willow Inn

294 N. Cherokee Rd.   404-464-0599
Social Circle, GA   LD | $$

Having spent our adult lives driving several million miles around the country looking for memorable regional restaurants, we can say without hesitation that the Blue Willow Inn is one of the best. In a spacious room of multiple serving tables, customers pile plates with meals that define Sunday supper southern-style.

The place itself is magnificent: a grand Dixie mansion that is said to have inspired Margaret Mitchell to conceive of Tara in *Gone with the Wind*. And although meal service is help-yourself, the serving staff couldn't be more gracious. "We have two rules," says the waitress when you are seated at a table and receive your sweet iced tea (known as the champagne of the South). "Rule one is that no one goes home hungry. Rule two is that everybody has to have at least two desserts."

Guests are given a plate and invited to return to the serving tables as often as possible to help themselves. The beautiful vista of food includes such must-eats as fried chicken, exemplary fried green tomatoes, collard greens that are long-cooked to porky tenderness, chicken and dumplings, and, of course, biscuits. Using a recipe from Sema Wilkes's legendary boarding house in Savannah, the Blue Willow kitchen creates tan-crusted domes with fluffy insides and a compelling fresh-from-the-oven aroma. Their tops are faintly knobby because the dough is patted out rather than rolled.

For dessert, there are pies, cakes, cookies, and pudding, but the one we recommend (assuming you have a smidgen of appetite by the end of the meal) is warm fruit cobbler. The inn provides rocking chairs on its broad front porch for postprandial snoozing.

The Crab Shack

40 Estill Hammock Rd.   912-786-9857

Tybee Island, GA   LD | $$

It may not be the most romantic come-on in the restaurant world, but what Roadfooder could resist the Crab Shack's catchphrase, "Where the Elite Eat in Their Bare Feet"?

Need we say that this is not a formal dining room? Park among heaps of oyster shells and eat off paper plates at picnic tables to the sound of Jimmy Buffett tunes. Toss your shells and refuse into big garbage bins provided. The deckside view of the broad tidal creek is lovely—a true waterside picnic—but even lovelier are the great heaps of sloppy, hands-on seafood that Savannahians come to gobble up with beer and/or frozen margaritas.

The fundamentals include boiled shrimp (served the low country way with corn, potatoes, and sausage), steamers by the bucket, raw oysters on the half-shell, crawfish in season, and your choice from a list of four kinds of boiled crab: Alaskan, blue, golden, or, when available, stone crab (claws only, of course). In addition to these simple seafoods, the Crab Shack offers deviled crabs, crab stew, and shrimp and crab au gratin. Couples can always opt for a shellfish feast for two: mountains of whatever's in season accompanied by corn, potatoes, and sausage.

Dillard House

Off US 441   706-746-5348

Dillard, GA   BLD | $$

Dillard House is the Disney World of restaurants—it is huge, it is fun, and you'll likely wait in line. Located in the beautiful foothills of the Blue Ridge Mountains, it is a vacation complex that includes a motel, riding stables, and an amazing family-style eatery where large groups of people sit at large tables and help themselves to large bowls of food.

You never know exactly what you'll be served in the Dillard House dining room. The menu, which is written on a blackboard that you can watch as you wait for a table, changes as all the pork cutlets are eaten up and country steak takes their place, or as fried okra is erased and replaced with butter beans. It is almost certain that among the three entrees always available there will be fried chicken and country ham. Vegetables, many of which come from the Dillard family garden, are served in abundance, and you will have your choice from among at least a half-dozen, including squash soufflé, black-eyed peas, and stupendously rich steamed cabbage. Don't miss the calico salad, a refreshing mix of pickled tomatoes and cucumbers. Also, there are dinner rolls, biscuits, peach cobbler for dessert, and iced tea in Mason jars.

Lunch and dinner are deeply satisfying. Breakfast at Dillard House is awesome. Eggs are merely a minor note in a repertoire that includes sausage, ham with red-eye gravy, bacon, and pork tenderloin, fried potatoes, grits, stewed apples, biscuits with sausage gravy, cinnamon rolls, and blueberry muffins. Like the other meals, it is an all-you-can-eat affair; and it is an excellent opportunity to store up ballast if you plan to spend the day whitewater rafting on the nearby Chattooga River.

Don's Bar-B-Que

217 E. US 80   912-748-8400
Pooler, GA   LD | $

"I'm most certainly a barbecue snob," wrote Meg Butler in her recommendation of Don's, which she described as a "tiny shack, great for lunch." If, indeed, one were a Deep South barbecue snob, Don's might prove a little disconcerting, as the meat served here is more North Carolina–style—pulled pork hacked to smithereens, dressed with a thin, tangy pepper sauce, and best eaten in a bun. On the side you want onion rings and the thing to drink is sweet tea served as per local custom in gigantic portions.

Don's is a minuscule place with barely room for a dozen people inside. But there is plenty of room for al fresco dining at outdoor picnic tables.

Edna's

Hwy. 411 S   706-695-4968
Chatsworth, GA   LD | $

Mobbed at lunch with locals and visitors to Georgia's northern mountains, a little less crowded at suppertime, Edna's is a meat-and-three feast.
That means that every day there is a short list of entrees and a long list of
vegetables, from which you choose one main course and three side
dishes. In many meat-and-three restaurants, it is the vegetables that matter, and some customers forget the meat altogether, getting a four-
vegetable plate for lunch.

At Edna's the all-vegetable strategy would be a big mistake. We don't
know about the meat loaf or the country-fried steak, but we can tell you
that the fried chicken is delicious, a fact that becomes apparent if you
look around the restaurant and note that probably half the clientele
choose it. Edna's logo is a chicken wearing a chef's toque with the procla-
mation, "Our chicken dinners are worth crowing about."

The side-dish list includes not only vegetables such as mashed potatoes, fried potatoes, green beans, pole beans, etc., but also mac and
cheese and Jell-O salads. And whatever you get, it comes with a corn
bread muffin that crumbles very nicely over a heap of cooked greens. For
dessert, the star of the show is Edna's peanut butter pie—a grand ode to
the Georgia goober.

The GA Pig

Route 17 and I-95 (Exit 29 for Jekyll Island)   912-427-2628
Brunswick, GA   LD | $

On the sign of the GA Pig you see a merry pig playing a fiddle and doing
a jig. You, too, will dance for joy when you eat at this oh-so-convenient
restaurant just yards from the exit ramp off Interstate 95. The perfume of
hickory and sweet meat that laces the air tells you that you are in pork
country; and GA Pig pork, slow-cooked over hickory wood, basted with
a tongue-teasing red sauce, then hacked into juicy hunks and shreds to be
served on a platter or stuffed into a sandwich, is soul-of-the-South classic. There are ribs, too, a joy to gnaw, and on the side, sorghum-sweet
barbecue beans.

A fun place to stop, the GA Pig is log-cabin rustic with picnic-table seating and a genuine pine grove set back from the road for al fresco dining. Eating here is a welcome break from the monotony of highway travel, or if you are really in a hurry, you can get anything to go and pig out as you drive along the highway. However you experience the GA Pig, we guarantee you will find a sweet place for it in your bank of culinary memories.

Harold's Barbecue

171 McDonough Blvd. SE   404-627-9268
Atlanta, GA   LD | $

Harold's is one of the South's grand old smoke pits, with a reputation built on velvet-soft sliced pork, racks of meaty ribs, and bowls of old-fashioned Brunswick stew. Outside a cheerful pig in sunglasses occupies the sign by the side of the road—a beacon of comfort in an otherwise scary neighborhood near Atlanta's federal prison. Although it is a stark building with bars on every window, Harold's interior has a comforting patina of age and hickory smoke. The wood-paneled walls are hung with earnest religious homilies, including this one above the door to the rear dining room: "God has time to listen if you have time to pray."

Tables are comfortable, but we much prefer seats at the worn black counter to the right as you enter. Here you see the wood-fired pit, where just-sliced barbecue is heated over hot coals and white bread for sandwiches is toasted until light brown. It is a mesmerizing sight, unchanged for decades.

The sliced pork is unbelievably tender and fairly glowing with the subtle perfume of wood smoke; pork ribs come as a magnificent rack—ultra-thick, heavily glazed with beguiling sauce, their crusty-lush meat pulling off the bone in messy strips. On the side of any platter come squares of excellent, gritty-textured corn bread and a small bowl of Brunswick stew loaded with meat, corn, and tomato shreds. A couple of items we've yet to try off Harold's menu, but hope to someday: barbecue salad (green salad topped with pork and sauce) and a stew dog (a hot dog blanketed in Brunswick stew).

Hot Thomas' Barbeque and Peach Orchard

3753 Hwy. 15

Watkinsville, GA

706-769-6550

LD Mon–Sat | $

Hot Thomas' used to be only a peach orchard. It's still in the middle of fruit-growing country, and inside the restaurant you can buy jams, chutney, and syrup made from peaches and bearing the Hot Thomas brand.

The main reason for coming to this sunbleached white building in Watkinsville, outside Athens, is to eat pork. Step up to the counter and order a plate, and while it is being assembled, nab yourself a Coke or Mr. PiBB from the cooler.

Find a seat and fork into delicious hickory-cooked pork, hacked to smithereens with a good measure of "Mr. Brown" (crusty dark meat from the outside) laced among the supple, sweet pieces from the center of the shoulder. Traditional Georgia side dishes to accompany this lovely entree (really, the only one on the menu) include Brunswick stew (a kind of tomato-onion-and-some-other-vegetable mélange with a mild pork flavor), sweet coleslaw, and soft white bread suitable for dunking in the stew and mopping up hot sauce. The sauce is available mild, hot, and extra hot, that last one being *extra* hot with a breathtaking pepper punch. Like the peach products, sauce is available in bottles to take home.

Len Berg's

240 Old Post Office Alley

Macon, GA

912-742-9255

L | $

A tip of our hats to Roadfooder Anne Peck, who clued us in to Len Berg's, which has been Macon's favorite downtown lunchroom since 1908. If we were to make a list of those restaurants that epitomize the glory of café lunch in Dixie, Len Berg's would be at the top—a great place to eat a civilized, inexpensive, and delicious southern meal.

The menu varies daily and as vegetables come in and out of season, but you can count on fried chicken with steamed cabbage and stewed apples on the side, meat loaf with mashed potatoes and a heap of likker-sopped turnip greens, shrimp Creole on rice with hamhock-flavored snap beans, creamed corn, and bright hunks of flavorful garden tomato. Every meal comes with warm yeast rolls and corn sticks.

For dessert, the macaroon pie can't be beat, and there is bright, sweet strawberry shortcake, but if you come anytime after June 1, there is only one proper way to end a meal—with Len Berg's fresh peach ice cream. Every summer, Macon citizens watch the newspaper for a small advertisement that says simply, "H.M.F.P.I.C. You know where." Translated, that means, "Home Made Fresh Peach Ice Cream" . . . and everyone who likes to eat for miles around does know exactly where.

Please note that the original Len Berg's is open only for lunch. A newer, take-out restaurant with the same good food (but without the vintage charm of the little dining rooms and white-coated waiters) is at 2395 Ingleside Avenue, and is open from 11:00 A.M. to 8:00 P.M., Monday through Saturday.

Love's Seafood

6817 Basin Rd.   912-925-3616
Savannah, GA   D | $$

Overlooking the Ogeechee River south of the city, Love's has been a destination for catfish lovers for some sixty years. It's been remodeled and expanded into a big, comfortable family restaurant with an especially inviting glass-enclosed porch with a dramatic sunset view.

The menu is huge, ranging from appetizers of alligator fingers and terrific calamari, crawfish étouffée and seafood gumbo, to steaks and seafood platters of all kinds, but it is catfish that's the big draw. For under $20, you can get an all-you-can-eat platter that is sweet and fresh and moist inside a crisp gold crust. It comes with potatoes, rice or grits, vegetables, and big steamy hush puppies. If you're here with a date who also has a big appetite, Love's offers a Captain's Platter for Two. That includes catfish and adds flounder, shrimp, oysters, scallops, and crab balls.

Warning: If you are impatient and want to eat on a weekend night, Love's can be a problem. A wait for a table of thirty minutes or more is not uncommon. Such is the price of success.

Mamie's Kitchen

1294 S. Main St. NE   770-922-0131
Conyers, GA   BL | $

Jack Howard started in the biscuit business in 1962 when he opened a small eat-shack in an industrial section of Atlanta. Named for a skillful cook he then employed who was able to fry sixty dozen eggs in a morning, Mamie's Kitchen has since expanded to four locations east of the city. "In the early days, I used to go to the mountains and buy big cakes of butter from the farmers," Jack recalls. "I brought jars of preserves they made and put them on my tables. My slogan was, 'I am rolling in dough.' "

When we ask Jack to explain why his biscuits are so good, he says, "We don't roll them with a rolling pin; we don't cut them with a can; we don't make them from a recipe." He lifts a hot one off its paper plate and cups it in one hand, using a deft twist of his other hand to separate its top and raise it like he's a Tiffany jeweler showing what's inside a ring box. A buttermilk-scented cloud of steam wafts up. "This is what you call a 'scratch biscuit,' " he continues. "It is made from nothing but White Lily flour, buttermilk, and lard. Pure, refined lard," he emphasizes. "Enough of each goes into a big bowl where your biscuit maker kneads the dough, but not too much. She knows when to pull one off, pat it out, and put it in the pan." Six days a week, 1,500 to 2,000 biscuits are made this way at Mamie's Kitchen of Conyers, from before the doors open at 5:30 A.M. until closing time at 2:00 P.M.

Any time you order a biscuit at Mamie's, it comes hot from the oven. Its knobby golden surface has a gentle crunch, and although the inside is fleecy, it is not fragile. While it is delicious plain or simply buttered, you can also get it topped with sausage gravy or sandwiching streak o' lean or fried chicken. Its greatest glory is to be pulled into two circular, gold-topped halves so it can sandwich a slice or two of deliriously flavorful country ham grilled until its rim of fat becomes translucent amber and the brick-red surface starts to turn crisp. The power of the ham—its complexity, its salty punch, its rugged chewy texture—is perfectly complemented by the fluffy biscuit around it.

Mary Mac's Tea Room

224 Ponce de Leon Ave.   404-876-1800
Atlanta, GA   LD | $$

We lifted a fried chicken breast off the plate and bit into it. As the crust crunched, juices spurted everywhere. Full-flavored, inside and out, dark meat or white, this just might be the best fried chicken in the South.

Mary Mac's Tea Room inspires superlatives. Originally opened in 1945, it is an old-fashioned urban lunchroom in the heart of Atlanta that offers a broad menu of dishes that exemplify Dixie cooking at its best.

You can start your meal with a bowl of pot likker—that's heaps of soft turnip greens wallowing in their flavorful cooking liquid—sided by a corn bread muffin. Entrees include such classics as baked chicken with cornbread dressing, pork barbecue with Brunswick stew, and country-fried steak with gravy.

The list of side dishes is a joy unto itself; many customers come to eat a four-vegetable plate with no meat at all. Stand-outs include a sweet potato soufflé that is spiced Christmas-sweet, macaroni and cheese in which the noodles are suspended in an eggy cheese soufflé, fried green tomatoes, hoppin' John, and crisp-fried okra.

An airy place with soothing pastel yellow walls and tables covered with white oilcloth, Mary Mac's offers old-style tea room service, which is great fun. When you sit down, you are given an order pad and menus. Once you've made your decisions, you write your own order and hand it to your waiter or waitress, who, in the meanwhile, has brought you an immense tankard of what the menu lists as the table wine of the South—sweet iced tea.

Melear's

Hwy. 85   770-461-7180
Fayetteville, GA   BLD | $

Melear has been a big name in Georgia barbecue since 1927, when John Melear opened a smokehouse in LaGrange. The Melear's south of Atlanta goes back more than forty years, and is open seven days a week, even for breakfast Monday through Saturday.

Pork is the meat of choice, chopped, mixed with a bit of peppery vinegar sauce, and served in a sandwich, on a tray, or as a dish with the irresistible name "bowl of pork." The sandwich is notable because it comes on grilled slices of bread (as opposed to barbecue's usual spongy-white companion slices), adding a nice crunch to the sandwich experience. The same pork, but more of it, is the anchor for a full-bore barbecue dinner that also includes potato chips, pickles, white bread, and rib-sticking Brunswick stew. Extra-hot sauce is available, and it is good, but Melear's pork has a fine, subtle flavor that we believe is better complemented by the mild version.

To accompany Melear's classic "Q" the proper beverage is iced tea—dazzlingly presweetened, as is the custom in this part of the country, presented in tumblers that are a full foot tall and about half again as wide at the mouth. When you get to the bottom of this tub, it is refilled on the house, and it will continue to be refilled for as long as you are parked in a high-backed chair at one of Melear's aged wood tables eating barbecue.

Mrs. Wilkes' Dining Room

107 W. Jones St.   912-233-8970
Savannah, GA   L | $

West Jones Street is a boulevard of antique brick houses with curving steps and graceful cast iron banisters. At eleven o'clock each morning a line begins to form at 107. Although there is no commercial sign outside, the serious student of Roadfood can tell you what is going on. At 11:30, the doors of 107 open and the lunch crowd finds seats at one of the large tables shared by strangers. And so begins the daily feast, boarding-house-style.

The tabletops are crowded with platters of fried chicken and corn bread dressing, sweet potato soufflés, black-eyed peas, okra gumbo, corn muffins, and biscuits. As at any southern feast worth its cracklin' corn bread, there are constellations of vegetable casseroles: great, gooey, buttery bowls full of squash au gratin and scalloped eggplant, cheese grits, corn pudding, pineapple-flavored yams topped with melted marshmallows, creamed corn enriched with bacon drippings, green rice (mixed with broccoli and celery); brown rice (with mushrooms and soy sauce); and the low-country legend, Savannah red rice (with tomatoes). The food comes fast, and everybody eats fast in a spirit of joyful camaraderie.

When Mrs. Wilkes first started serving meals in this dining room in 1943, there were many similar places in cities throughout the region, where boarders as well as frugal local citizens gathered to enjoy the special pleasure of a meal shared with neighbors and strangers. Now, the take-some-and-pass-the-bowl style of the old boarding house is a rarity. Mrs. Wilkes' is a prized opportunity to indulge in the delicious dining style of a culinary tradition that values sociability as much as a good macaroni salad.

Sconyers Bar-B-Que

2250 Sconyers Way   706-790-5411
Augusta, GA   LD Thurs-Sat only | $$

Sconyers is an immense barbecue complex with seating for hundreds in multiple dining rooms, plus drive-through service. Hams are cooked a full twenty-four hours over oak and hickory, resulting in meat that is ridiculously tender and bathed in its own smoke-perfumed juices. Curiously, it is a lot like Lexington-style barbecue, but with a sauce that has more of a pepper punch. It comes on a plate along with hash and rice, pickles and coleslaw, and plenty of nice soft white bread for mopping, or in a sandwich or à la carte by the pound.

If the luxury of traditional pork is too rich for your blood, Sconyers has added something called T-loin, which is billed as 96 percent fat-free, low sodium, and low cholesterol "choice pork." Someday perhaps we will try it. Ribs, chopped beef, turkey, and chicken are also available off the pit. Sweet tea is, of course, the most popular thing to drink.

Silver Skillet

200 14th St.   404-874-1388
Atlanta, GA   BL | $

The Silver Skillet is a charismatic blast from the past, a funky 1950s diner with glass windows that tilt outward like mid-century tailfins. Booths are upholstered in green and orange Naugahyde, tables topped with boomerang-pattern Formica, and the clientele ranges from blue-collar boys in overalls to visiting celebrities with entourage in tow.

The South gets hot. Refreshment is essential. One of the great warm-weather tongue-icers, popular at barbecues and in plate-lunch places throughout the region, is lemon icebox pie. There is none better than the one served at the Silver Skillet. And we do mean the one, because most days there is only a single pie available, and after it is sliced and served (often before noon), you are out of luck. Cool, creamy, and neatly poised between sugar-sweet and lemon-zesty, this pie is a superlative exclamation point after a meal of country ham, biscuits, and red-eye gravy.

The Varsity Drive-In

61 North Ave.   404-881-1706
Atlanta, GA   BLD | $

Anyone who loves all-American food and has spent any time in Atlanta knows about the Varsity Drive-In . . . and most people have their own personal stories about wonderful meals and good times they've had there. These extravagant tales tend to relate to the fact that the Varsity is huge and it is fast, the thrills commencing when you step up to the counter and an order-taker accosts you with the command, "What'll ya have?"

Hot dogs are the house specialty—little pink tube steaks served in steamy-soft buns, begging to be dolled up with condiments. The prime adornment is chili, a finely pulverized brew that perfectly complements either dog or burger. Chili dogs are customarily served with a line of mustard across their tops, and they are known among the staff as Yankee dogs, for their yellow streak. Dogs are customarily accompanied by cardboard boats full of crusty onion rings and/or excellent French fries.

To drink, there's a full menu of reliable southern favorites: ice cold buttermilk, gigantic cups full of Coke, PCs, and FOs. PC is Varsity lingo for chocolate milk ("plain chocolate") as opposed to a chocolate milkshake (with ice cream). FO means frosted orange, which is the Varsity version of a California smoothie, reminiscent of a Creamsicle-in-a-cup. With or without chili dogs, frosted oranges are one heck of a way to keep cool.

Lest you have any doubts, this is health food. Varsity founder Frank Gordy, who lived well into his seventies, once proclaimed, "A couple of chili dogs a day keep you young."

Bon Ton Café

401 Magazine St.   504-524-3386

New Orleans, LA   LD | $$$

Magazine Street was laid out in 1788; the building holding the Bon Ton Café is slightly newer, going back to the 1840s. The restaurant opened in 1953. Its menu is old-time Cajun, which means a rustic Louisiana cuisine that is *not* kicked up a notch, not overspiced or overhyped or blackened or infused, but simply delicious. This is the place to know the joy of crawfish étouffée, an unspeakably luscious meal especially in May, the peak of the season when crawdads are plumpest. You can have étouffée as a main course or as one part of a wonderfully monomaniacal meal of bisque, étouffée, Newburg, jambalaya, and an omelet, each of which is made with crawfish. Or you can start dinner with an appetizer of fried crawfish tails. They look like little fried shrimp, but taste like shrimp's much richer relatives.

Dinner begins with the delivery of a loaf of hot French bread, tightly wrapped in a white napkin. When the napkin is unfurled, the bread's aroma swirls around the table. Then comes soup—either peppery okra gumbo made with shrimp and crab or turtle soup into which the waitress pours a shot of sherry. Other than crawfish in any form, the great entree is redfish Bon Ton, which is a thick fillet sautéed until just faintly crisp, served under a heap of fresh crabmeat and three gigantic fried onion rings. For dessert, you want bread pudding, which is a dense, warm square of sweetness studded with raisins and drenched with whiskey sauce.

A big, square, brick-walled room with red-checked tablecloths, Bon Ton is soothingly old-fashioned. There is no music, just the sounds of knife, fork, and spoon and happy conversation, interspersed with the occasional ringing of the pay phone at the back near the bar. Service, by a staff of uniformed professionals, is gracious and Dixie-sweet. As we prepared to take a picture of our redfish, a waitress rushed over and insisted on taking the picture herself, so she could include the two of us along with the lovely meal.

Borden's

1103 Jefferson   337-235-9291

Lafayette, LA $

"What is a frappe?" we asked as we studied the drink section of the posted movable-letter menu above the counter at Borden's dairy bar.

"That's frapp-AY," replied the mixologist, a soda-fountain veteran to whom the differences among a shake, malt, freeze, flip, frappe, and soda are elementary. She explained that here in Lafayette, a frappe is four scoops of ice cream and your choice of flavor, blended together. It is like a milkshake without the milk. "You eat it with a spoon," she advised.

Nice as that sounds, we went for a traditional chocolate malt. It was a pleasure to watch her assemble ingredients in the tall cup with aplomb, then tend the cup as the mixer strained to whir them all together. It was a lot of work rearranging it round and round, up and down and at a cant so that unblended clods of ice cream were hit by the blades. The ultimate result: a classic malt, served with spoon and straw, with nary a single hunk of unmixed ice cream.

Sundaes are masterfully made, too—but served, alas, like the shakes, in paper cups rather than traditional soda fountain glassware. Among the broad choice of toppings, we are partial to hot fudge, marshmallow cream, and syrupy "wet nuts."

This old ice cream shop with its deco-stucco exterior is a blast from the past, and not only for the soda-jerking expertise of the lady behind the counter. It is in fact a genuine Borden's dairy store, complete with cartoon images of mascot Elsie the Cow above the entryway and seating at five booths upholstered in lipstick-red leatherette.

Boudin King
906 W. Division St.   337-824-6593
Jennings, LA   BLD | $

Yes, the boudin at Boudin King is wonderful—densely packed, spicy, and deeply satisfying. Buy it mild or hot, by the link; it is a Cajun classic. But so is just about everything else on the menu of this unlikely source of greatness. We say "unlikely" because Boudin King appears to be a fast-food restaurant, even including a drive-through window. Meals are served on disposable plates. Prices are little more than McJunkfood.

And yet here is stupendously good gumbo, smoky-flavored and thick with sausage and big pieces of chicken. And speaking of chicken, we would rate the fried chicken served by Boudin King as some of the most delicious in southern Louisiana, a part of the world where frying chicken is a fine, fine art. Other specialties include crawfish in the spring and nice fried pies for dessert.

The late Ellis Cormier, who founded this place back in the 1970s, once told us, "Nowhere else in America, except perhaps where the Mexicans live, is food properly spiced." Monsieur Cormier was one of the leading lights in America's rediscovery of its regional food, of Cajun food in particular. It was primarily thanks to his good cooking that in 1979 the Louisiana State Legislature proclaimed Jennings "The Boudin Capital of the Universe."

Brenda's Diner
409 W. Pershing   337-367-0868
New Iberia, LA   BLD | $

Brenda's brought tears of joy to our eyes. "It doesn't get better than this," we agreed out loud halfway through lunch of fried chicken, fried pork chops, red beans with sausage, rice and gravy, candied yams, and smothered cabbage. Each dish Brenda Placide had cooked was the best version of itself that we have had since, maybe, forever. The pork chop was audibly juicy with a tender taste that had us gnawing to the bone. The chicken's fragile crust shored in juice-dripping meat. The red beans were

New Iberia *hot;* the smothered cabbage, speckled with nuggets of garlicky sausage, brought high honor to the vegetable kingdom.

We ate this soul-stirring food in a tidy little dining room where a CD of southern gospel music set a rapturous tone. There are seats for no more than twenty people. The neighborhood is run-down, but the diner is immaculate inside; the walls are a gallery of Brenda's gratitude: prints and posters celebrating African American culture, as well as photos marking the achievements of Brenda's kin (graduations, weddings, reunions).

We had to ask her how she cooks such magnificent food, but we weren't surprised when she had no satisfactory answer. "It's from my mamma's kitchen," she said. "I cannot tell you how to do it because she never taught me to measure anything. You add seasoning and spice until it's right." It occurred to us that even if we studied Brenda as she cooked, taking scrupulous notes about every grain of every ingredient she used, we couldn't in a lifetime make food like this. It would be like watching Isaac Stern play the violin, then copying his every move.

Café des Amis

140 E. Bridge St.   337-332-5273
Breaux Bridge, LA   BLD | $$

A sign in the window of Café des Amis boasts that it is "the essence of French Louisiana." It's the real deal, all right, a French-accented mix of South and Soul, with a dash of Caribbean spice and Italian brio. But it's ridiculous to try to define it by its roots; better to describe what it is.

At breakfast, it is beignets, little crisp-edged twists of fried dough under an avalanche of powdered sugar, or *Oreille de Couchon*, a long strip of fried dough named because it resembles a pig's ear, available plain or filled with boudin, also spread with powdered sugar. Also at breakfast, it is biscuits topped with crawfish étouffée, omelets filled with tasso ham, and cheese grits with andouille sausage.

The menu for lunch and supper is a veritable encyclopedia of local favorites, including turtle soup, andouille gumbo, barbecue shrimp, corn bread filled with crawfish tails, softshell crab, and crawfish pie. Desserts include bread pudding with rum sauce, which is more of a New Orleans thing than a Cajun one, and *gateau sirop*, which is extremely local. Made from sugarcane—grown and processed all around here—it is a block of moist spice cake with the distinctive smoky sweetness of cane sugar.

A friendly old brick-wall storefront that has been renovated to serve as an art gallery and live-music venue as well as a restaurant, Café des Amis is a gathering place for locals (who love swilling the excellent strong coffee) and an easy destination for passersby, just a short drive off I-10. If you are looking for a full, true, and joyous taste of Acadian Louisiana, you'll find none more satisfying than this.

Café du Monde

813 Decatur St.	504-581-2914
New Orleans, LA	Always open | $

Café du Monde is a New Orleans institution, serving café au lait and beignets to locals and tourists for more than a century and a half. It is always open, and the characters you'll meet here—any time of day, but especially at odd hours in the middle of the night—are among the Crescent City's most colorful. The best seating is outdoors, where the chances are you will be serenaded by street musicians of the French Quarter as you sit under the awning and watch life go by.

There is not much to the menu: chickory coffee, either black or au lait (with a lot of milk), white or chocolate milk, orange juice, and beignets. Beignets are wonderful: square, hole-less donuts, served hot from the fry kettle and heaped with powdered sugar.

After leisurely coffee-sipping and beignet-eating, you can buy New Orleans souvenirs inside the restaurant, then stroll across Decatur Street to the place where fortune tellers, tarot card readers, and palmists set up shop every evening and, for the right price, reveal your future.

Casamento's

4330 Magazine St.	504-895-9761
New Orleans, LA	LD (closed in summer) | $$

Oyster loaves are served throughout New Orleans and the Cajun country of the South, and we've yet to find one that's bad. But for the best, loaf-lovers go to Casamento's. Oysters aren't the only item of note on the menu of this spanking-clean neighborhood oyster bar that closes for a long vacation in summer, when oysters aren't in season. You can also have fried fish and shrimp and springtime soft-shelled crabs, and there's even a plate of that arcane Creole Italian meal, daube, which is flaps of pot roast in gravy on spaghetti noodles.

Casamento's oyster loaf is nothing short of magnificent: a dozen crackle-crusted hotties piled between two big slabs of what New Orleans cooks know as pan bread, aka Texas toast. Each single oyster is a joy, its brittle skin shattering with light pressure, giving way to a wave of melting warm, briny oyster meat across the tongue. When we asked proprietor Joe Gerdes what made his oysters so especially good, he modestly replied that his method is "too simple to call a recipe." Of course he uses freshly shucked local oysters, and he does recommend frying in lard, but the real secret is ineffable. "Everything is fried by feel and sound," he said. "It requires a lot of personal attention and experience."

Central Grocery

923 Decatur St.   504-523-1620
New Orleans, LA   LD | $

The name "muffuletta" once referred only to a chewy round loaf of bread turned out by Italian bakeries in New Orleans. Grocery stores that sold the bread got the fine idea to slice it horizontally and pile it with salami, ham, and provolone, then top that with a wickedly spicy mélange of chopped green and black olives fragrant with anchovies and garlic. The place that claims to have done it first is the Central Grocery on Decatur Street.

While it has become something of a tourist attraction and muffulettas are the only sandwich on the menu, the Central Grocery still feels like a neighborhood store, its yellowed walls decorated with travel posters, the air inside smelling of garlic and sausage and provolone cheese. Shelves are stocked with imported olive oils, sauces, and pasta—reminders that New Orleans' largest ethnic group (as well as some of its best Creole cooking) is Italian.

There is no table service at the Central Grocery. You step up to the counter and give your order, at which time the sandwich makers go to work assembling it—an exacting process you can watch from where you stand. Once the sandwich is ready, it is cut into quarters (enough for four normal appetites) and wrapped, at which point you can take it to a counter toward the back of the store to unwrap and eat it.

Champagne's Breaux Bridge Bakery

105 Poydras St.

337-332-1117

Breaux Bridge, LA

BL | $

This charming nineteenth-century one-room bakery in the crawfish capital of the world caused us to stomp the brakes as we drove past early in the morning. The smell of just-baked bread was irresistible. Inside the door, a small card table was arrayed with loaves. They are the familiar-looking south-Louisiana torpedoes, like French baguettes but about half the weight. Some are wrapped in paper, the others in plastic bags. "You want soft, you get the plastic," advised the gent behind the counter. "For crisp, paper." Our paper-wrapped loaf had a refined crunch to its crust and ineffably feathery insides. It's delicious just to eat, but oh, how well this would scoop out to be become a seafood boat filled with fried oysters or shrimp!

Cooked meat pies were displayed along the bakery counter, and good as they looked, we hesitated about getting one because who wants a cold meat pie? "We have a microwave," said the woman behind the counter.

"Lots of people, they come in and they take two or three hot, to eat," said the man who had been our bread counselor. The warmed one we took out to the car was nothing short of spectacular: rich, moist, and vividly spiced.

We also walked away with a bag full of sugar cookies and one big, flat cookie filled with coconut. Delicious!

D.I.'s

Hwy. 97

337-432-5141

Basile, LA

LD | $$

Big round beer trays heaped with crawfish emerge from the kitchen trailing hot spiced steam through the dining room as accordion notes with a triangle beat bounce from the bandstand. Set back from the two-lane in the middle of nothing but rice fields and crawfish ponds, far from any town or major highway, D.I.'s is a brimful measure of Acadian pleasure. If it hadn't been for Sulphur, Louisiana, policeman and good friend Major Many McNeil, we never, ever would have come across it. When we told Many we were on the lookout for a true Cajun eating experience, he said D.I.'s was it.

Daniel Isaac ("D.I.") Fruge has been known to neighbors for his well-seasoned crawdads since the 1970s. He was a rice and soybean farmer who began harvesting the mudbugs, boiling and serving them on weekends to friends and neighbors: $5 for all you could eat. They were served in his barn the traditional way—strewn in heaps across bare tables—with beer to drink on the side.

D.I. and his wife, Sherry, now run a restaurant with a full menu that includes steaks, crabs, oysters, frog legs, flounder, and shrimp, but vividly spiced crawfish are the star attraction. The classic way to enjoy them is boiled and piled onto a beer tray—a messy meal that rewards vigorous tail-pulling and head-sucking with an unending procession of the vibrant sweetwater richness that only crawdads deliver. You can have them crisp-fried into bite-size morsels with a salty crunch, and there are crawfish pie, étouffée, and bisque.

No longer a makeshift annex to Monsieur Fruge's barn, D.I.'s is a spacious destination with multiple dining rooms and dance floor. The Cajun music starts at 7:00 P.M., with an open-mike jam session Wednesday.

Domilise's Po-Boys

5240 Annunciation St.   504-899-9126
New Orleans, LA   L | $

You won't likely drive past Domilise's bar/sandwich shop by accident, for it is located in a very unscenic blue-collar neighborhood by the river, and if you did accidentally drive by, you'd never guess that it was source of some of New Orleans's best sandwiches. From the outside it looks like a small, no-frills neighborhood tavern, and in some ways, that is what it is. We guess it would be possible to walk in, sit at the bar, and knock back longnecks or boilermakers all day long. To do so, you'd have to have no sense of smell, for the air of this tavern is wildly perfumed with its true claim to fame: great po-boy ingredients. Shrimp, oysters, and catfish are heaped hot from the fry basket onto loaves of bread. Po-boys are also available made from all manner of cold cuts.

When you walk in, you may have to take a number before you can place your order. At the height of lunch hour, Domilise's is packed, for its superior po-boys attract eaters from all over the city; table space is precious (strangers often share); and the house phone rings unanswered.

For the newcomer, a little delay is a good thing because it provides an opportunity to read the menu on the wall and to observe the sandwich makers construct various types of po-boys before deciding which is the right one for you. Hot smoked sausage with gravy is the one we recommend above all others. Get it "dressed," meaning topped with tomato, lettuce, and grainy Creole mustard. A large one is constructed on a length of bread so long that it must be cut in thirds to fit on its paper plate. While the sandwich is being made, buy your drink at the bar and hope that by the time you are ready to eat, space at a table is available.

Dupuy's Oyster Shop

108 S. Main St.   337-893-2336

Abbeville, LA   LD (closed Tues) | $$

There's a broad menu at Dupuy's, including sirloin steak, fried catfish, pastas, and wonderful onion rings, plus a bountiful Sunday brunch, but as the full name of the place suggests, oysters are the star attraction. The very best way to have them is raw on the half-shell by the dozen, served on a tray of ice with a full complement of condiments. Or, if you like things cooked, have them fried and stuffed into bread with mayonnaise and mustard. In addition, there is oyster stew and an intriguing grilled oyster salad.

The one other dish that is essential to eat at this friendly, always-crowded town café is Cajun seafood gumbo, a boldly spiced stew that you can practically eat with a fork.

When Dupuy's opened in 1869, the price of a dozen just-shucked oysters was a dime. Today, a dozen will cost you no more than five dollars.

Dwyer's Café

323 Jefferson St.   337-235-9364

Lafayette, LA   BL | $

No one makes lunch sound as good as Mike Dwyer does. You will hear his pitch as you approach the cafeteria area of Dwyer's Café, where he enumerates the day's choices, one by one, with enough pride and exuberance to make stomachs growl. It's a joy to hear him, but in fact, this food needs no hard sell. It is a superlative plate lunch.

Parenthetically, Dwyer's hamburgers are excellent. But it's the hot lunches we love. Dwyer's is a meat-and-three affair, the daily meats including such expertly cooked stalwarts as smothered pork chops, lengths of pork sausage, roast beef with dark gravy, and chicken-fried steak with white gravy. One day in the winter, Mike was pitching crawfish fettuccine, a fabulous cross-cultural Franco-Italian-Cajun noodle casserole loaded with crawdads. Among the notable side dishes are dirty rice, eggplant casserole, red beans, and sausage jambalaya. On cold days, you can get gumbo or chili.

Dwyer's is also a notable breakfast opportunity. We love the tender sweet potato hotcakes with their faintly crisp edge (which Mike says he added to the menu for low-carb dieters!). When you order pancakes, the waitress will ask what kind of syrup you want: cane or maple. Sugar cane is a major crop around here, and the pancake syrup made from it is thick, dark, and resonantly sweet—but not at all white-sugar sweet.

Lasyone's Meat Pie Kitchen

622 Second St.	318-352-3353
Natchitoches, LA	BLD | $

Lasyone's meat pie is a mash of pork and beef, onions and parsley, enclosed in a deep-fried half-moon pastry. Similar to a Cornish pasty but more piquant, it is practically a meal unto itself. Natchitoches used to have many places to buy meat pies—from street-corner vendors and from ladies who made them in their home kitchens and sold them from the back porch. But by the time James Lasyone opened his restaurant in 1967, meat pies were hard to find. Mr. Lasyone missed the food of his childhood, and so he rescued the idea and began making and selling his own meat pies, using a recipe that took him two years of experimentation to develop.

James Lasyone's meat pie is a vividly seasoned mélange enclosed in a crust and deep-fried until golden crisp. Most people get one for lunch, sided by "dirty rice" and a typical southern vegetable such as okra or greens, but it's not uncommon to see someone at 7:00 A.M. having a meat pie alongside a couple of fried eggs and a pile of warm grits, glistening with melted butter.

Lasyone's true Louisiana menu also lists fried seafood (shrimp, oysters), red beans and rice with spicy sausage, and such non-Creole Dixie classics as catfish platters and chicken and dumplings with corn bread and black-eyed peas. We have eaten first-rate banana pudding for dessert, but the sweet tour de force here is a dish invented by Mrs. Lasyone called Cane River cream pie—a variant of Boston cream pie, but with gingerbread instead of white cake.

Louisiana Seafood Exchange

428 Jefferson Hwy.   504-834-9395

Jefferson, LA   BL | $$

Along Jefferson Highway between two sets of train tracks, the Louisiana Seafood Exchange is a wholesale and retail seafood market with a fairly nondescript café in front. Inside this café you can eat extraordinary seafood, especially in sandwiches.

Po-boys are available normal-size (eight inches long) or king-size (foot-long), the latter big enough to feed a hungry couple, especially if filled with oysters. There must be two dozen crisp-crusted ones heaped into the loaf so copiously that you can barely see the bread beneath them. Likewise, the shrimp sandwich is overloaded with so many crisp-fried and impeccably seasoned shrimp that you want to ask for a whole other length of bread into which you can pile the overflow. And oh, the seafood muffuletta! That's shrimp and oysters and fish inside a big muffuletta loaf, dressed, preferably with lettuce, tomatoes, and mayo.

Most folks know this place as a sandwich shop; indeed, non-seafood sandwiches are as good as anywhere. But beyond sandwiches, LSE serves New Orleans plate lunches to remember: grilled tuna or tilapia, definitive jambalaya, and seafood gumbo are all on the menu, as is bread pudding for dessert.

Middendorf's

US 51 N   985-386-6666

Pass Manchac, LA   LD (closed Mon) | $$

As you might expect at a Tangipahoa Parish seafood house situated among a string of bait shops and take-out stands, Middendorf's is extremely casual, noisy, and fun. Its crowded dining rooms have long been the great country catfish destination restaurant of New Orleans, good reason to drive forty-five minutes north of town, then stand in line waiting for a table.

Middendorf's catfish is the big allure. There is nothing like it, whether you get thick or thin. Thick is a meaty cross-section of fish, similar to a steak wrapped in breading. It is sweet-smelling and has a freshwater taste that is unlike any saltwater fish. Thin catfish is more elegant than thick. Sliced into a diaphanous strip that is sharply seasoned, lightly breaded, and quickly fried, a thin cat fillet crunches loudly when you sink your teeth into its brittle crust, which is sheer enough to let the rich flavor of the fish resonate. With the catfish, thick or thin, there are perfectly good and unsurprising companions: French fries, hush puppies, and coleslaw salad.

Beyond catfish, just about any seafood on the menu is well worth eating. We have had some great gumbo here, made with shrimp and crabmeat, which was surprisingly delicate compared to the more overpowering versions sold in the city's famous gumbo houses. There are sautéed soft-shelled crabs, po-boy sandwiches, and Italian salads loaded with olives and spice.

Mosca's

4137 US 90 W   504-436-9942

Avondale, LA   D | $$$

Mosca's reopened in the summer after Hurricane Katrina, but when you drive out here to dine, you'd never even know there had been any damage. All the great things about the place are just as they were, including oysters Mosca—a festival of garlic, olive oil, Parmesan cheese, and bread crumbs—and the deliriously refreshing crabmeat and olive salad. Old-time air conditioners in the window still groan. The parking lot remains a gravel wreck, and the wait to get in at dinner is frequently an hour or longer.

It's quite a drive out to the swamp that is Mosca's location, but serious eaters from New Orleans have been doing it since 1946. If it's your first time, we guarantee you will think you are lost. And even when you find it, you will wonder: can this two-room joint with the blaring jukebox really be the most famous Creole roadhouse in America? Once oil and butter from the spaghetti bordelaise begin dripping down your chin and you inhale the fragrant bouquet of chicken à la grandee, you will know you are having a culinary epiphany. Rude as it is, roadside food gets no better, or more garlicky, or heartier, than this. Go to Mosca's with friends: the bigger the group, the more different wonders you can sample, and besides, everything is served family-style.

Mother's

401 Poydras St.
New Orleans, Louisiana

504-523-9656
BL (closed Sun & Mon) | $

Mother's remains what it has been since it opened in 1938: a blue-plate lunchroom where, for a few dollars, New Orleaneans from every rung of the social ladder come to feast. Morning grits are usually available with "debris," pronounced "day-bree," which is all the pieces of beef that fall into the gravy when a roast is carved. At lunch, in addition to definitive po-boy sandwiches, Mother's is known for red beans and rice (Tuesday), gumbo (Wednesday), jambalaya, spaghetti pie, and bread pudding with brandy sauce for dessert.

It's an everyday place where everybody waits in the cafeteria line and the staff treats each customer with nonchalant disrespect. If you are coming for lunch, we recommend visiting early. The first lunchtime customers have the opportunity to avail themselves of a lagniappe, such as cracklin's from the "black ham"—little amber squiggles and crusty sweet chunks from the outside of the baked meat—which are a brilliant addition to almost any hot lunch or sandwich.

You can have your po-boy hot or cold, made with anything from fried oysters to bologna. The most famous of Mother's po-boys and one of the Crescent City's definitive sandwiches is known as a Ferdi's special: ham, beef, debris, and gravy, preferably dressed with pickle slices, lettuce, Creole mustard, and possibly even "my'nez," which is how you say mayonnaise in New Orleans.

Prejean's

3480 I-49 N
Lafayette, LA

337-896-3247
LD | $$

"I love to eat!" wrote Louisiana Roadfooder Laura B., who told us that the next time we were in Cajun country, we needed to try the gumbo and crawfish enchiladas at Prejean's.

Thank you, Laura, for a recommendation we gladly pass on to anyone who loves to eat to the beat of a Cajun band. Located in North Lafayette, where there are good Cajun eateries galore, Prejean's is big and noisy (the live music starts every night at 7:00 P.M., and be sure to wear your dancing shoes), and the food is classic Cajun. In some other part of the country, a restaurant this brash might seem too "commercial" to qualify for Roadfood—walls hung with Acadiana, a stuffed alligator in the center of the dining room, a gift shop with tacky souvenirs—but for all its razzle-dazzle, Prejean's is the real thing, a fact about which you can have no doubt when you dip a spoon into the chicken and sausage gumbo or the dark andouille gumbo laced with smoked duck.

The menu is big and exotic, featuring dozens of dishes you won't find on menus outside Louisiana, from crisp-fried crawfish boudin balls and catfish Catahoula (stuffed with crawfish, shrimp, and crab) to eggplant "pirogues" (canoes), hollowed out, fried, and filled with crawfish and red snapper fillet, and drizzled with buttery lobster sauce. Laura's recommendation of crawfish enchiladas is a good one. The crawdads are rolled with chilies and cheese in flour tortillas, baked, and smothered in crawfish sauce with zesty "dirty rice" on the side. It is also possible to get a monomaniacal all-crawfish meal of crawfish bisque, fried crawfish, crawfish étouffée, crawfish pie, crawfish boulettes, and a salad dotted with crawfish. The one dessert you need to know about is bread pudding with Jack Daniel's sour mash sauce.

Robin's

| 1409 Henderson Hwy. | 337-228-7594 |
| Henderson, LA | LD \| $$$ |

It occurred to us as we traveled through southern Louisiana that a vast majority of restaurants have names with the possessive apostrophe. It makes sense, because these places tend to be defined by the personality of the owner/chef whose possession they are. Robin's is a perfect example. This is Lionel Robin's restaurant, with a menu that reflects his culinary taste and expertise. And chances are good that if you make any sort of inquiry about the menu or cooking techniques, you will meet Robin himself, who loves to come out of the kitchen to chat with strangers about his current culinary adventures, whether they be frozen and ready-to-heat crawfish étouffée or Tabasco ice cream.

Monsieur Robin cooks some of the most distinctive restaurant meals in swamp country. Year-round, but especially in crawfish season from early in the year through spring, this is the place to have them either simply boiled or in all the many ways Cajun chefs like to celebrate it. A crawfish dinner starts with bisque, which is smoky, complex, and rich. You then move on to a few boiled and fried ones, étouffée over rice, boulettes, stuffed pepper, and a superior pie in which the little crustaceans share space with vegetables and plenty of garlic in a translucent-thin crust.

The one crawfish dish we might not recommend here is gumbo—not because it isn't good (it is), but because the shrimp and okra gumbo is even better. And chicken and sausage gumbo, while containing none of the seafood for which Robin's is renowned, is wonderful—brilliantly spiced and thick with sausage you will remember for a long time.

Russell's Short Stop Po-Boys

119 Transcontinental Dr. 504-885-4572
Metarie, LA BLD | $

Here is a place to have gumbo and jambalaya, which in our experience are very, very good, or a po-boy, which is even better than that. In fact, this is one of the best po-boys in New Orleans. The sandwich is available in one of three sizes and comes loaded with whatever meats and/or cheeses you wish, top of the heap being the "Four Meat Special." Meatball po-boys are wonderful, but our preference is basic roast beef—king-size, please—which is a heap of moist beef that is guaranteed to ooze and tumble from the crusty length of bread as you hoist the sandwich.

There are no reservations and service is do-it-yourself in this humble 1966-vintage Creole lunchroom, but credit cards are welcomed.

Mississippi

Abe's Bar-B-Q

616 State St.　　　　　　　　662-624-9947

Clarksdale, MS　　　　　　　LD | $

Folklore designates the crossroads of Highways 61 and 49 in Clarksdale as the spot where Robert Johnson sold his soul to the devil in exchange for guitar mastery. In 1924, when Johnson was thirteen, Abraham Davis began selling sandwiches in Clarksdale. He opened Abe's Bar-B-Q at the infamous crossroads in 1937, and today his grandson Pat Davis runs the place, which is known for pecan-smoked pork and hot tamales.

Abe's barbecue is Boston butt that is first cooked over pecan wood, then allowed to cool overnight, then sliced, then heated again on the griddle when it is ordered. While it is getting heated, the pork gets hacked into a rugged hash. The process results in meat with lots of juicy buzz in its pale inside fibers and plenty of crusty parts where it has fried on the hot iron of the grill. You can have it on a platter or in a sandwich, the latter available in two sizes—normal and "Big Abe," which is twice the pork heaped into a double-decker bun. Clarksdale is close enough to Memphis that it is served city-style, i.e., with the slaw inside the bun.

One of the things that makes these sandwiches so especially delicious is the sauce, which is dark red and tangy, with the resonance of pepper and spice, a sublime companion for the meat. Pat Davis told us that it is made from the original recipe his grandfather developed, except for one ingredient, which he swears he doesn't use anymore. We wondered aloud if that secret ingredient might be opium, considering its addictive qualities. Pat denied it with a sly smile.

Served three to an order, with or without chili on top, Abe's tamales are packed into cayenne red husks, their yellow cornmeal moist with drippings from a mixture of beef and pork. The recipe is Abe Davis's, unchanged. "No doubt granddaddy got it from someone in town," Pat suggests, reminding us that Abe had come to the U.S. from Lebanon, where tamales aren't a big part of the culinary mix. Why Abe thought they would sell well in his barbecue place is a head-scratcher. "There were no Mexican restaurants here then," Pat says. "And as far as I know, not many Mexicans."

Blue and White Restaurant

1355 US 61 N   662-363-1371
Tunica, MS   BLD | $

Tunica has changed dramatically in the years since it went from being cotton farms and shotgun shacks to a coven of casinos and all the vulgarity that goes with them. But out on Highway 61, the old Blue and White Restaurant is operating pretty much the same way it's been doing things since opening day in 1937. The gas pumps out front are gone, so it is now only a restaurant, not a full-service travelers' stop, but if you are looking for good, southern food at reasonable prices in an atmosphere that is more down-home than high roller, this is the place to go.

We were lucky enough to visit on the cusp of breakfast and lunch hour. "You have ten more minutes to order breakfast," our waitress warned. "Then the lunch buffet will open." Naturally, we did both. For breakfast we had a classic country ham plate, the vigorous, well-aged slab of pig accompanied by eggs, biscuits, chunky sausage cream gravy, coffee-flavored red-eye gravy, and a bowl of stout, buttery grits. What a great morning meal!

When the buffet opened up, we helped ourselves to chicken and dumplings, which was superb: powerfully chickeny, loaded with meat, and laced with free-form mouthfuls of tender flavor-infused dough. On the side, we spooned up black-eyed peas, creamed corn, escalloped potatoes, and some of the most amazing turnip greens we've ever eaten. These greens were oily, salty, luscious, and rich, more like the pork that was used to flavor them than the green vegetable they appear to be. On the side of this meal came a sweet-dough yeast muffin and a crisp corn stick: both oven-hot and delicious.

We paid extra for an order of that weird specialty invented a few decades ago in the Delta, fried dill pickles. Blue and White's are ultra-thin slices with a veil of crust, nearly weightless, served with ranch dressing as a dip. Light as they are, the pickles have a resounding brine flavor that induces mighty thirst. If you are a beer drinker, you will have instant cravings.

Crystal Grill

423 Carrollton Ave.   662-453-6530
Greenwood, MS   LD | $$

Years ago, the Crystal Grill was known for a neon sign that glowed "Never Sleep." Open from 4:00 A.M. until midnight, it hosted the locals for their predawn coffee klatch as well as C&G Railroad men who'd stop their train on the tracks just across the street for late-night supper. Breakfast is no longer served; at lunchtime, townsfolk flock here with the gusto of celebrants arriving at a church picnic. Multiple remodelings over the years have created a labyrinth of small dining rooms that can seat over two hundred people in neighborly surroundings.

The menu is an eclectic spectrum of local treasures (peppery Delta tamales, Biloxi flounder, Belzoni catfish) and such saccharine Dixie eccentricities as pink velvet frozen salad (crushed pineapple, Cool Whip, cherry pie filling, and condensed milk) and "fruit salad" that is canned pear halves topped with grated yellow cheese. Proprietor John Ballas said that the recipe for his kitchen's aromatic yeast rolls came from a friend's mother who was a Home-Ec teacher at Greenwood High and that the spaghetti sauce is made from a recipe that his father obtained years ago by writing a letter to Heinz. Our favorite dishes on the menu are shrimp and crab Newburg, fried oysters, turnip greens, and sweet, sweet tea. And pie.

Annie Johnson started working here twenty-eight years ago and has been the pie maker for the last fifteen. Her legendary mile-high meringues are built upon a fragile crust that she rolls out from lard-laced dough, the recipe for which she shared with us using such measurements as "a big handful of baking powder" and a "little palm of salt." She makes the meringue by adding her simple syrup in a way that causes the egg whites to "jump out of the pot and whoop to a peak." Coconut pie and chocolate pie are always on the menu, and it is one of the great gastronomic joys of the South to be in the front dining room during lunch and watch the breathtaking dome-topped beauties carried out of the kitchen to a counter behind the register, where the cashier expertly severs them into wedges that are taller than they are wide.

The Dinner Bell

229 5th Ave.   601-684-4883
McComb, MS   L | $$

The Dinner Bell's reputation for grand southern meals has never flagged since it opened in 1945. Now run by the Lopinto family, who took over in 1981, it is the South's last bastion of revolving table dining.

In the center of each round table is a lavish lazy susan. Service is boarding-house-style: spin the lazy susan and take what you want. When any serving tray starts getting empty, out comes a full one from the kitchen. Grab as much as you want and eat at your own speed.

It isn't only quantity and convenience that make Dinner Bell meals memorable. This is some mighty marvelous food: chicken and dumplings, catfish, ham, corn sticks, sweet potato casseroles, black-eyed peas, fried eggplant, and fried okra. The dishes we cannot resist are the flamboyant vegetable casseroles supercharged with cheese and cracker crumbs—our kind of health food. Spinach casserole enriched with cream cheese and margarine and cans of artichoke hearts is good for the soul, not to mention the fact that it is scrumptious. To drink with all this good food, there is only one proper libation: sweet, sweet tea.

Doe's Eat Place

502 Nelson St.   662-334-3315
Greenville, MS   D | $$$

Located on the wrong side of town in the back rooms of a dilapidated grocery store, Doe's does not look like a restaurant, much less a great restaurant. Many of the dining tables are in fact located in the kitchen, spread helter-skelter among stoves and counters where the staff dresses salads and fries potatoes in big iron skillets. Plates, flatware, and tablecloths are all mismatched. It is noisy and inelegant, and service—while perfectly polite—is rough and tumble.

Doe's fans, ourselves included, love it just the way it is. The ambience, which is at least a few degrees this side of "casual," is part of what makes it such a kick. Mississippians have eaten here since the 1940s; for regular patrons the eccentricity makes the experience as comfortable as an old shoe. Newcomers may be shocked by the ramshackle surroundings, but Doe's is easy to like once the food starts coming.

Start with tamales and a brilliant salad made of iceberg lettuce dressed with olive oil and fresh-squeezed lemon juice. Shrimp are usually available, broiled or fried, and they are very, very good, but it's steak for which Doe's has earned its reputation. "Baby Doe" Signa, son of the founder, tells us that it is merely "U.S. Choice" grade, which, frankly, we don't believe. To us, it tastes like the primest of the prime, as good as any steak we have eaten anywhere, booming with flavor, oozing juice, tender but in no way tenderized. The choices range from a ten-ounce filet mignon up to a four-pound sirloin. Our personal preference is the porterhouse, the bone of which bisects a couple of pounds of meat that is very different in character on either side of the bone. The tenderloin side is zesty and exciting; the other side seems loaded with protein, as deeply satisfying as beef can be. With steak come some of the world's most delicious French fries—dandy to eat "neat," even better when dragged through the oily juices that flow out of the steaks onto the plate.

Giardina's

314 Howard St.	662-455-4227
Greenwood, MS	D | $$$

Opened in 1936, Giardina's started as a fish market but soon became a restaurant popular among cotton growers and known for its private curtained booths where bootleg booze could be drunk in secrecy. As King Cotton lost its economic hegemony late in the twentieth century, Giardina's fortunes waned along with those of Greenwood, the South's cotton capital. But then the Viking Range Corporation came to town in 1989 and the presence of the stove maker turned everything around. The Mississippi Heritage Trust awards Viking has won for the rehabilitation of local properties include the transformation of the historic Irving Hotel from a ratty embarrassment to a stylish boutique hotel called the Alluvian. What we like about the Alluvian, beyond its feather beds and 300-thread-count sheets, is the fact that it is the new home of Giardina's (pronounced with a hard *G*).

Giardina's is stylish, modern, and expensive. Service is polished. Tables are outfitted with thick white cloths and snazzy Viking cutlery. The wine collection—stored in state-of-the-art Viking wine cellars—is impressive. And yet for all that, the dining experience is down-home Delta. When you enter, Mary Rose Graham, a second-generation Giardina, will escort you to a private dining compartment just like in Prohibition days. The menu is upscale cotton-country fare, including hefty steaks and elegant pompano, hot tamales, and a bevy of dishes that reflect the powerful influence of Italian immigrants on Greenwood's cuisine. These include garlicky salads and a marvelous appetizer called Camille's bread, which our waiter described as "like a muffuletta but without the meat"—a hot loaf stuffed with olives, sardines, and cheese.

Hicks'

305 S. State St. 662-624-9887
Clarksdale, MS LD | $

"I am sixty-one years old, and I made my first tamales at age sixteen," Eugene Hicks told us a few years ago when we asked him why the ones he makes are so especially good. Rich and with a hard kick of pepper spices, each one is hand-wrapped, and they are available by threes, sixes, or twelves. A plate of three is served with chili and cheese, baked beans, and Italian-seasoned coleslaw.

Tamales are what put Hicks' on the map, but there is a whole menu of ribs, rib tips, and chopped pork shoulder cooked over flaming hickory logs and topped with house-made sauce. In addition, there are Hicks'-made pork sausages, fried catfish, and a fourteen-inch "Big Daddy" sandwich that is made with a combination of sliced barbecued pork and smoked turkey.

The first day we stopped in, a sign by the drive-up window advertised hog maws at $3.69 a pint. While the car ahead of us loaded up what looked like a meal for twelve, we debated for a moment what, exactly, hog maws are. Jane was sure maws were some part of a pig's mouth (inferred from the expression "shut your maw"); Michael believed they came from the far other end of the animal. When it came our turn Jane asked the woman behind the window, "Is this maw you are serving a mouth or a rectum?" She looked at us wide-eyed and explained that they are parts of a pig's stomach. For us, they turned out to be an acquired taste we have yet to acquire.

Lusco's

722 Carrollton Ave.	662-453-5365
Greenwood, MS	D	$$$

To occupy one of Lusco's back-room private dining booths, into which waiters sidle through Sears-catalog floral-print curtains, and to hear the plaint of blues musicians that floats from the sound system above the partitions that segregate each party of diners, are a weird and compelling taste of cotton-country history.

Planters around Greenwood came to know Charles "Papa" Lusco in the 1920s when he drove a horse-drawn grocery wagon to their plantations, bringing supplies from the market he and Marie "Mama" Lusco ran. Mama sold plates of her spaghetti at the store, and Papa built secret dining rooms in back where customers could enjoy his homemade wine with their meals.

Mama and Papa were Italian by way of Louisiana, so the flavors of the kitchen they established are as much Creole as they are southern or Italian. Gumbo, crab, and shrimp are always on the menu, and oysters are a specialty in season—on the half-shell or baked with bacon. The menu is best known for its high-end items. Lusco's T-bone steaks are some of the finest anywhere: sumptuous cuts that are brought raw to the table for your approval, then broiled to meaty succulence. Pompano has for many years been a house trademark (when available, usually the spring), broiled and served whole, bathed in a magical sauce made of butter, lemon, and secret spices.

The sauce for Lusco's broiled shrimp is nearly as far-famed as that used on pompano and trout. Firm, plump crescents are served in a silky translucent bath of buttery juice that has the zing of vinegar and pepper, and also a fusillade of strange, beguiling spices (could that be cardamom we taste?).

Lusco's is also known for its New Orleans–style salad of iceberg lettuce dolled up with anchovies, capers, and olives and liberally sopped in a fragrant vinaigrette, but third-generation Lusco Karen Pinkston is a serious salad buff who has made it her business to concoct more modern alternatives. One evening's choices included Mediterranean salad, made with feta cheese; traditional Caesar salad; and a salad billed as Gourmet's Delight, made with arugula, radicchio, endive, red lettuce, and spinach. "Andy [Karen's husband] likes to tease me about that one," Karen said about the latter. "He tells me it's just weeds I've picked by the side of the highway. But the fact is that the Delta is different now than it used to be, and the new people have more educated palates. Even this place has to change with the times."

For its pompano, for cut-to-order steaks, for gumbo and garlic-charged Italian salads, this seventy-two-year-old ex-grocery store on the wrong side of the railroad tracks, run by a fourth generation of the Lusco family, earns highest honors in the Roadfood pantheon.

Phillips Grocery

541-A E. Van Dorn Ave.   601-252-4671
Holly Springs, MS   L | $

Located in a two-story wood-frame house built as a saloon in the nine-teenth century, Phillips became a grocery store in 1919 and has earned a huge reputation for hamburgers since the 1940s. Some customers buy them to go, but there are comfy seats here, too—a short counter with stools, a handful of old wooden school desks, and a few odd tables (in-cluding one really odd one made from the cross section of a huge tree trunk). Outside on the front porch, a couple of picnic tables provide a view of the railroad depot.

The menu is written on a blackboard that lists side dishes, including fresh-from-the-freezer Tater Tots and morsels of deep-fried, bright green okra enveloped in a golden crust. Corn nuggets are something special—bite-size fritters with lots of kernels packed inside a sweet hush puppy–like jacket. You can get spicy or regular French fries. And if a Moon Pie off the grocery shelf isn't your dish for dessert, Phillips also of-fers fried pies for a dollar apiece. A fried pie is a folded over half-circle of dough fried until reddish brown and chewy, enclosing a heavy dollop of sugary peach or apple filling.

Hamburgers are presented wrapped in yellow wax paper inside a bag for easy toting, and when you peel back the wrapping, particularly on a half-pound Super-Deluxe, you behold a vision of beauty-in-a-bun. It is a thick patty with a wickedly good crunch to its nearly blackened skin. In-side, the meat is smooth-textured and moist enough to ooze juice when you gently squeeze the soft bun wrapped around it. The flavor is fresh, beefy, and sumptuous: an American classic.

Ramon's

535 Oakhurst St.	662-624-9230
Clarksdale, MS	D	$$

We thank Roger and Jennifer Stolle, infallible tipsters for all things relating to food and culture in the Mississippi Delta, for taking us to Ramon's. It's not the sort of place anyone would find accidentally. But it is a Roadfood treasure. "I wouldn't tell everyone to eat here," Roger said, pointing at the water-damaged acoustical ceiling tiles and explaining that local lore blames a lax landlord on the decomposition that makes the place a bona-fide dump. Still, Thomas and Barbara Ely, the couple who run Ramon's, valiantly create a pleasing milieu in the form of empty fifths of Jack Daniel's and three-liter jugs of Taylor Chablis that have been made into decorative lamps, and they serve magnificent butterflied fried shrimp nearly as big as moon pies. "We were taking bets in the kitchen if you all would be able to finish," the waitress admitted when Michael, dispossessed of all appetite, left two of his dozen shrimp uneaten on the plate.

Roger said his favorite thing to eat was a plate of chicken livers and spaghetti, a reminder of the significant Italian influence in Delta cooking. The livers are sensational: unspeakably rich and luxuriously crunchy. They are so filling that we barely forked into the heap of noodles that came alongside them.

South Carolina

Beacon Drive-In

255 Reidville Rd.   864-585-9387
Spartanburg, SC   LD | $

The South's drive-in trail leads to barbecue, fried chicken, boudin sausage, and biscuits stuffed with streak o' lean. At the Beacon, before the car window is halfway down, you will be accosted by a curb boy ready virtually to sing a menu that ranges from gizzard plates to banana sandwiches. We recommend Pork a-Plenty, which is chopped and sauced hickory-cooked hot barbecue on a bun that also contains cool coleslaw. The sandwich comes buried under a mountain of intertwined deep-fried onion rings and French fries. And of course the only correct libation to accompany this tremendous meal is sweet tea, served in a tall tumbler over crushed ice so cold that gulpers run the risk of brain-freeze headache. The Beacon claims to sell more tea than any other single restaurant in the USA.

Drive-in service is swell, but any newcomer must avail her- or himself of the serving line inside. Here, the Beacon is the most intense restaurant you will ever visit. The moment you enter and approach the counter, an employee behind it will demand, "Call it out!" The grand old man of the ritual is J. C. Stroebel, who used to insist that customers say what they want to eat and say it quickly, or else he instructed them to stand back and allow other, swifter folks to say their piece. On a good weekend day, the Beacon serves five thousand people.

Once you manage to convey your order, it is shouted back to the huge open kitchen, then you are asked in no uncertain terms to "Move on down the line!" Grab a tray and by the time you have moved twenty paces forward, there your order will be—miraculously, exactly as you ordered it, with or without extra barbecue sauce, double bacon on the burger. A bit farther down the line, you get your tea, lemonade, or milkshake and pay the cashier, then find a seat. Total time from entering to digging in—maybe two minutes.

Bookstore Café
1039 Johnnie Dobbs Blvd.   843-720-8843
Mt. Pleasant, SC   BL | $$

As a rule, creamy grits is the luxury starch of the low country, and the Bookstore Café serves some doozies along with tasso ham and sweet potato biscuits. But no potato lover can ignore the kitchen's chippers, which look to us like cottage fries: circular potato slices thick enough that they have been fried crisp, yet that still bend rather than break. You can have chippers alongside any breakfast, or, better, use them as the foundation for an Island Casserole, each of which is a great pile of good things to eat named after one of the local barrier islands. The chippers are topped with sautéed onions, peppers, and mushrooms, then you select from among such choices as sausage gravy and melted cheddar cheese (Kiawah Island), grilled shrimp, sausage, and Creole sauce (Edisto Island), or black beans, banana peppers, sour cream, and cheese (Isle of Palms).

"The Classics" section of the menu includes biscuits with sausage gravy and buttermilk or apple oatmeal pancakes. "Best Sellers" are shrimp and grits, a four-cheese omelet, eggs atop fried green tomatoes with country ham gravy, and various omelets. The Bookstore Café is also proud of its hash, and as hash devotees, we must say that the spicy tasso ham hash we ordered was terrific: rugged and chunky, at once spicy and sweet, topped with buttery fried eggs. When we return, we're going to try the traditional corned beef hash . . . or maybe the sweet potato–chicken hash . . . or the salmon–red potato hash.

Charlie's Steakhouse

18 Coffee St.   864-232-9541
Greenville, SC   D | $$

Dinner at Charlie's is built upon time-honored rituals that citizens of Greenville (and their parents and grandparents) have come to know and appreciate since this fine old steak house opened in 1921: apply-your-own dressing service for salad or slaw (the latter just a huge heap of cut cabbage), a bottle of Charlie's own steak sauce on every table, thick china plates rimmed with a pattern of magnolias, silver presented wrapped in thick linen napkins, and tables cushioned so well that highball glasses wobble as you slice into a steak.

The arrival of any steak is a glorious event, for it comes on a hot metal plate (resting on a wood pallet), sizzling and sputtering so loud that all conversations stop in wonderment. It is nice meat, dense and juicy, although like so many modern steaks, it lacks the intense beef taste of a good old prime cut. Still, who could resist a menu that boasts "All beef shipped direct from Waterloo & Des Moines, Iowa; St. Joe & Kansas City, Mo."? The roster includes a T-bone, a filet mignon, and a porterhouse for one, but many regulars who come in groups opt for a jumbo sirloin cut into portions for two, three, or four people.

Charlie's is a low-key sort of place—polite, but not overly impressed by itself and not ridiculously overpriced like the national prime-steak chains. Waitresses are friendly as can be, but also real pros, constantly positioning and repositioning the dressings, sour cream bowl, bread plate, and butter-pat dish on the table so everything is arrayed for maximum convenience. As we photographed an extra-large thick sirloin for our "What We Ate" picture album, our waitress suggested that when we get back to Wisconsin, we send her a copy so everyone at Charlie's could sign it. Earlier in the meal, we had told her we were from Connecticut, but we figure that to a lot of citizens of the Deep South, the difference between Connecticut and Wisconsin is a non-issue.

Diana's

155 Meeting St.	843-534-0043
Charleston, SC	BLD | $$

Diana's adjoins a downtown Day's Inn, but when we asked our waitress, Marie, if it was affiliated, she was adamant: "We are not connected to the hotel!" she said. "No way, whatsoever, not at all!"

It's apparent when you see the food that it is multiple levels above what one would expect in a chain-hotel snack shop. When you taste that food, you realize you are the beneficiary of master cooks. At breakfast, for example, if you order French toast you don't just get a couple of slabs of fried, egg-dipped bread. You get huge chunks of currant-berry bread stuffed with apples, cooked to a crisp outside, floating in an amber pool of apple cider syrup. Sausage gravy is served over luscious homemade biscuits. And the low country favorite, shrimp and grits, is amended with crawfish, too, and topped with some of the most delicious fried green tomatoes we've eaten anywhere—thinly veiled in crust, cooked al dente with a vivid tang.

Tipster Susanne Hupfer told us not to miss the southern fried chicken, served with chipotle whipped potatoes, and she was right. This is chicken with a rugged crust and succulent insides. Susanne also alerted us to Diana's pastries, which are on display as you enter the neat-and-tidy split level café. A glass case holds such wonderments as red velvet cake, white coconut layer cake, and yellow butter cake with chocolate whipped frosting. Here also are handsome pies: coconut cream, lemon meringue, chocolate cream, and pecan. Everything we've sampled from this case has been outstanding.

Of special note are Diana's coffees. The back of the breakfast menu is devoted to beverages, with more various ways to have your caffeine than at a Starbucks. Fat-free variations of café mocha and café mocchiatto are available, and we were in heaven with a double-shot red-eye, here known as a "shot in the dark."

Duke's

789 Chestnut St.	803-534-9418
Orangeburg, SC	LD Thurs-Sat only | $

When connoisseurs of southern food refer to Orangeburg-style barbecue, they mean Duke's. Here is a definitive eastern South Carolina barbecue parlor, including—please note—the very limited hours of operation, Thursday through Saturday. The limited schedule hearkens back to an old-fashioned pig pickin', which was a weekend celebration at which hogs were enjoyed from beard to tail, or "barbe à queue."

There's nothing at all charming about Duke's décor, at least not in an HGTV sort of way. It is a stark place with a single purpose: to celebrate hickory-smoked pork. Hacked into chunks at a cutting board in back, it is pork with a complex flavor that is just faintly smoky. Each piece is a tender mouthful that is a joy to savor in the peace of this room, where the only music is the cadence of more pork being hacked into hunks back in the kitchen.

You get the pork from a serve-yourself buffet line that also includes rice, hash (a stewlike mixture made from pig innards), a choice of red sauce that is four-alarm hot or yellow mustard sauce that is sweet and tangy (unique to central South Carolina), and pickles. Dish out as much as you want in your partitioned plate, grab a plastic fork, and find a place at one of the long picnic tables in the cavernous eating hall.

The drink of choice is presweetened iced tea, and each table is outfitted with a few loaves of Sunbeam bread, which is just the right thing for mopping a plate of all its good sauce.

Fishnet Seafood

3832 Savannah Hwy.   843-571-2423
Johns Island, SC   LD | $

A fundamental rule for finding good things to eat while traveling is to look for restaurants located in former gas stations. We don't know why, but they're some of the best Roadfood stops. To wit: Fishnet Seafood. It isn't really a restaurant at all; it is a fish market with no tables, not even provision for stand-up eating. But if you point to just about any fish in the house, the staff will bread it and fry it to order, and in this part of coastal South Carolina, frying is a fine art. Flounder is particularly wonderful, sheathed in a brittle gold crust, its sweet white meat moist and tender. If you order it as a sandwich, you get one huge, melt-in-your-mouth fillet with two token slices of white bread: finger food, for sure!

Another fine dish is Jesus crab, which is the management's name for what other places refer to as deviled crab. When we inquired about the name, a woman behind the counter explained that the dish was simply too good to be named for the prince of darkness. Indeed, Fishnet is a very religious place, its décor featuring not only the expected panoply of nautical nets and buoys, but signs everywhere reminding guests of Jesus's goodness and His ultimate importance. We've seen a lot of barbecues where religion is a fundamental aspect of the dining experience, but not so many seafood places. This is one where the original fisher of men is the star of the menu.

Gullah Cuisine

1717 Hwy. 17 N   843-881-9076
Mt. Pleasant, SC   LD | $$

"Food that speaks to ya" is the motto of Gullah Cuisine, a restaurant on a laudable mission. Its purpose is to celebrate the cuisine (and the culture) of coastal South Carolina, known as the low country. Gullah is the culture handed down by sea-island dwellers so isolated from the mainland that they developed their own African-American recipes distinct from the rest of the South. As you enter, you'll notice elegant woven sweetgrass baskets for sale near the cash register—they are a time-honored Mt. Pleasant craft—and you will also see little jars of "Gullah seasoning," which is the spice that gives so much of this food an indescribable zing.

You'll taste the zest in Gullah's gumbo, which is dense with shrimp, chunks of spicy sausage, and pieces of chicken. It is thickened with okra, which gives it a brilliant vegetable bite, and it has a perfume that will make you dizzy with hunger even before you spoon it up. Gumbo is optional, but Gullah rice is essential, available as a meal unto itself or as a side dish for such entrees as fried shrimp, smothered pork chops, or oxtail stew. It is a stunning dish, chockablock with shrimp, shreds of chicken, discs of sausage, and nuggets of vegetables, the rice itself tinted a glistening mahogany color and fairly radiant with peppery flavor.

As balm for a tongue with taste buds humming from all that spice, there is a wonderful broccoli casserole, and we must say that we were as impressed by it as by the more complex Gullah specialties. It is a real southern dish—broccoli transformed from a plebeian vegetable into something that is rich and full-flavored by the addition of cheese, bread crumbs, and seasoning. Far, far from modern al dente broccoli, this casserole is soft and profoundly comforting.

Other not-to-be-missed local specialties include she-crab soup with a slick of high-proof sherry floating on top, crunchy low country fried shrimp and oysters, and superb soul-food pumpkin pie for dessert.

Hominy Grill

207 Rutledge St.   843-937-0930
Charleston, SC   BLD | $$

Our first meal at the Hominy Grill was breakfast, and it was spectacular. The sausage patties that came alongside our sunny-side-up eggs were rugged and crusty and brilliantly spiced—a joy to eat when pushed through some yolk or sandwiched inside the tall biscuit that came along-side. Bacon was excellent, too—double-thick, crisp, and full-flavored, just begging to be cosseted in that hefty biscuit or eaten in alternating mouthfuls with a forkful of smooth-textured grits.

We were equally impressed when we returned for lunch and plowed into thick shrimp gumbo and a serving of Brunswick stew sided by good corn bread. And who could resist a distinctly southern BLT made with crunchy discs of fried green tomato? Buttermilk pie was the perfect dessert.

The Hominy Grill building was at one time a barber shop, and the striped poles that signify the tonsorial profession still flank the front door (on the inside). It's a spacious room with an old stamped tin ceiling, wood-slat walls, and slow-spinning fans overhead.

Hyman's Seafood

213 Meeting St.   843-723-6000
Charleston, SC   LD | $$

What we didn't eat one recent evening at Hyman Seafood: amberjack, cod, flounder, mahi, mako, monkfish, snapper, hokie, salmon, tilapia, trout, tuna, and black drum. Those were the fish of the day on the black-board, and below them were grouper, stuffed wahoo, and fried lobster tails, which we didn't sample either. Local oysters were coming in and available on the half-shell or fried, and we didn't even have appetite enough for them. The point is that Hyman has a big, big menu—mostly seafood, with a few token meats and pastas—and it's bound to be a little frustrating to pass up so many good things.

What we did have was swell: she-crab soup that is ridiculously thick, rich as cream sauce itself and loaded with meat; a broad dish with thirty steamed spiced shrimp; and a house specialty, crispy flounder. This is one large, beautiful fish that has been scored in a diamond pattern and broiled so the fork-size sections of meat develop a crusty edge and virtually seem to lift off the bone. This is one of the East Coast's top fish-eating experiences.

Hyman's is a tremendously popular place, frequented by tourists and locals alike. If you're looking for a funkier setting, Charleston and vicinity have plenty, but for a large-party ambience and impeccable local seafood, Hyman's is a good choice.

Jestine's Kitchen

251 Meeting St.   843-722-7224
Charleston, SC   LD | $$

Jestine's opened about ten years ago, but its recipes go back decades. Some were contributed by the kitchen staff, but most were bequeathed to proprietor Dana Berlin by Jestine Matthews, the African-American woman who raised her and for whom the café is named. Ms. Matthews passed away in 1997 at the age of 112.

A hospitable Meeting Street storefront with a soundtrack of old-time jazz singers and décor that includes vintage cast-iron skillets, flour sifters, and juice squeezers, Jestine's has a homey feeling that attracts guests from all walks of life. "This is my all-time, number-one restaurant," boasts a young seaman from the nearby naval base to his date one afternoon as he guides her to a booth and chivalrously unwraps her silver from the clean green washcloth that serves as a napkin, then orders a pound of spiced, steamed shrimp and a basket of corn bread for them to share.

"Lunch, Dinner, Supper?" asks the menu. "Whatever you call it, we serve it all day." That can range from the so-called Blue Collar Special of a peanut butter and banana sandwich to a big pork chop plate, fried seafood platter, or half-pound slab of meat loaf. There isn't a nicer table anywhere to taste the time-honored coastal delights of shrimp and grits or shrimp Creole, as well as such stupendously seasoned low country vegetables as okra gumbo and red rice or fried green tomatoes with sweet pepper relish. Even common side dishes are uncommonly delicious: mashed potatoes pack eye-opening zest, macaroni and cheese is threaded with chewy strips from the top of the casserole, cabbage is cooked with plenty of pork until its leaves are limp and sweet. Vegetarian vegetables (cooked without ham bone or hock) are also available. There are beer and wine to drink, but the proper beverage to accompany this powerfully flavored food is listed on the menu as "Jestine's table wine"—cool, sugary tea served in shapely tumblers.

The Old Post Office

Hwy. 174 at Store Creek   843-869-2339

Edisto Island, SC   LD | $$$

We don't know of another restaurant where the table setting includes bags of raw grits. The Old Post Office is renowned for grits prepared low country–style, meaning they are long- and slow-cooked, attaining a pleasant rugged texture but also a creamy quality from all the butter and milk they absorb. They come alongside virtually every meal served here, and they are especially wonderful as part of that favorite low country duet, shrimp and grits.

Grits bags on the table are important not only because the grits at the Old Post Office taste so good, but because grits are fundamental to low country cooking, and here is a restaurant where the food traditions of the region are honored with brio. Ask any food-savvy person from Edisto, Charleston, or beyond where to eat meals that sing of South Carolina's coastal culture, and chances are good you will be directed to this unlikely place on Edisto Island.

Chef Philip Bardin changes his menu to reflect the spectacular vegetable crops of Edisto, as well as the seafood caught around here. That means that if it's oyster season (fall through early spring), you will likely have the opportunity to fork into Oyster Skillet, a dish the menu describes as "low country Escargots," but that puts smelly old canned snails to shame. A cast-iron skillet filled with small local creek oysters swimming in a pool of butter, their own liquor, garlic, and parsley, it comes with a toasted baguette that is great for shoveling heaps of oysters up from the skillet, as well as for sopping up those intoxicating juices.

The wide-ranging menu goes well beyond local seafood to include delicious roast duck, a "fussed over pork chop" that's a good reminder of just how important pork is in these parts, and "P.B.'s Ultimate Filet Mignon" (P.B. = Philip Bardin).

The key lime mousse was a winning variation on key lime pie, and we were brought to our knees by Coca-Cola cake, a southern home cook's dish that is rare in restaurants.

Ruby Seahorse Grill

108 Jungle Rd.   843-869-0606

Edisto Beach, SC   LD | $

When Philip Bardin, chef at the Old Post Office (p. 282), recommends a place to eat, we listen. Philip knows good food, and when we asked him where to go on Edisto Island, other than his own restaurant, "The Ruby Seahorse" was his instant answer. And what should we eat? Again, no hesitation: "A pimiento burger."

We found ourselves on Jungle Road near the ocean at a breezy eatery that looks pretty much like a million hamburger joints in other places. The short menu included a few salads and sandwiches, including an excellent French dip known as the Jacques Chirac and a classic grilled Reuben. Chicken wings are available by the dozen: medium, hot, teriyaki, and calabash.

However, Philip's recommendation was quite specific, so we directed our attention to the hamburger menu. Here we found bacon-cheese, chili-cheese, and mushroom-Swiss burgers, but it was the "Original Dairy Bar Pimiento Burger" for which we came. This house specialty is a handsome, good-size hamburger mounded with a huge spill of mostly melted pimiento cheese—a good-tasting mess. And if you want to make it even messier, you'll ask for it "all the way," which means mayonnaise, mustard, lettuce, tomato, onion, and pickle chips.

Suitable to a hamburger, the dining experience is extremely informal. You wait in line at an order window through which the kitchen is visible. Once you've ordered and paid, you wait for the meal to be assembled on throwaway dishware, then carry it to a rickety table on a back porch where the perfume of the ocean provides priceless ambience.

SeeWee Restaurant

4808 US 17 N   843-928-3609

Awendaw, SC   LD | $$

A former grocery north of Charleston along US 17, SeeWee is now a hugely popular restaurant that includes a lovely outdoor area for al fresco dining. It still looks a bit like a roadside store—shelves stocked with supplies, and a higgledy-piggledy décor of nautical bibelots. But Charlestonians now come here for local seafood, down-home vegetables, and magnificent cakes.

Daily specials are chalked up on a board: country-fried steak, whole catfish, Jamaican jerk chicken, Buffalo shrimp or oysters (fried in a spicy Buffalo-wing style), fish stew by the cup or bowl. We are partial to the regular menu and its roster of fried seafood. In this part of the world, frying shrimp, scallops, and oysters is a fine art. You can get a platter or a sandwich with very good extra-large French fries and coleslaw on the side. Our shrimp were snapping firm and veiled in a fine, crisp crust.

One of the great only-in-the-South meals to get here is an all-vegetable plate. Choose four from a list of more than a dozen available, including such local faves as red rice, butter beans, fried squash, fried okra, and rice and gravy. We went for fried green tomatoes (deliciously al dente with a tangy smack), sweet potato casserole (super spicy), macaroni and cheese (dense and thick with cheese), and collard greens (salty, oily, luxurious).

As you walk in the restaurant you will see a shelf of the day's layer cakes, and desserts are listed on a blackboard. When we saw chocolate cake with peanut butter icing, we knew we had to have a piece. So we ordered it as we ordered lunch. The cake came before the meal. "I cut this for you because I was worried there wouldn't be any left by the time you were ready," our waitress kindly explained as she set it down with our sweet teas. We are grateful she was watching out for us, because this cake was superb, as was our caramel layer cake and goober pie.

No bill arrives after the meal. When you're done eating, the waitress will instruct you to go up to the cash register and tell the man your table number. He's got your check and will tally it up and get you squared away.

Breakfast is served Saturdays only.

Sgt. White's Diner

1908 Boundary St.	843-522-2029
Beaufort, SC	LD | $

Immediately upon entering this little diner you are faced with the steam table from which the server puts together your plate. While it is possible to order off a menu—and the fried chicken and shrimp therefrom are exemplary—we cannot resist the array of barbecue and side dishes in the trays. You get either pulled pork, which is a medley of velvet-soft shreds from inside and crunchy strips from the outside of the roast bathed in the Sergeant's brilliant tangy-sweet sauce, or ribs, which are crusty and unspeakably luscious, also caked with the good sauce. Each side dish is a super-soulful rendition of a southern classic: smothered cabbage richer than ham itself, broccoli gobbed with cheese, brilliantly seasoned red rice, a vivid mix of collard and turnip greens, real mashed potatoes, candied yams, etc., etc. A normal meal is one meat and two sides, served with a block of corn bread on top. Even that corn bread is extraordinary: rugged-textured and sweet as cake.

Sergeant White, by the way, is a U.S. Marine, a former drill instructor, who offers business-size cards at the counter to remind guests of the Marine code of Honor, Courage, and Commitment.

Shealy's Bar-B-Que

340 E. Columbia Ave.   803-532-8135

Leesville, SC   LD (closed Wed & Sun) | $

We found out about Shealy's thanks to tipster Paul McCravy, who wrote that "the vegetables surpass any I've had at the three family reunions I attend each year in Pickins County." Greens and beans, boiled, fried, and mashed, served plain and in elaborate casseroles, make up the awesome array of vegetables. And they are merely the side dishes to some magnificent meals of great fried chicken with cream gravy, including wishbones for those who are feeling lucky.

For us, the main attraction is pork barbecue, which is presented at the buffet with all the glory of a traditional South Carolina barbecue feast, meaning you will find just about every part of the pig from the rooter to the tooter. That includes meat, ribs, hash, skin, gravy, and a rather bizarre creamy-spicy mush apparently quite popular in these parts known as liver nips. Of special interest on the tender shreds of smoked pork is Shealy's sauce (available by the bottle), an alluring mustard-tinged sweet-and-sour condiment unique to the South Carolina Midlands.

Summerton Diner

33 Church St.   803-485-6835

Summerton, SC   BLD (closed Thurs) | $

Since Lois Hughes opened it for business in 1967, this little café on the outskirts of town has been a favorite of locals and a beacon for travelers along I-95. After Lois's daughter Lynelle Blackwell took over in 1987, she enlarged and remodeled it, but today the diner has the feel of an age-less eatery: well-worn Formica counter, blond wood-paneled walls, each table set with bottles of hot vinegar peppers for brightening up orders of collard greens.

There's a full menu, and such items as fried chicken or steak and quail are always available, but at lunchtime the thing to order is the special. For well under $10, you get an entree, three vegetables, dessert, and tea. Plus corn bread and biscuits. The Monday we stopped in a while back, the meats included calves liver with onions and gravy, baked ham, beef stew, and baked chicken supreme. We love that chicken! It is crusty and fall-apart tender; the waitress asks if you want white or dark meat. Like all entrees, it comes on a partitioned plate along with two of the vegetables you choose. (The third vegetable, for which the plate has no room, comes in its own bowl.) As you might expect in a true-South café such as this, the side dishes are superb: earthy fresh rutabagas, spicy stewed apples, porky sweet greens that still have an al dente oomph to their leaves, mashed potatoes blanketed in gorgeous, beef-shred gravy, hefty blocks of macaroni and cheese with crusty edges and creamy insides, rice infused with soulful gravy. Et cetera!

The serving of pudding is small but classic: balmy custard in which sliced bananas and softened vanilla wafers are suspended, all under a Kewpie-doll spiral of whipped cream.

Note that the Summerton diner is closed Thursdays. It is open for three meals a day the rest of the week.

The Wreck

106 Haddrell Point   843-884-0052
Mt. Pleasant, SC   D | $$

The docks at Shem Creek in Mount Pleasant, just north of the city, are lined with seafood restaurants, all quite pleasant-looking and with similar shoreline menus, but if you meander farther along the water, out Live Oak Road to Haddrell Point, you will find a Roadfood jewel in the rough. And we do mean find, for the restaurant known as the Wreck (formally named the Wreck of the Richard and Charlene for a boat hit by Hurricane Hugo) has no sign outside—it's tucked between the Wando Seafood Company and Magwood and Sons Seafood—and we also mean in the rough, for it is located in a former bait locker, and décor is mostly piles of cardboard beer cartons. Seats are plastic lawn chairs at tables clothed with fish-wrapping paper (but romantically lit by candles at night). If the weather is cool, you are warmed by a couple of fireplaces in the concrete-floored dining room. The view of docked shrimp trawlers couldn't be more picturesque. And the food is impeccable.

Place your order by using a marking pen to circle what you want on the paper menu. Meals begin with a bowl of soft boiled peanuts—an addictive reminder that peanuts are in fact not nuts but legumes. She-crab soup is served in the traditional manner with a shot of sherry to pour on top just before dipping in a spoon. Then come crunchy fried shrimp, scallops, oysters, or broiled fish accompanied by zesty slaw and tubular hush puppies. Depending on your appetite, you can get a meal either "Richard-sized" (copious) or "Charlene-sized" (normal portion). Everything is presented on cardboard plates with plastic utensils; beer comes in the bottle. Dessert is a choice of key lime bread pudding or banana pudding.

If you are a fish-frowner, the Wreck does offer London broil. However the menu warns, "This is a seafood house claiming no expertise in the preparation of red meat. So, when you order red meat it is yours . . . No returns!!!!!"

Midwest

Illinois * Indiana * Iowa * Michigan * Minnesota *

Missouri * Ohio * Wisconsin

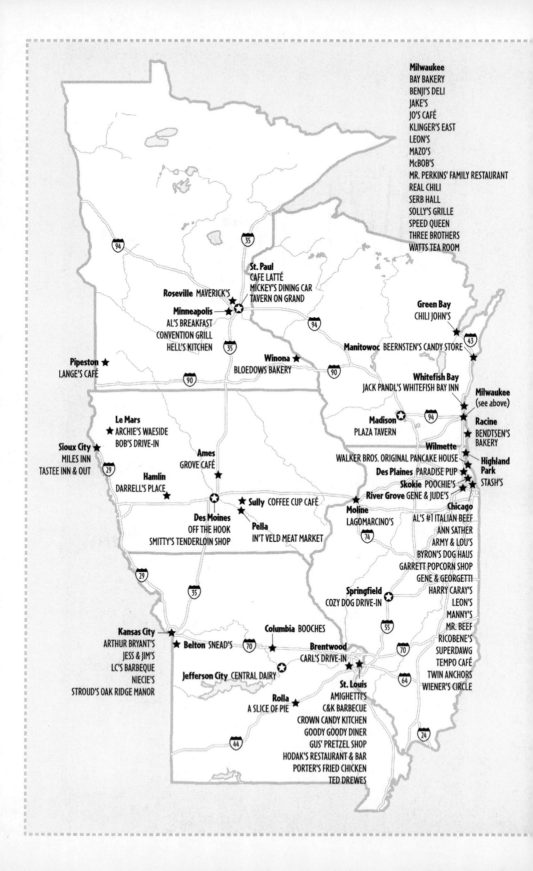

Milwaukee
BAY BAKERY
BENJI'S DELI
JAKE'S
JO'S CAFÉ
KLINGER'S EAST
LEON'S
MAZO'S
McBOB'S
MR. PERKINS' FAMILY RESTAURANT
REAL CHILI
SERB HALL
SOLLY'S GRILLE
SPEED QUEEN
THREE BROTHERS
WATTS TEA ROOM

St. Paul
CAFÉ LATTÉ
MICKEY'S DINING CAR
TAVERN ON GRAND

Roseville MAVERICK'S

Minneapolis
AL'S BREAKFAST
CONVENTION GRILL
HELL'S KITCHEN

Green Bay
CHILI JOHN'S

Manitowoc BEERNSTEN'S CANDY STORE

Pipeston ★
LANGE'S CAFÉ

Winona ★
BLOEDOWS BAKERY

Whitefish Bay
JACK PANDL'S WHITEFISH BAY INN

Milwaukee
(see above)

Le Mars
★ ARCHIE'S WAESIDE
BOB'S DRIVE-IN

Madison
PLAZA TAVERN

Racine
BENDTSEN'S
BAKERY

Sioux City ★
MILES INN
TASTEE INN & OUT

Ames
GROVE CAFÉ

Wilmette
WALKER BROS. ORIGINAL PANCAKE HOUSE

Des Plaines PARADISE PUP

**Highland
Park**
STASH'S

Hamlin
DARRELL'S PLACE

Sully COFFEE CUP CAFÉ

Skokie POOCHIE'S

River Grove GENE & JUDE'S

Des Moines
OFF THE HOOK
SMITTY'S TENDERLOIN SHOP

Pella
IN'T VELD MEAT MARKET

Moline
LAGOMARCINO'S

Chicago
AL'S #1 ITALIAN BEEF
ANN SATHER
ARMY & LOU'S
BYRON'S DOG HAUS
GARRETT POPCORN SHOP
GENE & GEORGETTI
HARRY CARAY'S
LEON'S
MANNY'S
MR. BEEF
RICOBENE'S
SUPERDAWG
TEMPO CAFÉ
TWIN ANCHORS
WIENER'S CIRCLE

Springfield
COZY DOG DRIVE-IN

Kansas City
ARTHUR BRYANT'S
JESS & JIM'S
LC'S BARBEQUE
NIECIE'S
STROUD'S OAK RIDGE MANOR

Belton SNEAD'S

Columbia BOOCHES

Brentwood
CARL'S DRIVE-IN

Jefferson City CENTRAL DAIRY

St. Louis
AMIGHETTI'S
C&K BARBECUE
CROWN CANDY KITCHEN
GOODY GOODY DINER
GUS' PRETZEL SHOP
HODAK'S RESTAURANT & BAR
PORTER'S FRIED CHICKEN
TED DREWES

Rolla ★
A SLICE OF PIE

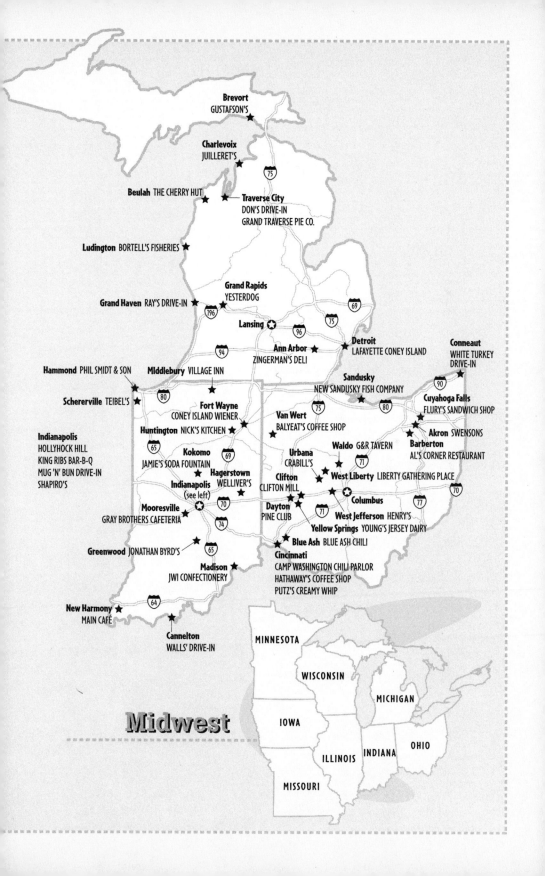

Brevort
GUSTAFSON'S

Charlevoix
JUILLERET'S

Beulah THE CHERRY HUT

Traverse City
DON'S DRIVE-IN
GRAND TRAVERSE PIE CO.

Ludington BORTELL'S FISHERIES

Grand Rapids
YESTERDOG

Grand Haven RAY'S DRIVE-IN

Lansing

Detroit
LAFAYETTE CONEY ISLAND

Conneaut
WHITE TURKEY
DRIVE-IN

Ann Arbor
ZINGERMAN'S DELI

Hammond PHIL SMIDT & SON

Middlebury VILLAGE INN

Sandusky
NEW SANDUSKY FISH COMPANY

Cuyahoga Falls
FLURY'S SANDWICH SHOP

Schererville TEIBEL'S

Fort Wayne
CONEY ISLAND WIENER

Van Wert
BALYEAT'S COFFEE SHOP

Akron SWENSONS

Huntington NICK'S KITCHEN

Waldo G&R TAVERN

Barberton
AL'S CORNER RESTAURANT

Indianapolis
HOLLYHOCK HILL
KING RIBS BAR-B-Q
MUG 'N' BUN DRIVE-IN
SHAPIRO'S

Kokomo
JAMIE'S SODA FOUNTAIN

Urbana
CRABILL'S

West Liberty LIBERTY GATHERING PLACE

Hagerstown
WELLIVER'S

Clifton
CLIFTON MILL

Indianapolis
(see left)

Columbus

Mooresville
GRAY BROTHERS CAFETERIA

Dayton
PINE CLUB

West Jefferson HENRY'S

Yellow Springs YOUNG'S JERSEY DAIRY

Greenwood JONATHAN BYRD'S

Blue Ash BLUE ASH CHILI

Cincinnati
CAMP WASHINGTON CHILI PARLOR
HATHAWAY'S COFFEE SHOP
PUTZ'S CREAMY WHIP

Madison
JWI CONFECTIONERY

New Harmony
MAIN CAFÉ

Cannelton
WALLS' DRIVE-IN

MINNESOTA

WISCONSIN

MICHIGAN

IOWA

ILLINOIS

INDIANA

OHIO

MISSOURI

Midwest

Al's #1 Italian Beef

1079 W. Taylor St.   312-733-8896

Chicago, IL   LD | $

To dine well at Al's, it helps to know the lingo.

"Big beef, double-dipped!" is the call for an extra-large sandwich of thin-sliced, gravy-sopped, garlic-charged beef that, once loaded into a chewy length of Italian bread, is reimmersed for approximately one second in a pan of natural gravy so the bread is soaked through.

"Beef with hot" is a request for the relish known as giardiniera, an eye-opening garden mélange of finely chopped marinated vegetables, capers, and spice that is roast beef's perfect complement. Al's giardiniera is made in thirty-gallon batches and fermented three to four days before it's ready. "With sweet" is what you say if you prefer the popular alternative to giardiniera: big, tender flaps of roasted green bell pepper with a charcoal taste.

"Combo!" or "half and half!" is a call for a sandwich that contains not only beef but also a plump, four-inch length of Italian sausage, retrieved from the appetizing haze that hovers over the hot metal grate just behind the order counter. Taut-skinned, succulent, and well-spiced, the sausage is itself a major lure for many customers who sidestep beef altogether and order double-sausage sandwiches, hot or sweet.

Al's is a small shop in old Little Italy that offers no seats for dining. You eat at waist-high counters along the wall or off the trunk of your car in the parking lot. After lunch, stroll across the street to Mario's Italian ice shop for the perfect dessert.

Ann Sather

929 W. Belmont Ave. 773-348-2378
Chicago, IL BL Mon & Tues, BLD Wed-Sun | $

This legendary Chicago restaurant started in 1945 as a Belmont Avenue diner run by a Swedish immigrant named Ann Sather. She finally sold the place in 1981 to Tom Tunney after Mr. Tunney apprenticed with her for a year. He expanded the business (there are now five Ann Sathers in Chicagoland), but kept the cinnamon rolls, which are spectacular. You get two big fluffy rolls per order, each one blanketed in a sweet glaze.

Among Ann Sather's other breakfast icons are Swedish pancakes, which are folded-over crêpes with a lace edge and fine, steamy-sweet flavor. They are available with a cup of lingonberry sauce, with a side of eggs, or with a couple of meatballs. The potato pancakes are superb, as is the French toast with peach compote. But the item that rivets our attention is the waffle, two waffles to be exact, Swedish waffles, the menu says. We're not exactly sure what makes them Swedish, but we do know that they are not big fat Belgians. They are thin, crisp, and aromatic waffles, baked in an iron that gives them a fetching scalloped shape and served two to an order.

Although most Chicagoans think of it (rightly) as a breakfast place, there are few places that offer such wonderful comfort-food supper. Chicken croquettes with candied sweet potatoes, anyone? There is roast tom turkey with all the fixin's, broiled Lake Superior whitefish, shepherd's pie, and roast loin of pork with caraway seed sauerkraut. And, of course, there are Swedish meatballs.

Army & Lou's

422 E. 75th St. 773-483-3100
Chicago, IL BLD | $$

A friendly storefront open since 1945, Army and Lou's is the place to go for soul food—breakfast, lunch, or dinner, and, Friday evenings, jazz performed by South Side artists. We were the only white people in the place the day we went for lunch, and wall décor is exclusively pictures of African Americans. It is said that the city's first black mayor, Harold Washington, ate here all the time.

While the menu features a wide array of soul food, including chitterlings (served with spaghetti!) and ham hock with mixed greens, there are plenty of items that appear to be just what you'd expect in any neighborhood café, black or white. We say "appear" because the smothered pork chops we ordered were soulful to the nth degree, and the fried chicken would never, ever be mistaken for KFC's flabby bird parts.

All entrees come with a choice from a long list of appetizing side dishes, including candied sweet potatoes and corn bread dressing with giblet gravy. Dessert is a choice of fruit cobbler (ooey-gooey peach the day we were here), sweet potato pie, or bread pudding with lemon sauce.

Byron's Dog Haus

1017 W. Irving Park Rd.   773-281-7474
Chicago, IL   LD | $

As plump Polish sausages sizzle on the grill, the Dog Haus counterman dips a ladle into the fryolator (whence commeth the French-fried potatoes) to get some hot fat to pour over the grilling tube steaks. The grease helps give them a blackened, crisp skin; it also gives them a look of glistening, sinfully swollen avoirdupois. These are some of the most cumbrous Polish sausages in a city where Polish sausages, along with their all-beef brothers, hot dogs, are matters of serious culinary consideration. If you are a Polish sausage fanatic, it isn't likely you will be blasé about the big, charred tubes they serve up at Byron's Dog Haus; you will love them or hate them.

The hot dogs are more civil, and we can recommend them to anyone who likes a substantial, all-beef frank. They are Vienna-brand beauties, steeped to plump succulence, with a faint crackle as you sink your teeth into them. Our only complaint is about the buns. They are a bore—small, plain (no poppy seeds), forked right out of their plastic-wrapped container (not well-warmed), and therefore redolent of cardboard and plastic wrap.

On the other hand, Dog Haus condiments are fine: eleven different toppings that include strips of green pepper, cucumber discs, piccalilli, squeeze-on yellow mustard, onions, sport peppers (hot!), and a whole tomato cut into slices. Yes, there resting atop your hot dog and all its other condiments is one sliced tomato, and because the slices don't go all the way through, it stays in one piece . . . until you try to eat the dog, at which time everything falls into a splendid mess. The tomato is customarily gilded with a sprinkle of celery salt.

Alongside this good specimen of frankfurter pulchritude, you want French fries. They are skinny and crisp—a suitable spuddy companion to the highly seasoned sausages that are this restaurant's specialty. Unless you really love French fries, one order is plenty for two.

Cozy Dog Drive-In

2935 S. 6th St.	217-525-1992
Springfield, IL	LD | $

Route 66 from Chicago to St. Louis has become Interstate 55 and the Cozy Dog Drive-In is now situated where the old Abe Lincoln Motel used to be, but the motto of this mid-century Mother Road treasure still holds absolutely true: "One calls for another."

Invented during World War II by Ed Waldemire when he was stationed in the Air Force in Texas, the corn-clad, deep-fried pup was originally called Crusty Cur and was a big hit with flyboys at the Amarillo PX. After the war, Waldemire's wife convinced him that his wiener needed a more appealing name, and in 1946, they opened the first Cozy Dog (so christened because no one eats a single, lonely one). You don't have to be a street food connoisseur to know the difference between a cozy dog and an ordinary corn dog. The cozy's batter jacket has a vivid crunch and earthy corn flavor; the dog within is plump with juice. Family baskets include four cozy dogs and a large order of (freshly cut) French fries.

Garrett Popcorn Shop

670 N. Michigan Ave.	312-944-4730
Chicago, IL	$

The management of Garrett Popcorn Shop insists that the product it makes is *not* caramel corn. It is CaramelCrisp, a trademarked name for a foodstuff that, to us, looks a lot like caramel corn. In any case, we have no desire to argue with the place that makes our all-time favorite caramel-coated, popcorn-based snack. Whatever you call it, Caramel-Crisp is simply sensational.

Generally speaking, candy-coated popcorn is frivolous junk food. CaramelCrisp is serious and soulful, its taste and texture dramatically more important than any other kind of candied corn. In fact, it doesn't really taste candied at all. The popcorn itself is a tender, earthy note within its caramel sheath, which is deeply buttery and has a dark flavor that teeters at the edge of tasting burned. Like the singed crust atop a well-made crème brûlée, the corn's coat smacks of fire more than sugar.

Another thing that makes it good is that it is always served hot and fresh. Once mixed with caramel, it is spilled into an L-shaped trough against the front wall where a woman worries it with two large scoops, ensuring the caramel corn doesn't clump into pieces larger than three or four popped kernels. As it achieves a perfect consistency, it is shoveled forward into the other end of the trough, where it is scooped into wax-paper bags that are weighed out for customers.

Almost equally excellent is Garrett's cheese corn, which is impossible to eat without your fingers turning bright orange from the cheese that coats and infuses the hot popped kernels. It is hilarious to stroll along Michigan Avenue, known as the Magnificent Mile for all its high-end shopping, and see otherwise dapper folks whose hands are the color of a school bus. Even knowing the mess that inevitably results, including orange stains on jeans and jackets, lips and chins, we cannot stop eating it once we start. The vivid cheese immeasurably enhances the starchy corn flavor of the puffy kernels, making a savory snack that is almost unimprovable.

But it can get better. Instead of ordering either CaramelCrisp or cheese corn, you can ask one of the women working the counter for a "mix," also known as a "Chicago mix." She fills a bag half full with caramel corn, then tops it off with cheese corn and shakes. The combo—which stains fingers only half as bad—is a giant taste sensation that seems to cover the whole spectrum of what a tongue can appreciate: salty, sweet, buttery, earthy, crisp, and chewy. Frankly, even a mini-mix, which is a mere eight ounces, exhausts our ability to eat anything else for hours. It is, for us, a perfect food.

The only negative thing to say about this place is that it is so insanely popular among Chicagoans that the wait in line to buy the product can be thirty minutes or even an hour. There are a handful of other Garretts around the Chicago Loop, and they tend to be a little less crowded.

Gene and Georgetti

500 N. Franklin St.   312-527-3718

Chicago, IL   LD | $$$

Gene and Georgetti's sirloin, filet mignon, and T-bone are all benchmarks by which other steaks should be measured. Perfectly cooked as ordered (medium rare, please), with a glistening charred crust and velvet pink-to-red insides dense with full-flavored juice, these are the hunks of meat we dream about anytime we are on the way to Chicago.

It is all too tempting to precede a steak with garbage salad, a piled-high plate that is a mishmash antipasto of cured meats, cheeses, olives, peppers, one big shrimp, and lettuce all in a garlicky marinade. Too tempting we say because a whole garbage salad is a big meal. Even a half is mighty filling if you've got steak and potatoes on the way.

On the side of G&G's steaks, the top starch is cottage fries, big round disks with crisp edges and soft centers. There is a large menu beyond beef: lamb chops are excellent; shrimp de Jonghe (or lobster de Jonghe) is surely the most buttery version of the dish anywhere in the city. We also love G&G's chicken Vesuvio, a mountainous plate of winey, garlicky roasted chicken wallowing in pan juices along with chunks of potato.

Impeccable meals are delivered by a staff of professional waiters who are all business. No fawning service here, no annoying "is everything okay?" will interrupt your dinner conversation. Gene and Georgetti is no nonsense, all quality.

Gene and Jude's

2720 N. River Rd.   708-452-7634

River Grove, IL   LD | $

We owe a debt of gratitude to Glen Stepanovic, who wrote imploring us to visit Gene and Jude's. Somehow, this estimable hot dog stand just a few minutes the *other* side of O'Hare had eluded our radar. It is hugely popular—Glen said it's the largest purveyor of Vienna hot dogs on Earth—but it's a relatively small place. There are no tables or chairs at all; as is Chicago custom, the eatery offers a counter to which you may bring your meal, unwrap it, and eat standing up. When you're finished, use the wax paper in which the food was served to gather up any scraps and heave them into one of the large garbage cans provided in the corners of the room. We find this arrangement comfortable and eminently practical for eating extremely messy food; however, many customers choose to dine in their cars in the parking lot.

You get a hot dog or a double dog. The natural-casing, all-beef Vienna-brand tube steaks are slim and snappy; they are inserted into soft buns and dressed with mustard, onions, piccalilli, or little hot "sport peppers" as you request. Glen told us that some hot dog historians consider this the "original" Chicago-style dog, before the more baroque garnishes of pickle spear, tomato slice, and celery salt.

A fine, fine hot dog . . . but wait, there's more! Whatever toppings are included, each dog gets heaped with a large fistful of some of the best French fries in Chicago. Fresh? Forget about it! As you wait for your hot dog to be prepared, you can watch the counter folks peel and cut whole potatoes, then fry them, drain them, and pile them onto waiting dogs. They spend a good long time in the bubbling oil, emerging a dark brown with some pieces crunchy through-and-through, others thick and potato-creamy inside.

Harry Caray's

33 W. Kinzie St.   312-828-0966

Chicago, IL   LD | $$$

We tend not to frequent sports bars because the food is usually less important than what's on TV. Harry Caray's is one huge exception. It is the sports bar to end all sports bars—especially heavenly for Chicago team fans—and it is loaded with memorabilia not only from the Cubs, but from the life of legendary announcer Harry Caray.

Beyond his antics in the broadcast booth, Caray was known as a man who loved to eat. And the place he opened is testimony to that passion, too. This is one truly great Chicago restaurant. For example, there is not a better prime steak in Chicago. We like the sirloin best, grilled in a coat of cracked peppercorns. Other highlights of the menu include such familiar Italian specialties as lasagna, veal parmigiana, and a risotto of the day.

Among the "Italian" dishes is one that we've found only in Chicago, and it is magnificent: chicken Vesuvio. Chicken Vesuvio is several bone-in pieces of chicken, sautéed then baked to utmost succulence, encased in a dark, red-gold crust of lush skin that slides from the meat as the meat slides off its bone. Is it tender? Yeah, baby! The dark meat in particular sets new standards for chicken tenderness. Piled among the chicken are wedges of potato, long-sautéed in a bath of white wine, garlic, olive oil, and spice until they are soft as mashed inside, but develop crunchy edges. Even if you don't get chicken Vesuvio, "Vesuvio" potatoes are available as a side dish to go with any steak or chop. The only problem about ordering them is that you likely won't also be ordering Harry Caray's garlic mashed potatoes, which are superb.

The setting is vintage: a 1895 Dutch Renaissance–style limestone building now on the National Register of Historic Places, its interior a luxuriously muscular space of mahogany woodwork and broad tables covered by thick white napery. Although a sumptuous place to which many customers come in pinstriped business suits, there is a democratic feel about this dining room that makes any decently dressed customer feel right at home. Harry Caray was a people's hero, and that's the way he liked it.

Lagomarcino's

| 1422 5th Ave. | 309-764-1814 |
| Moline, IL | LD \| $ |

Started as a Moline candy store in 1908, Lagomarcino's is still renowned for hand-dipped chocolates, as well as fancy fruit baskets. You won't find better sponge candy anywhere. (Sponge candy is crunchy chunks of spun molasses enrobed in dark chocolate, also known as "fairy food," "seafoam," and "violet crumbles.") And the chocolate-dipped fruit repertoire includes orange, apricot, pineapple, pear, and kiwi.

What we like best is the hot fudge sundae, its fudge made from a recipe acquired in 1918 from a traveling salesman for the princely sum of twenty-five dollars. It is a bittersweet, not-too-thick elixir that just may be the best hot fudge in this solar system or any other. When you order a sundae, the great, dark stuff is served in a manner befitting its distinction: in a small pitcher alongside the tulip glass full of ice cream and whipped cream, so you can pour or spoon it on to taste. This serving technique provides a fascinating demonstration of how one's soda fountain habits reflect one's personality. Do you pour on all the fudge at one time, willy-nilly, risking that some will spill over the sides of the serving glass? Do you pour it on spoonful-by-spoonful, carefully ensuring that every bite will have just the proper balance of ice cream and fudge? Or do you eat all the ice cream, with maybe just a dash of fudge poured on, so you can then conclude your snack by downing all the hot fudge that remains in one dizzy chocoholic binge?

Leon's

1640 E. 79th St.   773-731-1454
Chicago, IL   LD | $

For the Roadfooder traveling through town, Leon's is a huge pain in the neck. That's because the food it serves is some of the messiest barbecue anywhere, and there is no place to eat it. Everything at Leon's is take-out. On a pleasant afternoon, it would be great to dine standing up off the trunk of one's car, but local gulls are wise, and as soon as any food is out in the open, they start flocking and squawking and making threatening dives toward your meal. While we have never actually been attacked, these birds make outdoor dining feel downright dangerous. So you eat in your car, winding up with sauce on your fingers, the steering wheel, the seats, the gear shift, everywhere.

Rant over. The fact is, we love this place. The food is Chicago soul barbecue at its finest. Ribs, rib tips, and hot links are insanely luxurious, the rib meat pulling from its bones in long, savory strips, the hot link a real Chicago-style sausage, very soulful but with a distinct Italian accent. All these things are available with mild or hot sauce, the latter a serious lip-tingler. They are served in a cardboard boat, the meat topped with French fries, the fries sopped with sauce, the whole pile crowned with a few pieces of spongy white bread, the purpose of which is to absorb sauce and rib juice.

Customers and staff are separated by bulletproof glass. As in a bank, you slide your money through a slot, and when your meal is packed, they send it out via a lazy susan that ensures you can't shoot them, or we suppose, vice versa. But our experience is that Leon's looks scarier than it is. We wouldn't likely visit at midnight, but every lunch we've had here has been a totally pleasant experience, the staff helpful and clientele friendly. It's only the birds in the parking lot that feel threatening.

(Leon's other locations in Chicago are 8249 S. Cottage Grove, 1158 W. 59th St., and 4550 S. Archer Ave.)

Manny's

1141 S. Jefferson St.   312-939-2855
Chicago, IL   BL | $$

We usually return to our favorite Chicago cafeteria-style deli with the vow of not having corned beef sandwiches. There are so many other good-looking things to eat in the line. On a recent visit, for instance, we gazed upon such day's delights as kasha and bowtie noodles, chop suey, short ribs of beef, oxtail stew, and pierogies, not to mention the everyday matzoh ball soup, blintzes, and potato latkes. But once again, the beauty of the warm corned beef, thin-sliced before one's eyes and piled between slices of good, glossy-crusted rye bread in a pile of rosy-red cured-meat moistness, won out and that's what we ate . . . sided by potato latkes.

Gino Gambarota, Manny's corned beef man for the last ten years, will cut the meat the way you like it—lean, fatty, or regular—but he will not cut it thick. "The art of cutting corned beef is to cut it as thin as possible, and against the grain," Gino says. His slices are shaved so thin they verge on disintegration, but they stay intact and miraculously succulent.

Handfuls of this magnificent meat are stuffed into sandwiches so large that many customers eat one half and take the other back to the office. When a diminutive woman in a business suit asks Gino if he can make her only half a sandwich, he sasses back, "Lady, this isn't Highland Park!" (Highland Park is a hoity-toity suburb on the North Shore.) The sandwiches get made and sold so quickly that during busy mealtimes Gino always sets up four or five ready-made with a potato pancake on the plate, so customers in a hurry can bypass the hot food at the beginning of the cafeteria line and nab what they want without fuss at the sandwich counter. No prepared sandwich remains on the counter longer than forty-five seconds before a customer speeds past and pulls it down onto a tray.

Manny's charm goes far beyond its great deli sandwiches and inviting hot meals. At the edge of Chicago's Loop, not far from where the everything-goes bazaar known as Maxwell Street once thrived, it remains a magnet for Chicagoans of every stripe. Dining room tables are occupied by politicians and businesspeople, wise guys and university professors, and cured-meat lovers from distant suburbs. When a newspaper photographer joined us at a recent meal, a nearby Chicago cop just couldn't resist coming over to investigate the reason the camera was out. When he saw the photog focusing on a corned beef sandwich, he beamed with understanding and gave us the high sign.

Mr. Beef

666 N. Orleans St.   312-337-8500
Chicago, IL   LD | $

Mr. Beef is a premier source for the Second City's number one street food, Italian beef. Great heaps of ultra-thin-sliced, garlic-infused beef are piled into a length of muscular Italian bread that gets soft as beef juices soak into it, but retains the oomph to stay in one piece even if you order your sandwich "dipped," which means double-soaked in gravy. An important choice you'll need to make is whether or not you want your sandwich topped with roasted red peppers or the peppery vegetable mélange known as giardiniera, which is crunchy, spicy, and a brilliant contrast to the full-flavored beef.

Sausages here are excellent as well—cooked on a grate until taut and bursting with juice. You can get a sausage sandwich in similar configurations as beef, and it is also possible to have a combo, which is a length of sausage and a pile of beef loaded into the bread.

Accommodations are minimal. There is an adjoining dining room with actual tables at which to sit as well as a counter up front with stools, but the Italian beef connoisseur's choice is to stand at the chest-high counter that rims the perimeter of the main room. Here, the wax paper that wraps the sandwich can be unwrapped to catch all the spillage and keep it at handy plucking distance while you dine.

Paradise Pup

1724 S. River Rd.   847-699-8590
Des Plaines, IL   L | $

The name is Paradise Pup and the hot dogs are indeed excellent—Chicagoland classics that are available topped with a wheelbarrow's worth of condiments. And the Italian beef sandwiches are top-tier. But the Pup's primary claim to fame is its cheeseburger. A hefty patty charcoal-grilled to crusty succulence, all the more delicious when ordered with a sheaf of bacon on top or perhaps raw or grilled onions, it comes on a seeded kaiser roll. You get your choice of cheese—American, mozzarella, or the connoisseur's choice, Merkt's, which is a tangy Cheddar from Wisconsin that matches perfectly with the beef.

Seasoned French fries are excellent, too, whether you order them plain or loaded, which means heaped with cheese, bacon, and sour cream. To drink: a cream-rich milkshake.

Dining accommodations are virtually nonexistent—a handful of counter seats and outdoor tables with umbrellas—and the small eat-shack is almost always crowded. Expect to wait.

Poochie's

3832 Dempster St.	847-673-0100
Skokie, IL	LD | $

Poochie's red hots are all-beef Vienna franks boiled to perfect plumpness and served in tender, seeded Rosen's-brand buns. Char dogs, cooked over coals, are crusty, blackened versions thereof. Polish sausages are plumper, porkier variants that are slit in a spiral pattern to attain maximum crunchy surface area. And if one in a bun of any of these tube steaks is insufficient for your appetite, you can get either a jumbo dog or a double. Our personal favorite meal is a jumbo char dog with Cheddar fries (super fries!) on the side.

Poochie's is proud of its char-cooked hamburgers, and we like them very much, especially piled high with those sweet grilled onions. But if you are passing through Chicago and stop at Poochie's with time for only one street-food indulgence, make it a red hot with the works and a side of fries. It is an only-in-Chicago meal, and a jewel in the crown of America's Roadfood.

Ricobene's

252 W. 26th St.	312-225-5555
Chicago, IL	LD | $

Italian beef gets all the glory when Chicago street food is discussed, and Ricobene's serves a fine beef sandwich with natural gravy, but the main claim to fame of this 1946-vintage Bridgeport eatery (now in modern quarters) is its breaded steak sandwich. An Italian-American neighborhood invention, the sandwich is a vast, pounded-thin sheet of meat that is lightly breaded and fried, then rolled into a bundle and stuffed inside a long loaf of Italian bread with a coat of red gravy (tomato sauce). Favored garnishes include fried hot peppers, spicy giardiniera vegetable medley, or shredded mozzarella. It is a meal—no, two meals—in a bun.

Beyond its bodacious breaded steak sandwich, Ricobene's serves virtually all the great Chicago street foods, including Italian beef, pizza, and hot dogs, as well as a delectable "Vesuvio Italian Classic" sandwich. This is a quick-eats version of the meal known in more upscale restaurants as chicken Vesuvio (garlic-flavored chicken with cooked-soft hunks of potato). In this case, you get a crisp breaded cutlet dressed with onions, lettuce, tomato, and mayo stuffed into a length of Italian bread.

Whatever else you order, be sure to get an order of French fries, either plain or gobbed with molten Cheddar cheese. These are some of the city's best—dark, skin-on, and crisp.

Stash's

610 Central Ave.   847-432-6550

Highland Park, IL   LD | $

If you are north of the city and in need of a great Chicago hot dog, find Stash's in Highland Park. It's not a charming location, located in Port Clinton Square along with a bunch of mall-style businesses, but the red hots and French fries are first rate.

You can have your all-beef frank steamed, but we prefer ours charred, meaning its surface gets crusty all around the edges, while the inside still drips juice. It is pocketed in a fresh Rosen's brand poppy-seed bun and topped with a choice of nine different condiments, from mustard and relish to hot peppers and celery salt. If you get it "dragged through the garden," the hot dog itself will be completely eclipsed by long pickle spears, tomato slices, onions, etc. This is a beautiful wiener, and delicious. There are jumbo dogs and Polishes, too, as well as double dogs in a single bun, but it's our opinion that one of Stash's normal dogs, garnished with a plentiful supply of condiments, is one perfect food.

Beyond hot dogs, Stash's has a vast menu that includes a pasta bar from which the management will create whatever sort of dish you want from ten kinds of noodles, six different sauces, and all sorts of vegetable and cheese toppings. In addition, there are hamburgers, beef sandwiches, gyros, wraps, pockets, and quesadillas. We've never tried any of these things, but we do have one other important recommendation to make: French fries. With a Stash's dog, they are essential. These are four-star potatoes with a creamy center and crunchy edge. Cheddar cheese is available as a topping, but in this case, all we want is a sprinkle of salt.

Superdawg

6363 N. Milwaukee Ave.   773-763-0660
Chicago, IL   LD | $

In the Windy City, all-beef hot dogs rule, and Superdawg serves some of the finest: taut-skinned tube steaks in steamed-soft buns, available with the complete panoply of condiments. Everything at Superdawg really is super, including crisp-edged Superfries, Superonion chips, Superburgers, Supershakes, and Whoopskidogs (the house name for a Polish sausage).

You'll have no trouble spotting Superdawg as you approach along Milwaukee Avenue: a pair of ten-foot statues of a male and female wiener (Flaurie and Maurie) wear leopard-skin togas and stand high atop the roof, winking electrically. Opened in 1948, this Roadfood landmark still features the once-modern "Suddenserver" automated order system and serves its dogs in cardboard boxes that announce, "Your Superdawg lounges inside contentedly cushioned in Superfries, comfortably attired in mustard, relish, onion, pickle, and hot pepper."

Tempo Café

6 East Chestnut St.   312-943-4373
Chicago, IL   Always open | $

Open all the time and just a short walk from upscale Michigan Avenue, aka the Magnificent Mile, Tempo Café is a haven for cops, night-beat reporters, and people who have nowhere else to go when the bars close. Specialty of the house is the egg skillet omelet, served in its own metal pan. Variations include the Michigan (which includes Cheddar cheese and diced apples), the State Street (broccoli, ham, mushrooms, tomato), and the Jamaican (banana, walnut, honey). The eggs are presented atop a bed of crunchy fried potato disks and accompanied by thick slabs of sesame-dotted toast with a globe of sweet butter and a ramekin of housemade, fine-cut marmalade. Before breakfast is served, everybody gets a single pitted prune and a wedge of orange. Corned beef hash is terrific, too. Coffee cups are constantly refilled, and the caffeine menu includes latte and cappuccino.

Twin Anchors

1655 N. Sedgwick St.   312-266-1616

Chicago, IL   D | $$

Pop culture devotees know Twin Anchors for two big reasons: it was a favorite hangout of Frank Sinatra when he came to the toddlin' town, and it was transformed into O'Reilly's Italian Restaurant for the Bonnie Hunt melodrama *Return to Me.*

Foodies know it for just one reason: ribs. Here are the best baby back ribs in a city obsessed with rib excellence. They are succulent beyond description, tender enough that teeth are optional to eat them, and basted with a wonderful "zesty sauce" that is just hot enough to tease even more sweet pork flavor from the meat. (Mild sauce is also an option.) For the record, this type of rib is significantly different from the spare ribs commonly offered in soul food barbecues, the latter being larger, denser, and a good exercise for healthy dentition. We would not call Twin Anchors ribs soulful, but we would definitely say they're delicious.

There is a full menu beyond ribs, including steaks, fried chicken, and sandwiches. They look fine . . . on other people's plates. When we come to Twin Anchors, we know nothing but ribs.

The place is a charming corner tavern in Old Town dating back to the early twentieth century. It was a soda pop store (i.e., speakeasy) during Prohibition, then christened "Twin Anchors" in 1932 by a proprietor who had twin sons whom he considered his anchors to reality. Today the walls are festooned with nautical knickknacks and abundant pictures of the Chairman of the Board.

Walker Bros. Original Pancake House

153 Green Bay Rd.   847-251-6000

Wilmette, IL   BLD | $$

One of a nationwide chain of the Original Pancake House, which has defined pancake excellence since 1953, Walker Brothers is clean, polite, comfortable, generous, and delicious. Name your favorite restaurant accolade, and this place sets the standard . . . except for "fast." There is usually a wait for a table, a long wait on weekends.

Everything served is eye-opening good, from fresh orange juice and dark coffee (with a pitcher of heavy cream) to thick-sliced bacon and chicken-apple sausage. Order eggs and you may exclaim, as we have, "I forgot how good a fresh egg, cooked in pure butter, can taste!" Granted, it is difficult to order eggs when the pancakes are so good. The plainer ones are simple excellence—rich buttermilk cakes, tangy sourdough flapjacks, old-time buckwheat—and the snazzy crepe menu includes banana crepes and Cherry Kijafa crepes, and there is lavish seafood Newburg with crusty potato pancakes.

Our favorite meals, and the kitchen's showstoppers, are baked pancakes: the German pancake and the apple pancake, magnificent skillet creations of egg-rich batter that puff high above the plate. The apple pancake is a breakfast mountain running rivers of cinnamon. The German pancake is a vast mesa that totally covers its plate. On the side come lemon wedges and powdered sugar to spread across it and create a fine, sweet-tart syrup. This is pancake perfection!

The Wiener's Circle

2622 N. Clark St.
Chicago, IL

773-477-7444
LD | $

The name of the Wiener's Circle is a typically Chicagoan bit of culinary wordplay, but there is no joke about the red hots served here. They are among the city's best, presented in steamy soft Rosen's-brand poppy seed buns and topped with flawless condiments.

The mustard is classic yellow, the piccalilli is brilliant green and vividly pickly, the tomatoes are small and flavorful—four or five fresh-cut slices per dog. And there are grilled onions or raw, hot peppers, and a sprinkle of celery salt. Have your frankfurter as you like it, from naked to loaded, and you will not be disappointed. The major decision to make, dog-wise, is whether you want it boiled or charred. At many of Chicago's red-hot joints, we recommend boiled or steamed because it yields the plumpest, tautest skin, but here at the Wiener's Circle, charred is the way to go. Cooked on the grate just behind the order counter, the char dogs get a good crunch from the flames; and for us, that rugged tube steak nestled in its super-tender bun is essential Chicago.

Don't get a hot dog without French fries. These are beauties: hand cut, freshly fried, served in ridiculously large amounts that totally overflow their cardboard boat and fall all over the wax paper on which the boat is pushed toward you out the order window.

Inside, the perimeter of the Wiener's Circle is outfitted with counters and stools well-suited for hot-dog eating and for gazing out the window at Clark Street. Orders are taken and food delivered by one of several gals at the open-kitchen window. "Char Dog!" one calls out to a customer, using what he ordered as his name, then continuing her conversation as the bill is paid by calling him Sweetheart, Honey, and Darling. On other occasions, it is not unheard of for the staff to speak to customers the way baseball fans yell at umpires who have made a controversial call. Such personality is an extra condiment that helps make Wiener's Circle hot dogs something special.

Coney Island Wiener

131 W. Main St. 219-424-2997
Fort Wayne, IN LD | $

Coney Island wiener shops abound throughout the Midwest, "Coney Island" being the old term for hot dog, which folks in the Heartland used
to associate with New York. Fort Wayne's Coney Island, a Main Street
storefront formally known as the Famous Coney Island Wiener Stand,
was established in 1914, and has built its reputation on the classic Greek-
American frankfurter: a modest-size bright pink weenie nestled in a soft
bun and topped with Coney sauce, which is a fine-grind chili with a rainbow of seasonings and a fetching sweetness. Although all condiments are
technically optional, everyone orders their hot dogs with Coney sauce, as
well as a line of mustard and a good sprinkle of chopped raw onion. The
only other things on the menu are baked beans, chili (more a soup than a
stew), and hamburgers.

Seating is at counter stools, many of which offer a nice view not only
of the doings behind the counter and between staff and customers, but
also through the big window out onto Main Street.

Tipster Brett Poirier, who encouraged us to eat Fort Wayne's famous
Coney Islands, pointed out that it makes a great way station for anyone

traveling America's original coast-to-coast thoroughfare, the Lincoln Highway.

Gray Brothers Cafeteria

555 S. Indiana St.	317-831-5614
Mooresville, IN	LD | $

Gray Brothers is gigantic, and quite deluxe as far as cafeterias go: leaded glass windows in the doors, plenty of tasteful décor. Almost any time you walk in, it will be crowded, but that's no problem because the cafeteria line moves really fast, and besides, your wait takes you along the "preview line," which allows you to study the dozens and dozens of food items from which you will soon be choosing. The trays are big ones, but if you're at all like us, you'll find yours fully occupied well before you get to the rolls and beverages at the end of the line.

It's hard to know what to recommend because we've never had anything at Gray's we didn't like. Among the most memorable dishes are chicken and noodles, meat loaf (with mashed potatoes, natch), chicken livers, and fried chicken with an ultra-flavorful crust that pulls off the bird like strips of pork cracklin'. The way things work in Gray's line is that you tell the servers what entree you want; they put it onto a nice flower-patterned partitioned plate then slide the plate down to the vegetable area, where it is piled with whatever sides you desire.

Who can resist the corn bread stuffing? Or mac 'n' cheese? We also love the heartland salads, especially the ones composed of creamy peas and of carrots, raisins, and marshmallows. Desserts are dazzling, with whole pies arrayed on shelves below the individual slices (many pies get bought and taken home). Fruit pies abound, of course, and there are swell butterscotch, banana cream, and pumpkin flavors, but the Indiana favorite, and a specialty of Gray's, is sugar-cream pie . . . as simple and pure and good as the name suggests.

Hollyhock Hill

8110 N. College Ave.	317-251-2294
Indianapolis, IN	D | $$

In 1928, on a quiet street at the northernmost outskirts of Indianapolis, a restaurant named the Country Cottage started serving family-style chicken dinners. The city has grown around it and the name was changed to honor the hollyhock bushes on the lawn, but the specialty of the house is still fried chicken dinners.

The time to fully experience the bedrock character of this place is Sunday, after church. Pastels on the ladies echo the flowery murals in the pastel dining room, which is partitioned with trellises and wrought iron the color of Easter eggs. Tables are draped with linen, and some of the really big ones have lazy Susans in the center so members of big families can spin the wheel and grab what they want.

The meal people come to eat is a ritualized banquet that begins with pleasant enough but unmemorable pickled beets and cottage cheese and salad with sweet and sour vinaigrette then upshifts to unforgettably good chicken. Fish, shrimp, and steak are options, but this chicken is skillet-fried and wonderful, served with pan gravy. To go with it there are bowls of mashed potatoes, green beans, and corn niblets, as well as hot breads with apple butter. All these trustworthy selections are replenished for as long as anyone at the table wants to keep eating them, but it's only the chicken that makes you want to eat 'til you bust.

Dessert is ingenuous and fun: make your own sundae. Sauces of butterscotch, crème de menthe, and chocolate are provided to dollop as desired on your ice cream. The default ice cream flavor is vanilla, but true Hoosiers opt for the state favorite, peppermint.

Jamie's Soda Fountain

307 N. Main St.   765-459-5888
Kokomo, IN

Jamie's is a genuine, old-fashioned Main Street soda fountain where there are enough syrups on hand to offer a near-infinite variety of drawn-to-order drinks. Chocolate Coke? How about a diet chocolate Coke? Or a cherry ginger ale or a vanilla root beer or a diet vanilla-strawberry phosphate? Of course there are green rivers and black cows and black-and-white sodas and pink lemonades. Plus shakes, malts, sundaes, and floats. The swankiest shakes are made with hot fudge and/or black raspberry flavoring.

Beyond a festival of confectionery beverages and desserts, Jamie's food menu is a catalog of lunch-counter fare. The fried ham sandwich is excellent. Hoosier tenderloins are available breaded and fried or grilled. There are hamburgers, cheeseburgers, bacon cheeseburgers, and burger baskets (including fries). If you wish to exercise knife-and-fork, you can have chicken and noodles or gravy-blanketed hot beef Manhattan. For breakfast, which is served all day, the choices range from bacon and eggs and wraps and sandwiches to biscuits and gravy.

Good French fries are available on the side, as are hot potato chips and deep-fried macaroni and cheese.

Jonathan Byrd's Cafeteria

I-65 and Main St. (Exit 99)   317-881-8888
Greenwood, IN   LD | $

Jonathan Byrd's boasts that it is America's biggest cafeteria, a claim with which we would not argue. The serving line is eighty-eight feet long with a minimum of twenty entrees at any one time (serving continuously from 10:45 A.M. to 8:45 P.M. daily) as well as countless vegetable side dishes, Jell-Os, salads, desserts, bread and rolls. In need of comfort food when we stopped by, we dined on turkey potpie and a bowl of chicken and noodles, the latter an especially salubrious bowl of thick, soft pasta and shreds of chicken in just enough broth to keep it all moist.

Among the memorable side dishes were macaroni and cheese with a good portion of crusty, chewy top-cheese mixed in with the creamy noodles from below, a buttermilk drop biscuit that was a textural joy, and bread pudding laced with slices of cooked-soft apple and plenty of sweet caramel sauce.

Jonathan Byrd, the founder and proprietor, is a man on a mission from God. "I was impressed by how many significant biblical events involved people eating together," he wrote for a story in *Guideposts* (reprints of which are available in the vestibule). As a matter of principle, he serves no liquor in the cafeteria, not even in its banquet rooms, and the Jonathan Byrd function rooms regularly play host to gospel concerts.

JWI Confectionery

207 W. Main St.   812-265-6171
Madison, IN   L | $

A beautiful restoration, complete with nostalgic photos of long-gone high-school days on the wall, makes a visit to this old soda parlor an irresistible taste of history as well as a worthwhile detour for Roadfood of the sweetest kind. The building that houses JWI Confectionery was built when Andrew Jackson was president—in 1835! Madison is an Ohio River town with a great historical feel to it, and this Main Street storefront shop, which old-timers know as Betty Mundt's Candies, dates back to 1917. JWI still makes candies from heirloom recipes in vintage molds, and the ice cream is manufactured in a machine at the back of the store.

Lunch is served from about 11:00 A.M. until early evening, and the meals we've seen look dandy—meat loaf, roast beef, cold-cut sandwiches, soups, quiche, etc.—but to be honest, we've only seen them. When we come to JWI, we want pie, cake, candies, cookies, and ice cream. The ice cream is especially excellent, ranging from cones and single scoops in a dish to sundaes topped with real whipped cream. Of course we could not resist the top-of-the-line pig's dinner known as the '37 Flood—a ten-scoop, multitopping extravaganza that JWI says will feed four to six people.

King Ribs Bar-B-Q

4130 N. Keystone Ave.	317-543-0841
Indianapolis, IN	LD | $

King Ribs is a former automobile garage with no dining facilities. All business is drive through, walk up, or home delivery. It is the sort of barbecue you smell before you see. The scent of more than a dozen drums lined up, smoldering wood inside them, and pork sizzling atop the wood perfumes the neighborhood for blocks.

The house motto is "Fit for a King," and of all the regal meals to eat here, ribs top the list. They are tender enough so that the meat pulls from the bone in heavy strips, barely glazed with sauce, but chewy enough that the pork flavor resonates forever. It is a pure, sweet flavor, just faintly tingling with the smoke that has infused the meat.

Side dishes include macaroni and cheese that is thick as pudding and intensely cheesy, with noodles so soft they are almost indistinguishable from the cheese. Also baked beans, fine-cut slaw, and white bread for mopping. For dessert, there is a choice of sweeties: chess pie or sweet potato pie.

Main Café

520 Main St.	812-682-3370
New Harmony, IN	BL | $

The southern Indiana countryside for miles around New Harmony is farmland: no business or industry, no malls, no convenience stores, no chain restaurants. Just rolling green landscape and two-lane roads. A former utopian community created by folks who sought heaven by living simply, New Harmony remains a bucolic small town that happens to have a dandy little Main Street café. Just sitting here is a Roadfood delight. Despite lively table-to-table conversations (everybody who eats here knows everybody else), it is a meditative sort of place, ideal for getting centered, as well as nicely fed, before or during a day of travel along the Ohio River Valley.

In truth, the breakfast menu is not all that interesting, the baking powder biscuits are slightly overweight, and dairy products are virtually unheard of (buttery spread for biscuits, powdered creamer for coffee). But we relished the very piggy, crisp-fried tenderloin that came alongside our plate of eggs. And on a return trip, we delighted in the ploughman's lunch of ham, beans, and corn bread. And the pies—coconut cream and chocolate cream—are blue-ribbon beauties.

Mug 'n' Bun Drive-In

5211 W. 10th St.   317-244-5669
Indianapolis, IN   LD | $

The mug is root beer; the bun is the fried pork cutlet sandwich known as a Hoosier tenderloin. Together they are a paradigmatic Midwest drive-in meal. This timeless drive-in not far from the Indianapolis Motor Speedway gives customers a choice of eating off the dashboard or at outdoor picnic tables umbrellaed by radiant heaters for cold weather. In-car diners blink their lights for service and food is presented by carhops on window trays. People seated at tables summon the kitchen by using a buzzer that adjoins the posted menu.

We were tipped off to Mug 'n' Bun by journalist Dale Lawrence, who described its root beer as "legitimately creamy, yes, but also smoky, carrying hints of vanilla fudge and molasses, as rich and smooth as a dessert wine." In other words, not like your average soda pop! It truly is delicious root beer, served in thick frosty mugs and in sizes that include small, large, giant, quart, half-gallon, and gallon.

As for the tenderloin, it too is big, if not the juiciest in town. We were more fond of the double cheeseburger that filled out its bun with meat to spare. Also, the onion rings are something special: battered thick, crisp, and sweet.

Nick's Kitchen

506 N. Jefferson St.   260-356-6618

Huntington, IN   BLD | $

The tenderloin is one of America's great regional sandwiches; historians believe it was invented here in Huntington. The story is that Nick Frienstein started frying breaded pork cutlets in 1904 to sell in sandwiches from a street cart in town; four years later he opened a small café called Nick's Kitchen. His method of preparing the fried pork cutlets was finessed one winter shortly after Nick moved to the café and his brother Jake suffered such severe frostbite that he lost his fingers. Jake, whose job it was to bread the slices of pork, found that his stumps made good tools for pounding the meat to make it tender. Since then, a tenderloin (no need to say pork tenderloin) has been defined as a sandwich of pork that has been either beaten tender (with a wooden hammer) or run through a mechanical tenderizer (or both).

Now run by Jean Anne Bailey, whose father owned the town café starting in 1969, Nick's Kitchen lists its tenderloin on the menu with a challenge that's more than a little ironic considering its culinary history: "Bet You Need Both Hands." Two hands are barely adequate for hoisting the colossal sandwich, which is built around a wavy disk of audibly crunchy pork that extends a good two to three inches beyond the circumference of a five-inch bun, virtually eclipsing its plate. Soaked in buttermilk, which gives a tangy twist to the meat's sweetness, and tightly cased in a coat of rugged cracker crumbs (not the more typical fine-grind cracker meal), the lode of pork inside the crust fairly drips with moisture. Jean Anne tells us she buys the meat already cut and cubed. She pounds it, marinates it, breads it, and fries it.

Nick's Kitchen isn't only a tenderloin stop. It's a wonderful three-meal-a-day town café with big breakfasts and a noontime blackboard of daily specials. We loved our plate of ham, beans, and corn bread, and we were bowled over by Jean Anne's pies. "My father served frozen ones," she says. "I knew I wanted something better." Made using a hand-me-down dough recipe that incorporates a bit of corn syrup, her fruit pies have a flaky crust that evaporates on the tongue, melding with brilliant-flavored rhubarb or black raspberries. Butterscotch pie—which she learned to cook from her grandmother—is more buttery than sweet, nothing at all like cloying pies made from pudding filling. Sugar-cream pie, an Indiana signature dessert, is like cream candy in a savory crust.

Phil Smidt and Son

1205 Calumet Ave.
Hammond, IN

800-FROGLEG
LD | $$

The primary reason to come to Smidt is pan-fried perch, the formal name for which is "a mess of perch." It is available whole, boned, buttered, or boned and buttered. Old-timers do their own boning and make it look easy. The rest of us get fillets, swimming in butter. They are small sides of fish, pan-crisped, firm, freshwater luscious. Plates of perch are preceded by five relish trays, lined up in formation on the table: potato salad, kidney bean marinade, pickled beets, slaw, and cottage cheese.

If perch is not your dish, the other house specialty is frog legs, either crisp-fried or sautéed. They are messy and delicious and make chicken wings seem like second-class appendages. Smidt offers half-and-half plates of perch and legs, as well as a full menu of more traditional lake seafood, steaks, and chicken. For dessert, the one thing to know about is gooseberry pie, served warm and available à la mode.

It was about one hundred years ago that Smidt started in business as a fisherman's shanty. Not too many fishermen are left in this industrial neighborhood, and Smidt has become a majestic restaurant with weekend entertainment and banquet rooms. It's not a Roadfood diamond in the rough, but it is a Midwest culinary jewel.

Shapiro's

808 S. Meridian St.
Indianapolis, IN

317-631-4041
BLD | $

For a century, this "granddaddy of delis" in Indianapolis has been a source of excellent, authentic Jewish food, ranging from lox and onion omelets in the morning to gefilte fish and matzoh ball soup. Not a typical urban delicatessen, Shapiro's serves meals cafeteria-style. In addition to a full repertoire of traditional kosher-style fare, its menu includes such Midwestern specialties as buttered perch plates (Friday) and Hoosier sugar-cream pie.

The corned beef sandwich is as good as any corned beef sandwich from the best delis of New York, Chicago, and L.A. The meat itself is lean but not too much so; each slice is rimmed with a thin halo of smudgy spice and is so moist that it glistens. The slices are mounded between slabs of Shapiro's own rye bread, which has a shiny, hard, sour crust.

Slather on the mustard, crunch into a dill pickle to set your taste buds tingling, and this sandwich will take you straight to deli heaven.

Get some latkes (potato pancakes), too. They are double-thick, moist, and starchy—great companions to a hot lunch of short ribs or stuffed peppers. Shapiro's supplements ordinary latkes with cinnamon-scented ones—wonderful when heaped with sour cream. And soup: bean, lentil, split pea, and chowder are daily specials; you can always order chicken soup or red beet borscht.

Shapiro's does big take-out business: sandwiches, salads, whole loaves of bread, and cakes. We try never to leave without a babka.

Teibel's

1775 Route 41	219-865-2000
Schererville, IN	LD | $$

Teibel's is one of a handful of restaurants that continue to serve the favorite big-eats Sunday-supper sort of meal so beloved in northern Indiana, buttered lake perch. When it opened in 1930, it was a mom-and-pop café, and today it is a giant-size dining establishment (run by the same family), but the culinary values that made it famous still prevail.

The ritual feast starts with a relish tray—scallions, olives, celery, and carrots—followed by a salad (superfluous), then a plate piled high with tender fillets of perch glistening with butter. It is a big portion, and this fish is full-flavored; by the time our plate was empty, we were more than satisfied. Our extreme satisfaction was due also to the fact that we had to have an order of Teibel's fried chicken, too. Perhaps even more famous than the perch, this chicken is prepared from a recipe that Grandma Teibel brought from Austria many years ago. It is chicken with a crumbly red-gold crust and juicy insides, in a whole other league from the stuff that comes in a bucket from fast-food franchises. Some other interesting items from Teibel's menu: frog legs (another local passion) and walleye pike. For fish- and frog-frowners, there is a turkey dinner.

After a family-style feed like this, what could be nicer than a hot apple dumpling? Teibel's flake-crusted, cinnamon-scented dumpling is served à la mode with caramel sauce on top.

Village Inn

107 S. Main St.   574-825-2043
Middlebury, IN   BL | $

The traffic patterns in Middlebury are frequently determined by the comings and goings of the somber black buggies driven by all the Amish people who live around here and visit town for trading and livestock auctions. If you are looking for a meal fitted to the mighty caloric needs of such hardworking people, we recommend a booth at the Village Inn.

Of course, you can have eggs and potatoes and toast, just as in any regular town café, but here you can also plow into a vast plate of cornmeal mush, accompanied by head cheese. Lunches are huge, too: chicken and noodles or meat loaf or beef stew and mashed potatoes, smothered steaks and stuffed peppers, all served with plenty of richly dressed slaws and salads and well-cooked vegetables enriched with bread crumbs, butter, and cheese.

You cannot say you have truly partaken of this monumental heartland cuisine unless you follow breakfast, lunch, or dinner by a piece or two of pie. The Village Inn offers a dozen different kinds daily, including blueberry (from locally picked berries), lattice-topped raisin, and the pie known among Indiana farm folks as O.F., meaning "old fashioned": little more than sugar, eggs, and cream, whipped into a jiggly custard perched atop a flaky pastry crust. Whole pies can be ordered in advance, to go.

Walls' Drive-In

Hwy. 66   812-547-8501
Cannelton, IN   LD | $

A sign above Walls' Drive-In along the Ohio River in southernmost Indiana announces that it is "Home of the Big Square Burger," a promise that drew our car into the parking lot like a magnet. Even without the sign, we would have wanted to eat at Walls'. It is a pretty little place by the side of the road, painted red, white, and blue outside, with picnic tables out back and order windows in the front.

The Big Square Burger turned out to be a patty of meat that is squared off at the edges, similar to Wendy's, but it isn't really all that big. It is a quarter-pound patty, available in the Big Square Box configuration, which means fully dressed with French fries and baked beans on the side. If you do arrive with an appetite for a really big one, we suggest you order a double or, better yet, a Wall Banger Special, which is a Big Square topped with melted cheese and a round of Canadian bacon.

Beyond hamburgers, Walls' has an exemplary fast-food menu featuring crisp-fried tenderloins (those are pounded-thin rounds of pork on a bun that are a passion in these parts), hot dogs, and plump Polish sausages. Good ice cream, too, either hard-packed or soft-serve.

Welliver's

40 E. Main St.	765-489-4131
Hagerstown, IN	LD | $$

Guy Welliver bought a restaurant on this location in 1946, hoping to realize his life's dream of becoming a haberdasher. The plan was to run the eatery for a while and when he made enough money, transform it into a hat store. But one night after an especially satisfying dinner at his mother-in-law's house, Guy changed plans and decided to serve meals like the ones she had served him: big and bountiful, with multiple main courses, lots of side dishes, and a choice of desserts.

So began Welliver's smorgasbord, which over the last six decades has become a well-loved bonanza for anyone the least bit hungry traveling along I-70 near the Indiana-Ohio border. Today's Welliver's is huge in every way. It has nine dining rooms—which can get so crowded on weekends that you will wait for a table—and the selection of food is awe-inspiring. Outstanding entrees include Hoosier chicken with cream gravy, fried chicken livers that connoisseurs believe to be the best in the Midwest, and heaps of succulent peel-and-eat shrimp. The selection of side dishes includes warm cinnamon bread that drips with sweet icing, "grandma's turnips," which are the best-tasting good-for-you vegetable imaginable, and world-class macaroni and cheese.

Iowa

Archie's Waeside

224 4th Ave. NE 712-546-7011
Le Mars, IA D | $$$

A steak-eaters' magnet since Archie Jackson started it in 1949, Archie's is now run by grandson Bob Rand, who is a fanatic for excellence. He loves to describe details of the dry-aging process—how the meat sheds moisture but absorbs the flavors of the marbling. But, technical details aside, your taste buds will tell you that the steaks served here are among the best in the Midwest, some of the best anywhere in America. They arrive a little crusty on the outside, overwhelmingly juicy and bursting with the full, resonating flavor of corn-fed beef. Even the filet mignon, usually a tender cut that is less flavorful, sings with the succulent authority of blue-ribbon protein. Bone-in rib eye is extravagantly succulent. And an off-the-menu item called the Benny Weiker (named for a good customer of years ago who used to be a cattle buyer in the Sioux City stockyards) is simply the most handsome piece of meat we have ever seen presented on a plate: an eighteen-ounce, center-cut, twenty-one-day dry-aged filet mignon.

Jack L. Holmes, the Iowa *fine bouche* who clued us in to Archie's, said that we would be shocked not only by the quality of the steak, but by its low price. He was right. Relatively speaking, in the realm of high-quality beef, Archie's is an incredible bargain. Our supper for three—the Benny Weiker, the ribeye, and a plate with a pair of immense Iowa pork chops (perhaps a pound-and-a-half of pork, total), plus onion rings, Mexican cheeseballs, and all the fixin's—cost a grand total of $75 plus tip.

And by the way, in the above paragraph, where we mention "all the fixin's," we need to say that the things that come before and during the beef course are pretty special at Archie's. Along with the salad you get a relish tray and a plate of cured-here corned beef: super-lean, high-flavored, beautiful to look at. The waitress suggested we do like regular customers do and shred the spicy beef on our salads. Available companions for meat include a well-browned patty of hash brown potatoes and a trio of substantial corn fritters.

Archie's is a big, pleasant restaurant with capacious booths and hordes of happy customers who come from miles around to enjoy what is a Siouxland prize.

Bob's Drive-Inn

Hwy. 75 S, at Hwy. 3   712-546-5445
Le Mars, IA 51031   L | $

In case you are from any one of the other forty-nine states where loose-meats is unheard of, know this when you come to northwest Iowa: loose-meats is a sandwich of ground beef that is cooked loose—unpattied—and served sauceless. Compared to a hamburger, it has a higgledy-piggledy character, but there is nothing scattered about its satisfying taste. It is customarily dressed with pickle, mustard, and a slice of cheese; and like grits, it is a food spoken of with singular/plural ambivalence. Usually one sandwich is a loosemeats; a batch in the kitchen or a bowlful without the bun are loosemeats.

You will not find loosemeats on the menu that hangs above the order window at Bob's Drive-Inn. That is because it is listed by one of its several aliases, a tavern. At many restaurants that serve it, loosemeats is called something else: tavern, Big T, Charlie Boy, or Tastee. When Roseanne Arnold opened her Big Food Diner over in Eldon out Ottumwa way, journalists unfamiliar with Iowa cuisine made a fuss over the fact that her menu did list loosemeats, a name that to outsiders sounds vaguely taboo. According to Marcia Poole, food writer at the *Sioux City Journal,* folks in Siouxland were righteously angry about Roseanne calling it that. "The other side of Des Moines, it should be called a Maid-Rite," Marcia told us, referring to the eponymous name for the similar sandwich and the Maid-Rite Restaurants that serve it, mostly between Des Moines and Dubuque. "Loosemeats are ours alone."

Loosemeats are so dominant in this area that Bob's menu doesn't even offer a hamburger. If you want beef, you get loosemeats. Browned, strained of fat, then pressure-cooked with sauce and spice, then drained again, the meat is moist, full-flavored, and deeply satisfying. Each sandwich is made on a good-quality roll from Le Mars's own Vander Meer Bakery.

If for some reason you don't want loosemeats, or if you, like us, need to sample every good hot dog that exists, get a couple of franks at this fine place. (At $1.35 apiece, the same price as a loosemeats sandwich, they are a bargain.) These dogs are natural-casing beauties with a real snap to their skin. They come from a sausage maker in West Point, Nebraska.

Root beer is house-made, and fruit shakes are made from real summer fruit.

Coffee Cup Café

616 4th St.   641-594-3765
Sully, IA   BLD | $

If you are southeast of Des Moines looking for the sort of town café where locals come to eat and schmooze, here's the place. Breakfast is lovely—plate-wide golden pancakes and big rounds of sausage; there are eggs and potatoes of course, and modest-size but big-taste cinnamon buns with a translucent sugar glaze, served warm with butter on the side. The meal we like best is lunch. The menu lists hot beef sandwiches and tenderloin steaks, and there is one square-meal special every day—last visit, it was baked ham with mashed potatoes and apple salad. Any time of day you can order Dutch lettuce, a locally preferred salad of crisp, cold iceberg leaves bathed in a warm sweet and sour creamy mustard dressing with pieces of bacon and slices of hard-cooked egg.

No matter what meal you eat, or what time of day you eat it, you must have pie at the Coffee Cup Café. Iowa is major pie country, and it is in just such inconspicuous small-town cafés that some of the very best are eaten. Looking for a good cream pie? Have a wedge of Coffee Cup banana cream. It quivers precariously as the waitress sets it down on the table, the custard jiggling like not-quite-set Jell-O, the foamy white meringue on top wafting like just-spun cotton candy. Below these ribbons of white and yellow is a thin, tawny crust that doesn't break when met with a fork; it flakes. The whole experience of cutting a mouthful, raising it to one's lips, and savoring it, is what we imagine it would be like to eat pastries on the moon or some planet where gravity is only a fraction of earth's; for the word "light" barely does justice to the refinement of this piece of pie.

Darrell's Place

4010 1st St.	712-563-3922
Hamlin, IA	LD | $

Darrell's Place looks more like a large utility shed than a restaurant, but aficionados of the tenderloin know that it is a culinary gem. Winner of the 2004 Iowa Pork Producers Association award for the best tenderloin in the state, Darrell's serves tenderloins that are thick and juicy, enveloped in a crisp, fine-textured crust that is more crunch than breading. The ribbon of meat is a good half-inch thick, making for an ultra-opulent eating experience. And while it is a very large sandwich, the crisp-edged patty extends only a bit beyond the bun, not outrageously far, meaning you can easily pick it up, even with one hand.

Hamlin is a tiny town with a population of less than three hundred. It's a charming place in the heart of farm country and seems light-years away from civilization. And yet it is just fourteen miles north of I-80, a supremely convenient detour for interstate travelers in the west of the state. While visiting, you might consider visiting Nathaniel Hamlin Park, home of the world's largest collection of nails.

Grove Café

124 Main St.	515-232-9784
Ames, IA	BL | $

When you order a pancake at the Grove Café, the word will take on a new meaning. In this place, a pancake truly is a pan cake—a good-size layer of cake that has been cooked in a pan, or in this case, on the grill. Nearly an inch thick in its center, it is wide as its plate—a round of steamy cooked batter that has an appealing orange hue. It comes with a couple of pats of butter and a pitcher of syrup (all of which this cake can absorb with ease). With some peppery Iowa sausage patties, one of these cakes is a full-size meal. Two of them, listed on the menu as a "short stack," are a breakfast for only the tallest of appetites.

Grove Café also offers omelets with hash browns and happy little slices of French toast for breakfast, as well as hamburgers, hot beef, and meat loaf at lunch. But to many of its longtime fans, including hordes of Iowa State alumni who have consumed tens of thousands of calories in these bare-tabled booths and at the low stools of the counter, pancakes are all that matter. To its most devoted fans, Grove Café is a pancake parlor.

Located in the old business district, it has a weathered character with faded cream-colored walls decorated with photos and mementoes from the riding exploits of the proprietor. Among them is a blue ribbon he won at the state fair showing Appaloosa horses. A large sign painted on the wall above the grill jokes, "Just Like Home: You Don't Always Get What You Want."

In't Veld Meat Market

820 Main St.   641-628-3440
Pella, IA   L | $

Most customers come to In't Veld to shop for meat rather than to eat, and even those of us who are just passing through will find such good travel companions as summer sausage, dried beef, and wax-wrapped cheeses. For those in search of regional specialties, the meat to eat is ring bologna, also known as Pella bologna because this town is the only place it is made. It is a tube of sausage about as thick as a pepperoni stick, curled into a horseshoe shape, smoked, and cured and ready to eat. It is delicious sliced cold with a hunk of cheese and a piece of bread; it's even better when you can warm it up and cut it into thick discs like kielbasa. Smoky, vigorously spiced, and firm-textured, this bologna is an only-in-Iowa treat.

For Roadfooders, what is especially good about In't Veld Market is that you can sit down right here and have a hot bologna sandwich: five thick slices on a fresh bakery bun—pass the mustard, please! In fact, a whole menu of meat-market sandwiches is available for eating here (or taking out) until midafternoon each day. In addition to the famous bologna, you can have house-dried beef on a bun, homemade bratwurst with sauerkraut on a hoagie roll, ham and Swiss, or a ground-here beefburger. Side orders are limited to potato salad, macaroni salad, beans, slaw, and Jell-O, and for dessert, we suggest a walk across the square to Jaarsma Bakery, a Dutch-accented shop with some of the most beguiling pastries, sweet cakes, and cookies in the Midwest.

Miles Inn

2622 Leech Ave.   712-276-9825

Sioux City, IA   LD | $

If you look through the Sioux City Yellow Pages for the Miles Inn, you won't find it under *R*, for "Restaurants." It is listed under *T*, for "Taverns." This makes sense in two ways. First, and most obvious, is that it is, in fact, a tavern—a place people come for long, leisurely afternoons or evenings sipping beer, watching the overhead TV, and kibitzing with one another. Built in 1925 by bricklayer John Miles, it is a sturdy edifice that sells suds by the case as well as by the draft. The only hot food you can get in this place is a sandwich, which the sign on the wall calls a Charlie Boy. That's reason number two that its listing under "Taverns" makes sense, because the Charlie Boy is known by many Sioux Cityans as a tavern.

In northwest Iowa, taverns are more popular than hamburgers. Dozens of restaurants serve them, and each has its own twist on the basic formula, which is ground beef that is gently spiced and cooked loose so it remains pebbly when put upon a bun. A scoop of meat is generally garnished with pickle chips and mustard, most often with cheese, and the sandwich is almost never served on a plate.

Miles Inn's definitive taverns (named Charlie Boys after Charlie Miles, who was founder John Miles's son) are served in wax paper that you unwrap and use to catch any drippings. They are rich and well-fatted with a concentrated beef flavor that even a sirloin steak cannot match. (Raise your hand if you agree with us that the one meal that most fully satisfies the deepest hunger for beef is a great burger, even more than a great steak.) Two or three Charlie Boys make a wonderful lunch, and the proper libation is plenty of draft beer from the tap.

Off the Hook

1100 E. 14th St.

515-265-1662

Des Moines, IA

LD | $

A pleasant, bare-tabled café and fresh fish market, Off the Hook specializes in meals based around fish, but not your typical middle-of-the-road, no-flavor fishes that people on diets tend to eat. Here you eat fish with character, like catfish with meat fairly dripping flavor, or buffalo fish that is as funky as the darkest dark-meat chicken, and carp encased in earthy cornmeal batter.

The fish-frowner among us Sterns declared the fried chicken to be some of the best she has eaten outside the Deep South—crisp-crusted and thoroughly tender. We both agreed that the vegetables that come alongside meals are soul-food classics. They include collard greens, an insanely opulent dish of fried cabbage, red beans and rice, fried green tomatoes, mac 'n' cheese, southern-fried potatoes (sliced and cooked with onions), and creamy-cool coleslaw.

For dessert: smooth, silky sweet potato pie.

Smitty's Tenderloin Shop

1401 SW Army Post Rd.

515-287-4742

Des Moines, IA

LD | $

"Home of the *real* Whopper" says a cartoon on Smitty's wall, and if you know the taste of Iowa, you know that in this case "Whopper" does not refer to a hamburger. It means a tenderloin: pork tenderloin, pounded thin and plate-wide, breaded and fried crisp and sandwiched in a bun. Smitty's Tenderloin Shop has been a pork connoisseur's destination since 1952, and its loyal clientele put it in the pantheon of sandwich shops.

Like all the top tenderloin restaurants, Smitty's is a humble setting. It has a scattering of tables and a friendly counter where locals sit and shoot the breeze at lunch hour. Although the menu includes a handful of other lunch-counter meals—hamburgers, double hamburgers, Coney Island hot dogs, a lovely corn dog, a bowl of chili—"King Tenderloin" is the dish to eat. Available in small or large sizes (small is large; large is nearly a foot across), Smitty's tenderloin is served on an ordinary burger bun. The bun is virtually irrelevant except as a method for keeping ketchup, mustard, onions, and pickles adjacent to the center section of the ten-inch-diameter cutlet, and as a kind of mitt to hoist the vast tenderloin from plate to mouth. It is a marvelous disk of food: its inside a soft and flavorful ribbon of pork succulence, its crust brittle and luscious.

For homesick Iowans who live in a place where pork tenderloins are not part of the food scene, Smitty's can ship them frozen by the dozen, ready to fry, to any of the lower forty-eight states.

Tastee Inn and Out

2610 Gordon Dr. 712-255-0857
Sioux City, IA LD | $

No one but the staff goes inside Tastee Inn and Out. Meals are procured at either a walk-up or drive-through window, and they are eaten either in the car or at a picnic table in the parking lot. Run by the Calligan family for over a half-century now, this ingenuous eatery specializes in what it calls a Tastee sandwich, known elsewhere in northwest Iowa as a tavern or a loosemeats: seasoned, barely sauced ground beef shoveled into a bun with a slice of bright orange cheese, pickle chips, and onion. It is sloppy and addictive; its only possible companion is an order of onion chips, which are bite-size, crisp-fried petals of sweet onion, customarily served with a creamy dip similar to ranch dressing.

Bortell's Fisheries

5510 S. Lakeshore Dr.   231-843-3337
Ludington, MI   L (summer only) | $

You catch it, they'll cook it. BYO seafood to this old fish market and smokehouse where the menu includes walleye, catfish, trout, and white-fish from nearby waters. Bortell's also imports ocean perch and Alaskan salmon; so even if you don't have your own catch, you will have a wide variety of flavorful smoked fish from which to choose. It is sold by the piece or pound.

On the road between Pentwater and Ludington and identified by a simple sign that says, "Fish," Bortell's is easy to drive right past, but if the car windows are open, you will likely smell sweet wood smoke in the air. Step up to the counter, place your order, and pay. There is no dining room and business is strictly take-out. Once you get your fish, find a picnic table outside to eat in the shade under the grove of ancient beech trees. Bring your own bread, beer, and cream cheese.

The Cherry Hut

246 Michigan Ave.
Beulah, MI

231-882-4074
LD Memorial Day-mid-Oct | $

Comfort-food lunch is grand at this 1920s roadside eatery: sandwiches, turkey dinner, lovely cinnamon rolls, and turkey salad brightened up with cherries. But it is pie baked from locally grown cherries that is the destination dish. Bright red fruit spills out the sides of each unwieldy slice—the cherries are a little sweet, a little tart, and the crust adds a luxurious savor. With a scoop of creamy vanilla ice cream, it's a perfect, all-American dessert.

Dining facilities include outdoor picnic tables as well as indoor tables, and part of the Cherry Hut experience is buying things to take home. The restaurant shop sells not only whole fresh pies (five hundred per day), but also jellies, jams, and a wide array of Cheery Jerry, the Happy Pie-Faced Boy, souvenirs.

Don's Drive-In

2030 N. Hwy. 31 N
Traverse City, MI

231-938-1860
LD | $

Don's is a real drive-in that opened the year Elvis joined the Army (1958). Selections on its jukebox evoke days of American mid-century car culture in its prime, and the ambience is rock-and-roll: hubcaps and album covers decorate the walls and you can dine inside or in your car, where meals are served to you on window trays. The menu is basically burgers and fries, featuring the old-fashioned "basket" presentation, meaning a sandwich sided by French fries and coleslaw.

The tough decision to make at Don's is whether to get a hamburger or a brace of Coney Island hot dogs. The burger is thick and juicy; a Coney, topped with chili sauce, is a Midwest paradigm. Whatever you get to eat, there should be no question about the beverage. Make it a milkshake. Don's blends its shakes to order, either large or small, both of which are big enough to fill at least a couple of glasses, and both of which are thick enough to require powerful suction with a straw. Chocolate and vanilla shakes are good all the time; in the summer, strawberry shakes are made with fresh fruit.

Grand Traverse Pie Co.

525 W. Front St.   231-922-PIES
Traverse City, MI $

One of the great sensory thrills of the upper Midwest is walking into Grand Traverse Pie Co. For those of us who enjoy eating, the smell in here is more devastating than any rare perfume. It is the unspeakably delicious aroma of baking crust and bubbling-hot fruit filling.

As the name suggests, it is a limited-service restaurant where pies are virtually all that matter. Indeed, other than coffee and a few kinds of cookie, pies are the only thing on the menu, and much cross-counter business is whole pies to go.

Although you can't come here for a square meal, there are a handful of tables inside and (when weather permits) outdoors, to which you can carry a warm, just-cut slice and appreciate the absolute goodness of a pie that is individually crafted out of raw fruit and sugar in a crust rolled from daily-made scratch dough.

Because northern Michigan is the fruit capital of the Midwest, where apples, cherries, and blueberries are harvested in abundance, the double-crust fruit pies are what we like best. Among the varieties available, most of them named after sights and places around Traverse Bay, are Suttons Bay blueberry, Front Street apple, Lakeshore berry, Union Street peach strawberry, and Long Lake berry cherry. Some thirty varieties are in the kitchen's repertoire (not all available every day), and in addition to fruit-filled ones, there are key lime, coconut cream, and (in season) autumn harvest pecan and Northport pumpkin.

Gustafson's

4321 US 2   906-292-5424
Brevort, MI   L | $$

The full name of this alluring roadside attraction is Gustafson's Smoked Fish and Beef Jerky. It is a gas station and party store that has delicious food that is oh-so-ready-to-eat, but does not offer full-service meals.

Even with your eyes closed, you'll find it as you cruise along the shore road (we don't recommend driving this way) because a sugar maple haze from a quartet of smoldering smokers outside clouds the air with the unbelievably appetizing smell of whitefish, trout, menominee, chub, and salmon turning gorgeous shades of gold. Inside, coolers are arrayed with the firm-fleshed beauties, which you can buy by the piece, wrapped in butcher's paper. Utensils and plates are unnecessary; it's a pleasure to use one's fingers to pick flavorful chunks of fish straight from the paper in which they're wrapped.

Beef jerky is also a specialty of the Gustafson family, who marinate strips of top round for a day-and-a-half, then slow-smoke it over maple for six hours. Jerky is made with a traditional smoky-sweet taste, Cajun-spiced, or barbecue flavored. Vacuum-packed jerky is available through the mail, by the pound.

Michigan's Upper Peninsula lends itself to waterside picnics. A few chaws of jerky, a moist hunk or two of freshly smoked freshwater fish, a fifty-cent stack of saltine crackers, a bag of fried cheese curds, and a beer, plus the scenic beauty of Lake Michigan's northern shore: what's better than that?

Juilleret's

1418 Bridge St.	231-547-9212
Charlevoix, MI	BLD | $

Frankly, it's frustrating to eat at Juilleret's. There are too many good things on the menu, and there are always some you won't have enough appetite to try. Just walking in the door is tough, especially in the morning. There before you is a case of just-baked loaves of cinnamon, cinnamon-raisin, white, banana-walnut, and whole wheat bread. Plus maple rolls, nutty rolls, and cinnamon raisin rolls.

The pancakes belong on our short list of the nation's best. They are large, so large that one is a nice-size meal, but amazingly they are not gross or doughy. In fact, each cake is a rather elegant piece of food, like a fine pastry but with all the good buttery character of a griddle-cooked flapjack. They are made plain or laden with raspberries or blueberries and available with house-made syrup, powdered sugar, honey, or peanut butter, or (for $1.50 extra), maple syrup from a nearby farm.

At lunch, mashed potatoes for the side of hot sandwiches are real and delicious, topped with homemade gravy. Local whitefish is broiled to a fine, fragile, crisp-edged succulence, sandwiched in Juilleret's good bread, and served with excellent pickly-sweet tartar sauce. Hamburgers are served on made-here buns; even the tuna salad, made fresh the Midwestern way with Miracle Whip, is a cut above.

Desserts? Couldn't be better. Juilleret's coconut cream pie is one of the best anywhere, its dense, coconut-chocked custard so intensely flavorful that you want to call it savory, its meringue topping light as a puff of steam.

Lafayette Coney Island

118 W. Lafayette Blvd.　　　　313-964-8198
Detroit, MI　　　　　　　　Always open | $

The Lafayette and the American are an adjoining pair of storefront Coney Island hot dog joints in Detroit (two of many Coney Islands in the area), and while we travelers might think their cuisine similar, if not identical, most of Michigan's Coney Island aficionados prefer one over the others. It's too fine a debate for us, but we are more than happy to find ourselves facing a brace of Lafayette weenies topped with chili, raw onions, and mustard. We also like chili by the bowl, with or without beans, but definitely with shredded cheese on top.

The chili is fine-grind, peppery, and fairly intense unless supplemented by the starch of beans and pleasant fatty mantle of bright orange cheese. The dogs are far from fancy, but in their déclassé way, they are mighty good: porky-sweet inside with a skin that has a nice little snap, their succulence perfectly complemented by the spongy bun that cradles them. In our opinion, the condiments are essential. A plain Coney is as erroneous as a pancake without syrup.

Tasty as the hot dogs are to the true frank-o-phile, ambience of Lafayette Coney Island is a big part of its charm. Open round the clock, and especially interesting in the wee hours of the morning when there is no place else to eat and the bars are closing, it is staffed by cranky old gents who have seen it all and who remember exactly what everyone eats and don't have to bother with written checks: everything is in their heads.

Ray's Drive-Inn

20 N. Beacon Blvd.　　　　616-842-3400
Grand Haven, MI　　　　　LD | $

A tipster who identified him/herself as Flame On Catering of Muskegon advised us exactly what to eat when we went to Ray's: a triple beefburger with only cheese. Flame On explained, "I would never order a burger with nothing else but cheese from anywhere else." Nor would we, as we are big fans of all sorts of burger condiments. However in this case, the suggestion was a good one. Ray's uses gobs of cheese, and while the beef itself is just fine, it's all that cheese that puts this one over the top. When you unwrap your triple, you will definitely see bun and cheese, but the meat itself is completely smothered. It is a delightful mess.

French fries are especially excellent, and while all the usual milk-shakes are available, we took good advice and ordered pineapple. A great drive-in meal!

Yesterdog

1505 Wealthy St. SE	616-336-0746
Grand Rapids, MI	LD | $

Courteous service? No way. Comfortable, modern accommodations? Not here. Neat and tidy meals? Not a chance! Excellent snappy-skinned boiled hot dogs loaded into steamed soft buns and smothered with sloppy chili sauce, cheese, onions, mustard, pickles, sauerkraut, and just about any other condiment you can name? This is the place. Pick your condiments one by one or simply ask for an ultra, which is some of nearly everything.

Yesterdog has been around for decades and today it is a self-consciously old-timey sort of place with vintage advertising signs all about (sharing wall space with pictures of happy customers wearing Yes-terdog T-shirts) and a pre-electric cash register for ringing up sales. It is almost always crowded, so much so that there is frequently a mob of peo-ple out on the sidewalk waiting to get in, and it doesn't empty out until long after midnight. Tips are given to the staff by tossing coins into the bell flare of a tuba.

Zingerman's Deli

422 Detroit St.	734-663-3354
Ann Arbor, MI	BLD | $

Here is a world-class deli that serves every kind of sandwich the human race has devised—from Italian salami subs to brisket-and-schmaltz on rye and a pile of hot pastrami parenthesized 'twixt two potato pancakes. We get dizzy thinking of Zingerman's smoked whitefish salad, redolent of dill and red onion, piled on slices of freshly made onion-rye bread. The immense menu is an hour's read, and ranges beyond sandwiches to such traditional specialties as noodle kugel (a sweet pudding), cheese blintzes (cheese-filled crêpes), and knishes (heavyweight dumplings). Or you can choose Thai noodle salad, Arkansas peppered ham, or ratatouille with polenta. Brash, crowded, and invariably delicious, this one-of-a-kind place is an essential stop for all traveling eaters.

Zingerman's stocks a tremendous inventory of smoked fish, meats, breads, coffees, etc. for retail sale. It also features a full-service mail-order department, selling such specialties as rugelach cookies (the best!), babkas, poppy-seed cake, brownies and blondies, cheeses, oils, vinegars, and multiple-item gift baskets.

Al's Breakfast

413 14th Ave. SE

Minneapolis, MN

612-331-9991

BL | $

Al's is the mother lode for those of us who spend our lives in search of great diner breakfasts. It is smaller than small, wedged perpendicular to 14th Avenue among the shops of Dinkytown, near the University of Minnesota. Customers waiting for one of the fourteen stools at the counter stand hovering just above and behind those who are seated and eating. In the narrow space between the counter and the back bar, where Al's hash slingers race to and fro with seasoned aplomb, décor consists of pictures of Elvis and Wayne Newton, foreign currency, and a sign that advises, "Tipping is not a city in China."

Al's makes a specialty of blueberry pancakes, poured from either a whole wheat or buttermilk batter, also available studded with walnuts or corn kernels. They have a barely sticky texture and a flavor that is a poised balance of sweet fruit and the faintly sour batter, a harmony well abetted by a drizzle of maple syrup. Get them as a short stack (2), regular stack (3), or long stack (4), and you can also have your waitress garnish them with sour cream and/or strawberries. Also of note: griddle-cooked corned beef hash with beautiful poached eggs on top.

The short-order chef up front spends his time poaching eggs, constructing omelets, and griddle-cooking corned beef hash and crisp hash browns. It is an old-fashioned pleasure to watch this guy work, handling about a dozen orders at a time, always snatching whatever he is frying, poaching, or grilling away from the heat at the peak of its perfection.

Bloedows Bakery

451 E. Broadway   507-452-3682
Winona, MN   B | $

Southwest Minnesota foodlore tells the story of the little, homegrown bakery (in business for some eighty years) that ran Krispy Kreme out of town. It was back in aught-three that the national chain moved in, setting up its products throughout town in groceries and convenience stores. But the interloper donuts did not impress Minnesotans who knew better. In less than two years, KK had vanished from the shelves and Bloedows reigned supreme.

It's a sweet story for those of us who prize eateries with genuine character over those cookie-cuttered in the corporate boardroom, and the fact is that the glazed and cake donuts, sweet rolls, maple-frosted long johns, and cookies at Bloedows (rhymes with Playdoughs) deserve their renown. We found out about the place thanks to Roadfood.com tipster Vanessa Haluska, who directed us to a Bloedows' specialty, the peanut butter roll. It's a big, circular pastry made with sweet dough and swirled with peanut butter where you might expect cinnamon. For PB lovers it is a very large taste of heaven, and so we salute Vanessa, who described this charming place as "the best small-town bakery that I have ever visited!"

Cafe Latté

850 Grand Ave.   651-224-5687
St. Paul, MN   LD | $$

We arrived in St. Paul mid-morning and headed straight to Grand Avenue for an early lunch. We had the cafeteria line at Cafe Latté all to ourselves. The ready-made salads were laid out, pretty as can be, as were ingredients for the made-to-order ones. If you like Caesar salad, this place is a dream, because you can get the classic version as well as a Caesar supplemented by artichoke hearts, Greek olives, or sliced tomatoes. Each individual salad is made to order, so you can specify if you want a little more of this or that. Breads from the prodigious bakery in the back of the store are arrayed along the line and regal cakes were on display at the beginning.

We'll be drooling on our computer keyboard if we try to describe too many of the cakes, so let's just say that the turtle cake, an intense mountain of chocolate, caramel, and pecans, is monumentally good. Other available layered chocolate wonders are chocolate-chocolate, orange blossom, German chocolate, and chocolate banana.

Whether you are in the mood for cake or a salad, a sandwich and soup, or just scones and espresso, this is a fine, inexpensive place to enjoy yourself.

Convention Grill

3912 Sunnyside Rd.   952-920-6881
Minneapolis, MN   LD | $

Here is a great American hamburger. Not the biggest or the best-dressed, not stuffed with foie gras like the $100 oddities made by show-off chefs, not so lean it's dry nor so greasy it is unctuous, this is a thick, bun-size patty sizzled to crusty perfection on an extremely well-oiled grill. It oozes juice and radiates beefy savor, and is especially good topped with a mantle of melted cheese and presented California-style (with lettuce, tomato, and mayonnaise). Other available toppings include bacon and mushrooms, or you can have a Plaza Burger, which comes with sour cream, chives, and chopped onions and is sandwiched in a dark bun. The menu boasts it is just like the one "featured in the Plaza Tavern of Madison, Wisconsin," but anyone who has eaten the original (p. 376) wouldn't be fooled. We much prefer the regular Convention Grill hamburgers.

For burgers alone, we'll happily make the pilgrimage to this 1934-vintage diner in Edina, but we can guarantee our California cheeseburgers will be accompanied by French fries. Beautiful fries, cooked until honey-tone brown, each portion a mix of cream-centered, full-size sticks and darkened crunchy little twigs and burnt ends of potato debris from when the spuds are hand-cut in the kitchen.

On the side you want a malt. Huge and so thick that they must be spooned from their metal beaker because pouring is impossible, Convention Grill malts are available in a rainbow of flavors: chocolate, wild blueberry, butterscotch, strawberry, coffee, banana, vanilla, caramel, honey, hot fudge, butterfinger, mint, and Reese's Peanut Butter Cup. For fifty cents extra, you can have fresh banana added. The only problem with ordering a malt is that it makes it less likely you will have the stamina to have a hot fudge sundae for dessert. That was our problem when we visited, but we couldn't help ogling the sundaes at the next table. They come in the typical broad tulip glass with plenty of fudge underneath the ice cream and a mountain of whipped cream on top, and on the side is a good-size cup of extra hot fudge to pour on as you eat your way through.

All this excellent Roadfood is dished out by a staff of white-uniformed waitresses who are utterly efficient and, in our experience, omnipresent. It was Lynne Rosetto Kasper, host of NPR's *The Splendid Table*, who said we needed to go here, and while Lynne is best known as an expert on Italian food, this suggestion alone earns her an exalted chair in the Burger Lovers' Hall of Fame.

Hell's Kitchen

89 S. 10th St.   612-332-4700
Minneapolis, MN   BLD | $$

Our first visits to Hell's Kitchen were for breakfast—some of the best breakfasts anywhere. Every table is supplied with chef Mitch Omer's magnificent preserves and marmalade and extra-luxurious chunky peanut butter, which are themselves a compelling reason to eat at this downtown hot spot. Among the stars of the morning menu include huevos rancheros of the gods—a huge plate of food that includes spicy beans, eggs, cheeses, sour cream, and fresh salsa on a crisp flour tortilla. Rosti potatoes come alongside, too; and they are available as a dish unto themselves. Chef Omer's rostis are less like the Swiss spuds that are their namesake than they are glorified hash browns, the shreds of potato mixed with bacon, onions, chives, and scallions and grilled in sweet cream butter. A few other breakfast specialties: lemon ricotta hotcakes, extra-spicy maple-glazed bison sausage, and a quarter-pound caramel pecan roll featuring extra-crunchy pieces of nut and a refined glaze that is a sweet tooth's dream.

The most unusual and perhaps the most delicious dish on the breakfast menu is Mahnomin Porridge, a recipe that the promethean Mr. Omer came up with from reading accounts of native Cree Indian meals that featured wild rice. His version includes nuts and berries and is topped with maple syrup and cream. What an amazing hot cereal!

The lunch menu is every bit as inviting. How about a walleye BLT made with cornmeal-dusted fillets and lemon tartar sauce instead of the homemade mayo the kitchen uses on its regular BLT? Who wouldn't love the ham and pear crisp sandwich on sourdough bread, draped with a mantle of Swiss and fontina cheeses? We instantly became addicted to the house Bread Bucket, which is all the chewy, freshly made baguette you can eat served along with sweet cream butter, Omer's preserves, and peanut butter.

Rather than rave on, let us simply say that if you are in Minneapolis and want to wow your taste buds, go to Hell's Kitchen. It is inspired and inspiring.

Lange's Café

110 8th Ave. SE (Route 23)   507-825-4488
Pipeston, MN   Always open | $

The moment we walked into Lange's Café, we looked at the case of caramel rolls and knew we had hit pay dirt. And sure enough, as we ate our way through as much of the menu as possible, we swooned with pleasure over and over again. Beef is the entree not to miss. Listed as roast beef if it comes on a plate with mashed potatoes, green beans, and gravy, and as hot beef if it is served in a sandwich with mashed potatoes on top and gravy all over, it is pot-roast-tender and deep-flavored. Mashed potatoes are the real thing; dinner rolls that come alongside are freshly baked.

The caramel rolls that so many people eat for breakfast must be sampled anytime they are available. They are immense blocks of sweet, yeasty dough—about three inches square—and they are bathed in buttery warm caramel syrup that has a burned smack to its sweetness.

Now, we have saved the best for last: sour cream raisin pie. It's a specialty of bakers in Minnesota, Wisconsin, and Iowa, and over the years we have made it our business to sample every SCR pie we come across. Lange's is built upon a custard that is dense, packed with raisins, creamy and sweet with the sour-cream edge that makes its sweetness all the more potent. Its meringue is air-light; the crust flakes when poked by a fork. It was our supremely lucky day, for we walked into Lange's about 10:00 A.M. and the SCR pie had been out of the oven only a short while. Our pieces were faintly warm, like baby food, and as we ate, we declared this the best sour cream raisin pie ever made, 10 on a 1 to 10 scale, the crème de la crème, the mother lode.

Not too long after we included this great place in the last edition of *Roadfood*, we got a note from Peg Lange saying, "We have breathed *new life* and commitment into our business: new sign, new canopy, new landscaping, new atrium glass, new display cabinet, and new uniforms." We're thrilled at the renaissance, but even more thrilled to report that the food hasn't changed at all. This is still southwestern Minnesota's premier café.

Maverick's

1746 N. Lexington Ave.	651-488-1788
Roseville, MN	LD | $

Maverick's specialty is roast beef sandwiches: soft, pink, velvety slices cut to order and piled into a soft white bun while the meat is still hot and moist. Rick Nelson of the *Minneapolis Star-Tribune* told us that the restaurant concept was inspired by the proprietor's desire to improve on Arby's. If that was his goal, he has more than succeeded, for this is a super roast beef sandwich—simple, pure, and satisfying.

It is served cafeteria-style, along with a short menu of other beefy things, including brisket (offered on a dark pumpernickel bun) and barbecued beef, plus pulled pork, ham, chicken, and fish fillets. When we stopped by, open-face roast beef sandwiches were the day's special: the same good beef piled on a plate with the roll on the side and a couple of mounds of mashed potatoes. While the beef in this one was the same as in the simple sandwich, we much preferred Maverick's crisp French fries to the ersatz mashed potatoes.

Ambience at this inconspicuous strip-mall eatery is that of a workman's café. Once you get your food, you stop by a condiment bar where the choices range from horseradish and horseradish cream to hot peppers, ketchup, mustard, and pickles. Then you find a place at one of the four-tops along the side of the room or at the long banquet table that runs down the middle. We walked out happy and satisfied.

Mickey's Dining Car

36 West 7th St.	651-222-5633
Saint Paul, MN	BLD | $

The best thing about Mickey's Dining Car is Mickey's Dining Car itself—a stunning yellow-and-red enamel streamliner built by the Jerry O'Mahony company in 1937. Although it has been well used over decades of twenty-four-hour service, it is still in magnificent shape. Complementing the Deco dazzle of the diner (which is listed on the National Register of Historic Places) is a jukebox featuring Elvis and Del Shannon, and a staff of waiters and waitresses who have honed the art of service with a snarl. It's not mean service, and it's not bad service; in fact, it is efficient and polite . . . unless you are one of the frequent gawkers (we plead guilty) who come in to look around at the handsome joint and its colorful regular denizens. We who are too preoccupied to place our order swiftly and with no hesitation can find ourselves at the mercy of the hash slingers, one of whom once told us, in no uncertain terms, "A museum, it's not. You gonna eat or kick tires?"

We're not going to tell you that the cuisine at Mickey's Dining Car rates four stars. There are some things they serve we wouldn't recommend at all. The pies, for example, are more easily identifiable by their color (red, yellow, blue) than by their designated ingredient (could it be fruit?).

On the other hand, breakfast is foursquare. Eggs are whipped up in a flash, blueberry-buttermilk pancakes are pretty fine, and the hash brown potatoes are available O'Brien-style, meaning mixed with diced ham, onion, and green peppers. We like the French toast made from the diner's extra-thick white bread, and the morning special of pork chops or steak and eggs. While these chops bear little resemblance to the thick, tender ones you'll get for supper in a high-priced restaurant, they have a flavorful hash-house charm all their own. The milkshakes are real, blended to order. And how many other joints do you know that still offer mulligan stew?

Tavern on Grand

656 Grand Ave.   651-228-9030
St. Paul, MN   LD | $$

Walleye sandwiches are a big deal in Minnesota, the best of them, no doubt, made at North Country campfires by walleye fishermen. For those who don't catch and cook their own, the place to go is Tavern on Grand in St. Paul.

Billing itself as "Minnesota's State Restaurant Serving Minnesota's State Fish," this friendly place will start you off with an appetizer of sautéed walleye cakes or a walleye basket of deep-fried bites. The sandwich is a fillet—grilled or fried—served on a length of French bread with tartar sauce that does a marvelous job of haloing the sweet meat of the lake fish. You can get a walleye plate for lunch (with steamed vegetables and red potatoes, known as a "shore lunch") or a walleye supper of one or two fillets with the works. There is even a Lakeshore Special that is a single fillet accompanied by a half-pound sirloin steak. On the side of almost anything, turkey wild rice soup is essential. To accompany your meal, there are beers galore, domestic and imported, on tap and by the bottle.

Tavern on Grand feels like the right place to enjoy a true Minnesota meal. It is designed to resemble a log cabin lodge in the woods, and no matter where you sit in the bar, you have a good view of one of the many TVs positioned for everyone to watch whatever game is currently broadcast. You'll know it by the big neon fish in the front window.

Amighetti's

5141 Wilson Ave.   314-776-2855
St. Louis, MO   LD | $

Amighetti's is a serve-yourself sandwich shop that has become a beloved culinary institution on "The Hill," St. Louis's old Italian neighborhood. Eating here is casual and fun, especially on a pleasant summer day. Place your order at the window and wait for your name to be called. Find yourself a seat on the sunny patio, and feast on an Italian sandwich.

Amighetti's bakes its own bread—a thick-crusted loaf with sturdy insides ready to be loaded with slices of ham, roast beef, Genoa salami, and cheese, garnished with shreds of lettuce and a special house dressing that is tangy-sweet. All kinds of sandwiches are available, including a garlicky Italian hero, roast beef, and a three-cheese veggie sandwich—all recommended primarily because of the bread on which they're served.

Each sandwich is wrapped in butcher paper secured by a tape inscribed with Amighetti's motto: "Often Imitated, Never Duplicated."

Arthur Bryant's

1727 Brooklyn Ave.   816-231-1123
Kansas City, MO   LD | $

Arthur Bryant used to shock reporters by calling his esteemed barbecue restaurant a "Grease House." Although the master of Kansas City barbecue passed away in 1982, his business heirs, bless them, never tried too hard to shed that moniker. The original location of the "House of Good Eats" (another of Mr. Bryant's appellations) remains a cafeteria-style lunchroom with all the decorative charm of a bus station. (There are branches at the Kansas City Speedway, Ameristar Casino, and airport.)

Because Arthur Bryant and his brother Charlie (who started the smokehouse) hailed from Texas, it makes sense that the smoked brisket—a Texas passion—is the best meat in the house. It drips flavor. It is sliced into fall-apart lengths that get heaped into white-bread sandwiches, or if you come as a large party, you can order a couple of pounds of beef and a loaf of bread and make your own at the table.

The pork ribs are wonderful, too, glazed with blackened burned edges and lodes of meat below their spicy crust. The skin-on French fries are bronze beauties and the barbecue beans are some of Kansas City's best.

What makes Arthur Bryant's unique is the sauce. It is beautiful—a gritty, red-orange blend of spice and sorcery that is not at all sweet like most barbecue sauces. It packs a hot paprika wallop and tastes like a strange soul-food curry, a unique complement to any meat. Once you've tasted it, you'll understand why this old Grease House is a foodie legend.

Booches

110 S. 9th St.   573-874-8772 or -9519
Columbia, MO   LD | $

A billiard parlor/tavern where the beverages of choice are beer (in a bottle) and iced tea (in a pitcher), or maybe Coke in a paper cup, Booches is a magic name to hamburger aficionados. The hamburgers—known among old-timers as "belly bombers"—are thick, juicy, and maddeningly aromatic, served unceremoniously on a piece of wax paper. It is difficult to say what exactly makes these hamburgers so especially delicious. They are normal-size, available with or without cheese, and the condiments are standard-issue onions, pickles, mustard, or ketchup; yet their smoky/meaty flavor is extraordinary from first bite to last. In 1999, Booches won kudos from the *Digital Missourian* as an especially earth-friendly eatery, not only because each hamburger is cooked to order (thus, no meat is wasted), but because "no one can leave a Booches burger half-eaten."

Some of the food's charm is no doubt due to the offhand way in which it is served in colorful surroundings. Booches is the oldest pool hall in Columbia, and it is likely your burger—or good chili dog—will be eaten to the wooden clack of pool shooters as well as the noise of whatever sports event is blaring on the television. Décor is a combination of sports memorabilia, kudos from famous artists who have enjoyed the beer and burgers, and some delightful politically incorrect humor, including one sign that advises, "Parents—keep your ankle-biting little crumb-gobblers on a leash or I will put them in the cellar to play with the rats."

C&K Barbecue

4390 Jennings Station Rd. 314-385-5740
St. Louis, MO D | $

St. Louis has always been a great barbecue town; C&K represents the best of this tradition. It is a small, out-of-the-way place with no seating (all take-out) and late-night hours, well-suited to those of us who get a craving for ribs after midnight.

Ribs, rib tips, chopped meat, even chicken, all bathed in proprietor Darryle Brantley's exclamatory red sauce, are served in Styro boxes with sweet potato salad and soft white bread that makes a good sponge for drippy extra sauce. These are extremely messy meals, so even though each order is packed with napkins, we recommend getting extras.

In addition to all the expected smokehouse specialties, C&K offers a few rarer items such as snoots (pig snouts baked until crisp and bathed in sauce) and ears (yes, pig ears, cooked until butter-soft and served between two slices of white bread, with or without sauce). These items are for the advanced barbecue connoisseur. We recommend the first-time visitor start with a slab of ribs!

Carl's Drive-In

9033 Manchester Rd.
Brentwood, MO

314-961-9652
LD (closed Sun & Mon) | $

A tiny sixteen-stool diner on old Route 66, Carl's is the place to belly up for elegant-oily hamburgers and foot-long hot dogs that stretch far beyond the bun and come smothered with chili. The burgers are mashed flat on the grill so that their edges turn into a crisp lace of beef, and they are thin enough that a double or a triple makes good sense, as does the addition of cheese. Ketchup is supplied in small paper cups.

Burgers are the main attraction, but Carl's is also a source for three-way chili and tamales topped with chili or sauce. Shoestring French fries are a great companion for any meal, and the beverage of choice is house-brewed root beer drawn straight from the barrel, served in a frosted mug. (Root beer floats are not to be missed.)

Expect to wait for a seat at lunchtime. But not too long. The turnover is quick, and it is an amazing thing to watch the staff juggle cooking for sit-down customers, take-out customers, and call-in customers whose orders come in via the house pay phone.

Central Dairy

601 Madison St.
Jefferson City, MO

573-635-6148
L | $

Missouri is a dairy state, and Central Dairy is one of its top bottlers, turning out seven million pounds of milk per month, and known to local sweet tooths for its repertoire of outstanding ice cream. The ice cream tastes great, but what's truly amazing about it is the way it is portioned out at the old-fashioned soda fountain store in the capital city's downtown. Ask for a cup and you get a pint container nearly full! Never make the mistake of having a banana split in a flimsy low-rimmed boat, from which vast amounts of ice cream and syrup will spill over the edge onto the table of your Formica booth as you spoon into it. Instead, ask for your split or sundae in a quart container. It, too, will brim over the top, but once the first dozen or so spoonfuls are consumed, the quart is a good holding vehicle for the remaining pounds of ice cream and syrup.

Sundaes and splits are the pièces de résistance—especially the behemoth known as the Rock and Roll Sundae, made with four kinds of ice cream and a bunch of toppings, but for those who don't have time to plow in at a table, it is possible to get a tall triple-dip ice cream cone, then face the challenge of trying to lick enough off the pile of cool, creamy globes before they start to melt down one's wrist. Ice cream sodas are grand-size, too, and we want to thank Roadfooder Tony Gawienowski, our Central Dairy tipster, for pointing out that the ice water tap serves cold soda water—just what ice cream–sated taste buds require!

Crown Candy Kitchen

1401 St. Louis Ave.   314-621-9650

St. Louis, MO   LD | $

The Crown Candy Kitchen is an old-time sweet shop that makes its own chocolate candy and serves all kinds of malts, shakes, sodas, and sundaes. We are especially fond of the chocolate banana malted and the hot fudge malted, not to mention the excellent house policy of giving five malts free—to anyone who can consume them in thirty minutes.

Other than excellent ice cream treats, Crown has a nice lunch-counter repertoire of sandwiches, chili, and chili mac. Two items of special interest from the kitchen are the BLT, which the menu promises is made with Miracle Whip, and the giant gourmet chili dog. We have yet to see the latter, but intend to give it a whirl next visit.

Goody Goody Diner

5900 Natural Bridge   314-383-3333

St. Louis, MO   BL | $

Breakfast is served all day (until closing mid-afternoon) Wednesday and Friday at Connelly's Goody Goody diner, and other days only until 11:00 A.M. The menu is vast, ranging from omelets, breakfast sandwiches, pancakes, waffles, and French toast to boneless catfish fillets with eggs and one amazing dish known as the Wilbur. "We're bringing a popular St. Louis diner breakfast to Goody Goody's," the menu notes in its description of the Wilbur. Known in other local diners and chili parlors as a slinger, the Wilbur is an omelet filled with chili, fried potatoes, peppers, onions, and tomatoes. It is a soulful meal, profoundly satisfying . . . although not necessarily what we crave to eat early in the morning!

The chili that gives the Wilbur its avoirdupois can be ordered as a side dish. It is stout and salty, made with chunks of beef, and it is the fundamental element in a once-popular but now rare Midwestern diner dish, chili mac. Goody Goody's chili mac is prepared with blunt hash-house style: well-cooked spaghetti noodles are topped with chili and crowned by a mass of shredded Cheddar cheese.

"We've changed many items on our menu over the years," the Goody Goody credo goes. "But the way we prepare our hamburgers will never change. They're not fancy—they're just *good!*" We agree. Regulars and doubles, patty melts and cheeseburgers, slawburgers and barbecue slawburgers are all outstanding, available with sides that include onion rings, French fries, cheese fries, and, of course, chili. Each burger is mashed down hard enough on the grill that it becomes a thin, rugged patty with a lacy-crisp circumference, its rugged nature nicely gentled by the soft yellow bun in which it is served.

Gus' Pretzel Shop

1820 Arsenal St. 314-664-4010
St. Louis, MO L | $

St. Louis is a serious pretzel town, and Gus' has been known for excellent soft pretzels since 1920. Gus' pretzels are soft, chewy, and slick-crusted. They are available as twists or sticks, numbers and letters, and—best of all—as the casing for sausage, i.e., pigs in blankets. The varieties of sausage available inside the pretzel include a diversity typical of St. Louis's savory ethnic heritage: Italian salsiccia, German bratwurst, and all-American hot dogs.

To complement its first-class pretzel repertoire, Gus' offers cups of Dijon mustard and melted Cheddar cheese, plus servings of Ted Drewes ice cream. The proper method of dining is to dip one's pretzel, bite by bite, in the little cups, swilling a mug of beer on the side. The only problem is finding a place to do this. Gus' has no tables or counter; business is all take-out, for eating at home, in the car, or on the sidewalk. Frozen cooked pretzels are available, as are bags of "Bake UR Owns."

Hodak's Restaurant & Bar

2100 Gravois Rd. 314-776-7292
St. Louis, MO LD | $

Boasting that it has been "St. Louis' premier stop for chicken lovers since 1962," Hodak's started as a corner bar, but the proprietor's wife used to bring in fried chicken for the customers, and the customers liked it so much that it became part of the bar's attraction. Relocated to its current location, remodeled and renovated many times over the years and now under new management, it is still a good place to drink as well as to have a nice family supper.

The single-digit-priced chicken platter includes four pieces, each encased in a thin, crunchy crust that shores in very juicy meat; on the side come crinkle-cut French fries and coleslaw, and for forty cents extra you can get hot barbecue sauce for dipping. Hodak's also has a broad menu of steaks, roast beef, ribs, and seafood as well as such appetizers as seasoned wings, chicken strips, and, of course, toasted ravioli.

Jess and Jim's

517 E. 135th St. 816-941-9499
Kansas City (Martin City), MO LD | $$$

Jess and Jim's, a Kansas City landmark that opened in 1938, is all about beef. This is apparent even from a distance when you spot the huge statue of a bull atop the roof of the restaurant. Steaks arrive from the kitchen exuberantly sputtering, crusty from an iron griddle. The top-of-the-line KC Playboy Strip is two inches thick, and unlike the super-tender bacon-wrapped fillets, it demands some serious chewing. Not that it is tough, but neither is it a cut of meat for milquetoasts. Dense and intense, this is steak-lover's steak, which is not to say that the T-bones and porterhouses are anything less than excellent.

On the side of regal meat, excellent potatoes are essential. There are cottage fries, French fries, and immense bakers available, of course, with sour cream, bacon, and shredded cheese as condiments. The sleeper on the menu here is fried chicken. It's a reminder that as much as it is a beef lode, Kansas City is a serious fried chicken town.

Note: On weekends especially, this place gets very crowded. Call-ahead seating is available, and strongly advised.

LC's Barbeque

5800 Blue Pky. 816-923-4484
Kansas City, MO LD | $$

A sandwich at LC's is quite ridiculous. You get a heap of sauce-sopped meat piled onto a puny slice of white bread and topped with another slice. The bread underneath has disintegrated before it arrives at your table, so this sandwich cannot be lifted by hand from its Styrofoam tray. You either use plastic utensils or pick at it by hand. (All tables are outfitted with rolls of paper towels.)

Beef, ham, turkey, pork, sausage, and ribs are all pit-cooked, and among the "specialty meats" listed on the menu is burnt ends. These are crisp, chewy, extra-luscious nuggets of meat cut from the outside edges of smoked brisket. Many pieces are laced with an obscenely delicious amount of fat; there are chewy pieces and crunchy pieces, and while the ends might be dry all by themselves, LC's excellent sauce makes them sing.

LC's is a no-frills barbecue parlor with a tile floor and acoustical tile ceiling. There is a TV in one corner of the room and a few dusty game-animal trophies on the wall. The tables are, of course, unclothed, and all dishware and utensils are disposable.

Niecie's

5932 Prospect Ave.	816-444-6006
Kansas City, MO	BLD | $

Niecie's is a long-running soul-food café opened by Denise Griffin Ward in 1985. Since then it has become a sort of community center, and every morning except Sunday you can expect to see a gathering of a dozen or more Baptist and Holiness Church pastors assembled for breakfast and conversation. As we sat down in a booth one day, a couple nearby were praying over their fried pork chops before digging in.

We really like the breakfast of chicken and waffles; in this case it is three jumbo wings, beautifully fried with lots of gnarled crisp skin, along with a waffle and a big plastic jug of Hungry Jack syrup. Other breakfast choices include biscuits and gravy (we're not all that fond of the biscuits), pancakes, country ham, and eggs with grits on the side.

Among the daily lunch specials are salmon croquettes on Monday, a legendary smothered chicken Tuesday, short ribs Friday, and fried catfish Saturday. An everyday specialty of the house we highly recommend is Niecie's grilled wings. They're seasoned and cooked with onions and are powerfully flavorful. If you order them, expect a twenty- to thirty-minute wait.

The most exotic item on the menu, at least for those of us who don't have easy access to southern Midwest soul-food specialties, is the pig ear sandwich. "You get two ears!" beamed waitress Ms. Myra C., whose badge identified her as having nineteen years of service at Niecie's. Yes, indeed; it is two whole ears in a bun. We got ours with the works: lettuce, tomato, onion, and ultra-hot horseradish. We've got to admit that ears are a little scary, not so much because they're the worst part of the pig— there are plenty of parts that are far worse on the ick! scale. The problem is that they look exactly like what they are: large, pointy porker ears. Their taste is not objectionable; it's something like the fatty parts of bacon or streak o'lean, but the gelatinous texture is, to say the least, a little weird.

Porter's Fried Chicken

3628 S. Big Bend Blvd.   314-781-2097
St. Louis, MO   LD | $

Note the name of this restaurant. While the menu lists hamburgers, fish dinners, fish sandwiches, and even fish buckets—and we can tell you that the catfish nuggets are pretty darn good—it is chicken that is the big allure. The repertoire is a lot like familiar franchised chicken restaurants and the ambience is zilch, but the food is a cut above.

Encased in a medium-thick batter that is extremely luscious and yet nearly grease-free, white meat is moist and full flavored; dark meat drips juice. In addition to wings, breasts, drumsticks, and thighs, you can have dinners of liver or gizzards, wings, and tenders. On the side, in addition to mashed potatoes, French fries, onion rings, and coleslaw, you can have a twelve-piece order of that St. Louis favorite, toasted ravioli, served with red sauce for dipping.

A Slice of Pie

601 Kingshighway   573-364-6203
Rolla, MO   LD | $

The pies are glorious: velvet-cream meringues, Boston cream, and Tahitian cream are especially noteworthy, that last one being a layered pie of sliced bananas, pudding, and pineapple with a mantle of toasted coconut on top. Phillip Quintana, the tipster who directed us to this little eatery halfway between St. Louis and Springfield, said that his favorites were apple and peach with cinnamon cream, as well as any of the pies filled with fruit. We did our best to sample some of everything, but there are far too many pies (not to mention cakes and cheesecakes!) for even two big appetites to try some of everything in just a few visits.

The problem of eating one's way through the dessert menu is compounded by the fact that lunch and supper at A Slice of Pie are hearty. After bowls of wonderful homemade creamy tomato soup and potato soup with bacon, we forked into a pair of flake-crusted chicken mushroom potpies. After polishing off those savory potpies, it took some mustering of appetite to ask for several sweet pies, a dilemma compounded by the fact that each slice served is enormous!

Snead's

1001 E. 171st St. 816-331-7979
Belton, MO 64012 LD (closed Mon & Tues) | $$

"What are these rumors about Snead's closing soon?" we asked the woman who led us to a booth.

"Just that," she replied. "Rumors." For some reason, Snead's impending demise has been talked about among foodies for years.

What a relief it is to believe that it will continue on, because Snead's is one of the greats, if not the greatest, among Kansas City barbecue restaurants.

A low, rustic dining room decorated with quilts, farmy pictures, and a small collection of vintage wooden coat hangers, it is way out in the country where urban sprawl hasn't yet arrived. One customer with whom we chatted recalled coming here as a child when the place opened in the mid-1950s on the corner of Bill Snead's farm.

Snead's meats are cooked in large kettles in a brick pit fueled only by hickory wood. The result is barbecue with supreme tenderness and powerful smoke flavor. Most indulgent of all are the brownies, aka burnt ends, pieces stripped of the ends of brisket and/or ham. Pork is sliced thin but so moist that sauce is optional. Beef is a little dry, so sauce is a good idea. Snead's offers two variations: a slightly sweet mild sauce and a vigorously peppery orange brew that is reminiscent of Arthur Bryant's, and not at all sweet.

Stroud's Oak Ridge Manor

5410 N.E. Oak Ridge Dr.   816-454-9600
Kansas City, MO   D | $$

Stroud's makes the most delicious fried chicken in America.

It is fried in a heavy iron skillet and arrives at the table a shade of gold that is breathtakingly beautiful. Each piece is audibly crusty, but not the least bit bready; there is just enough of an envelope of crust to shore in all the chicken juices. The crust itself is thin, brittle, and as flavor-packed as bacon, but in this case, with essence of chicken and spice. Once you crunch through it, juices flow down your chin and fingers and forearm: you are an unsightly mess, but you don't care because the juices are ambrosia.

The mashed potatoes are fluffy-textured, with an intense flavor of pure potato. As you fork up mouthfuls of these spuds you learn new respect for real mashed potatoes and new intolerance for bogus ones. The only way these lovelies can be improved is if you ladle some of Stroud's gravy on them. It is zesty, pan-dripping gravy, redolent of chicken and powerfully peppered.

At the risk of sounding hysterical, we must tell you that the cinnamon rolls that accompany this meal are fantastic, too. Tasting more of yeast and cinnamon than sugar, they are big, swirly things with a layer of caramelized cinnamon butter around the base.

The original Stroud's, a funky wood-floored roadhouse that began as a fireworks stand, is long gone. The new place is a gracious frontier homestead with a dining room that looks out over grassy lawns. It's very crowded most mealtimes and you will likely wait for a table; then, once you are seated, there's another wait for the chicken, which is pan-fried to order. This is one place we don't mind waiting. There is no better chicken dinner.

Ted Drewes

6726 Chippewa St.   314-481-2652
St. Louis, MO   (Closed in winter) | $

For anyone in search of America's most delicious ice cream (and who is not?), here's a name to put on the short list of candidates for greatness: Ted Drewes. Drewes's frozen custard is fresh, pure, and tons of fun, manufactured only as vanilla, but mixable with your choice from a list of dozens of different flavoring agents from chocolate and strawberry to fudge, cherries, cookies, nuts, and candy bars.

The best-known dish in the house is called a concrete, which is a milkshake so thick that the server hands it out the order window upside down, demonstrating that not a drop will drip out! Beyond concretes, there are sundaes, cones, floats, and sodas.

Ted Drewes has two locations (the second is at 4224 S. Grand Blvd., phone: 352–7376), both of them mobbed all summer long with happy customers spooning into huge cups full of the creamy-smooth delight. In winter, the custard operation closes and Ted goes into the Christmas tree business.

If you are far away and seriously crave this superb, super ice cream (as is the case for many St. Louis expatriates), Ted Drewes is equipped with dry ice to mail-order its custard anywhere you need it.

O h i o

Al's Corner Restaurant

545 W. Tuscarawas Ave.   330-475-7978

Barberton, OH   L Mon-Fri | $

Cruising around a strange town or city, whether or not we find a place to eat, we often wonder about great restaurants that we may not have noticed and blithely drove past. That might have been the case in Barberton, for Al's Corner Restaurant doesn't look too intriguing from the outside and we had Barberton chicken on our minds. But we were guided here by infallible Akron food authority, Jane Snow, and the moment we walked in, we knew we had hit Roadfood paydirt.

The immaculate storefront luncheonette, open only for weekday lunch, is a treasure-trove of blue-plate Hungarian meals at blue-collar prices. Service is cafeteria-style. Step to the right when you enter where one of the servers will show you what's to eat, put it on a plate, and then a tray. Dine either at a table or the long U-shaped counter in the center of the room.

Lunch specials, at well under $10 each, include the likes of chicken paprikash with dumplings, pierogies, cabbage and dumplings, and Al's sausages. The sausages are made down the street at Al's Quality Market, and they are stupendously delicious: taut, muscular, and oozing savory juices. Jane, whose father was a Hungarian epicure and taught her well, declared the paprikash to be one of the best she ever ate: creamy with a real paprika punch, the chicken falling-off-its-bone tender. The only problem we had was deciding which starch to eat more of: the dumplings are buttery and satisfying; the mashed potatoes are . . . buttery and satisfying, too!

Balyeat's Coffee Shop

131 E. Main St.   419-238-1580
Van Wert, OH   BLD (closed Mon) | $

Outside, a lovely neon sign advertises "Young Fried Chicken Day and Night." Good as the chicken is, it is just the lead item on a menu that is an honor roll of mid-America square meals. Balyeat's is the place to sit down for a plate of roast pork or roast beef, cooked that morning, served hot and large, with piles of mashed potatoes and gravy. Sauerkraut and sausage is on the menu every day but Friday, and you can usually count on a choice from among barbecued ribs, meat loaf, and liver and onions. If mashed potatoes don't ring your chimes, how about the fine alternative, escalloped potatoes?

Ahh, dessert! Pie is king in this part of the world, and Balyeat's pies are pastries to behold. There are cream pies, fruit pies, custard pies, and pecan pie, but our personal favorite is the one known as "old-fashioned pie" (OF pie). It is like custard, but tawnier, and with a sort of layered effect that happens as its cream rises to the top. It is pure, simple culinary synecdoche for Balyeat's Coffee Shop.

Blue Ash Chili

9565 Kenwood Rd.   513-984-6107
Blue Ash, OH   LD | $

The way to order chili in Cincinnati is to build a plate, layer by layer. It is, for instance, possible to order merely a dish of spaghetti (traditionally, the bottom layer) or a bowl of chili (the meat sauce that usually goes atop the spaghetti. You can get a dish of only chili and spaghetti, or you can get a three-way (chili, spaghetti, and cheese), four-way (chili, spaghetti, cheese, and raw onions), or five-way (add beans). You can even get a five-way, hold the onions, extra cheese. The possibilities are nearly endless, all the way up to what the menu lists as a gallon of chili (to go, we assume!) for $20.

A layered plate of three- to five-way is a beautiful thing. The chili meat is dark and resonant, not too spicy but with complex character, and the spaghetti noodles are always fork-friendly: not overly long, and squiggly enough that they stay on the tines of a fork with virtually no slippage.

Good as the chili is at Blue Ash, we think of this Naugahyde-and-linoleum eat-place more as a sandwich shop; for the sandwiches are nothing short of spectacular. "We think we have the best sandwiches in town," the menu advises, and in Cincinnati, sandwiches are a very big deal, almost as big as chili. As in every Cincinnati chili parlor, double-deckers reign. A double-decker means two ingredients of your choice are sandwiched in three slices of bread, making a sandwich that is so tall it is a challenge to lift from its plate. Ingredient choices for double-deckers range from bacon and egg to hot ham and cheese, turkey, beef, and bacon. Any combo is possible, including "turkey and turkey," "beef and beef," etc., meaning your double-decker is simply a double load of a favorite ingredient. We are fond of hot ham, which is sliced thin and packed into the bread in moist clumps, especially when paired with American cheese, lettuce, tomato, and mayo. Bacon is quite wonderful in any double-decker; it is thick and smoky—great with turkey, eggs, or cheese.

Camp Washington Chili Parlor

3005 Colerain Ave. 513-541-0061
Cincinnati, OH BLD | $

When we met John Johnson in 1977, he was beaming with pride, having just bought Camp Washington Chili Parlor from its founders, his uncle Steve Andon and Anastasios "Fred" Zarmbus. John had worked at Camp Washington since his arrival in America in 1951, so he knew the secrets of five-way chili as well as any cook in the chili-crazed city of Cincinnati, and he explained to us with conspiratorial glee that when he took over, he actually tinkered with the hallowed recipe and improved it! The result was an American success story—a restaurant beloved by Queen City eaters for decades, now recognized far and wide as a Road-food original.

Camp Washington sets the standard for Cincinnati's unique style of chili, and John Johnson, God bless him, has maintained his prototypical Midwest urban chili parlor as the open-all-night, democratic joint it always has been. He's kept the menu simple, too. Of course there is chili, available three-, four-, or five-way, or as a "haywagon" (only spaghetti, chili, and cheese, named because fluffy grated yellow cheese dominates the *mise-en-plat*), and there are Coney Island hot dogs heaped with chili, cheese, and onions, and double-decker sandwiches.

The basic principle of the double-decker, which is a staple in most local chili parlors, is similar to that of five-way: a layered mountain of ingredients as impressive for its looks as for its multilevel tastes. The difference is that a double-decker sandwich, theoretically, requires no utensils. In reality, while half of a well-made double-decker can indeed be picked up in two hands, it cannot be eaten like a normal sandwich, i.e., all strata going into the mouth at one time. It must be nibbled at, top to bottom, or bottom to top, in such a way that some bites are more the top layer and others more the bottom.

Clifton Mill

75 Water St.   937-767-5501
Clifton, OH   B&L | $$

A genuine water-powered grist mill—the largest in the United States— Clifton Mill is the place to come for such country comforts as cornmeal mush, buckwheat cakes with coarse-textured sausage, and biscuits the size of softballs, accompanied by a vast bowl full of creamy sausage gravy.

The mush is swell: three tiles of cornmeal fried into crunchy squares with a sticky interior—great with a little syrup poured on top. Biscuits and gravy is a daunting meal, although we did watch a ten-year-old boy at a nearby table polish off the whole thing with precise strategy, mopping the last of the gravy with his last piece of biscuit. The assortment of pancakes, made from grain ground on premises, is vast, including whole wheat, buttermilk, buckwheat, cornmeal, apple-cinnamon, banana-walnut, and oat bran–honey. Blueberries, raisins, or chocolate chips can be added to any kind you like. Lunch specials include hamburgers, buffalo burgers, and ostrich burgers. Sandwiches are made on baked-here bread.

You can buy the mill's grains as well as country-style souvenirs in an attached gift shop. Christmas aficionados should note that Clifton Mill puts on a display that is *way* over the top: 2.5 million lights on the building, in the gorge, and in the waterfall that powers the mill, plus a collection of three thousand different Santa Clauses, and a live Santa who goes up the chimney every half hour. Starting the day after Thanksgiving and continuing through New Year's, the light display goes on every night at 6 and runs until 9:30 P.M., weather permitting.

Crabill's

727 Miami St. 513-653-5133
Urbana, OH L | $

Size matters, but when it comes to hamburgers, bigger isn't necessarily better. In fact, some burger hounds prefer minuscule two-bite "sliders." The best place we know in Ohio to gobble such mini-burgers is at the counter of Crabill's, where fifty-cent hamburgers are served on itty-bitty buns, with small squares of cheese if desired, and with mustard and/or relish for a few cents extra. Eating one of these gems is a unique experience: Cooked in deep oil on the grill, it has an outside surface with delicious crunch, and it is so skinny that there is virtually no interior! Six or eight make a decent meal, but if you have a competitive spirit, you might want to try to beat the single-sitting record-holder, Dave Woods, who ate thirty-one on February 22, 2001.

Flury's Sandwich Shop

1300 Sackett Ave. 330-929-1315
Cuyahoga Falls, OH BL | $

This tiny diner seats scarcely over a dozen people and there is nothing revolutionary on the menu, but if you are in greater Akron and looking for a hospitable slice of Americana, we highly recommend it. There is always a pancake of the day—we've enjoyed cornmeal and banana-nut—and lunch opportunities include nice meat loaf sandwiches and creamy mac 'n' cheese, preceded by proprietor Kim Dunchuck's homemade soup. For dessert, choose from among Kim's homemade cookies and shortcake laced with blueberries or blackberries.

G&R Tavern

103 N. Marion St. (off US 23)   740-726-9685
Waldo, OH   BLD | $

Waldo, north of Columbus, is known as the town with the fried bologna sandwich. Since 1962, the G&R has built its reputation on bologna sandwiches that put pale, pink, thin-sliced supermarket bologna sandwiches to shame. In this family-friendly sports bar, the bologna is dark and smoky, firm as a knoblewurst salami, and sliced as thick as a good-size hamburger patty. It is fried until its exterior turns a bit crisp, and loaded into a sandwich with sweet pickles and onion (a great condiment combo), or your choice of mustard, mayonnaise, or tomato. Fitting side dishes include a variety of deep-fried vegetables and curly fries.

If for some reason you are a fried-food-frowner, G&R also offers a bologna salad sandwich, and because this bologna is so much better than the spongy packaged stuff, the salad reminds us of something made with good ham, but smoother.

While you stand along the bar waiting for a seat (at mealtimes, you will likely wait), your appetite will be whetted by the sight of the kitchen staff carrying great big logs of this very special bologna into the kitchen.

Hathaway's Coffee Shop

441 Vine St.
In the Carew Tower Arcade   513-621-1332
Cincinnati, OH   BL | $

When we called our Cincinnati friend Mary Beth Brestel at seven o'clock one morning and asked her where to eat breakfast, she directed us to Hathaway's for waffles. Like us, Mary Beth is a fan of slim, small-tread waffles—as opposed to the bloated Belgians that have been a plague on American restaurant menus ever since they were introduced at the New York World's Fair of 1964. She said that Hathaway's, a vintage coffee shop in the Carew Tower Arcade downtown, made the elegant, old-fashioned kind. It had been her bad luck that the last time she had breakfast there, the waffle iron had been broken, so she joined us this morning for a redo.

We sat at the lunch counter, perfunctorily perused the menu, and ordered waffles. "It's broken again," the waitress said. "No waffles today!"

Reassured that this was only a temporary problem, we ordered pancakes and French toast with goetta—a fried-crisp tile of pork-and-pin-oats loaf that is unique to Cincinnati—on the side. The French toast was especially good: cinnamon-accented, dusted with powdered sugar and running rivulets of melting butter. The goetta was melt-in-the-mouth good. And on the side came a metal pitcher of syrup nearly too hot to pour.

So we cannot tell you about Hathaway's waffles. But we can say it is an endearingly civilized urban dining experience reminiscent of downtown coffee shops half a century ago. Seating is at one of three U-shaped counters or at a steel-banded dinette table against the wall. Waitresses patrol the low-ceilinged room in white-collared mauve uniforms, refilling coffee cups as required. Meals are handsome and inexpensive. After breakfast, lunch items range from grilled cheese to half-pound cheeseburgers, triple-decker club sandwiches, salad plates, and a hot-plate special of the day (fried chicken Monday, hot roast beef Tuesday, spaghetti Wednesday, meat loaf Thursday, and battered fried cod with macaroni and cheese Friday). Hathaway's has a full soda fountain menu of sundaes and banana splits, plus traditional malts and yogurt shakes. These latter include a banana whisk, a pink cloud (made with strawberries), and a crème sickle (orange juice and milk). The menu touts yogurt shakes as "Healthful Pick Me Uppers," for when one needs that sweet supercharge in the middle of the shopping day.

Henry's

6275 Route 40　　　　　　　614-879-9321
West Jefferson, OH　　　　　 LD | $

No traveler in a hurry wants to be on Highway 40, the side road parallel to I-70, but anyone with an appetite for home cooking needs to make the detour. Here, set back from the south side of the road, is what looks to be a defunct gas station. The pumps are long gone, but the on-premises restaurant is alive and well and a delightful slice of Roadfood heaven.

The meals are country-style fare: baked ham, hot roast pork sandwiches with mashed potatoes and gravy, creamed chipped beef on cornbread. But it's not the hot meals that put this unlikely knotty pine–paneled roadside café on the map. It is pie. Here are some of the best pies in Ohio, in the Midwest, anywhere. Every day, baker Shelly Kelly has a list of six or eight she has made: peach, banana, chocolate, peanut butter, cherry, coconut, etc. The butterscotch pie is thick and dense, full flavored the way only real (not from a mix) butterscotch can be, and it comes topped with a creamy meringue. Custard pie is modestly thin, a sunny yellow wedge dusted with nutmeg. It is balmy, lightweight, melt-in-the-mouth tender. The flavor of the rhubarb pie is as brilliant as bright summer sun, intensely fruity, sweet but not cloying, and balanced by a crust that flakes into luscious shards.

On the way out, for the road, we took a small oval zucchini loaf Shelly Kelly had pulled from the oven just hours before. It was glorious. No doubt about it: she is a baker with a magic touch.

Liberty Gathering Place

| 111 N. Detroit St. | 937-465-3081 |
| West Liberty, OH | BLD \| $ |

While waiting for the Pine Club (p. 364) to open for supper one day, we drove north of Dayton into the farmland around Urbana and West Liberty. We marveled at the Crystal Sea and the Devil's Tea Table (formed from stalactites and helactites) in the Ohio Caverns; we toured Mac-A-Cheek and Mac-O-Chee, two late-nineteenth-century Gothic-style castles filled with sublime woodwork and surrounded by waves of cornfields; and we came upon a stupendously good lunch at the Liberty Gathering Place.

"We have girls who come in at four in the morning to make the coleslaw and macaroni salad," the Gathering Place waitress boasted when we asked if the side dishes were good. "Good" turned out to be not a good enough word to describe them, for the little bowl of macaroni salad set before us was inspired: blue-ribbon, church-supper, Independence Day–picnic fabulous! It was creamy with a pickle zip, dotted with hunks of hard-cooked egg and a few crunchy shreds of carrot, the noodles themselves cooked just beyond al dente but not too soft.

Noodle rapture proved to be a paradigm for the dining experience at what appears to be a typical Main Street café, but is in fact an extraordinary one. During a week in Dayton, the Gathering Place became our destination lunch stop for moist ham loaf and deep-flavored smoked pork chops sided by mashed potatoes and bread crumb–enriched escalloped corn. We were astounded by the fried tenderloin sandwich—totally unlike the brittle-crisp, foot-wide 'loins typical of Midwest cafés. Here, the tenderloin is a thick pork steak with only hint of crust—a slab of meat that is folded over inside the bun so you get a double layer of pork as juicy as a pair of chops. For dessert, we had cool coconut and peach crunch pie, the latter served hot and veined with melted butter.

New Sandusky Fish Company

235 E. Shoreline Dr.   419-621-8263
Sandusky, OH   LD | $

Virtuoso Roadfooders Bruce Bilmes and Sue Boyles turned us on to this little take-out only shack that offers sandwiches and whole dinners at single-digit prices. Located on Lake Erie's southern shore, it boasts fresh yellow perch and walleye and that locally loved specialty, frog legs. All are fried to golden-crusted tenderness, and the fish fillets (also including catfish and bass) are piled into buns with abandon. The frog legs are available only at dinner, with sides of fries, onion rings, hush puppies, etc. We are especially fond of the mellow freshwater savor of the perch and the soft, milky meat of the whitefish.

Many customers are anglers who bring their catch here to have it cleaned (in a building out back) and have a sandwich while they wait. While all business is take-out, for travelers like us who prefer outside-the-car dining there are nice bench seats in a gazebo across the street.

The Pine Club

1926 Brown St.   937-228-7463
Dayton, OH   D | $$$

The Pine Club is paradise for meat eaters. You have your choice of filet mignon, porterhouse, or sirloin, each cut and aged on premises and cooked on a grill so the outside gets a good dark crunch and the inside is stunningly juicy. Perhaps even more wonderful than steak is chopped steak, made from a mix of prime beef and dry-aged lamb, its succulence as luxurious as steak tartare, but with the added pleasures of dripping juice and a crusty skin.

Regulars know to begin a meal with scallops—sweet, firm nuggets with a pale light crust and breezy sea taste. Brilliant tartar sauce comes on the side. All meals are served with a basket of dinner rolls, and steaks come with a handful of onion rings and choice of potatoes that includes Lyonnaise: a crunchy, plate-wide pancake of shredded taters woven with veins of sautéed onion. As for salad, although a mesclun mix was added

to the menu a while ago, the traditional Pine Club salad is iceberg lettuce—cold, crisp chunks served "red and bleu," which is French dressing
loaded with enormous clods of dry blue cheese.

Dessert? There is none. If you're in dire need of something sweet and
don't necessarily want a high-proof libation such as a grasshopper or a
Golden Cadillac, you go next door to the Ben & Jerry's store.

The Pine Club is a true and pure Midwest supper club, open only in
the evening, until midnight on weekdays, 1:00 A.M. on Friday and Saturday. No reservations, no credit cards, no nonsense.

Putz's Creamy Whip

Putz Place and West Fork Rd.
Exit 17 off I-74   513-681-8668
Cincinnati, OH   LD (closed in winter) | $

Putz's is a drive-up stand with a menu of hot dogs, foot-longs, burgers,
and barbecue, but it's ice cream that stars. Smooth and rich, it is an ivory-
hued soft-serve custard that is great swirled into a sugar cone or waffle
cone or heaped into a cup and enjoyed for its simple, pure, creamy goodness. Or you can have it whipped up for an extra-thick milkshake or malt
or mixed into a soda.

The best way to enjoy Putz's Creamy Whip, in our opinion, is to
come for a sundae or banana split. Banana splits are long plastic boats
that hold three mounds of ice cream plus all the toppings. Sundaes are
medium-size plastic cups filled with custard and topped with whatever
you like. The best of all sundaes is the turtle, for which the bottom of the
cup is filled with caramel, the caramel is topped with custard, then the
custard is topped with chocolate syrup. And the chocolate syrup is
mounded with whipped cream, chopped nuts, and a cherry.

Putz's is just off the highway in a little grove all its own (on a street
that was rechristened to honor the longtime favorite destination-dessert
place). There are pleasant picnic tables alongside that are an ideal place
to spoon into creamy-whip perfection. For us, a sundae here defines summer in Cincinnati.

Swensons

18 S. Hawkin Ave.   330-864-8416

Akron, OH   LD | $

Pull into a space and flash your lights. Out sprints a curb boy to take your order. Apparently, most customers know the kitchen's repertoire so well that menus are superfluous—we didn't get one until we requested it. And besides, the vast majority of customers get what Swensons is famous for: hamburgers.

Top-of-the-line is the Galley Boy, a double cheeseburger dressed with two sauces, one mayonnaisey with bits of onion added, the other zesty barbecue. Optional condiments include ketchup, relish, sweet pickles, horseradish, Worcestershire, Tabasco, cocktail sauce, Coney sauce, honey mustard, tartar, and Cajun spice. Garnish choices are tomato, lettuce, olives, grilled onions, hot peppers, bacon, and coleslaw.

Beyond burgers the menu lists a quarter-pound all-beef bologna sandwich, salads, soups, fried chicken, and shrimp. Among the beverages are milkshakes and malts, something called a California (it reminded us of Kool-Aid), and half-and-half (tea and lemonade). French fries, which we didn't try, are listed as "Only Idaho's," the dubious apostrophe apparently having migrated from the restaurant name, Swensons, which doesn't contain one on the outdoor sign or menu.

Swensons has no indoor seats. Meals to be eaten here are presented on sturdy trays that clip onto the inside of car windows in such a way that it's possible to dine in comfort even when it's raining.

White Turkey Drive-In

388 E. Main Rd.   440-593-2209

Conneaut, OH   LD (Mother's Day through Labor Day) | $

"If you find yourself along Lake Erie in the northeast corner of Ohio, pull into the White Turkey, a seriously vintage drive-in." So wrote a Roadfood tipster in a note with no return address and no ID. So we don't really know who to thank for this suggestion, but we sure would like to! This Richardson's Root Beer stand is a quintessential Roadfood stop along old US 20, offering seats at high stools where you can feel a lake breeze and watch the cars cruise past while you dine on true mid-America, mid-century drive-in fare.

The namesake turkey sandwich is the real thing. No turkey loaf here! You can get a plain one or a "Large Marge," which also includes cheese and bacon. And beyond turkey, there are Big Ed one-third-pound burgers, hot dogs, and chili cheese dogs.

While only one flavor of ice cream is available—vanilla—the variety of soda fountain drinks and desserts is mesmerizing. Of course there are cones, shakes, and malts; there are sundaes topped with your choice of pineapple, cherry, chocolate, hot fudge, butterscotch caramel fudge, strawberry, grasshopper, or mint. You can get a black cow (here, a blend of root beer and ice cream). And the root beer floats are divine, available in sizes from kiddie (80 cents) to Super Shuper, created with a quart of root beer and a quantity of ice cream to match.

Young's Jersey Dairy

6880 Springfield-Xenia Rd.   937-325-0629
Yellow Springs, OH   BLD | $

There's something for everyone at Young's Jersey Dairy: a goat-petting zoo, a farm-themed gift shop, a miniature golf course (Udders and Putters), a picnic grounds where you can have catered meals, summertime wagon rides around the farm, a serious restaurant (just up the road) that serves local produce, identified by which farm it came from, and a June-to-October art exhibit of statuary cows painted by local artists. Recently, a gourmet coffee shop was added, offering espresso drinks, gelato, and wireless Internet access. All great stuff, but for us, Young's will always be the place to get a milkshake.

Using ice cream and milk from their own farm, Young's blends regular shakes and extra-thick shakes (spoon required), as well as bullshakes that are extra-large, extra-thick, and come with one additional scoop of ice cream floating on top. There are exotic flavors galore, but give us a vanilla or chocolate shake every time, preferably with plenty of malt powder added. There's none better. The dairy store counter is also a fine source of sundaes, banana splits, and bowls of ice cream from a choice of more than two dozen flavors. And you can have a nice little meal here, too: breakfast of sausage gravy and biscuits or pancakes, or lunch-counter hamburgers and sandwiches.

Bay Bakery

423 E. Silver Spring Dr.   414-332-5340
Milwaukee, WI $

Here in the state with license plates that proclaim it "America's Dairy-land," good pastries made with butter are not uncommon. But those made at Bay Bakery are some of the best we have eaten anywhere. Known to many customers as a place that makes elaborate celebration cakes, it is, for us, an opportunity to get bags and boxes full of sour cream donuts, cupcakes, fruit flips, caramel buns, single-serving bundt cakes, and fritters.

Fresh-baked bread is also outstanding. There are warm loaves on the shelf every morning, but the day we like stopping in is Friday, when you can count on caraway rye. We would describe this rye as "heaven on toast," but in fact we've never had the opportunity to toast it. We buy a loaf and tear at it as we drive around Milwaukee looking for other good things to eat.

Mostly a take-out store, Bay Bakery does have a couple of tables for customers desperately in need of eating pastries *now.*

Beerntsen's Candy Store

108 N. 8th St.　　　　　　　920-684-9616
Manitowoc, WI　　　　　　　LD | $

In the back of Beerntsen's, past the confectionery shelves and through an elaborately carved archway, handsome wooden booths are occupied by customers who come for such ice cream fancies as a Sweetheart (caramel, vanilla ice cream, marshmallow, crushed nuts) or a Sunset (strawberry and vanilla ice cream, pineapple, marshmallow, crushed nuts). Up front are more than a hundred different kinds of hand-dipped candy, including a chocolate cosmetology set (brush, mirror, hair dryer), smoochies (like Hershey's kisses, but bigger), raspberry and vanilla seafoam dainties and—the pièce de résistance—a bonbon known as fairy food, which is a two-inch square of gossamer spun sugar molasses shrouded in deep, dark chocolate. The chocolate is dense and luxurious. The molasses melts into nothing but flavor. We are very happy we live nowhere near Manitowoc, Wisconsin, and that fairy food is too delicate to be shipped; otherwise, we'd be addicts.

Bendtsen's Bakery

3200 Washington Ave.　　　　262-633-7449
Racine, WI　　　　　　　　　L | $

Bendtsen's calls its kringle "the world's finest Danish pastry," a claim with which we would not disagree. If you don't know what kringle is, think of an ordinary Danish, like you have with morning coffee. Now, imagine its crust buttery and feather-light, almost like a croissant, and fill it with a ribbon of pecan paste and chopped nuts, or a layer of almond macaroon paste, or a tunnel of cherry and cheese. Picture it as big as a Christmas wreath, a ring that is about a foot-and-a-half across and iced with sugar glaze or flavored frosting. Finally, imagine it served warm with butter melting on top, accompanied by a leisurely pot of coffee. There you have one of the great breakfast (or teatime) treats in America, a dish that is virtually unknown outside the city of Racine, Wisconsin.

Bendtsen's has pictures on the wall that show the time they made the world's largest kringle, but size isn't what makes their pastry so wonderful. Each kringle made here, whether simply filled with apricot jam or fancy-filled with a mash of cranberries and walnuts, is a beautiful sight—

a broad oval rather than a perfect circle, quite flat, and ready to slice into small pieces (of which you'll want three or four).

There is no place to eat at Bendtsen's, although samples of kringle are often available for tasting on the counter. And we must warn you that this is not really car food. It's rather a mess to eat (it crumbles and the filling oozes), and it really should be served warm, buttered, and with hot coffee. Nevertheless, we have been known to devour the better of two whole rings between Racine and Chicago, leaving a hail of crumbs on the seat and floor of our rental car.

Benji's Deli

4156 N. Oakland Ave.   414-332-7777
Milwaukee, WI (in Shorewood)   BLD | $$

Benji's is an old-fashioned Jewish-style deli in a modern shopping area. It is an authentic taste of Milwaukee, by which we mean it offers a reassuring menu of old country ethnic dishes (chicken-in-the-pot, cabbage rolls, fried matzoh) along with plenty of Midwestern Americana, such as a Friday night fish fry, a deluxe hamburger plate with French fries, a French dip sandwich on a poppy-seed roll, and that mysteriously named heartland meal-in-a-skillet, Hoppel Poppel, for which no ethnic group we know has ever taken credit. Hoppel Poppel is a griddle-cooked breakfast mélange of chewy salami chunks, scrambled eggs, tender potato chunks, and (optional) onions. Benji's offers it also in a "super" version that adds peppers, mushrooms, and melted cheese to the formula. Either way, it's delicious.

The other specialties of the house are deli food: piled-high corned beef sandwiches on rugged-crusted sour rye bread, lox-and-bagel platters, sweet-and-sour cabbage borscht, buttery warm blintzes (available filled with cheese, cherries, or blueberries), and crisp potato pancakes, served with applesauce. For dessert, we recommend noodle kugel (a cheesecake-rich block of cooked egg noodles and sweetened cheese), served hot with sour cream. And for a beverage to drink with your meal, Benji's offers true melting pot variety: domestic or imported beer, kosher wine, Dr. Brown's in cans, Sprecher's soda in bottles, and chocolate phosphates (seltzer water and chocolate syrup).

Chili John's

519 S. Military Ave.   920-494-4624
Green Bay, WI   LD | $

In 1916, "Chili John" Isaac devised a recipe for ground beef cooked with a rainbow of spice. The way he served it at his little eat-place, in concert with spaghetti noodles, beans, and cheese, the heat became part of a well-balanced plate of food. Today, it is served with spoon-size oyster crackers, which were invented at Chili John's request. The story is that sometime in the 1920s, he came to believe that the old-fashioned store cracker, at least an inch in diameter, was too unwieldy to garnish his chili, so he convinced cracker manufacturers to downsize.

Although some locals still call the multilayered configuration Texas-style chili (an appellation Texas chiliheads no doubt would abhor), variations of the formula are now known throughout the state as Green Bay–style chili, and the legendary chili parlor Chili John created has become a culinary beacon.

Jack Pandl's Whitefish Bay Inn

1319 Henry Clay St.   414-964-3800
Whitefish Bay, WI   LD | $$

Jack Pandl's (since 1915) serves German-flavored Dairyland cuisine in a friendly, wood-paneled dining room with a wall of windows that look out over elegant Lake Drive. Waitresses wear dirndl skirts and there is lots of old-world memorabilia for décor (including one of the planet's biggest collections of beer steins), but the menu is at least as Midwestern as it is middle European. At lunch, when the steel-banded tables are set with functional paper place mats, you can eat a julienne salad or a Reuben sandwich made with Wisconsin cheese, or pork chops, or a Denver omelet. In addition to superlative broiled whitefish ("always purchased fresh," the menu guarantees), there is that lean but luscious local specialty, walleyed pike, filleted and broiled to perfection. This being Milwaukee, Friday is fish fry night, of course. Pandl's perch is lovely—whole fish filleted so their two halves hold together, encased in a golden crust and accompanied by first-class potato pancakes.

We love schaum torte for dessert. That's a crisp meringue dolloped with freshly made custard. On the other hand, we never can resist the German pancake. It's not really a dessert item, and many people have it as their main course, but somehow it makes a grand conclusion to a meal. This gorgeous edible event, a Jack Pandl's specialty, is a big puffy cloud of batter similar in texture to Yorkshire pudding, but slightly sweeter. It arrives at the table piping hot and shaped like a big bowl, its circumference crisp and brown, risen high in the oven, its center moist and eggy. Dust it with a bit of powdered sugar and give it a spritz of lemon, creating a sophisticated syrup, then dig in immediately. It is a big plate of food, a pleasure to share with friends.

Jake's

| 1634 W. North Ave. | 414-562-1272 |
| Milwaukee, WI | L | $ |

It took us a long time to realize that Milwaukee was a major corned beef city, but if we had any doubts, Jake's erased them. Here is a vintage urban deli where the hand-sliced corned beef is steamy-moist, unbearably tender, and vividly flavored.

Proprietor Michael Kassof suggested that one reason for his beef's deliciousness might be that a dozen or more briskets are boiled together, their pot becoming a slurry of spice and beef flavor that reinsinuates itself into the fibers of the meat. Just as the counterman prepares to slice a whole brisket for sandwiches, it is sprinkled with paprika, adding a little extra jolt to the taste. The beef is sliced medium-thick then piled into slick-crusted, Milwaukee-made Miller bakery seeded rye: not an outrageously huge sandwich like you might get in Chicago or New York, but in no way skimpy, either. We see the meat-to-bread ratio as perfect.

There are a few other items on Jake's menu: pastrami, turkey pastrami, hard salami, hot dogs, and soups-like-mama-should-have-made, and you can have the corned beef as part of a Reuben with sauerkraut and cheese. But for us, and for generations of Milwaukeeans, Jake's is synonymous with corned beef on rye.

With its pale yellow walls, its tables topped with worn linoleum, its ancient wood booths equipped with out-of-order buzzers once used to summon service, Jake's exudes faded charm. It has been around since 1935, when the neighborhood was mostly Jewish. Original proprietor Reuben Cohen sold it to Jake, who sold it to Michael Kassof's dad in 1967, and now Michael runs the place—the last Jewish business in a neighborhood that is mostly African American. Superlative corned beef is a cross-cultural infatuation.

Jo's Café

3519 W. Silver Spring Dr. 414-461-0210

Milwaukee, WI BL | $

Hoffel poffel (also known as hoppel poppel) isn't widely known any-where in the United States that we are aware of, although we have seen versions of it in Iowa. It is one gigantic breakfast plate of a few eggs scrambled with chunks of potato, some onions, and, at Jo's, lots of nuggets of spicy salami and, optionally, some cheese on top. The only rea-son we would recommend not getting it for breakfast at Jo's is that the *other* kind of potatoes—the thin-cut hash browns—are delicious. Cooked in a flat patty until brittle-crisp, they, too, are available under a mantle of melted cheese. Actually, either sort of potato dish will leave precious little room for Jo's terrific pecan rolls and cinnamon rolls; nor should a first-time visitor miss out on one of the large omelets cooked on Jo's griddle.

We generally think of Jo's for breakfast, but lunch is not to be ignored. Blue-plate cuisine is the order of the day, including such daily specials as meat loaf, beef stew, pork chops, and country-fried steak with real (of course!) mashed potatoes, homemade gravy, and a yeasty fresh-baked din-ner roll. Every day you can order good barbecued pork ribs or chicken.

Klinger's East

920 E. Locust St. 414-263-2424

Milwaukee, WI D | $$

When we went to Milwaukee on a mission to eat its best fish fries, our buddies Jessica Zierten and Brad Warsh, both lifelong Milwaukeeans, in-sisted that any significant expedition needed to include a visit to their fa-vorite tavern in the Riverwest neighborhood, Klinger's East. We're glad they recommended it, because this shadowy bar is not one that we would necessarily feel obliged to enter. It doesn't look like a great place to eat.

Despite the fact that half of Klinger's East is a pool hall and the bleak décor shadowed by the dining room's dropped acoustic tile ceiling in-cludes a sickly green rug and tables covered with matching green oilcloth, it's a cozy place, even for out-of-towners like us. Customers include wholesome-looking families you'd never see dining in such an establish-ment in other parts of the country. But in Milwaukee, taverns aren't just for drinkers; they are community centers.

The fish fry is brilliant. Of course cod is on the menu, sheathed in a crunchy coat of beer batter. You can also get smelt, which Brad informed us is properly pronounced "shmelt" hereabouts. It is a fish-lover's fish with vivid oily character—a heap of crunch-coated two-inch sprats well-accompanied by a short stack of silver-dollar-size potato pancakes. The night we visited, the potato-slicing machine was broken so fresh-cut French fries were unavailable. Bartender Tammy Galioto apologized for their absence, but wanted to know if we agreed that the fish was fantastic. "People say it should be patented!" she exclaimed. When we asked how to ID her for this story, she pondered a moment and said, "How about 'An East Side Sicilian Icon'?" But she didn't kid around when we asked her to describe Klinger's East. "You are in a neighborhood tavern," she declared. "This is what makes the city of Milwaukee what it is."

Leon's

3131 S. 27th St.
Milwaukee, WI

414-383-1784
$

There is no place to eat at this neon-rimmed, Eisenhower-era hangout other than in your car or standing in the parking lot along with other happy pilgrims who have come for the ultimate frozen dessert. Leon's menu is all custard: cones, cups, sodas, sundaes, malts, pints, and quarts. (Hot dogs are available, but they are irrelevant.)

Milwaukee is fanatical about custard, which is heavy, smooth, and pure—denser than the richest superpremium ice cream and nothing like wan frozen yogurt. As made by Leon's, Milwaukee custard is egg-rich, sweet but not cloying, and uncomplicated. No mix-ins, no silly names for flavors, no cookie dough or brownie chunks. Choose vanilla, chocolate, strawberry, or butter pecan. Have it in a cone or cup. Or have a sundae topped with sauce of your choice and some of the most delicious toasted nuts on the planet: pecan halves that have a wicked crunch, a salty punch, and an earthy flavor that only helps accentuate the heavenly clarity of the superior custard itself.

Mazo's

3146 S. 27th St.
Milwaukee, WI

414-671-2118
BLD Tues-Sat | $

One of Milwaukee's lesser-known culinary attractions is its hamburgers. Some connoisseurs believe Mazo's serves the best. It is a tiny place now run by Nick Mazo, whose grandparents started it in 1934, and if you come at lunchtime, prepare to wait a while once you find a precious seat in the dining room. These burgers are *not* fast food, but they are worth the wait.

They are not spectacular; they are very normal patties of good ground beef that are grilled in butter—the Milwaukee way!—and served in lovely toasted buns. Available toppings include fried onions, sautéed mushrooms, and, of course, a layer of cheese. Other choices for dressing up the burger are bacon, lettuce, and tomato as well as Thousand Island dressing. On the side, have coleslaw, French fries, or baked beans.

Bonus: Mazo's is directly across the street from the excellent Leon's custard stand (p. 374).

McBob's

4919 W. North Ave.	414-871-5050
Milwaukee, WI	LD | $$

Roadfood.com users Jessica Zierten and Brad Warsh said we needed to come to McBob's a few years ago when we were in their home city of Milwaukee looking for excellent fish fries. Thumbs-up to that! Every Friday, McBob's offers three choices—perch, walleye, or grouper—or you can have a combo of perch and walleye, or a super combo of all three. With the fish come American fries or potato pancakes, coleslaw, and bread. "This is the real deal!" Brad proclaimed, "All fresh, all real." Each fish fillet is encased in a highly seasoned, fragile crust. The walleye is light and ephemeral; the grouper is mild with a sweet oily flavor. The perch is snowy white. If you get the meal with potato pancakes—you should!— the pancakes are fanned out on the plate as a kind of edible trivet for the fish. They are laced with bits of onion and have a potato flavor that perfectly complements the crisp fish.

If you happen to be a fish-fry-frowner, McBob's has another treasure. Every day of the week it is a source of terrific corned beef. Big chunks of steamy-hot meat from a super-tender spiced brisket are piled into a sandwich of plain rye or in toasted rye with sauerkraut, horseradish mustard, and Swiss cheese (a Reuben). The meat is extraordinarily lean and yet veritably dripping with flavor. The ideal condiment is horseradish mustard.

McBob's is a very popular place after work, and the thank-God-it's-Friday crowd with whom we bent elbows and ate fish and corned beef made our meal there a memorable party.

Mr. Perkins' Family Restaurant

2001 W. Atkinson Ave.   414-447-6660

Milwaukee, WI   BLD | $

Mr. Perkins' is a city lunchroom with a mostly African American clientele, but all visitors are made to feel welcome at this counter and in these booths. With a large menu (and a reliable rotation of daily specials, i.e., neckbones every Wednesday), this neighborhood café is a Milwaukee landmark.

While certain dishes may be an acquired taste—chitterlin's, for example—many specialties are comfort food for anyone. Baked chicken with dressing is tender and vividly spiced; meat loaf is firm and satisfying; those pork neckbones on Wednesday are some trouble to eat (they're little), but the meat virtually falls from the bone as you savor it. We must also mention the fried perch, which is a plate of about three large boneless fillets encased in a sandy cornmeal crust. The meat of the fish is amazingly juicy, with flavor as lusty as beefsteak.

One of the most delightful aspects of lunch and supper at Mr. Perkins' (which also serves breakfast) is choosing side dishes. Macaroni and cheese has a perfect balance of tender noodle and crusty edges; fried okra is vegetable-sweet; fried green tomatoes are tangy and brittle-crisp; there are pot-likker-sopped turnip greens *or* turnip bottoms, made into an intriguing squash-like mash with butter and sugar. Cornbread is Tennessee-style, i.e., a griddle-cooked cake that is buttery, tender, golden-colored, and an ideal tool for mopping gravy and vegetable drippings from a plate. Desserts include pineapple coconut cake, individual-size fried peach pies, sweet potato pie, or a plate of sweet yams. And to drink, the beverages of choice are lemonade and iced tea, both served southern-style, i.e., supersweet!

Plaza Tavern

319 N. Henry St.   608-255-6592

Madison, WI   LD | $

We found out about the Plaza Tavern at Minneapolis's Convention Grill, which boasts that its hamburger is modeled after the one served in Madison. We were intrigued by the one we had in Minnesota, so next time we were driving west of Lake Michigan, we stopped at the source to check it out.

Not merely intriguing, a Plazaburger is downright delicious, addictively so. What makes it different from a regular hamburger (which is also available) is the secret-sauce condiment that drenches the patty. It is thinner than ketchup and its texture reminded us of some eastern North Carolina barbecue sauces, although it doesn't have the vinegar tang. It's spicy but not even three-alarm hot, and in addition to infusing the meat with flavor, it gets deeply imprinted into the tawny bun on which the burger is served. Connoisseurs have it on their French fries, too. You can buy a cupful for sixty cents.

The Tavern menu is an otherwise unremarkable array of sandwiches, plus, of course, cheese curds. Beers are sold by the pint and pitcher. Ambience is pure Midwest saloon: long bar, tight booths, and wall murals depicting scenic Wisconsin.

Real Chili

419 E. Wells St. 414-271-4042

Milwaukee, WI BLD | $

Real Chili serves bowls of chili mild, medium, or hot, with spaghetti or beans, or spaghetti *and* beans, the latter arrangement known as the Marquette Special (to honor the many Marquette University students who are frequent chili eaters). Atop this heap of food, you can have your choice of sour cream, cheese, or onions, and on the side, you'll get some oyster crackers to crumble on top or to eat as a palate-cleanser between bites of chili.

This déclassé joint is the kind of beanery you once could find in big cities throughout the region. With the exception of Cincinnati, the Midwest has lost most of its chili parlors, and although heartland chili gets little respect from gastronomes who prefer the southwestern kinds, Real Chili is a true culinary adventure. Sit at a counter or at one of two communal tables with backless stools; uniformed waitresses dole out second helpings at half price, and the preferred beverages are beer or cherry Coke. If you need a bumper sticker for your car, you can get one here that says, "Real Chili: It's Not Just for Breakfast Anymore."

Serb Hall

5101 W. Oklahoma Ave.   414-545-6030

Milwaukee, WI   D Fri only | $$

Serb Hall is the largest fish fry in the United States. The chandelier-crowned eating stadium seats 950 people at hundreds of four-tops and dozens of big-party tablelands as a loudspeaker voice reverberates above the dinner din with announcements of birthdays and anniversaries and clusters of diners cheer from a hundred yards away. By 6:00 P.M., the South Side banquet hall is filled and the line of people waiting outside stretches for city blocks.

Fish fries are the only meal regularly served, fifty-two Fridays per year, Good Friday being the big blowout when over two tons of fish are served along with a ton-and-a-half of French fries and seventy-three gallons of tartar sauce. Most people come here to eat Icelandic cod—thin-crusted blocks of soft white meat served in a plastic basket with French fries, tart coleslaw, and rye bread on the side. Beer-battered cod is frequently available, its hopsy coat shoring in an abundance of cream-rich fish juices.

When we inquired about Serb Hall serving hours, our very busy waitress took time to carefully explain that the doors close precisely at 8:00 P.M., but customers already seated are allowed to finish eating and drinking.

Solly's Grille

4629 N. Port Washington Rd.   414-332-8808

Milwaukee, WI   BLD Tues-Sat | $

Here is the great butter burger of Milwaukee, a city where burgers are a passion and butter is the staff of life. It is a fairly thin patty of beef, cooked through, served on a bun literally dripping with butter. Not margarine, not flavored oil: pure, dairy-rich, delicious butter. You can get a Super burger (two patties, and a good idea; to us, a single one is overwhelmed by its bun) or a Super Special, which adds lettuce, tomato, and mayonnaise to the mix (also a good idea), as well as cheeseburgers and burgers topped with mushrooms, onions, and Monterey Jack cheese. The biggest of all burgers is the Cheesehead, which is a half pound of sirloin with Swiss and American cheeses, stewed onions, raw onion, and mushrooms. It is virtually impossible to eat with one's hands, but it's fun to try!

There are a few other kinds of sandwiches on Solly's menu, none of which we've tried, also omelets and fish fries, excellent crinkle-cut French fries, and made-here pie. If you've got a sweet tooth, we recommend you reserve it for a milkshake, which is Dairy State–rich and made in flavors that include chocolate, hot fudge, strawberry, pineapple, vanilla, and the superb fresh banana malt. Another confectionery alternative is a black cow made with Sprecher's root beer. And, this being a city where ice cream is even more beloved than butter burgers, there is a full array of sundaes, too.

Seating is at two horseshoe-shaped counters with stools, and the staff of uniformed waitresses still go about their business with well-seasoned hash-house aplomb.

Speed Queen

1130 West Walnut St. 414-265-2900
Milwaukee, WI LD | $

Speed Queen is Milwaukee's best barbecue, serving pork, beef, and turkey cooked until ridiculously tender and served in a glaze of spicy sauce. The mild sauce is robust and slightly sweet. Hot sauce is explosive, a dark orange emulsion that reminds us of Arthur Bryant's dizzying potion in Kansas City. For many customers, the mild is a little too mild, the hot is too lip-burning, so it is not uncommon to hear orders for "half and half." (Sauce is sold in bottles to take home: *highly recommended!*)

There are two kinds of pork available: shoulder or outside meat. Shoulder is thick slices that are almost chunks, tender as velvet. Outside meat is a motley pile of nearly blackened shreds and nuggets, some of which are tender, some of which are crusty, and some of which quite literally melt on the tongue. It is smokier-tasting than inside meat, like essence of barbecue. A favorite way to eat at Speed Queen is to order a half-and-half plate (ribs and outside, rib tips and shoulder, etc.) that consists of meat, sauce, a couple of slices of spongy white bread (necessary for sopping sauce), plus a cup of coleslaw. Beans and potato salad cost extra. You can also get a sandwich, but beware: these "sandwiches" are, in fact, lots of meat and sauce piled onto white bread in such a way that it is inconceivable to hold it in your hands like a sandwich.

Everything is delivered at the order window in a Styrofoam container, and while most business is take-out, Speed Queen offers a row of functional booths for dining-in. Décor is minimal, consisting of two identical photo murals of the Wisconsin Dells on opposite walls. While there is a jukebox, it seems seldom to be plugged in or playing. Room tone is a hush punctuated by lip-smacks, sighs of pleasure, and the quietest kind of reverential conversation—the pensive hush induced by truly wonderful barbecue.

Three Brothers

2414 S. St. Clair St.   414-481-7530
Milwaukee, WI   D | $$

The story of Three Brothers is a dramatic one. "My father bought this tavern in 1950," recalls proprietor Branko Radiecevich. "He chose the name Three Brothers in anticipation of his three sons coming to the United States. Alexander, Milutin, and I escaped Yugoslavia in 1956. It was a real reunion; I had not seen my father for fourteen years, when we were separated in a Nazi concentration camp."

Branko's family restaurant has become a Milwaukee landmark that attracts eaters from all walks of life and all ethnic groups. Accommodations are polite but humble—dine at a bare-top, steel-banded table—and the ethnic food is grand. We started with lemon-and-wine marinated rice-stuffed grape leaves, which were served with black olives and firm sticks of nut-sweet *kashkaval* (a goat's milk cheese) and a "Serbian salad" of tomatoes, green peppers, and onions showered with finely grated *Bryndza*, a soft goat's-milk cheese.

One autumn a while ago when we came for supper, Branko reminded us that it was leek season and brought out a savory pastry pie layered with caramelized peppered leeks. He was even more enthusiastic about roast lamb, a Three Brothers signature dish that is basted four hours in its own juices with tomato, pepper, onion, and garlic, and served just barely on the bone. Poke it with fork tines, and bite-size hunks of meat separate from the haunch and fall into the juice on the plate. The menu describes it as a must for the lamb lover, but we suspect that even non-lamb lovers might find its refined taste irresistible.

The building in which Three Brothers serves these fine meals is a corner tavern that was built in 1897 and was owned and operated for decades by the Schlitz Brewing Company. The Schlitz insignia—a globe—still crowns the peak of the roof. There are no longer seats at the old bar, which runs the length of the front room and is now a service area, but the wood-floored saloon retains the warmth of a community gathering place.

Watts Tea Room

761 N. Jefferson St.   414-291-5120

Milwaukee, WI   BL&T Mon-Sat | $

When we wrote the cookbook *Square Meals* in 1984, we described the ritual of ladies' lunch as culinary history. We were wrong. At the Watts Tea Room, on the second floor of George Watts and Son fine china shop, ladies' lunch is alive and well, along with afternoon tea and lovely breakfasts of ginger toast and hot chocolate.

Such a pleasant place! At the front door downstairs, you are greeted by a member of the staff and directed to the elevator. Past display cases of Limoges and Wedgwood, you find yourself on the second floor in a broad lunchroom with a window view of Jefferson Street below. The tables are well-worn bare wood, the floral carpet is a muted blue. Coffee is served in Royal Worcester Hanbury pattern cups, and napkins are white linen. Of course, waitresses wear tidy uniforms.

Sandwiches are served on tender-crumb homemade whole wheat bread, and while we adore the mixed green and black olive salad sandwich, and the BLT is exemplary, and a quiche of the day is always available, what dazzles us about the menu is its many ways with chicken. You can have chicken salad, minced chicken, all-white chicken, sliced chicken, or chicken salad Polynesian, that last one mixed with coconut shreds, pecans, and a citrus vinaigrette.

To drink, there are tea and lemonade, and the wonderful house specials known as a Waterford spritzer (lemonade, lime, and sparkling water) and a cold Russian (coffee, chocolate, and whipped cream). Dessert is splendid: filled sunshine cake, made from a decades-old recipe for triple-layer sponge cake with custard filling and seven-minute frosting.

Great Plains

Idaho * Montana * Nebraska *

South Dakota * Wyoming

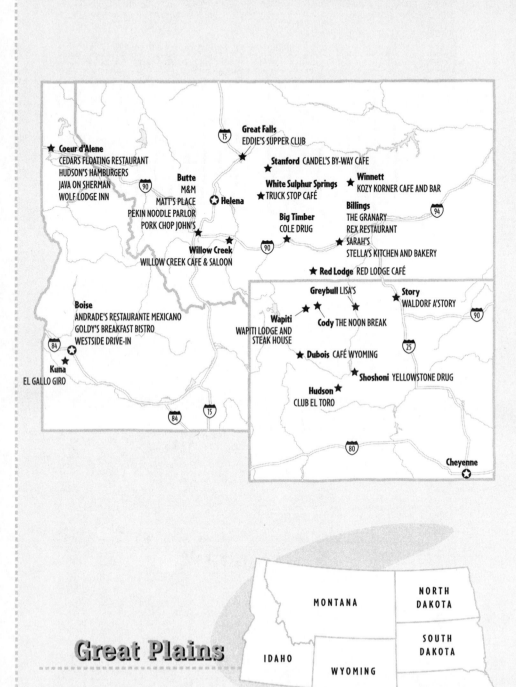

Coeur d'Alene
CEDARS FLOATING RESTAURANT
HUDSON'S HAMBURGERS
JAVA ON SHERMAN
WOLF LODGE INN

Great Falls
EDDIE'S SUPPER CLUB

Stanford CANDEL'S BY-WAY CAFE

Winnett
KOZY KORNER CAFE AND BAR

Butte
M&M
MATT'S PLACE
PEKIN NOODLE PARLOR
PORK CHOP JOHN'S

White Sulphur Springs
TRUCK STOP CAFÉ

Helena

Billings
THE GRANARY
REX RESTAURANT
SARAH'S
STELLA'S KITCHEN AND BAKERY

Big Timber
COLE DRUG

Willow Creek
WILLOW CREEK CAFE & SALOON

Red Lodge RED LODGE CAFÉ

Boise
ANDRADE'S RESTAURANTE MEXICANO
GOLDY'S BREAKFAST BISTRO
WESTSIDE DRIVE-IN

Greybull LISA'S

Story
WALDORF A'STORY

Wapiti
WAPITI LODGE AND
STEAK HOUSE

Cody THE NOON BREAK

Kuna
EL GALLO GIRO

Dubois CAFÉ WYOMING

Shoshoni YELLOWSTONE DRUG

Hudson
CLUB EL TORO

Cheyenne

Great Plains

MONTANA

NORTH
DAKOTA

IDAHO

SOUTH
DAKOTA

WYOMING

NEBRASKA

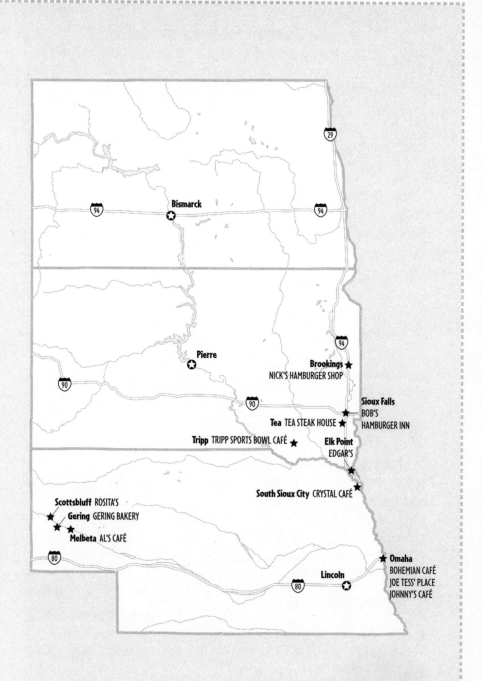

Bismarck

Pierre

Brookings
NICK'S HAMBURGER SHOP

Sioux Falls
BOB'S
HAMBURGER INN

Tea TEA STEAK HOUSE

Tripp TRIPP SPORTS BOWL CAFÉ

Elk Point
EDGAR'S

South Sioux City CRYSTAL CAFÉ

Scottsbluff ROSITA'S
Gering GERING BAKERY
Melbeta AL'S CAFÉ

Omaha
BOHEMIAN CAFÉ
JOE TESS' PLACE
JOHNNY'S CAFÉ

Lincoln

Andrade's Restaurante Mexicano

2137 Broadway Ave.   208-424-8890
Boise, ID   LD | $$

We used to think that the only good food to eat while traveling through southern Idaho was Basque. But Mexican food also abounds, and one of the best places to enjoy it is Andrade's Restaurante Mexicano in Boise (with a second location in Meridian). It's a pretty, hospitable place with bright-colored murals on the walls and a shady patio for al fresco dining.

Javier Andrade is known for his salsa bar, where diners help themselves to chunky salsa roja, pico de gallo, four-alarm habañero purée, and a large variety of other tongue-tinglers that are just right for dipping tortilla chips. Our one caution is to note that the salsas are not clearly labeled, so it's hit and miss, heat-wise, and in our experience, some of these are hair-raising.

Two great ways to start a meal are fish tacos and chori queso, the latter a dense, delicious cheese melted and mixed with chorizo sausage. Favorite dinners include a powerhouse chicken mole, carne asada with grilled onions, and puerco Michoacan, which is pork stewed in a tomato sauce with peppers, onions, and sweet corn.

Cedars Floating Restaurant

1 Marine Dr. (Blackwell Island)   208-664-2922

Coeur d'Alene, ID   D | $$$

Rugged as it is, the landscape of northern Idaho can be irresistibly romantic—especially when appreciated at dinner hour from a table in Cedars Floating Restaurant, which is one of the few eateries that take full advantage of the city's auspicious setting at the north end of Coeur d'Alene Lake. In fact, Cedars is located in the lake, moored about a hundred yards out at the head of the Spokane River and reachable by a walk down a long, narrow gangplank from the parking lot. Permanently berthed on 300 tons of concrete, the dining room does not bob with the waves (as the original structure did in the 1960s!), but the window tables are virtually on the waterline. Our first visit was on a drizzly September evening when the lake was steel gray, reflecting stormy skies and low clouds creeping down over a forested horizon.

A crackling fire and the lively sounds of an open kitchen provide cozy ambience to the spacious circular dining room, where every seat affords a view of waterfowl skimming over waves and the distant rocky shoreline. Cedars specializes in fresh fish from Pacific waters. Salmon, ahi, sea bass, halibut, shark, and mahimahi are some of the frequently available choices; they are cut into thick fillets and charcoal broiled, served with a choice of clear lemon butter caper sauce, tropical fruit salsa, or cucumber dill sauce.

We started our meal with a pound of steamed clams lolling in a garlicky wine broth and accompanied by toasted French bread and a plate of fresh-seared calamari with garlic aioli and red pepper remoulade. Our fillet of Hawaiian wahoo was a handsome piece of meat, well over an inch thick: firm and sweet-fleshed with a savory crust from the grill. It was accompanied by a baked potato with tawny skin and flavorful insides. "An Idaho potato?" we asked the waitress. Blushing, she confessed the spud was grown in Washington State. On a subsequent visit, we decided to try the beef and were thrilled by a one-pound prime rib, roasted for twelve hours and rubbed with herbs. A marinated "biergarten" filet mignon was butter-knife tender . . . if somewhat painfully priced at $35.95.

The dessert list is short, but it includes huckleberry cheesecake and Cascade Creamery huckleberry ice cream.

El Gallo Giro

482 W. 3rd St.   208-922-5169

Kuna, ID   LD | $

A cheerful restaurant whose name translates as "the fighting rooster,"
this Treasure Valley gem southwest of Boise and just a few minutes from
I-84 serves superb true-Mex food. Start with hominy-pork soup (pozole),
campenchana (octopus and shrimp in a garlic-lime marinade), or freshly
made guacamole accompanied by chips and salsa. Quaff a Mexican beer
or creamy-sweet horchata (rice milk), then move on to a beautiful plate
of chicken mole blanketed with intense chile-chocolate sauce or fish tacos
on soft tortillas. We loved our *carne borracha*, which is shredded beef
with hot peppers, onions and tomatoes; anything mixed and served in a
molcajete—a lava rock bowl—is a dining event. Even the refried beans
are extra-good, sprinkled with crumbled cotija cheese.

From what we could see on other people's tables, the more familiar
Tex-Mex meals are mighty tempting: enchiladas, chimichangas, fajitas,
etc. El Gallo Giro's little tacos, selling for a dollar apiece, are local legend.
You can have them filled with steak, pork, goat, cheek, tongue, chicken,
or tripe.

One reason people return again and again, other than the food, is the
hospitality of Enrique Contreras, who is known for circulating around
the dining room throughout mealtime to say hello to old friends and welcome new ones.

Goldy's Breakfast Bistro

108 S. Capitol Blvd.   208-345-4100

Boise, ID   BL | $$

Who couldn't love Goldy's "Create Your Own Breakfast Combo"? Select
a main course, which can be eggs, chicken-fried steak, or a salmon fillet,
then take your pick from long lists of meats, potatoes, and breads.
Among the not-to-be-missed meats are habañero chicken sausage,
Basque chorizo, and pork sausage infused with sage. The potato roster
includes not only hash browns and sweet potato hash browns but also
red flannel hash (spuds, beets, and bacon) and also cheese grits. The six
available breads include sourdough, cinnamon raisin walnut, and fresh-
baked biscuits.

Hollandaise sauce is fantastic: smooth and fluffy with an ethereal lemon perfume. It comes on several variations of eggs Benedict. There's eggs Blackstone (black forest ham and tomato); a dilled salmon fillet blanketed with slivers of cucumber and sauce; even a veggie Benny, which is hollandaise sauce over broccoli, asparagus, and tomato. Other choice breakfast items include frittatas, breakfast burritos, cinnamon rolls and sticky buns; a full-service espresso bar offers cappuccinos, lattes, and flavor shots from amaretto to passion fruit. Orange juice is freshly squeezed.

A stylish little place with an open kitchen that affords diners a view of breakfasts being cooked and plated, Goldy's can be maddeningly crowded, making meal service less than speedy; on weekends you will likely wait for a table. But if your goal is having the best breakfast in Boise, this is the place to go.

Hudson's Hamburgers

207 Sherman Ave.   208-664-5444
Coeur d'Alene, ID 83814   L | $

"Pickle and onion?" the counterman will ask when you order a hamburger, a double hamburger, or a double cheeseburger at Hudson's, a counter-only diner that has been a Coeur d'Alene institution since 1907, when Harley Hudson opened a quick-eats lunch tent on the town's main drag.

Your garnish selection is called out to grillman Todd Hudson, Harley's great-grandson, who slices the raw onion to order, using his knife blade to hoist the thin, crisp disk from the cutting board to the bun bottom; then, deft as a Benihana chef, he cuts eight small circles from a pickle and arrays them in two neat rows atop the onion. When not wielding his knife, Todd hand-forms each burger, as it is ordered, from a heap of lean ground beef piled in a gleaming metal pan adjacent to his griddle. All this happens at warp speed as customers enjoy the mesmerizing show from the sixteen seats at Hudson's long counter and from the small waiting area at the front of the restaurant, where new arrivals watch for stool vacancies.

Each patty is cooked until it develops a light crust from the griddle but retains a high amount of juiciness inside. One in a bun makes a balanced sandwich. Two verge on overwhelming beefiness. Chef Hudson sprinkles on a dash of salt, and when the hamburger is presented, you have one more choice to make: which condiment? Three squeeze bottles are deployed adjacent to each napkin dispenser along the counter. One is hot mustard, the other is normal ketchup, the third is Hudson's very spicy ketchup, a thin orange potion for which the recipe is a guarded secret. "All I can tell you is that there is no horseradish in it," the counterman reveals to an inquisitive customer.

There are no side dishes at all: no French fries, no chips, no slaw, not a leaf of lettuce in the house. And other than the fact that a glass case holds slices of pie for dessert, there is nothing more to say about Hudson's. In nine decades, it has been honed to a simple perfection.

Java on Sherman

324 Sherman Ave.   208-667-0010
Coeur d'Alene, ID   BL | $

Several years ago during a week in Coeur d'Alene, we started every day at Java on Sherman, and fell in love with it. We sampled breakfast at other cafés and diners around town, but none were as compelling as this stylish storefront coffeehouse (one of a handful of Idaho Javas) where Seattle-level caffeine connoisseurship combines with muffin mastery. All the usual drip-brewed and espresso-based beverages are expertly made, supplemented by house specialties that range from the devastating "Keith Richards," made from four shots of espresso and Mexican chocolate, to the sublime "bowl of soul," which is a balance of coffee and espresso with a tantalizing sprinkle of chocolate and cinnamon served in a big ceramic bowl.

Java offers a repertoire of hot breakfasts, including bulgur wheat with apples and raisins, non-instant oatmeal, and eggs scrambled then steamed at the nozzle of the espresso machine, but it's the baked goods that have won Idahoans' hearts: handsome scones, sweet breads, and sour-cream muffins, plus a trademarked thing known as a "lumpy muffin"—big chunks of tart apple with walnuts and raisins all suspended in sweet cinnamon cake. Considerably more top than base, this muffin breaks easily into sections that are not quite dunkable (they'd fall apart), but are coffee's consummate companion.

Westside Drive-In

1939 W. State St.   208-342-2957
Boise, ID   LD | $

A drive-in owned by "Chef Lou" Aaron, who has a regular cooking segment on Boise television and is creator of a dessert called the Idaho Ice
Cream Potato, Westside is a place people come to eat (off their dash-
boards or on the patio's picnic tables) and to take home such Chef Lou
specialties as prime rib, pastas, and salads. The drive-in fare includes
crisp-fried shrimp and fish 'n' chips and a roster of extraordinary made-
to-order hamburgers that are thick and crusty and juicy inside, nothing
like franchised fast-food junkburgers. There are doubles, deluxes, Cajun
burgers, guacamole burgers, and Maui burgers. We like a good ol'
cheeseburger, preferably with lettuce and tomato. It comes wrapped in
wax paper for easy eating.

In honor of his home state, Chef Lou offers "the biggest bakers in the
valley," which are one-pound potatoes available simply saturated with
butter or loaded with chili, cheese, and onions. To drink, there are fine
milkshakes, including huckleberry and black raspberry.

Wolf Lodge Inn

12025 E. Frontage Rd.
Exit 22 off I-90   208-664-6665
Coeur d'Alene, ID   D | $$

Here are meat-and-potatoes meals of legendary scale. A vast red barnboard roadhouse just yards from the highway, this exuberant Wild West
domain features oilcloth-clad tables and walls festooned with trophy animal heads, bleached bovine skulls, antique tools, old beer posters, and
yellowing newspaper clippings of local-interest stories. It is a sprawling
place with miscellaneous booths and dining nooks in several rooms; at
the back of the rearmost dining area is a stone barbecue pit where tama-
rack and cherrywood burn a few feet below the grate. On this grate sizzle slabs of beef ranging from sixteen-ounce sirloins and filets mignon to
porterhouses well over two pounds. (Seafood is also available, cooked
over the wood.)

Cowboy-cuisine aficionados start supper with a plate of "swinging
steak"—sliced and crisp-fried bull testicles, served with cocktail sauce
and lemon wedges. We relished a bowl of truly homey vegetable beef

soup that was thick as stew with hunks of carrot, potato, beef, green pepper, and onion. All dinners come with saucy "buckaroo" beans, a twist of krebel (fried bread), and baked or fried potatoes, the latter excellent steak fries, each of which is one-eighth of a long Idaho baker that has been sliced end-to-end and fried so that it develops a light, crisp skin and creamy insides. We split a forty-two-ounce "Rancher"—exquisite beef, not too crusty, but loaded with juice, well-seasoned with salt and pepper, and redolent of the burning wood over which it was cooked.

As we exited into the brisk autumn air, we noticed that whenever the Inn's front door swings open, a cowbell clangs.

Candel's Byway Café

36619 US Hwy. 87   406-566-BYWA

Stanford, MT   BLD | $

We arrived at Candel's Byway Café mid-morning, just as the pies had come out of the oven. They are homely pies and each piece fell apart on its way from tin to plate, but the sour cream raisin pie turned out to be one of the best anywhere, with a wicked tangy-sweet character. The crust underneath the warm peach pie is the melt-in-mouth kind, so good we found ourselves hunting stray little slivers on emptied plates, gathering them up by pressing down with our forks' tines.

"Why are these pies so good?" we called out from our counter seats, ecstatic about finding them. Sheila Candelaria, who runs the place with her husband, Mike, credited them to her mother, from whom she learned to bake growing up on a ranch seventeen miles south of town. But it turned out that pies aren't the only reason to inscribe this place on the honor roll.

"We cut the steaks, we make our seasoning mixes, even our chicken fingers are from scratch," Sheila told us, singing especially high praises of the chunky, garlic-studded salsa that accompanies the Mexican food Mike makes. At this point, post-pie lunch seemed essential.

Mike's beef-and-bean burrito is smothered with orange-hued chili Colorado that tastes like nothing more than pure peppers and spice. We could hear our chicken-fried steak getting pounded tender through the pass-through window to the kitchen, and rather than coming sheathed in the typical thick batter coat and smothered under gluey gravy, this one has a thin, brittle crust. It sits atop a puddle of refined white gravy with a pepper punch.

Sitting at a table where the view out the front window is the fronts of pickup trucks pulled up in the lot and Highway 87/200 beyond them, a few everyday customers told us just how much they appreciate this place. Opened long ago as the Byway Café, it was closed for six years, reopened for one year as Bubba's, then closed again until the Candelarias bought it, cleaned it up, and reopened it in 2004 as a family enterprise, with all four of their kids on duty. Everyone in town comes here to eat and to meet, and the ones we met feel comfortable lingering at a table over coffee and conversation. As we paid our bill at the cash register we noticed a book of blank, nonpersonalized checks from the Basin State Bank: for customers who don't have cash.

Cole Drug

136 McLeod St.   406-932-5316
Big Timber, MT

Cruising through the lovely little town of Big Timber, we could not resist stopping at the good old lunch counter in Cole Drug store. The menu remains the same as it was ten years ago when we first faced the challenge of a Big Timber sundae (nine scoops of ice cream and all the toppings in the house). This time we ate more modestly and enjoyed a perfectly made black-and-white soda and a huckleberry sundae. Huckleberries are big in the Plains states, and their bright, sweet, fruity flavor makes for an ideal ice cream topping. We were also impressed with the good crunch of the nuts on top.

It was a quiet, soul-satisfying pleasure to sit at the boomerang-pattern Formica counter and chat with the soda-fountain mixologists and a few other customers who walked in for sodas and sundaes. This is a nice place in a nice town in a very nice part of the world.

Eddie's Supper Club

3725 2nd Ave. N　　　　　　　　　406-453-1616

Great Falls, MT　　　　　　　　　LD | $$

Eddie's is supper-club heaven, loved by generations of Montanans and visitors (it opened in 1944) as a comfortable place to go for cocktails and campfire steaks. There are two halves to it: a coffee shop, which is lighter-feeling, more casual, and with a varied menu that includes sandwiches, and the more serious restaurant, which is atmospheric and has a big-deal menu of beef and seafood.

We like sitting in the supper club if only for its décor: large, handsome pictures of horses, all kinds of them: trotters in action, a bucking horse tossing a cowboy, western horses at work tending cattle. The picture at the back of the room, which has a horse's head in the foreground and a herd of cows in back, is especially beguiling. "We call him Mr. Ed," our waitress said. "His eyes follow you all around the room."

Booths are supremely comfortable, lights are low, and the staff are able pros. Steaks are grand. "Tastes just like that old Marlboro Cowboy cooked it over the campfire," advises the menu. Our waitress told us that the secret of the steaks is not the fire over which they are cooked, but the house's special wine marinade. This seeps into the meat and gives it a special tang, also coating the surface so the exterior of the steak develops a crunchy caramelized crust as it cooks. The T-bone we ate was spectacularly good. And an off-the-menu hamburger, which has the marinade folded into the meat, was wildly flavorful.

The Granary

1500 Poly Dr.　　　　　　　　　406-259-3488

Billings, MT　　　　　　　　　　LD | $$$

The Granary is a beautiful old building that was part of Billings Polytechnic Institute before World War II, but lay empty from the mid-1940s into the 1970s. It was then made into a fancy restaurant, and again in 2004 it was bought, remodeled, and reconceived to be what it is today: the finest place in Billings to dine. Suave service, comfortable accommodations, a serious wine list, and a contemporary menu are its hallmarks.

The interior décor is chic log-cabin West and meals are urbane and sophisticated but with a western twist. That twist is primarily in the variety and quality of beef on the menu. It is Misty Isle Farms aged Northwest Black Angus, cooked at 1,700 degrees in the broiler. We had a sirloin, which was one of the best in a land of really good steaks. You can also get a rib eye, tenderloin, prime rib, or Kobe New York strip (for $49). Non-beef entrees include the likes of Thai orange salmon, maple leaf duck breast, and a pineapple green chili bone-in pork chop. We started our meal with an excellent Caesar salad.

The dessert menu is strange for its dearth of chocolate, but fancy-pants sweet tooths will have no problem choosing from among such luxuries as a caramelized blueberry napoleon, a banana tower on a mousse-filled caramel crisp, passion fruit mousse, and a crème brûlée trio (lemon, strawberry, and vanilla bean).

The cocktail list is tempting indeed. Jane loved her pomegranate mojito; there are different margaritas and three champagne cocktails: rosé royal, French (with gin), and a Kir Imperial.

Kozy Korner Cafe and Bar

1 S. Broadway	406-429-2621
Winnett, MT	BL | $

A tipster told us that we needed to go to Winnett, Montana, for big pancakes. His note said he couldn't remember the exact name of the restaurant that served them, but he assured us we would have no problem finding it. When hunting an eatery in such situations, the thing to do is look for the place where the cars and pickup trucks are gathered, but at 6:45 A.M., there was not a single vehicle parked anywhere at the crossroads that is town.

A guy on a bicycle loaded with a rack trunk and side panniers pulled up to a faded building that looked like it was a gas station long ago and, more recently, a place labeled Kozy Korner Cafe and Bar. "Pancakes?" we asked as he removed his helmet and secured the bicycle next to a phone booth outside the front door.

"Pancakes!" he answered, explaining to us that he was on a westward trip from St. Louis and was really looking forward to carbo-loading a Petroleum County tall stack to start the day's ride.

A neon "open" sign in the window lit up exactly at 7:00 A.M. and Buck Wood unlocked the Kozy Korner door, wordlessly pointing us down a short hall into the dining room. His wife, Ellen, waved a nonchalant hello from the open kitchen, where she was mixing batter in a metal bowl. As we found ourselves a table, Buck poured coffee.

After a while, Buck came from the kitchen with two pancake stacks that looked like layer cakes. Kozy Korner pancakes are a half-inch thick but not heavy, their substantial insides girded by a fragile skin. They have a buttermilk tang that demands the complement of syrup, of which they can seemingly absorb endless amounts.

The person who had told us about the awesome pancakes also mentioned that the same restaurant was known for "damn good pies." As we paid for breakfast ($4 for three pancakes), we watched Ellen at the kitchen counter cutting shortening into flour, adding salt and a dash of vinegar and cold water to make the dough for crust for that day's berry pies. We told her we were on our way to Great Falls, but if we happened to drive back through Winnett tomorrow, would she save us a couple of pieces of pie? Of course she would. We got waylaid and didn't get back that trip, but sure look forward to a return visit.

M&M Bar and Café

9 N. Main St.   406-723-7612
Butte, MT   BLD | $

It was a sad day when the M&M closed in 2003, but a great one when it reopened two years later. The place Jack Kerouac once described as "the end of my quest for an ideal bar" is a radiant vision of the West—chrome, with a dazzling neon sign looming over the street. The interior is a fluorescent-lit, high-ceiling cavern, weathered by decades of use. Here indeed is the consummate drinking person's bar, its stools occupied by a clientele of regulars and irregulars including part-time cowboys, old-time miners, frocked and unfrocked priests, ladies and women who used to be ladies, winners and losers; their faces are a stunning group portrait of a town long ago known as the Richest Hill on Earth.

At the lunch counter, customers eat husky slabs of liver and onions, hot roast beef sandwiches with mashed potatoes, swollen spaghetti noodles topped with strong red sauce and accompanied by a roasted quarter chicken, and Whatzit burgers (with cheese, bacon, lettuce, and tomato) accompanied by lanky French fries. Thursday is pasty day, when steaming behemoth baked dough crescents filled with beef, potatoes, and onions are served under a puddle of brown gravy with a cup of vegetable soup and a dish of thick, cream-style coleslaw. Service is lightning-fast and diner-friendly and prices are rock-bottom.

Matt's Place

Montana St. and Rowe Rd.   406-782-8049

Butte, MT   LD | $

Opened in 1930, Matt's Place is Montana's oldest drive-in restaurant, featuring beautiful old murals of the Rocky Mountains on the wall, a short curved counter, and an ancient, bright red, waist-high Coke machine—the kind in which the green glass bottles tinkle when you pry open the top to fetch one. The soda fountain behind the counter is fully equipped: six wands for blending milkshakes, dispensers for syrup, and three tall seltzer spouts. The menu features a root beer float, ice cream sodas, malted milks, and nut sundaes, plus "hot Silex coffee." To eat, there is the Montana classic, a pork chop sandwich, and all sorts of hamburgers, including a Wimpy special (two patties on one bun), a hamburger with an egg on top, and a nutburger with ground peanuts mixed into the meat. On the side of any sandwich, you want Matt's fine onion rings.

Pekin Noodle Parlor

117 S. Main St.   406-782-2217

Butte, MT   D | $

Pekin Noodle Parlor is a relic of Butte's boom days as a mining town, when the small street out back was known as China Alley. An ancient sign on the wall says "Famous Since 1916." Climb a small dark staircase to the second floor and you will be escorted to your own curtained dining cubicle. The setting suggests exotic intrigue, like an old Montana version of the Shanghai Express. When the food comes from the kitchen, it is announced by the rumble of the waitress's rolling trolley along the wood-plank floor; the curtain whisks aside, and behold! Here is a vista of foreign food the likes of which most devotees of Asian cookery forgot about fifty years ago.

Chop suey and chow mein are mild, thick, and harmless; fried shrimp are girdled by a pad of breading and served on leaves of lettuce with French fried potatoes as a garnish; sweet and sour ribs drip pineapple-flavored syrup, and the house specialty—noodles—come in a shimmering clear broth with scallions chopped on top. Get the noodles plain or accompanied by strips of pork, beef, or chicken served on the side in a little bowl with half a hard-boiled egg.

The after-dinner drink-menu-that-time-forgot includes separators, stingers, White Russians, and pink squirrels. The thing to drink before a meal is a ditch—Montanese for whiskey and water.

Pork Chop John's

8 Mercury St.　　　　　　　406-782-0812
Butte, MT　　　　　　　　L | $

Pork chop sandwiches are now sold in many Montana restaurants. The place they were invented, and the cognoscenti's choice, is a hole-in-the-wall on Mercury Street in Butte known as Pork Chop John's. Although minuscule, John's is easy to spot by its sign hanging out over the street: a portrait of three smiling pork chops named Wholesome, Healthful, and Delicious.

The sandwiches are patties of ground pork, breaded and fried to a crisp and served "loaded," which means topped with pickle chips, mustard, and onions. (Mayo, cheese, and ketchup are also available, but must be specified.) They are a savory splurge, crunch-crusted and luscious inside. Enjoy them at John's small counter or at one of three al fresco tables on the sidewalk, from which you have a view of the cramped back street that was the heart of Butte's once-thriving (but now extinct) Chinatown.

Red Lodge Café

16-18 S. Broadway　　　　　406-446-1619
Red Lodge, MT　　　　　　　BLD | $

The Red Lodge Café is a good reflection of the character of Red Lodge, Montana: eager to please with all modern facilities, yet ingenuous and charming like a mid-twentieth-century tourist stop. The town (once, the home of mountain man Jeremiah Johnson) has been discovered by skiers and tourists heading down through Montana on the scenic route to Yellowstone Park, but it has not been overrun. Here is the real West, and this colorful café serves food to match.

For breakfast, you'll want to eat jumbo omelets or blueberry buckwheat pancakes, and sip coffee long enough to eavesdrop on the conversations of locals and passers-through. The lunch menu features such stalwart items as country-fried steak and potatoes and buffalo burgers, as well as some fine deluxe hamburgers. For dessert, everybody has pie: apple or berry pie or, best of all, banana cream pie, which is a tender pillow of pale yellow custard that eats better with a spoon than a fork.

The restaurant itself has a western theme, but there is something for everyone from morning to night: keno, weekend karaoke, and the strangest-shaped pool table we've ever seen. Lighting fixtures above the dining room are made of wagon wheels, the ceiling is stamped tin, and the walls are bedecked with painted wooden totem poles and spectacular murals of scenery along the 11,000-foot Beartooth Highway that leads from here to Yellowstone. The two-lane highway is closed by snow in the winter, but once it's open, it is a spectacular trip. Charles Kuralt once called it "America's most beautiful road."

Rex Restaurant

2401 Montana Ave.   406-245-7477
Billings, MT   LD | $$

Montana Avenue in Billings has become something of a restaurant row with a handful of trendy places drawing people back downtown for dinner. One of the old reliables in the area is the Rex, a vintage hotel dining room that has been cleaned up but not drastically modernized to be one of the city's most respected upscale eating establishments. Unless you sit on the breezy patio, accommodations are dark and clubby, all varnished wood, brass, raw brick, and cut glass under an old stamped tin ceiling.

Beef is king, and the prime rib we had was one of the best around: thick, juice-laden, and full-flavored. For those not intent on ingesting maximum red-meat protein, the menu includes pizzas made to order, sandwiches and big salads, shrimp, crab, and lobster. Lunch can be as inexpensive as a $7.95 burger or Vietnamese noodle salad; big beef dinners range to near $30.

We were introduced to the Rex many years ago by a local saddle maker whose doctor had told him he needed to eat less beef, so he ordered cream-sauced pasta, which looked to us like it was richer than a rib eye steak!

Sarah's

310 N. 29th St.   406-256-5234
Billings, MT 59101   BLD | $

We hit Billings eager to have lunch at El Burrito, our favorite Mexican blue-plate lunchroom in Montana . . . and El Burrito was gone! We panicked for a moment until it dawned on us that the restaurant now occupying the same location, Sarah's, looked a whole lot like the old establishment that used to call itself "The Working Person's Eating Place." In fact it is one and the same, renamed Sarah's to honor one of the three sisters who founded it back in the 1980s, but passed away six years ago. It is still in the family, though, Sarah's two sisters running it efficiently and cordially, even if meal service is a little strange.

Here's the way it works. Upon entering, go to the back of the room to an order window. At the right of the window is a large posted menu. Choose your burritos, tacos, or enchiladas and tell the nice lady who steps out of the kitchen what you want. Then go to the cash register and pay for it. Now move over to the condiment bar and help yourself to Styrofoam cups full of hot sauce or mild sauce, onions, or jalapeños to carry to a table, where a basket of chips is set out along with lots of napkins. When you are halfway through the chips, the meal arrives.

We especially love the taquitos, which would be called flautas in much of the Southwest: tightly wrapped, crisp-fried tortilla tubes containing moist shredded beef. They are served with a cup of garlicky guacamole.

The order-taker grinned broadly when we said we wanted a red smothered beef burrito, telling us it was the most popular dish in the house. It is a monumental meal, the burrito loaded with big hunks of beef. Our one complaint is that the plastic forks provided are only barely up to severing the tortilla wrap and beef inside.

Sarah's is a hangout for locals, young and old. It is open for three meals a day, and at high noon, it is mobbed. As the lunch-hour crowd cleared out, one table in the center of the room was occupied by a group of teenagers carrying skateboards. Toward the front of the room was a family having a quiet discussion with each other in a language that sounded like Spanish, but wasn't. And we were busy plowing through some fine Mexican meals, grateful that nothing here has changed except the name.

Stella's Kitchen and Bakery

2525 1st Ave. N

Billings, MT

406-248-3060

BL | $

Stella's cinnamon rolls are legendary, each one bigger than a softball and enough breakfast for two or more hungry people. The rolls are made fresh each day, but when you order one, it is microwaved so a big glob of butter set atop it is melting when the roll arrives at the table. Heating also tends to give the caramel glaze on top a good, chewy texture that makes it a fork-and-knife pastry. Even bigger than the cinnamon roll is Stella's giant white caramel roll—fourteen ounces of sweet dough served with a small tub of whipped butter.

Everything is large at Stella's, especially pancakes, which are known as monster cakes. "You've got to see 'em to believe 'em," the menu boasts. Each one is a good twelve inches, edge to edge; and yet they have a nice light texture that makes it easy to eat a couple, or maybe even three. You have your choice of buttermilk or wheat batter; and if you can polish off four of them in a single sitting, you get a free cinnamon roll! We are especially fond of the very small print underneath the pancake listing on the menu: "Diet Smuckers jelly & syrups available upon request." So these would qualify as diet food?

There are normal-size breakfasts at Stella's: omelets, hot cereals (oatmeal, seven-grain, and Stella's homemade grits), and egg sandwiches, and the lunch menu includes such regular-size items as club and sub sandwiches, chili by the bowl, and a French dip as well as hamburgers that range up to the half-pound Ziggyburger, served on an outsized bun to match.

For dessert? Bread pudding made with Stella's homemade breads, please.

Truck Stop Café

511 E. Main   406-547-3825

White Sulphur Springs, MT   BL | $

We would not go out of our way to eat at the Truck Stop Café, but it is a convenient waystation if ever you find yourself halfway between Glacier and Yellowstone along Highway 89 and hunger strikes. It's a funky sort of operation with wood-paneled walls, a counter, upholstered booths, and some really odd wood-slat booths located near the front windows. Other clientele when we stopped in one morning included a family with a large motor home outside and a trio of bikers who arrived on thundering Hogs.

The waitress told us that the biscuits and pie were not made here, so we went for the sweet roll, which is, and for the pancakes. The latter were quite nice, served with both corn and boysenberry syrup. The sweet roll was immense: a huge, doughy mountain gooped with icing, probably seven thousand calories' worth of breakfast.

Willow Creek Café and Saloon

21 Main St.

Willow Creek, MT

406-285-3698

LD (reservations advised) | $$

Reservations advised? In Willow Creek, population 209?

Yes, indeed. Here is a way-way out of the way restaurant that attracts customers from Three Forks, Manhattan, and even Bozeman, some fifty miles away. They come for pillowy beef steaks and chicken-fried steaks, hamburgers and homemade soups, pies and cakes made that day, even such upscale suppers as pork marsala and saltimbocca. There's always prime rib on weekend nights, but the one never-to-miss meal is barbecued ribs, anointed with a brilliant honey mustard glaze that teases maximum flavor from the pork. A chalkboard lists the day's specials and featured wines, which oenophile friends tell us are a good deal.

The place itself is a hoot: a sunflower-yellow house that started life in 1912 as the Babcock Saloon and has been a pool hall, barber shop, and butcher shop. Dining facilities are small indeed, with room for only a few dozen customers at a time. The old-fashioned print wallpaper and antique wood fixtures make it feel like a trip back in time. If you're heading for Willow Creek, don't worry about finding it. It is the only business in town.

Al's Café

205 Main St.
Melbeta, NE

308-783-1133
L Mon-Fri | $

We recommend you go to Al's very soon. If proprietor Ruth Neal, age ninety-two, decides to retire, the place will close. Because she has been here since 1952, and maybe because the people of Scotts Bluff County love it so much, the restaurant gets a pass on certain health department rules that might otherwise close it. Oh, it's neat as a pin, and clean. However the semi-open kitchen with its household stove and refrigerator and vintage counters and adjoining bedroom are vestiges of simpler and less regimented times.

Open only for lunch Monday through Friday and with a daily customer count of about twenty, Al's is as small-town an eatery as we ever have visited. It is located in a former gas station and while no breakfast is served, it is a gathering place each morning for a good cadre of Melbeta's men. They come to gab with one another and to make sure Ruth is doing okay. Each day she makes a couple of specials: fried chicken and baked ham the Thursday we stopped in—as well as two kinds of pie—we had apple and pecan. The chicken was deliciously homey. It was served, like the ham, with terrific mashed potatoes and gravy, creamed corn, and a small green salad topped with Ruth's sweet dressing.

We complimented Ruth on her pie crust, which has a brittle, sugary surface, and asked her secret. She advised that it was using half white Crisco, half yellow Crisco, the latter giving it a buttery savor. "People tell me to use a mixer when I make the crust, but I do it with my hands," she said. "How can you feel the dough with a mixer?"

As we forked up the last crumbs of pie from our plates a regular customer down the counter made us promise to return on a Monday, when Ruth makes banana cream pie that he described as "the best on earth." If ever there was a restaurant we have yearned to return to, Al's is it.

Bohemian Café

1406 S. 13th St.
Omaha, NE

402-342-9838
LD | $$

The Bohemian Café is an immensely cheerful place, a vast, multiroom eating hall decorated with colorful old-country woodwork and pictures of men and women in traditional peasant attire; tables are patrolled by veteran professional waitresses in bright red dirndl skirts. "*Vitáme Vás*," meaning "we welcome you," is the house motto of this 1924-vintage Omaha landmark. Whether you are an old-timer who came with your parents decades ago or a visiting fireman who wants a fun-time meal with polka music setting the beat in the dining room, you will feel welcome.

The traditional way to begin a meal is with a cup of liver dumpling soup; we also love the plain-dumpling, chicken-stock soup that is often available as an alternative. Every meal begins with a basket of chewy sour rye bread. The big menu includes American-style steaks and seafood, a quartet of specials every day, and traditional Czech specialties. Foremost among the kitchen's accomplishments is roast duck—half a bird with crisp skin and flavorful meat that pulls off the bone with ease. We are particularly fond of the sauerbraten, which is a stack of pot-roast-tender hunks of beef that are a joy to pull apart with the tines of a fork. We also like the Czech goulash, a vivid red, smoky pork stew. There is a large choice of side dishes, but the two for which the Bohemian Café is best known are dumplings and kraut. The former is a pair of saucer-size slices of doughy matter covered with whatever gravy your main course demands; the latter is a fetching sweet and sour mix, thick as pudding, dotted with caraway seeds. Whatever entree you choose, it will come flanked by dumplings and kraut—an awesome presentation that is a challenge to all but the mightiest appetite.

Paper place mats remind diners that this restaurant is home of the Bohemian Girl Jim Beam commemorative bourbon bottle (there is a huge collection of Jim Beam commemoratives in the entryway), and the mats also list the lyrics to the house song, which has been used in radio advertisements:

> Dumplings and kraut today
> At Bohemian Café
> Draft beer that's sparkling, plenty of parking
> See you at lunch, Okay?

Crystal Café

4601 Dakota Ave.   402-494-5471
South Sioux City, NE   Always open | $

At 8:30 in the morning at the Crystal Café, the sour cream raisin pie comes out from the kitchen too hot to slice. At the counter and in the booths, men and women who are starting the day (and some finishing a long night) converse about issues that include jackknives, deadheading, log books, and speed traps. They are professional truckers; the Crystal Café is where they come not only to eat, but for fuel and over-the-road supplies. It is an open-all-night truck stop just west of the Missouri River.

Each place is set with a clean overturned coffee cup and a water glass. The waitress flips your cup right-side up and pours coffee and refills throughout breakfast; pour your own water from a pitcher on each table. The cuisine is haute highway: big food, served in abundance. Plate-wide buttermilk pancakes, chicken-fried steak with a patty of oily hash browns, sausage gravy on big, crumbly biscuits are some of the morning specials. The Texaco Deluxe is an omelet with ham, bacon, or sausage plus cheese, tomato, onions, and green peppers. The morning item we especially like is the caramel sweet roll, which is thick and goopy.

The lunch menu features breaded pork tenderloin, bowls of chili, and hamburgers that include one-third-pounders and a ten-ounce king-of-the-road Texaco Burger. We never did get to try the sour cream raisin pie, but the chocolate pie was grand. It was exciting to watch the waitress cut a piece, using a moistened warm knife to slide down through a full eight inches of whipped topping, then balance a taller-than-wide slice on a plate.

This is a great spot to hobnob with over-the-road pros. An unusual souvenir from our visit is a booklet we picked up in the adjoining truckers' store entitled *Beef Spotter: A Guide to Midwest Feed Lots.* And we love the truck-stop humor evidenced at the penny bowl by the cash register. Above it, a handwritten sign reads, "Need a penny . . . take a penny. Need 2 pennies . . . get a job!"

Gering Bakery

1446 10th St.	308-436-5500
Gering, NE	BL | $

A small sign in the window of the Gering Bakery advertises cabbage burgers. Considering that we were in Nebraska, home of the Runza and the bierock—bread pockets stuffed with ground beef, cabbage, and spice—the sign caused us to come to a sudden halt and investigate. Runzas and bierocks are nineteenth-century immigrant fare, but in the mid-1950s, the name Runza was trademarked and is now the lead item at the eponymous restaurant chain. Runza's runzas are okay, but the monotony of the identical restaurants makes us depressed.

Gering Bakery, on the other hand, is the real deal. Sure enough, the advertised cabbage burger is a non-corporate Runza, and a delicious one at that. Available in bulk to take home or one at a time and heated up by the kind lady behind the counter, they are fully enclosed pillows of tender bread inside of which is a spill of juicy beef and peppery bits of cabbage and onion. Delicious comfort food.

Our hearts won over by the cabbage burger, we had to sample some of the good-looking sweet pastries on the bakery shelves. We liked the crisp-edged old-fashioned cake donuts and fell instantly in love with something called a peanut butter pretzel. That's a twisted piece of pastry dough generously frosted with sweet peanut butter icing.

Most business is take-out, but Gering Bakery offers a few window tables as well as help-yourself coffee and a cooler full of soda for those who want to dine here.

Joe Tess' Place

5424 S. 24th St. 402-731-7278
Omaha, NE LD | $

Roadfood warriors Bruce Bilmes and Sue Boyle discovered Joe Tess' Place, which bills itself as "Home of the Famous Fish Sandwich." It is a restaurant, tavern, and fresh seafood market on the south side of Omaha that serves a fish little-known on dining tables outside the region: carp. Like the herring that swim upriver in North Carolina, carp are fish-flavored fish that get deep-fried long enough that their fine bones become part of the soft, juicy flesh underneath the crunchy batter crust. The fried pieces of carp are available on rye in the famous sandwich or doubled up in the double fish sandwich. (The connoisseur's condiment is hot pepper sauce.) Or you can have a dinner-size portion bedded on rye on a plate with coleslaw and discs of fried potato, the latter known here as jacket fries. Catfish is another specialty. Like the carp, mudpuppies are trucked in live from Minnesota and you can see them swim in the tanks of the live fish market. For those with a less adventurous palate, the Joe Tess menu offers chicken (white or dark), grilled salmon, and fried shrimp.

There is a full bar's worth of beverages to drink, plus the western working man's version of a bloody Mary, known as red beer: beer and tomato juice. Bruce and Sue noted "any restaurant that serves upside-down cake gets bonus points from us." Beside pineapple upside-down cake larded with pecans, the dessert menu includes a swell cream cheese bundt cake.

Ambience is all-fish, all the time and everywhere. The bar is shaped like a boat and walls are decked with taxidermized fish of every size and shape as well as pictures, posters, and nautical memorabilia celebrating underwater life.

Johnny's Cafe

4702 S. 27th St. 402-731-4774
Omaha, NE LD | $$

Johnny's has been Omaha's steak house since 1922. At the edge of the stockyards, it was once a café for cowboys and cow shippers. Now it is a grand-scale restaurant with well-upholstered chairs, broadloom carpets, and modernistic chandeliers. We love the baronial ambience, especially because it is balanced by service that is as folksy as in any small-town café, courtesy of waitresses unafraid to scold you if you don't finish your T-bone but then want dessert.

Beef is king in this dining room. Steaks, chops, ribs, liver, even, on occasion, tongue or oxtail are the things to order. You can splurge at dinner and eat the finest filets mignons or chateaubriands for miles around, and pay accordingly, or at lunch, for well under ten dollars, you can have yourself a superb downsized slab of prime rib.

Dessert is corny and ingratiating, including crème de menthe sundaes and clear blocks of Chuckles-colored Jell-O. Turtle pie is a weighty affair—a frozen block of the same ingredients used in candy turtles, with the addition of ice cream: chocolate, nuts, and caramel. Johnny's serves it still fairly well frozen, so you will have all sorts of merry fun trying to fork off a piece. Once defrosted, it is gooey and sweet as candy, but even richer.

Rosita's

1205 E. Overland	308-632-2429
Scottsbluff, NE	LD | $

In this friendly sit-down café with festive south-of-the-border décor, every dish is made to order, even the corn chips—particularly the corn chips. Amazing chips they are, nearly as three-dimensional as a sopaipilla, fried so they puff up and become airy triangles with fragile skin. An order arrives almost too hot to handle; they come plain or as the foundation for the house specialty called panchos—a circle of chips topped with frijoles, melted cheese, guacamole, and jalapeños. Panchos are like nachos, but the chips' refined texture and their perfect poise between breakable and bendable give panchos character far more satisfying than any bar grub.

The same quick-fry technique makes Rosita's taco shells an ideal crispy-chewy wrap for beef or chicken with plenty of garnishes. Flat tostadas are made the same way, and even taco salad includes the fine, fluffy chips.

Proprietor Rosemary Florez-Lerma credits her mother-in-law with the recipes that make Rosita's food stand out in an area with an abundance of Mexican restaurants (legacy of field workers who came to pick beets). The cinnabar-red, garlic-charged salsa that starts every meal and chunky pico de gallo that dresses up any dish with a stunning spicy punch are especially memorable. We are also fond of Rosita's garlicky menudo, thick with puffs of posole and strips of tripe, sparkling with fresh-squeezed lemon juice. Menudo is known as a great hangover cure, but even if your head isn't aching, we guarantee it will make you feel better.

(Rosita's has a second location in Scottsbluff, at 710 W. 27th St.)

South Dakota

Bob's

1312 W. 12th St.
Sioux Falls, SD

605-336-7260
BLD | $

Fans of diner food will think they've entered heaven the moment they walk into this place and sniff bacon sizzling and burgers grilling. A tiny diner with a curvy counter and a mere dozen seats, all with a view of the grill, Bob's specializes in plentiful hash-house breakfasts, burger baskets, broasted chicken, fried shrimp, and slabs of ribs.

If your life is dull and you need a challenge, may we suggest the Megabob? On a blackboard behind the counter, the names of those who have tried and succeeded are written in chalk . . . just waiting to be erased by a newer, faster gun in town. What is the Megabob Challenge, you ask? Eat a three-quarter-pound hamburger, three-quarters of a pound of French fries, and a cookie, plus drink a large bottle of soda pop faster than anyone else and you get it free. How good are the hamburgers? Proprietor Bob Weiland sent us a copy of his customer comment book, which included these reviews: "Best burger between Seattle and Chicago" . . . "Oh, boy, that was delicious!!!" . . . "It's the bomb!" . . . "The best reason to be in S. Dakota."

Although it is a minuscule space, Bob's specializes in cooking vast amounts of food for big parties, and will deliver in the Sioux Falls area. The menu includes such mega-listings as a ninety-piece order of broasted chicken, a whole broasted turkey, and slabs of ribs by the dozen.

Edgar's

At Pioneer Drug
Business Route 29   605-356-3336
Elk Point, SD 57025   L | S

Soda jerking is a fine art at Edgar's. Have a seat on one of the steel-banded counter stools and watch a soda being made. This is no haphazard process. First, syrup and a little ice cream are smooshed together at the bottom of the deep vase-shaped glass to form a kind of sweet-shop roux; next, soda is squirted in and mixed vigorously; penultimately, a globe of ice cream is gingerly floated on top; finally, a crown of whipped cream is applied and, to that, a single cherry. It's a beautiful sight, and while much of the soda will drip and spill down the sides of the glass as soon as it is touched by a spoon, one cannot help but admire the confectionery perfectionism.

The same high standards apply to tulip sundaes, malts, and shakes, and a long roster of more elaborate daring delights that range from the relatively familiar turtle sundae (vanilla ice cream with hot caramel, chocolate syrup, and pecans) to the Rocket, a vertical banana split that the menu promises "will send you for a blast!"

With its pink-and-white tin ceiling, quartet of creaky wood booths, and steel rod chairs and scattering of tables, Edgar's is an absolutely charming little place inside the Pioneer Drug store on the main street of Elk Point. Its nucleus is a soda fountain that was first installed in Schmiedt Drug in Centerville in 1906. In the 1960s, the old marble fountain was removed and put into storage. It was only recently discovered by Edgar Schmiedt's granddaughter, Barb Wurtz. Barb brought it to Elk Point where it is once again part of a pharmacy (run by Barb's pharmacist husband, Kevin) and general store.

The back of Edgar's menu is a marvelous page from soda-fountain history that features practical how-to articles taken from the 1906 *Standard Manual of Soda and Other Beverages*. Among the suggestions are that a soda fountain attendant "should never display soiled towels or dirty sponges," "should never stand watching the patrons drinking," and "should study each customer's desire and endeavor to remember the particular way in which he likes his drinks mixed and served." The year all this was written, the *Centerville Journal* declared Edgar's soda fountain one of the finest in the state. Over a century later, it is once again.

Hamburger Inn

111½ E. 10th St.   605-332-5412

Sioux Falls, SD   L | $

Mel "Nels" Nelson and his wife, Bev, are no longer at the helm of this charming Depression-era twelve-stool diner; and for several weeks early in 2006 it was closed altogether. But hail Jason Bensen and Kelly Torberson, who took over and have promised to keep the Sioux Falls hamburger landmark running for at least a few more decades. They have increased the size of the hand-formed hamburgers from sliderhood to patties well over a quarter pound, making the old tradition of getting triples or even quadruple burgers in one bun somewhat ridiculous, although doubles still are available. Still, we prefer a couple of single original cheeseburgers or, better yet, bacon cheeseburgers with a side of onion rings. To drink? A lovely chocolate milkshake made the old-fashioned way and served not too thick. A coterie of regulars are loyal to the egg burger, which includes a fried egg on top. Other optional dressings include bacon, onions, cheese, lettuce, tomato, and mayonnaise.

Nick's Hamburger Shop

427 Main Ave.   605-692-4324

Brookings, SD   LD | $

We get a lot of enthusiastic tips from Roadfooders, but few were as insistent as the one that came from April Carlson about Nick's. "This is the perfect destination for you two," she wrote. "Get in the car and go. You won't be disappointed. Promise. Why haven't you left yet?"

It took us a while, but we went, and we understand April's zeal. Nick's is a Roadfood landmark, actually on the National Register of Historic Places, famous for itty-bitty hamburgers since 1929. The price of a Nickburger has gone up from a nickel to $1.18 in the last three-quarters of a century, but it's still the same twenty-two-stool shack inviting customers to "buy 'em by the sack." We'd say that three to five Nickburgers make a nice meal. The ingestion record is twenty-two in a single sitting, set by a Mormon missionary who was passing through town a few years ago. Owner Dick Fergen says that anyone who can beat the record will eat free.

The burgers are sliders: small, hand-formed patties cooked on a grill with so much oil that they are virtually deep-fried. Onions are part of the formula, so the burger as well as Nick's itself is perfumed with the sweet smell of onions caramelizing. The only way to have one (or, preferably, several) is with relish. They're small and wieldy enough that plates are extraneous; Nickburgers are presented on wax paper.

Tea Steak House

215 S. Main St.   605-368-9667
Tea, SD   LD | $$

When we first ate at the Tea Steak House several years ago, it was in the middle of nowhere. Just about ten miles south of Sioux Falls, nowhere has become somewhere as houses go up in the countryside all around. Still, this combination restaurant and bar in the community of Tea has a rural character that adds an especially appealing flavor to supper.

Start with onion rings or deep-fried cheese balls, then move on to an iceberg lettuce salad that you dress yourself from a caddy that contains ranch, Thousand Island, and French dressing. A selection of bland white rolls and cellophane-wrapped crackers is the standard steak-house breadbasket in this region.

We love the pound-plus T-bone, a cushiony slab of meat that oozes juice at the first poke of a knife. It's a good thing to order hash brown potatoes on the side to soak up the beef's seepage; they are great potatoes in their own right (much better than the foil-wrapped baked potato or uninteresting French fries). We also ordered filet mignon, which came splayed open and wrapped in bacon, and it was amazing just how different these two cuts of beef were: each excellent, but while the T-bone had a vivid, almost gamey smack and tight-knit texture that rewarded serious chewing, the filet practically melted on the tongue.

The Tea Steak House serves more than steak. You can eat chicken or ham, halibut, perch, lobster tails, or a Saint and Sinner supper of one lobster tail and one small sirloin. Don't ask us how any of the other stuff tastes. When we're in Tea, we'll eat beef. And don't ask about dessert, either. This place doesn't bother making any. You need something sweet, you go next door to O'Toole's Bar and have a grasshopper or pink Cadillac.

Tripp Sports Bowl Café

210 S. Main St.   605-935-6281

Tripp, SD   L | $

Tripp is a small town in the middle of big country. A short jog off the highway takes you to Main Street, where the town bowling alley and town café are one. We love this place where the locals eat (few travelers pass through Tripp at all), and where décor includes not only the bowling alleys themselves, but tropies won by the likes of Doug Janssen (a 300 game!) and Dorothy Schnabel (267). The day we came across it, a blackboard in the dining area listed the day's specials as creamed chicken on toast, which was delicious—quintessential comfort food—but we were also intrigued by a menu item listed as the Dakota Burger.

The Dakota Burger turned out not to be a hamburger at all—at least if you define hamburger as a patty of ground beef—but rather, Tripp's version of that upper Midwest pleasure, hot beef. Junellia Meisenhoelder, chef and proprietor at the Sports Bowl Café, didn't tell us why the sandwich is known as a burger, but there is no point quibbling about labels; it is swell. Hot beef served with mashed potatoes and gravy is a frequent daily special at the Sports Bowl Café, and the Dakota Burger is a somewhat more wieldy variation on the theme: chunks of ultra-tender roast beef, warm enough to melt a slice of bright orange cheese placed atop them, piled into a grill-warmed bun. Simple and excellent!

Cafe Wyoming

106 E. Ramshorn St.   307-455-3828
Dubois, WY   LD | $$

"Very Wyoming" is how our California tipster described this log cabin adjoining a True Value hardware store parking lot overlooking Horse Creek. The note said that the chef made deluxe dinners every night for which reservations were advised. It sang of homemade soups and salad dressings, and a whole repertoire of house-smoked meats.

While the menu is broad, it's ribs that made a deep impression on us. They are beautiful racks of bones heavy with smoke-infused meat and spiced and sauced with brio. A smoked pork chop was equally delicious, and the steaks that others around us were eating looked great. Sandwiches are served on homemade bread, and there are a BLT and a catfish sandwich in particular that are numbers one and two on our list to eat next time we visit.

Club El Toro

132 S. Main

Hudson, WY

307-332-4627

D | $$

Sixteen different cuts of beef are listed on El Toro's menu, including a rib eye as big as its plate. The house specialty is prime rib, which is available in four sizes. The top-of-the-line Royal cut is a mesa of meat weighing well over two pounds. Heavy with juice and so tender that a butter knife glides through with ease, it has enough flavor to win over even those of us who generally prefer the more assertive character of steak. On the side comes a cup of dark juice for dipping. And of course you want potatoes: French fries or a foil-wrapped baker or, best of all, cowboy fries, which are what some know as jo-jo potatoes: spiced potato logs accompanied by ranch dressing as a dip.

Every dinner starts with a relish tray and a salad, then hot appetizers—individual plates with two spicy ravioli in tomato sauce and a small portion of *sarma* on each. *Sarma* is an unusual treat, a staple of the Serbian kitchen—and of Hudson's two great steak houses (Svilar's being the other one). It is a thick, boiled-tender leaf of pickled cabbage rolled around a tightly packed filling of ground pork and beef with onions.

Club El Toro is a spacious restaurant brimful of character. One large room is set up with a U-shaped banquet table and flags for meetings of the Marine Corps League. Adjacent to the bar is a room that is mostly dance floor, where Carl F. Baxter performs on keyboard weekend nights, occasionally joined by volunteer locals on sax or drums. Mr. Baxter's repertoire of 554 selections is mimeographed and bound in clear plastic so patrons can choose their favorites, ranging from "Misery and Gin" and "Heartaches by the Number" to "Coca Cola Cowboy."

Lisa's

200 Greybull Ave.

Greybull, WY

307-765-4765

BLD (Breakfast served only in the summer) | $

As you cruise down west of the Big Horn Mountains—or prepare to head east into them—the town of Greybull offers all sorts of attractions. These include a sprawling Museum of Flight and Aerial Fire Fighting with countless decommissioned airplanes on display, an awesome museum of taxidermy, Probst's Western Wear Shop, in business since the 1940s, and Lisa's restaurant.

"In Wyoming when we say hearty, we mean hearty!!" Lisa's menu crows. But it isn't so much the generous size of meals that makes this roadside café a worthwhile stop; it is the taste. We've only had breakfast, but wow, was it good: chunky corned beef hash made from full-flavored slices of spiced brisket, warm biscuits with luxurious sausage gravy, "puff scrambles," which are eggs stuffed into puff pastries and topped with hollandaise sauce, and a side order of crisp Indian fry bread. Other tempting breakfast items include Breakfast Charlotta, which is a tortilla stuffed with potato hash and eggs, pork chile and polenta, huevos rancheros, pancakes, and French toast made from homemade bread.

Lisa and Brad Dalin, the proprietors, call their place "a tribute to the original cowboy camp cook as well as the Native-American way of cooking on our Western Plains." In keeping with that theme, décor includes Navajo rugs, Mexican tiles, and walls of stucco and wood; a tree-shaded outdoor patio offers the opportunity to dine al fresco in crisp mountain air.

The Noon Break

927 12th St. 307-587-9720
Cody, WY BL | $

The Noon Break remains for us what it has been for years: the place to go first whenever we hit Cody. It is a sweet, friendly, funny town café just off the main drag where the made-to-order food is delicious and the prices are reasonable (the latter is not true of too many things in Cody).

One of these days we will veer away from the menu of Mexican specialties, but probably not too soon. The chile, burritos, tacos, and tamales are all exemplary. The chips that start each meal are hot and salty; the salsa that accompanies them is redolent of fresh garlic. Two varieties of chili are available, served by the cup or bowl with tortillas on the side for dipping and mopping: regular and Code Ten. Regular is mild. Code Ten is incendiary, a classic southwestern stew, meaning there are no beans or other frippery. It is pork and green chile peppers, a viscous meal for chili-lovers only. Other lunchtime items include posole (hominy soup), enchiladas made with blue corn tortillas, burritos, and soft-shell tacos. There is a soup of the day, a hamburger, and even a veggie burger.

Smothered tamales are a frequent lunch special. You get your choice of hot pork or mild chicken tamales, smothered with green chili in one of three degrees of hotness: mild, medium, or Code Ten. We chose one of each kind of tamale and medium-hot chili. A magnificent tamale plate!

Décor is a hoot: license plates from every state in the union, amusing gewgaws hanging from the ceiling, and newspapers and magazines scattered about to read while you dine. Open at seven in the morning, it's a great place to come for biscuits and gravy or a breakfast burrito.

Waldorf A'Story

In the Piney Creek General Store
19 North Piney Rd.   307-683-2400
Story, WY 82842   BLD | $

The jam-packed place known as the Piney Creek General Store in the tiny town of Story (between Sheridan and Buffalo) is a place to buy groceries, wine (fine or cheap), beer (domestic or imported), to rent DVDs, and to hobnob with locals. Built of pine logs and featuring some gorgeous outdoor accommodations in the form of benches and tables made of rough-hewn wood, it has the comforting feel of a base camp commissary, where you can stock up on any provisions you might need for hunting, fishing, camping, or otherwise enjoying the beauty of the Big Horn Mountains.

As you enter the retail commotion, look to the left and you see Waldorf A'Story, a small dining room with mismatched tables where locals come to greet the day with biscuits and gravy, fresh-baked coffee cake, or a superb breakfast sandwich of bacon, eggs, cheese, tomatoes, and onions on French bread crisped on the grill.

The lunch menu ranges from single- and double-decker sandwiches, soup, and chili to hot wings with blue cheese dressing and celery sticks. Daily specials include theme-meals of Mexican huevos rancheros for Sunday morning, Chinese egg rolls with fried rice, and Native-American "Indian tacos" made on crisp fry bread. Saturday the merry little eatery becomes a "Happy Moose Rib Shack" with a mix 'n' match menu of baby backs, smoked brisket, sausage, and chicken accompanied by potato salad, barbecued beans, and French pan toast.

Take-out meals are also available, and the menu lists the Waldorf's phone number as 683–2400–I–AIN'T–COOKIN'.

Wapiti Lodge and Steak House

3189 Yellowstone Hwy. 307-587-6659
Wapiti, WY D | $$

The drive out to Wapiti Lodge from Cody is a beautiful half-hour along the Shoshone River, past the Buffalo Bill Reservoir and Dam toward Yellowstone Park. The Lodge shares a building with the post office, which, other than a school, seems to be the only public building in the small settlement of Wapiti.

The Lodge is an old, rustic place with a log cabin feel and décor that includes a lot of hunting trophies and western memorabilia. Of course, beef is big on the menu, from a Rocky Mountain oyster hors d'oeuvre to a long list of various-size sirloins and filets mignons as well as prime rib from twelve to twenty ounces. The rib-eye steak we had was smoky-flavored and luxuriously fatty, as luscious as prime rib. Jane declared her lamb chops to be four-star. Blackened food, including chicken breast and red snapper, is a house specialty. Although we've tried neither, we can tell you that the blackened prime rib is delicious. Many people come to eat racks of baby back ribs, tender little riblets presented under a glaze of good barbecue sauce.

Dinner includes a wonderfully old-fashioned relish tray that comes with a ramekin of what tastes like California dip (made from Lipton's onion soup) as well as a curious salad that was surprisingly modern, i.e., contained no iceberg lettuce, but did contain radicchio and a few Northwest cherries.

Yellowstone Drug

127 Main St. 307-876-2539
Shoshoni, WY L | $

Yellowstone Drug is a wonderful attraction with something for everyone: cowboy clothing for sale, including hats, boots, and spurs; an inventory of tack including roping saddles and a few stunning horsehair bridles made by inmates at the state prison; bumper stickers that say "Christian cowboys have more fun"; and bookends and rifle racks that proprietor Ted Surrency makes from horseshoes and spurs. It has a patent medicine display and vintage (unlocked) security vaults (from when the building was the First National Bank of Shoshoni) available for impromptu walk-in visits.

The most important of Yellowstone Drug's assets is a large assortment of ice cream. The ice cream is available by the cup or cone, in sodas, floats, and sundaes, but nearly everyone comes for the milkshakes. Since it opened in 1909, a sign in Yellowstone Drug has boasted that this is home of "the best malts and shakes in the state." Made with a triple-wand shake maker behind the long counter, they are impressive—served with a spoon because their thickness defies a straw. Chocolate is the most popular flavor, followed by strawberry, vanilla, and chocolate peanut butter. Our personal choice is the locally beloved huckleberry. Altogether, there are fifty-nine flavors available, from almond to wild cherry, and you can mix any two, allowing a connoisseur to taste a different shake every Sunday from now until the middle of the century and beyond.

Southwest

Arizona * Colorado * Kansas * Nevada *

New Mexico * Oklahoma * Texas * Utah

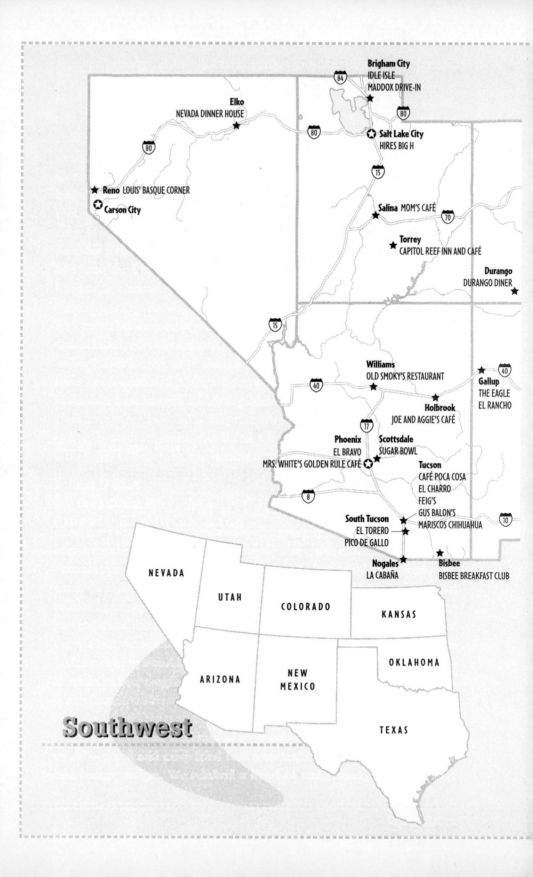

Brigham City
IDLE ISLE
MADDOX DRIVE-IN

Elko
NEVADA DINNER HOUSE

Salt Lake City
HIRES BIG H

Reno LOUIS' BASQUE CORNER

Carson City

Salina MOM'S CAFÉ

Torrey
CAPITOL REEF INN AND CAFÉ

Durango
DURANGO DINER

Williams
OLD SMOKY'S RESTAURANT

Gallup
THE EAGLE
EL RANCHO

Holbrook
JOE AND AGGIE'S CAFÉ

Phoenix   **Scottsdale**
EL BRAVO   SUGAR BOWL
MRS. WHITE'S GOLDEN RULE CAFÉ

Tucson
CAFÉ POCA COSA
EL CHARRO
FEIG'S
GUS BALON'S
MARISCOS CHIHUAHUA

South Tucson
EL TORERO
PICO DE GALLO

Nogales
LA CABAÑA

Bisbee
BISBEE BREAKFAST CLUB

NEVADA

UTAH

COLORADO

KANSAS

ARIZONA

NEW
MEXICO

OKLAHOMA

TEXAS

Southwest

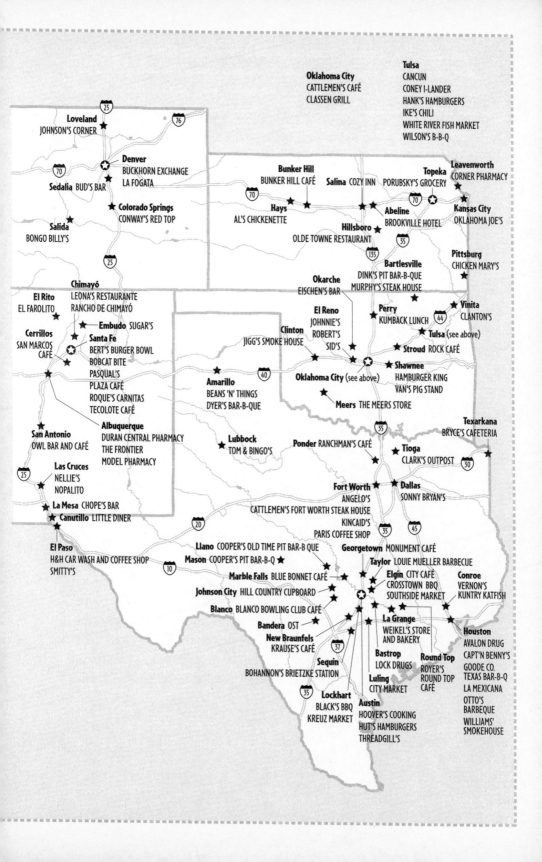

Bisbee Breakfast Club

75A Erie St.   520-432-5885

Bisbee, AZ 85603   BL (closed Tues & Weds) | $

The Bisbee Breakfast Club is the sort of place that makes traveling with an appetite so much fun: it is loved by locals and serves personality-plus food at low prices. Opened by Pat and Heather Grimm on Good Friday in 2005, it has since become a magnet for people from as far away as Douglas and even Tucson. But most customers are regulars from Bisbee. The everyday clientele reflects the curious population of a community that has gone from mining town to hippie enclave to artist colony and is now becoming coveted sunbelt real estate.

You cannot spend more than $10 for a meal, and for $3.25 you can enjoy one of the heartiest breakfasts ever: two jumbo oven-warm biscuits split and topped with sausage cream gravy seasoned with crushed chiles, black pepper, Tabasco sauce, and sage. Gooey sticky buns, made weekends only, have earned legendary status. The everyday menu includes broad, free-form wally cakes (pancakes with walnuts) and a juicy chicken-fried steak topped with the same crazy-spiced gravy used on biscuits. It is not uncommon to follow breakfast with a lofty wedge of pie. Of the several we sampled, the most amazing was lemon cheese, a citrus-perfumed cross between lemon meringue pie and cheesecake, stacked upon a soft-as-cookie crust.

Attention, coffeehounds. If visiting the Bisbee Breakfast Club, make it a point to head toward the heart of old Bisbee, where, among the cluster of Victorian buildings on streets as inclined as those of San Francisco, you will find Old Bisbee Roasters at 7 Naco Road. Here, brewmeister Seth Appell roasts some of the most delicious coffees anywhere. While it is not a formal restaurant, tasting cups are often available and beans are sold by the pound, as are Mr. Appell's devastating house-made chocolates. Most business is done via phone (866–432–5063) and at www.old bisbeeroasters.com.

Café Poca Cosa

110 E. Pennington St.   520-622-6400
Tucson, AZ   LD | $$$

Café Poca Cosa has moved to a dramatic new location in a parking garage on East Pennington in downtown Tucson. Gone is the explosion of colorful folk art that set the tone in the razzle-dazzle dining room back at the old Santa Rita Hotel. In its place is a sweeping, stylish space with objects of Mexican art on display as if in a museum. "Upscale a little bit, with the times," is how chef Suzana Davila described the new quarters. "It has that chic-iness to it, a click to it. It has the feeling of the big city."

The new place is a cooler environment than before, perhaps not as welcoming as it once was. But the black-clad staff was nothing if not polite and solicitous, and more important, the food has not changed. It is at the same level of excellence that originally put this place on the map of great southwest restaurants.

Davila is an inspired chef, with a menu that morphs throughout meal times to reflect what chiles, spices, vegetables, and ingredients are at that moment available in the kitchen, and what her whim dictates. When you are seated, you are shown a portable blackboard with about a dozen choices on it, virtually all of which need to be explained. Nothing on this menu is familiar; certainly, there are no tacos, enchiladas, or burritos! Nor are there appetizers and side dishes from which to choose. Each dinner comes complete on a plate with exactly what the chef believes should be there.

You will find some glorious chicken moles, or perhaps the variant of mole known as *pollo en pipian*, for which boneless chicken is cosseted in sauce made from bitter chocolate, crushed red chiles, Spanish peanuts, pumpkin seeds, and cloves. You will always find a tamale pie (*pasatel de elote*) on the menu as a vegetarian alternative. Even if you are a devoted meat-eater, you must have it, for this tamale pie is creamy comfort food supreme, tender as a soufflé, always dressed up a little differently, topped with vivid green chili purée or a sweet mango sauce.

There is shredded beef (*deshebrada*) infused with smoky chile flavor; there are seafood dishes and pork, too. Each entree is presented heaped upon a plate along with a bright, fresh salad, so that whatever your main course is, it mixes with the greens and makes a happy mess of things. On the side come small warm corn tortillas, and for dessert, do not neglect the cinnamon-tinged Mexican chocolate mousse or the soft, custardy square of flan, floated on a dish of deliriously sweet burned-sugar syrup.

El Bravo

8338 N. 7th St.   602-943-9753
Phoenix, AZ   LD | $$

Chuck Henrickson recommended we visit El Bravo for the "best tamale in Arizona." Yes, indeed, the chicken and green corn tamales we sampled are earthy, just zesty enough to perk up taste buds, and impossible to stop eating.

Add to that the other AZ-Mex fare on this merry menu and you have a restaurant that is hard to resist. It's not much for looks: décor is piñatas and beer signs. But who needs mood-making ambience when you can choose from among chiles relleños, enchiladas, burritos, and a fragile-crusted Navajo red beef popover that are all dishes to remember? On the side come super-savory refried beans. We are especially fond of the *machaca*, aka dried beef, that is available in tacos, burritos, and flautas. For dessert? How about a chocolate chimichanga?

Service is homey, meaning sometimes slow and sometimes brisk. The grandma in residence is friendly, but not cloyingly so.

El Charro

311 North Ct.   520-622-5465
Tucson, AZ   LD | $$

El Charro opened in 1922 and created many of the dishes that are now taken for granted as classic Mexican-American fare. The tostada grande, first made here by founder Monica Flinn, is a broad cheese crisp known on local menus as a Mexican pizza. Most people get it with a veneer of creamy melted cheese on top; other options include green chiles, guacamole, air-dried beef, and refried beans. El Charro's round-the-world version is a majestic appetizer, served on a pedestal, garnished with fresh basil leaves.

El Charro's *carne seca* (dried beef) is cured high above the patio in back of the restaurant, where strips of thin-sliced tenderloin hang in an open metal cage. Suspended on ropes and pulleys, the cage sways in the breeze over the heads of customers, wafting a perfume of lemon and garlic marinade into the Arizona air. Sautéed after it is air-dried, *carne seca* is customarily served in concert with sweet onions, hot chiles, and tomatoes, making an explosion of flavor like no other food. El Charro has a full menu of tacos, enchiladas, and chiles rellenos, plus such rarer regional specialties as enchilada Sonorese (a patty of fried cornmeal garnished with chili) and chalupas (small cornmeal canoes filled with chili, meat, or chicken and whole beans). Beyond the indisputable goodness of these meals, the kitchen offers a full repertoire of nutritionally enlightened fare—lo-cal, lo-fat, good for you, and good tasting!

El Charro is noisy and sociable, almost always packed with tourists, Tucsonians, health nuts, and burrito hounds who spoon up fiery salsa picante with corn chips and drink Tecate beer served in the can with a wedge of lime on top. Mariachi music sets the mood as the sturdy wood floors virtually shake with the crowds and the air fills with the inviting aromas of hot tostadas grandes. Wall décor is a kaleidoscope of vintage south-of-the-border advertisements, straw sombreros and rawhide bullwhips, and many years' worth of El Charro calendars, many of which feature melodramatic scenes of Mexican horsemen (known as *charros*), proud steeds, and pretty maidens all making flirty eyes at each other amidst stormy landscapes. The calendars are a house trademark, and a good memento of the high spirits of an El Charro meal.

El Torero

231 E. 26th St. 520-622-9534
South Tucson, AZ LD (closed Tues) | $$

South Tucson is surrounded by the City of Tucson but legally and culturally separate. In this part of town, buildings are festooned with brilliant painted tiles, streets hum with low riders cruising in their chopped-roof custom *caruchas*, and at least a dozen different restaurants serve Mexican food that most of us gringos have never encountered.

One of the best is El Torero, a place that is all too easy to drive right past. Despite a sign on 4th Avenue, a set-back location off 26th Street makes it seem nearly hidden. If you do realize that it exists, chances are good that you will assume it isn't open for business. The front door of the pink-painted building, far at the back of the parking lot, is inconspicuous to say the least. From the outside, it looks like a tiny place, perhaps abandoned a while back.

Once you push that door open, you instantly realize you have entered a very inviting region of Mexican-food heaven. The jukebox will likely be belting out party tunes; the bar you walk past to get inside may be occupied by happy people knocking back longneck beers; and at the tables in the brightly lit dining room, where the walls are decorated with bullfighter paintings and one large stuffed swordfish, people are plowing into gorgeous plates of expertly prepared true-Mex food.

Start with a wafer-thin tortilla crisp of cheese and green chile strips, presented on a silvery pedestal so all at the table can pull away slices. This crisp is among the thinnest and tastiest in a neighborhood full of excellent crisps. The main menu is a broad one, featuring all the familiar tacos, burros, enchiladas, and chimichangas, plus a few items that are truly special. These include off-the-bone turkey topped with a spectacular spicy-rich dark mole sauce or, on occasion, the similar sauce known as *pipian*, which includes pumpkin seeds. Our Tucson friends the Sparks, who directed us to this out-of-the-way gem, are hooked on the shrimp or flounder Vera Cruz and they also insisted on ordering a *topopo* salad— an amazing sight. *Topopo* means "volcano," and El Torero's *topopos* are great conical mounds of lettuce and other vegetables packed with your choice of chicken, shrimp, chili, guacamole, or *carne seca*, the sides of the mound columned by logs of hard cheese.

Feig's

5071 E. 5th St.   520-325-2255

Tucson, AZ   L | $

Feig's is a kosher grocery store, and while people come here to shop, they also come to eat. At the back of the store is a counter where you stand to order lunch. The short menu includes baked chicken quarters, stuffed cabbage rolls, gefilte fish and chopped liver, matzoh ball soup and knishes. There are smoked-fish salads and baked-here bagels and bialys.

We came for the corned beef sandwich because food authority David Rosengarten had proclaimed it America's best (and a large sign hanging above the grocery shelves reiterates his claim). We tried a jumbo, regular fat (you have the option of getting it cut lean). It arrived surrounded by excellent dill pickles. We had not specified what kind of bread—the menu lists rye, marble rye, and pumpernickel, all made here—and this one arrived on marble rye that was fresh and attractive, but fairly flaccid. The corned beef itself was sliced medium-thin. It was warm, tender, and juicy, mildly spiced. It is good corned beef, probably the best in Tucson and for miles around . . . but in our opinion, it is not in the same league as what you'll get at Katz's in New York, Manny's Coffee Shop in Chicago, or Shapiro's Deli in Indianapolis.

Other sandwich ingredients available include tongue, brisket, pastrami, corned beef, and salami, and all-beef hot dogs are served in made-here rolls.

Gus Balon's

6027 E. 22nd St.   520-747-7788
Tucson, AZ   BL | $

According to Tucson tipster Ron Spark, customers arrive in discrete groups throughout the day at Gus Balon's. First come the police and firefighters, after them other municipal employees, then office workers, and, by lunchtime, teachers. We haven't hung around this excellent breakfast-and-lunch café long enough to have seen the procession ourselves, but we've had enough breakfasts to recommend it as one of Tucson's bests.

There is nothing exotic or odd on the menu, unless you count the size of the huge signature sweet roll that is served warm with a big glob of butter on the plate. And we don't know any other place that can elevate an ordinary breakfast sandwich into the stratosphere the way Gus does. It's sausage, egg, cheese, and bacon, all of which are fine, but the homemade bun makes all the difference. Eggs come with American fries that include some crunchy bits from the griddle.

Gus Balon's is also known as a source of first-rate pie. One day's list included banana, chocolate banana, chocolate peanut butter banana, chocolate peanut butter, chocolate, coconut, lemon, butterscotch, blueberry, peach, raspberry, peanut butter, pineapple, apple, cherry, raspberry, peach, and raisin. Plus the crumb-topped ones: apple-cranberry, peach, raspberry, apple, apple-raisin, cherry, and pumpkin!

Aside from breakfast, commendable baked goods, and inexpensive lunches served in a bare-bones coffee-shop setting (counter and booths), Gus's is notable for its waitstaff, a team of uniformed pros who serve the food and coffee almost faster than you can speak the words to order it, and who refer to newcomers as well as friends as Hon, Sweetheart, and Doll. Last time we visited—about three years after our most recent Gus Balon's breakfast—waitress Pat exclaimed, "You're back!" She then recalled exactly where we had sat the last time and what we had ordered!

Joe and Aggie's Café

120 W. Hopi Dr.   520-524-6540
Holbrook, AZ   BL | $

At the front of Joe and Aggie's, cases and shelves display souvenirs of Route 66: playing cards, key rings, hats, and nostalgic books about the "Mother Road" that took travelers through Holbrook long before Interstate 40 bypassed the town. Despite the interstate, Holbrook remains one of those places where you can get a real feel for what life was like along western roads in the two-lane days. It still has the famous Sleep in a Wigwam motel; there are some fascinating pawnshops and Native-American jewelry emporia; and at Joe and Aggie's you can have a real old-fashioned roadside diner meal.

Tables are outfitted with squeeze bottles of honey for squirting onto sopaipillas (puffy triangles of fried bread), and meals begin with a basket of chips and an empty bowl in which you decant some hot, pepper-flecked hot sauce for dipping. The sign on the front window boasts of Mexican and American food, but in fact, the menu at Joe and Aggie's is not quite either; it is a blend of Mexican and American that is unique to the southwest. After the chips and salsa, you move on to such main courses as enchiladas made with red or green chile, big stuffed burritos, crisp tacos, or chicken-fried steak with potatoes and hot sopaipillas on the side. Roadfood.com user "icrmg" posted a gorgeous photo showing breakfast of green chile-topped huevos rancheros sided by a cake of hash browns and a side of cheese-dripping refried beans.

Joe and Aggie's is the oldest restaurant in Holbrook, dating back to 1946, the year Bobby Troup headed west in his Buick convertible and wrote "(Get Your Kicks on) Route 66."

La Cabaña

840 N. Grand Ave. #12   520-287-8208

Nogales, AZ   BLD | $

Our South Arizona friend Margaret Bond took us to La Cabaña when we asked her and her husband, Paul (the estimable boot maker), where to go in Nogales to get a real local meal. Margaret walked into the inviting little cantina with us in tow and she was greeted warmly by the staff, who know her as a regular.

Hostess Lupita had a worried look on her face when we sat down around 10:30 in the morning, between breakfast and lunch. Lupita knows what Margaret likes to eat when she comes here, and she warned us, "The chiles relleños are not ready yet. Can you wait ten minutes?" For relleños like these, we are happy to wait longer than that. They are packed with deep green-chile flavor, oozing melted cheese, and enrobed in a luscious fried crust.

The meal started with made-to-order guacamole, a bowl of chunky mashed avocado mixed with little bits of cheese and tomato. Margaret advised that we might want to spruce it up with a dab of the hot salsa provided to every table, as well as a spritz of tiny Mexican limes. We also sampled steamy corn tamales, spicy enchiladas, a crisp-crusted taco, and a beef burrito filled with meat that was moist and pot-roast tender. Among the most memorable flavors on the table were the simple flour tortillas, served in a bread basket. They are suitable for mopping one's plate of sauce and refritos, but just by themselves, these are superb tortillas: warm, delicate, with an earthy wheat flavor so rich they taste buttered.

La Cabaña is an inconspicuous little adobe restaurant/bar in a cluster of shops on the main drag. It is outfitted with tables and a couple of comfortable booths. For serious eating, we recommend the booths, where you can lounge like royalty.

Mariscos Chihuahua

2902 E. 22nd St.   520-326-1529

Tucson, AZ   LD | $$

Mariscos Chihuahua is a big, bright place with sunlight streaming in picture windows all around, illuminating a tempestuous seascape mural that covers one wall. The staff is friendly and the tape player belts out Mexican tunes that make every meal feel like a celebration. Seafood stars on this menu: oysters raw or cooked, fish grilled or fried, stews and soups. And oh, such shrimp! The menu lists a dozen different styles including cool cocktails and "drowned raw," meaning ceviche-style, i.e., cooked by immersion in a lime marinade, as well as breaded and fried.

We stuck to the basics and got an order of cooked shrimp in garlic sauce and an order of shrimp *endiablados*, which means extremely hot. The shrimp are presented in a most appetizing way, strewn across a field of crisp French fries on a broad fish-shaped plate that also holds a mound of rice, a green salad, and a warm tortilla wrapped in foil. They are served with the hard tail still on, providing a nice handle for nabbing one good mouthful. What's great about the presentation is that whatever the shrimp are sauced with—be it garlic butter, soy sauce, oyster sauce, or that devilish *endiablados*—seeps down and flavors the French fries that are their bedding.

Beverages include excellent presweetened (and lemon-flavored) iced tea as well as horchata, the locally flavored sweetened rice milk. A large cooler in the center of the dining area holds bottles and cans of Dos Equis, Tecate, Corona, and Bud and Bud Light.

(There are two other Mariscos Chihuahua in Tucson. They are located at 1009 N. Grande Ave. and 3901 S. 6th Ave.)

Mrs. White's Golden Rule Café

808 E. Jefferson St.	602-262-9256
Phoenix, AZ	L until 5:00 P.M. | | $

Looking for inexpensive home cooking in downtown Phoenix? This is the place. A destination lunch for citizens from all social strata, Mrs. White's is a concrete bunker that usually gets mobbed shortly after opening at 11:00 A.M. But don't worry if you have to wait. Meals are served quickly and customers don't linger. The cuisine is southern-style soul food, including smothered pork chops, catfish, and crunch-crusted fried chicken, always accompanied by hunks of corn bread. On the side come such vegetables as creamed corn, escalloped cabbage, stewed tomatoes, and salubrious, pork-flavored greens. For dessert, spoon into a bowl of warm peach cobbler or fork up sweet potato pie.

We love the do-it-yourself décor of this ramshackle little eatery, where strangers instantly feel right at home. The menu is written on the wall and no checks are given at the end of a meal. Simply go to the register and tell the cashier what you've eaten. She rings it up and you pay (cash only).

Old Smoky's Restaurant

624 W. Bill Williams Ave. (Old Route 66)   520-635-2091

Williams, AZ   BL | $

Before Interstate 40 replaced Route 66, Williams was known to travelers along great Mother Road as the "Gateway to the Grand Canyon." For vacationing families as well as hungry long-haul drivers, it was an oasis, an opportunity to buy souvenirs, spend the night, establish a base camp, and eat a good meal. There are two restaurants in town, both opened in 1946, that maintain the flavor of the old road. At Rod's Steak House, you eat big meat-and-potatoes supper, and at Old Smoky's, you fuel up for the day on stacks of three hotcakes starting at six o'clock every morning.

Old Smoky's is a cozy, wood-paneled diner where tourists and truckers rub elbows at the counter and exchange news over the backs of wellworn upholstered booths. Open only through the lunch hour, it has a midday menu of chili cheeseburgers and bowls of homemade chili topped with biscuits, but it's breakfast—served anytime—that pulls our car into the lot like a magnet.

Bread is featured on the front of the menu: white, wheat, rye, cheddar-wheat, and Swiss rye, all of which are available by the halforder, whole order, or 2½-pound loaf. In addition to these savory selections, there is a long roster of sweet breads available: cinnamon raisin, banana nut, banana chocolate chip, pumpkin raisin, apple walnut, etc. Select your toast to accompany a scramble of chorizo sausage and eggs, a green chile cheese omelet, or huevos rancheros on a corn tortilla. French toast is available made from any of the loaves, and of course there are pancakes—buttermilk or buckwheat—as well as a Billy Hatcher omelet made from the kitchen's red chili, cheese, and beans (named for the Chicago Cub who came from Williams).

We were strangers when we first stepped in the door of Old Smoky's several years ago, but were soon drawn into conversations among the staff and pancake eaters about everything from the current price of cranberries to major detours on the road ahead. Before we knew it, we had put away about a dozen cups of coffee and the morning was mostly gone. It was just the sort of genial café experience that makes Route 66 through Arizona a necessary course for any Roadfood scholar.

Pico de Gallo

2618 S. 6th Ave.   520-623-8775
South Tucson, AZ   LD | $

People are always asking us to name our favorite restaurant. It's an impossible challenge, akin to asking Hugh Hefner to single out his favorite Playmate. It is hardly any easier to name number one in any one category of eatery (barbecue, fried chicken, meat-and-three), but we have little difficulty choosing the single Mexican restaurant we like most in all the USA. It is Pico de Gallo in South Tucson.

This informal, stand-in-line-and-place-your-order tacqueria started as a street-corner taco stand and has grown into several small dining rooms. Nothing about the increase in size has impacted the magnificent food. Tacos, constructed in rugged made-here corn tortillas, are magnificent, available with *carne asada* and *birria* (meat stew) or more exotic ingredients such as tongue, manta ray, and beef cheeks. We love the *coctel de elote* (corn cocktail), which is not quite the beverage its name suggests. It does come in a large Styrofoam cup, the cup filled with an extraordinary stew of warm corn kernels, drifts of soft melted cheese, hot chili, and lime. Spoon it up like soup; it is corn-sweet and lime-zesty. The menu also lists burros, quesadillas, and tamales by the dozen.

Marshaled in a refrigerated case at the counter are plastic red cups filled with the restaurant's namesake, pico de gallo. In this case, the "beak of the rooster" is a salty chile powder mix that is sprinkled on top of a gorgeous bouquet of giant chunks of watermelon, coconut, pineapple, mango, and jicama, the whole shebang stuck with four or five long wooden picks for fetching the pieces you want. The red-hot spice elicits the fruit's sweetness and packs its own lip-tingling punch. It is a heady culinary collusion like nothing else we've ever eaten.

In addition to house-made lemonade and *horchata* (rice milk), the beverage selection includes Coca-Cola imported from Mexico. It's very different from the U.S. kind: spicier and more syrupy, a good companion for hot food.

Next door to Pico de Gallo is a place that we have a hard time defining because no one there speaks a bit of English, but we highly recommend it for dessert. We believe it is called Paleteria Diana. It is two separate rooms, one of which serves some hot food and big cups of ice topped with sweet-syrup fruits and fillings, the other serving homemade ice cream bars and Mexican ice cream in countless flavors.

Sugar Bowl

4005 N. Scottsdale Rd.　　　　602-946-0051

Scottsdale, AZ　　　　　　　　LD | $

A while back, Roadfood.com user Charlene Kingston wrote to tell us, "The Sugar Bowl is the name of the ice cream counter that [cartoon character] Dennis the Menace visits, named after this restaurant. Hank Ketcham [Dennis's creator] used to come and visit Bill Keane (creator of the syndicated cartoon *Family Circus*), who lived in Scottsdale near this famous local landmark, and he used the name in his strip as an inside joke with Keane." So not only is it a good place to eat ice cream: it is a cultural landmark, too!

The Sugar Bowl has been Old Town's go-to source for soda fountain treats since 1958. With its pink-upholstered booths and counter stools and a swift young staff who look so cheerful carrying Raspberry Glaciers (Sprite and sherbet), Golden Nuggets (Sprite, sherbet, and ice cream), and Turkish coffee sodas, it is the quintessential ice cream parlor. In particular, we recommend the Camelback sodas, made with either vanilla or coffee ice cream, and the "extra luscious malts," which are infused with marshmallow and fudge or caramel sauce.

There are sandwiches, soups, and salads, too, which look just fine, but in truth, when we walk into this happy place, we instantly become too obsessed with eating ice cream to consider anything else.

Bongo Billy's

300 W. Sackett Ave.   719-539-4261

Salida, CO   BL | $

Thanks to Chuck Henrikson for tipping us off to this cute little sandwich shop in Salida—one of two Bongo Billy's in Colorado. (The other is in Buena Vista.) It bills itself as a café, but it has more of a coffeehouse spirit, with all sorts of whole beans and coffee (and tea) drinks available, as well as an inventory of coffee makers, mugs, and T-shirts. The walls are decorated with a changing display of work by local artists, and bluegrass and folk musicians regularly perform in the evenings. A deck overlooking the Arkansas River provides customers a wonderful opportunity for meditative caffeination.

The menu is a sprightly selection of salads, sandwiches, and such Mexican-accented dishes as a Three Sisters Quesadilla (corn, beans, squash, tomatoes, and cheese) and breakfast burritos. Our pick dish is the Blue Moon Harvest Salad, which is a mesclun mix topped with blue cheese, spicy toasted walnuts, dried cranberries, and sweet peppercorn dressing. On the side comes a length of French baguette.

Beyond coffee, espresso drinks, and tea, drinks include smoothies, imported Italian sodas, cider, wine, beer on tap, and microbrews by the bottle.

Buckhorn Exchange

1000 Osage St.   303-534-9505

Denver, CO   LD | $$$

Holder of Colorado Liquor License no. 1 (issued in 1893), outfitted with antique firearms and furniture, and hung with a dazzling menagerie of some five hundred game animal trophies shot by former owner Shorty Zietz and his progeny, the Buckhorn Exchange is not only a frontier-themed restaurant for tourists. It happens to be a good place to eat the cuisine of the Rockies.

At lunch, hamburgers, salads, and sandwiches are consumed without ado by a cadre of regular customers inured to the stare of a thousand glass eyes and the creak of wood floors where Buffalo Bill once trod. Tourists like us cannot help but gape and wonder—and then tuck into a seriously carnivorous meal. Those who want to eat really wild western fare can start with Rocky Mountain oysters (sliced, fried calf testicles) or rattlesnake marinated in red chile and lime. For the main meat you can choose buffalo tenderloin, elk medallions, Colorado lamb, beefsteaks, or pork ribs. If there's more than a single passionate meat-eater at the table, the dish to have is "The Big Steak," a strip steak sized for two to five appetites and carved tableside.

Top it all off with a broad slab of hot crumb-topped apple pie with cinnamon rum sauce, and you have eaten a true-West meal.

Bud's Bar

5453 N. Manhart St.   303-688-9967

Sedalia, CO   LD | $

Bars tend not to be great places to look for satisfying food, but if it's a hamburger you seek, they're worth putting on the hit-list. For a first-rate bar-burger, we suggest heading south on Highway 85 out of Denver to the town of Sedalia and finding a mid-twentieth-century watering hole named Bud's. Here is served what tipster Mindy Leisure described as "one of the best burgers you will ever eat." It is juicy with a good crust, modest-size, and served with no unusual toppings. Pickles and onion are the only garnishes available. You have a choice of a single or a double with or without cheese. There's no deep-fryer on premises, so the menu advises patrons, "We don't have no damn fries." Instead, you get a bag of potato chips.

As you might guess by the extremely limited menu—there's nothing to eat other than burgers—Bud's attracts a lot of people for whom the hamburgers are a side dish to the main course, which is beer.

Conway's Red Top

1520 S. Nevada Ave.   719-633-2444
Colorado Springs, CO   LD | $

Conway's motto, referring to its hamburger, is "One's a Meal." The colossi they dish up in these restaurants are genuine whoppers—a half a foot across, served on broad-domed buns, accompanied by shoestring French fries and titanic pitchers of soda. Panavision-wide but not gourmet-thick, they are happy lunch-counter patties with enough of an oily smack to imprint the bun with their savor. They are sold whole or half, topped with cheese (Cheddar, Velveeta, American, mozzarella, or Pepper Jack), chili, mushrooms, or hickory-flavored barbecue sauce.

One definitely is a meal, especially if accompanied by good, shrivel-tipped French fries, onion rings, or a combo known as frings. But it would be a shame to visit the Red Top without a taste of the soups and stews that are still made from Grandma Esther's (Phyllis Conway's mom) original recipes. The navy bean soup, for example, is a stout brew with a profound, long-simmered flavor redolent of hickory-smoked ham and spice. With its accompanying sourdough roll, it is hearty enough to be a filling lunch (with a minuscule price tag). Beef stew is another homespun delight—hours in the making, so all the juices of the beef and vegetables have a chance to mellow and blend and soften. It is so thick you need only a fork to eat a bowlful. You can also have a bowl of spicy green chile (made with pork) or a split, grilled hot dog served on a broad burger bun.

The Red Tops have been a family operation since 1962, when Norb Conway bought the hamburger shop he worked in and he and his wife and ten children went to work. The Conways instilled an unshakable pride in the business that is as much a part of this restaurant's charm as are the giant hamburgers. After all, the Red Tops aren't really much more than hamburger shops, with waitresses in red hats and blue uniforms who deliver the check with your meal and provide the kind of quick service one expects. The honest menu, homemade food, and genuine hospitality are delightfully oldfangled.

(There are four other Red Tops in Colorado Springs, at 1228 E. Filmore, 390 Circle Dr., 3589 N. Carefree Circle, and 5865 Palmer Park Blvd. And there is one in Pueblo at 112 W. 2nd St.)

Durango Diner

957 Main Ave.
Durango, CO

970-247-9889
BLD | $

It was pancakes that made us fall in love with the Durango Diner—plate-wide pancakes, preferably with blueberries, glistening with butter and running rivers of syrup. We branched out to other breakfasts, and liked them plenty, especially the "half and half" plate of biscuits with gravy and green chile, and the big warm cinnamon roll. Breakfast is a particularly good meal to eat in this Main Street hash house; you will share it with some locals who claim to have been having coffee at these seats for more than thirty-five years.

Then we discovered hamburgers. If you are a connoisseur of hamburger excellence, put Durango on your treasure map, for here they make one really wonderful variation known as the Bonus Cheeseburger Deluxe: one-half pound of meat under a mantle of melted Swiss cheese and a heap of diced green chiles, French fries on the side. We love the Durango Diner's bacon double cheeseburgers almost as much as we love the chiliburgers (available red or green), and although some customers combine all these toppings on one mound of meat, we must confess that bacon and chili together atop a cheeseburger are just too much for our delicate palates.

Johnson's Corner

2842 S.E. Frontage Rd. (Exit 254 off I-25)
Loveland, CO

970-667-2069
Always open | $

A favorite truckers' stop along Highway 87 between Denver and Cheyenne since before there was an interstate, Johnson's Corner is known for round-the-clock breakfast and is famous for its plate-size cinnamon roll. The roll is the most bang for your buck, a monument of dough blanketed with what seems like a full cup of sweet white icing and sided by a helping of buttery spread. But when seeking maximum flavor along with maximum calories, we prefer chicken-fried steak with eggs, crunchy hash browns, and a biscuit with gravy. The breakfast menu contains all the usual suspects—omelets, pancakes, corned beef hash—as well as buffalo sausage and a breakfast burrito. Non-breakfast highlights include pot roast dinner, hot turkey sandwich, steaks, and pork chops. There are cream pies and fruit pies and a full-service soda fountain offers shakes, floats, malts, and one heck of a handsome banana split.

Recently remodeled, the dining area offers hugely spacious booths and counter service. And for truckers and other travelers who want to stay connected, it is a Wi-Fi hot spot.

La Fogata

5670 E. Evans Ave.	303-753-9458
Denver, CO	BLD | $
(2nd location in Denver at 8090 E. Quincy Ave.	720-974-7315)

La Fogata means "the bonfire"; however, the green chile stew served in this bilingual establishment isn't really all that hot. But it is quite delicious: zesty, glowing with sunny chile flavor, and packed with the punch of cumin. If you are looking for excellent Mexican food in Denver, this is the place to be.

Many items on La Fogata's menu are nationally familiar Tex-Mex staples—enchiladas, chiles relleños, tamales—expertly made and served in abundance; but this is also an opportunity to be adventurous. If you are blasé about beef in your taco, you can order tacos filled with crisp-roasted pork (wonderful!) or with beef tongue (spicy!), or ceviche tostadas, or you can spoon into a bowl of *menudo*, the Mexican tripe-and-hominy stew that is alleged to have magical powers to cure a hangover. To drink, there are imported beers, plenty of tequila cocktails, and the true-Mex nonalcoholic favorite, horchata, which is sweet rice milk.

This is a fun place to dine, where the crowd is equal measures of downtown business executives, blue-collar beer drinkers, and foodies who appreciate a rare taste of high-quality but unpretentious and inexpensive Mexican food.

Al's Chickenette

700 Vine St.   785-625-7414

Hays, KS   LD | $

We salute *The Splendid Table* listener named Craig who wrote to tell us that Al's Chickenette is "a great Roadfood place . . . fantastic, everything freshly made, piping hot, and slender, fresh-cut French fries, a rarity in that part of the country."

We agree. If you are traveling in western Kansas along I-70 with any degree of appetite as you approach Hays, do yourself a favor and find Al's. It will be especially easy to find if it's after dark, for this sixty-year-old eatery has a beautiful vintage neon sign glowing outside. Indoors, the walls are covered with evocative pictures of Kansas railroad history and a huge collection of chicken figurines.

Of course, the thing to eat is chicken, fried. You can buy it by the quarter or half bird, tenders or nuggets, a breast fillet or a giblet dinner of livers and/or gizzards. This is not fast-food chicken. It will take a while for your order to cook, which is one reason it is so good. As your teeth crack through the chicken's crunchy skin, wafts of aromatic steam erupt into the air. It is delicious plain, but the way Al's customers know to eat it is to take a squeeze bottle of honey and drizzle some across the crisp skin (as well as on the excellent French fries). The honey's sweetness sings mellifluous harmony with the chicken's salty crust.

Brookville Hotel

Lafayette St.	785-263-2244
Abeline, KS	LD | $$

Buffalo Bill slept at the Brookville Hotel in the small town of Brookville, as did untold numbers of cowboys when Kansas was the end of the line for trail drives up from Texas. It was opened in 1870, and it has built a reputation for its bountiful family-style chicken dinners since 1915.

The old Brookville Hotel closed a few years ago and a new version opened in Abeline. It's a modern building with a design reminiscent of the old facility; however, the charms of the old railhead town of Brookville are absent. For travelers who considered the restaurant part of a visit to genuine old Kansas, the reborn facility will be a disappointment—more like a theme park. Still, the menu remains the same one that made Brookville a destination for generations of hungry Kansans who think nothing of driving two hours each way for Sunday supper. Fried chicken is the main attraction—a half a bird, skillet-fried and served with mashed potatoes and chicken gravy, with side dishes of corn, cottage cheese, baking powder biscuits with sweet preserves, sweet-and-sour slaw, and ice cream for dessert.

Bunker Hill Café

6th and Elm Sts.	785-483-6544
Bunker Hill, KS	D Weds-Sat | $$$

Located in a blink-and-you-miss-it crossroads community, the Bunker Hill Café is a rugged limestone building that opened as a drugstore then became a pool hall. Today it is a destination steak house, open for supper only Wednesday through Saturday. It's a small place, no more than a dozen tables, with a menu that includes shrimp, catfish, chicken, and even a vegetarian dinner, but red meat is the café's raison d'être. Filet mignon is available in sizes that range from 2 to 16 ounces, sirloin from 4 to 16. There's also bacon-wrapped ground beef and occasionally Kansas elk and buffalo. Our sirloins were laden with juice, tender but not at all tenderized, a joy to slowly savor. It was late summer, and on the side came beautiful, full-flavored tomatoes and corn on the cob, as well as the house specialty, honey bread (available for puchase by the loaf).

Décor is Plains rustic: lots of mounted trophies and naturalist pictures on the wall and a couple of wood-burning stoves for warmth in cool weather. As seating is limited, reservations are advised.

Chicken Mary's

1133 E. 600th Ave.	620-231-9510
Pittsburg, KS	D | $$

"It's crazy, isn't it," Chicken Mary's son mused to us one hot summer day many years ago. "What's all this fried chicken doing out here anyway?"

It was a rhetorical question. The man knew perfectly well why the narrow lane off Highway 69 between Frontenac and Pittsburg, Kansas, is known as the Chicken Dinner Road, but he also knew that a couple of strangers hightailing up toward Kansas City had to wonder: why, in the middle of nowhere, are there two flourishing restaurants—Chicken Mary's and Chicken Annie's (not to mention Chicken Annie's Annex)—that specialize in nearly identical dinners of deep fried chicken?

Mary and Annie have long ago gone to their reward, so Mary's son—no spring chicken himself—explained that in the hard times of the 1930s, his father and Annie's husband both worked in a nearby mine. In 1934, Annie's husband lost a leg in a mine accident. To make ends meet, Annie opened a little restaurant and served her specialty, fried chicken. Only a few years after that, Mary's husband had to quit work, too, because of a bad heart. "There were three of us kids to feed," the old man recalled. "And my mother could see how well Annie was doing selling chicken dinners out here. She took a hint and opened her own place, Chicken Mary's, just down the road."

A tradition was begun. The rivalry has made this unlikely farm road a chicken-lover's mecca for six decades. The meals are ritualized family-style feasts: plenty of ultra-crunchy deep-fried chicken and mashed potatoes or German potato salad, with side dishes that include German coleslaw, green beans, baked beans, and spaghetti, plus ice cream for dessert. (Poultry-frowners can order chicken-fried steak.)

Note: Chicken Annie's is a short walk up the road, at 1143 E. 600th Ave. We've never eaten at both in the same trip, nor do we feel we have done enough research to rate one place above the other.

Corner Pharmacy

429 Delaware St.   913-682-1602

Leavenworth, KS   BL | $

Located in a well-tended Victorian building that dates back to the beginning of the twentieth century, the Corner Pharmacy is a trip back in time not only for its soda fountain treats and breakfast-served-all-day (to 6:00 P.M., closing time), but for the low-single-digit prices for meals. A cup of coffee costs less than a dollar, including refills.

Have a seat on a bentwood stool. The countertop is a faux marble, but the food is real. Watch the mixologist create a Green River or a phosphate and see milkshakes assembled scoop by squirt, then whirled in the multiwand mixer and served in their ice-frosted silvery canisters. Hamburgers are lunch-counter paradigms—thin and just greasy enough to leave a savory imprint on the bun. A plate of biscuits and gravy is one of the best dollars-for-calories deals in the nation.

Beyond the counter is a full-service drugstore, where pharmacist Ron Booth was quoted as saying, "My customers are also my friends and neighbors. They can come in and talk to me about anything."

Cozy Inn

108 N. 7th St.   785-825-9407

Salina, KS   LD | $

Back when the McDonald Brothers opened their first hamburger stand in California after World War II, the Cozy Inn had already been around a quarter-century. This is one of America's original hamburger stands; and although its management has changed over the years, and it was threatened with extinction (saved by a consortium of local hamburger patriots!), it serves burgers that are pretty much the same as they were in 1922.

The first great thing about Cozy burgers is their aroma. As you step up to the Cozy Inn, the smell of grilling onions and beef with a hint of dill pickle tickles your senses like some exotic hash-house perfume. Sit at the Cozy counter on one of the six stools for a twenty-minute lunch of maybe a half dozen little sliders and a bag of potato chips, and that smell will saturate your clothes and stay with you the rest of the day. Freeze a bag of Cozies, then heat them in the microwave oven six months later, and their perfume will billow out when you open the oven door.

The other exceptional thing about them is their taste. These are no Salisbury steaks or even quarter-pounders. They are thin-as-a-nickel patties in little buns that somehow form a perfect combination with pickle, mustard, and ketchup. It is a configuration so consecrated that, according to Cozy Inn folklore, some years ago when a Cozy cook tried to put a piece of cheese on his own, personal burger, he was fired on the spot.

The best way to eat a Cozy burger is straight from the grill (which holds fifty-five at one time), at the counter in Salina, any time between 9:30 in the morning and 11:00 at night, Monday through Saturday, and 11:00 to 11:00 on Sundays. (It has been reported that the management will ship Cozy burgers packed in dry ice to desperate people elsewhere in the country, but it is not a house policy.) As always, the price is right: A single Cozy burger, which sold for a nickel when the Inn opened in 1922, now goes for seventy-five cents. Inflation accounts for most of the price rise, but not too long ago, new owners also increased the size of each hamburger, from $\frac{1}{25}$ of a pound to $\frac{1}{16}$.

Oklahoma Joe's

3002 W. 47th Ave.	913-722-3366
Kansas City, KS	LD | $

Championship pennants adorn the walls of Oklahoma Joe's, whose proprietor, Jeff Stehney, has proven his skills in barbecue cook-offs throughout the region. The meats are slow-smoked until ridiculously tender, and his sauce is a beautifully balanced emulsion that is sweet with a pepper kick that will have your lips tingling long after you walk out the door.

Pulled pork is the specialty: variegated shreds and chunks that are just smoky enough to halo the sweet flavor of the meat. Other choices include turkey, ham, and sausage, and Joe's offers a number of interesting specialty sandwiches such as the Z-man, which is brisket and provolone cheese topped with onion rings, and Hog Heaven, which is pulled pork *and* sliced sausage. They are presented atop butcher paper on small square trays. Service is immediate in the cafeteria line; however, at meal times, you can expect to wait to get to the line. This is one very popular place.

A lot of Oklahoma Joe's charm has to do with its one-stop nature. It is not only a barbecue restaurant; it is also a gas station and convenience store, as well as a place to buy such smoke-cooking essentials as Night of the Living Bar-B-Q Sauce, Squeal Hog Rub, and T-shirts that say, "I Got Smoked to the Bone at Oklahoma Joe's."

Olde Towne Restaurant

126 N. Main St.   316-947-5446
Hillsboro, KS   BL Tues-Sat. D Fri & Sat, Sun supper | $$

In a big old limestone building on Main Street in downtown Hillsboro, Olde Towne Restaurant really is olde! Located in what was built in 1887 as the town's bank (with a vault in the basement), it served for many years as an egg factory where women candled, sorted, and crated eggs. Lower-story décor includes vintage egg crates made of wood as well as antique farm implements and a mural of old Hillsboro showing the great yellow bank building.

Olde Towne is the one nice restaurant in Hillsboro, and so it has a menu with something for everyone, from sandwiches, soups, and hamburgers every day at lunch to an all-you-can-eat Mexican buffet on Friday nights and a Saturday night Low German smorgasbord. Hillsboro is the heart of America's Mennonite community, and many of today's three thousand citizens descended from Germans who came to the USA (some via Russia). One of those who upholds the culinary heritage is Linden Thiessen, proprietor of Olde Towne Restaurant, and a man who makes a point of serving such melting-pot dishes as *verenika* (cottage cheese dumplings), zwiebach bread, and beet borscht as well as locally made German whole-hog sausage and slow-smoked beef brisket reminiscent of Texas Hill Country cuisine (where many of the original settlers were German). Dessert measures up to grandmotherly standards and includes an array of cream pies, bumbleberry pie, hot fruit cobbler, and elegant cream puffs.

Porubsky's Grocery

508 N.E. Sardou Ave.   785-234-5788
Topeka, KS   L Mon-Thurs | $

For a half a century, customers have been coming to the dining room at the side of Porubsky's Grocery store to eat cold-cut sandwiches and chili (the latter during cold-weather chili season only—October to March). Curiously, no coffee is served for the simple reason that this is an eat-it-

and-beat-it type of establishment where few midday customers have long lunch hours to while away sipping coffee. Regulars include a large blue-collar crowd as well as Kansas politicians and other public figures whose autographed pictures, inscribed with praises of the place and the family who has run it since 1950, line the walls.

The sandwiches are fine, but it's the extras that make lunch worth a detour off Highway 70. The most famous of the extras are Porubsky's pickles. These big, firm disks, which start as dills but are then infused with horseradish, mustard, and hot peppers, are guaranteed to snap your taste buds to attention. They are a favorite complement, along with crumbled saltine crackers, atop a bowl of Porubsky's chili.

Note: Lunch is served only Monday through Thursday. The Porubsky family likes to keep the store aisles clear on Friday and Saturday to make way for deliveries as well as for local residents who come to shop for groceries.

Louis's Basque Corner

301 E. 4th St.   775-323-7203

Reno, NV   LD | $$

We ate at Louis's Basque Corner on our first trip across the USA in the early 1970s. At the time, Louis's was only about five years old—Mr. and Mrs. Louis Erreguible, who had only recently come to Reno from southwestern France, were ebullient hosts in their new-world dining room. After supper, we walked out utterly inspired, thinking that someone really ought to be writing about marvelous local restaurants in unlikely places across the country. We've been writing about such restaurants ever since, and Louis's Basque Corner continues to serve what Mrs. Erreguible described long ago as "simple food cooked to perfection."

By average-American-meal standards, the food at Louis's is far from simple. What you eat at the long, family-style tables are copious feasts that start with soup, salad, bread, and beans, then move on to a plate of beef tongue, paella, oxtails, lamb stew, or Basque chicken. That's the first course! After that comes the serious eating: an entree of sirloin steak, paella, pork loin or pork chops, lamb chops, or a fish of the day. Dessert is inconsequential, but do consider a glass of Picon punch, the bittersweet Basque digestif with bitter orange flavor.

Louis's is a colorful place with waitresses outfitted in native attire and walls decorated with travel posters of the Pyrenees as well as pottery from Ciboure. Its clientele is a mix of travelers passing through for whom a meal here is a special treat as well as plenty of Renoans who make Louis's a regular part of their week.

Nevada Dinner House

246 Silver St.   775-738-9925
Elko, NV   LD | $$

The emblem of the Nevada Dinner House is a shepherd drinking wine from a bota bag. It is not necessary to drink wine to enjoy a meal in this family-style eatery on Silver Street in Elko's old downtown, but it is the sort of meal that makes you want to celebrate.

A casual tavern/dining room decorated with paintings of life in the Pyrenees, the Dinner House is also a spacious bar, where it is a joy to linger before or after dinner over Picon punch, the high-octane Basque very-adult beverage made of brandy, bitter orange Picon liqueur, and a twist of lemon. At capacious tables in the dining area a speedy waitstaff serves meals that are fundamentally western, but with Basque seasonings. Simply put, that means nearly everything but the liquor and after-dinner ice cream is shot through with garlic. The ritual of big-feed starts with powerhouse salads—no exotic greens or any such wussy ingredients; just good ol' iceberg lettuce—glistening with lemony vinaigrette. From that, you move on to old-world "first course" casseroles, then pork chops, lamb, sirloin steaks, prime rib, shrimp, halibut, or falling-off-the-bone garlic chicken accompanied by mouthwatering mashed potatoes.

After supper, Elko is a great place to stroll; its attractions include a casino reminiscent of Las Vegas in the pre-Disneyfication era, where farmers, cowboys, and visitors came to whoop it up at the gaming tables.

Bert's Burger Bowl

235 N. Guadalupe St.   505-982-0215

Santa Fe, NM   LD | $

Bert's says it invented the green chile cheeseburger, and while we cannot confirm or deny the claim, we can tell you that the one made here is a doozy. Flat patties of beef are sizzled on a grate over charcoal, from which flames lick up and flavor not only the meat, but also the bright orange cheese laid upon it. Dollops of fiery minced green chile are mounded atop the cheese from a bucket near the fire, and unless you say otherwise, your burger will come dressed with mustard, pickle, lettuce, onion, and tomato. Experienced customers, who dine under umbrellas on a sun-drenched patio overlooking Guadalupe Street, gradually peel back the wax paper in which the sandwich is wrapped as they eat, thus avoiding too much spillage.

Other popular burger configurations include BBQ and mayo/relish, and if the normal one-quarter pounder seems insufficient, a half-pound hamburger is available. Anyone who eats four half-pound burgers in thirty minutes gets them free. The menu also lists taco carnitas, flautas de pollo, chili dogs, and Fritos pie.

Bert's is a quick-order joint, but the food doesn't come right away.

You tell them what you want, and they take your money and give you a number. Then you hang around listening to hamburgers sizzle. Each one is cooked to order. A sign on the cash register advises: "All our food at Bert's is specially made for you and the approximate wait is 12 minutes once order is placed."

Bobcat Bite

420 Old Las Vegas Hwy.   505-983-5319
Santa Fe, NM   LD | $

The chile pepper (spelled with an *e*) is the official state vegetable of New Mexico (along with the pinto bean) and yet few restaurants in the state serve chile con carne as a meal. Instead, you'll savor puréed chiles atop enchiladas, whole ones stuffed and battered and fried into chiles rellenos, and chopped ones as part of a brilliant dish called the green chile cheeseburger.

While some hash slingers put chiles atop the cheese, at Bobcat Bite, a neon-lit diner on the outskirts of Santa Fe, the cook secrets a lode of fire-flavored chopped chile underneath the cheese. The creamy cheese melts among the peppers and into the crevices of the crusty burger down below to create a fusion flavor that is pure Land of Enchantment.

Bobcat Bite is itself an extremely enchanting place, offering lovely rib-eye steaks in addition to the legendary burgers. It is a close-quarters roadside diner packed with customers through the dinner hour, with a sign-up board outside for those willing to wait. Inside there are about a half dozen seats at the counter and five or six tables and not much room to move around. Throughout the mealtime, there is a considerable amount of shuffling sideways at the counter seats so parties of two can sit together.

Since it opened in the middle of the last century, Bobcat Bite has maintained a country coziness that makes newcomers and old friends always feel at home. For us, the experience of eating here has a strong nostalgic air, as though we've somehow stepped into a shipshape roadside diner in the mid-1950s. In its modest way, it is a beautiful place with clean varnished wood tables and counter and pictures of bobcats and other wildlife on the walls.

Chope's

Route 28
La Mesa, NM

505-233-3420
LD | $

Cecilia Benavides, whose father, Chope, was born and raised in the building that is now the family restaurant, and whose grandmother started selling enchiladas to La Mesa farmers in 1915, buys her year's supply of New Mexico chiles—about three tons—during the autumn harvest from a farmer who, she says, "knows what we like—not too hot, not too mild. He plants it, grows it, picks it, then takes it to a man outside Las Cruces who roasts it."

The Mesilla Valley's long greens are best savored in Chope's relleños. Stuffed with mild cheese, battered and crisp-fried, the fleshy walls of the pod have a strapping vegetable punch. As for red chiles, their ultimate taste is in the purée that is made in the kitchen each Monday. Cecilia told us that starting with commercial powdered chile inevitably makes a bitter brew. She de-stems, de-seeds, soaks, and blends whole red ones to create a cream-thick opaque vermilion liquid with flavor as clear as fruit nectar, and fairly hot—the kind of lip-searing hot that any restaurant outside New Mexico would warn customers about. But in this area, it's normal. The really hot stuff on the table is green salsa, made entirely from Mesilla Valley jalapeños. Chope's will oblige those who insist on maximum heat by offering special four-alarm chile in a bowl or on enchiladas. The chile-centric menu also includes gorditas, tacos, plates of chile con carne, tamales, and green chile-draped cheeseburgers.

Located among verdant fields of pepper plants and vast precision-planted orchards of pecan trees, Chope's is a bar and a restaurant with a deservedly high reputation among planters, horticulturalists, and all aficionados of the state vegetable of New Mexico.

Duran Central Pharmacy

1815 Central Ave. NW
Albuquerque, NM

505-247-4141
BL | $

One of our favorite views in the scenery-rich Southwest is from a stool at the lunch counter in Duran Central Pharmacy. To the right is the kitchen, where you can view one of the staff using a dowel to roll out rounds of dough into broad flour tortillas that are perfect tan circles. Straight ahead is the grill where they are cooked. To see them puff up from the heat and blister golden-brown, then to smell the warm bready aroma fill the air, is to know for certain that good food is on its way.

These superlative tortillas, available plain or glistening with butter, come on the side of most lunches, including the wondrous Thursday-only *carne adovada* (chile-marinated pork). They are used to wrap hamburgers and as the base of quesadillas. We like them best as a dunk for Duran's exemplary red or green chile, which is available either plain (nothing but chiles and spice) or loaded with your choice of ground beef, beans, potatoes, or chicken. The green is hugely flavorful, hot and satisfying with an earthy character; the red is pure, essence of plant life, liquefied with a full measure of sunshine.

Duran, by the way, is a full-service pharmacy.

The Eagle

220 W. Route 66	505-722-3220
Gallup, NM	BLD | $

With its pea-green walls, high ceiling, and décor consisting of cutout images of a taco, a chicken basket, a hot dog, a hamburger, and French fries, the Eagle is a humble place favored by locals and visitors who come to buy or sell at the venerable Richardson's Trading Post next door. The menu is Southwest-café cuisine, including hamburgers, Navajo tacos, and enchiladas. And lamb. Lamb is part of the culinary heritage of this region, primarily thanks to Navajo shepherds who have raised it for millennia, but it isn't all that common on café menus. That is why we felt compelled to order a bowl of Eagle café lamb stew one afternoon for a snack.

"It'll be kinda huge," the waitress warns. Huge it is, and unforgettable. A stark dish with hominy and spuds on the side, it is little more than a bowl full of seasoned meat, much of it still on the bone, soft and tender and rich as cream. The bones necessarily make it finger food, so there is no way to eat this meal fast. To work through it at the ancient porcelain counter with the big neon "Welcome" sign on the back wall and the beveled mirrors that look like something from an Edward Hopper painting is to have a dining experience that could happen only on Route 66.

El Farolito

1212 Main St.   505-581-9509

El Rito, NM   LD | $

El Rito is a long way from almost everywhere, and we never would have come across El Farolito had it not been for a great Roadfood tip from Michelle Sullivan, who wrote to praise the green chile. The trip from Santa Fe was an adventure in itself, a drive through a glorious landscape of awesome rock formations, sagebrush, and grazing cows. The town is little more than a single street with a general store on one side and El Farolito on the other. It's a small restaurant, hardly bigger than a house trailer, with seven picnic tables up front and the kitchen in back.

For native New Mexican food, you won't find a better place at a better price. Chiles relleños, tacos, enchiladas, and green chile cheeseburgers are featured on the menu (which also offers ordinary hamburgers and hot dogs for chilephobes). The green chili is especially excellent: a luxurious stew of bite-size pieces of pork, tomato, and slivers of ultra-hot green chile. Red chile is more a sauce, nothing but puréed chiles and spice, and it is used on burritos and enchiladas. But if you'd like a "bowl of red" as a meal, the Trujillos will add beef and/or beans to create a thick, power-house stew.

We cannot resist El Farolito's Fritos pie. Dominic Trujillo, son of founders Carmen and Dennis, told us that some customers who get their pies to go have the corn chips packed separately so they don't get too soft by the time dinner is ready to eat. The way it normally comes from the kitchen, there is a thick layer of relatively mild-mannered red chili spread atop a foundation of corn chips, the chili garnished with melting shredded cheese, lettuce, and tomato. It's the whole food pyramid in a single bowl!

El Rancho Restaurant

1000 E. Route 66   505-863-9311

Gallup, NM   BLD | $

Built by D. W. Griffith's brother so early Hollywood filmmakers would have a place to stay when shooting westerns on location, the El Rancho Hotel has been revived and spiffed up and is a nice place to stay, albeit rather rugged and modest. The lobby is loaded with western artifacts and movie colony memorabilia that includes autographed pictures of the stars who stayed here.

Aside from celebrity connections and colorful non-chain accommodations, El Rancho earns its place on the Roadfood map for an excellent hotel restaurant. The menu is a mélange of western Americana, New Mexican standards, and a bit of Tex-Mex thrown in. For breakfast, we have enjoyed huevos rancheros and swell plates of steak and eggs with crunchy hash brown potatoes, and a lunchtime chicken enchilada was lovely. The bar is especially inviting, considering its history, and the margaritas are renowned.

The Frontier

2400 Central Ave. SE
Albuquerque, NM

505-266-0550
Open 24 hours except 1:30 A.M.–4:00 A.M.,
Fri & Sat | $

A Roadfood landmark on old Route 66 across from the University of New Mexico, the Frontier boasts that it is "home of the latest in broiled food and the Frontier sweet roll." We're not up on broiled food trends, and frankly, the famous butter-dripping Frontier sweet roll, while awesomely sized, is on the doughy side. Nevertheless we love this place—not only because it is cheap, informal, and open round-the-clock, but because the New Mexican food is outstanding.

At breakfast, for instance, huevos rancheros are available with a choice of four toppings: salsa, green chile stew, red chile, and green chile. The last one is the hottest, with a full-tilt chile punch, giving the plate a roasted, earthy aroma that is insanely appetizing. Cheddar cheese is technically an option, but should not be left out of this big platter that looks like a mess but eats like a dream. On the side comes a puffy, just-cooked flour tortilla (you can watch the man make them behind the counter) that is almost too hot to handle. Orange juice is freshly squeezed. Quart pitchers of coffee are available for $2—a good deal for students who come to pore over books early in the morning.

The lunch menu includes such Land of Enchantment specialties as a *carne adovada* burrito, green chile stew and, naturally, a chile cheeseburger, here dubbed the Fiesta Burger. Homemade lemonade is available to drink.

One thing that makes dining at the Frontier fun is its breakneck pace. Because meals are ordered fast, cooked fast, and served instantaneously, you are guaranteed that things that are supposed to be hot are piping hot; we've gotten hamburgers still sizzling from the grill. Although many students come to linger over coffee and homework, it is possible to be in and out, with a good meal under your belt, in five minutes. The system is serve-yourself. While you wait in line, study the overhead menu and make your decision. When the green light flashes, indicating someone is ready to take your order, step up to the counter and say what you want. Approximately two minutes later, you are carrying your meal to an open table.

Leona's Restaurante

4 Medina Lane
Chimayó, NM

505-351-4569
LD (closed Tues & Weds) | $

The village of Chimayó is off a winding road in the foothills of the Sangre de Christos, but it isn't obscure. Generations of weavers have made its cloth a western legend, and its early-nineteenth-century Santuario is a destination for religious pilgrims who believe that dirt from the earthen floor has miraculous healing powers. For four decades, hungry travelers have come to Chimayó to eat Leona's tortillas.

Leona Medina-Tiede knows wheat. When she was growing up, her mother grew it and harvested it with a sickle. "We rubbed it on a screen to get off the thistles," she remembers. "We'd hurt our hands bad doing that. Then we'd pick it up and the wind blew the thistles away." She and her mother took the wheat to the Chimayó mill where, Leona recalls, "They wouldn't grind it too well, so you'd get little crispy nuggets of unground wheat in your flour. It was so good!" Leona's mother rolled out fresh tortillas three times a day for her and ten siblings.

The first time we drove through New Mexico in the mid-1970s, Leona had a roadside stand on Highway 76 where she sold tortillas and chiles. At harvest time in the fall, you could pull over and get a sandwich of just-roasted chiles wrapped in a fresh tortilla—one of the great roadside snacks of all time. She now makes and sells flavored tortillas (apple cinnamon for breakfast; onion, garlic, piñon, or pesto) and she runs a little restaurant, shaded by an ancient catalpa tree just below the Santuario. Here she serves tamales that radiate corn flavor, red and green chile stew, posole, and the traditional hangover cure of posole and tripe known as *menudo*.

Leona's serves exceptional burritos stuffed with fiery *carne adovada* (chile-marinated pork), rice and beans, or chicharrones (rendered pork fat like nuggets of bacon, only piggier). The one that knocks our socks off is the chile relleño burrito. Relleños, which are cheese-stuffed, breaded-and-fried chiles, are popular throughout New Mexico, but too often the chile and its crust turn to mush. Leona's has crust with crunch; the chile pod it sheaths is al dente and full-flavored, with enough mellow melted cheese inside to balance the heat. Wrap it in one of her tortillas and you have what Leona calls a "hand-held burrito," meaning it's easy to pick up and eat with no utensils. This is a valued quality to pilgrims for whom Leona's sanctuary is a blessed part of the walk through Chimayó.

Model Pharmacy

3636 Monte Vista Blvd. NE   505-255-8686
Albuquerque, NM   L | $

You enter this neighborhood pharmacy past the drug counter, navigate along perfumes, soaps, and sundries, then find the little lunch area: a few tables scattered about and a short marble counter with a Pueblo-Deco knee guard of colorful enamel tiles. If you are like us, your attention will be drawn to the right of the counter, where the cobblers are displayed under a spotlight. Three or four are made every day—geological-looking strata of flaky crust atop syrupy tender hunks of apricot, peach, blackberry, or a mix thereof—and they are available simply warm or warm with a globe of ice cream melting on top.

The soda fountain is impressive: a fully stocked armory of milkshake mixers, syrup dispensers, and soda nozzles, plus a modern espresso machine (so you can get an espresso milkshake—mmm). As for lunchtime entrees, locals love the walnut chicken salad, and some come to eat hamburgers and cold-cut sandwiches, but we'll choose green chile stew every time. It is more a soup, actually, chockful of carrots, tomatoes, and bits of green chile with good flavor and alarming heat.

Nellie's

1226 W. Hadley Ave.   505-524-9982
Las Cruces, NM   BL | $

A passing police officer was suspicious when he spotted us loitering outside of Nellie's one morning before the café's 8:00 A.M. opening.

"We're waiting to eat," we responded to his inquiry about our intentions.

Good answer. He broke into a big grin and said, "Best chile in town!"

In Las Cruces, the heart of chile country, such an avowal is no casual observation.

Inside the cozy cinder-block and glass brick restaurant, a sign on the wall confirms the kitchen's priorities: "A day without chile is like a day without sunshine."

Danny Ray Hernandez, Nellie's son, makes vivid salsas using five to seven different types of chile and specializes in such eye-opening breakfasts as huevos à la Mexicana (scrambled with jalapeños) and eggs with chile and meat. For the latter you can get red or green or a combination of the two (known as Christmas). The red tastes of pure pod; the green is hot enough to require tongue-tamping with the kitchen's pulchritudinous sopaipillas. Mr. Hernandez speculated that dry growing conditions over recent years have produced chiles in which the heat is more concentrated.

Years ago, Nellie's and its offspring, Little Nellie's Chile Factory, served dinner. Today it is strictly a breakfast-and-lunch eatery.

Nopalito

310 S. Mesquite St.   505-524-0003
Las Cruces, NM   LD | $

Nopalito is a family-run restaurant (actually two restaurants; the other is at 2605 Missouri) where you can count on excellent New Mexican food. Not Tex-Mex nor Arizona-Mex nor California-Mex nor Sonoran-Mex, but the unique cuisine of New Mexico. That means that chile peppers star and the question of red or green is one you will confront at every meal. There is no rule about which is hotter. The day we came to Nopalito (which means "little cactus"), the waitress assured us that green was the hot stuff, but that red was more delicious. What to do? "Christmas!" she replied, which is the term for a dish topped with both.

We had ours on a stacked enchilada with the works, meaning beans and cheese and a fried egg on top and rice and salad on the side. We also savored excellent chiles relleños, fried to a crisp and oozing warm cheese.

Before the main course, everybody gets crisp, warm tortilla chips and a set of salsas, red and green. The green is served hot (temperature-wise), but is fairly mild. The red is served cool but is very, very hot. We also ordered what the menu lists as avocado salad, but looked and tasted a lot like chunky guacamole.

The broad, airy dining room with its adobe mission–style décor is a pleasant place to relax and enjoy native foods. The staff was kind and helpful, seats were comfortable, and we relished the aroma of other people's chile-focused meals—gorditas, con carne, tacos, tamales, rolled as well as stacked enchiladas—wafting past us on their way from the kitchen to tables.

Owl Bar and Café

Hwy. 380   505-835-9946
San Antonio, NM   BLD | $

"Masterpiece! Masterpiece!" sings the waitress at the Owl Bar as she carries a green chile cheeseburger from the kitchen to the bar at 8:30 A.M. While the menu does have a couple of egg-and-bacon breakfasts as well as steaks and sandwiches, the unique New Mexico hamburger is what puts this out-of-the-way watering hole on the Roadfood map. Since at least the early days of atomic bomb tests at nearby White Sands, when scientists used to come here for nuclear-hot burgers, the Owl Bar has built such an exalted reputation that aficionados drive from Texas and Colorado to eat 'em two by two.

Crusty, gnarled patties of beef are covered with chopped hot green chiles and the chiles are in turn topped with a slice of cheese that melts into them and the crevices of the hamburger. Customary condiments include raw onion, chopped lettuce, sliced tomato, and pickle chips. It is a glorious package, and while we have never compared this one side-by-side to the excellent green chile cheeseburger up at Bobcat Bite in Santa Fe, there can be no doubt that the Owl Bar's version is among the state's best.

While we ate ours at breakfast time, the stools at the bar were occupied by a few regular customers having their own all-liquid breakfasts in the form of Coors Light.

Pasqual's

121 Don Gaspar Ave.   505-983-9340

Santa Fe, NM   BLD | $

Pasqual's is a modest corner café with terrific food. At any mealtime in this crowded, split-level dining room, you are lucky to find a seat at a small table or at the large shared one, where a local or a stranger from just about any part of the world might break bread with you.

For breakfast, we love the pancakes, the blue and yellow cornmeal mush, big sweet rolls, and giant bowls of five-grain cereal with double-thick cinnamon toast on the side, accompanied by immense bowls—not cups—of latte. And for lunch, we can never resist the expertly made soups. Little things mean so much: fresh bread for sandwiches, flavorful roasted chiles on quesadillas, even the coffee is a tasty surprise.

After a few meals at Pasqual's, it is easy to feel affection for its unpretenious, sometimes clamorous ambience; this is a restaurant with character that perfectly complements the good stuff from the kitchen.

Plaza Café

54 Lincoln Ave.   505-982-1664

Santa Fe, NM   BLD | $

Opened in 1918, the Plaza is the oldest restaurant in Santa Fe. Its interior is a blast from the past, especially attractive to those of us who appreciate traditional diner ambience, but the tidiest version imaginable. At the back of the room is a neon-edged map of New Mexico. The floor is lovely tiny-tile checks, and tables are chrome-banded luncheonette-style.

The Plaza seems not to be impressed by itself as a piece of history or an example of classic counter culture. It is an easygoing kind of café, one of the last vestiges of the Santa Fe Plaza as a town gathering place. The menu is an appetizing combination of Americana (burgers, chicken-fried steak, hot turkey sandwich), Greek diner standards (lamb meat loaf, souvlaki, Greek salad), and real New-Mex specialties including chiles rellenos, posole with pork, *menudo*, and pure red chile or green chile stew. Every day starting at 11:00 A.M., the Plaza kitchen turns out what may be the city's most delicious sopaipillas. Fresh and hot and cloud-soft, these golden pillows of quick-fried bread are served with a squeeze bottle of honey to sweeten them, and they are simply wonderful to eat plain or on the side of red or green chile. The Plaza's green chile is a slippery stew with chunky vegetables; red is thicker and hotter.

More than any other downtown restaurant, the Plaza feels like a real part of day-to-day Santa Feans' lives. Locals eat here, but so do travelers in search of a good square meal. Below the clock on the wall is a movable-letter board on which are spelled out "Important Phone Numbers," which include the mayor, the governor, the representatives in Congress, the president of the United States, and the police chief, as well as a New Mexico road conditions report.

Rancho de Chimayó

Route 520   505-351-4444
Chimayó, NM   LD | $$

North of Santa Fe, through the foothills of the Sangre de Cristo Mountains, the road leads toward the ancient village of Chimayó. It is a beautiful journey, past apple stands and adobe homes draped with bright red chile *ristras* (ropes of pods) hung out to dry. Built a century ago by the Jaramillo family, whose ancestors arrived in the 1600s, Rancho de Chimayó is a spacious home of wide wood planks and low-beamed ceilings, hammered tin chandeliers, and a capacious fireplace. It became a restaurant in 1965, and since then it has gained fame not only for its charm and ambience, but for a kitchen that exalts the cuisine of New Mexico.

Native New Mexicans seldom sit down for a "bowl of chili." In fact, chili as a meal isn't listed on the Rancho de Chimayó menu. But there are few dishes this kitchen makes in which the chile pepper doesn't play a vital role. New Mexican cooks use their native pod in stews and omelets, on top of steaks, stuffed into sopaipillas, and as a marinade for the fire-breathing native specialty known as *carne adovada*—pork infused with a pepper bite. If you are coming to Rancho de Chimayó only once, and if you like hot food, *carne adovada* is the dish to order. The pork glistens red, and has turned tender from its long marinade in a sauce made from hot red chile pods. On the side of this fiery pork the kitchen provides a mound of posole (hominy corn)—mild little lumps of tenderness to soothe the tongue.

For those who want something a little less inciendiary, Rancho de Chimayó's menu also offers sopaipillas relleñas, in which the triangular fried breads are stuffed with beef, beans, tomatoes, and Spanish rice, and topped with red or green chili sauce. There are flautas, too—rolled corn tortillas filled with chicken or pork and fried crisp, topped with cool sour cream.

For us, it is a special joy to to drive to Rancho de Chimayó through the foothills of the Sangre de Christo mountains in the cool of an autumn evening, when *ristras* decorate adobe homes and late-day autumn light makes sagebrush shimmer. Candlelit tables are arrayed on a stepped patio outdoors, strolling guitarists strum southwestern tunes, and the air smells of sagebrush and native cooking.

Roque's Carnitas

Washington and Palace

Sante Fe, NM   L (closed in winter) | $

Roque's is a jolly little chuckwagon that serves one thing: a sandwich made of a sturdy flour tortilla that has been heated on a grate over a charcoal fire. The warm tortilla is folded around succulent beef, and plenty of it—thin slices of marinated top round sizzled on a grate—along with onions and chiles. Atop the beef goes fiery jalapeño salsa.

As soon as you peel back the foil and try to gather up the tortilla for eating, chunks of salsa tumble out, meat juice leaks, onions slither, and plump circles of earth-green chile pop free. There is a tall garbage can near the carnitas wagon, and it is not unusual to see two or three well-dressed customers gathered around it, bending over at the waist and chomping on their sandwiches so that all its spillage falls right into the trash. The choice location for eating, though, is a bench in the nearby Plaza, which is the heart of the old city. Here you can sit and lean far forward as you dine, thus sparing your shirt and lap, and providing resident pigeons the carnitas banquet to which they are now accustomed.

Roque, a fifth-generation Santa Fean and a fount of local lore, goes to Mexico each winter, where he runs a pizzeria. To our noses, the smell of his sizzling carnitas on the Santa Fe Plaza is as much a sign of spring as singing robins and blooming lilacs.

San Marcos Café

3877 State Road 14   505-471-9298

Cerrillos, NM   BL | $

The San Marcos Café is a popular destination eatery and a convenient stop for folks on their way to Cerrillos or Madrid. If you plan on eating here on a weekend morning, it's best to call ahead and make sure there's room. Breakfast can be a mob scene. We were thrilled with the cinnamon rolls—taller than they are wide, and rather than being dense and doughy like so many others, they are crisp and lightweight, almost croissant-like in character. Other dandy breakfast items are eggs San Marcos, which is a large serving of fluffy scrambled eggs wrapped inside a tortilla and sided by beans, chili, and guacamole under a mantle of melted cheese; biscuits topped with spicy sausage gravy; and *machaca* (beef and eggs with pico de gallo).

A cozy, charming ranch house decorated in country-kitchen style (old enameled stoves, wooden cupboards, knickknacks galore), the café also happens to be a veritable bird jungle. Peacocks and peahens, wild turkeys, and roosters all cavort around the front and back, and while they are not allowed inside the restaurant, there are pictures on the wall of the most famous chicken of them all, a leghorn rooster named Buddy, who served long tenure as unofficial maitre d'. Dressed in black tie, Buddy cheerfully greeted guests at the door and crowed through the breakfast hour. Years ago, when Buddy passed away, customers mourned. And although a few other roosters have been named to take his place, none has ever had the people skills that Buddy had.

Sugar's

1799 Hwy. 68   505-852-0604
Embudo, NM   LD | $

Sugar's is a tin-sided house trailer by the side of the road with a small cluster of picnic tables on an adjoining open patio. Sugar herself is gorgeous: a big, muscular bulldog bitch whom you can usually see in the yard to the left of the tin trailer where you place your order at a window then wait while they cook it inside. Her picture also adorns the wall-mounted menu, which is a roadside roster of burgers and green chile cheeseburgers, corn dogs, burritos, and Fritos pie.

We have never tried any of those things because we go straight to Sugar's excellent barbecue. It's brisket, slow-cooked until pot-roast tender, ridiculously juicy, and infused with the flavor of smoke. Basically there are two ways to have it: in a sandwich, with tangy red sauce, or wrapped in a tortilla with green chiles and cheese. We prefer the latter because, in our opinion, that sweet-tangy sauce on the sandwich distracts from the lovely, subtle taste of the brisket. On the other hand, the barbecue burrito is an inspired creation: thick shreds of beef accented by the snap of peppers and even further enriched by melted cheese. We could eat these burritos all day long. But alas, where we live, they are nothing but a memory. Such a fine cheap-eats meal is an only-in-New-Mexico experience.

During the summer, Sugar's also offers barbecued ribs and sausage. The winter smokehouse menu is strictly brisket.

Tecolote Café

1203 Cerrillos Rd.   505-988-1362
Santa Fe, NM   BL | $$

When Bill and Alice Jennison opened Tecolote in 1980, they did so with a sense of mission. Their goal, stated on the back of the menu, was "to serve a wholesome, tasty meal, at a reasonable price, in a comfortable and cheerful environment." On occasion they have opened up for evening meals, but the Jennisons' specialty, and the distinction of Tecolote, is breakfast. Lines of morning customers waiting to get in are testimony to their fulfillment of the mission.

Personally, we like Tecolote's *atole piñon* hotcakes best of all. Made with blue cornmeal and studded with roasted piñon nuts, they actually resemble wide, low-rise cakes more than ordinary flattened-out flapjacks. Pale blue inside with a faintly crusty exterior from the grill, each cake is ethereally fluffy, and gosh, what joy it is to bite into a little lode of those roasty-rich nuts! There are blueberry hotcakes, too, made with a similar, from-scratch batter, and plain ones—each available singly, as a short stack (two), or a full stack (three).

Of course there are omelets galore and eggs of every kind, including shirred on a bed of chicken livers, as the crown of corned beef hash, and "rancheros" style—fried on a corn tortilla smothered in red or green chile and topped (at your request) with cheese. One non-traditional meal we hold dear at Tecolote is a gallimaufry called Sheepherder's Breakfast—new potatoes boiled with jalapeño peppers and onion, cooked on a grill until crusty brown, then topped with two kinds of chile and melted cheddar cheese.

Tecolote, by the way, is an Aztec word that means "owl," chosen by the Jennisons because Bill had been fascinated by a nearly deserted village of that name in northern New Mexico. "We like to think of him as our 'wise friend,'" says the Tecolote menu, "and hope that you will think of those of us at Tecolote Café that way."

Oklahoma

Cancun

705 S. Lewis Ave.   918-583-8089
Tulsa, OK   LD (closed Weds) | $$

Cancun is a neighborhood Mexican restaurant where English is a second language. It is a welcoming place with a handful of tables, those along the front window offering a view of the parking lot. We plowed into a super burrito stuffed with *carnitas* (shredded pork), rice, and beans, smothered with shredded cheese and warm salsa, and decorated with dabs of sour cream and guacamole. It's a grand meal, the savory roast pork packing heaps of flavor. On the side you can have horchata, the cool sweet rice beverage that is so refreshing with spicy food, Jarritos-brand mandarin orange soda or, of course, beer.

The menu is frustratingly tempting for those of us just passing through town with time for a single meal. Beyond the big burrito, choices include tacos filled with a wide range of ingredients from spicy pork to tongue, cheek meat, tripe, fish, chicken, and goat. Other temptations: enchiladas, chile verde and chili Colorado, fajitas, and chimichangas. Seafood specialties include *camarones al Tequila* (shrimp with green salsa and tequila) and *pescado frito* (whole fried fish).

Cattlemen's Café

1309 S. Agnew Ave.   405-236-0416

Oklahoma City, OK   BLD | $$

A sign outside says "Cattlemen's Cafe," and yes, indeed, this is the café to which people who work in and around the Oklahoma stockyards come for breakfast, lunch, and supper. And yet, it is also a top-end steak house, serving some of the best cuts of beef you will find anywhere in the West.

Top-of-the-line on Cattlemen's menu is a sirloin steak as luxurious as anything served on the white-clothed tables of New York's steak row or in the premier beef houses of Chicago, Omaha, and Kansas City. It is a boneless crescent of meat that comes from the kitchen alone on a white crockery plate, surrounded only by a puddle of its translucent pan juice. It is charred on the outside, but not drastically so, and you can see by its glistening, pillowy form—higher in the center than around the rim—that this hefty slab has been seared over a hot flame. Cattlemen's provides each customer a wood-handled knife with a serrated blade. The blade eases through the meat's crust and down into its warm red center—medium-rare, exactly as requested. You don't really need the sharp edge—a butter knife would do the job—but it sure is mouthwatering to feel the keen steel glide through beef that, although tender, has real substance.

Two other specials worth knowing about are steak soup, which is fork-thick, crowded with vegetables and beef, and lamb fries. The latter are testicles that are sliced, breaded, and deep-fried. Gonads are a highly regarded delicacy in much of the West; when young livestock is castrated on the range, it is traditional for cowboys to fry their harvest as a treat at the end of the day. Cattlemen's lamb fries are served as an appetizer: a mound of them on a plate with a bowl of cocktail sauce for dipping and a half a lemon to squeeze on top. They are earthy tasting inside their golden crust, almost custardy with nut-sweet savor.

While you can spend $20 to $30 on a steak dinner, lunch can be one-third that price. We like the steak burger in particular. It is juicy and radiant with good beef flavor, served on a nice bun with lettuce, tomato, and pickles, and all the condiments on the side. While dinner patrons tend to be a dress-up group, the crowd at lunch is an amazing mix of rich ranchers in 100x beaver hats and fancy boots, huge blue-collar guys in overalls, and skinny blue-haired ladies out with their friends.

This place is a real taste of old Oklahoma City!

Clanton's

319 E. Illinois

Vinita, OK

918-256-9053

BLD | $

When Sweet Tater Clanton opened for business in 1927, most of the road out front was not yet paved, and legend has it that to attract customers Mr. Clanton used to walk out the front door and bang a pot and pan together when he spied someone about to drive past. Today Sweet Tater's great-granddaughter Melissa and her husband, Dennis Patrick, have a crowd of breakfasters so predictable that those who frequent the big "public table" toward the back of the dining room never look at menus and never place an order. When Lowell walks in the door, a waitress calls "Lowell!!" back to the kitchen and the cook starts preparing what Lowell eats. Same for Jim B., Freddy, and Glen.

Clanton's chicken-fried steak starts with what the Patricks call an "extra tenderized" cube steak they get from Tulsa. The beef patty is dipped in a mixture of egg and buttermilk, then dredged once in seasoned flour. "If you double-dip," Patrick says, referring to a common practice of repeating this process a second time, "you will get a steak that looks bigger. But it takes you farther away from the flavor of the beef." The steak is cooked on a flat griddle in vegetable oil until the blood starts rising up through the flour, then flipped and finished. The edge of a fork will sever it effortlessly into a bite-size triangle with beefy, crisp-crusted taste that is ineffably amplified when it's pushed through mashed potatoes and peppery cream gravy.

Sightseers who get off the interstate to explore the original roadbed of Route 66 often find their way to Clanton's, which is known for the tourist-friendly tradition of giving fifty-cent pieces as change. But the Patricks relish the fact that their place is a town café with standards set by local taste. Dennis says, "If our gravy is a little off, if the biscuits aren't as fluffy as usual, if there's too much salt in the dressing that goes with roast chicken, they will let us know!" He points out that one of the most popular dishes on the menu is calf fries—not exactly tourist fare—and that the pie crust recipe hasn't changed for decades. Melissa did share the ingredient that ensures the foundation underneath Clanton's chocolate cream, coconut cream, and banana cream pies is ineffably fragile and flaky—ice water, icy, icy ice water.

Classen Grill

5124 S. Classen Circle   405-842-0428

Oklahoma City, OK   BLD | $

Classen Grill has been our breakfast destination in Oklahoma City since the earliest editions of *Roadfood*. We love to start the day with a glass of fresh-squeezed orange juice and a plate of *migas*, the Mexican egg scramble that includes strips of tortilla, chunks of tomato, nuggets of sausage, and a mantle of melting shredded cheese. Chinook eggs are salmon patties topped with poached eggs and accompanied by a block of cheese grits. Taquitas are tortilla-wrapped packets of eggs, cheese, and vegetables. When we arrive with insatiable appetites, we go for "biscuits debris"—two big ones split open and mounded with gravy chockablock with ham and sausage chunks and cloaked with melted cheddar cheese.

On the side, it is possible to enjoy some serious potatoes—either home fries or the specialty known as Classen potatoes, which are mashed, seasoned with garlic, and rolled into little balls, then deep-fried until brittle gold on the outside. The result is a kind of prairie knish.

The place is an ultra-casual, one-room café with paintings of fruit and other gastronomical items posted on its pink stucco walls. During our Sunday breakfast, nearly half the customers sat at tables reading the morning paper while leisurely enjoying their meals.

Coney I-Lander

7462 E. Admiral Pl.   918-836-2336

Tulsa, OK   LD | $

In 1926, Christ Economou came to Tulsa from Texas, where he had run a few hot dog restaurants, and opened the city's first Coney I-Lander. There are now a handful of these cheap chili-dog restaurants in Tulsa and environs, all based on the formula of a small hot dog in a steamed bun topped with mustard, raw onions, and no-bean chili. Shredded cheese is a popular option, and some folks get theirs with a sprinkle of cayenne pepper.

The chili is vividly spiced but not combustible, and it is nothing like the stuff you would spoon up from a bowl as a meal. It is more a beef paste that is both hot (cayenne pepper) and sweet (cinnamon), eminently suited as a dressing for a snappy little weenie or as a topping for a plate of tamales. A Coney I-Lander Coney is a two- or three-bite affair. Three or four are a modest meal in the single-digit price range; big eaters think nothing of having a half-dozen for lunch. It's not uncommon to see a runner from a nearby business walk out with several dozen to take back for lunch with colleagues.

Ambience is drive-in, fast-food plain. Service is immediate. The menu is minimal. One dandy alternative to a Coney is the Southwest's beloved hot lunch, a Fritos pie.

Dink's Pit Bar-B-Que

2929 E. Frank Phillips Blvd.   918-335-0606
Bartlesville, OK   LD | $$

Dink's barbecue selection is broad. Hickory-cooked pig dinners (pork loin), ham, turkey, chicken, sausage, spareribs, brisket, and back ribs all are available, and while the menu advises that brisket is the specialty, we like pork better. The brisket can be a bit dry—not a horrible problem, considering that an application of Dink's red-orange sauce revives it and adds a welcome tangy punch. The spareribs were so good that we left only denuded bones on the plate, and the pig dinner is succulence squared.

Dinners include a choice of two side dishes from a roster that includes baked beans, pinto beans, green beans, coleslaw, curly-Q fries, baked potato, potato salad, and cottage cheese, plus bread, pickles, green onions, and sauce. The sauce is available regular or hot; we liked the latter so much that we dipped our toasted bun in the bowl, bite for bite.

A Bartlesville fixture since 1982, Dink's is a family-friendly, multi-room establishment, occupied the night we dined by a widely varied clientele of couples and families, a large group of festive square dancers, a table of local ambulance personnel, some guys in overalls, others in pressed slacks and button-down shirts. Décor is cowpoke-style, meaning mounted steer horns, pictures of hunters, cowboys, and Indians, and displays of the "Barbed Wire that Fenced the West."

Eischen's Bar

108 N. 2nd Ave.   405-263-9939
Okarche, OK   LD (closed Sun) | $$

Opened in 1896 and touted as the state's oldest bar, Eischen's is a Wild West bonanza a half-hour northwest of Oklahoma City. The brick-front bar is patronized by locals at lunch and is almost always crowded with pilgrims at suppertime, especially weekend nights, when it is not uncommon for strangers to share the big tables in the back dining room. Everybody comes for fried chicken of succulent meat and bacon-rich skin that is made to be eaten by hand (plates and silverware are nonexistent). The chicken comes in a pile with fried okra that is easy to pop in the mouth. The beverage of choice is cold beer from the tap. The only other thing on the menu is chili-cheese nachos, another no-utensil food.

Classic road-trip tunes blare from the jukebox and when you wait for a seat, you may be able to avail yourself of one of the two pool tables to pass the time.

Hamburger King

322 E. Main St.   405-878-0488
Shawnee, OK   LD (closed Sun) | $

There used to be a handful of Hamburger Kings in Oklahoma; now there is only one other, in Ada, and it is no longer owned by the same family. We love the look of this vintage lunchroom with its tall ceiling and long rows of tables, each equipped with a direct phone line to the open kitchen. The menu refers to this as the "electronic order system" and advises customers to lift the receiver and place their order with the operator. "And we will bring it to you."

The walls are decorated with pictures that show the history of Oklahoma in general and Hamburger King in particular, the showstopper being a blown-up photo of founder George Macsas flanked by King of Western Swing Bob Wills and movie star Jack Hoxie. Wills once wrote a song to celebrate his favorite eatery, its lyrics reading:

> When you're feelin' blue, and hungry too
> Here's a tip to make you sing.
> Pick up your hat, close your flat
> Go down to the Hamburger King.

When Macsas opened in 1927 he sold large hamburgers for a nickel apiece, extra-large for a dime. Today's prices are $3.05 for a regular burger ($3.70 for a basket with potato wedges) and $3.80 for a double, with cheese 20 cents extra. Baskets, which include potato wedges, add 60 cents to the price.

The burgers are beautiful. Right up front behind the counter and cash register, where the broad, medium-thick patties sizzle on the grill, you can watch each one assembled by a cook skillful enough to bun, dress, and garnish one faster than it takes to name its components. The result is a classic lunch-counter hamburger: not too thick, not thin, oily enough to leave a delicious beefy imprint on the bun bottom, crusty enough to provide textural contrast to the lettuce, tomato, and pickle on top.

While hamburgers are its raison d'être, this vintage lunchroom has a broad menu that also includes catfish dinners, Fritos pie, stew (served with saltines or hush puppies), chili, and "redtop stew," which is stew topped with chili.

Hank's Hamburgers

8933 East Admiral Pl.   918-832-1509
Tulsa, OK   LD | $

Hank's has been in business since 1949 and it is one of countless restaurants in Oklahoma where burgers rule. The menu also lists Fritos pie, corn dogs, onion rings, and French fries, and there are even made-here chocolate-covered peanut butter bonbons for dessert, but hamburgers are what matter.

You can get a single, a double, a triple, a Big Okie (four patties), or a Hank's Special, which is a single half-pound patty. Each normal patty is a quarter pound, and while the avoirdupois of a Hank's Special is awe-inspiring, nevertheless we prefer the multiple-patty configurations. The interleaved meat and cheese, especially on the one-pound Big Okie, provide a textural adventure that a large single patty cannot. Unless you say otherwise, each hamburger is dressed with mustard, pickle, grilled onion, raw onion, lettuce, and tomatoes.

Hank's is a tiny place with just a few booths around the counter, which is high enough that no seat affords a good view of Mr. Felts, chef and owner, orchestrating events at the griddle. We recommend standing up, or going to the walk-up to-go window at the front, because watching him create his burgers is a scene of beauty. As is the custom down in El Reno, onions are pressed hard onto the surface of each patty before it hits the hot surface so that as the burger cooks under a heavy iron, the onions caramelize and virtually become one with the hamburger itself. When the iron is lifted and the burger is flipped, Felts sprinkles on some of his secret seasoning, then cheese. If he is creating a double, triple, or quadruple, he applies the bun top on one patty, uses a spatula to lift it onto another, and so forth until the pile is ready to be placed onto the bottom half of the bun, which has been arrayed with all other condiments.

Even the largest creation is presented as a tidy package, but by the time you are halfway through, onions and tomatoes will be slithering out and patties will be slipping out of alignment, creating an extremely delicious mess.

Everything is cooked to order, and while the half-pound hamburger takes a full fifteen minutes to cook, even the quarter-pounders are not served lightning-quick. "Please allow us a few minutes to prepare your order for you because we don't cook ahead," the menu asks. "Please call early and tell us what time you would like your order. We will try our *best* to have it ready for you right on time and *fresh* off the grill." A sign above the counter advises, "We will call your name and bring your food to you as fast as possible . . . Hank's a lot."

Ike's Chili

5941 East Admiral Pl.   918-838-9410
Tulsa, OK   L | $

According to a 1936 article in the *Tulsa Daily World* reprinted on the back of Ike's menu, "When the original Ike Johnson established his first modest little 'parlor' down by the old Frisco depot twenty-five years ago, there was no lowlier food than chili. . . . It was openly sneered at by the Social Register and the hot dog was much higher up on the social scale." To this day, chili maintains a plebeian aura, and there's no better place to savor that aura, and a classic bowl of chili con carne, than Ike's. We thank Tulsan Jim Oakley for tipping us off to this excellent southwestern chili parlor.

Made from a recipe supposedly secured from a Hispanic Texas employee named Alex Garcia, Ike's chili is a dish of ground beef and a peppery jumble of spice. It comes plain in a bowl, with spaghetti noodles, or three-way, meaning with noodles and beans. Cheese, jalapeño peppers, and onions are extra-cost options, but even a three-way with everything will get you change from a five-dollar bill. Chili is also the star of Ike's Fritos pie and Coney dog. The latter is described on the menu as being built upon a "large Oscar Meyer."

Jiggs Smoke House

Route 2 Box 42 (exit 62 off I-40) 580-323-5641
Clinton, OK   L | $

Jiggs's beef jerky is tough as shoe leather. Ordinarily, that would not be an encomium we'd use for food we love, and if you are dentally challenged, Jiggs's jerky must be cut into matchstick-size pieces that won't hurt weak teeth. But if your jaw is strong and your tongue salivates for that mystic combination of beef and smoke, there are few eating experiences more emphatically satisfying than tearing off a plug from a foot-square sheet of Jiggs's dried meat and worrying it like a happy dog with a hunk of rawhide.

The place looks the way an Okie smokehouse should: a weather-beaten wood shack with creaky wood steps and a front porch where you can sit in the shade and chew your meat. Inside, two construction spools are used as tables opposite the butcher counter, and there are a few kitchenette tables in an adjoining cubicle where the paneled walls boast odes to such meat-eaters' heroes as John Wayne, Bob Wills, and Marty Robbins, along with countless business cards from travelers and local fans.

Unlike the formidable jerky, Jiggs's barbecue is tenderness incarnate and easy to eat. Ribs actually are available boneless—in a "pigsickle," which is rib meat, cheese, and barbecue sauce in a bun. Beef sandwiches are huge and delicious, and the notorious "kitchen sink" is nothing short of astonishing. It's a somewhat ridiculous combo of beef, sausage, and ham sandwiched between—are you ready?—a pair of sirloin steaks. A meal of which the late Dr. Atkins would have approved.

Johnnie's

301 S. Rock Island 405-262-4721
El Reno, OK   BLD | $

Ah, the onion-fried burger of El Reno, Oklahoma! A sphere of beef is slapped onto a hot griddle. Onto the beef goes a fistful of thinly sliced yellow onions—about the same volume as the beef. The grill man uses a spatula to flatten the onions and the meat together, creating a broad circular patty with an uneven edge; he presses down three or four times, slightly changing the angle of attack with each press, and pressing only one-half to two-thirds of the patty each time. The ribbons of onion get mashed deep into the top of the soft raw meat, which assumes a craggy surface because of the uneven, overlapping use of the spatula. Once the underside is cooked, the burger is flipped. The air around the grill clouds with the steam of sizzling onions. After another few minutes, the hamburger is scooped off the grill with all the darkened caramelized onions that have become part of it and it is put it on a bun, onion side up. Lettuce, tomato, mustard, and pickles are all optional if you like them, but no condiment is necessary to enhance this simple, savory creation.

Beyond four-star onion-fried burgers, Johnnie's is a good place to eat El Reno's own version of a Coney Island hot dog, topped with meaty chili and a strange, soupy slaw that local epicures hold dear. (Some customers get this slaw on their burger, too.)

We also like breakfast at Johnnie's, when the little place is packed with locals eating Arkansas sandwiches (that's a pair of pancakes layered with a pair of eggs) and three-dollar all-you-can-eat platters of biscuits and gravy. It was at breakfast one day that we decided we had to stick around El Reno for a midmorning pie break, for as we were finishing our coffee, in walked Everett Adams, Johnnie's baker, wedging his way through the thirty-seat restaurant toting a battered tray above his head on which were set the coconut meringue pies and Boston cream pies he had made that morning for the lunch crowd.

Kumback Lunch

625 Delaware   580-336-4646
Perry, OK   BLD | $

Kumback Lunch was founded in 1926 in a town created by the Cherokee Strip land run of 1893, when the U.S. government sold property to homesteaders who got there first. So says the very informative menu, which also notes that among the interesting moments in Kumback history is the night in the early 1930s when gangster Pretty Boy Floyd came in brandishing a gun—not to rob the place, but to demand that proprietor Eddie Parker cook him the biggest steak in the house. Mr. Parker is something of a legend in these parts, known for giving free steak dinners to soldiers returning home after World War II as well as to sluggers on the town's semi-pro baseball team every time one hit a home run.

Fascinating history and beautiful Art Deco façade aside, Kumback Lunch is a swell place to eat. And everyone in the town of Perry (and beyond) seems to know that fact, because when we walked in midmorning one weekday, the place was packed with happy eaters and coffee drinkers having late breakfast or early lunch.

We had some of both: a tall stack of brawny pancakes, a crisp-crusted chicken-fried steak, a swirly warm cinnamon roll, biscuits and sausage gravy, and a couple of pieces of lofty meringue pie—all home-made, all excellent. What a fine town café meal! Highlights of the breakfast menu include egg-stuffed burritos, stacks of pancakes with pecans or blueberries, and daily homemade cinnamon rolls. At lunch and dinner you can choose from among a dozen different hamburgers, barbecued ribs and brisket, and a selection of Mexican meals that includes a baked potato stuffed with seasoned beef, cheese, and salsa.

As we dined, we gazed with wonder at Kumback's walls, which are covered with pictures and memorabilia of "Perry Heroes," including local athletes, several governors of the state, and Oklahoma Highway Patrol officer Charlie Hanger, who captured Oklahoma City bomber Timothy McVeigh and brought him to the county jail in Perry.

The Meers Store

Hwy. 115   580-429-8051

Meers, OK   BLD | $

Tulsa World magazine once declared the hamburger at the Meers Store the best burger in Oklahoma, which is a bold pronouncement indeed. Border to border, Oklahoma is crazy for all kinds of interesting and unusual burgers, including the unique giants—seven full inches across!—known as Meersburgers.

A Meersburger is special not only for its size, but because it is made exclusively from Longhorn cattle that are locally raised. Longhorns are less fatty than usual beef stock and supposedly have less cholesterol than chicken, and yet the meat has a high-flavored succulence for which no excuses need be made. In addition to Meersburgers the Meers Store has a menu of steak, chicken-fried steak, prime rib, and barbecue, plus a salad bar, and, being the only place in town, it also serves breakfast: biscuits or pancakes with sausage, cured ham, or thick-sliced smoked bacon.

Meers itself is a sight. In the southwest corner of the state, it is a ghost town that sprung up in the wake of a gold strike in the 1890s, but is now populated by exactly six citizens—the Maranto family, who run the Meers Store. The Store is the only open business, located in what was once a mining-camp emporium. Its walls are blanketed with antiques, memorabilia, pictures of famous and not-so-famous customers, and business cards left behind by happy Meersburger and Meerscheeseburger eaters.

Murphy's Steak House

1625 W. Frank Phillips Blvd.   918-336-4789
Bartlesville, OK   LD | $

Murphy's calls itself a steak house, but to us it looks more like a diner: counter and stools, bare-tabled booths, and a staff of superquick waitresses. The menu does include a bevy of steaks in the double-digit price range—sirlons, filets mignon wrapped with bacon, T-bones, and rib eyes—and those that we've seen on other people's plates look good. Nevertheless, it's not for steak that we recommend a visit to this 1940s-era eatery just east of the Osage Indian reservation. It is for a hot hamburger.

If you picture in your head some sort of beef patty in some sort of bun, erase that image and consider this: pieces of toasted white bread spread out on a plate topped with a large hamburger that has been hacked into pieces, the burger topped with a mountain of French fries, and the French fries topped with a large spill of dark, beefy gravy as rich as Mexican mole. It's a magic combination, especially the way the crisp logs of fried potato soften in places where the gravy blankets them, imbibing a rich beefy savor for which squiggles of onion (an optional component) are an ideal accent. Even folks who come for steak instead of chopped-up hamburger know to order a side dish of fried potatoes with gravy.

Variations on the theme include a hot cheeseburger, hot beef, hot steak, and hot ham. Extra gravy is available at thirty-five cents per bowl.

The front of Murphy's menu is emblazoned with a motto that is one of our favorites: "Gravy Over All." When anyone orders a hot hamburger, the motto becomes a question. The waitress asks, "Gravy over all?" We can't imagine saying no.

Robert's

300 S. Bickford Ave.　　　　　　405-262-1262
El Reno, OK　　　　　　　　　　BL | $

Robert's is a museum-piece town café, El Reno's oldest hamburger shop, going back to 1926. Starting at six in the morning, its fourteen-stool counter is occupied by regulars who come for coffee and eggs and home fries or—even at dawn—a brace of onion-fried burgers. Proprietor Edward Graham, who started in the business by slicing onions as a kid, slaps a round of beef on the grill and cooks it with a fistful of onions until the onions become glistening, limp squiggles that only partially adhere to the meat and tend to fall from inside the bun as soon as the sandwich leaves its plate. The hamburger, infused with the sweet taste of onions, is juicy and rugged-textured. Some people add bacon and cheese, but we recommend this burger au naturel.

Robert's is a good place to sample El Reno's second passion (after onion-fried burgers), slaw-topped hot dogs, which are known here as Coney Islands. Mr. Graham makes a coarse, pickly slaw that seems to be an ideal complement for the chili sauce that tops the dog.

As for ambience at Robert's, there is none, other than pure, unadulterated American hash house. Décor is nothing more than a picture of the pro stock race car that Robert's cosponsored along with Don's Muffler Shop in 1995.

Rock Café

114 W. Main St.　　　　　　　918-968-3990
Stroud, OK　　　　　　　　　　BLD | $

The Rock Café opened in 1939 when the last stretches of the Oklahoma section of Route 66 were paved. While most of the historic road from Chicago to Los Angeles has vanished, as have the colorful tourist courts, service stations, and short-order diners that once made it a festival of highway kitsch, this solid little restaurant is a vision out of the past.

Just as the Rock Café's heavy sandstone walls have endured, so has its original grill, which cook and proprietor Dawn Welsh describes as having been "seasoned for eternity." She credits the old grill with the shattering-crisp crust that hugs her chicken-fried steak as well as with the moistness of the thick ribbon of beef inside. "The moment you put something in a deep-fryer [the typical way to make a bad chicken-fried steak], you can see the juice start coming out of it," she says, adding that her chicken-fried steak made with beef, delicious though it may be, isn't all that popular any more. She and her customers have found something better.

Dawn used to be married to a man from Switzerland whose mother made such good pork jagerschnitzel that when she bought the Rock Café thirteen years ago, she put it on the menu. "Locals love it," she says. "They like it so much that a while back some of them started asking me if I would make their chicken-fried steak from the jagerschnitzel pork." The resulting beef-free chicken-fried pork now outsells chicken-fried steak ten to one. Although it sounds similar to the tenderloins popular in the Midwest heartland, this one is thicker and spicier and fathomlessly juicy, sporting a complex bouquet of flavor from its tenure on the venerable grill.

Dawn tells us she has nightmares about losing the grill. When we stopped in for breakfast, she had just the night before dreamed that it cracked beyond repair. Running a spatula across the dark, timeworn surface to clear away crumbs, she worries aloud if a few more decades of scraping might eventually wear it out. She tells of the day a few years ago that a woman from New York came to visit and asked if she could watch Dawn make chicken-fried steaks. The woman observed, then offered to buy the grill so she could bring it back east with her. The offer was generous, big enough to buy a modern replacement, but Dawn refused what she considered a Faustian bargain. The soul of the Rock Café was not for sale.

Sid's

300 S. Choctaw Ave.	405-262-7757
El Reno, OK	LD | $

Sid's onion-fried burgers are mouthwatering, cooked so the onions mashed into the patty of meat are charred from their time on the grill, giving the sandwich a sweet and smoky zest. Non–burger eaters get two or three Coney Islands, which are bright red weenies topped with chili and a superfine slaw with a mustard punch. Milkshakes are so thick that they are served with a spoon as well as a straw.

Other than the exemplary burger-shop menu, Sid's is noteworthy for its interior décor. Because he is a history buff, proprietor Marty Hall has filled the place with photographs of life in and around El Reno going back more than a century. Using eleven gallons of clear epoxy to seal some 450 pictures onto the top of the counter and the tops of tables, he arranged his visual gallery in chronological order starting at the far left of the restaurant. Here are pictures of the Oklahoma land lotteries and cowboys on horseback, as well as nostalgic ephemera from the early days of car culture, when El Reno was a major stop along Route 66. No matter where you sit at Sid's, images of olden days in Oklahoma will surround you.

Van's Pig Stand

717 East Highland   405-273-8704

Shawnee, OK   LD | $$

It is said that the secret of any great barbecue is time—time the meat spends on the pit—but here is a case where greatness is also owed to the long time that Van's has had to perfect the menu, the side dishes, the whole operation. Opened in 1928 in Wewoka, Van's now has four locations in Oklahoma, including one in Norman, one in Moore, and another in Shawnee; this particular place on East Highland has been a Pig Stand since 1935 and is the oldest family-owned barbecue in Oklahoma. We love the rustic, wood-paneled eatery with its volumes of graffiti on the wooden booth backs (and a warning to customers not to inscribe any on the tabletops!). Each table is outfitted with a roll of paper towels and plenty of toothpicks—both essential for happy barbecue eating. And of course, the aroma in and around the old building is the irresistible perfume of sweet pork smoking.

We have not eaten our way through the menu, and some day we will try the smoked turkey breast, the hot links, the Polish sausage, the brisket, the chicken dinners available only on Sunday, and maybe even the double-meat hamburger. But for now, let us salute the two essential items made here: pork ribs that are muscular and yet velvet-tender, crusty with glaze, and packed with flavor, and the pig sandwich, which is vividly sauced hacked hunks of pork in a bun with Van's own zesty relish. These are two of the best barbecue dishes anywhere. Superb sides include Curlie Q Fries, which are a variegated tangle of honey-tone twigs, and a bacon-flavored, twice-baked potato invented by the current Van's grandma and listed as "Vanized" in the menu.

"The pie lady goofed," said the girl taking our order at Van's counter. "She put coconut meringue on the chocolate pie and regular meringue on the coconut pie." This heinous error—which, in fact, made the chocolate pie extra-good—was the worst thing that happened during an exemplary meal at one of the great barbecue outposts of the Southwest.

If you like barbecue, you need to eat at Van's.

White River Fish Market
1708 N. Sheridan Rd.   918-835-1910
Tulsa, OK   LD | $$

Surrounded by light industry and warehouses out by the airport, the White River Fish Market is not where anyone would expect to eat well. Outside, it looks like a hardware store in a strip mall; inside, there is no printed menu—just a posted list of items on the wall above the counter where customers stand in line to place orders. Meals come at fast-food speed to boomerang-pattern Formica tables, some of which are private, some communal; the brightly lit dining room sounds like a rowdy factory mess hall, occupied by blue collars and Oxford shirts, blacks and whites and Native Americans. For all its indecorous democracy, this unlikely outpost serves the most elegant fish in Tulsa, maybe the best in the state. We know, that's a funny assertion given that Oklahoma is the heart of the beef belt and has no reputation for seafood other than excellent catfish. But you'll have a hard time naming a place in Charleston or Mobile with as wide a variety of beautiful fish so perfectly prepared.

What's very wonderful is that you choose exactly what you will eat. At the order counter just inside the front door is a long glass case with trays of raw sea scallops from Boston, catfish live-hauled from Arkansas, rainbow trout from Idaho, red snapper, frog legs, colossal shrimp and popcorn shrimp, salmon steaks, tilapia, orange roughy, perch and whole Gulf Coast flounders. Select what you want and tell the server your preferred cooking method. If you want it fried, the piece or pieces you have chosen are immediately dipped into salted cracker meal; if it is to be broiled, your selection is put directly onto a broiling tray. The ready-to-cook order is then handed through a large pass-through portal straight to the kitchen. Meanwhile, you pay and find a seat. The servers will make note of where you've gone, and by the time you're comfortable and sipping sweet tea, the meal will be carried from the kitchen trailing wisps of savory smoke.

The dish at the top of our must-eat list is broiled flounder. It is one fish, weighing over a pound and wider than a large dinner plate. Its flesh is scored in a diamond pattern, making the display of several raw ones on ice in the glass case resemble a shimmering ocean jewel box. When broiled, the flesh firms up and contracts so it forms a pattern of bite-size diamonds of meat arrayed neatly atop the skeleton. The tail, hanging over the side of the large oval plate on which it is served, is blackened by flame and provides its own smoked scent; and each juicy nugget you lift—using the gentlest upward pressure of a fork slid underneath—has a delicate ocean sweetness that forbids fancying up.

Wilson's B-B-Q

1522 East Apache St. 918-425-9912

Tulsa, OK LD | $

A recording of Chicago blues emanated into the parking lot at Wilson's on East Apache, a Tulsa street that sports a handful of interesting barbecue parlors. Inside the door, the blues were louder, but another rhythm was even more compelling: the whack-thud-whack of a meat cleaver hacking hickory-cooked beef into shreds. "U Need No Teeth to Eat Our Beef" is one of Wilson's several mottos (others being "U Need a Bib to Eat Our Ribs" and "U Need No Fork to Eat Our Pork"), and sure enough, that hacked-up beef is outlandishly tender. Moist, velvet-soft shreds are interspersed with crusty strips from the outside of the brisket; the flavor is quintessentially beefy, well salted, and fatty. Wilson's sauce is tongue-stimulating hot with vintage savor that reminded us of fine old bourbon.

We have not sampled either the ribs or barbecued bologna (the latter an Oklahoma favorite), but we did get hot links with the beef and they are terrific: snapping-taut, dense, and peppery. Another house specialty is a huge smoke-cooked spud that is presented splayed open and lightly seasoned, available plain, with just butter and sour cream, or stuffed with your choice of brisket, cut-up hot links, or bologna.

J. B. Wilson, who opened the place in 1961, passed away in 2004, but it is now run by Amos Adetula, whom the menu describes as "a good friend to J.B. [carrying on] the same values and traditions." It is now a modern two-room eat-place with wood-paneled walls, table service, and a counter where people come for take-out orders. Décor includes signs that read, "Our cow is dead. We don't need no bull"; and "The bank and I have an agreement. They will not sell bar b que and I will not lend money or cash checks." Tulsa law enforcement officials who dine at Wilson's are entitled to a 10 percent discount for their public service.

Angelo's

2533 White Settlement
Fort Worth, TX

214-332-0357
LD | $

"You are in the Land of Brisket," proclaims the counterman when an out-of-towner arrives at the head of Angelo's line and innocently asks what type of meat is served on the beef plate. You can watch the brisket being cut from the order counter. As the knife severs the dark crust and glides into the meat's tender center, each slice wants to disintegrate. But slices hold together enough to make it intact onto a Styrofoam plate, where they are accompanied by beans, potato salad, coleslaw, a length of pickle, a thick slice of raw onion, a ramekin of sauce, and two pieces of the freshest, softest white bread in America. Tote your own meal to a table, and if you pay an extra twenty-five cents, you can stop at the bar along the way and fill a small cup with scorching hot peppers to garnish the meat.

Sliced brisket stars at Angelo's, but the hickory pit also yields pork ribs with meat that slides easily off the bone, as well as zesty hot link sausages, ham, and salami. In the relatively cooler months of October through March Angelo's posts a sign below its regular menu advertising chili. Strangely, a simple bowl of red is hard to find in modern Texas. The kind Angelo's serves is an unctuous soup/stew of ground beef and plenty of pepper, here served in a plastic bowl with plastic spoon and little bags of oyster crackers on the side. Most people get an order to accompany a rib or beef plate or a few sandwiches—along with a few of Angelo's huge, cold mugs of beer.

Avalon Drug

2417 Westheimer Rd.   713-527-8900
Houston, TX   BLD | $

One morning at the counter of Houston's Avalon Drug and Diner, as members of the ad hoc Breakfast Club start to swirl around on their stools, leaving behind tips alongside emptied coffee cups, we get into a conversation with Don Compton, a seven-day-a-week regular, who tells us that in his profession as jury consultant, this is the best possible place to be. "Here, people say what they really think," he explains. "If you're curious about what's on people's minds, sit at this counter a few days and there is nothing you will not know."

Although it is in the deluxe neighborhood of River Oaks and extravagantly manicured, big-haired ladies come to lunch, the Avalon is categorically plebeian. A single inconspicuous door near the kitchen leads from pharmacy to a dining area where the lunchtime din is like a party. Eating here is a happy event—for singles, couples, families, and businessmen who toss their ties over their shoulders to shelter them from burger-juice drippings.

The lunch counter dates back to 1938, and although this new location is in a modern strip of stores around the corner from the original, the inside looks ancient, especially the booths upholstered in out-of-date, white-piped green leather. While there is a full menu including the likes of smothered pork chops, chicken-fried steak, mustard greens, and candied yams (as well as the Dixie favorite, pimiento cheese sandwiches), the Avalon is known for consummate lunch-counter hamburgers. They are modest-size, just thick enough that a hint of pink remains in the center, and their crusty outsides glisten with oil from the griddle. The configuration is deluxe, meaning fully dressed with tomato, lettuce, pickle, onion, mustard, and mayonnaise. The bun has been butter-toasted crisp on the inside but is ineffably soft outside. Burgers are available with American cheese, of course, as well as with Swiss, and their possible companions include French fries, chili fries, chili cheese fries, wet fries (topped with brown or cream gravy), and onion rings.

Avalon is one of our favorite Houston breakfast spots, mostly because it serves elegant, small-tread waffles, all the better to hold countless pools of swirled-together syrup and melted butter. Not-to-be missed beverages include vibrant squeezed-to-order lemonade and handsome milkshakes served in the silvery mixing container.

Beans 'N' Things

1700 Amarillo Blvd. E   806-373-7383
Amarillo, TX   BLD | $

We came across Beans 'N' Things a few decades ago when it was run by Wiley Alexander, a marine whose no-nonsense personality dominated the barbecue parlor. Mr. Alexander is gone, but this Amarillo lunchroom is still a fine stop for plates of hickory-smoked brisket with sides of pinto beans and coleslaw. Two sauces are available—hot and mild; beer is the preferred beverage.

It's good barbecue, but a recent visit reminded us that Amarillo is also a significant Fritos pie place. Beans 'N' Things' version is a Southwest classic, heaped with cheese that melts into the meat, which softens the chips directly underneath.

Beans 'N' Things opens at 7:00 A.M., so if you're blasting along old Route 66 and need a quick breakfast, it's a good place to stop for egg-centered burritos.

Black's Barbecue

215 N. Main St.   512-398-2712
Lockhart, TX   LD | $

Most barbecue restaurants sell little more than meat, bread, and beans, but at Black's, you can stroll through the cafeteria line and choose hard-boiled eggs stuck on toothpicks, little garden salads in bowls, and fruit cobbler for dessert. You can even have the man behind the counter put your meat into a sandwich and your sandwich on a plate—a "deluxe" presentation unheard of in more traditional barbecues where meat is sold by the pound and accompanied by a stack of white bread or saltine crackers. Furthermore, Black's dining room actually has décor—another smoke-pit oddity—in the form of game trophies and pictures of the high-school football team on its knotty-pine walls.

All these luxuries, nice though they may be, have no bearing on the superiority of Black's pork ribs, the meat of which pulls from the bone in weighty strips, sausage rings that burst with flavor, and brisket slices bisected by an ethereal ribbon of translucent fat that leeches succulence into every smoky fiber of the meat. Black's has been one of Lockhart's great smokehouses since 1932, and if you want to know why Texas barbecue inspires rapture, here is a place that will make you understand.

Black's will ship ribs overnight to most places in the United States. Although the cost of sending them is nearly as much as the ribs themselves, this is a good emergency source to know about when the craving for great barbecue strikes.

Blanco Bowling Club Café

310 Fourth St. 830-833-4416
Blanco, TX BLD | $

The Blanco Bowling Club Café is a real bowling alley where the nine-pin league gathers at night. The rest of the day the alleys are curtained off, although customers in the back dining room do enjoy such décor as bowling trophies, racks of balls, and ball bags piled atop league members' lockers. Accommodations are basic: wood-grain Formica tables set with utensils wrapped in paper napkins. There is a short counter in the front room with a view of the pass-through to the kitchen and one big table where locals come and go for coffee, cinnamon buns, and glazed donuts all morning.

The lunchtime menu includes hamburgers and hot beef sandwiches and an array of tacos, chalupas, and enchiladas. Pies are spectacular, with meringue tops that rise three times as high as the delicious fillings. Coconut pie has an indescribably creamy flavor, accented by little bits of toasty coconut scattered across the top of the meringue. Fudge pie is dense, rich, and super-chocolaty. If you are a pie fancier, put this bowling alley on your must-eat list. Meringue pies get no better.

Blue Bonnet Café

211 Hwy. 281   830-693-2344
Marble Falls, TX   BLD | $

The Blue Bonnet Café menu has something for everyone, from salads and sandwiches to big beautiful hot plates of chicken-fried steak, pot roast, and rib-eye steaks accompanied by a choice of three vegetables from a long and inviting list. Our favorites are fragile-crusted fried okra, pork-rich pinto beans, and butter-sopped leaf spinach.

Lunch and supper begin with a basket of excellent rolls, including four-by-four-inch yeast rolls with a bakery sweetness that perfumes the whole table as soon as you tear one apart. With the rolls are coarse-grain corn-bread muffins. At breakfast, eggs are accompanied by hash-brown potatoes or grits and your choice of thin toast, biscuits, or double-thick Texas toast.

The only problem about eating breakfast at the Blue Bonnet Café is that the pies may not be ready to serve until after 11:00 A.M., and in this place it behooves diners to heed the sign posted on the wall that implores "Try Some Pie"! Eight or ten are available each day, plain or à la mode; and while we enjoy the apple pie and pecan pie, the one we'll come back for is peanut butter cream. Smooth and devilishly rich, topped with a thick ribbon of whipped cream, it is accompanied by a small paper cup full of chocolate sauce to either pour on or use as a dip for each forkful: an inspired condiment!

Bohannon's Brietzke Station

9015 Fm 775   830-914-3288
Seguin, TX   BLD | $

A while back Cheryl Speakman wrote to tell us about a place we had to visit on our next trip to Texas. "If you think you have already experienced pie bliss, you haven't yet experienced one of Mutsie's pies." What a great tip! Although the official address of the café is Seguin, in fact it is in New Berlin, a Guadalupe County mini-municipality so small it doesn't have its own zip code. To say Brietzke Station is an inconspicuous eatery hardly does justice to its humble looks. Driving past, you might think it was just a gas station, but a small sign on the wall outside says "Café."

Opened in 1977 by John and Mutsie Bohannon, it is a treasured town gathering place where citizens come for coffee and homemade biscuits every morning, and for meals of chicken and dumplings, steak and gravy, and fish specials every Wednesday and Friday night. Half the pleasure of eating here is getting to know Big John and Mutsie. Mutsie, who was recognized as New Berlin's Citizen of the Year in 2005, is known to regular patrons as the "town mom."

Her cream pies are modest but masterful. The one that made us swoon was chocolate: not spectacular to look at and not at all sinfully fudgy, but totally satisfying in an old-fashioned milk-chocolate way.

Bryce's Cafeteria

2021 Mall Dr. (Interstate 30, Exit 222) 903-792-1611
Texarkana, TX LD | $

There are few more appetizing preludes to a meal than waiting in line at Bryce's Cafeteria. Before you reach the food, you will snake through the "preview line," past arrays of pies, salads, a dozen entrees, a couple dozen side dishes, breads and biscuits, muffins, and beverages.

In addition to cheesey macaroni casserole and rice casseroles, there are more vegetables than most Yankees see in a year: purple-hulled peas, fried green tomatoes, red beans, turnip greens cooked with chunks of ham, buttered cauliflower, sauced broccoli, pickled beets, etc., etc. Main-course highlights include fried chicken that is stupendously crunchy and big slabs of sweet ham sliced to order. There also are roast beef and gravy, turkey with all the fixin's, and fried and broiled fish. Among the multitude of pies, we like Karo-coconut and chess pies. Excellent pie alternatives include hot fruit cobbler with a savory crust and traditional banana pudding made with meringue and vanilla wafers.

Bryce's has been a Texarkana landmark since it opened downtown in 1931. Now in modern quarters with easy access from the interstate, it remains a piece of living culinary history. They don't make restaurants like this any more. Among amenities are a smartly uniformed dining room staff (to help old folks and invalids with their trays, and to bus tables) and servers who address men as "sir" and ladies as "ma'am." For travelers in a big hurry, Bryce's even offers drive-through service.

Capt'n Benny's

8506 S. Main St.   713-666-5469
Houston, TX   LD | $$

First, the bad news: this literally ship-shaped little building is generally so crowded that unless you are an offensive lineman, you may have trouble getting from the door to a place inside where you can eat. Bankers and bus drivers crowd together sliding fat, glistening, just-opened oysters down the hatch and freshening their palates with cold beer. Longtime fans know also that Benny's fried catfish is the best in town—snowy-white, sweet, and moist with a positively elegant crust, and the boiled shrimp and spicy gumbo are not to be missed.

Note: There are a few other Benny's around town, but this is the flagship.

Cattlemen's Fort Worth Steak House

2458 N. Main St.   817-624-3945
Fort Worth, TX   LD | $$$

Full-body black-and-white portraits of monumental Herefords, Anguses, and Brahmans decorate the walls at Cattlemen's Fort Worth Steak House, located in the historic stockyards district since 1947. At the back of the main dining area, known as the Branding Room, raw steaks are displayed on a bed of ice in front of a charcoal fire where beef sputters on a grate. Before placing a dinner order, many customers stroll back toward the open broiler to admire the specimens on ice and compare and contrast rib eye and T-bone, demure filet mignon and ample porterhouse, K.C. sirloin strip, and pound-plus Texas strip.

Texas sirloin is the steak-lover's choice, a bulging block of aged, heavy beef with a charred crust and robust opulence that is a pleasure simply to slice, and sheer ecstasy to savor. Sweet dinner rolls make a handy utensil for sopping up juices that puddle onto the plate. Start with a plate of lamb fries—nuggets of quivery organ meat sheathed in fragile crust, get the zesty house dressing on your salad, plop a heap of sour cream into your baked potato, and accompany the big feed with frozen margaritas, longneck beers, or even a bottle of Texas's own Llano Escatado cabernet sauvignon. It's a one fine cowtown supper.

City Café

19 N. Main St.   512-281-3663
Elgin, TX   BLD | $

The City Café is an ancient building on a raised-sidewalk street with a big awning out front for shade. It has been remodeled in recent years, but its brick walls resonate with a century of history. First a drugstore, then a bakery and barber shop before it became a café in 1910, it used to be the place in town to which cowboys rode in from cattle-punching for a cool beer late in the day.

History aside, we treasure this place for its chicken-fried steak, one of the best in Texas. Gnarled and crusty, golden brown with a brittle crust and a lush ribbon of tender meat inside, it is a beautiful thing. It comes sided by chunky peppered mashed potatoes and sweet carrots, as well as a basket of moist corn-bread muffins.

The City Café menu goes beyond such country classics as chicken-fried steak and chicken 'n' dumplings to include modern salads, fajitas, hamburgers, and all-vegetable plates with a choice of four from a repertoire of at least a dozen. Our favorites, other than the sweet carrots and mashed potatoes, are black-eyed peas and fried okra.

City Market

633 E. Davis St.   830-875-9019
Luling, TX   LD | $

The dining area at the City Market in Luling is cool and comfortable with faux-granite tables and clean tile floors. To fetch the food, however, you must walk into hell. A swinging door leads into a back-room pit, a shadowy, cave-like chamber illuminated by the glow of burning logs in pits on the floor underneath the iron ovens. It is excruciatingly hot, but pit men, apparently at ease in their sweltering workplace, assemble meats on pink butcher paper with gracious dispatch. They take your money, then gather the edges of the paper together so it becomes a boat-like container you easily can carry back into the cool, pine-paneled dining room. City Market's specialties are circular rings of sausage with chewy skin and coarse-chopped all-beef filling as well as overwhelmingly succulent pork ribs.

Uncharacteristically (for Texas), the City Market also makes significant barbecue sauce—a spice-speckled, dark orange emulsion that is so coveted by customers that signs on the wall above every booth implore "Please Leave Sauce Bottles on Tables." One-serving Styrofoam sauce containers are available to go for forty cents apiece; if you need more, the management finds a clean empty jar, fills it, and charges you accordingly.

Clark's Outpost

101 Hwy. 377 (at Gene Autry Dr.)   940-437-2414
Tioga, TX   LD | $$

Clark's Outpost, a good hour north of Dallas, is a Lone Star legend patronized by local horse breeders, city folk hungry for a country meal, flamboyant high rollers who arrive by helicopter in the field across the road, and good-food pilgrims from all over the United States in search of Texas on a plate.

Its fame is built on brisket, slow cooked for days until it becomes beef and smoke laced together in exquisite harmony that words cannot convey. Rimmed with a crust of smoky black, each slice is so supple that the gentlest fork pressure separates a mouthful. The warm barbecue sauce, supplied on the side in Grolsch beer bottles, is dark, spicy, and provocatively sweet. Pork ribs are another treasure, rubbed with a seasoning mix and cooked until tender. Rib dinners arrive at the table severed into individual bones, each one lean and smoke-flavored, glistening with its own juice but also begging for some of that good sauce.

Country-style side dishes include crisp-fried okra, jalapeño-spiked black-eyed peas, and a marvelous oddity, French fried corn-on-the-cob. Lengths of corn, unbattered and unadorned, are dipped in hot oil about a minute or so, just long enough for the kernels to cook and begin to caramelize. The result is corn that is cooked and crunchy and astoundingly sweet. Each piece is served with blacksmith's nails stuck in its ends to serve as holders.

Despite success and renown, Clark's is pleasingly rustic. Located in a town that is little more than a farmland crossroads, it is a small agglomeration of joined-together wood buildings surrounded by a gravel parking lot and stacks of wood for the smoker, with the flags of Texas and the United States flying above.

Cooper's Pit Bar-B-Q

502 San Antonio St.   915-347-6897

Mason, TX   LD | $$

At the northern edge of the Hill Country in Mason County is a grand barbecue shrine, Cooper's, where the ritual is that you eyeball the meat on its grate, tell the pit man what you want, and he hoists it off. Once it is sliced and priced, you find a seat at one of a handful of tables inside the cinder-block dining room (or at a picnic table outside) and feast. The repertoire of meats is huge, including brisket, all-beef sausage, pork chops, pork tenderloin, and lamb ribs. The brisket is among the best in the state: moist, radiant with beefy flavor, and so tender that it literally falls to pieces when you lift it toward your mouth. There's a tangy sauce that is delicious, but we recommend a few good samples of this meat au naturel. Sided by coleslaw and jalapeño-spiked pinto beans, it is the foundation of an only-in-Texas feast.

(Although they were originally related and do business pretty much the same way, this Cooper's is now an entirely different operation from the one in Llano. The Llano one tends to be much more crowded at mealtime, and while some local connoisseurs consider this Mason store to be far superior, we've had great meals at both.)

Crosstown BBQ

211 Central Ave.   512-285-9308

Elgin, TX   LD | $$

Crosstown BBQ is a relative newcomer in the world of Texas smoked meats, located in Elgin across the street from where the venerable Southside Market was before it moved to the outskirts of town. It is a stark tin building with little decorative charm, outside or in, but the allure of pit smoke is a seductive perfume impossible to resist.

Service is cafeteria-style. Tell the man what sort of meat you want, and how much you want of it. He slices it, puts it on a plate, and sides it by white bread and, if desired, beans. The available choices are ribs, brisket, mutton, and sausage. They're all exemplary, and we would recommend the ribs, brisket, and sausage to anyone. Mutton has a sharp flavor and isn't as fall-apart tender as the beef, but if you are a serious barbecue person, you will find it immensely satisfying.

We took our place at the long communal table in the center of the room and dug into vast platters of meat, using the bread to mop juices, slaking our thirst with tall cups of iced tea. In the corner of the big dining room, a television was tuned to a show of celebrity gossip from Hollywood, but everyone was way too interested in what was on their plates to pay attention to such nonsense.

Dyer's Bar-B-Que

Wellington Sq.   806-358-7104
Amarillo, TX   LD | $$

Dyer's is a family-friendly barbecue that is especially convenient for travelers along Interstate 40. When we walked in on a Sunday at noontime, it seemed that every single person in the room was dressed in church clothes. Tables were occupied by large, multigenerational groups of happy Texans all plowing into big plates of ribs and brisket. Décor is Lone Star rustic, including bare wood tables, a brick floor, paintings on the walls of such regional icons as roadrunners, the Alamo, and a stagecoach. Catch ropes and branding irons also share wall space with a few neon beer signs.

A good choice for one-time visitors passing through is a combo plate that includes beef brisket, Polish sausage, and a rib. Strangely enough, this being Texas, the brisket was a disappointment: although tender, it was pretty dry. Sweet-and-sour barbecue sauce, presented warm in a Corona beer bottle, did a good job of rehydrating it, but it still did not attain succulence of really great Hill Country brisket. Sausage, on the other hand, was fine: a taut, full-flavored section that needed no sauce whatsoever. And the rib was delightful, its surface sticky with cooked-on sauce, its meat moist and succulent, pulling easily in long strips from the bone. All meals come with the house apricot sauce, which the waitress suggested I use to garnish the meat. It's a curious condiment—not necessarily an idea whose time has come.

Goode Co. Texas Bar-B-Q

5109 Kirby Dr.   713-522-2530
Houston, TX   LD | $$

Goode Co. isn't exactly a little-known name in the Houston food world. Driving south on Kirby from the city center, you pass Goode Co. Seafood and Good Co. Tacqueria, and there is another branch of Goode Co.

Bar-B-Q on Katy Freeway. The place on Kirby is a large eating barn (with a nice covered outdoor patio) surrounded by stacks of wood and the perfume of smoldering mesquite. Inside, there's always a line leading to the cafeteria-style counter, but the line moves fast, because nearly everyone knows exactly what he or she wants when they come here. Once you've eaten at Goode Co. Bar-B-Q, chances are good you will return for more.

Goode Co.'s fame is well deserved, especially for its brisket. This long-smoked meat is velvet-soft and radiant with essential beef flavor. It is so moist and delicious that sauce is superfluous, although Goode Co. does offer fairly spicy red stuff to pour on it if you wish. You can get this beef as part of a platter with superb, slightly sweet baked beans, potato salad, and jambalaya, or you can have it in a sandwich. While blah bread is de rigueur in most great barbecue parlors, Goode Co. offers a fantastic alternative: thick slices of fresh, soft jalapeño corn bread that makes a first-rate mitt for the smoky beef.

Other than brisket, the smoke-pit menu lists Czech sausage, pork sausage, lean pork ribs, ham, chicken, sweet water duck, spicy pork, turkey breast, and turkey sausage. The pecan pie served for dessert is legendary.

Mesquite, pecan, and oak wood are available by the bundle, in chunks or logs, for do-it-yourselfers to take home.

H&H Car Wash and Coffee Shop

701 E. Yandel Dr.   915-533-1144
El Paso, TX   BL | $

If you are hungry and your car is dusty from traveling Southwest roads, the place to go is the H&H Car Wash and Coffee Shop, where table seats in the little joint afford a view of your vehicle being scrubbed and dried. We prefer counter stools with a vista of chiles relleños getting battered and fried and huevos rancheros being topped with a curious buttery gravy flecked with onions and hot peppers. Artimisa, who has been a waitress here for years, frequently conjures up her own special salsa which capsicum addicts know to request. "It will hurt you," warns proprietor Kenny Haddad, who offers curious visitors a few spoonfuls in a saucer. It is flecked with seeds and pod membrane (the hottest parts) and glistens seductively. Artemisa, who is normally a stern sort of person, broke into a broad grin when she watched us wipe the last of it up with warm tortillas, then wipe the beads of perspiration from our brow with napkins.

Not everything posted on H&H wall menu is four-alarm. You can eat ordinary eggs for breakfast or a hamburger for lunch (the café closes at 3:00 P.M.). Burritos are available seven ways: stuffed with chile rellenos, egg and chorizo sausage, picadillo, red chile, green chile, *carne picada,* or beans. Specials include chicken mole, red and green enchiladas, and—always on Saturday—*menudo*, the tripe and hominy stew renowned for its power to cure a hangover.

Hospitality at the well-worn cook shop is enchanting. If you speak Spanish, so much the better: you will understand the nuances of the chatter. But if, like us, you are limited to English, you will still be part of the action. The day we first visited, many years ago, we were wearing ten-gallon hats, so we soon became known to one and all as the cowboys. "*Vaqueros*," called a waitress as we headed out the door, "*Vaya con dios*." With our car newly cleaned and the radio tuned to the rollicking Mexican polka rhythms of Tejano music, we vamoosed north along the Rio Grande.

Hill Country Cupboard

Hwy. 281	830-868-4625
Johnson City, TX	BLD | $

Like Diogenes searching for an honest man, we are forever on the lookout for the perfect chicken-fried steak. We've found many excellent ones (and too many mediocre ones); one of the finest anywhere is served at the Hill Country Cupboard. This big barn of a restaurant claims to serve the world's best. Two sizes are available: regular and large, the latter as big as its plate. Neither requires a knife; a fork will crack through a golden brown crust that is rich and well-spiced, a perfect complement to the tender beef inside. Alongside the slab of crusty protein comes a great glob of skin-on mashed potatoes; and of course, thick white gravy blankets the whole shebang.

Beyond chicken-fried steak, Hill Country Cupboard has a full menu of southwest eats: barbecued beef, sausage, turkey, and ribs, catfish fillets, and grilled chicken with jalapeño cheese sauce. There are even salads, available topped with hunks of chicken-fried steak or chicken-fried chicken!

The Cupboard is where locals eat. Two airy dining rooms are crowned with circulating fans, illumination provided by fluorescent tubes shaded by what appears to be burlap feed-sack material. Service is no-nonsense; checks are put down on the table along with the meal.

Hoover's Cooking

2002 Manor Rd.   512-479-5006
Austin, TX   LD | $$

Chef Hoover Alexander says, "I am an Austin native with deep Central Texas roots that run from Manchaca and Pilot Knob to little ol' Utley, Texas. All of the recipes we use here were inspired by both my mother Dorothy's good cooking and the styles and spices native throughout Texas itself. I grew up on home cooking—nicely seasoned vegetables, smoked foods, pan-fried dishes, and spicy foods with a nod toward Tex-Mex and Cajun. I also have never forgotten eating a lot of Mom's fresh baked rolls, corn bread, and desserts. . . . After you've had one of our freshly made meals and washed it down with a nice cool beverage, you'll understand why I like to call the restaurant my 'Smoke, Fire, and Ice House!' "

We knew we were in for a bigger-than-life treat as soon as our glass of lemonade arrived. In fact, it arrived not as a glass, but as a pitcher with a straw. We had to ask if a glass would be forthcoming; our waitress told us that the pitcher *is* the glass: a quart of lemonade to be drunk straight from the tankard. And it is good lemonade—sweet, fresh-squeezed, and refreshing.

The choice of meals is wide. Hoover's has its own smokehouse, perfuming the parking lot outside, from which come pork ribs, Elgin sausage, highly spiced Jamaican jerk chicken, and regular-spiced barbecue chicken. In addition to smoked fare, the menu lists chicken-fried steak, meat loaf, catfish, and an array of sandwiches that range from a meatless muffuletta (made with a portobello mushroom) to half-pound hamburgers. On the side of any meal, choose from a large selection of vegetables that includes chunky mashed potatoes, macaroni and cheese, black-eyed peas, sweet and hammy mustard greens, crisp-fried okra, and jalapeño-accented creamed spinach. The vegetables are so good, and served in such abundance, that Hoover's offers a three- or four-vegetable plate, with no meat at all.

Hut's Hamburgers

807 W. 6th St.   512-472-0693
Austin, TX   LD | $

Hut's is a burger joint with nineteen different varieties of hamburger listed on its menu (not to mention the options of buffalo meat, chicken breast, or veggie burgers), each one topped with a different constellation of condiments that range from hickory sauce (delicious!) to cheeses of all kinds to guacamole to chipotle mayonnaise. We are particularly fond of the Buddy Holly Burger with the works, the double-meat Dag burger, and the Hut's favorite with bacon, cheese, lettuce, and mayonnaise. The French fries are excellent and the onion rings have a peppery zest that makes them a joy to overeat. Beyond burgers, there are other sandwiches, a different blue-plate special every day (chicken-fried steak, meat loaf, catfish, etc.), and a beverage list that includes cherry Coke, pink lemonade, and a root beer float.

Decorated to the rafters with neon beer signs, team pennants, and clippings celebrating its long-standing fame—since 1939—it is a small place that is always overstuffed with people, with noise, and with a spirit of fun. You will likely wait for a seat in the small vestibule or on the sidewalk outside, but once seated, the food comes fast.

Kincaid's

    4901 Camp Bowie Blvd.   817-732-2881

    Fort Worth, TX   L | $

Kincaid's serves a half-pound hamburger, lean yet juicy, sandwiched between halves of a big warm bun that oozes a surfeit of onions, tomato slices, and shreds of lettuce. What an unholy mess it is, compounded by the fact that Kincaid's accommodations are—how shall we say it?—less than deluxe.

In fact, it is the ambience of Kincaid's that gives these hamburgers their extra pizzazz. Kincaid's is not quite a normal restaurant. It started as a grocery store and is still configured that way. The old grocery shelves were cut down to approximately chest high and surfaced so customers can find a convenient place to stand and scarf down lunch. Many years ago when we first discovered the place, we saw one old couple arrive with their own folding chairs, wait in line at the counter, get their burgers, find an unoccupied length of shelf space, tuck napkins into their collars, and dig in with gusto. They told us they eat lunch at Kincaid's at least three days every week. Since then, tables and chairs have been added so people can dine more normally, but somehow this place makes us want to dine the old-time way, standing up.

Kreuz Market

619 N. Colorado St. 512-398-2361
Lockhart, TX LD | $$

Kreuz (rhymes with bites) started as a downtown meat market over a century ago, and it was one of the places that defined Texas barbecue. A short while back, owing to a complicated family feud, it moved out of town to an immense roadside dining barn with all the charm of an airplane hangar.

But if it lacks the ambience of a good old Texas pit, there is absolutely no denying that its pit-cooked prime rib is among the most carnivorously satisfying foodstuffs on earth. Brisket, sausage, and ribs all are superb. Despite its modern facilities, Kreuz has maintained pit-cook tradition: a limited menu that is meat, bread, and condiments (plus ice cream cones at a separate counter), and tote-your-own service from a ferociously hot pit where meat is sliced to order and sold by the pound.

La Mexicana

1018 Fairview St. 713-521-0963
Houston, TX 77006 BLD | $

Sometimes we feel sorry for our friend Jim Rains. He's got a beautiful wife, a great job, and a bucolic home, but he's a Texan and he lives in Connecticut. Not that there's anything wrong with that, but Jim grew up eating excellent Mexican food whenever he wanted it. And in our neighborhood—and virtually the entire Northeast—it is a rarity. Well, Jim's loss was our gain, at least on a trip we took to Houston, where he highly recommended we stop into a restaurant called La Mexicana. "It's nothing fancy," he warned. "It's plain and it's cheap—and it's goo-ood." We had it in our crosshairs as soon as we arrived in the Lone Star State.

It used to be a corner grocery store and now offers sit-down meals in a festively decorated dining room and bar as well as take-out meals from a cafeteria line, and all sorts of interesting pastries from the in-house bakery. When you sit down for a lunch or dinner, a waiter (outfitted in white shirt and tie) brings a basket of thin, elegant tortilla chips, still warm, along with a mild red sauce and a hotter, lime-tinged green pepper sauce. The chips are large and somewhat fragile; if you eat your way through half the basket so that only smaller, broken half-chips remain, the old basket is whisked away and a new one of full-size, warm chips takes its place.

The menu is huge, including fajitas à la Mexicana, for which the beef is stewed rather than grilled, tacos, flautas, tamales, enchiladas, and chiles rellenos. We began with an order of chile con queso, which comes with a large bowl of jalapeño slices to heat it up, then went on to an all-seafood meal: fish tacos made with succulent strips of grilled (not deep-fried) mahimahi, and shrimp in a chipotle chile sauce. The tacos were light, refreshing, and hot (we asked for them that way), the fish, cabbage, tomato, and cilantro laced with little nuggets of tongue-searing pepper. They were accompanied by Mexican rice and a bowl of creamy-smooth, blue-black refritos.

For dessert, we indulged in chocolate cake topped with flan and fudge-coated coconut macaroons. And for the road, we took a bag of heart-shaped cinnamon-sugar cookies.

La Mexicana's breakfast starts at 7:00 A.M. and the choices include all sorts of huevos rancheros, eggs scrambled with chorizo (Mexican sausage), *migas* (a sort of tortilla omelet), and, on Saturday and Sunday only, *menudo*, which is a bowl of stewed honeycomb tripe. *Menudo* has long been considered a sure cure for hangovers.

Little Diner

7209 7th St.   915-877-2176
Canutillo, TX   LD | $

Lourdes Pearson's Little Diner, also known as the Canutillo Tortilla Factory, is far off I-10 in an obscure residential neighborhood north of El Paso, and yet her crisp-skinned gorditas (stuffed cornmeal pockets) are worth getting lost to find. The normal filling is ground meat, but the great one is chili con carne. Tender shreds of beef become an ideal medium for the brilliant red chili that surrounds them with a walloping flavor of concentrated sunshine. You can also get the chili con carne in a bowl—one of the few classic "bowls of red" still to be found in all of Texas. Its flavor is huge, and you wouldn't think of adding beans or rice to this perfect duet. Of course, you do want to tear off pieces from Lourdes's wheaty flour tortillas to mop the last of the red chili from the bottom of the bowl.

We love everything about this friendly diner, where you step up to the counter and place your order before sitting down. The tortilla chips that start each meal have a rich, earthy character and are not at all salty—all the better to taste the essence-of-red-chile salsa served with them. Flautas are crunchy little fried tortilla tubes (like flutes, which is what the name means) packed with moist shreds of chicken or succulent pot roast. The last time we visited the green chili was even hotter than the red (this varies with the harvest); the Little Diner adds potatoes and onions to the basic meat-and-chile formula.

The broad Tex-Mex menu includes burritos, enchiladas, tapatias, and tacos. Tamales—red chile pork, green chile cheese, green chile chicken, and green chile chicken with cheese—are generally made once a week, but Lourdes told us that in December, they are a menu item every day.

Lock Drugs
1003 Main St.   512-321-2422
Bastrop, TX $

Texas food fans know Route 183 as an essential detour off I-10 between San Antonio and Houston into the town of Lockhart, which is to Lone Star barbecue what Milwaukee is to Dairy State butter burgers: source of the best. Of Lockhart's world-class smoke pits, which include Kreuz Market, Smitty's, and Black's, only Black's offers meaningful dessert (hot cobbler), so we recommend travelers save their sweet tooth for a half-hour's drive northeast to Bastrop, where you will find Lock Drugs.

In this 1905-vintage drugstore that still displays its remedies in exquisite carved wood fixtures, the marble counter up front is strictly for soda fountain fare; there are no sandwiches or hot food. The menu warns that "malts and shakes cannot be made with ice cream that has nuts, as it will break our machine," but that's fine with us, because we're ordering a magnificent black-and-white soda (topped with crunchy fresh chopped peanuts) and an item we've seen nowhere else, a frosted Coke. The latter is built just like a milkshake with an ice cream of your choice (smooth ice cream, please!) and flavored syrup, but it is blended with Coca-Cola instead of milk. The result isn't as thick as a regular shake, but it is rich and effervescent and candyland sweet—essence of soda fountain.

Louie Mueller Barbecue

206 W. 2nd St.　　　　　　　512-352-6206
Taylor, TX　　　　　　　　　LD | $$

Louie Mueller's has a modern dining room that does not have the smoky patina of the old, brick-walled restaurant, but no matter where you eat in this august barbecue, the flavor is historic. Here is a restaurant where beef brisket (as well as sausage, ribs, and mutton) is cooked and served the way Texas pitmasters have been doing it for decades. Step up to the counter behind which you have a view of the old smoke pits. Order your meat by the pound or plate. Carry it yourself to a table.

Louie Mueller's brisket is a thing of beauty. It is sliced relatively thick, salt-and-pepper crusted, each individual slice halved by the ribbon of fat that runs through a brisket, separating the leaner, denser meat below from the more luscious stuff on top. It is served with a cup of sauce reminiscent of au jus, and there is some hotter sauce set out on the table, but forget sauce, forget side dishes. Other than great hot sausages, everything but the brisket is inconsequential.

Note: Another Louie Mueller's has opened on Manor Road in Austin. Although operated by a member of the same family, it is not officially affiliated with the original location. This is a point the folks in Taylor are quick to point out; the explanation has something to do with the sort of family feud that seems to be part and parcel of Texas barbecue culture.

Monument Café

1953 S. Austin Ave.　　　　　512-930-9586
Georgetown, TX　　　　　　　BLD | $$

Three meals a day are served at the Monument Café, and we recently enjoyed a swell chicken-fried Kobe steak for a mere $11 and a whole fried catfish ($14), but it is breakfast we like best. The kitchen's *migas* are exemplary: eggs scrambled with cheese, diced tomatoes, and small ribbons of tortilla that variously soften and turn crisp depending on where they are in the pan, giving the dish an earthy corn flavor. On the side comes a nice red salsa to heat it up, if desired, along with grits or hash browns and a soft flour tortilla that is good for mopping and pushing food around on the plate. Pancakes and waffles are lovely, as are the big squarish biscuits; the pastry that makes us swoon is sour cream coffee cake, its top blanketed with sugar and frosting, its inside layered with local pecans.

"Our pies, cakes, and cookies are made here fresh every day," the menu notes. "We use only the best ingredients, including real butter, yard eggs, and real whipping cream." Of this boast, you will have no doubt if you order a piece of cream pie. Here is some of the best pie in Texas, some of the best anywhere! Chocolate pie with a toasted pecan crust is inspired and devilishly chocolaty. Coconut cream pie is equally amazing, but at the opposite end of the pleasure spectrum: angelically light, silky, fresh, and layered on a flaky gold crust.

Oh, one more thing: lemonade, limeade, and orange juice are fresh. You can watch the fruits squeezed if you sit at the counter, which is also a great place to view beautiful plates of food as they are sent out the pass-through window from the kitchen.

OST

305 Main St.	830-796-3836
Bandera, TX	BLD	$$

Even die-hard Texans have to agree that the majority of chicken-fried steaks served in restaurants are tough, spongy, and tasteless and have given the dish a bad reputation. But anyone who is a chicken-fried-steak skeptic only needs to come to Texas Hill Country to realize there is another way. Dine at OST (Old Spanish Trail) and you will understand just how wonderful a well-made chicken-fried steak can be. It is the platonic ideal of the dish, a tantalizing balance of crunch and tenderness with gravy that is cream-soft but pepper-sharp.

OST has been Bandera's town café since 1921, and its cypress bar stools and roomy booths made of western saddles make it an especially appealing destination for hungry travelers in search of cowboy culture. One whole wall is devoted to images of John Wayne; its spur collection includes rowels dating back to frontier days; and the buffet is set out under a downsized covered wagon. The buckaroo trappings make a lot of sense in Bandera, which is surrounded by dude ranches and has proclaimed itself "The Cowboy Capital of the World."

Otto's Barbecue

5502 Memorial Dr.	713-864-2573
Houston, TX	BLD | $

There are two good reasons to come to Otto's: the hamburger and the brisket. Each is served in its own half of this bifurcated restaurant that has two separate entrances and two entirely different dining areas. Up front on Memorial Drive at Otto's burger bar, the patties are blue-plate delights: grilled thin and well, served on spongy, lightly toasted store-bought buns, with potato chips the only possible accompaniment. They are not gourmet burgers, that's for certain, but in their less-is-more way, they are perfect.

There is no doubt about what's special at the back entrance of Otto's: you smell smoke and meat long before you even get to the door. Inside, the dining room seems itself to have been well-aged in smoke, its pine-paneled walls now a gallery of encomia from the press and from the restaurant's greatest fan, George H. W. Bush, for whom Otto's barbecue was heaven on a plate. In fact the most expensive dish in the house, at $9.49, is the Bush Plate, a medley of sliced brisket, ribs, and hot links with potato salad and beans. It's the brisket we like best for its soft, subtle flavor and a beef character that could almost be described as dainty. Barbecue, of course, is mostly thought of as crude food; indeed the ribs here are big hefty bats, the hot links virtually vibrate with spice, and the condiment bar is replete with hot, hot sauce and jalapeño pepper chips. And yet this tender brisket, its edge rimmed with blackened crust, its pale, roseate center heavy with beef juices, is shockingly mild. To bring it to the peak of perfection there is a tangy, rust-colored sauce to apply yourself.

Otto's breakfast menu, available every day from 7:00 to 10:30 A.M., includes buttermilk pancakes, French toast, a taco fiesta (tortillas stuffed with eggs and your choice of omelet ingredients), and biscuits with sausage gravy.

Paris Coffee Shop

700 W. Magnolia Ave.	817-335-2041
Fort Worth, TX	BL | $

The day starts early in cattle country, so it should be no surprise that Fort Worth has always been a good breakfast town. By 7:00 A.M., the Paris

Coffee Shop on the south side is bustling, and many mornings you will have to wait for a table (seldom for too long, though). An airy, wood-paneled room with a counter, booths, and tables, Paris smells delicious in the morning, its air fragrant with the smell of sausages, bacon, pork chops, and corned beef hash, as well as tangy biscuits smothered with gravy. Beyond biscuits, breadstuffs include soft, glazed cinnamon rolls and a choice of eight-grain, sourdough, or sun-dried-tomato toast.

The Paris Coffee Shop is also a legendary lunchroom (since 1926), known for meat loaf, fried chicken, and chicken-fried steak with mashed potatoes and gravy as well as one of the best bowls of chili in the Metroplex. The café's signature dish is an "Arkansas Traveler": hot roast beef on corn bread smothered with gravy. Such Lone Star comfort fare is accompanied by your choice from a wide variety of southern-style vegetables such as turnips and/or turnip greens, pole beans, and butter beans. And every meal *must* be followed by a piece of Paris pie. One morning, when we spotted a single piece of custard pie we wanted behind the counter and ordered it for breakfast, the waitress warned, "It's not today's." (Today's pies were still in the oven.) But then she thought a while and agreed with our choice, declaring, "Hey, yesterday's egg custard pie is better than no pie at all!"

Ranchman's Café (aka Ponder Steakhouse)

110 W. Bailey St.   940-479-2221
Ponder, TX   D (reservations advised) | $$

In a sleepy encampment by the train tracks at the northern fringe of the Dallas/Fort Worth Metroplex, the Ponder Steakhouse (actually named Ranchman's Café) has been a destination meat house since 1948. Since that date, indoor bathrooms have been added, but the steaks are still hand-cut, and the ambience is Lone Star to the core.

There's a full menu that ranges from quail quarters and Rocky Mountain oyster hors d'oeuvres to fabulous made-from-scratch buttermilk pie, but it is big, butter-glistening steaks that motivate us for the drive. Porterhouse, T-bone, club, rib eye, and sirloin are sizzled on a hot griddle until they develop a wickedly tasty crust. Although tender, they are not the silver butter-knife cuts of expense-account dining rooms; they are steaks of substantial density that require a sharp knife and reward a good chew with plenty of flavor. French fries come on the side, but if you call an hour and a half ahead, they'll put a baked potato in the oven and have it ready when you arrive.

Royers' Round Top Café

On the Square   877-866-7437
Round Top, TX   LD | $$

Royers' is a vintage forty-seat café on the square in the small town of Round Top (population 81). Bud Royer describes his menu as "contemporary comfort food." In fact, no one category of cuisine begins to describe this kitchen's boundlessly creative bent. Some of the choice things to eat are grilled pork tenderloin topped with peach and pepper glaze, crabmeat-and-shrimp-stuffed jalapeño peppers, a huge BLT sandwich made with grilled shrimp, and a boneless quail stuffed with cilantro-flavored grilled shrimp. Entrees come with a choice of down-home vegetables that include black-eyed peas, mashed potatoes, and buttered corn—or one of Round Top's creamy pasta dishes. Among the available seafood meals are red snapper either grilled or "stacked," the latter being a fillet crowned with a mantle of crabmeat and shrimp.

If you know Royers' Round Top, then you know that we haven't even mentioned the single item that has made it a beacon for food pilgrims from miles away. The moment you walk into the café and look at the counter in back, you can see what the specialty of the house is: pies. Lined up on that back counter are a few dozen country-style beauties with ribbons of baked fruit oozing out over the edge of knobby crusts. Royers' café is a pie-lover's paradise, with a repertoire that goes from classic apple to butterscotch Toll House and coconut chess. We believe the pecan pie, made with giant halves of Texas-grown nuts, is one of the best pecan pies anywhere—a perfect balance of toasty nut flavor and syrupy sweetness. Royers' is so deeply into pies that the menu jokes, "We reserve the right to charge you for pie and Häagen-Dazs even if you don't order it! It is a matter of principle . . . You don't drive all this way and not eat pie!!!!!" If you are a small group of people (i.e., two or more), you can get a "pie sampler" for dessert, which is a choice of *four* kinds of pie with ice cream, for $16.95. And if you are not able to come to Round Top, the café is set up to mail-order pies anywhere in the United States.

Smitty's

6219 Airport Rd.
El Paso, TX

915-772-5876
LD | $

Smitty's is a kick-ass barbecue favored by soldiers stationed at Fort Bliss, and it makes an easy quick-stop for people on their way to or from the El Paso Airport. Take-out orders are a specialty, as is custom barbecue: "You bring it, we'll BBQ it!" The spacious dining room smells of smoke from the pit; décor is a combination of beer signs and Wild West imagery, and the background music is just right for knocking back longnecks and engaging in full-volume palaver with tablemates.

The meat selection is vast: regular or lean beef brisket, corned beef or lean corned beef, ham, turkey breast and turkey sausage, chicken, sliced pork and chopped pork, pork chops, and pork and beef ribs. Most of these items can be had on a lunch plate or larger dinner plate (with German fried potatoes, slaw, and beans), in a sandwich or stuffed into a burrito, or on the "high protein special" plate, which is multiple meats accompanied by a Styrofoam cup full of Smitty's opaque sweet sauce and a few slices of soft white bread.

Iced tea (unsweetened) is presented to each table in a large pitcher so you can pour your own refills as you dine.

Sonny Bryan's

2202 Inwood Rd.
Dallas, TX

214-744-1610
LD | $ (other locations around Dallas)

Sonny Bryan's signature sandwich is brisket bathed in hickory smoke until moist and flavorful and painfully tender. Piled high in a bun, it needs no condiment, but Bryan's sauce happens to be marvelous—tangy and complex, a great beef companion. Turkey, ham, pulled pork, pork ribs, and sausage are also on the menu, available in a sandwich or on a plate with a couple of side dishes, and each one is superb: French fries, onion rings, barbecue-sauced beans, potato salad, black-eyed peas, fried okra, mac 'n' cheese, coleslaw, and in-season corn on the cob. One plate can include three different meats, and you can add cheese to a sandwich. But if you are coming to Sonny Bryan's for the first time, please have brisket—chopped or sliced, it doesn't matter—and you will understand why Texans are passionate about barbecue.

The Bryan barbecue dynasty goes back to 1910, when Elijah Bryan, Sonny's grandfather, opened a smoke shack in Oak Cliff. The Sonny Bryan's on Inwood Road opened in 1958, and it still features awkward but irresistibly charming school-desk seating. Sonny Bryan himself has since passed on, but the family tradition of great barbecue continues at about a dozen Sonny Bryan restaurants all around the Metroplex.

Southside Market

1212 Hwy. 290   512-281-4650

Elgin, TX   LD | $

In the geography of American barbecue, no town name is more sacred than Elgin (with a hard G, as in "gut"), known for hot beef sausages (known as "hot guts") since the Southside Market opened in 1882. Elgin sausage is renowned throughout the west, and the old Market, a creaky, sawdust-floored store downtown, was a beacon for beef lovers through most of the twentieth century.

About ten years ago, the Southside Market moved from its original location to a huge, spanking clean, barn-size building on the outskirts of town. While the new place lacks the charm of a well-aged and charmingly dilapidated house of barbecue, it still has a working butcher shop on premises, and it still smokes sausage and beef brisket the old-fashioned way, in big iron pits over slow-smoldering post oak wood. Order your meat by the pound at the pit and carry it to a table.

The sausage is spectacular—vividly spiced, taut, and moist beyond description, but don't ignore the sliced beef; it too is luscious and flavorful, needing no companion other than a few slices of white bread just to mop up its juices.

Threadgill's

6416 N. Lamar Blvd.   512-451-5440

Austin, TX   LD | $

In the years we've been eating at Threadgill's, portions have gotten noticeably smaller. Now one full meal is big enough to feed only two or three people. Despite downsizing, this boisterous culinary giant of a restaurant remains a bonanza for endless appetites, particularly for those of us smitten with southern and/or Texas cooking.

The menu features chicken-fried everything (steak, pork chops, even chicken) as well as a long list of vegetables, from virtuous (okra with tomatoes) to wicked (garlic cheese grits). Many hungry customers come to Threadgill's to eat *only* vegetables, accompanied by big squares of warm corn bread. If you choose right, a meal of five vegetable selections is, in fact, every bit as satisfying as a few pounds of beef. Among the excellent choices from the regular list are the San Antonio squash casserole, turnip greens, and definitive crisp-fried okra.

As for entrees, we tend to pull out all stops and go for chicken-fried steak or an impossibly rich plate of fried chicken livers with cream gravy. Those of lighter appetite can choose a very handsome (albeit quite gigantic) Caesar salad piled with grilled chicken, and there are a couple of unfried fish items. Bottom line: this is not a great place for meager appetites.

Aside from big, good food, Threadgill's is worth visiting for its history (the Austin music scene started here; Janis Joplin used to be a waitress) and its Texas-to-the-max ambience. Although the original beer joint/gas station that Kenneth Threadgill opened in 1933 burned down twice and virtually none of it remains, the restaurant today has the feel of a genuine antique: creaky wood floors, wood-slat ceilings, and a devil-may-care floor plan that gives the impression that the sprawling space just kept growing through the years. The main decorative motif is beer signs.

Tom and Bingo's

3006 34th St.   806-799-1514
Lubbock, TX   L | $

A wood-slat shack surrounded by a parking lot, Tom and Bingo's serves heaps of tender, moist beef brisket in a bun. That's the menu. Plus chips. And, of course pickles and onions and relish, if you'd like. Sauce is available, and it's good, but hardly necessary to enhance the taste of this succulent meat. Seating is spare, along benches that line the walls.

Whole briskets are available if you order them in advance, and Meg Butler, who tipped us off to this place, reported that she and her husband shared four sandwiches at Tom and Bingo's. They were so enthusiastic that they bought one to carry home. "Security screeners at the airport didn't blink," she said.

Vernon's Kuntry Katfish

5901 W. Davis St. 409-760-3386

Conroe, TX LD | $

Hugely popular—you will wait for a table any weekday at lunch—Vernon's Kuntry Katfish serves not only Mississippi-raised catfish, but also a passel of country-style vegetables every day. Mustard greens or turnip greens, white northern beans, field peas, fried okra, mashed potatoes, and cheese-enriched broccoli are some of the selections, and crunchy, dark-cooked hush puppies, studded with bits of onion and jalapeño pepper, are accompanied by bowls of pickled green tomatoes.

If catfish is not your dish, try the chicken-fried steak. It's a Texas benchmark, gilded with pepper gravy and served with biscuits or cornbread squares on the side.

Dessert is significant: fruit cobbler, banana pudding, or an item known as "good pie," which is a uniquely American pastry edifice of pineapple chunks, bananas, cream cheese, nuts, and chocolate syrup.

Weikel's Store and Bakery

2247 W. State Hwy. 71 979-968-9413

La Grange, TX BL | $

A Danish-like pastry with Czech lineage, the *kolache* has become a tasty symbol of the Eastern European roots that have helped make this part of Texas such a culinary adventureland. One of the least-likely places to find superior *kolaches* is Weikel's Store and Bakery, a convenience store attached to a gas station by the side of the highway. While it might at first look like any other quick-shop highway mart, bakery cases toward the back tell a different story. Here are handsome cakes, rolls, and cookies, plus several varieties of *kolache* from a house repertoire of about a dozen. Prune, cream cheese, apricot, and poppy seed are plentifully crumbed coffee companions.

You know Weikel's is serious about its kolaches when you consider the house motto: "We Got'cha *Kolache*." In addition to its pastry treasures, one other house specialty worth sampling is the house-made pig-in-a-blanket. It is a taut-skinned, rugged-textured kielbasa sausage fully encased in a tube of tender-crumb bread that is finer than any hot dog bun we've ever eaten.

Williams' Smoke House

5903 Wheatley St.   713-680-8409

Houston, TX   LD Tues-Sat | $

If you need ribs in Houston, take a drive fifteen minutes north of downtown into the area known as Acres Homes, a tumbledown rural neighborhood that seems a hundred miles from the city. Here you'll find a cabin by the side of the road that Willie and Hattie Williams opened back in the 1980s. Since then it has become many Houstonians' favorite barbecue. It's a shipshape little place with an order window by the door and a cluster of well-varnished tables in the wood-paneled dining room. A lot of business is takeout, but there's a special pleasure eating here, listening to the fall of the cleaver in the kitchen as chef chops meat, and inhaling the smell of the smoke that makes this food so good.

The ribs in particular are marvelous. They are served severed into individual bats, each one with a heavy lode of meat that still bears a crust from the dry rub that is put on them before they bask for hours over the smoke of oak wood. They come glazed with a pretty-darn-hot sauce, but it's the pork itself that makes Williams' bones so good. This meat is supremely tender, except at the tips and edges, which reward a good chew, and it is packed with the sweet flavor that only smoked pork can deliver.

We also believe that the brisket is some of the best in town, and if you order hot links, you now have a choice of beef or pork. We picked the former and were rewarded with disks of zesty, muscular sausage that paired perfectly with Williams' sauce.

At the order window, we asked for sweet potato pie and pecan pie for dessert at the same time we ordered our meal. When the waitress brought everything out to our table in the dining room, the pies came in take-away Styrofoam containers. In fact, all food is presented on throwaway plates with disposable plastic utensils. But the waitress felt obliged to explain that she put the pies in take-out containers because most people who order a full meal and pie with it wind up lacking sufficient appetite to eat the pie here, and so take it home for later. That is what we did, and that night in the hotel room, with the scent of smoky barbecue still on our fingers, we enjoyed outstanding dessert.

Capitol Reef Inn and Café

360 West Main St.   435-425-3271

Torrey, UT   BLD | $$

At the west end of the town of Torrey in the wilds of southcentral Utah, the Capitol Reef Inn and Café is a rare oasis of good food and elevated cultural consciousness. It is not only a restaurant, it is a lovely (and inexpensive) motel with hand-hewn furniture in the rooms; it is a bookstore featuring practical and meditative volumes about the West; and it is a trading post with some intriguing Native-American jewelry and rugs.

The restaurant serves three meals a day and appears to be as informal as any western motel dining room, except for the fact that you are likely to hear the gurgle of an espresso machine in the background and Bach played to set the mood. The house motto is "Local, Natural, Healthy," and while it is entirely possible to sit down to a breakfast of bacon and eggs, you can also choose to have those eggs accompanied by smoked local trout, or you can have an omelet made with local cheeses, with fresh-squeezed juice to drink.

At lunch and dinner as well as breakfast, the Capitol Reef dining room is a blessing for traveling vegetarians. A few notable meatless menu items include spaghetti with marinara sauce (also available with meat), fettuccine primavera, and plates of steamed, stir-fried, or shish-kebabed vegetables. Beef, chicken, and seafood are always available for vegetable-frowners (that trout, broiled with rosemary, is what we recommend), and desserts include a hot-fudge sundae and/or apple pie.

Hires Big H

425 S. 700 East   801-364-4582
Salt Lake City, UT   LD | $

Ever since the success of nickel-a-glass root beer at A&W stands during Prohibition, "the temperance beverage" has been an axiomatic drive-in drink. At Hires Big H, with three curb-service outlets in Salt Lake City, Utah, it comes in five sizes, from "baby" to "large," and of course there are root beer floats, or you can sip a limeade or a marshmallow-chocolate malt.

The juicy quarter-pound Big H burger is available plain or topped with bacon, ham, pastrami, Roquefort cheese, grilled onions, or a trio of crunchy onion rings and it is brought to the car in a wax paper bag that makes a handy mitt. The bun is a not-too-sour sourdough with a floury top (as opposed to what the combative menu describes as "some preservative-enhanced, wilted crust studded with obnoxious seeds"), and French fries and onion rings are served with dipping sauce reminiscent of French dressing. Hires even accommodates beef-phobes with its Harvest H, a mock hamburger made of oats, barley, and vegetables, but garnished like the real thing with sauce, lettuce, tomato, and melted American cheese.

Hires Big H also has locations at 835 E. Fort Union Blvd. in Midvale and 2900 W. 4700 S. in West Valley.

Idle Isle

24 S. Main St.   435-734-2468
Brigham City, UT   BLD | $

The third-oldest restaurant in Utah (since 1921), Idle Isle is the sort of cordial town dining room once found on Main Streets everywhere. In the twenty-first century, its charm is a rarity. Although the confectionery that was once part of the business has separated and moved across the street and the café has expanded and modernized to a small degree, dining here is a sweet trip back in time.

You can have a lovely burger and a malt at the marble and onyx soda fountain; and there is a slightly more boisterous back room with oilcloth-covered tables where regulars congregate at noon, but the choice seats, at least for us travelers, are in polished wood booths up front, each outfitted with a little ramekin of Idle Isle apricot marmalade for spooning onto the fleecy rolls that come alongside dinner. Before taking your order, a waitress sets down a little card that says, "Your Server Is . . . " with her name written on it, then she guides you through a menu of blue-plate fundamentals, including divinely tender pot roast with lumpy mashed potatoes shaped like a volcano crater to hold gravy as well as such daily specials as Wednesday braised beef joints, Friday trout, and Saturday prime rib.

Serving sizes are temperate, so you will have room for Idleberry pie—a resonating purple blend of blue-, black-, and boysenberries—or baked custard pudding, which is simply the tenderest food imaginable. "I'm sorry," says our waitress, Cariann, when she places a jiggly bowl of it before us. "The pudding might still be a little warm. They just took it from the oven." An apology is hardly necessary: balmy, smooth, golden-sweet, this is food fit for the god of comfort.

Maddox Drive-In

1900 S. Hwy. 89	801-723-8845
Brigham City, UT	LD | $

The Maddox Drive-In, attached to the Maddox Steak House, serves lots of hamburgers, but specializes in another drive-in delight, the chicken basket: fried chicken and French fries piled into a woven plastic basket. The beverage of choice is known as "fresh lime," which tastes something like Sprite doctored with lime juice and extra sugar. The long, covered tramway where you park at Maddox is festooned with enthusiastic signs apparently meant to stimulate appetites: "We serve only grain-fed beef. . . . We invite you to visit our entire operation." What we remember best about this mid-century showpiece is the huge, spinning sign high above the restaurant, where futuristic letters boast of Maddox Fine Food.

The steak house next door boasts "Over 4,000 head of choice beef used annually." There used to be a feedlot right in back, allowing customers to look out the window at future steaks on the hoof as they dined. Today the cows are gone, but pound-plus T-bones remain the order of the day, accompanied by a basket of crunchy cornpones and glasses of pure drinking water drawn from Maddox's own well. Beef alternatives include skinless fried chicken, chicken-fried bison, and turkey steak.

Mom's Café

| 10 E. Main St. | 435-529-3921 |
| Salina, UT | BLD \| $ |

At the crossroads in the old cowboy town of Salina, Mom's Café isn't really all that motherly, but it's been a great Roadfood stop since long before we hit the road many years ago. In fact, this square brick edifice has been a gathering place for travelers and ranchers for more than seventy years now, and it bears the well-weathered look and seeming permanence of the rock mesas that surround the town.

Mom's offers a full menu, including excellent liver and onions at supper, but we like breakfast best, for that is when the scones are fresh and hot. The scone is a Utah specialty, and always on the menu in this true Utah café. It is similar to New Mexican sopaipillas and to the Indian fry breads served at roadside stands throughout the Southwest, but generally big enough and weighty enough to be a nice little meal all by itself.

As the sun rises, Mom's fills up with breakfasters for whom the close quarters are an invitation to socialize with one another. Our dining companions one morning included ranch hands with rodeo-trophy belt buckles, Paiute Indians wearing spectacular porcupine-quill hatbands, and a pair of German-speaking tourists with backpacks on their way to hike around Bryce Canyon. The waitress used hand gestures to explain to the foreigners the difference between "over easy" and "sunny-side-up"; the cowboys showed the newcomers how to dip their biscuits in the thick, white gravy; and a Native-American coffeehound demonstrated that a squeeze bottle of honey-butter on the table was put there so they could frost their scones.

The German couple bombarded with all the good advice looked a little confused. But finally they beamed with joy when their chicken-fried steak arrived. This was food they recognized!—the ranch kitchen cook's version of a wiener schnitzel—made perfectly at Mom's, the pounded-tender slab of meat encased in a luscious meltaway crust. At eight in the morning, the two well-fed travelers finally topped things off with wide slices of blueberry sour cream pie, then headed out the door for a day of hiking.

West Coast

California * Oregon * Washington

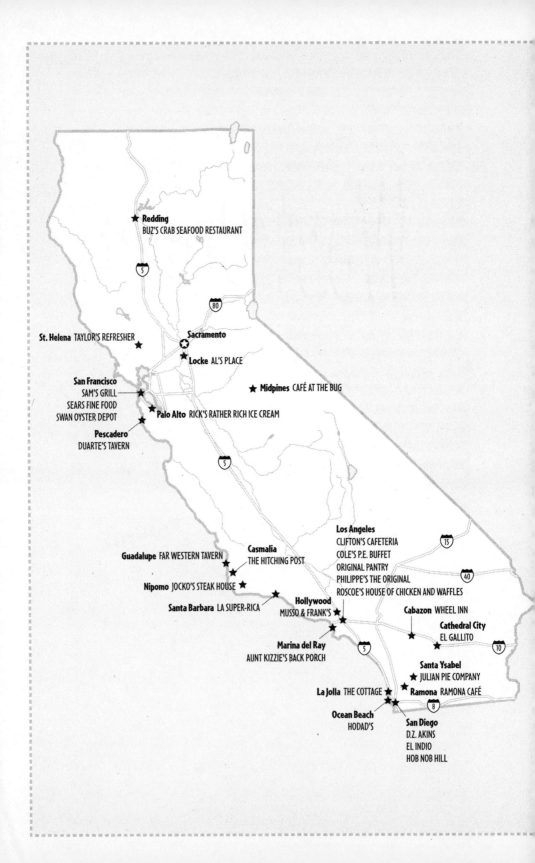

★ **Redding**
BUZ'S CRAB SEAFOOD RESTAURANT

St. Helena TAYLOR'S REFRESHER ★

★ **Sacramento**

★ **Locke** AL'S PLACE

San Francisco
SAM'S GRILL ★
SEARS FINE FOOD
SWAN OYSTER DEPOT
★ **Palo Alto** RICK'S RATHER RICH ICE CREAM

★ **Midpines** CAFÉ AT THE BUG

Pescadero
DUARTE'S TAVERN

Los Angeles
CLIFTON'S CAFETERIA
COLE'S P.E. BUFFET
ORIGINAL PANTRY
PHILIPPE'S THE ORIGINAL
ROSCOE'S HOUSE OF CHICKEN AND WAFFLES

Guadalupe FAR WESTERN TAVERN ★

Casmalia ★
THE HITCHING POST

Nipomo JOCKO'S STEAK HOUSE ★

★ **Hollywood**
MUSSO & FRANK'S ★

Cabazon WHEEL INN
★

Cathedral City
EL GALLITO
★

Santa Barbara LA SUPER-RICA ★

Marina del Ray
AUNT KIZZIE'S BACK PORCH

Santa Ysabel
★ JULIAN PIE COMPANY

La Jolla THE COTTAGE ★
★ **Ramona** RAMONA CAFÉ

Ocean Beach
HODAD'S

★ **San Diego**
D.Z. AKINS
EL INDIO
HOB NOB HILL

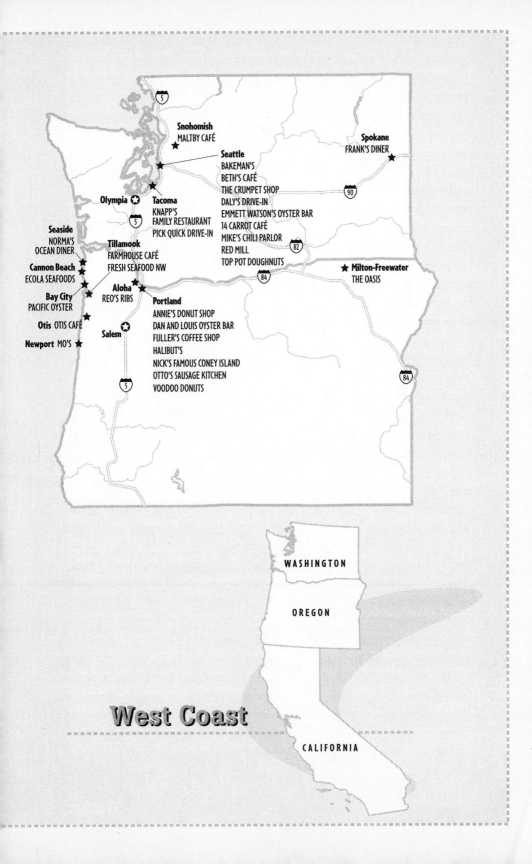

Snohomish
MALTBY CAFÉ

Spokane
FRANK'S DINER

Seattle
BAKEMAN'S
BETH'S CAFÉ
THE CRUMPET SHOP
DALY'S DRIVE-IN
EMMETT WATSON'S OYSTER BAR
14 CARROT CAFÉ
MIKE'S CHILI PARLOR
RED MILL
TOP POT DOUGHNUTS

Olympia

Tacoma
KNAPP'S
FAMILY RESTAURANT
PICK QUICK DRIVE-IN

Seaside
NORMA'S
OCEAN DINER

Tillamook
FARMHOUSE CAFÉ
FRESH SEAFOOD NW

Milton-Freewater
THE OASIS

Cannon Beach
ECOLA SEAFOODS

Bay City
PACIFIC OYSTER

Aloha
REO'S RIBS

Otis OTIS CAFÉ

Portland
ANNIE'S DONUT SHOP
DAN AND LOUIS OYSTER BAR
FULLER'S COFFEE SHOP
HALIBUT'S
NICK'S FAMOUS CONEY ISLAND
OTTO'S SAUSAGE KITCHEN
VOODOO DONUTS

Newport MO'S

Salem

WASHINGTON

OREGON

West Coast

CALIFORNIA

Al's Place

13936 Main St.   916-776-1800
Locke, CA   LD | $$

If you are traveling the Central Valley in search of tasty meals served with heaps of personality, locate Locke, a hidden-away little town in the Sacramento Delta. Originally built by and for Chungshan Chinese, the old levee community was once notorious for its gambling halls, houses of ill repute, and last—maybe least—of its pleasures, Cantonese food. Locke's weathered main street of wood-plank sidewalks and shuttered emporia with swayback second-story balconies remains a magical sight. In the middle of it is Al's Place.

Al's opened in 1934 when Al Adami, fresh out of prison as a convicted bootlegger, opened up the only non-Chinese restaurant in town. Al had no menu—he asked you how you liked your steak, which was the only thing to eat amid the slot machines and card tables in the dining room behind the front-room bar. Legend says that at some point in time, a hungry crop duster came in with jars of peanut butter and marmalade and asked Al for some toast to spread them on. Al liked the idea, and started putting peanut butter and marmalade on every table, a tradition that endures.

Today run by Stephen and Lorenzo Giannetti, Al's Place still feels illicit. You enter past the beer and shooter crowd who occupy a dimly lit bar hung with dusty game trophies and memorabilia, into a bright backroom dining area lined with worn laminate tables equipped with shared benches instead of chairs, seating anywhere from two to eight friends or strangers, depending on how crowded Al's is.

The menu remains simple, now including hamburgers, cheeseburgers, steaks, and one amazing steak sandwich. It is amazing because it is only barely a sandwich. In fact, what it is is a sandwich-size steak on a platter accompanied by a second plate of toasted pieces of sturdy Italian bread. Horseradish or a dish of minced garlic are available to spread on the meat. "Most people put the peanut butter or jelly on their toast," Stephen advises us when we ask him what to do with it. "But I've seen some spread peanut butter right across their steaks!"

By the way, Al's is known to regular customers as Al the Wop's. When we asked Mr. Giannetti if he hears any complaints about that, he answered flatly, "No," as if only some sort of dimwit pedant would worry about such a nonissue. He then continued: "I am Italian, and I don't mind. It's all in how it is said, anyway. WOP simply means 'without papers.' What's wrong with that?"

Aunt Kizzy's Back Porch

| 4325 Glencoe Ave. | 310-578-1005 |
| Marina del Rey, CA | LD | $$ |

The back porch is actually just inside the door at this unlikely shopping-center restaurant with a sign outside that boasts of "down-home cooking." Inside, the menu located underneath each glass tabletop offers such comfort-food classics as chicken and dumplings, meat loaf, and barbecued ribs served with collards, black-eyed peas, green beans, smothered cabbage, and/or mac and cheese. We are particularly fond of the crisp-fried catfish, sided by a pair of sweet-corn hush puppies. Lemonade is served in Mason jars.

Sweet potato pie is not to be missed—unless you prefer the rococo allure of pineapple coconut cake or the avoirdupois of bread pudding.

Ambience is a curious Los Angeles mix of neighborhood soul and photos of celebrities, especially of the Lakers from when they used to play in Inglewood.

Buz's Crab Seafood Restaurant

2159 East St.   530-243-2120
Redding, CA   LD | $$

Thanks to Roadfooders Karen Meyer and Paul Duggan for clueing us in to Buz's as one of the essential Roadfood experiences of northern California. They especially recommended cracked Dungeness crab (fresh from November through May), fish and chips, and charbroiled salmon, and they noted that Buz's kitchen is supplied by its own fishing boats out of Eureka on the coast. Calling itself "Redding's own Fisherman's Wharf," Buz's truly is a seafood bonanza, being not only a restaurant, but a fish market, a deli, a crab-feed caterer, and a mail-order source of cooked crab, smoked salmon, and sourdough bread.

In the restaurant, you'll find something on the menu for every kind of seafood fancier (and even charbroiled chicken and chicken nuggets for fishphobes), ranging from the glorious fisherman's stew known as cioppino to fish tacos and salmon burgers (the latter advertised as low fat and low cal). When Dungeness crab is coming in fresh from the cold Pacific, that's all we care to know about, but any other time of year, we will gladly plow into one of Buz's umpteen different kinds of fried seafood basket, featuring prawns, oysters, catfish, and calamari (or all possible combinations thereof). In addition, there are seafood wraps, salads, sandwiches, and burritos, and a long list of fish available charbroiled with barbecue sauce, teriyaki sauce, garlic sauce, or lemon butter.

To accompany meals, Buz's "almost famous" sourdough bread is baked in outdoor ovens throughout the day.

Café at the Bug

6979 Hwy. 140   209-966-6666
Midpines, CA 95345   BLD | $

If you are coming to Yosemite to hike, bike, swim, or otherwise savor the wilderness, but want to stay in a room or tent cabin for the evening, you won't do better than the Yosemite Bug Mountain Resort. And if you're looking for a nice place to eat other than around a campfire, the Café at the Bug is swell.

It's a three-meal-a-day place with outdoor patios and a glassed-in deck for scenic dining and a menu with choices that range from carnivorous to vegan. You can start the day with a giant buckwheat pancake (available vegan or not), muesli, or eggs or tofu egg substitutes. And while you are having breakfast you can have the kitchen prepare a boxed lunch for the trail. We relished our dinner of stuffed trout with rice and seasonal vegetables and a handsome sirloin steak with potatoes. We were especially fond of the chocolate cake served for dessert; while we cleaned the last of it from our plates, we listened to neighbors rave over their cheesecake.

Service is casual, semi-cafeteria-style. Order at the counter and pick your own table. It is customary for customers to bus their own tables at the end of a meal.

Clifton's Cafeteria

648 S. Broadway　　　　　　　213-627-1673

Los Angeles, CA　　　　　　　LD | $

Clifton's cafeteria is an amazing place to eat. Built to represent the Golden State's redwood forests, its interior décor includes granite cliffs and boulders, babbling brooks, walls that resemble tree trunks, and stunning (if faded) murals of forest scenes. The food line is immense, with choices that include fried chicken with buttermilk biscuits, oxtail stew, turkey and dressing, side dishes ranging from whipped or fried potatoes to "cranberry jewel gelatin," and cheerfully corny desserts such as fruit cocktail torte and strawberry pie. For those with fond memories of school lunch, Clifton's also offers grilled cheese sandwiches cooked crisp and pressed flat as a pancake.

We like Clifton's plenty, but its surroundings stink. When it opened in 1935, Broadway was a fashionable thoroughfare. Today the street can be an intimidating place to walk, especially at night. Once you get to Clifton's, though, you cannot help but love Los Angeles all over again, especially when you gaze down at the sidewalk below its marquee. Here, a magnificent tile mosaic in a sunburst pattern shows the many scenic wonders that once made southern California such an alluring place: the Rose Bowl, the Hollywood Bowl, the oil fields, the deserts, the missions, City Hall, the movie studios, and Catalina Island. To walk across this magic picture and enter the redwood forest dining room, then tuck into a tray of meat loaf, mashed potatoes, and gravy, with millionaire pie for dessert (mounded with whipped cream, crushed pineapple, and pecans), is to taste an optimistic city where the world seems honest and new at every meal.

Cole's P.E. Buffet

118 East 6th St.   213-622-4090
Los Angeles, CA   BLD | $

Cole's P.E. Buffet claims to have invented the French dip sandwich in 1908, ten years before Philippe's (p. 536). The story here is that a hungry man with sore gums was so impressed by the way Cole's chef Jack Garlinghouse carved a roast that he beseeched him to make a sandwich he could chew without pain. The compassionate Mr. Garlinghouse dunked a hard roll in natural gravy to soften it and filled the roll with tender flaps of beef. The soft and juicy sandwich required little in the way of dental might.

Cole's also claims to be the city's oldest restaurant, a boast that seems irrefutable when you descend a short flight of stairs into the commissary where wood-paneled walls are imbued with the savory aroma of countless steam-table meals. Decor includes panoramic photos of Miss California contests held long ago in the Santa Monica sun. The cash register at the end of the cafeteria line goes only as high as $9.99, and there is one table that always has a Reserved sign on it—for police officers who favor the robust food and neighborhood air of the vintage landmark. Tables in some of the cloistered back dining areas are made of oak salvaged from the sides of Pacific Electric Railway Red Cars, source of the "P.E." in Cole's full name: Cole's P.E. Buffet. When it opened, and until the Pacific Electric ended service in 1953, Cole's clientele was mostly commuters traveling what used to be the world's largest interurban rail line.

The French dip is particularly well-executed here, where carvers stab slabs of hot brisket from the steam box and hand-slice mounds of thick, juicy pieces, spearing each half of the sliced roll and holding it in a pan of dark gravy long enough to fully flavor the soft part of the chewy bread but leave the crust crisp. The moistened bread melds with the mellow beef inside, and the result is a delicious mess. Cole's is a great place for outmoded hot lunch other than carved meat on French rolls: oxtails, meat loaf, and turkey à la king with such sides as chili, mac 'n' cheese, and baked beans. The dessert menu features apple pie, cherry pie, and Jell-O.

The Cottage

7702 Fay Ave.   858-454-8409
La Jolla, CA   BL | $$

Here is the quintessential southern California restaurant: supremely casual with food that is always fresh and delicious. Located on a quiet corner in the village of La Jolla, it offers vividly flavored meals in either a sun-drenched dining room or a breezy outdoor patio.

Breakfast is especially wonderful. As you walk in the door, look right. There's the bakery case holding nut-topped cinnamon rolls, muffins, and buttermilk coffee cake with cinnamon and walnut crumb topping. The pastries are superb, but so are hot meals. In particular, we recommend Cottage Irish oatmeal, served with a full complement of brown sugar, sliced bananas, raisins, milk, and a dish of sensational sticky-crunchy carmelized walnuts. Also grand are meat loaf hash crisped with cottage-fried potatoes and topped with eggs, French toast stuffed with strawberry compote and mascarpone, and crab Benedict, which is like eggs Benedict, but heaped with pure rock crab instead of Canadian bacon. Cottage granola is extra-special—dark and toasty, a delightful chew.

Lunch is an opportunity to taste a high-tone version of San Diego's favorite fast food, the fish taco, here built around grilled mahimahi, dressed with cilantro-avocado sauce, and accompanied by bowls of creamy black beans and chunky papaya relish. The pork and beef chili has a true-southwest pepper zest, and the hamburger is a So-Cal classic, served with an abundance of Cheddar cheese, tomato, lettuce, onion, and mayo. The BLT, augmented with avocado, reigns supreme.

The restaurant is in a bungalow that was built early in the last century and served as a private home in the days La Jolla was a little-known community of sun-and-surf worshippers. It still exudes end-of-the-earth charm that makes this seaside community so appealing.

Duarte's Tavern

202 Stage Rd.   650-879-0464
Pescadero, CA   BLD | $

Duarte's is a 100-plus-year-old small-town tavern where locals come to eat three square meals a day at mismatched tables and chairs in a knotty-pine-paneled dining room. When it's crowded, as it usually is at mealtime, strangers share tables. Geezers hold court, babies squall, townsfolk trade gossip, and travelers are made to feel right at home.

Here is down-home dining, California-style: pork chops served with homemade apple sauce and chunky mashed potatoes; pot roast; beef stew; roast turkey with sage dressing. Seafood is something special, including big servings of Dungeness crab cioppino, calamari, sea scallops, and oysters baked in puddles of garlic butter. Even the house salad—a perfunctory gesture in so many restaurants—comes topped with beets, pickled beans, and tomatoes that come directly from Duarte's gardens.

The farmland around Pescadero is thick with the thistle-topped stalks of artichoke plants, and artichokes are a Duarte's specialty. You can get them simply steamed or elaborately stuffed (with fennel sausage), in utterly wonderful omelets at breakfast, or as the foundation of cream of artichoke soup, which several travelers have declared to us is simply the best soup in the world.

To conclude any meal at Duarte's, you want pie—blue-ribbon pie made from local olallie berries, rhubarb, apricots, or apples heaped into feather-light crusts that are all the more delicious for being homely rather than symmetrical.

D.Z. Akins

6930 Alvarado Rd.   619-265-0218
San Diego, CA   BLD | $$

As folks who frequently complain that urban delis aren't what they used to be, we were thrilled the moment we walked into D.Z. Akins. The air was perfumed with spiced beef and the bakery shelves up front held a spectacular array of ryes, pumpernickels, bagels, hard rolls, and challahs, plus countless macaroons and cookies, all baked right here. The sandwiches we got were fantastic: hot, fat-striated corned beef radiant with flavor, cut thick and piled between two slices of the best rye we've had in years: soft inside with a nice sour smack and a hard savory crust. Full-flavored roast beef was presented in a poppy-seed-spangled hard roll that was also impeccably fresh. And the kosher salami (Vienna brand, the choice deli's choice) packed a garlic wallop.

We liked our sandwiches so much that we returned to D.Z. Akins for breakfast and plowed into a platter of matzoh brei that was nearly as good as the brei Michael makes (and he makes the best), homemade blintzes, and a plate of bagels and lox. Nothing was short of excellent.

This full-service restaurant also features a soda fountain, the menu of which includes sundaes and sodas of all kinds, from a traditional banana split to one called Prenatal Silliness: chocolate ice cream and pickles, with your topping of choice!

El Gallito

68820 Grove St.   760-328-7794
Cathedral City, CA   LD | $

So popular that it is frequently wait-for-a-table crowded, El Gallito has been serving California-style Mexican food in the Coachella Valley since 1978. It has a broad menu of familiar dishes such as tacos, chiles relleños, enchiladas, and burritos. They're all quite good, in our experience, but we are especially fond of daily specials that include *carnitas* (shredded pork) every Thursday, chicken mole (Friday), and *menudo* (Saturday). The mole is smoky with a pepper zest, cosseting on-the-bone chicken that is ridiculously tender.

We also like El Gallito's bowls of chili. They are not fire-hot, and they are mighty tasty: either chili Colorado, which is bite-size pieces of beef in a peppery red sauce, or chili verde, which is beef cooked with green peppers, onions, and shreds of tomato. The El Gallito Especial is a half-and-half plate of both kinds of chili. It is also worth nothing that breakfast is available, but starting at 10:00 A.M., when the restaurant opens: huevos rancheros, shredded beef and scrambled eggs, and egg burritos with rice and beans.

El Gallito is an extraordinarily clean and tidy place, outfitted in classic Mexican-restaurant décor (serapes, sombreros, velvet paintings). It operates according to a lot of rules that are posted throughout the dining room and written in the menu. A sign above the cash register warns, "Cash only." A placard hanging over the dining room notes: "If you have reservations, you are at the wrong place." To discourage unsavory clientele, a sign in the entryway advises: "We are not a bar. Beer/wine is only served to those who dine with us." And on the menu, the management notes that daily specials are in limited supply, so customers who want them should come early; it is further noted that "It is impossible to debone the chicken entirely, so it is possible that you may find a bone in your chicken entree." Finally, be advised that there is a limit of three drinks per customer, and "persons who seem to have been drinking will not be served."

El Indio

3695 India St.   619-299-0333

San Diego, CA   BLD | $

A San Diego destination since 1940, El Indio is a quick-service, cafeteria-style taqueria adjacent to Interstate 5. Meals are served on Styrofoam plates with throwaway utensils. There are a few shared seats at a counter and some tables to the side of the order line, but many people choose to eat on the sunny, fenced-in patio across the street. Here, one is serenaded by vehicles passing on the raised highway.

The menu is classic Cal-Mex. An on-premises tortilla press turns out big, warm wheaty ones for burritos and chimichangas; there are freshly fried, hot corn tortillas and deliciously crunchy taquitos; and there are all sorts of combo plates topped with gobs of sour cream. One of the best things to eat is the San Diego specialty, a fish taco. El Indio's version is a hefty meal served in a foil wrapper along with a wedge of lime. When the foil is pulled back, you find a double layer of warm corn tortillas loosely wrapped around a log of crisp-fried cod with a golden crust. The fish is nestled on a bed of ruggedly shredded cabbage, a few tomato shreds, and a faintly peppery pink sauce. Give it a spritz or two from the wedge of lime provided—an ideal complement for the sweet meat of the white fish and its savory crust.

Above the windows where you order your food at El Indio are portraits of fierce Mayan gods, including the god of war, the gods of rain and wind, and the god of Mexican food, who according to this portrait goes by the name of El Indio. We are not up to date on our Mayan theology, but there is no doubt in our minds that El Indio is indeed the reigning deity of San Diego Mexican food.

Far Western Tavern

899 Guadalupe St.   805-343-2211

Guadalupe, CA   LD | $$

The Far Western Tavern is a place to eat barbecue, California cowboy–style. The dining room features a spectacular suite of hairy brown-and-white cowhide curtains and meals are served on cowboy-fantasy dishware festooned with little images of brands, spurs, and cows' heads. The wall across from the bar is one sweeping painted mural of ranch life; other displays include a portrait of Will Rogers, a poster that shows how to break a wild pony, an autographed 8 X 10 of Ralph Edwards (from *This Is Your Life*) praising the steaks, and a photograph of the all-woman bowling team sponsored by the Tavern along with a display of their trophies.

Specialty of the house is a bull's eye steak, a boneless rib eye cooked over flaming oak wood, served Santa Maria–style, meaning sided by firm piquinto beans, French bread, and salsa. Fillets, strips, sirloins, and chopped steaks also are available, as are buttered sweetbreads, pork chops, rack of lamb, and baby back ribs. The bull's eye is available for late-morning breakfast and Sunday brunch in a smaller version, served alongside eggs, hash browns, beans, and biscuits.

The Hitching Post

| 3325 Point Sal Rd. | 805-937-6151 |
| Casmalia, CA | D \| $$$ |

The Hitching Post's top sirloin is pungent with age, oozing juice, effortless to chew; but the filet mignon is even better. Its delicate fibers seem to glow with the flavor of burning wood, and with the smack of a wine vinegar and oil marinade that is applied as the meat cooks. "We've had people throwing $100 bills at us to try to get the recipe for that marinade," proprietor Bill Ostini says of the magic potion developed by his father. "But the real trick is in how the steaks are handled. You've got to know how to cook which steak which way—some are made to be cooked rare, some well-done; it depends on the marbling, and how much age they have. It takes two to three years to train a cook to do it the right way. Cutting and cooking steaks is practically a lost art."

Steak at the Hitching Post is part of a full dinner, which is the archetypal Santa Maria repertoire of relish tray with sweet peppers and chile peppers, celery ribs, carrot sticks, and olives, plus shrimp cocktail made with teensy-weensy shrimp, a green head-lettuce salad, garlic toast, and potatoes, either baked or French fried.

Ambience is cattle country supreme: a big, dimly lit roadhouse with linoleum floors and red tablecloths, each table supplied with a basket full of cellophane-wrapped saltines. Above the bar, a TV is always playing; the mirror is plastered with decals from NASA, the *Voyager* space shuttle, and the Army Corps of Engineers; a bison head on one wall wears a Buffalo Bills cap. In the dining room, which affords a view of the kitchen, there are mounted deer heads and old black-and-white family photos of young Bill and his brother on hunting and fishing trips with their dad when they were young. The hallway that leads to the restrooms is lined with cattle hides.

Hob Nob Hill

2271 First Ave.   619-239-8176
San Diego, CA   BLD | $

The California coffee shop is a unique style of square-meal restaurant, but there aren't a lot of them left. Hob Nob Hill is classic, a three-meal-a-day place where the food is homey, the service fast, and the prices low. At mealtimes, especially breakfast, chances are you will have to wait in line. But the line moves quickly, and once you are seated you are set upon by a team of waitresses who could not move faster if they flew through the aisles—taking orders, filling coffee cups, making sure everyone is happy.

Hob Nob Hill's repertoire is broad, and there isn't a clinker on the menu. There are pecan waffles, pigs in blankets (buttermilk pancakes rolled with ham, sausage, and sour cream), blueberry hotcakes, grilled smoked pork chops, etc.—plus a bakery's worth of coffee cakes, muffins (try carrot), and a not-to-be-missed pecan roll. Even little amenities are special: syrup is served warm; jelly comes in hollowed-out orange halves; coffee is strong and rich.

At dinner, it's meat-and-potatoes time: leg of lamb with sage dressing and mint jelly, chicken and dumplings, roast tom turkey with giblet gravy, corned beef and cabbage, pot roast and buttered noodles every Sunday. There are turkey croquettes with cranberry sauce, a nursery-food breast-of-chicken curry, and baked ham with fruit sauce and yams on Thursday. Accompaniments are such comfort-food side dishes as warm applesauce (homemade, of course), marinated bean salad, and puffy yeast rolls.

Hodad's

5010 Newport Ave.   619-224-4623
Ocean Beach, CA   LD | $

Hodad's motto, on a sign above the cash registers: "No Shirt, No Shoes, No Problem!"

This ultra-casual beachside eatery offers hamburgers in three sizes (mini, single, and double), cheeseburgers, and bacon cheeseburgers. They come solo or as part of a basket with a pile of French fries, and they are sights to behold. The double, which is two good-size patties, is huge beyond belief, piled inside a broad sesame-seed bun with lettuce, tomato, onion, pickle, mayonnaise, mustard, and ketchup. The menu warns that all burgers come with all condiments "unless you say otherwise"; and frankly, we suggest that unless you are allergic, all the way is the way to go.

The hamburger is presented partially wrapped in yellow wax paper, which provides a way to hoist it from the table and to keep it relatively together as you try to eat it. The French fries in the basket are thick wedges of potato with pleasantly tough skins and creamy insides. To drink on the side, we recommend a milkshake or malt (vanilla, chocolate, strawberry) served in a glass and the silver beaker with a straw and a necessary spoon.

Just getting to Hodad's is a blast. Lined with palm trees, and with a gorgeous ocean view, Newport Avenue is a colorful part of the city. It is occupied by surf shops, alternative hair salons, juice bars, and high-proof bars, and this rockin' joint fits right in. Its walls are festooned with vanity license plates from around the nation; surfboards are strung above the dining room. Seating includes hardwood booths and a counter along the wall with stools, plus a special booth made from the front end of a VW minibus. Each booth is outfitted with a cardboard container that once held a six-pack of beer bottles. The half-dozen compartments are now used to store sugar and sweeteners for coffee.

Jocko's Steak House

125 N. Thompson Ave.   805-929-3686

Nipomo, CA   BLD | $$

We found Jocko's many years ago while we were students at Gary Leffew's bull-riding school north of Santa Barbara. (That's another story. . . .) When the week of riding rank bulls was over, cowboys who hadn't broken too many bones and had some jingle in their jeans headed for Nipomo to eat beef at Jocko's on Saturday night.

Nipomo isn't much of a town, but cars from afar crowd around Jocko's on weekends, and even if you've made a reservation (highly recommended), you will likely wait for a table. Waiting allows time to belly up to the bar and imbibe a colorful tavern atmosphere of taxidermized animal heads on the wall and the good-time shenanigans of California country folk (a whole 'nother breed from those who live in the big cities). Although the steaks are first-class, the experience of dining at Jocko's is absolutely nothing like a meal in one of the high-priced, dress-up steak house chains. Wear your jeans and boots and Stetson or John Deere cap and you'll feel right at home.

Meat is the only thing to eat. (One Roadfooder wrote to us suggesting that this must be the place where bad vegetarians go when they die, for it truly is a kind of beef-frowners' hell, where smells of roasting meat permeate the air.) Shockingly thick steaks and hefty lamb chops and pork chops are cooked on an open pit over oak wood and served Santa Maria–style, meaning accompanied by tiny pinquita beans and salsa. It's a great, filling meal, and even if you get a relatively modest-size filet mignon, chances are you'll be taking meat home in a doggie bag for lunch the next day.

Julian Pie Company

21976 Hwy. 79
Santa Ysabel, CA

760-765-2400
$

Apple pie is the specialty of the Julian Pie Company, a sweet oasis at the western edge of the desert. Merely walking into the big modern building is an olfactory joy—the air is thick with the aroma of cooked apples, cinnamon, and hot crust. You can watch the pies being made behind the counter; you can buy whole pies to take home; or you can get a single slice and a cup of coffee and find a seat at the counter and indulge.

Varieties of apple pie in the Julian repertoire include Dutch apple with a crumb top, boysenberry apple crumb, natural strawberry apple, and apple rhubarb. Also on the regular menu are peach, peach melba, blackberry, and pecan. Basic apple pie with a pastry top is the classic, and we can't think of a better pie anywhere. Its crust is flaky, and the insides powerfully fruity/sweet. If you dine here, you have the à la mode option, which is nice, but unnecessary.

While not a full-service restaurant by any means, this bakery does have a few other excellent food items worth knowing about. One unusual snack is pie crust—two-bite-size, heart-shaped pieces of crust that are baked with a sprinkling of cinnamon sugar; these irresistibly delicious cookies fall into flakes as you bite. The other handsome things in the glass display cases are plump cider donuts enrobed in either cinnamon sugar, chocolate, or supersweet (and super-good!) maple frosting.

La Super-Rica

622 N. Milpas St.   805-963-4940
Santa Barbara, CA   LD | $

La Super-Rica is barely a restaurant. It is a taco stand where service is do-it-yourself and customers are expected to clean their own tables when they're finished eating. All plates and utensils are disposable; and seating is at wobbly tables on a semi–al fresco patio. Since Isidoro Gonzalez opened for business in 1980, this extremely modest eatery has built a reputation as the source for some of the very best Mexican food anywhere in the USA.

Tacos cost between two and five dollars each and the roster includes basic beef, beef with green chile and cheese, and a "chorizo especial" of spicy sausage, melted cheese, and tomato. We are especially fond of the taco *adobado* (grilled pork) and the frijol Super-Rica (chorizo and pinto beans with bacon and chile). In addition to tacos, La Super-Rica makes some sensational tamales, and beverages of choice include *horchata* (sweet rice milk), hibiscus tea, and Mexican beer. Each of the three kinds of salsa is excellent: chunky tomato, spicy red chile, and even spicier green chile.

Expect to wait in line at mealtime. The line is actually a good thing. La Super-Rica has no signs outside, so the crowd of people you see on N. Milpas Street will let you know you have arrived.

Musso and Frank's

6667 Hollywood Blvd.   213-467-7788
Hollywood, CA   LD | $$

When Musso and Frank opened for business in 1919, Hollywood was young and fresh and Hollywood Boulevard was a magic address. The boulevard went to honkytonk hell in a handbasket and is now trying to rebirth itself with entertainment complexes and shopping malls competing for attention with cheap souvenirs and hookers' wig shops, but the moment you step inside Hollywood's oldest restaurant, the battle of the lifestyles is left behind.

In fact, now that meat and potatoes have enjoyed a well-deserved renaissance, this vintage eatery almost seems trendy. The menu is printed every day, but Musso's is known for dowdy kinds of meals: thin flannel cakes (for lunch), Welsh rarebit, chicken potpie on Thursday, classic corned beef and cabbage every Tuesday, lamb shanks, baked ham, chiffonade salads.

There are so many things we love to eat from the extensive repertoire, but pay special attention, please, to the potatoes. Ten different kinds occupy the menu, from mashed and boiled to lyonnaise and candied sweet. Steaks and chops—cooked on an open broiler where those sitting at the counter can watch—are grand. From the dessert list, note bread-and-butter pudding, and its deluxe variant, diplomat pudding, topped with strawberries.

Many adventurous gourmets of our acquaintance do not understand the appeal of Musso and Frank's. They compliment its antique Tudor decor and comfortable red leather booths but complain that the food is ordinary. Yes, indeed! It is some of the tastiest ordinary food anywhere.

Original Pantry

877 S. Figueroa St.   213-972-9279
Los Angeles, CA   Always open | $

Not far from the Staples Center, the Original Pantry is a choice stop for fans after Lakers' games. Never having closed its doors since opening in 1924, this round-the-clock temple of honest eats is renowned for buckwheat hotcakes and full-bore egg breakfasts accompanied by sourdough toast, thick slabs of bacon, and piles of really excellent hash brown potatoes. OJ is fresh-squeezed and the coffee keeps coming. At supper, you can't go wrong with a steak platter or such stalwarts as roast beef or liver and onions; and the great dessert is hot apple pie with rum sauce. Sourdough bread and coleslaw are served with every meal.

When the Original Pantry was threatened by developers in 1980, former Mayor Richard Riordan bought it, and His Honor's aura helped make it a destination for city politicians, bigwigs, and wannabes, especially at breakfast, when people-watching is a sport. A relatively small place, it is always bustling and service, by hash-house pros, is nearly instantaneous.

Philippe's the Original

1001 N. Alameda St.   213-628-3781

Los Angeles, CA   BLD | $

Genesis, according to Philippe's: One day in 1918 Philippe Mathieu was preparing a beef sandwich at his proletarian eat-place when the roll fell into gravy. Fetched out with tongs, the drippings-sopped bread looked good enough that an impatient customer said, "I'll take it just like that." And so the French dip sandwich was created.

Los Angelenos considered the "French dip" sandwich theirs alone for decades, and while no one knows for sure how it got its Gallic name in L.A., similarly configured sandwiches throughout the Midwest and West are known as wet beef, beef Manhattan, hot beef, and dipped beef. The sandwich is all-American, and the term French dip is so widespread on modern menus that few people think of it as a Los Angeles creation any more.

Philippe's remains a sawdust-on-the-floor, people-watcher's paradise. It moved from its original location in 1951 when the freeway was built, and the current quarters are reminiscent of an urban hash house from a mid-century film noir. Place your order with a carver at the counter, then carry it to a tall chairs at a chest-high communal table where your dining companions will range from racetrack touts and refugees from the nearby court house to So-Cal creative types desperately seeking a dose of old-fashioned reality.

The sliced beef is soft and tender, the roll is fresh, and the gravy is radiant with protein savor. Philippe's also offers French-dipped lamb and ham, available with cheese on top and sided by pickles, coleslaw, and potato or macaroni salad. The one essential add-on is Philippe's own mustard, a roaring-hot emulsion that is beef's best friend. In addition, customers can select from a full array of such old-fashioned bar-room grub as pickled eggs and pigs' feet. The price of coffee is a dime per cup.

Ramona Café

628 Main St.   760-789-8656

Ramona, CA   BLD | $$

Here is a menu that honors potatoes. No mere side dish, Ramona Café's glistening chunks of home-fried potato are the underpinnings of whole breakfasts piled into ceramic skillets. Design your own, selecting four toppings from a list that includes ham, bacon, taco meat, chorizo sausage, four kinds of cheese, crushed garlic, and jalapeños. Or choose the Kitchen Sink, which is a panful of hunky home fries loaded with some of everything, including sausage gravy and a couple of eggs, and sided by an immense squared-off biscuit. If you want a meal that is less complicated, but nearly as satisfying, consider Ramona Café's blue-ribbon cinnamon roll: a half-pound circle of hot, sweet pastry veined with cinnamon sugar and accompanied by two paper cups of butter.

Other good breakfast options include omelets of all kinds. Of special note is the Gilroy Omelet, named for the California town that has proclaimed itself the garlic capital of the world: ham, bacon, mushrooms, Cheddar and Jack cheeses, plus lots and lots of garlic.

While breakfast is the meal by which many travelers know Ramona Café, it also happens to be a fine place for hearty lunch. There are good-size cheeseburgers, hot meat loaf sandwiches, turkey potpie, and fine fried chicken that is crusted with breading made from the café's breakfast biscuits. The list of pies is a long one, including apple and rhubarb and a chocolate peanut butter pie that we once had as dessert for breakfast before a long drive inland, where good eats grow scarce.

By the way, we were clued into this place many years ago by singing cowboy Roy Rogers, who used to stop by regularly for hamburgers and milkshakes on his way out to the desert. Roy told us how much he enjoyed dunking hot home fries into the yolks of over-easy eggs.

Rick's Rather Rich Ice Cream

3946 Middlefield Rd.   650-493-6553
Palo Alto, CA $

Do not for a moment believe the name of this 1958-vintage ice cream parlor. True, Rick's sorbets may not be rich, but the ice creams are loaded! Exotic flavors rule in the congenial parlor decorated with paintings of cows, but even such "Rick-o-Mendations" as white chocolate ginger and saffron pistachio impress you foremost with their creaminess. For us, the most compelling flavor in the house is chocolate ginger, but it's hard not to explore such oddities as kulfi (saffron and pistachios), Computer Chip (chocolate chips in chocolate-orange ice cream), and Industrial Chocolate (fudge and cookie dough).

Roscoe's House of Chicken and Waffles

5006 W. Pico Blvd.　　　　　　　323-934-4405
Los Angeles, CA　　　　　　　　BLD | $

Waffles, which have nearly vanished from lunch and supper menus, used to be a staple at tea rooms, department-store lunch counters, and home-cooking diners. One of the few places that honors waffles as something more than the Belgian monstrosities that have become a breakfast cliché is Roscoe's of Los Angeles. As far as we know, it is America's only one-of-a-kind waffle house. And what a treasure it is.

There are five Roscoe's in Southern California. The one we know and love is on West Pico in Los Angeles—a location movie buffs know from its appearance in *Pulp Fiction*. A soulful eatery that looks a little scary from the outside but takes good care of customers, Roscoe's dishes out thin, crisp, butter-dripping waffles with a bit of cinnamon in the batter as a companion to pieces of crisp-skinned fried chicken. Whatever pieces you like are available: breasts, thighs, legs, wings, livers and giblets, even chicken sausage, and the menu offers all sorts of ready-made combos of chicken parts and side dishes. The latter include candied yams, red beans, mac and cheese, corn bread, and biscuits. We think collard greens provide ideal soulful harmony to the chicken and waffle combo. Of course, gravy is available; but butter and syrup are the preferred condiments at a Roscoe's meal.

Sam's Grill

374 Bush St.　　　　　　　　　415-421-0594
San Francisco, CA　　　　　　　LD Mon-Fri | $$$

With time for only one meal in San Francisco, we were asked by *Sacramento Bee* writer Dixie Reed where we most wanted to go. The answer was easy: Sam's. While food trends come and go and hot restaurants pop up and fizzle, Sam's remains our echt San Francisco eating experience. Open since 1867, it is at once deluxe and informal, featuring high-priced, top-quality ingredients prepared simply. It looks the way you want a great old California restaurant to look: outfitted with yards of thick white linen, brass hooks for coats, and private wooden dining booths for intimate meals.

The daily-printed menu is divided into such enticing categories as "Fish (Wild Only)" and "From the Charcoal Broiler," and the big rounds of sourdough bread brought to table at the beginning of the meal are among the best we've ever had. It's a frustrating place to eat because the menu lists so many things that are intriguing, from the unknown (what is chicken Elizabeth? what are prawns Dore?) to such bygone classics as hangtown fry (oysters and scrambled eggs) and mock turtle soup to ultra-exotic (fresh abalone meuniere at $50 per plate). It is possible to order charcoal-grilled steaks and chops, sweetbreads done three ways, or short-ribs of beef with horseradish sauce, or just bacon and eggs, but nearly everybody comes to Sam's for the seafood.

During our visit with Dixie, we feasted on a plate of Rex sole fillets glistening with butter—perhaps the tenderest seafood we've ever slid onto the tines of a fork; we hefted hunks of clean and meaty charcoal-broiled petrale sole, and enjoyed delicately fried fillet of sole.

Sam's is quirky, the way venerable oldsters are entitled to be. Open only on weekdays, only until nine at night, it caters to a clientele of people who work downtown and come every day for lunch or for an early dinner before heading home. At noon, it is mobbed with successful-looking types jockeying for a table, or crowding three deep against the bar. Once you are seated, it is an immensely comfortable place to eat. The staff of impeccably dressed waiters are consummate professionals, treating us out-of-towners in jeans with as much respect as the important guys in business suits.

Sears Fine Food

439 Powell St.	415-986-0700
San Francisco, CA	BLD | $$

It was worrisome late in 2003 when it looked like Sears was about to vanish from the San Francisco landscape. While not the most exciting or innovative restaurant in town, nor an undiscovered gem, this comfortable storefront facing the cable cars on Powell Street has been Old Reliable since it opened in 1938, especially for breakfast. In fact, three meals a day are served and the lunch and dinner menus are extensive; but like most other tourists who find their way here, when we think of Sears we think of little Swedish pancakes served eighteen to a plate, sourdough French toast as tender as custard, non-Belgian waffles (from an old Fannie Farmer cookbook recipe), and thick, crisp bacon or plump sausage links alongside.

Happily, reports of Sears's death were greatly exaggerated; and while new owners took over in 2004, the traditional specialties remain reassuringly unchanged and the vintage dining room décor still sets a cozy tone.

Swan Oyster Depot

1517 Polk St.   415-673-1101

San Francisco, CA   L | $$

Swan's is an urban seafood shack that is a combination oyster bar and storefront market. Seating is limited to a nineteen-seat counter, where your chances of walking in and finding a seat at mealtime are near zero. It is relatively expensive, uncomfortable, and noisy. And yet somehow its inconvenience is part of its charm (as is the ebullience of the Sancimino family, who have run the lunch counter since 1946). For many devotees, this is simply the best place in San Francisco to eat fresh seafood. Fans have been crowding in for nearly a century to feast on oysters from the East and West Coasts, whole lobsters, salads of shrimp or crab, smoked trout or salmon, and New England–style chowder. The marble counter is strewn with condiments: Tabasco sauce, lemons, oyster crackers.

Dungeness crab is served in season (generally, mid-November through May), available "cracked," meaning sections of cooked, cooled claw, leg, and body ready to be unloaded of their sweet meat. Crab Louie is a regal dish (invented in San Francisco) in which large chunks of sweet meat are cosseted in a sauce compounded from lemony mayonnaise spiked with relish and olive bits, and enriched by hard-cooked egg.

Side your meal with sourdough bread and wash it down with Anchor Steam beer.

Taylor's Refresher

933 Main St.   707-963-3486

St. Helena, CA   LD | $$

Cocoa-rich, coffee-strong, and so thick that it is served with a spoon, the espresso bean milkshake alone would secure a place for Taylor's Refresher in America's drive-in pantheon. This picnic-table oasis opened in St. Helena in 1949 and has since earned a stellar reputation for one-third-pound hamburgers (topped with bacon, cheddar, barbecue sauce, mushrooms, and mayo, please!), chicken and fish tacos, chili-cheese dogs, and to-die-for garlic French fries. In a Napa Valley spirit of culinary enlightenment, the menu also features a seared-rare ahi tuna burger with ginger wasabi mayo and Asian slaw; a winter salad that includes candied walnuts, sliced pears, and blue cheese; and, naturally, California wine by the glass.

Wheel Inn

50900 Seminole Dr.   951-849-7012

Cabazon, CA   Always open | $

The Wheel Inn is the great American truck stop, featuring round-the-clock hours and full-size, walk-in statues of a Tyrannosaurus Rex and a Brontosaurus out back. In the minimart adjacent to the restaurant, travelers can buy candies, smokes, and sundries; the knotty-pine walls of the café are arrayed with merchandise for sale: fancy cowboy-style belt buckles, novelty clocks, scenic handmade oil paintings (some on velvet). There is a short counter facing the pie case, and leatherette-upholstered booths are outfitted with Formica on which the wood-grain pattern has been worn away in places by decades of heavy plates and diners' elbows.

Pie is the specialty of the house. They are truck-stop pies—not elegant or fancy, but satisfying in a big, extra-sweet sort of way. We like the banana cream filling, the sturdy apple pie, and the fresh strawberry.

Much of the food on the Wheel Inn menu is shockingly real. In a diner where the seasoned highway traveler would expect to find a kitchen using fast-food shortcuts, you find instead Karel Kothera, the seasoned chef who bought the Wheel Inn in 1992 and now runs it alongside his wife, Marie, who serves as hostess. The Kotheras are a class act, both in the dining room and the kitchen, and their efforts transform a basic truck stop into a really fine place to eat. The hot turkey sandwich is a good example. It is made of meat from a roasted bird (not from a "turkey loaf"), and it is accompanied by mashed potatoes actually made from potatoes (not dehydrated potato flakes). French fries to accompany hamburgers or other sandwiches are delicious, served hot and salty, just oily enough to make perfect culinary sense alongside a half-pound Dino burger (two quarter-pound patties) on a whole-wheat sesame bun with tomato slices, lettuce, pickle, a small cup of Thousand Island dressing, and (optionally) raw or grilled slices of onion.

The preferred beverage for many of the working clientele is coffee, which is served in a bottomless cup, but if you want a true local treat here at the edge of the Coachella Valley, order a date shake. It's a milkshake supercharged with shreds of locally grown dates.

O r e g o n

Annie's Donut Shop

3449 N.E. 72nd Ave.   503-284-2752

Portland, OR   B | $

There's been a donut renaissance in the Pacific Northwest. Seattle and Portland are bonanza cities for sinker lovers, especially those who like their morning pastry with excellent coffee. For all the new, fashionable, retro, and Goth donuts available in both cities, we have a soft spot for traditional ones that go great with morning coffee (not latte!), especially for those you'll find at Annie's. They're made here daily, and the variety is tremendous. Old-fashioned cake donuts have the concentric circle-within-a-circle shape so popular in the Northwest that provides nearly twice the crunchy exterior of a simple round one. Glazed and maple-frosted OFs are especially swell, and although the price is plebeian, the taste and mouth feel are aristocratic. Cream puffs are light and impeccably fresh, the only way a cream puff should be. The wickedest variety we sampled was a raspberry fritter—unctuous, super-sweet, slightly fruity, and monumentally filling.

Annie's has none of the amenities of upscale coffee and donut shops: no art on the walls, no Wi-Fi, no couches or lounge chairs and, of course, no baristas. You sit in molded plastic booths that look out on the parking lot and are served by a staff with no attitude other than pride in the donuts they make and sell.

Dan and Louis Oyster Bar

208 S.W. Ankeny St.	503-227-5906
Portland, OR	LD | $$

Warm milk, melted butter, and lots of little oysters: This is Dan and Louis's oyster stew, one of the unaffected seafood specialties of the Northwest. According to the menu, it was invented by Louis Wachsmuth long ago on a cold, winter day. Its oysters are Yaquinas from the restaurant's own beds. On the half shell, they are ocean-sweet; in a stew, they are little pillows of oceany aplomb. While it is possible to get the stew with a double dose of oysters, we prefer having a half-dozen or a dozen on the half shell, then having the stew with its normal number.

If we're really hungry, we'll follow that with a plate of pan-fried oysters. Yaquinas fry up beautifully with a toasty golden crust. They are sent to the table with ramekins of tartar sauce and Thousand Island dressing, as well as a pile of lettuce shreds heaped with small shrimp and a length of chewy sourdough bread.

Beyond oysters, Dan and Louis sells Dungeness crab, Shrimp Louis, halibut fish and chips, even a hamburger for those who accidentally find themselves in this thoroughly nautical eat-place. Among the non-oysters items, we are especially fond of the dowdy creamed crab on toast, a dish that could have been served in a department store lunchroom seventy-five years ago.

The interior of Dan and Louis is mesmerizing, its handsome sailing-ship wood walls bedecked floor to ceiling with an inexhaustible accumulation of nautical memorabilia and historical pictures, notes, and maps that tell of Portland since Louis started serving food here.

Ecola Seafoods

208 N. Spruce St.	503-436-9130
Cannon Beach, OR	LD | $$

Cannon Beach is one of the most picturesque places on the Oregon coast, known for the awe-inspiring haystack-shaped rock a couple hundred yards out beyond the shoreline. It is a quiet hamlet and a grand destination for eaters because of Ecola Seafoods (named for nearby Ecola State

Park). Ecola is total Roadfood—extremely casual and extremely local, a no-frills seafood market and restaurant where fresh is all. We love simply browsing the cases full of Dungeness crab, oysters, scallops, and flat fish that we seldom see back east. And for those who arrive with a good appetite, what fun it is to choose from a broad menu of "fish and chips," the former part of the equation including Willapa Bay oysters, Oregon albacore tuna, razor clams, and troll-caught Chinook salmon, Pacific cod, halibut, jumbo prawns, and ocean scallops. Each is available as a lunch or dinner (bigger portion), and you can get the cod, halibut, salmon, or oysters fried up and put into a toasted, buttered bun with lettuce, tomato, and a couple of lemon wedges.

We feasted on a crab cocktail, which was a sweet pile of cool, pearly meat in a bowl along with zesty red cocktail sauce. And we liked the chowder, too: fine-textured, creamy but not heavy, its ocean savor highlighted by a fine jolt of pepper.

For picnickers, sandwiches and whole ready-to-eat dinners are available to go, as are all manner of cook-it-yourself fish.

Farmhouse Café

4175 US 101   503-815-1325
Tillamook, OR   BLD | $

Tillamook cheese is a hard Cheddar rich with a creamy essence that makes it just right for eating by the piece, especially with a crisp apple. It grates well into shreds that are dense but fluff up nicely, and is therefore our favorite way to top a plate of Cincinnati five-way chili. Depending on how long it is aged, its character varies from svelte (sixty days) to stout (fifteen months).

Tillamook is available around the country, but if you want to wallow in it, the place to go is the source, Tillamook, where the Tillamook County Creamery Association runs a store and the Farmhouse Café, in which the product is infinitely celebrated. On the store shelves are more cheese products than we ever have imagined could exist, all made from the local pride: loaves, baby loaves and junior baby loaves, white and yellow, sharp and mild, Jack and Pepper Jack, snack bars, dips, spreads, and curds.

While the menu at the Farmhouse Café is a little less cheesecentric (you can get a BLT or a grilled chicken sandwich), the cheeseburgers are excellent and there is a long list of sandwiches devised to celebrate the glory of Cheddar. We are especially fond of cheese, bacon, and tomato on toasty sourdough bread.

While it can get mobbed with noisy tourists and certainly is not the hidden-away treasure that many travelers crave to find along Oregon's beautiful coast, this big roadside enterprise is nonetheless a fun place to stop if you are in need of ice cream, milk, cheese, smoked meats, or a quick education in regional industry.

Fresh Seafood NW

3800 Hwy. 101 N   503-815-3500

Tillamook, OR   L | $

The name of this restaurant is accurate. "My parents are my whole-salers," said cook and proprietor Kari McGrath. "We get everything off the boats in Garibaldi." That means steamers, mussels, and prawns, lo-cal oysters, and Dungeness crab. It is all available raw to take home and cook, but late in 2006 Kari finally heeded pleas from travelers to offer something to eat right here.

There's nothing fancy, mind you. Virtually everything on the menu is an ode to what local waters yield, with a happy nod to the excellent cheese made here in Tillamook. The best way to combine those two elements is in a grilled cheese sandwich that also contains bay shrimp and/or Dungeness crab. The combination of sweet marine meat and creamy, slightly sharp cheese is inspired, especially when the bread is but-tery and toasted to a golden crisp. Kari also sells whole crabs for do-it-yourselfers as well as picked crabmeat for those who need immediate gratification.

We've also sampled her crab cakes, which have a good creamy tex-ture but are a letdown after a cocktail of nothing but pure, cool crab-meat. That great crabmeat is also available as an addition to a green salad or a wonderful roasted garlic Caesar salad, and if you ask, Kari will likely add a few pieces to decorate the top of your bowl of chowder.

Fuller's Coffee Shop

136 N.W. Ninth Ave.   503-222-5608

Portland, OR   BL | $

Off the tourist path but loved by locals, Fuller's is a taste of the sort of high-quality urban hash house now nearly vanished from most American cities. A man sitting near us at one of the two U-shaped Formica counters mopped the last of some yolk off his plate with a forkful of pancake and declared that he used to eat at Fuller's nearly every day thirty-two years ago, and as far as he could see, nothing has changed but the prices. "This is a diner where they know how to fry bacon!" he declared. Yes, indeed. An order of bacon is four medium-thick ribbons that are crisp but retain enough pliability so they don't break at first bite. And the hash browns are a short-order delight, fried so they are a mix of golden crust and soft, spuddy shreds of buttery potato. The pancakes are good, too, and the cinnamon roll, baked fresh each day, is yeasty and tender.

Our favorite thing at Fuller's is the bread, white or whole wheat. These slices are simple and perfect, especially so when toasted and buttered and accompanying a big, well-rounded breakfast. Jelly and marmalade are set out in ramekins along the counter.

Lunch consists of such blue-plate specials as hot beef and gravy (on the good bread) with mashed potatoes and a corned-beef sloppy joe. There is always interesting seafood: salmon steaks in season, batter-dipped fish and chips, fresh-fried oysters, and big, slightly scary (but easy to eat) egg-battered, fried razor clams with French fries and coleslaw.

Halibut's

2525 N.E. Alberta St.   503-808-9600

Portland, OR   LD | $$

The best fish and chips in the West? This very well might be the place. When we walked in owner Dave Mackay was at the left side of the restaurant behind the counter, where the row of fry kettles are, proclaiming aloud the beauty of a particular side of salmon. Vivid pink with dense, meaty flesh, it was from the Copper River, of course (Alaska's coldest). While broiling or grilling it would be grand, this restaurant's deep-fry skills are equally brilliant, encasing the kingly meat in a thin, fragile crust that is amazingly grease-free and only enhances the essential taste of the fish within. Dave cut the side of fish with practical skill, creating chunks about 2 X 2 X 4 inches for frying.

All kinds of fish are fried here. Halibut comes as four heavy blocks that are moist and sweet, big white hunks of flesh flake off with pieces of crust when you poke a fork into the basket that also contains crunch-crusted French fries. (Malt vinegar is supplied for dressing the spuds.) Also of note on the menu are Dungeness crab cakes, four flat ones, very crabby and nicely spiced with a red-gold crust. The restaurant's subtitle is "Fish/Chips and Chowder," and the chowder is not to be missed. It is ridiculously thick with clams and potatoes and a surfeit of bacon, available plain in a bowl or with Alaskan bay shrimp added.

Halibut's is a casual bar with raucous blues playing on the speakers (or performed live many nights). There is a happy hour menu and a long list of such whoop-de-doo cocktails as the ultimate margarita, a mai tai, and a refreshing lemon drop, made with fresh-squeezed lemons, Absolut Citron, triple sec, and Bacardi Limon and served in a goofy-stemmed martini glass.

Mo's

622 S.W. Bay Blvd.　　　　541-265-2979
Newport, OR　　　　　　　LD | $$

Surrounded by a dockside sprawl of fish markets, seafood-packing companies, and stores that advertise they will smoke any fish, meat, or fowl you bring in, Mo's is famous for its chowder. Thick and creamy, it is stocked with pieces of clam and has a faintly smoky taste. A good variation on the theme is Mo's slumgullion, which is the chowder enriched with shrimp—a terrific combination, and with a salad and a hunk of bread, a royal supper. Comfort-food aficionados will want to know about scalloped oysters, a lavish baked-together combination of butter, cream, crackers, and oysters. You can also order oysters "barbecued"— sauced, smothered with cheese, and baked.

Across the street from the original Mo's is Mo's Annex, with the same fine seafood menu, including a mighty bouillaibasse thick with clams, shrimp, oysters, crab, cod, halibut, and salmon in a light tomato sauce, plus a wonderful view of Yaquina Bay, where diners look out over the water and the commercial fleet berthed at its dock, and watch sport fishermen cleaning their day's catch.

Nick's Famous Coney Island

3746 S.E. Hawthorne Blvd.　　　503-235-4024
Portland, OR　　　　　　　　　LD | $

Portland is a great sausage city; its highlights including Otto's Sausage Kitchen and the Dog House. And then there is Nick's. We cannot tell you that the hot dog served at Nick's is a gourmet's treat, but it would be a shame to come to town and not experience it. Unlike the fingerling Coneys of the East and Midwest, it is big—a foot long and as thick as a kielbasa, weighted into a bun by a spill of so much chili sauce (and if you know what's good for you, chopped raw onions) that the dog and bun are eclipsed. It's a piggy, fatty link, and the chili sauce is unctuously beefy. No doubt, the proper companion beverage is several long draughts of Nick's on-tap beer.

One of these bad boys is a nice-size meal, but the repertoire also includes doubles and triples smothering a single bun as well as a "home run," which is four dogs piled onto two buns. That last one costs $12, but cook/bartender Herbie, who has been the man at Nick's for over thirty years, claims that it is so much food that "$12 is giving it away." Herbie also recommends Nick's chiliburger, which is the same idea but with the option of beans mixed into the Coney sauce. He told us that a lot of his customers are businessmen from Chicago and Cincinnati who tell him that what they get at Nick's is just like home.

A 1930s-era neighborhood tavern in a neighborhood that has yuppified around it, Nick's is a wonderful anachronism. For us, even a single Coney is daunting, but we love sitting at the counter and listening to Herbie regale customers about the history of hot dogs, chili, Portland, and the world.

Norma's Ocean Diner

| 20 N. Columbia St. | 503-738-4331 |
| Seaside, OR | LD \| $$ |

Seaside is a semi–honky tonk town in a divinely beautiful location along Oregon's Pacific shore. You can buy all kinds of T-shirts, fudge, and salt water taffy; and at Norma's, you can have a real Northwest meal.

We knew we were going to like this place the moment we walked in and saw the chalkboard near the pass-through window to the kitchen. It lists which fresh seafoods are available and where they are from: salmon from the Oregon coast, steamer clams and oysters from Willipa Bay, halibut from Alaska, and local petrale sole. Even the featured wine was Oregonian: Duck Pond Merlot.

The waitress congratulated us on our choice of petrale sole mid-April: "Oooo, it's in season right now," she said. And it was wonderful: delicately flavored, buttery-rich, ocean-sweet. Nor could we resist Dungeness crab, which is available here in all sorts of ways. We chose the

Louis presentation, which turned out to be about a dozen big, pearly hunks of white meat arrayed atop a pile of lettuce with all the proper garnishes, plus garlic toast made from fresh-baked bread, and a ramekin of excellent house-made Thousand Island dressing.

People at a nearby table were all eating fish and chips. The menu lists cod, salmon, halibut, and even albacore available as the fish part of the equation. We asked our dining-room neighbors how they liked it. Between bites, they were able to exclaim that this was the best fish and chips they had eaten anywhere, any time.

The Oasis

85698 Hwy. 339   541-938-4776
Milton-Freewater, OR   BLD | $$

A short detour off the main road at the Washington State line leads to the Oasis, a sprawling roadhouse that seems to have expanded room by room over the last seven decades. It is ramshackle and rugged, a favorite destination for locals in search of meat and potatoes served with maximum cowboy atmosphere.

Sirloin steaks come branded with a neat field of cross-hatch char marks on their surface. These are cuts of beef with some chaw to them, available in all cuts and sizes, ranging from $13.50 on up.

We like lunch at the Oasis, when we can get a hot beef sandwich made from slices of prime rib. The meat reminded us of the best kind of school lunch—soft and gray with an appetizing institutional-kitchen aroma. It is piled atop slices of velvety white bread that seem able to absorb ten times their weight in gravy. We prefer Oasis French fries to the blah mashed potatoes; the fries are crusty red with good potato flavor. Hash browns, laced with onions, are better yet, especially when juices from a nearby steak seep their way.

Many customers who come from afar to dine at the Oasis make a grand night of the occasion by treating themselves to the most celebratory of all restaurant meals, surf and turf, which is such a house specialty that an entire section of the menu is devoted to its various permutations. Prime rib or sirloin is available with a ten- to twelve-ounce Australian lobster tail or with prawns, scallops, or grilled oysters.

Breakfast at the Oasis is a roll-your-sleeves-up kind of meal, served all day with the exception of pancakes and biscuits, which are available only until 11:00 A.M. The biscuits are extraordinary, a single order consisting of three behemoths and a cascade of thick gravy. This is a meal of caloric content suited to the eater who plans to flex muscles all day.

Otis Café

1259 Salmon River Hwy.   541-994-2813
Otis, OR   BLD | $

The Otis is a tiny roadside diner serving large meals. Located next to the post office, featuring a picnic-table patio as well as counter-and-table seats inside, this modest eat-place has received national acclaim for great pies and lumberjack's (or more accurately in this case, fisherman's) breakfasts. Sourdough pancakes have a tang beautifully complemented by lots of melting butter and a spill of syrup. Eggs come with hash browns, the potatoes preferably blanketed with melted cheese, and excellent homemade black molasses bread or a jumbo cinnamon roll.

Our lunch was a two-fisted BLT made with full-flavored slices of beefsteak tomato plus a bonus layer of cheese, and a goopy cheeseburger on a hefty bun with Otis's homemade mustard. On the side were dreamy fried red potatoes. Pies are gorgeous, especially the West Coast rarity, marionberry. A more intense, supremely aromatic blackberry, the marionberry was made to be baked in a pie. That the crust here is crisp and aristocratic makes it all the more perfect a dessert.

Otto's Sausage Kitchen

4138 S.E. Woodstock Ave.   503-771-6714
Portland, OR   L | $

A few years ago, we got a note from Diane Chaffin that said, in part: "When we moved into the neighborhood, we did not have to concern ourselves with good schools anymore, we wanted to live near Otto's. If our realtor had said 'huh?' we would have fired him for sure. We give directions to our house: just turn left at Otto's, but buy some dogs on your way."

While it is a full-scale meat market and smokehouse with sausages of all kinds to take home and cook, Otto's is also a fantastic place to eat lunch. When the outdoor grill starts up late in the morning, a smoky sausage aroma perfumes the area for blocks around—an aroma, Diane wrote, that sometimes creates traffic jams along Woodstock Avenue.

Whether you choose an ordinary beef-and-pork hot dog (with snap to its skin that is far from ordinary) or an extra-large sausage made from chicken or pork, you might just find yourself amazed, as we do, by just how much better these fresh, homemade tube steaks taste than factory-made ones from the supermarket. The progeny of Otto Eichentopf, who opened this neighborhood meat market in 1927, maintain the highest standards of old-world sausage making. The beauty of the links they make for lunch is that you really taste the meat from which they are made. Spices are used to accent, not overwhelm, the primary ingredient. Served in soft buns with a choice of onions, kraut, relish, mustard, or ketchup for you to apply yourself, Otto's sausages can be enjoyed with a beverage chosen from a vast cooler full of local soft drinks and imported and regional beers.

Otto's appeal has a lot to do with its casual ambience. Dining facilities are simply a bunch of wooden tables arranged on the sidewalk outside, as well as a handful of places to sit indoors. It's a neighborhood picnic every lunch hour.

Pacific Oyster

150 Oyster Dr.   503-377-2323

Bay City, OR   BLD (closed Sat) | $$

Attached to a very large oyster-processing plant on the ocean side of Route 101 is a charming little bare-table dining area and fish market where you can find a table and feast on Northwest seafood.

All kinds of raw oysters are available: mediums, petites, or the alluring little Kumamotos—freshly opened and served on the half shell or in shooter glasses for easy gulping. And of course, there are oyster stew, fried oysters, and even an oyster burger (four fried ones on a bun). Dungeness crab is available in a crab melt made with Oregon's own Tillamook Cheddar cheese. Another treat is a salmon stick, a staff of salty/sweet smoked salmon that is like beef jerky, but easier to chew.

Reo's Ribs

17385 S.W. Tualatin Valley Hwy.   503-356-1452

Aloha, OR   LD | $$

Although we weren't looking for it, and had no idea it was there, it would have been impossible for us to drive past Reo's Ribs in Aloha without noticing that there was some serious barbecuing underway. Appetizing smoke signals were emanating from huge black cookers at the side of the front parking lot, where the pit man used a garden hose to spritz the exterior of the metal drums so they smoked all the more.

Lured in by the scent, we found spectacular barbecue: certainly the best ribs we've eaten west of Chicago, maybe the best ribs anywhere. They are big, muscular spare ribs, not the weenie-size baby backs that, by comparison, seem all too easy to eat. Meat does not fall from these bones. You tug it off with your teeth or pull it with sauce-drenched fingers. It comes off easily, though, and is a pleasure to chew, deeply flavored with Reo's vibrant sauce.

Beyond ribs, Reo's is a bonanza of soul-food barbecue that reflects the proprietor's southern roots. Side dishes include collard and mustard greens simmered with ham hocks, fried okra, red beans and rice, butter-sopped yams, and macaroni and cheese, plus big hunks of freshly made corn bread for the side and sweet potato pie for dessert.

Voodoo Donuts

| 22 S.W. 3rd Ave. | 503-241-4704 |
| Portland, OR | B \| $ |

When Roadfood.com user Mr. Chips wrote to tell us that Voodoo Donuts, a block away from the estimable Dan and Louis Oyster Bar (p. 543), was a "great place to view Portland's strong Goth culture as well as sample tasty donuts," we were intrigued. We generally don't think of Goth culture as a source of good eats, and while we cannot say for sure if the ambience of this brick-walled ex-warehouse indeed is true Goth, we can tell you with certainty that the donuts are dandy.

There are beautiful old-fashioned cake donuts with crunchy crust and creamy insides, puffy raised donuts, one glazed behemoth as big as a pizza labeled a Tex-Ass donut (and costing $3.95), and donuts topped with powdered sugar, multicolored jimmies, and all sorts of flavored glazes. The menu listed many mysteries that we shall have to return to explore, including a no-name donut, a dirt donut, a dirty snowball, and a diablos rex. Our favorite item on the menu above the counter was "nonexisting fritter," its cost null. We suspect that may be Goth humor.

The one pastry we shan't forget is a bacon-maple bar. It is a substantial buttermilk long john frosted with maple glaze and festooned with strips of bacon that somehow, magically, retain a welcome crunch. What a great all-in-one breakfast!

Washington

14 Carrot Café

2305 Eastlake Ave. E   206-324-1442

Seattle, WA   BLD | $

Ownership of the 14 Carrot Café has changed a few times since we first wrote about it back in the late 1970s, but its character (and menu) remains familiar and eater-friendly. If there is such a thing as a typical Seattle café, this is it: casual and comfortably disheveled, nutritionally enlightened, and perfumed inside and out by coffee. One new feature, for those who are in desperate need of a quick caffeine fix when there are no seats available inside (a likely situation on weekend mornings) is barista John Hornall's coffee cart on the sidewalk outside. Seattle's coffee cognoscenti consider the latte from this particular cart to be the city's best.

Although lunch is served every day, and it includes some excellent salads and soups as well as vegetarian plates and no-beef hamburgers, most fans of the 14 Carrot Café consider it a breakfast place. Omelets are big and beautiful, served with good hash browns and a choice of toast, English muffin, or streusel-topped coffee cake. The coffee cake itself is something to behold: a moist crumble-topped block, served with a sphere of butter as big as a Ping-Pong ball. Other notable breadstuffs include blueberry muffins and cinnamon rolls. The latter, described as "large and gooey" by our waiter, is a vast doughy spiral with clods of raisins and veins of dark brown sugar packed into its warm furrows. It, too, comes blobbed with a ball of melting butter.

If eggs aren't your dish, how about hotcakes, sourdough or regular, with sliced bananas, apple slivers, or blueberries, with bacon on the side or cooked into the cakes? You can order hot oats with soy milk, dates, and cashews; homemade granola; sourdough French toast; or a grand version of French toast known as Tahitian toast, gilded with a thin layer of sesame butter.

Bakeman's

122 Cherry St.
Seattle, WA

206-622-3375
L Mon-Fri | $

A working-class cafeteria with a menu that is pretty much limited to soup and sandwiches. Bakeman's is open only for lunch, Monday through Friday. Its raison d'être in this book is the turkey sandwich on white or whole wheat. The bread is homemade, stacked up at one end of the cafeteria line. It is not spectacular bread. It is bread for sandwiches: tender slices that come to life when spread with mayo and/or mustard and/or cranberry and/or shredded lettuce, then heaped with turkey or—almost as wonderful—slabs of meat loaf.

If meat loaf is your dish, we recommend it on whole wheat with ketchup and shredded lettuce. The meat is tightly packed but tender, gently spiced, with a delicious aroma. As for turkey, get it any way you like, because this is superb, *real*, carved-from-the-bird turkey with homey flavor. The dark meat is lush; the white meat is moist and aromatic; and both varieties have an occasional piece of skin still attached, a nice reminder of just how real it is. The way we like it is, in the words of the countermen who hustle things along at breakneck pace, "white on white, M&M," which means white meat turkey on white bread with mustard and mayonnaise. You can also get it dressed with shredded lettuce and an order of cranberry relish. Turkey sandwiches get no better than this!

Bakeman's offers a couple of good soups each day, such as turkey noodle or beef vegetable plus a nice chili, or, on one memorable occasion, Chinese eggflower—an egg-drop variation. There are not-so-interesting Waldorf or potato salads and such, but dessert can be wonderful—carrot cake, cookies, or chocolate or lemon poppy-seed cake, sliced like bread.

Beth's Café

7311 Aurora Ave. N　　　　　　206-782-5588

Seattle, WA　　　　　　　　　Always open | $

Are you hungry? Really, really hungry? If so, eat at Beth's. Order the twelve-egg omelet. Yes, that's an even dozen, served not on a puny plate but on a pizza pan. If you're only half-hungry, Beth's offers six-egg omelets. Each comes with a heap of hash brown potatoes—all you can eat—and, if desired, bacon strips that have been cooked under a weight so they arrive flat and fragile. Biscuits-and-gravy is another of Beth's monumental meals, but if you arrive with only a tiny appetite, the menu offers mini breakfasts that are merely a single egg with hash browns and your choice of bacon or sausage.

At lunch the flagship meal is a half-pound Mondo burger with cheese, bacon, lettuce, and tomato, fries on the side. There's a great big Reuben sandwich as well as normal-size burgers, BLTs, and French dips.

Beth's is open round the clock and is not a place to please a fastidious epicure. It is what some have called an "alternative greasy spoon," attracting wee-hours diners from the fringes of city life. And in Seattle, those fringes are pretty far out!

The Crumpet Shop

1503 1st Ave.　　　　　　　　206-682-1598

Seattle, WA　　　　　　　　　BL | $

The Crumpet Shop is a great place to kick back and take a break from the frenetic food bazaar that is the Pike Place Market. Located on 1st Avenue at the very entrance, it is a small tea shop that serves crumpets for breakfast, brunch, and lunch. In case you don't know, a crumpet resembles an English muffin. Here it is cooked fresh from batter on a griddle, coming off chewy and flavorful with a craggy-textured surface that begs to be heaped with butter and fruit-clotted marmalade. You can have one simply buttered, or with butter and maple syrup, or with your choice from among nearly two dozen different sorts of sweet and savory toppings, including honey, Nutella, local jams, ham, cheese, and smoked salmon. On the side, have espresso, cappuccino, or, better yet, imported tea. If crumpets are not your cup of tea, the Crumpet Shop also bakes terrific loaves of bread, including a rugged groats bread that is an apt foundation for a hefty sandwich.

And do bring home some edible or potable souvenirs! The shelves are filled with exotic teas from around the world as well as a fabulous assortment of honeys and preserves, oatmeals, grains, and cereals from the Northwest and the British Isles. Crumpets are available, too, already cooked, sold by the six-pack, ready to take home, heat, and eat. We bought one of our all-time favorite kitsch souvenirs here many years ago: a clock in the shape of a toaster, with plastic slices of toast that went up and down as the second hand ticked.

Daly's Drive-In

2713 Eastlake Ave. E   206-322-1918
Seattle, WA   LD | $

Why, exactly, Daly's calls the salmon burger a burger, we cannot say. It is not the patty of mealy, ground-up salmon we expected when we first saw it listed on the menu of this family-owned drive-in that opened during the World's Fair of 1962. It is in fact a broad, thick slab of grilled salmon presented on a whole wheat bun with lettuce, tomato, and tartar sauce. The meat is pink and juicy, densely flavorful and protein-rich.

The menu also boasts of flame-broiled hamburgers, so even though our general mission is to eat more local cuisine (such as the salmon burger or excellent crisp-fried halibut and chips), we could not resist trying one. It turned out to be a slim, modest patty with a neat pattern of cross-hatch grill marks and no pretensions whatsoever. If we were in a serious hamburger mood, we'd more likely go for a double or, better yet, a double deluxe, which is two patties, cheese, lettuce, tomato, onion, pickles, relish, and mayonnaise.

French fries are excellent in a raunchy-crunchy way and milkshakes are flavored with fresh, in-season fruit. We are especially fond of the ultra-casual air of Daly's. Meals are presented on plastic cafeteria trays. Carry your own to a seat, preferably at the counter or, better yet, on the patio with a magnificent view of Lake Union.

Emmett Watson's Oyster Bar

1916 Pike Pl., Suite 16   206-622-7721
Seattle, WA   LD | $$

A laid-back eatery just across the street from the Pike Place Market in a back-street nook inside the Soames-Dunn Building, Emmett Watson's can be maddening if you are an efficiency nut in a hurry. For leisurely enjoyment of oysters, clams, and mussels, or baskets of fish and chips, or wonderful soups and chowders, this brash little place is a Seattle treasure. There is a sunny, flower-adorned courtyard behind the building for warm-weather dining at rickety little tables, and an indoor area with small booths.

For many regular customers, Emmett Watson's is a place to come for several beers accompanied by oysters on the half shell, either raw or broiled. We have spent many a happy afternoon at a patio table enjoying a drawn-out "grazing" meal of oysters, then shrimp, then a cup of chowder, and an occasional order of garlic bread. For appetites in search of well-balanced meals, we recommend anything fried (fish, clams, shrimp, oysters) or the steamed mussels or clams in garlic broth. Soups are notable, too, including a spicy shrimp soup Orleans, Puget Sound salmon soup, and a classic cioppino stew of cod, shrimp, clams, and mussels. Meals are accompanied by slices of excellent French bread and butter, and there is good key lime pie for dessert.

Frank's Diner

1516 W. Second Ave.   509-747-8798

Spokane, WA   BLD | $

Hungry in Spokane? Really, really hungry? If so, we have a meal for you: a King of the Road omelet at Frank's Diner. This big boy is made from six eggs, ham, Cheddar and Swiss cheeses, peppers and onions, and is served with hash brown potatoes and toast.

Not quite that hungry? How about a Joe's Special, named in honor of the "New Joe Special" that is so popular in the San Francisco Bay area. At Frank's, the Joe's special is a mere three eggs scrambled with ground beef, spinach, and onion and flavored with Parmesan cheese. There are plenty of normal-size breakfasts, too, from hefty biscuits and gravy to eggs Benedict, and from silver-dollar pancakes to French toast made with cinnamon swirl bread. The breakfast menu boasts that Frank's serves 12,000 eggs per month.

Our tipster, Charlie, told us that breakfast is the meal to eat at Frank's, but the lunch selection looks pretty inviting, too. It includes, and we quote from the menu, "the best hot turkey sandwich ever," made from turkey roasted in Frank's kitchen, as well as a grilled meat loaf sandwich, chicken potpie, and a large assortment of one-third-pound

Vista Cruiser Burgers made with assorted combinations of cheese, dressings, bacon, and barbecue sauce.

Grand food! But what will strike you even before you eat is the place itself, which is the state of Washington's oldest diner. It really was a railroad diner, Car 1787, built in 1906, and now completely restored in hash-house configuration with a counter that provides a view of the grill. Frank's was located in Seattle from 1931 to 1991, at which point it lost its lease and was moved to Spokane.

Knapp's Family Restaurant

2707 N. Proctor St.   253-759-9009
Tacoma, WA   BLD | $

All kinds of people give us all kinds of suggestions of places to eat, but when one of the nation's great restaurateurs tells us where to go, we pay special attention. It was Hap Townes, who for many years ran an estimable cafeteria-style lunchroom in Nashville, Tennessee, who tipped us off to Knapp's. "It's your kind of place," Hap said with assurance born of watching us eat many of his fine meals.

The setting of Knapp's in the Proctor District helps create an aura of small-town charm in the midst of big-city life. Walking into the old brick building is like going back half a century. The dining room is patrolled by teams of waitresses who wait tables for a living—pros, who refill coffee and replace needed silverware with the grace of a four-star sommelier.

The menu is nostalgic, too. This is a place to have a platter of liver and onions or turkey with sage-flavored dressing and a pile of mashed potatoes with a ladle of gravy on top. Every Tuesday, Knapp's serves corned beef and cabbage, every Wednesday, roast pork loin. Begin your meal with a shrimp cocktail or an iceberg-lettuce salad, and finish it off with homemade peach pie. It is an all-American experience, not necessarily for the fussy epicure, but a treasure for aficionados of square meals.

Maltby Café

8809 Maltby Rd.   425-483-3123
Snohomish, WA   BL | $

If ever we write a book called *Really Big Food*, the Maltby Café would be featured for breakfast. It's cinnamon roll is not so much a "roll" as it is a loaf—a massive circular coil of sweet pastry scattered with bits of walnut. It is served on a dinner plate, which it fits edge-to-edge, and it is at least a couple of good breakfasts unto itself.

You must get a cinnamon roll at the Maltby Café, but there are some other terrific meals, too, and while none is quite so flabbergastingly immense, they are satisfying in the extreme. The Maltby omelet, for example, is another plate-filler, loaded with ham, beef, peppers, and onions. Maltby oatmeal is served with melted butter running all over the top of the bowl; the French toast is double-thick; and—lest we forget—the strawberry jam on every table is homemade.

After breakfast, there is lunch, which looks good . . . although we must admit that cinnamon rolls and omelets have pretty much put lunch out of the question for us. The menu includes pasta plates, homemade soup, and a piled-high hot Reuben sandwich.

The Maltby Café is a most unusual place (a former school cafeteria) in an amazing little town of nostalgic mise-en-scène that includes strategically situated old farm machinery, a few windmills, and uncounted number of vintage gasoline station signs. Other than the café, the town has a few knickknack shops and a drive-through espresso stand shaped like a big gulp cup.

Mike's Chili Parlor

1447 N.W. Ballard Way   206-782-2808
Seattle, WA   LD | $

We salute Gregg Simonsen of WhereGreggEats.com for tipping us off to Mike's, which is one of an endangered breed of restaurant, the urban chili parlor. Other than in Cincinnati, where chili culture still thrives, there are precious few good proletarian eateries where chili is king.

Outfitted with a billiards table, a few video games, an ATM station, and pull-tab lotto, decorated with beer signs and festooned with announcements warning that only cash is accepted and touting such specials as a Big Ass Bowl of Chili, this joint is the real deal. Seats are available at a couple of communal tables in the center of the room, at the counter and in a few booths. Customers are a ragtag bunch and the staff doesn't bow and scrape, but we felt completely welcome and well taken care of.

As for the chili itself, let us simply say that this is *not* gourmet–yuppie–celebrity chef type chili. It is rugged beef with plenty of savory fat—delicious even if nutritionally incorrect. Beans are optional, as are grated cheese and chopped onions.

An old article posted on the wall describes Mike's chili as "Mexican with a touch of Chicago and a pinch of old Greece." The Chicago touch is evident in the item listed on the menu, strangely, as chili pasta: chili served atop a bed of limp spaghetti noodles, a gloss on the Windy City's chili mac. Greek spice pervades the meat, which is more Mediterranean sweet than Mexican hot.

Mike's hamburgers looked great in a hash-house way, and next time we intend to try some. Meanwhile, we recommend the chili dog topped with cheese and onions. And to drink, if beer is not your choice, have some lemonade. It's fresh-squeezed!

Pick Quick Drive-In
4306 Pacific Hwy. E   253-922-5599
Tacoma, WA   L (closed in winter) | $

Here's a roadside blast from the past (1949 to be precise), especially alluring in nice weather when you can sit outside and enjoy a triple cheeseburger, chili fries, and milkshake—all of that still in the single digit price range.

The hamburgers, though not contenders for our Best of the Northwest burger awards, have a nice savor from the well-aged grill and come dressed quite royally with mustard, mayonnaise, relish, pickles, onion, lettuce, and tomato. Of course, bacon, cheese, and grilled onions are options. French fries are very good and the milkshakes can be extraordinary, as they are made from fresh fruit in season—strawberries, blueberries, blackberries, cherries, raspberries. Any time of the year, you can have fresh banana added to your shake or malt.

Pick Quick is a minuscule establishment that originally served as the canteen for a now-defunct drive-in movie theater. There is plenty of dining room in the great outdoors with picnic tables of all shapes and sizes.

Red Mill
1613 W. Dravus St.   206-284-6363
Seattle, WA   L | $

A diner called the Red Mill opened in Seattle in 1937 and survived for thirty years. Twenty-seven years after it closed, a new Red Mill opened in

Phinney Ridge, and a hamburger legend was born. No doubt, Seattle is a significant burger city and many of its connoisseurs believe Red Mill's rate near the top. Flame broiled to a smoky savor, they come in many configurations from basic to deluxe (lettuce, tomato, pickle, onion, and sauce) and include patties topped with blue cheese or barbecue sauce. You can get a double—that's a half-pound of meat—and you even can get a meatless garden burger. We are fond of the verde burger, which is topped with roasted green chiles, Jack cheese, red onion, lettuce, tomato, and the Red Mill's proprietary sauce. Condiments and dressing are applied in abundance, so while the meat patty itself is good, it's all those extras that put it over the top.

On the side, onion rings are essential. They are big crunchy hoops with ribbons of sweet, caramelized onion inside. And there is a whole menu of milkshakes and malts, plus fresh-squeezed lemonade.

And as if burgers, o-rings, and shakes weren't enough reason to love this place, we should also add that it has a strict no–cell phone policy, allowing all of us to dine well and in peace.

Top Pot Doughnuts

2124 5th Ave.	206-728-1966
Seattle, WA	$

Thanks to several Roadfood.com users who tipped us off to Top Pot, and to Seattleite Rebekah Denn, who took us there, our donut consciousness has been raised. No longer can we blithely claim that all top-tier donuts are made in New England, because that claim would exclude those made in Seattle, and not to count Top Pot's among the nation's best would be a crime against taste buds.

Behold a plain one. First and foremost, there's the crunch of its skin, crisp enough to feel like your teeth are breaking something, after which they slide into the creamy cake interior just below the golden crust. Now, encase the top half in silky dark chocolate, coconut shreds, maple frosting, or a glistening thick sugar glaze and this modest-size circular pastry becomes sheer ecstasy.

They call them "gourmet donuts" at Top Pot, of which there are three shops now in Seattle, and if "gourmet" means better than average, the term is apt. There's nothing froufrou or pretentious about them. They are good ol' cake donuts, the kind you want to have with morning coffee, but by any meaningful standard—taste, texture, heft, even good looks—

they are world-class, far superior to any of the national chains and in a league with those of Dottie's Diner in Connecticut, Allie's in Rhode Island, and Butler's Colonial in Massachusetts.

The downtown Top Pot we visited is a beautiful, airy space with book-lined walls and retro décor that includes a vintage TV and a handsome old espresso machine. The nice guy behind the counter told us that Top Pot has a bakery but not a retail shop in Portland, where they make donuts for Starbucks. We asked if the owners of Top Pot planned to create an empire. He doubted that was their goal. Whatever the future of Top Pot, anyone who considers a great donut one of life's essential pleasures needs to come to Seattle and feast, right now.

JANE and MICHAEL STERN are the authors of more than forty books, including *Square Meals*, *Chili Nation*, and six previous editions of *Roadfood*. They write the "Roadfood" column in *Gourmet*, the winner of three James Beard Awards for Best Magazine Series, and are regulars on public radio's *The Splendid Table*. They host the interactive Web site Roadfood.com, which Yahoo! declared "site of the year," and frequently contribute book reviews to the *New York Times*. They live in Connecticut.

TAKE A DELICIOUS TOUR IN RECIPES THROUGH EVERY STATE IN *Chili* NATION

THE ULTIMATE CHILI COOKBOOK
with Recipes from Every State in the Nation

FROM FEROCIOUS FOUR-ALARM TEXAS RED

TO GENTLE COMFORT-FOOD CHILI STEW

AND FROM MANLY CHAIN-GANG CHILI

TO VEGETARIAN BOWLS OF GOODNESS

Chili NATION

JANE & MICHAEL STERN
Authors of *Eat Your Way Across the U.S.A.*

Chili may have started in the Lone Star State, but today it's become the one-dish wonder that unites all Americans. Now Jane and Michael Stern present the best regional interpretations of this national favorite gathered on their coast-to-coast rambles in a cookbook guaranteed to surprise and delight chili fans (and incite more than a few cook-offs).

TAKE YOUR LOVE OF CHILI TO AN ALL NEW STATE OF SATISFACTION WITH...

- ✪ Maryland's Chesapeake Bay Chili
- ✪ Nevada's Cowboy Poetry Chili
- ✪ Louisiana's Mardi Gras Vegetable Chili
- ✪ Michigan's Cornish Miner Chili Pasties
- ✪ D.C.'s Serious Capital Punishment Chili
- ✪ And 45 more great recipes!

VISIT THE STERNS AT WWW.ROADFOOD.COM

Available wherever books are sold